Linux Mint 18.2

Desktops and Administration

For my mother Cecelia
and her love for books
1919-2017

Linux Mint 18.2: Desktops and Administration

Richard Petersen

Surfing Turtle Press

Alameda, CA

www.surfingturtlepress.com

Please send inquires to: editor@surfingturtlepress.com

ISBN 1-936280-92-2

ISBN-13 978-1-936280-92-6

Copyright Richard Petersen, 2017

All rights reserved

Copyright 2017 by Richard Petersen. All rights reserved. Printed in the United States of America.

Except as permitted under the Copyright Act of 1976, no part of this publication may be reproduced or distributed in any form or by any means, or stored in a database or retrieval system, without the prior written permission of the publisher, with the exception that the program listings may be entered, stored, and executed in a computer system, but they may not be reproduced for publication.

Information has been obtained by Surfing Turtle Press from sources believed to be reliable. However, because of the possibility of human or mechanical error by our sources, Surfing Turtle Press, the author Richard Petersen, or others, Surfing Turtle Press does not guarantee the accuracy, adequacy, or completeness of any information and is not responsible for any errors or omissions or the results obtained from use of such information.

Limit of Liability and Disclaimer of Warranty: The publisher and the author make no representation or warranties with respect to the accuracy or completeness of the contents of this work and specifically disclaim all warranties, including without limitation warranties of fitness for a particular purpose. The information and code in this book is provided on "as is" basis. No warranty may be created or extended by sales or promotional materials. The advice and strategies contained herein may not be suitable for every situation. This work is sold with the understanding that the publisher is not engaged in rendering legal, accounting, or other professional services. Surfing Turtle Press and anyone else who has been involved in the creation or production of the included code cannot and do not warrant the performance or results that may be obtained by using the code.

Trademark Acknowledgements

UNIX is a trademark of The Open Group

Microsoft and MS-DOS are registered trademarks of Microsoft Corporation

IBM and PC are registered trademarks of the International Business Machines Corporation

Fedora is a trademark of Red Hat, Inc.

Linux Mint is a trademark of Canonical, inc.

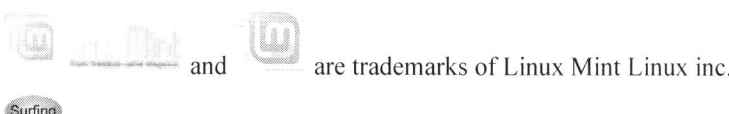 and are trademarks of Linux Mint Linux inc.

is a trademark of Surfing Turtle Press

Preface

This book covers the Linux Mint 18.2 release, focusing on desktops and administrative tools. The emphasis here is on what users will face when using Linux Mint, covering topics like installation, applications, software management, the Linux Mint desktops (Cinnamon, Mate, KDE, and Xfce), shell commands, network connections, and system administration tasks. Linux Mint 18.2 introduces several new features, as well as numerous smaller modifications. It is based on the Ubuntu 16.04 long-term support release. The Cinnamon, Mate, and KDE desktops are examined in detail. Cinnamon and Mate have custom Linux Mint menus to manage access to applications and devices. Advanced components are also examined such as PulseAudio sound configuration, systemd service management, and Linux Mint software management applications (Software Manager and Update Manager).

The Linux Mint Cinnamon desktop is developed and maintained by Linux Mint, with several desktop configuration tools and a System Settings dialog. The Mate desktop is based on GNOME 2, with the traditional panel and applets implementation. The KDE Linux Mint desktop, which uses KDE, provides a very different interface using plasma containers to support the panel, menu, desktop, configuration tools, and plasmoid applets. Each desktop has its own file manager. The Cinnamon desktop uses Nemo, which is based on the Ubuntu GNOME 3 version of Nautilus. The Mate desktop uses Caja, which is based on the GNOME 2 file manager. KDE Linux Mint uses the KDE Dolphin file manager.

Part 1 focuses on getting started, covering Linux Mint information and resources, using Linux Mint Live DVD/USB discs, installing and setting up Linux Mint, upgrading Linux Mint, basic use of the desktops (Cinnamon, Mate, and KDE), and connecting to wired and wireless networks. Repositories and their use are covered in detail. Software Manager and Synaptic Package manager, which provide easy and effective software management, are both discussed. The new X-Apps are also reviewed, including Xplayer, Xed, and Xviewer. In addition, a listing of office, multimedia, mail, Internet, and social media applications is presented.

Part 2 covers the Cinnamon, Mate, and KDE desktops. The Cinnamon desktop retains popular GNOME 2 features, such as panels and applets. It also has the Cinnamon menu with a favorites sidebar similar to the Ubuntu launcher. The Mate desktop is derived from the GNOME 2 desktop, but with a more advanced applications menu. The KDE desktop has features such as plasmoids, activities, panels, menus, and KWin desktop effects. The shell interface is also explored, with its command editing, directory navigation, and file operations.

Part 3 deals with administration topics, first discussing system tools like the GNOME system monitor, the Disk Usage Analyzer, and Disk Utility (Udisks). Then a detailed chapter on Linux Mint system administration tools is presented, covering tasks such as managing users and file systems, Bluetooth setup, and network folder and file sharing. The network connections chapter covers a variety of network tasks, including manual configuration of wired and wireless connections, and firewalls (the Gufw and FirewallD).

Part 4 focuses on shared resources such as Samba, NFS, and CUPS, and covers how **systemd** manages services using unit and target files. Shared resources are also examined, including the CUPS printing server, the NFS Linux network file server, and Samba Windows file and printing server. Printer administration and installation are discussed, including configuration for local and remote printers.

Overview

Preface	5
Overview	7
Contents	9

Part 1: Getting Started

1. Linux Mint 18.2 Introduction	27
2. Installing Linux Mint	39
3. Usage Basics: Login, Desktop, Network, and Help	59
4. Installing and Updating Software	99
5. Applications	129

Part 2: Desktops

6. Cinnamon Desktop	155
7. Mate Desktop	217
8. KDE Linux Mint (KDE)	261

Part 3: Administration

9. System Tools — 307

10. System Administration — 327

11. Network Connections — 375

12. Shell Configuration — 421

Part 4: Shared Resources

13. Managing Services — 441

14. Print Services — 481

15. Network File Systems and Network Information System: NFS and NIS — 513

16. Samba — 531

Table Listing — 559

Figure Listing — 563

Index — 577

Contents

Preface 5

Overview 7

Contents 9

Part 1: Getting Started

1. Linux Mint 18.2 Introduction 27

Linux Mint 18.2 28
Linux Mint Editions 28
Linux Mint Live DVD 30
    Linux Mint Live DVD 30
    Linux Mint Live USB drive 31
Linux Mint Software 32
Linux Mint Help and Documentation 32
Ubuntu 34
Linux documentation 35
Open Source Software 36
Linux 36

2. Installing Linux Mint 39

Upgrading directly from Linux Mint 18 40
Install Discs 40
Installing Multiple-Boot Systems 40
Installation Overview 41
Installation with the Linux Mint DVD 42
    Welcome and Language 43
    Preparing to install (third party software) 44
    Installation type 44
        No detected operating systems 45

- Use LVM ... 46
- Encrypt the disk ... 46
- Detected Linux Mint operating system ... 46
- Detected other operating systems with free space ... 47
- Detected other operating system using entire disk (resize) ... 47
- Something else ... 47
- Creating new partitions on a blank hard drive manually ... 48
- Reuse existing Linux partitions on a hard drive ... 52
- Where Are You? ... 53
- Keyboard Layout ... 53
- Who Are You? ... 54
- Install Progress ... 56
- Recovery, rescue, and boot loader re-install ... 56
- Recovery Mode ... 56
- Re-Installing the Boot Loader ... 57

3. Usage Basics: Login, Desktop, Network, and Help ... 59

- Accessing Your Linux Mint System ... 60
  - GRUB Boot Loader ... 60
  - The LightDM Display Manager ... 61
- Login Window Preferences ... 63
  - Lock Screen and Switch User ... 65
  - Shut down and Logging out ... 65
  - Accessing Linux from the Command Line Interface ... 66
- The Linux Mint Desktops ... 67
  - Cinnamon ... 67
  - Mate ... 71
  - KDE Linux Mint ... 73
  - Xfce Desktop ... 75
  - Linux Mint Debian Edition (LMDE) ... 78
- Accessing File Systems and Devices ... 78
  - Accessing Archives from GNOME: Archive Mounter ... 80
  - File Manager CD/DVD Creator interface ... 80
  - Burning ISO images from the file manager ... 81
  - Brasero Disc Burner application interface ... 81
- Laptop Power Management and Wireless Networks ... 81
- Network Connections ... 81

Network Manager wired connections	82
Network Manager wireless connections	83
System Settings Network, Cinnamon (GNOME and proxies)	84
Display Configuration and Device Drivers	87
Device Drivers	88
Display (resolution and rotation)	89
Hi-DPI	90
Color Profiles	90
Private Encrypted Directories (ecryptfs)	91
Help Resources	92
Linux Mint User Guide	92
Application Documentation	94
The Man Pages	94
The Info Pages	94
Terminal Window	95
Command Line Interface	97

4. Installing and Updating Software 99

Installing Software Packages	100
Linux Mint Package Management Software	101
Linux Mint Software Repositories	101
Repository Components	102
Ubuntu Software Repositories	102
Repository Components	102
Repositories	103
Linux Mint Repository Configuration file: sources.list.d/ official-package-repositories.list	103
Software Sources managed from Linux Mint	104
Codec packages on Linux Mint (mint-meta-codecs)	107
Updating Linux Mint with Update Manager	107
Managing Packages with Software Manager (mintinstall)	111
Synaptic Package Manager	115
Properties	118
Installing packages	118
Removing packages	119
Search filters	119
Software Manager for separate DEB packages	119
Installing and Running Windows Software on Linux: Wine	120

Source code files 121
Software Package Types.. 121
DEB Software Packages.. 122
Managing software with apt-get 123
    Updating packages (Upgrading) with apt-get 124
Command Line Search and Information: dpkg-query and apt-cache tools 125
Managing non-repository packages with dpkg 126
Using packages with other software formats 127

5. Applications 129

X-Apps.. 130
Office Applications 131
    LibreOffice 131
    Calligra 132
    GNOME Office Applications 133
    Document Viewers, and DVI) 133
    Ebook Readers: FBReader and Calibre.. 134
    Editors.. 134
    Database Management Systems 135
        SQL Databases (RDBMS) 136
        LibreOffice Base 136
        PostgreSQL... 136
        MySQL... 136
        MariaDB 136
Mail (email) and News 137
    Mail Clients 137
    Usenet News.. 138
Graphics Applications 139
Multimedia.. 141
    Multimedia support 142
    GStreamer.. 142
        GStreamer Plug-ins: the Good, the Bad, and the Ugly 143
    Music Applications 143
    Video Applications 143
        Video and DVD Players... 145
        Videos Plugins (Xplayer and Totem).. 145
        PiTiVi Video editor 145

TV Players	146
DVB and HDTV support	146
Xvid (DivX) and Matroska (mkv) on Linux	147
CD/DVD Burners	147
Internet Applications	148
Web Browsers	148
Java for Linux	149
BitTorrent Clients (transmission)	149
FTP Clients	149
Network File Transfer: FTP	150
Web Browser–Based FTP	150
GNOME Desktop FTP: Connect to Server	151
Social Networking	152

Part 2: Desktops

6. Cinnamon Desktop 155

Cinnamon Desktop	156
Desklets	158
Hot Corners	160
Keyboard and Mouse Shortcuts	160
Menu	162
Windows	166
Minimizing, Maximizing, and Closing Windows	168
Resize and tiling Windows	170
Switching Windows with the Windows QuickList	170
Switching Windows with the Scale Screen and Alt-Tab	171
Effects	172
Workspace Selection with Hot Corners (expo) and expo applet	173
The Linux Mint Panel	176
Linux Mint Applets	179
Panel Launchers Applet	180
Nemo File Manager	181
Home Folder Sub-folders and Bookmarks	181
File Manager Windows	182
File Manager Sidebar and Bookmarks	183
Tabs	185

Contents

- Displaying Files and Folders 185
- File manager menus and tools 187
- Navigating in the file manager 189
- Nemo File Manager Search 191
- Nemo Plugins and Extensions 192
- Managing Files and Folders 192
  - Using a file's pop-up menu 193
  - Renaming Files 193
  - Grouping Files 194
  - Opening Applications and Files MIME Types 194
- File and Directory Properties 194
- Nemo Preferences 196
- System Settings 196
  - Appearance 200
    - Backgrounds 200
    - Fonts 202
  - Themes 202
  - Preferences 204
    - Preferred Applications and Removable Media 205
    - Time & Date Settings (Calendar applet) 206
    - Screensaver 208
    - Languages 209
  - Accessibility 210
  - Startup Applications 210
  - Hardware 211
    - System Info 211
    - Mouse and Touchpad 211
    - Power Management 212
    - Keyboard Settings 214
    - Notifications 215
    - Privacy 216

7. Mate Desktop 217

- The Mate Desktop 218
  - Mate Components 219
  - Drag-and-Drop Files to the Desktop 219
  - Desktop Settings 220

- Applications on the Desktop 221
- The Desktop Menu 221
- Windows 221
  - Window List 223
  - Workspace Switcher 224
- Linux Mint Menu for Mate 225
  - Linux Mint Menu Preferences dialog 227
- Mate Panel 229
  - Panel Properties 230
    - Displaying Panels 230
    - Moving and Hiding Expanded Panels 231
    - Unexpanded Panels: Movable and Fixed 231
    - Panel Background 231
  - Panel Objects 232
    - Moving, Removing, and Locking Objects 232
    - Adding Objects 232
    - Application Launchers 232
    - Adding Drawers 233
    - Adding Menus 233
    - Adding Folders and Files 234
  - Adding Applets 234
- Caja File Manager 234
  - Home Folder Sub-folders and Bookmarks 234
  - File Manager Windows 235
  - File Manager Side Pane 238
  - Tabs 239
  - Displaying Files and Folders 240
  - File manager tools and menus 241
  - Navigating in the file manager 241
  - Caja File Manager Search 244
  - Managing Files and Folders 245
    - Using a file's pop-up menu 245
    - Renaming Files 245
    - Grouping Files 245
    - Opening Applications and Files MIME Types 245
  - File and Directory Properties 247
  - Caja Preferences 248
- Control Center 248

Mate Preferences 249
    Mouse and Keyboard Preferences 251
    Configuring your personal information 252
    Appearance 252
    Desktop Themes 252
    Desktop Background 254
    Fonts 254
        Configuring Fonts 255
        Adding Fonts 255
    Mate Power Management 256
    Preferred Applications for Web, Mail, Accessibility, and terminal windows 257
    Default Applications for Media 258
    Screen Saver and Lock 259
    Assistive Technologies 259

8. KDE Linux Mint (KDE) 261

KDE Plasma 5 262
KDE Linux Mint 18.2 263
Installing KDE Linux Mint 263
SDDM 264
The KDE Desktop 265
    The KDE Help Center 266
    Desktop Backgrounds (Wallpaper) 267
    Themes 268
    Leave KDE 269
    KDE Kickoff menus 271
    KDE Application Dashboard menus 273
    Krunner 274
    Removable Devices: Device Notifier 275
    KDE Network Connections: Network Manager 276
    Desktop Plasmoids (Widgets) 277
        Managing desktop widgets 277
        Folder and Icon Widgets 279
        Activities 280
    KDE Windows 282
    Applications 284
    Virtual Desktops: Pager 284

KDE Panel	286
KDE Panel Configuration	288
Desktop Effects	289
KDE File Manager: Dolphin	294
Navigating Directories	298
Copy, Move, Delete, Rename, and Link Operations	299
Search Bar and Filter Bar	299
Search Bar	300
Filter Bar	300
KDE Configuration: KDE System Settings	301

Part 3: Administration

9. System Tools 307

GNOME System Monitor	308
Managing Processes	309
Scheduling Tasks	310
System Log Viewer	311
Disk Usage Analyzer	312
Virus Protection	313
Hardware Sensors	314
Disk Utility and Udisks	315
Plymouth	317
Sound Preferences	318
Sound menu (volume control and player access)	319
Sound: PulseAudio	320
PulseAudio applications	322
dconf editor	325

10. System Administration 327

Administrative Tools	328
Controlled Administrative Access	329
PolicyKit	330
sudo	331
sudo command	331
sudo configuration	332
pkexec	333

Contents

- Root User Access: root and su 335
- Nemo with elevated privileges on Cinnamon desktop 336
- /etc/hostname and hostnamectl 337
- Users and Groups (cinnamon-settings-users) 338
- Users and Groups (Mate) 341
  - New Users (Users and Groups) 344
  - Groups (Users and Groups) 345
  - Passwords 346
- Managing Services 346
- File System Access 346
  - Access to Internal Linux File Systems 346
  - Access to Windows NTFS File Systems on Local Drives 347
  - Access to Local Network Shared File Systems (Windows) 347
  - Shared Folders for your network 349
  - File and Folder Permissions 351
  - Automatic file system mounts with /etc/fstab 352
- Bluetooth 353
- DKMS 356
- Editing Configuration Files Directly 357
- GRUB 2 357
- Backup Management 360
  - Backup Tool (mintBackup) 361
  - Deja Dup 362
  - Individual Backups: archive and rsync 364
  - BackupPC 365
  - Amanda 365
- Logical Volume Manager 366
  - LVM Structure 366
  - LVM Tools: using the LVM commands 367
    - Displaying LVM Information 367
    - Managing LVM Physical Volumes with the LVM commands 367
    - Managing LVM Groups 368
    - Activating Volume Groups 369
    - Managing LVM Logical Volumes 369
  - Steps to create a new LVM group and volume 370
  - Steps to add a new drive to an LVM group and volume 370
  - Using LVM to replace drives 371
  - LVM Snapshots 372

OpenZFS 373

11. Network Connections 375

Network Connections: Dynamic and Static 376
Network Manager 377
    Network Manager menu 378
Network Manager manual configuration using GNOME Network (Network Settings)
.... 379
Network Manager manual configuration using the nm-connections-editor (Network
Connection) 383
    General tab 384
    Wired Configuration 385
    Wireless Configuration 387
    DSL Configuration 388
    Mobile Broadband: 3G Support 389
    PPP Configuration 390
    Network Manager VPN 391
    Managing Network Connections with nmcli 393
Dial-up PPP Modem Access: wvdial 397
Configuring a network with systemd-networkd 399
Firewalls 403
    Important Firewall Ports 403
    Setting up a firewall with ufw 404
    Gufw 404
    ufw commands 408
    ufw rule files 409
    FirewallD and firewall-config 409
GNOME Nettool 414
Predictable and unpredictable network device names 415
    Network device path names 415
    Renaming network device names with udev rules 417
    Renaming network device names for systemd-networkd with systemd.link 418

12. Shell Configuration 421

Shell Initialization and Configuration Files 422
Configuration Directories and Files 423
Aliases 424
    Aliasing Commands and Options 424

    Aliasing Commands and Arguments 425
    Aliasing Commands 425
Controlling Shell Operations 426
Environment Variables and Subshells: export 426
Configuring Your Shell with Shell Parameters 428
    Shell Parameter Variables 428
        Using Initialization Files 429
        Your Home Directory: HOME 429
        Command Locations: PATH 429
        Specifying the BASH Environment: BASH_ENV 431
        Configuring the Shell Prompt 431
        Specifying Your News Server 433
    Configuring Your Login Shell: .profile 433
        Exporting Variables 434
        Variable Assignments 434
        Editing Your BASH Profile Script 435
        Manually Re-executing the .profile script 436
        System Shell Profile Script 436
    The System /etc/bash.bashrc BASH Script 437
    The BASH Shell Logout File: .bash_logout 438

Part 4: Shared Resources

13. Managing Services 441

systemd 442
    systemd basic configuration files 443
    units 443
    unit file syntax 445
    special targets 447
    Modifying unit files: /etc/systemd/system 449
    Execution Environment Options 450
    service unit files 450
    System V Scripts and generated systemd service files: /etc/init.d and
    /run/systemd/generator.late 452
    On Demand and Standalone Services (socket) 453
    Path units 455
    Template unit files 455

Contents

- Runlevels and Special Targets 456
  - systemd and automatically mounting file systems: /etc/fstab 458
  - systemd slice and scope units 460
- System V: /etc/init.d 460
- Shutdown and Poweroff 460
- Managing Services 462
  - Enabling services: starting a service automatically at boot 462
  - Managing services manually 463
  - The service Command 463
  - /etc/default 463
  - Service Startup Management with rcconf 463
- Network Time Protocol, NTP 464
  - The ntp server 465
  - The ntp.conf configuration file 465
    - NTP access controls 465
    - NTP clock support 467
- AppArmor security 467
  - AppArmor utilities 468
  - AppArmor configuration 469
- Remote Administration 470
  - Puppet 470
  - The Secure Shell: OpenSSH 471
    - Encryption 471
    - Authentication 472
    - SSH Packages, Tools, and Server 472
    - SSH Setup 473
    - Creating SSH Keys with ssh-keygen 474
    - Authorized Keys 475
    - Loading Keys 476
    - SSH Clients 476
    - Port Forwarding (Tunneling) 478
    - SSH Configuration 479

14. Print Services 481

- CUPS 482
- Printer Devices and Configuration 484
  - Printer Device Files 484

Contents

- Printer URI (Universal Resource Identifier) ... 484
- Spool Directories ... 485
- CUPS start and restart: cups init script ... 485
- Installing Printers ... 485
- Configuring Printers on the Desktop with system-config-printer (System Settings Printers) ... 485
  - system-config-printer ... 485
  - Editing Printer Configuration ... 488
  - Default System-wide and Personal Printers ... 490
  - Adding New Printers Manually ... 491
- CUPS Web Browser-based configuration tool ... 494
- Configuring Remote Printers on CUPS ... 497
  - Configuring Remote Printers on the Desktop with system-config-printer ... 498
  - Configuring remote printers manually ... 501
- CUPS Printer Classes ... 501
- CUPS Configuration files ... 502
  - cupsd.conf ... 502
    - Location Directives ... 503
    - Default Operation Policy: Limit Directives ... 504
  - cupsctl ... 506
  - printers.conf ... 506
  - subscriptions.conf ... 507
  - cups-files.conf ... 507
  - cups-browsed.conf ... 507
- CUPS Command Line Print Clients ... 508
  - lpr ... 508
  - lpc ... 508
  - lpq and lpstat ... 509
  - lprm ... 509
- CUPS Command Line Administrative Tools ... 509
  - lpadmin ... 510
  - lpoptions ... 510
  - cupsenable and cupsdisable ... 511
  - accept and reject ... 511
  - lpinfo ... 511

15. Network File Systems and Network Information System: NFS and NIS 513

- Network File Systems: NFS and /etc/exports 514
- NFS Daemons 514
- Setting up NFS Directories on the Desktop with shares-admin 517
- NFS Configuration: /etc/exports 519
  - NFS Host Entries 519
  - NFS Options 519
  - NFS User-Level Access 521
  - NFSv4 521
  - NFS /etc/exports Example 521
  - Applying Changes 522
  - Manually Exporting File Systems 522
- Controlling Accessing to NFS Servers 523
  - /etc/hosts.allow and /etc/hosts.deny 523
  - Portmap Service 523
  - Netfilter Rules 524
- Mounting NFS File Systems: NFS Clients 524
  - Mounting NFS Automatically: /etc/fstab 524
  - Mounting NFS Manually: mount 525
  - Mounting NFS on Demand: autofs 526
- Network Information Service: NIS 526
  - /etc/nsswitch.conf: Name Service Switch 528

16. Samba 531

- Samba Applications 533
- Starting up and accessing Samba 533
  - Firewall access 536
- Setting Up Samba on the Desktop 537
  - Samba Server Configuration 537
  - Samba Users 538
  - Samba Shares 539
- User-Level Security 540
  - Samba Passwords: smbpasswd 542
  - Managing Samba Users: smbpasswd and pdbedit 542
- The Samba smb.conf Configuration File 543

Contents

- Variable Substitutions ... 544
- Global Settings ... 545
  - Browsing/Identification ... 545
  - Networking ... 546
  - Debugging/Accounting ... 546
  - Authentication ... 547
  - Domains ... 548
  - Misc ... 548
- Share Definitions ... 549
  - Homes Section ... 549
  - The printers and print$ Sections ... 549
- Shares ... 550
- Printer shares ... 551
- Testing the Samba Configuration ... 552
- Samba Public Domain Controller: Samba PDC ... 552
  - Microsoft Domain Security ... 553
  - Essential Samba PDC configuration options ... 553
  - Basic configuration ... 553
  - Domain Logon configuration ... 554
- Accessing Samba Services with Clients ... 555
  - Accessing Windows Samba Shares from GNOME ... 555
  - smbclient ... 556
  - mount.cifs: mount -t cifs ... 557

Table Listing ... 559

Figure Listing ... 563

Index ... 577

Part 1: Getting Started

Introduction
Installation
Usage Basics
Managing Software
Applications

1. Linux Mint 18.2 Introduction

- Linux Mint 18.2
- Linux Mint Editions
- Linux Mint Live DVD and USB
- Linux Mint Software
- Linux Mint Help and Documentation
- Ubuntu Linux
- Open Source Software
- History of Linux and UNIX

Linux Mint aims to provide a user-oriented desktop system that is concise, elegant, and powerful. Linux Mint started in 2006 and is based on the Ubuntu distribution. Linux Mint has developed a desktop called Cinnamon, initially derived from GNOME 3. Though Cinnamon is developed and maintained by Linux Mint, it can also be installed on other Linux distributions, including Ubuntu, open SUSE, and Fedora.

You can think of Linux Mint as more like a portal to different underlying Linux implementations. Linux Mint directly supports desktops using Cinnamon and Mate. It also supports KDE and Xfce desktops. The desktops are based on the Ubuntu Linux distribution with many of the packages taken directly from the Ubuntu software repositories. It does not use the Ubuntu Unity desktop.

Following the Ubuntu releases, Linux Mint provides both long-term and short-term support releases. Long-term support releases (LTS), are released every two years. Short-term releases are provided every six months between the LTS versions. They are designed to make available the latest applications and support for the newest hardware. The long-term support releases are supported for three years for desktops and five years for servers, whereas short-term support releases are supported for 18 months. Linux Mint numbers its releases sequentially.

Installing Linux Mint is easy to do. A core set of applications are installed, and you can add to them as you wish. Following installation, additional software can be downloaded from online repositories. There are only a few install screens, which move quickly through default partitioning, user setup, and time settings. Hardware components such as graphics cards and network connections are configured and detected automatically. With Software Manager (installed by default on all systems), you can find and install additional software with the click of a button. The Linux Mint distribution of Linux is available at **https://www.linuxmint.com.** You can download the current release of Linux Mint Linux from **https://www.linuxmint.com/download.php**.

Linux Mint 18.2

Linux Mint 18.2 introduces several new features, as well as numerous smaller modifications (see Figure 1-1). You can find out what is new at:

```
https://linuxmint.com/rel_sonya_cinnamon_whatsnew.php
https://linuxmint.com/rel_sonya_mate_whatsnew.php
```

Linux Mint Editions

Linux Mint is released in several editions, each designed for a distinct group of users or functions. Editions install different collections of software such as the Cinnamon desktop, the Mate desktop, the KDE desktop, and the Xfce desktop. Table 1-2 lists the editions. You can download these editions from mirrors that you can link to from the download page, which you can access from the Linux Mint site by clicking on the Download tab. The download page is:

```
http://www.linuxmint.com/download.php
```

You can choose either the 32-bit or the 64-bit versions, and, for Cinnamon and Mate. The "no codecs" versions in previous releases have been replaced by a prompt on the second screen of the standard installation to install third-party codecs. If you live in a region that may require software patents and licenses, in particular, for multimedia codecs, you should not check this prompt.

Figure 1-1: Linux Mint 18.2 Cinnamon Desktop

The Cinnamon and Mate releases allow you to install the full range of available codecs for Linux, including mp3, DVD, and HDTV video support. The second screen of the installation process will prompt you to choose whether to install these third party codecs. If you choose to do so, you do not have to bother about installing additional codecs to make multimedia applications work. This policy differs from Ubuntu, which does not install such codecs initially, and have to be installed manually later.

If you already have Linux Mint 18 or 18.1, you can now upgrade directly to 18.2 using Update Manager. In Update Manager, first click the Refresh button and check for and install any updates to the **mint-update** and **mint-upgrade-info** packages. Then in the Update Manager, on the Edit menu, you will see the entry "Upgrade to Linux Mint 18.2 Sonya" (Edit | Upgrade to Linux Mint 18.2 Sonya). Select this entry to perform the upgrade. The upgrade does not install the 4.8 kernel or the LightDM display manager. For Upgrade instructions, see the article "How to Upgrade to Linux Mint 18.2" on the Linux Mint blog.

```
http://blog.linuxmint.com/?p=3306
```

You can perform a fresh upgrade or a package upgrade. The fresh upgrade is actually not an upgrade as such, but a completely new install performed after you make a backup of your data. It is the recommended form of upgrading. For a fresh upgrade, you first backup all your data to a separate drive, then install the new Linux Mint release, overwriting and erasing the old one. Then restore your backup to the new system. You do have to make sure that you backup all your data, including all configuration files, such as those for your Web browser.

A simple strategy for easily implementing a fresh upgrade is to set up a separate partition for your home directory (**/home**), which you then keep. Have the Linux Mint system installed on a separate partition (root partition, /), which you can overwrite to upgrade. Make sure to backup any configuration files, if any, that you may want from other partitions.

Linux Mint Editions	Description
Linux Mint Cinnamon	Live DVD and Install with the Cinnamon interface, **https://www.linuxmint.com/download.php**. Cinnamon has no-codecs versions for regions that support software patents. Add to other Linux Mint versions with the **mint-meta-cinnamon** metapackage.
Linux Mint Mate	Live DVD and Install with the Mate interface, **https://www.linuxmint.com/download.php**. Mate has a no-codecs version for regions that support software patents. Add to Linux Mint with the **mint-meta-mate** metapackage.
Linux Mint KDE	Live DVD and Install using the KDE desktop, instead of GNOME, **https://www.linuxmint.com/download.php**. Add to Linux Mint with the **mint-meta-kde** metapackage.
Linux Mint Xfce	Uses the Xfce desktop instead of GNOME, **https://www.linuxmint.com/download.php**. Useful for laptops. Add to Linux Mint with the **mint-meta-xfce** metapackage.

Table 1-1: Linux Mint Editions

Linux Mint Live DVD

All Linux Mint DVDs can operate as a Live DVDs, so you can run Linux Mint from any DVD-ROM drive. You can also install the Linux Mint DVD image to a USB drive. In effect, you can carry your operating system with you on a DVD-ROM or a USB drive. New users can also use the Live-DVD/USB to try out Linux Mint to see if they like it. The Linux Mint Cinnamon DVD will run as a Live DVD automatically using Cinnamon as the desktop. If you want to use the KDE desktop as your Live DVD instead, you would use the KDE Linux Mint DVD.

Linux Mint Live DVD

The Desktop Live DVD provided by Linux Mint includes a basic collection of software packages. You will have a fully operational Linux Mint system (see Figure 1-2) . You have the full set of administrative tools, with which you can add users, change configuration settings, and even add software, while the Live DVD is running. When you shut down, the configuration information is lost, including any software you have added. Files and data can be written to removable devices like USB drives and DVD write discs, letting you save your data during a Live DVD session.

When you start up the Linux Mint Desktop DVD/USB, the Live DVD desktop is then displayed (see Figure 1-2) and you are logged in as the **Linux Mint** user. On the left side, an install Linux Mint icon is displayed, along with the computer and home folder icons. Use the Cinnamon menu at the left side of the bottom panel to quit. Use the network manager menu on the right side of the bottom panel to configure network connections. Figure 1-2: Linux Mint Cinnamon Live DVD

You can save files to your home directory, but they are temporary and disappear at the end of the session. Copy them to a DVD, USB drive, or another removable device to save them.

All the Live DVD/USBs also function as install discs for Linux Mint, providing a basic collection of software, and installing a full-fledged Linux Mint operating system that can be expanded and updated from Linux Mint online repositories. An Install icon lets you install Linux Mint on your computer, performing a standard installation to your hard drive. From the Live DVD desktop, double-click the "Install Linux Mint" icon on the desktop to start the installation.

Figure 1-2: Linux Mint 18.2 Cinnamon Live DVD

Linux Mint Live USB drive

You can install the Linux Mint disc image using either the USB Image Writer or the USB Startup Disk Creator. The USB Image Writer will erase all data on the drive, but the Startup Disk Creator will not. The USB Image Writer is installed by default on Cinnamon, but you can download and install the Startup Disk Creator (**usb-creator-gtk**).

With the USB Startup Disk Creator utility, you can install any Linux Mint disc image on a USB drive. The USB Live/install drive is generated using the DVD image that you first have to download. The Startup Disk Creator displays the Make Startup Disk window with an entry at the top to select an ISO image and an entry below to select the USB drive to use. Click the Other button to locate a specific disk image to use. Then click the "Make Startup Disk" button to install the ISO on the USB drive.

The "Make Startup Disk" operation will not erase any data already on your USB drive. You can still access it, even Windows data. The Linux Mint Live OS will coexist with your current data, occupying available free space.

To boot from the Live USB, be sure your computer (BIOS) is configured to boot from the USB drive. The Live USB drive will then start up just like the Live DVD, displaying the install screen with options to try Linux Mint or directly install.

When you create the Live USB drive, you have the option to specify writable memory. This will allow you to save files to your USB drive as part of the Linux Mint Live operating system. You can save files to your Document or Pictures directory and then access them later. You can also create new users, and give those users administrative permission, just as you would on a normally installed OS. With the System Settings' Users and Groups tool, you could even have the new user be the automatic login, instead of the **Linux Mint** user. In effect, the Linux Mint Live USB drive becomes a portable Linux Mint OS. Even with these changes, the Linux Mint Live USB remains the equivalent of a Live DVD, just one that you can write to. There is no GRUB boot loader. You still use the install start up screen. In addition, you cannot update the kernel. One advantage of this approach is that your other data can coexist on the USB drive, accessible by other operating systems.

If you want a truly portable Linux Mint OS, just perform a standard installation to a USB drive, instead of to a hard drive. You will have to create a new clean partition on the USB drive to install to. You would either reduce the size of the current partition, preserving data, or simply delete it, opening up the entire drive for use by the new Linux Mint OS.

Linux Mint Software

All Linux software for Linux Mint is currently available from online repositories. You can download applications for desktops, Internet servers, office suites, and programming packages, among others. Software packages are distributed through the Linux Mint and Ubuntu repositories. Downloads and updates are handled automatically by your desktop software manager and updater.

The complete listing of Linux Mint software packages for a release can be found at:

`http://packages.linuxmint.com`

A more descriptive listing is kept at Linux Mint Community site at:

`https://community.linuxmint.com/software`

For the Ubuntu packages in the Linux Mint distribution, you can search the Ubuntu packages site at:

`https://packages.ubuntu.com`

All software packages in the Linux Mint and Ubuntu repositories are accessible directly with Software Manager and the Synaptic Package Manager, which provide easy software installation, removal, and searching.

Due to licensing restrictions, multimedia support for popular operations like MP3, DVD, and DivX are installed separately by the **mint-meta-codecs** package. If not already installed, choose "Install Multimedia Codecs" from the Sound & Video menu, or click the "Multimedia codecs" icon on the Welcome screen.

Linux Mint Help and Documentation

Help and documentation for Linux Mint are available on the Linux Mint site at **https://www.linuxmint.com** and at Linux Mint Community site at **https://community.linuxmint.com/** (see Table 1-2). The Linux Mint Community site provides extensive help resources. Here you will find detailed tutorials, package lists, hardware support information, and online chat for questions. You can also obtain help from the Linux Mint Forum at **https://forums.linuxmint.com**. The Linux Mint site (**https://www.linuxmint.com**) has a page where you can download the current user manual, which covers installation and basic desktop use.

Chapter 1: Linux Mint 18.2 Introduction   **33**

The Linux Mint User Guide is available as a browser application on your Cinnamon desktop. To start the Linux Mint User Guide, choose Help from the Accessories menu. The User Guide displays several links covering Linux Mint topics, such as installation, the desktop, and software management. Detailed documentation on applications, including X-Apps, is available from the All Documents list (Go menu).

Site	Description
https://www.linuxmint.com	Linux Mint site
http://packages.linuxmint.com	Linux Mint software package list
https://community.linuxmint.com/software	Linux Mint software package list, organized by name and more descriptive
https://forums.linuxmint.com	Linux Mint forums
https://www.linuxmint.com/download.php	Download Linux Mint Editions
http://developer.linuxmint.com	Cinnamon desktop site
Linux Mint User Guide	Help on the Accessories menu

Table 1-2: Linux Mint resources and help

Figure 1-3: Linux Mint Welcome dialog

After you install your system and login, a Welcome screen is displayed with icons that link to Linux Mint sites and resources (see Figure 1-3 and see Table 1-3). The "New features" icon links to either the Cinnamon or Mate What's new page, depending on the edition you installed. The Documentation icon links to the Linux Mint documentation page where you can download user guides for different editions. The Drivers icon opens the Driver Manager, where you can install display drivers. The Forums icon opens Linux Mint Community sites where you can ask questions, consult specialized tutorials, and comment on recommendations. The Chat room icon opens a chat application to the Linux Mint chat room. The Get Involved, Donations, and Sponsors icons link to the Linux Mint Project page. The Apps icon opens the Software Manager application, letting you install or remove applications. If you have not installed the additional third-party multimedia codecs, then a "Multimedia codecs" icon is displayed, which you can click to install the codecs.

Site	Description
New Features	The What's New page for the edition you installed. https://www.linuxmint.com/rel_sonya_cinnamon_whatsnew.php https://www.linuxmint.com/rel_sonya_mate_whatsnew.php https://www.linuxmint.com/rel_sonya_kde_whatsnew.php https://www.linuxmint.com/rel_sonya_xfce_whatsnew.php
Important Information	The Release Notes page for the edition you installed. https://www.linuxmint.com/rel_sonya_cinnamon.php https://www.linuxmint.com/rel_sonya_mate.php https://www.linuxmint.com/rel_sonya_kde.php https://www.linuxmint.com/rel_sonya_xfce.php
User Guide (PDF)	Linux Mint page for user guides (Cinnamon, Mate, and KDE), at the Linux Mint Download page, Documentation tab. https://www.linuxmint.com/documentation.php
Chat room	Opens the Hexchat IRC app to the Linux Mint chat room.
Forums	The Linux Mint forums with support for topics such as networking, desktops, installation, and newbie questions. https://forums.linuxmint.com
Tutorials	Tutorials provided by the Linux Mint community on topics such as edition upgrades and installing servers. https://community.linuxmint.com/tutorial
Hardware Database	A searchable supported hardware database provided by the Linux Mint community https://community.linuxmint.com/hardware
Idea Pool	A site provided by the Linux Mint community where users can propose ideas for Linux Mint development https://community.linuxmint.com/idea
Get Involved	The Linux Mint Project page, Get Involved tab https://www.linuxmint.com/getinvolved.php
Donations	The Linux Mint Project page, Donors tab https://www.linuxmint.com/donors.php
Sponsors	The Linux Mint Project page, Sponsors tab https://www.linuxmint.com/donors.php
Restore Data	Opens the Backup Tool to let you restore any backups.
Software Manager	Opens Software Manager (install and remove applications)

Table 1-3: Linux Mint Welcome Screen resources

Ubuntu

Ubuntu Linux is currently one of the most popular end-user Linux distributions (**https://www.ubuntu.com**). Ubuntu Linux is managed by the Ubuntu foundation, which is sponsored by Canonical, Ltd (**https://www.canonical.com/**), a commercial organization that supports and promotes open source projects. Ubuntu is based on Debian Linux, one of the oldest Linux distributions, which is dedicated to incorporating cutting-edge developments and features (**http://www.debian.org**). Mark Shuttleworth, a South African and Debian Linux developer, initiated the Ubuntu project. Debian Linux is primarily a Linux development project, trying out new features. Ubuntu provides a Debian-based Linux distribution that is stable, reliable, and easy to use.

Site	Description
https://help.ubuntu.com/16.04	Help pages and documentation for Ubuntu 16.04
http://packages.ubuntu.com	Ubuntu software package list and search
https://ubuntuforums.org	Ubuntu forums
https://askubuntu.com	Ask Ubuntu Q&A site for users and developers (community based)
http://planet.ubuntu.com	Member and developer blogs
https://blog.canonical.com	Latest Canonical news
http://www.tldp.org	Linux Documentation Project website
https://www.ubuntu.com/community	Links to Documentation, Support, News, and Blogs

Table 1-4: Ubuntu help and documentation

Ubuntu is designed as a Linux operating system that can be used easily by everyone. The name Ubuntu means "humanity to others." As the Ubuntu project describes it: "Ubuntu is an African word meaning 'Humanity to others", or "I am what I am because of who we all are." The Ubuntu distribution brings the spirit of Ubuntu to the software world." Ubuntu aims to provide a fully supported and reliable, open source and free, easy to use and modify, Linux operating system.

Table 1-4 lists several Ubuntu help and resource sites. Ubuntu-specific documentation is available at **https://help.ubuntu.com**. Here, on listed links, you can find specific documentation for different releases. Always check the release help page first for documentation, though it may be sparse and cover mainly changed areas. The Ubuntu LTS release usually includes desktop, installation, and server guides. For Ubuntu 16.04 the Documentation section provides the Ubuntu Guide (Ubuntu Help), the Ubuntu Server Guide, and Ubuntu installation.

```
https://help.ubuntu.com/lts/ubuntu-help/index.html
```

One of the more helpful pages is the Community Contributed Documentation page, **https://help.ubuntu.com/community**. Here you will find detailed documentation on the installation of all Ubuntu releases, using the desktop, installing software, and configuring devices. Always check the page for your Ubuntu release first. Ubuntu forums provide detailed online support and discussion for users (**https://ubuntuforums.org**).

Linux documentation

The Linux Documentation Project (LDP) has developed a complete set of Linux manuals. The documentation is available at the LDP home site at **http://www.tldp.org**. The Linux documentation for your installed software will be available in your **/usr/share/doc** directory.

Open Source Software

Linux is developed as a cooperative Open Source effort over the Internet, so no company or institution controls Linux. Software developed for Linux reflects this background. Development often takes place when Linux users decide to work together on a project. Most Linux software is developed as Open Source software. The source code for an application is freely distributed along with the application. Programmers over the Internet can make their own contributions to a software package's development, modifying and correcting the source code. As an open source operating system, the Linux source code is included in all its distributions and is freely available. Many major software development efforts are also open source projects, as are the KDE and GNOME desktops along with most of their applications. You can find more information about the Open Source movement at **https://opensource.org**.

Open source software is protected by public licenses that prevent commercial companies from taking control of open source software by adding modifications of their own, copyrighting those changes, and selling the software as their own product. The most popular public license is the GNU General Public License (GPL) provided by the Free Software Foundation. Linux is distributed under this license. The GNU General Public License retains the copyright, freely licensing the software with the requirement that the software and any modifications made to it are always freely available. Other public licenses have been created to support the demands of different kinds of open source projects. The GNU Lesser General Public License (LGPL) lets commercial applications use GNU licensed software libraries. The Qt Public License (QPL) lets open source developers use the Qt libraries essential to the KDE desktop. You can find a complete listing at **https://opensource.org**.

Linux is currently copyrighted under a GNU public license provided by the Free Software Foundation (see **http://www.gnu.org/**). GNU software is distributed free, provided it is freely distributed to others. GNU software has proved both reliable and effective. Many of the popular Linux utilities, such as C compilers, shells, and editors, are GNU software applications. In addition, many open source software projects are licensed under the GNU General Public License (GPL). Most of these applications are available on the Linux Mint software repositories. Chapter 4 describes in detail the process of accessing these repositories to download and install software applications from them on your system.

Under the terms of the GNU General Public License, the original author retains the copyright, although anyone can modify the software and redistribute it, provided the source code is included, made public, and provided free. In addition, no restriction exists on selling the software or giving it away free. One distributor could charge for the software, while another could provide it free of charge. Major software companies are also providing Linux versions of their most popular applications. (you can use Wine, the Windows compatibility layer, to run many Microsoft applications on Linux, directly.)

Linux

Linux is a fast, stable, and open source operating system for PCs and workstations that features professional-level Internet services, extensive development tools, fully functional graphical user interfaces (GUIs), and a massive number of applications ranging from office suites to multimedia applications. Linux was developed in the early 1990s by Linus Torvalds, along with other programmers around the world. As an operating system, Linux performs many of the same functions as UNIX, Macintosh, and Windows. However, Linux is distinguished by its power and flexibility, along with being freely available. Most PC operating systems, such as Windows, began their development within the confines of small, restricted personal computers, which have become more versatile and powerful machines. Such operating systems are constantly being upgraded to keep up with the ever-changing capabilities of PC hardware. Linux, on the other hand, was developed in a different context. Linux is a PC version of the UNIX operating system that has been used for decades on mainframes and is currently the system of choice for network servers and workstations.

Technically, Linux consists of the operating system program referred to as the kernel, which is the part originally developed by Linus Torvalds. However, it has always been distributed with a large number of software applications, ranging from network servers and security programs to office applications and development tools. Linux has evolved as part of the open source software movement, in which independent programmers joined to provide free quality software to any user. Linux has become the premier platform for open source software, much of it developed by the Free Software Foundation's GNU project. Most of these applications are also available on the Linux Mint repository, providing packages that are Debian compliant.

Linux operating system capabilities include powerful networking features, including support for Internet, intranets, and Windows networking. As a norm, Linux distributions include fast, efficient, and stable Internet servers, such as the Web, FTP, and DNS servers, along with proxy, news, and mail servers. In other words, Linux has everything you need to set up, support, and maintain a fully functional network.

Linux is distributed freely under a GNU General Public License (GPL) as specified by the Free Software Foundation, making it available to anyone who wants to use it. GNU (which stands for "GNU's Not Unix") is a project initiated and managed by the Free Software Foundation to provide free software to users, programmers, and developers. Linux is copyrighted, not public domain. The GNU General Public License is designed to ensure that Linux remains free and, at the same time, standardized. Linux is technically the operating system kernel—the core operations—and only one official Linux kernel exists. Its power and stability have made Linux an operating system of choice as a network server.

Originally designed specifically for Intel-based personal computers, Linux started out as a personal project of computer science student Linus Torvalds at the University of Helsinki. At that time, students were making use of a program called Minix, which highlighted different UNIX features. Minix was created by Professor Andrew Tanenbaum and widely distributed over the Internet to students around the world. Torvalds's intention was to create an effective PC version of UNIX for Minix users. It was named Linux, and in 1991, Torvalds released version 0.11. Linux was widely distributed over the Internet, and in the following years, other programmers refined and added to it, incorporating most of the applications and features now found in standard UNIX systems. All the major window managers have been ported to Linux. Linux has all the networking tools, such as FTP file transfer support, Web browsers, and the whole range of network services such as email, the domain name service, and dynamic host configuration, along with FTP, Web, and print servers. It also has a full set of program development utilities, such as C++ compilers and debuggers. Given all its features, the Linux operating system remains small, stable, and fast.

Linux development is overseen by The Linux Foundation (**http://www.linuxfoundation.org**), which is a merger of The Free Standards Group and Open

Source Development Labs (OSDL). This is the group with which Linux Torvalds works to develop new Linux versions. Linux kernels are released at **http://kernel.org/**.

2. Installing Linux Mint

Install Discs
Installation Overview
Installation with the Linux Mint DVD
Recovery
Re-Installing the Boot Loader

Installing Linux Mint Linux is a very simple procedure, using just a few screens with default entries for easy installation. A pre-selected collection of software is installed. Most of your devices, like your display and network connection, are detected automatically. The most difficult part would be a manual partitioning of the hard drive, but you can use automatic partitioning for fresh installs, as is usually the case. As an alternative, you can also install Linux Mint on a virtual hard disk on your Windows system.

Upgrading directly from Linux Mint 18

If you already have Linux Mint 18 or 18.1, you can now upgrade directly to 18.2 using Update Manager. In Update Manager, first click the Refresh button and check for and install any updates to the **mint-update** and **mint-upgrade-info** packages. Then in the Update Manager, on the Edit menu, you will see the entry "Upgrade to Linux Mint 18.2 Sonya" (Edit | Upgrade to Linux Mint 18.2 Sonya). Select this entry to perform the upgrade. The upgrade does not install the 4.8 kernel or the LightDM display manager. Your system will run fine with the 4.4 kernel and the Mint display manager (MDM), but you can manually install them if you wish. See the article "How to Upgrade to Linux Mint 18.2" on the Linux Mint blog for detailed instructions.

http://blog.linuxmint.com/?p=3306

If you want to upgrade from Linux Mint 17 to 18.2, you first must upgrade to Linux Mint 18. To do this you will have to first install the Linux Mint 17 **mintupgrade** tool. If you have an earlier version of Linux Mint, such as Linux Mint 16, first upgrade sequentially through to 17. The upgrade is available for Cinnamon, Mate, and Xfce (not KDE). See the instructions on the Linux Mint community tutorial.

http://blog.linuxmint.com/?p=3068
https://community.linuxmint.com/tutorial/view/2316

Install Discs

Installation is performed using a Linux Mint DVD that will install the Linux Mint, along with a pre-selected set of software packages for multimedia players, office applications, and games. The Linux Mint DVD is also designed to run from the DVD disc while providing the option to install Linux Mint on your hard drive. This is the disc image you will download from the Linux Mint download site. The Linux Mint DVD has both 32 and 64-bit versions. If you want to use the 64-bit version, be sure you have a CPU that is 64-bit compatible (as are most current CPUs). The 64-bit version is faster. The Linux Mint DVDs are available at:

https://www.linuxmint.com/download.php

You can download the ISO file directly from a mirror or by using a torrent file with a BitTorrent client like Transmission. Click on the Torrent link on the download page for the BitTorrent file.

Installing Multiple-Boot Systems

The GRUB boot loader already supports multiple booting. Should you have both Linux Mint and Windows systems installed on your hard disks; GRUB will let you choose to boot either the Linux Mint system or a Windows system. During installation, GRUB will automatically detect any other operating systems installed on your computer and configure your boot loader menu to let you access them. You do not have to perform any configuration yourself.

If you want a Windows system installed on your computer, you should install it first. Windows would overwrite the boot loader installed by a previous Linux Mint system, cutting off access to the Linux system. If you installed Windows after having installed Linux Mint, you will need to re-install the Linux Mint GRUB boot loader. See the section at the end of this Chapter on re-installing the boot loader. There are several ways you can do it, most very simple.

If you have already installed Windows on your hard drive and configured it to take up the entire hard drive, you can select the "Install alongside" option during installation to free up space and set up Linux Mint partitions.

If you do have an operating system installed, but the "Install alongside" message does not appear, then be sure to use the "Something else" option. Otherwise, you may overwrite and destroy your installed operating system. On some Windows installs with the EFI bios, the Windows install may not appear. Be sure to choose "Something else" and then manually configure your partitions for Linux Mint.

For EFI Bios systems with Windows installs, the GRUB 2 boot loader that is installed with Linux Mint, will detect the EFI bios partition and list Windows as a boot option when you start up your system.

Tip: You can also use the Linux Mint Live DVD to start up Linux Mint and perform the necessary hard disk partitioning using GParted.

Installation Overview

Installing Linux Mint involves several processes, beginning with creating Linux partitions, then loading the Linux Mint software, selecting a time zone, and creating new Users and Groups. The installation program used for Linux Mint is a screen-based program that takes you through all these processes, step-by-step, as one continuous procedure. You can use either your mouse or the keyboard to make selections. When you finish with a screen, click the Continue button at the bottom to move to the next screen. If you need to move back to the previous screen, click Back. You can also press TAB, the arrow keys, SPACEBAR, and ENTER to make selections.

Check the Linux Mint User Guide, Installation of Linux Mint chapter, for a review of how to install Linux Mint. The Linux Mint User Guide can be downloaded as a PDF file from:

https://www.linuxmint.com/documentation.php

Linux Mint uses the same installation application and procedure as Ubuntu Linux. You can check the Ubuntu Linux documentation for Ubuntu 16.04 installation for a more detailed explanation, at:

https://help.ubuntu.com/16.04/installation-guide/index.html

Installation is a straightforward process. A graphical installation is easy to use, providing full mouse support.

Most systems today already meet hardware requirements and have automatic connections to the Internet.

They also support booting a DVD-ROM disc, though this support may have to be explicitly configured in the system BIOS.

If you are installing on a blank hard drive or on a drive with free space, or if you are performing a simple update that uses the same partitions, installing Linux Mint is a simple process. Linux Mint also features an automatic partitioning function that will perform the partitioning for you.

A preconfigured set of packages are installed, so you will not even have to select packages.

For a quick installation, you can simply start up the installation process by placing your DVD disc in the DVD drive and starting up your system. Graphical installation is a simple matter of following the instructions in each window as you progress. Installation follows a few easy stages:

1. **Welcome**   A default language is chosen for you, like English, so you can usually just click Continue.
2. **Preparing to install**   On the "Preparing to install" screen your system is checked and you can opt to install third party software and multimedia codecs.
3. **Installation type**   For automatic partitioning you have different options, depending on what other operating systems may have been installed on your hard drive. For drives that have other operating systems installed, you can install alongside them or choose to erase the entire disk. In all cases, you can also choose to partition your disk manually instead.
4. **Installation type: partitioner**   Used for manual partitioning only, in which you set up partitions yourself. Otherwise, this is skipped.
5. **Where are you? Time Zone**   Use the map to choose your time zone or select your city from the drop-down menu.
6. **Keyboard Layout**   A default is chosen for you; you can usually just click Continue.
7. **Who are you?**   Set up a username and hostname for your computer, as well as a password for that user. You can also choose to log in automatically, as well as encrypt your home folder.

After the installation, the DVD disc ejects and you will be asked to remove it and press ENTER. This will reboot your system.

Installation with the Linux Mint DVD

The Linux Mint DVD is designed for running Linux Mint from the DVD (Live DVD) and installing Linux Mint. Most users will use the Linux Mint DVD to install Linux Mint. You can first start up Linux Mint, and then initiate an installation, or install directly. Just place the DVD disc in the DVD-ROM drive before you start your computer. After you turn on or restart your computer, the installation program starts up.

Tip: Most computers are already set up to boot first from the DVD-ROM drive. If your computer cannot boot the DVD disc, then the boot sequence may be set up in the wrong order. You may first have to change the boot sequence

setting in your computer's BIOS so that the computer will try to boot first from the DVD-ROM. This requires some technical ability and knowledge of how to set your motherboard's BIOS configuration.

On most screens, a Continue button is displayed on the lower-right corner of an installation dialog. Once finished with a screen, click Continue to move on. In some cases, you will be able to click a Back button to return to a previous screen. As each screen appears in the installation, default entries will be selected, usually by the auto-probing capability of the installation program. If these entries are correct, you can click Continue to accept them and go on to the next screen.

When the Linux Mint DVD first boots, a text screen first appears with the following options:

```
Start Linux Mint 18.2 Cinnamon 64-bit
Start Linux Mint 18.2 Cinnamon 64-bit (compatibility mode)
OEM install (for manufacturers)
Check the integrity of the medium
```

This menu is displayed for each edition. The Mate, KDE, and Xfce DVDs will have those names instead of Cinnamon. Use the compatibility mode if you are not sure your video card will support the Live DVD desktop. The OEM install starts up the install process in system manufacturer mode, letting you install the same configuration on several systems. There is no longer a separate OEM edition.

Welcome and Language

On the Live CD desktop, click the "Install Linux Mint" icon to start up the installation (see Figure 2-1). The Install window opens to the Welcome screen for choosing your language, but without the button for choosing to try Linux Mint. Click the Continue button to start the installation.

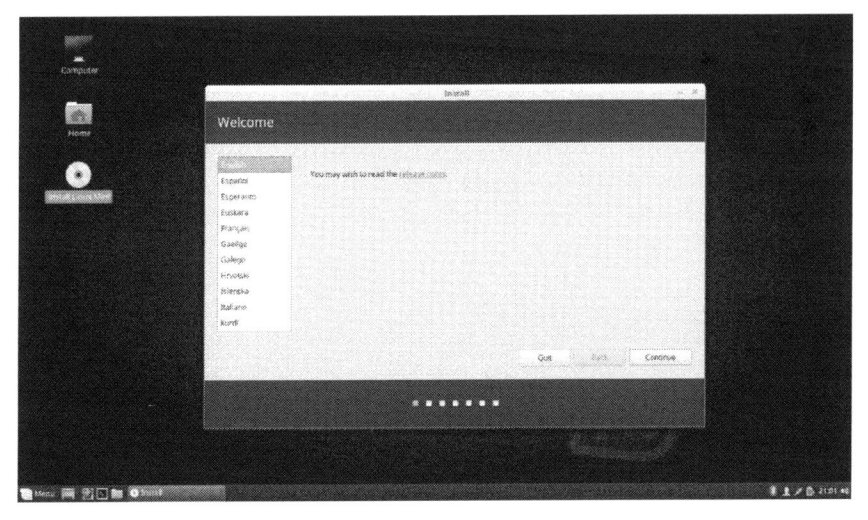

Figure 2-1: Live DVD (Desktop) with Install icon.

Preparing to install (third party software)

The "Preparing to install Linux Mint" dialog appears with an option to install third party software, such as multimedia codecs and Adobe Flash (see Figure 2-2). Leaving this option unchecked, installs the equivalent of the "no codecs" releases from earlier versions. If you live in a region that may require software patents and licenses, in particular, for multimedia codecs, you should not check this prompt. Checking the option installs all available codecs. Click the Continue button to continue.

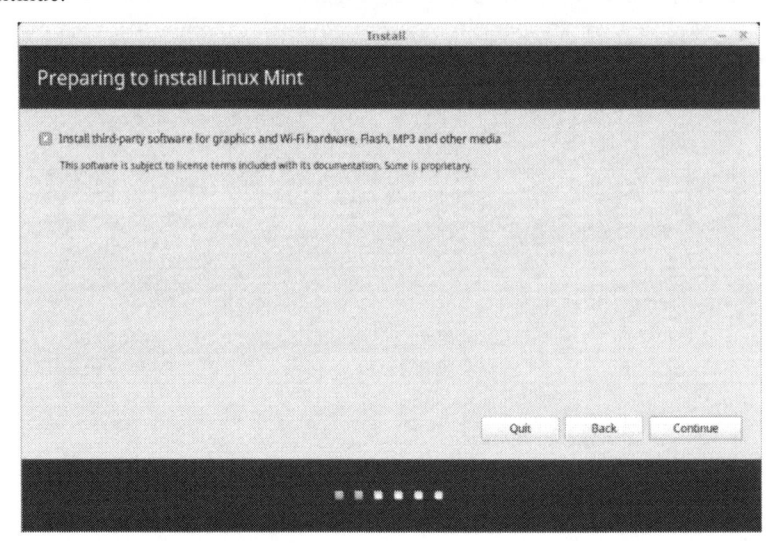

Figure 2-2: Install Third-Party Software

Click the Continue button to continue. Your system then detects your hardware, providing any configuration specifications that may be required.

Installation type

You are now asked to designate the Linux partitions and hard disk configurations you want to use on your hard drives. Linux Mint provides automatic partitioning that covers most situations, like using a blank or new hard drive and overwriting old partitions on a hard drive. Linux Mint can even repartition a system with an operating system that uses all of the hard drive, but with unused space within it. In this case, the install procedure reduces the space used by the original operating system and installs Linux Mint on the new free space. A default partition layout sets up a swap partition and a root partition of type **ext4** (Linux native) for the kernel and applications.

Alternatively, you can configure your hard disk manually (the "Something else" option). Linux Mint provides a very simple partitioning tool you can use to set up Linux partitions.

For multiple boot systems using Windows, Linux Mint automatically detects a Windows system.

No partitions will be changed or formatted until you click the "Install Now" button. You can opt out of the installation until then, and your original partitions will remain untouched.

Warning: The "Erase disk and install Linux Mint" option will wipe out any existing partitions on the selected hard drive. If you want to preserve any partitions on that drive, like Windows or other Linux partitions, always choose a different option such as "Install Linux Mint alongside ..." or "Something else".

You are given choices, depending on the state of the hard disk you choose. A hard disk could be blank, have an older Linux Mint operating system on it, or have a different operating system, such as Windows, already installed. If an operating system is already installed, it may take up the entire disk or may only use part of the disk, with the remainder available for the Linux Mint installation.

Tip: Some existing Linux systems may use several Linux partitions. Some of these may be used for just the system software, such as the boot and root partitions. These can be formatted. Others may have extensive user files, such as a /home partition that normally holds user home directories and all the files they have created. You should *not* format such partitions.

No detected operating systems

If no operating systems are detected on the hard drive, which is the case with a drive with only data files or a blank hard drive, you are given four choices: to use the entire disk, to additionally encrypt the entire disk, to use LVM instead of standard partitions, or to specify partitions manually (see Figure 2-3). Encryption and LVM are options that you can choose in addition to the "Erase disk and install Linux Mint option." They have square buttons. The message displayed on the Installation type dialog is:

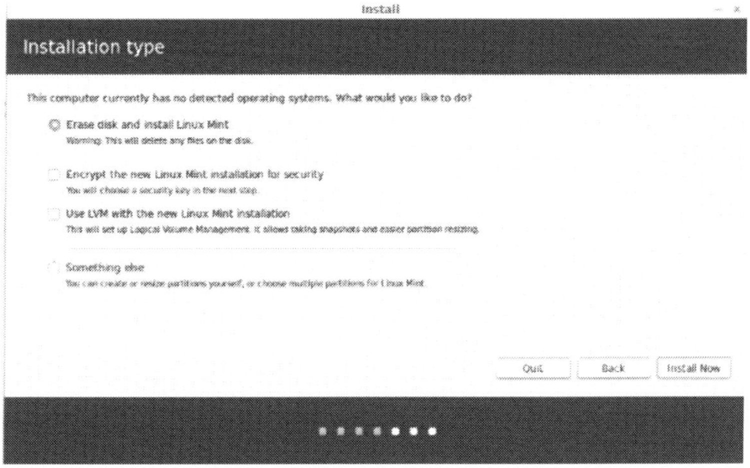

Figure 2-3: No detected operating systems

"This computer currently has no detected operating systems. What would you like to do?"

You are given four choices.

```
Erase disk and install Linux Mint
Encrypt the new Linux Mint installation for security
```

```
Use LVM with the new Linux Mint installation
Something else
```

If you choose to install Linux Mint without LVM, your hard drive is automatically partitioned creating two partitions, a primary partition for your entire file system (a root file system, /), and a swap partition. The swap partition is set up as a logical partition within an extended partition.

Use LVM

With the "Use LVM with the new Linux Mint installation" option, LVM partitions are set up using physical and logical volumes, which can be added to and replaced easily. A small standard ext4 partition is set up to hold the boot directory. Then an LVM physical volume is set up, which contains two LVM logical volumes, one for the swap space and one for the root.

Encrypt the disk

The "Encrypt the new Linux Mint installation for security" option lets you encrypt your entire system with a password. You cannot access your system without that password. The encryption option will destroy any existing partitions if there are any, creating new partitions. Your hard drive will then have only your new Linux Mint system on it. On the "Choose a security key" screen that follows you are prompted to enter a security key (password), along with the option to overwrite empty space. After installation, whenever you start up your system, you are prompted to first enter that security key.

Detected Linux Mint operating system

If you have another Linux Mint operating system on your disk, you will have the option to erase the Linux Mint system and replace it with Linux Mint 18.2. If the installed Linux Mint system is version 16, then you are also given the option to upgrade your system, preserving your personal files and installed software. You are also given the option to erase the installed operating system, and install the new system.

If the current system has enough unused space, you are also given an install alongside option, resizing the disk to free up space and installing 18.2 in added partitions on the free space. This will keep your original Linux system, as well as install the new one.

The message displayed on the Installation type dialog is something like this:

"This computer currently has Linux Mint 16 on it. What would you like to do?"

You are given three choices. The Upgrade Linux Mint option is selected by default.

If you choose to Erase Linux Mint and reinstall, you can also choose the options to encrypt the drive and to use LVM partitions.

On systems that also have Windows installed alongside Linux Mint, you are given the same options, but with an added option to erase everything including your Windows system. You are warned that both Windows and Linux Mint are installed on your system. Should you choose to erase Linux Mint 18.2 and reinstall (the first entry), your Windows system will be preserved.

Detected other operating systems with free space

If you have another operating system on your disk that has been allocated use of part of the disk, you will have an option beginning with "Install Linux Mint alongside" with the name of the installed operating system listed. For example, a system with Windows XP already installed will have the option "Install Linux Mint alongside Microsoft Windows ". This option is selected initially.

The message displayed on the Installation type dialog is:

"This computer currently has Microsoft Windows XP Professional on it. What would you like to do?"

If you do have an operating system installed, but this message does not appear, then be sure to use the "Something else" option. Otherwise, you may overwrite and destroy your installed operating system. On some Windows installs with the EFI bios, the Windows install may not appear. Be sure to choose "Something else" and then manually configure your partitions for Linux Mint.

Detected other operating system using entire disk (resize)

If you have another operating system on your disk that has been allocated use of the entire disk, you will have an option beginning with "Install Linux Mint alongside" with the name of the installed operating system listed. A system with Windows XP already installed will have the option "Install Linux Mint alongside Microsoft Windows XP Professional" (see Figure 2-12). This option is selected initially.

This option is designed for use on hard disks with no unallocated free space but with a large amount of unused space on an existing partition. This is the case for a system where a partition has already been allocated the entire disk. This option will perform a resize of the existing partition, reducing that partition, preserving the data on it, and then creating a Linux Mint partition on that free space. Be warned that this could be a very time-consuming operation. If the original operating system was used heavily, the disk could be fragmented, with files stored all over the hard disk. In this case, the files have to be moved to one area of the hard disk, freeing up continuous space on the remaining area. If the original operating system was used very lightly, then there may be unused continuous space already on the hard drive. In this case, re-partitioning would be quick.

On the "Install alongside" dialog two partitions are displayed, the original showing the new size it will have after the resize, and the new partition for Linux Mint 18.2 formed from the unused space. The size is automatically determined. You can adjust the size if you want by clicking on the space between the partitions to display a space icon, which you can drag left, or right to change the proportional sizes of the partitions.

Upon clicking the Install Now button, a dialog will prompt you with the warning that the resize cannot be undone, and that it may take a long time. Click Continue to perform the resize, or click Go Back to return to the "Installation type" screen. The time it will take depends on the amount of fragmentation on the disk.

Something else

All install situations will include a "Something else" option to let you partition the hard drive manually. The "Something else" option starts up the partitioner, which will let you create, edit, and delete partitions. You can set your own size and type for your partitions. Use this option to preserve or reuse any existing partitions. When you have finished making your changes, click the Install Now button to continue. At this point, your partitions are changed and software is installed, while you continue with the remaining install configuration for time zone and user login.

The partitioner screen displays the partitions on your current hard disk, and lists options for creating your Linux partitions. A graphical bar at the top shows the current state of your hard disk, showing any existing partitions, if any, along with their sizes and labels.

A Boot Loader section at the bottom of the screen provides a drop-down menu of hard drives where you can install the boot loader (see Figure 2-6). Your first hard drive is selected by default. If you have several hard drives on your system, you can choose the one on which to install the boot loader. Systems with only one hard drive, such as laptops, have only one hard drive entry.

The partitioner interface lists any existing partitions (see Figure 2-8). The graphical bar at the top will show the partition on your selected hard drive. The depiction changes as you add, delete, or edit your partitions. Each partition device name and label will be displayed. Unused space will be labeled as free space.

Each hard disk is labeled by its device name, such as **sda** for the first Serial ATA device. Underneath the hard disk graphics bar are labels for the partitions and free space available, along with the partition type and size. The partitions are identified by their colors. At the bottom of the screen are actions you can perform on partitions and free space. To the right are the "New partition table" and Revert buttons for the entire disk. To the left are add, delete, and edit buttons for partitions (+, -, and Change). Your current hard disks and their partitions are listed in the main scrollable pane, with headings for Device, Type, Mount point, Format, Size, and Used space for each partition.

Creating new partitions on a blank hard drive manually

To create partitions on a blank hard drive manually, choose "Something else". The partitioner interface starts up with the "Installation type" screen, listing any existing partitions. For a blank hard drive, the hard drive only is listed in the main pane.

For a new blank hard drive, you first create the partition table by clicking the New Partition Table button (see Figure 2-4). This displays a warning that it will erase any data on the drive. Click Continue. The warning dialog is there in case you accidentally click the New Partition Table button on a drive that has partitions you want to preserve. In this case, you can click Go Back and no new partition table is created.

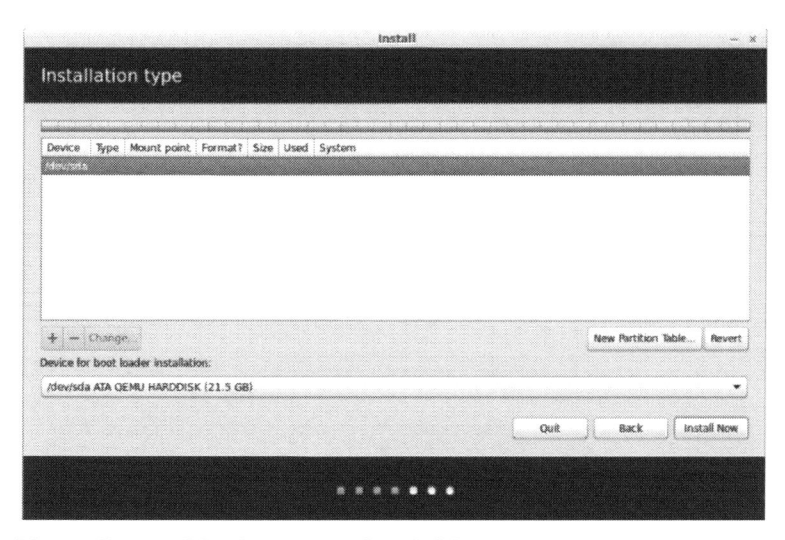

Figure 2-4: Manually partitioning a new hard drive

Once the new partition table is set up, the free space entry appears and a graphical bar at the top shows the free space (see Figure 2-5). If your system already has an operating system installed that takes up only part of the disk, you do not need to create a new partition table. Your free space is already listed (see Figure 2-6).

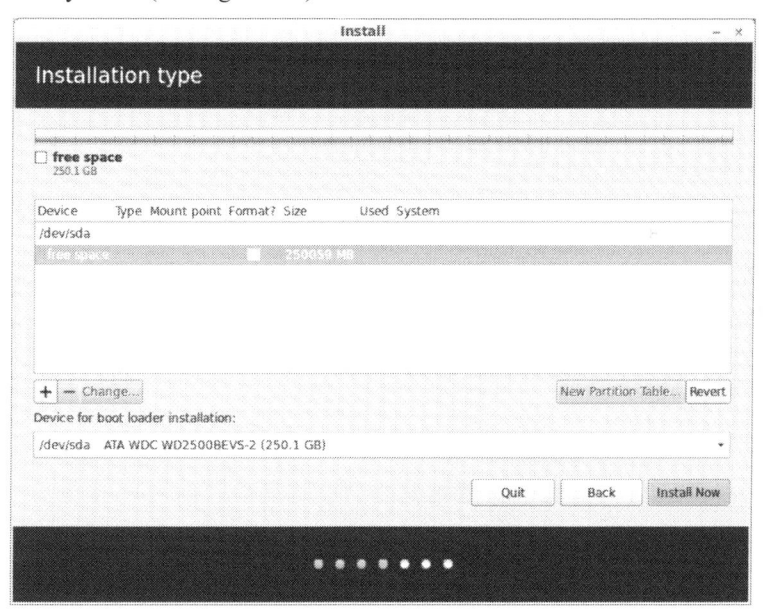

Figure 2-5: Select free space on a blank hard drive

50 Part 1: Getting Started

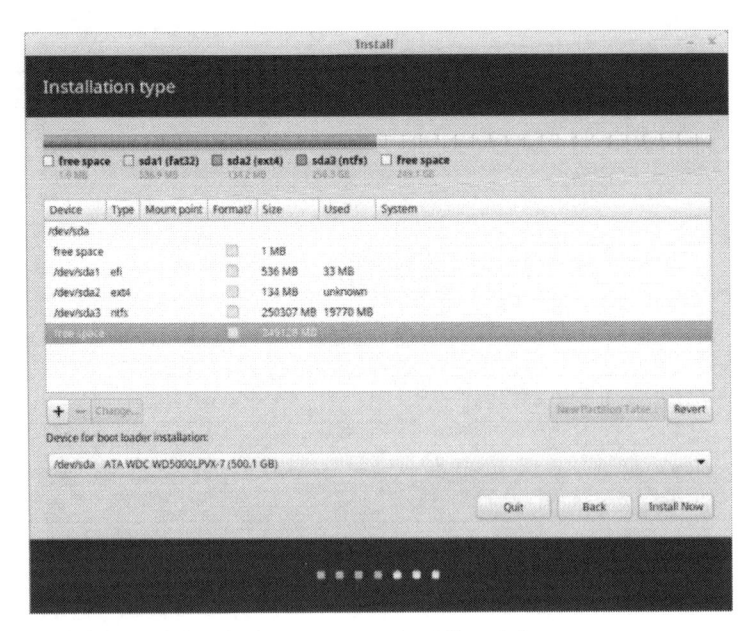

Figure 2-6: Hard drive with windows on part of the drive

For Linux Mint, you will have to create at least two partitions, one swap and the other a Linux partition, where your system will be installed. To create a new partition, select the free space entry for the hard disk (see Figure 2-5) and click the + button. This opens a Create Partition dialog where you can choose the file system type (Use as) and the size of your partition. Do this for each partition.

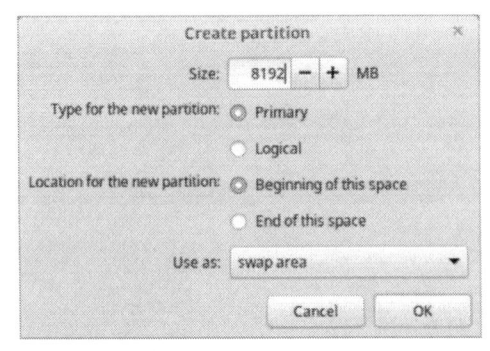

Figure 2-7: Create a new swap partition

The Create Partition dialog displays entries for the partition type (Primary or Logical), the size in megabytes, the location (beginning or end), the file system type (Use as), and the Mount point. For the partition type, the "Do not use" partition entry is initially selected. Choose a partition type from the drop-down menu. Select "Ext4 journaling file system" for the root partition and choose Swap for the swap partition.

The swap partition will have no mount point. You only set the size, normally to the amount of your computer's RAM memory (see Figure 2-7).

For the root partition, from the Mount point drop down menu choose the mount point /, which is the root directory (see Figure 2-8). This is where your system will be installed. The size of the partition is specified in megabytes. It will be set to the remaining space. If you have not already set up the swap partition, reduce the size to allow space for the swap partition.

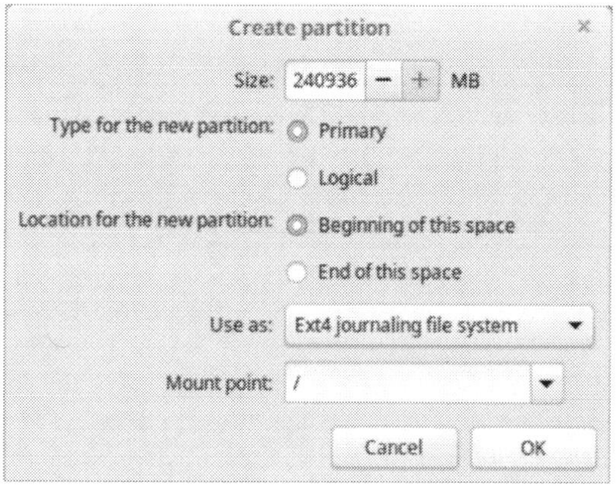

Figure 2-8: Create a new root partition

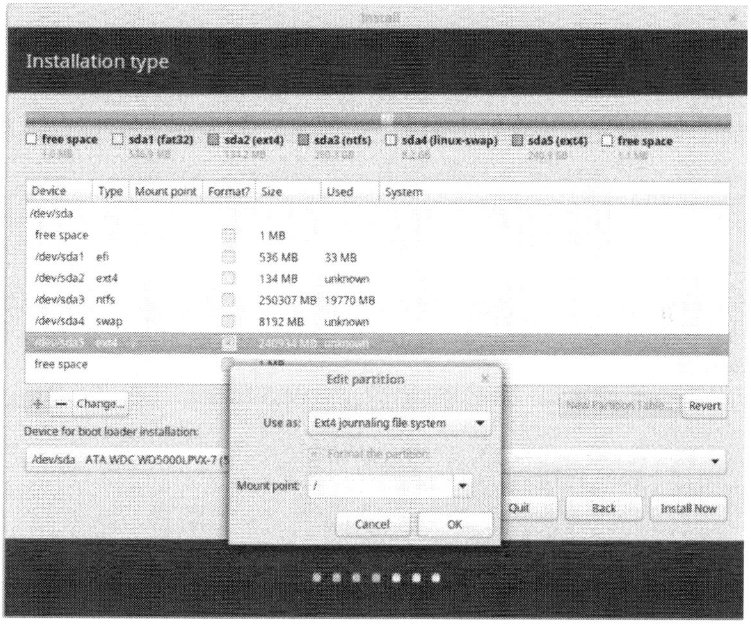

Figure 2-9: Manual partitions

If you make a mistake, you can edit a partition by selecting it and clicking the Change button. This opens an Edit partitions window where you can make changes. You can also delete a partition, returning its space to free space, and then create a new one. Select the partition and click the - button (delete). The partition is not actually deleted at this point. No changes are made at all until you start installing Linux Mint. The "Revert" button is always available to undo all the changes you specified so far, and start over from the original state of the hard disk.

When you have finished setting up your partitions, you will see entries for them displayed. The graphical bar at the top will show their size and location (see Figure 2-9). Most computers now use the EFI bios, which requires a small EFI boot partition on the hard disk. This partition is automatically added. You will see it listed along with the ext4 and swap partitions.

Click the "Install Now" button to perform the partitioning, formatting, and installation. A dialog opens that lists the changes to be made to the disk, specifying which partitions will be formatted. Click the Continue button to make the changes.

Reuse existing Linux partitions on a hard drive

If you already have a hard drive with Linux partitions that you want to reuse, you choose the "Something else" option on the "Installation type" screen. In this case, you have a hard disk you are using for Linux, with partitions already set up on the hard drive for your Linux Mint systems. However, you do not want to keep any of the data on those partitions. This situation occurs if you are using a previous Linux Mint version, but want a fresh install instead of an upgrade, and you do not want to perform any partitioning, keeping the current partition configuration. You can just overwrite the existing Linux Mint root partition. In effect, you just want to reuse those partitions for the new release, creating an entirely new install, but with the old partitions. With this action, all current data on those partitions will be destroyed. This procedure avoids having to change the partition table on the hard drive. You just keep the partitions you already have. In this case, you wish to overwrite existing partitions, erasing all the data on them.

This procedure is used often for users that have already backed up their data, and just want to create a fresh install on their hard disk with the new release. Also, a Linux system could be configured to save data on a partition separate from the root partition, like a separate partition for the **/home** directories. In this case, you would only need to overwrite the root partition, leaving the other Linux partitions alone.

Note: The New partition table becomes active whenever the top-level hard drive device name is selected instead of a particular partition. This will be initially selected when your Prepare partition screen is first displayed, activating the New partition table button. Do NOT click that button. It will wipe out any existing partitions.

To edit an existing partition, click on its entry and click the Change button. A dialog opens with entries for the partition type (Use as), a format checkbox, and the mount point.

To re-use partitions, all you have to do is edit your existing root partition. You will see your partitions listed. You can leave the swap partition alone.

You will have to know which partition is your root partition. It will have the type **ext4** and the mount point /. Once selected, the Change button will become active, which you click to open an Edit window. Select the type, which for Linux Mint 18.2 would be "Ext4 journaling file system", the **ext4** file system type. Then select the mount point, which, for the root partition, is /. The size remains the same. Once finished, you will see your Windows partition (**ntfs**) if there is one, as well as the swap and Linux root partition (**ext4**).

Once you have edited the root partition, you can click the "Install Now" button to continue on.

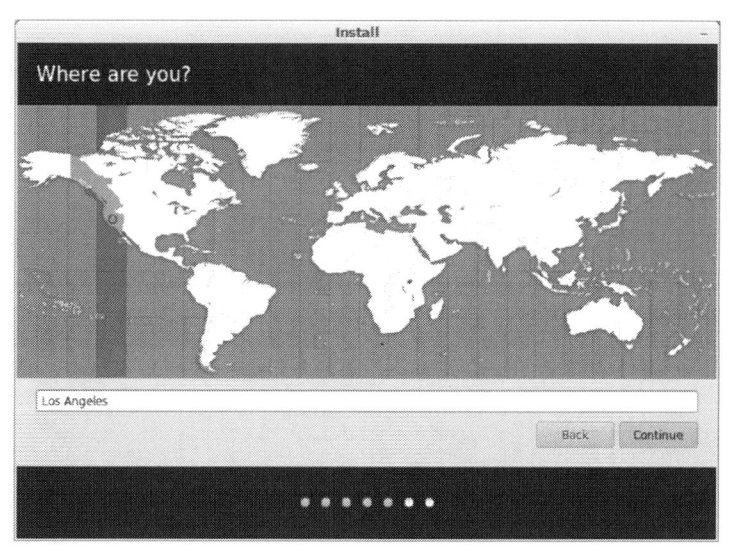

Figure 2-10: Where Are You, Time zone

Where Are You?

On the "Where are you?" screen, you can set the time zone by using a map to specify your location (see Figure 2-10). The Time Zone tool uses a map feature that displays the entire earth, with sections for each time zone. Click on your general location, and the entire time zone for your part of the world will be highlighted in green. The major city closest to your location will be labeled with its current time. The selected city will appear in the text box located below the map. You can also select your time zone entering the city in the text box below. As you type in the city name, a pop-up menu appears showing progressively limited choices. The corresponding time zone will be highlighted on the map.

Click the Continue button to continue.

At the same time as the "Where are you?" dialog appears, Linux Mint begins to format your partitions, copy files to your hard drive, and install the software. A progress bar at the bottom of the dialog shows the progression of the copy process. You can click an expansion arrow next to the progress bar to open a small terminal section that displays the install operations as they occur.

Keyboard Layout

You are then asked to select a keyboard layout, "Choose your keyboard layout." Keyboard entries are selected first by location in the left scroll box, and then by type on the right scroll box. A default is already selected, such as English (US) (see Figure 2-11). If the selection is not correct, you can choose another keyboard, first by location in the left scroll box, and then by type on the right scroll box.

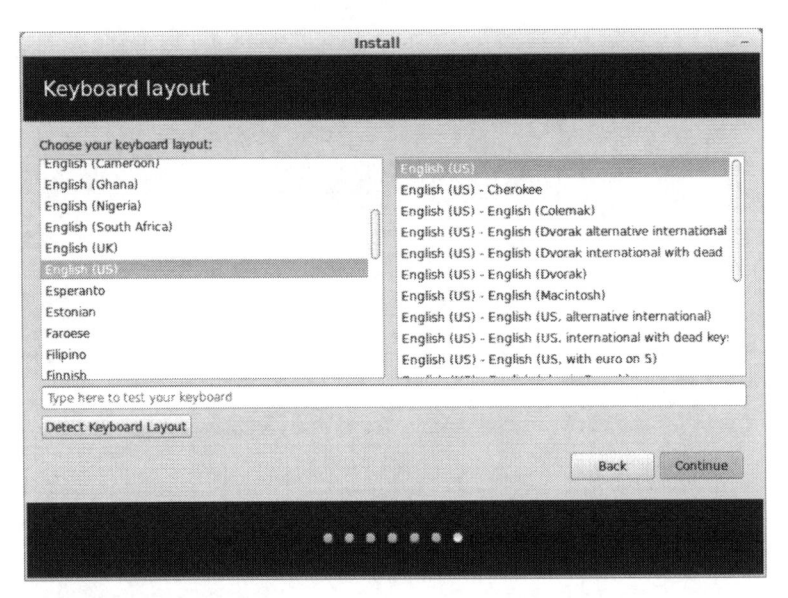

Figure 2-11: Keyboard Layout

To test your keyboard, click on the text box at the bottom of the screen and press keys, "Type here to test your keyboard."

The "Detect Keyboard Layout" button tries to detect the keyboard using your input. A series of dialogs opens, prompting you to press keys and asking you if certain keys are present on your keyboard. When the dialogs finish, the detected keyboard is then selected in the "Choose your keyboard layout" scroll boxes.

Click the Continue button to continue.

Who Are You?

On the Who are you? screen you enter your name, your user login name, and password (see Figure 2-12). When you enter your name, a username will be generated for you using your first name, and a computer name will be entered using your first name and your computer's make and model name. You can change these names if you want. The name for the computer is the computer's network hostname. The user you are creating will have administrative access, allowing you to change your system configuration, add new users and printers, and install new software. When you enter your password a Strength notice is displayed indicating whether it is too short, weak, fair, or good. For a good password include numbers and uppercase characters.

At the bottom of the screen, you have the options: "Log in automatically" and "Require my password to log in." The "Require my password to log in" option has an additional check box for "Encrypt my home folder." Choose the "Log in automatically" option to have your system login to your account when you start up, instead of stopping at the login screen. The "Require my password to log in" entry provides a standard login screen. If you choose "Encrypt my home folder" private directory encryption is set up for your home folder, encrypting all the home folder files and subdirectories.

Figure 2-12: Who are you?

If your computer supports a camera, the next screen will prompt you to choose an image to use for the user. You can choose an icon or snap a picture of yourself.

Note: Migration assistant for importing accounts from other operating systems is no longer supported in the installer.

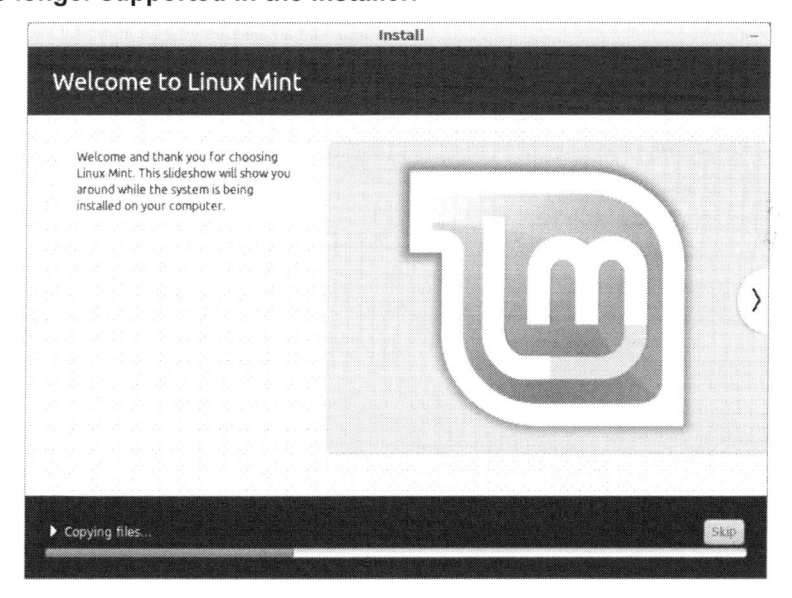

Figure 2-13: Install progress slide show

Install Progress

Your installation continues with a slide show of Linux Mint 18.2 features such as Web browsers, services, Software Manager, and photo editing. You can click on the arrow tabs at either end to move through the slide show manually (see Figure 2-13).

Once finished, the Installation Complete dialog appears. Click the Restart Now button to restart and reboot to the new installation. Your DVD disc is ejected, and a screen will appear prompting you to remove the disc, and then press ENTER. If you installed from the Live DVD session, you are also given the option to return to the Live DVD session.

Tip: Pressing ESC from the graphics menu places you at the boot prompt for text mode install.

Recovery, rescue, and boot loader re-install

Linux Mint provides the means to start up systems that have failed for some reason. A system that may boot but fails to start up, can be started in a recovery mode, already set up for you as an entry on your boot loader menu.

Recovery Mode

If for some reason your system is not able to start up, it may be due to conflicting configurations, libraries, or applications. On the GRUB menu first choose the recovery mode entry, the Linux Mint kernel entry with the (recovery mode) label attached to the end (see Figure 3-1). This starts up a menu where you can use the arrow and ENTER keys to select from several recovery options (see Figure 2-14). These include resume, clean, dpkg, grub, network, and root. Short descriptions for each item are displayed on the menu.

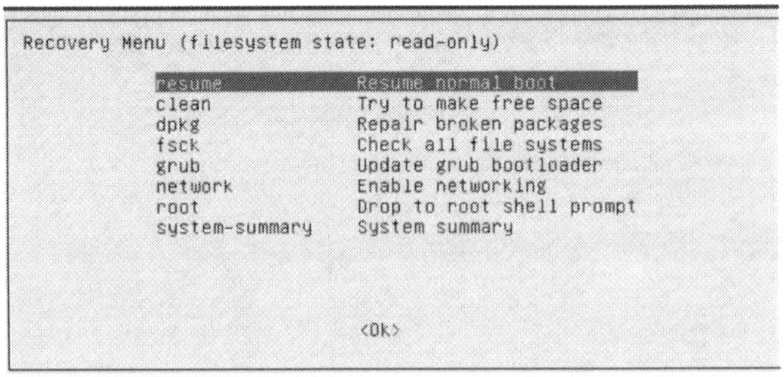

Figure 2-14: Recovery options

The root option starts up Linux Mint as the root user with a command line shell prompt. In this case, you can boot your Linux system in a recovery mode and then edit configuration files with a text editor such as Vi, remove the suspect libraries, or reinstall damaged software with **apt-get**.

The resume entry will start up Linux Mint normally, but into the command line mode.

The **grub** entry will update the grub boot loader. With GRUB2 your hard drive is re-scanned, detecting your installed operating systems and Linux Mint kernels, and implementing any GRUB configuration changes you may have made without updating GRUB.

To rescue a broken system, choose the **root** entry. Your broken system will be mounted and made accessible with a command line interface. You can then use command line operations and editors to fix configuration files.

Re-Installing the Boot Loader

If you have a multiple-boot system, that runs both Windows and Linux on the same machine, you may run into a situation where you have to reinstall your GRUB boot loader. This problem occurs if your Windows system completely crashes beyond repair and you have to install a new version of Windows, if you added Windows to your machine after having installed Linux, or if you upgraded to a new version of Windows. A Windows installation will automatically overwrite your bootloader (alternatively, you could install your boot loader on your Linux partition instead of the master boot record, MBR). You will no longer be able to access your Linux system.

You can reinstall your boot loader manually, using your Linux Mint DVD live session. The procedure is more complicated, as you have to mount your Linux Mint system. On the Linux Mint DVD Live session, you can use GParted to find out what partition your Linux Mint system uses. In a terminal window, create a directory on which to mount the system.

```
sudo mkdir mymint
```

Then mount it, making sure you have the correct file system type and partition name (usually **/dev/sda5** on dual boot systems).

```
sudo mount -t ext4 /dev/sda5 mymint
```

Then use **grub-install** and the device name of your first partition to install the boot loader, with the **--root-directory** option to specify the directory where you mounted your Linux Mint file system. The **--root-directory** option requires a full path name, which for the Linux Mint DVD would be **/home/mint** for the home directory. Using the **mymint** directory for this example, the full path name of the Linux Mint file system would be **/home/mint/mymint**. You would then enter the following **grub-install** command.

```
sudo grub-install --root-directory=/home/mint/mymint /dev/sda
```

This will re-install your current GRUB boot loader. You can then reboot, and the GRUB boot loader will start up.

3. Usage Basics: Login, Desktop, Network, and Help

Accessing your Linux Mint System

LightDM Display Manager

Linux Mint Desktops (Cinnamon, Mate, KDE, and Xfce)

Network Connections: wired and wireless

Help Resources

Command Line Interface

Terminal Window

Using Linux Mint is an intuitive process, with easy-to-use interfaces, including graphical logins and desktops, including the Cinnamon, Mate, and KDE Linux Mint desktops. Even the standard Linux command line interface is user-friendly with editable commands, history lists, and cursor-based tools. To start using Linux Mint, you have to know how to access your system and, once you are on the system, how to execute commands and run applications. Access is provided by a display manager that provides a graphical login.

Accessing Your Linux Mint System

You access your Linux Mint system using the GRUB bootloader to first start Linux Mint, and then use the display manager to log in to your account. Linux Mint, like Ubuntu, uses the systemd login manager, logind, to manage logins and sessions, replacing consolekit, which is no longer supported. You can configure login manager options with the **/etc/systemd/logind.conf** file. You can set options such as the number of terminals (default is 6), the idle action, and hardware key operations, such as the power key. Check the **logind.conf** man page for details.

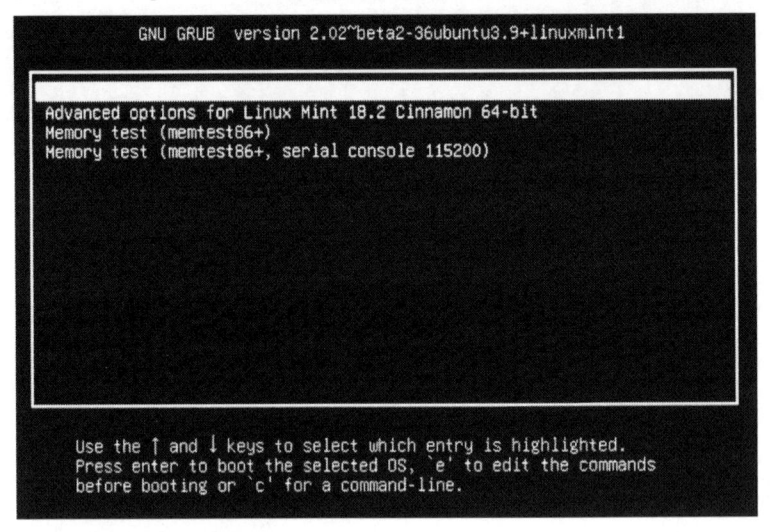

Figure 3-1: Linux Mint GRUB menu

GRUB Boot Loader

When your system starts, the GRUB boot loader will quickly select your default operating system and start up its login screen. If you have just installed Linux Mint, the default operating system will be Linux Mint.

If you have installed more than one operating system, you can select one using the GRUB menu. The GRUB menu is displayed for several seconds at startup, before loading the default operating system automatically. Press any key to have GRUB wait until you have made a selection. Your GRUB menu is displayed as shown in Figure 3-1. The recovery entry allows you to start Linux Mint in recovery mode.

The GRUB menu lists Linux Mint and other operating systems installed on your hard drive, such as Windows. Use the arrow keys to move to the entry you want and press ENTER

For graphical installations, some displays may have difficulty running the graphical startup display. If you have this problem, you can edit your Linux GRUB entry and remove the **splash** term at the end of the **linux** line. Press the **e** key to edit a GRUB entry (see Figure 3-2). To change a particular line, use the up/down arrow keys to move to the line. You can use the left/right arrow keys to move along the line. The Backspace key will delete characters and typing will insert characters. The editing changes are temporary. Permanent changes can only be made by directly editing the GRUB configuration **/etc/default/grub** file, and then running the following command:

```
sudo update-grub
```

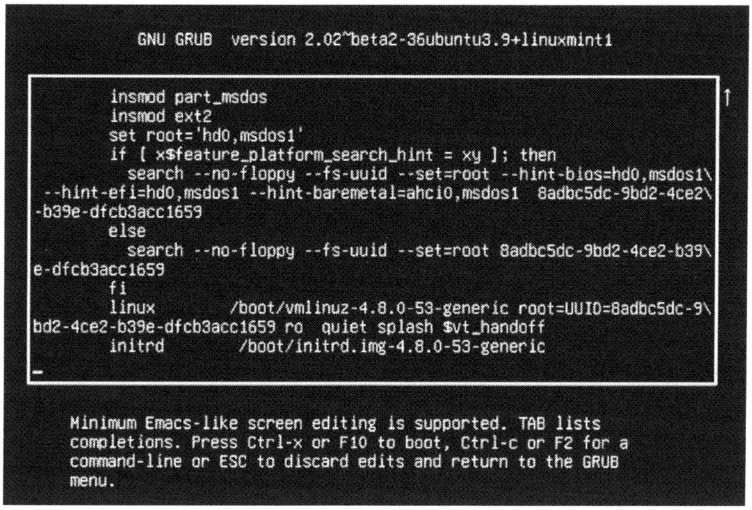

Figure 3-2: Editing a GRUB menu item

When your Linux Mint operating system starts up, a Linux Mint logo appears during the startup. You can press the ESC key to see the startup messages instead. Linux Mint uses Plymouth with its kernel modesetting ability to display a startup animation. The Plymouth Linux Mint logo theme is used by default.

The LightDM Display Manager

The graphical login interface displays a login window listing a menu of usernames. The currently selected username displays a text box where you then enter your password. Upon pressing ENTER, you log in to the selected account and your desktop starts up. Graphical logins are handled by the LightDM display manager. The LightDM manages the login interface along with authenticating a user password and username, and then starting up a selected desktop. LightDM replaces the older Mint Display Manager (MDM), though the Mint implementation of LgithDM uses a customized greeter called Slick Greeter. LightDM and Slick Greeter can be configured with the System Settings Login Window dialog. You can also configure Slick Greeter with the dconf editor (**x.dm.slick-greeter**).

From the LightDM, you can shift to the command line interface with the CTRL-ALT-F1 keys, and then shift back to the LightDM with the CTRL-ALT-F8 keys. The keys F1 through F6 provide different command line terminals, as in CTRL-ALT-F3 for the third command line terminal.

When LightDM starts up, it shows a list of users, displaying a dialog that lets you enter a username at the login prompt. You can use your mouse or arrow keys to move through the list of users, displaying a login dialog for the currently selected user (see Figure 3-3). The login dialog displays the user's proper name. Below the username is a text box for entering a password. Once the password is entered, press ENTER. The desktop then starts up. If you log out from a user desktop, you will return to the LightDM login screen.

Figure 3-3: LightDM Login Screen with user list

To top right corner of the screen shows a power icon. When you click this icon, a menu appears with entries Suspend or Quit. Clicking the Quit entry displays a dialog with Shutdown or Restart buttons. Click the close box to cancel (see Figure 3-4). To shut down your Linux Mint system, click the Shut Down icon. You can also shut down the system directly from the desktop. The top right corner also shows current keyboard, time, and an assistive technology button. Click on the assistive technology button to display a menu for the onscreen keyboard, high contrast display, and the screen reader (voice). The top left corner shows your computer's hostname.

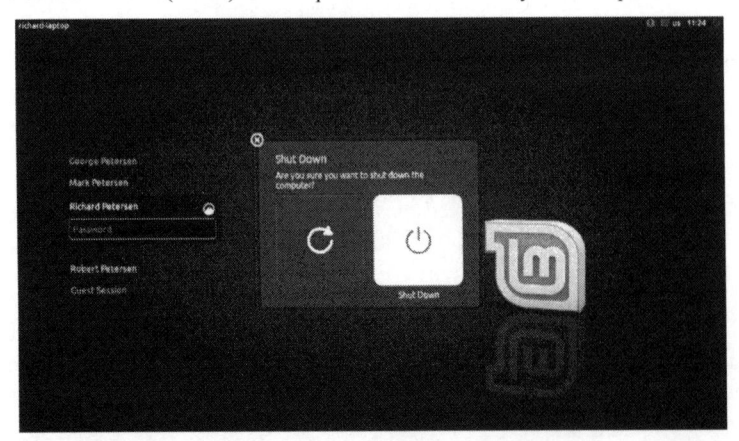

Figure 3-4: LightDM Login Screen with Shut Down options

In the top right corner of each login entry is a sessions button. The session button displays an emblem indicating the currently selected desktop. There are emblems for Cinnamon, MATE,

KDE, and Xfce. If you have installed more than one desktop interface, such as Linux Mint MATE, you can use the session menu to choose one. Click on the session button to display the session menu (see Figure 3-5) from which you can select the desktop interface you want to start up. The menu shows all installed possible desktop interfaces. Here you can choose MATE to use the MATE Desktop, "Xfce Session" to use the Xfce desktop or Cinnamon for the Cinnamon desktop. Use the arrow keys or mouse to choose a selection. Once you have made the selection click the back arrow to return to the login entry. A desktop option is not shown unless you have already installed that desktop, such as MATE (use the **mint-meta** packages to install a desktop, such as **mint-meta-mate** for MATE). The default session is the last desktop you logged out of.

Figure 3-5: LightDM Login screen with desktop choices

Login Window Preferences

You can configure your login screen using Login Window dialog, accessible from System Settings Login Screen and from the Administration menu as Login Window. The Login Window dialog shows display options such as the theme, bachground image, and logo (see Figure 3-6). You can choose a desktop (GTK) theme, and icon theme, a background image or color, and a background logo. The default theme is Mint-X. You choose an image for your background and logo. You can also decide whether to display your hostname, and to allow guest logins. Configuration files for LightDM are located in the **/etc/lightdm** folder

64 Part 1: Getting Started

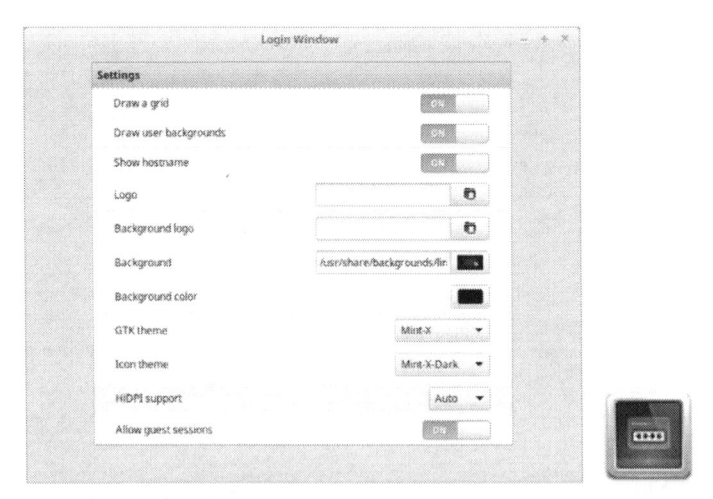

Figure 3-6: Login Window Preferences

Turning off the draw grid and show hostname options removes them from the login screen (see Figure 3-7).

Figure 3-7: Login Window with no grid and no hostname

To set up an automatic login for a user, you can edit the **/etc/lightdm/lightdm.conf** file and set the autologin options. The autologin-user sets the user to be automatically logged in and autologin-user-timeout sets a time delay, to allow login as another user. The autologin-guest option logins a quest user. It is set to false by default.

/etc/lightdm/lightdm.conf

```
[Seat"*]
autologin-guest=false
autologin-user=richard
autologin-user-timeout=0
```

Lock Screen and Switch User

You can choose to lock your screen and suspend your system by choosing the Lock entry in the desktop menu, or by pressing Ctrl-Alt-L. You are first asked to enter an away message. Click OK to start the lock screen. The Screen shows the time and date. To start up again, press the spacebar and the Lock Screen dialog appears (see Figure 3-8). Click the Unlock button to start up your desktop session again.

You can switch to another user by clicking the Switch User button on the Logout dialog or on the lock screen. The LightDM login screen starts up and you can login as another user. When you log out, you are returned to the lock screen and prompted for the last user that you switched from. To login as another user, click the Switch User button to display the LightDM login screen. Users already logged in will have a "Already logged in" note below their username on the face browser.

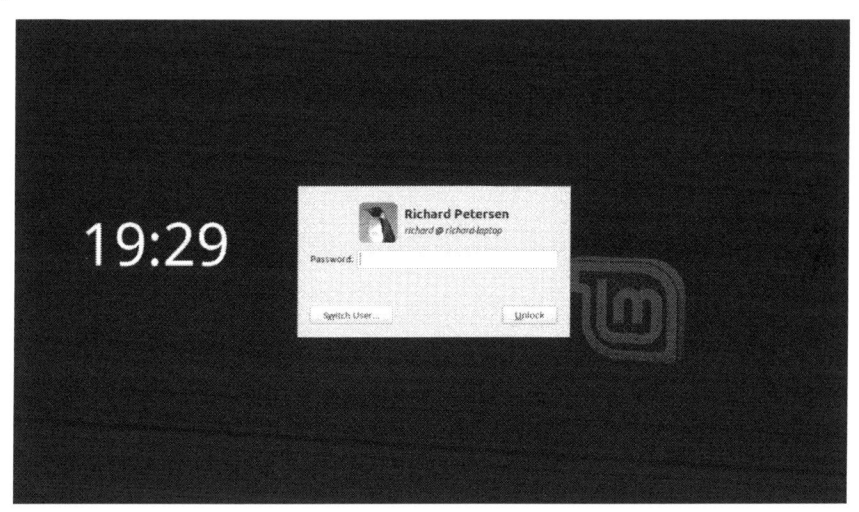

Figure 3-8: Lock Screen

Shut down and Logging out

To shut down from the Linux Mint, click the power button on the desktop menu (Cinnamon or Mate). A dialog opens with the shutdown options: Suspend, Hibernate, Restart, and Shut Down (see Figure 3-9).

There are several ways to shut down your system:

Click the power button on the desktop menu to display the shutdown dialog (see Figure 3-9).

On Cinnamon, choose the Power Off entry on the user applet menu.

Press the power button on your computer to open the shutdown dialog.

Should your display freeze or become corrupted, one safe way to shut down and restart is to press a command line interface key (like CTRL-ALT-F1) to revert to the command line

66 Part 1: Getting Started

interface, and then press CTRL-ALT-DEL to restart. You can also log in on the command line interface and then enter the **sudo poweroff** command.

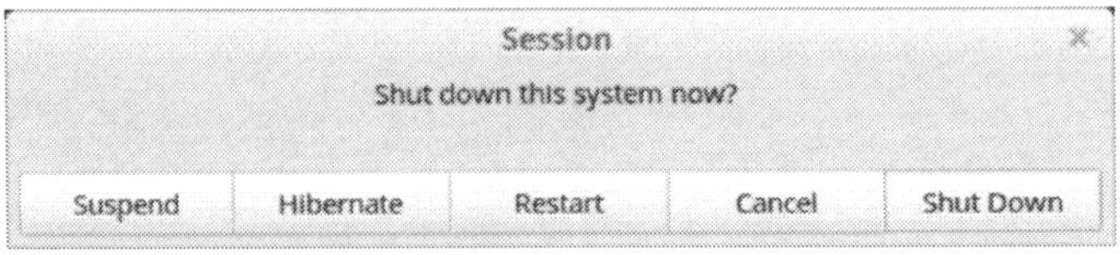

Figure 3-9: Shut Down and Restart dialog

To log out, you can use the Log Out button on the desktop menu (Cinnamon or Mate), which returns you to the log in screen where you log in again as a different user. A one-minute timer logs you out if you do nothing (see Figure 3-10). You also have the option to switch users.

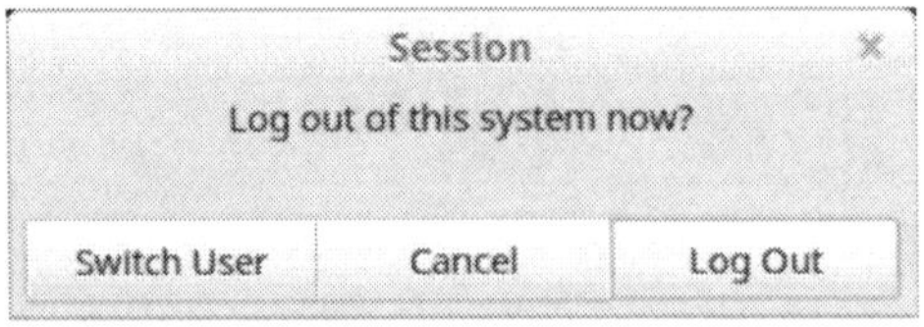

Figure 3-10: Log Out dialog

Use Suspend to stop your system temporarily, using little or no power. Press the space key to redisplay the locked login screen where you can access your account again and continue your session from where you left off.

Accessing Linux from the Command Line Interface

You can access the command-line interface by pressing CTRL-ALT-F1 at any time (CTRL-ALT-F8 returns to the graphics interface). For the command line interface, you are initially given a login prompt. The login prompt is preceded by the hostname you gave your system. In this example, the hostname is **richard-desktop**. When you finish using Linux, you log out with the **logout** command. Linux then displays the same login prompt, waiting for you or another user to log in again. This is the equivalent of the login window provided by the LightDM. You can then log in to another account.

Once you log in as a user, you can enter and execute commands. To log in, enter your username and your password. If you make a mistake, you can erase characters with the BACKSPACE key. In the next example, the user enters the username **richard** and is then prompted to enter the password:

```
Linux Mint 18.2 Sonya richard-desktop tty1

richard-desktop login: richard
Password:
```

When you type in your password, it does not appear on the screen. This is to protect your password from being seen by others. If you enter either the username or the password incorrectly, the system will respond with the error message "Login incorrect" and will ask for your username again, starting the login process over. You can then reenter your username and password.

Once you enter your username and password, you are logged in to the system and the command line prompt is displayed, waiting for you to enter a command. The command line prompt is a dollar sign (**$**). On Linux Mint, your prompt is preceded by the hostname and the directory you are in. The home directory is indicated by a tilde (~).

```
richard@richard-desktop:~$
richard@richard-desktop:~$ cd Pictures
richard@richard-desktop:~/Pictures$
```

To end your session, issue the `logout` or `exit` command. This returns you to the login prompt, and Linux waits for another user to log in.

```
richlp@richard-desktop:~$ logout
```

To, instead, shut down your system from the command line, you enter the **poweroff** command with administrative access (**sudo** command). This command will log you out and shut down the system.

```
richard@richard-desktop:~$ sudo poweroff
```

The Linux Mint Desktops

Linux Mint 18.2 supports four different desktops: Cinnamon, Mate, KDE, and XFCE. Linux Mint is derived from the Ubuntu Linux distribution. Many of its packages, especially in the case of servers, are taken directly from Ubuntu repositories. But its desktops are completely different. Cinnamon is a new desktop developed and maintained by Linux Mint. It is completely different than the Ubuntu Unity desktop. Mate is derived directly from the older GNOME 2 desktop.

You can add a desktop to any Linux Mint version you installed, by using the Software Manager to install the **mint-meta** package for the desktop you want. There are mint-meta packages for Cinnamon, Mate, KDE, and XFCE.

```
mint-meta-cinnamon
mint-meta-mate
mint-meta-kde
mint-meta-xfce
```

For the Linux Mint version of a desktop, be sure to install the **mint-mint** meta package for it, not the standard Ubuntu metapackage. The standard Ubuntu metapackage for KDE is **kubuntu-desktop**, which installs the Ubuntu version of the KDE desktop, not the Linux Mint KDE version, **mint-meta-kde**.

Cinnamon

The Linux Mint Cinnamon desktop is a new desktop that retains some of the features found in GNOME 2, such as applets and panels (see Figure 3-11). Some of the configuration dialogs are similar to those used for GNOME 3. The Cinnamon bottom panel displays the system applets. The left side of the panel is the Cinnamon menu and the window list applet, which shows buttons for the currently open windows.

Figure 3-11: Linux Mint Cinnamon desktop

The Cinnamon desktop prefers hardware acceleration support provided by the appropriate display driver. If your current graphics driver does not support hardware acceleration, you will be logged into Cinnamon using software rendering, which uses acceleration simulation with LLVMpipe on OpenGL running on the CPU. This can result in a slower system.

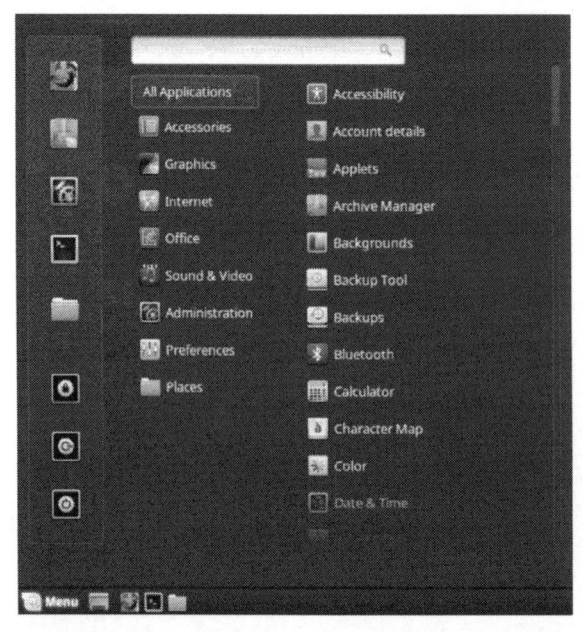

Figure 3-12: Linux Mint Cinnamon menu

The right side of the panel holds system applets for the network manager, sound volume, the user applet, updates, date and time (calendar), and the window list menu. When you open a window, a button for it is displayed on the bottom panel in the window list applet. Unique to Cinnamon is the Cinnamon menu, which incorporates a favorites bar similar to the launcher in Ubuntu Unity (see Figure 3-12).

Though you can use the Cinnamon menu to log out, shutdown, and access System Settings, you could use the user applet instead, as shown here. The user applet is modeled on the Ubuntu sessions menu, and has entries for Lock Screen, Switch User, Log Out, and Power Off. It is a very quick way to perform these tasks, without having to display the Cinnamon menu. You can also access System Settings (the Cinnamon desktop configuration tools), and System Settings Account details. The first entry displays the user's icon and name. Clicking on it displays the Account details dialog, where you can change the user icon, full name, and password.

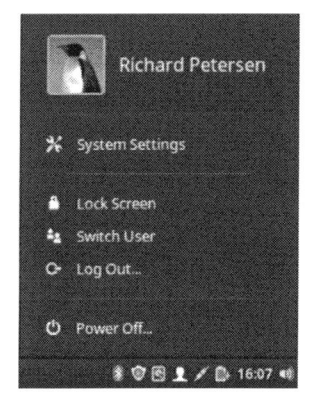

On the panel, the user applet displays a person icon. You can configure the applet (right-click on it and choose configure) to also display the user's full name.

Cinnamon places the window control buttons (close, maximize, and minimize buttons) on the right side of a window title bar, as shown here. There are three window buttons: an x for close, a dash (-) for minimize, and a plus (+) for maximize.

window buttons

To move a window, click and drag its title bar. Double-clicking the title bar will maximize the window. Many keyboard operations are also similar as listed in Table 3-1.

Cinnamon uses the Nemo file manager. You can access your home folder by clicking the Home Folder icon on the desktop, or the home folder button on the panel. A file manager window opens showing your home directory. Your home directory will already have default directories created for commonly used files. These include Pictures, Documents, Music, Videos, and Downloads.

Your office applications automatically save files to the Documents directory by default. Image and photo applications place image files in the Pictures directory. The Desktop folder will hold all files and directories saved to your desktop. When you download a file, it is placed in the Downloads directory.

Part 1: Getting Started

Keypress	Action
SHIFT	Move a file or directory, default
CTRL	Copy a file or directory
CTRL-SHIFT	Create a link for a file or directory
F2	Rename selected file or directory
CTRL-ALT-Arrow (right, left, up, down)	Move to a different desktop
CTRL-w	Close current window
ALT-spacebar	Open window menu for window operations
ALT-F2	Open Run command box
ALT-F1	Open Applications menu
Ctrl-F	Find file

Table 3-1: Window and File Manager Keyboard shortcuts

The file manager window displays several components, including a browser toolbar, location bar, and a sidebar showing devices, file systems, and folders. When you open a new folder, the same window is used to display it, and you can use the forward and back arrows to move through previously opened directories. The location bar displays folder buttons showing your current folder and its parent folders. You can click on a parent folder to move to it. Figure 3-13 shows the file manager window.

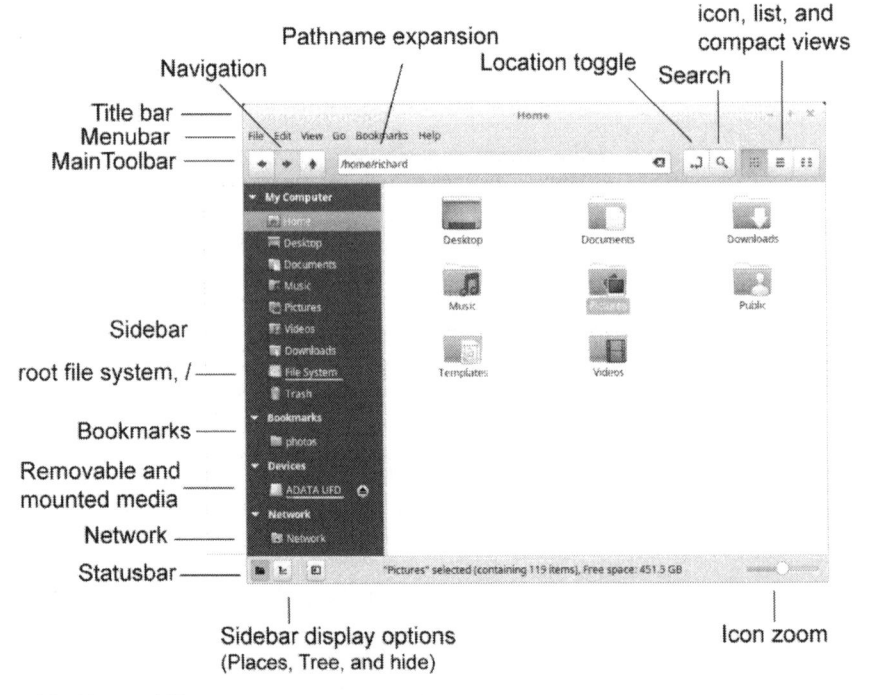

Figure 3-13: Nemo File manager

The file manager supports full drag-and-drop capabilities using combinations of key presses and mouse clicks. You can drag folders, icons, and applications to the desktop or other file manager windows open to other folders. The move operation is the default drag operation (you can also press the SHIFT key while dragging). To copy files, press the CTRL key and then click-and-drag before releasing the mouse button. To create a link (shortcut), hold down both the CTRL and SHIFT keys while dragging the icon to where you want the link to appear, such as the desktop.

Mate

The Mate desktop, though it appears similar to Cinnamon, is very much a GNOME 2 desktop (see Figure 3-14). The bottom panel displays applets. The left side of the panel is the Linux Mint menu for Mate. The right side of the panel holds system applets for the network manager, sound volume, updates, and the date and time. When you open a window, its button is displayed on the bottom panel in the window list applet.

Figure 3-14: Linux Mint Mate desktop

Unique to the Linux Mint version of Mate is the Linux Mint menu, which shows places and system sections, as well as a Favorites view for applications (see Figure 3-15).

Mate places the window control buttons (close, maximize, and minimize buttons) on the right side of a window title bar, using the same buttons as Cinnamon: an x for close, a dash (-) for minimize, and a plus (+) for maximize. Mate also displays a menu button at the left for the window menu.

window buttons

72 *Part 1: Getting Started*

To move a window, click and drag its title bar. Double-clicking the title bar will maximize the window. Many keyboard operations are also similar as listed in Table 3-1.

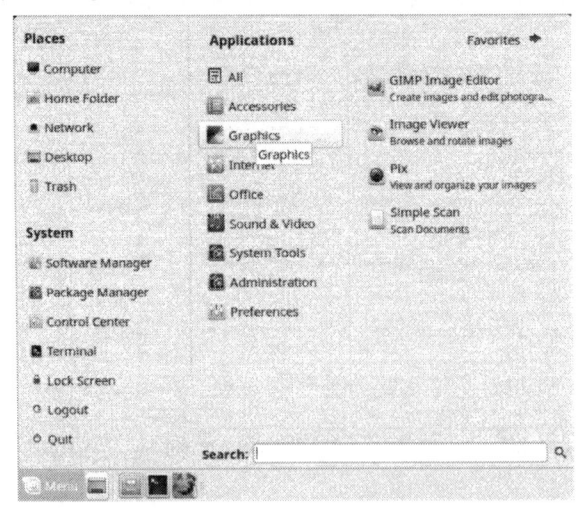

Figure 3-15: Linux Mint Menu (Mate)

Mate uses the Caja file manager. You can access your home folder from its entry in the Places section of the Linux Mint menu, or by clicking the Home Folder icon on the desktop. A file manager window opens showing your home directory. Your home directory will already have default directories created for commonly used files. These include Pictures, Documents, Music, Videos, and Downloads.

Your office applications automatically save files to the Documents directory by default. Image and photo applications place image files in the Pictures directory. The Desktop folder will hold all files and directories saved to your desktop. When you download a file, it is placed in the Downloads directory.

The file manager window displays several components, including a browser toolbar, location bar, and a side pane with several views including places, tree, and information. When you open a new folder, the same window is used to display it, and you can use the forward and back arrows to move through previously opened directories. The location bar displays folder buttons showing your current folder and its parent folders. You can click on a parent folder button to move to it. Figure 3-16 shows the file manager window.

The file manager supports full drag-and-drop capabilities using combinations of key presses and mouse clicks. You can drag folders, icons, and applications to the desktop or other file manager windows open to other folders. The move operation is the default drag operation (you can also press the SHIFT key while dragging). To copy files, press the CTRL key and then click-and-drag before releasing the mouse button. To create a link (shortcut), hold down both the CTRL and SHIFT keys while dragging the icon to where you want the link to appear, such as the desktop.

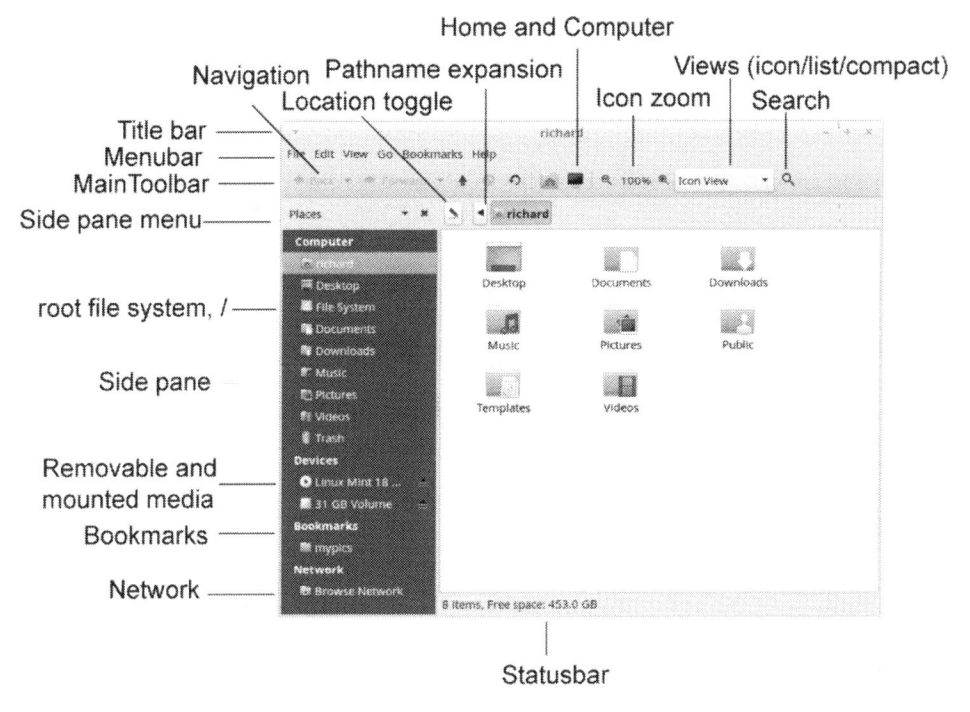

Figure 3-16: Caja File manager

KDE Linux Mint

KDE Linux Mint is based on the KDE desktop (see Figure 3-17). Configuration dialogs are the same as those used for KDE. The left side of the bottom panel displays the icons for the main menu, the Dolphin file manager, and the taskbar for open windows. The right side of the panel shows the time and date, and the system tray, which holds icons for the update manager, network manager, and sound volume. KDE Linux Mint uses the Linux Mint Software Manager for managing software, which is the same application used on the Cinnamon and Mate desktops.

KDE Linux Mint uses the same Kickoff menu for applications and places as KDE (see Figure 3-18). The default favorites are different, featuring the Firefox browser, Konsole terminal, and the Linux Mint Software Manager.

Kde uses the Dolphin file manager. You can access your home folder from the file manager icon on the panel to the left. A file manager window opens showing your home directory. Your home directory will already have default directories created for commonly used files. These include Pictures, Documents, Music, Videos, and Downloads.

Your office applications automatically save files to the Documents directory by default. Image and photo applications place image files in the Pictures directory. The Desktop folder will hold all files and directories saved to your desktop. When you download a file, it is placed in the Downloads directory.

74 Part 1: Getting Started

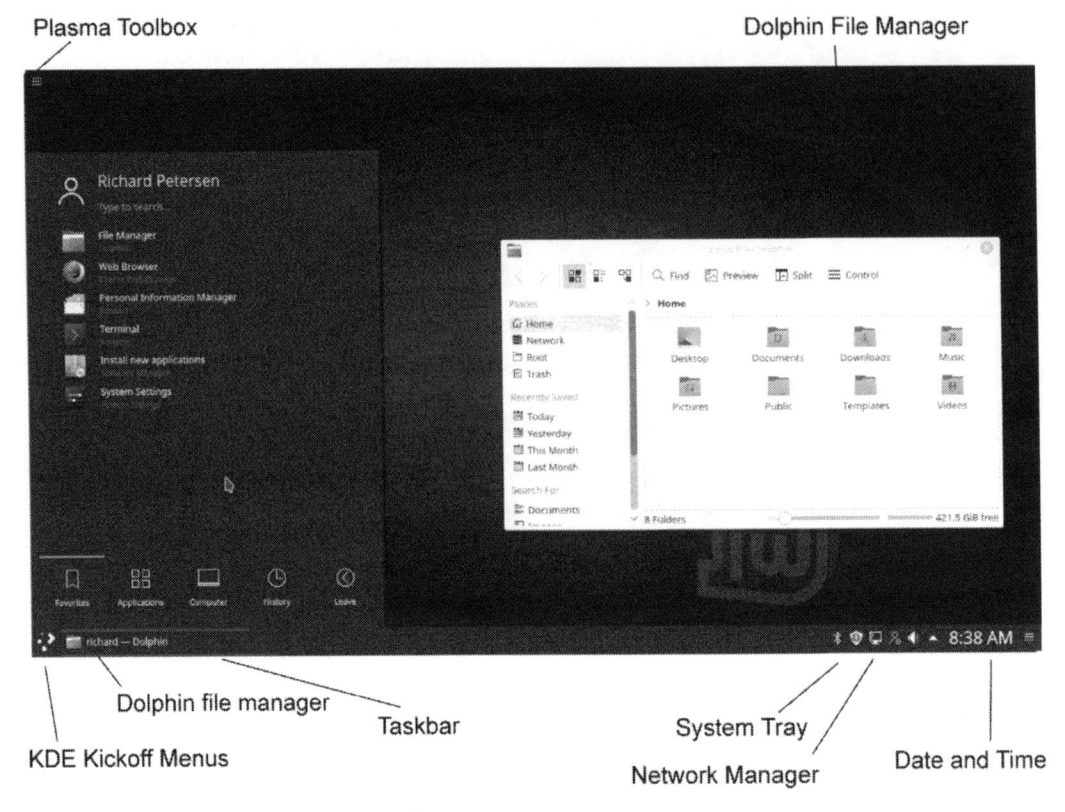

Figure 3-17: KDE Linux Mint desktop

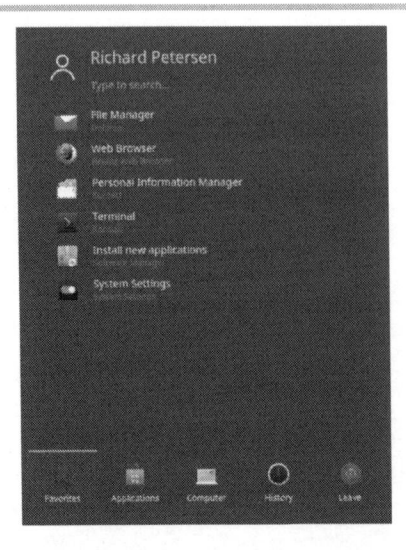

Figure 3-18: KDE Menu

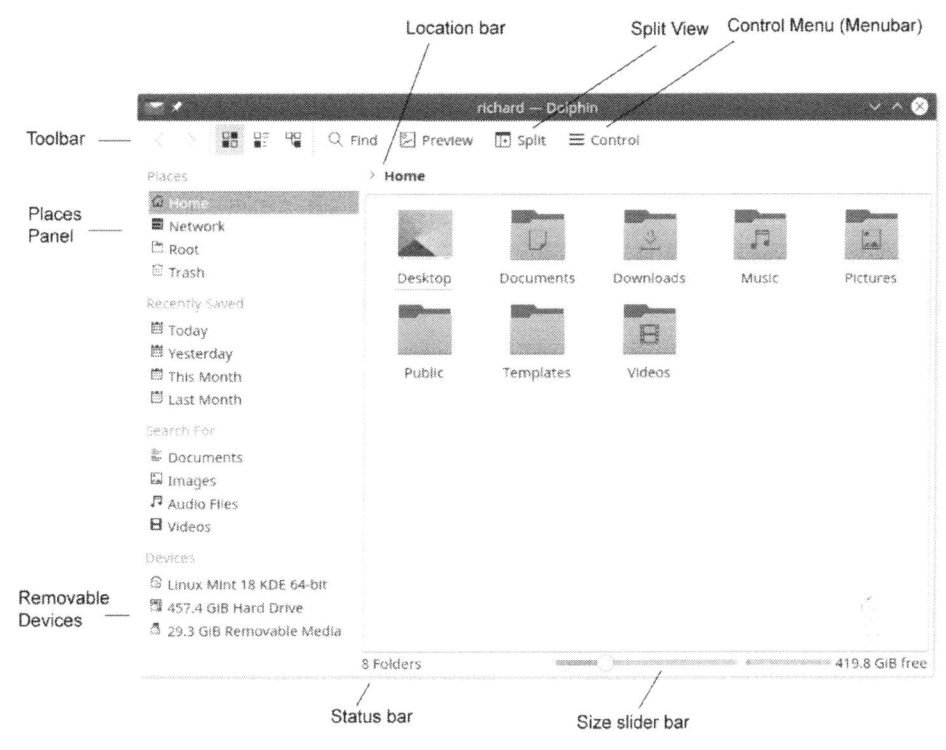

Figure 3-19: Dolphin File manager

The file manager window displays several components, including a browser toolbar, location bar, and a Places side panel showing devices, file systems, and folders. When you open a new folder, the same window is used to display it, and you can use the forward and back arrows to move through previously opened directories. The location bar displays folder buttons showing your current folder and its parent folders. You can click on a parent folder to move to it. Figure 3-19 shows the Dolphin file manager window.

The file manager supports full drag-and-drop capabilities using combinations of key presses and mouse clicks. You can drag folders, icons, and applications to the desktop or other file manager windows open to other folders. The move operation is the default drag operation (you can also press the SHIFT key while dragging). To copy files, press the CTRL key and then click-and-drag before releasing the mouse button. To create a link (shortcut), hold down both the CTRL and SHIFT keys while dragging the icon to where you want the link to appear, such as the desktop.

Xfce Desktop

The Xfce desktop is a lightweight desktop designed to run fast without the kind of overhead required for full-featured desktops like KDE and GNOME. You can think of it as a window manager with desktop functionality. It includes its own file manager and panel, but the emphasis is on modularity and simplicity. Like GNOME, Xfce is based on GTK+ GUI tools. The desktop consists of a collection of modules like the Thunar file manager, xfce4-panel panel, and the xfwm4 window manager. Keeping with its focus on simplicity, Xfce features only a few common applets on its panel. It small scale makes it appropriate for laptops or dedicated systems, that have no need for complex overhead found in other desktops. Xfce is also useful for desktops designed for just a few tasks, like multimedia desktops.

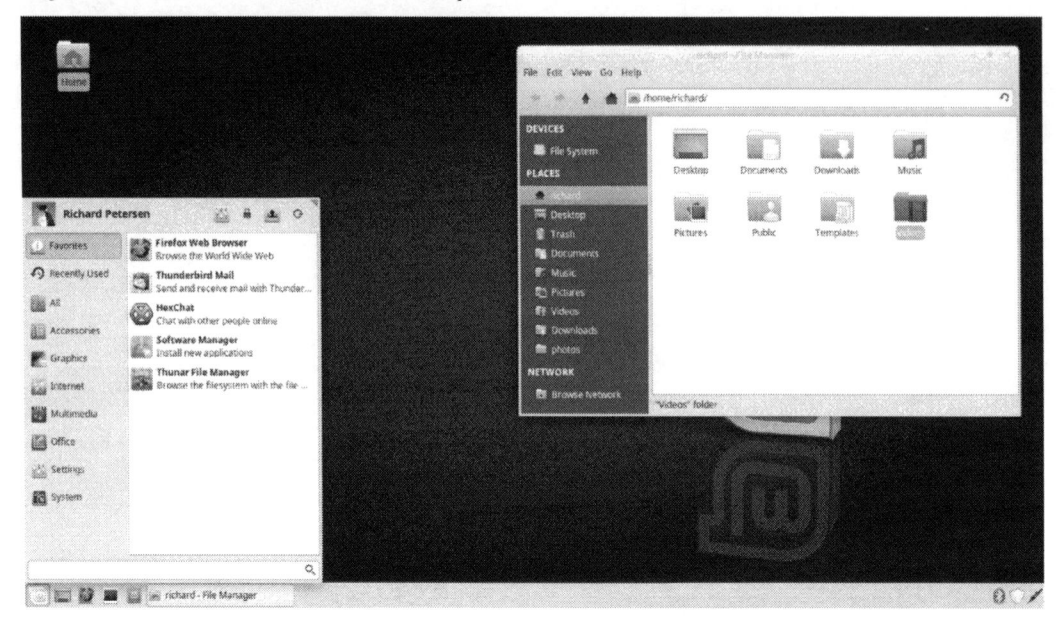

Figure 3-20: Xfce desktop

To install Xfce as an alternative desktop on a Linux Mint system, select the Xfce metapackage, **mint-meta-xfce**. This installs the Linux Mint Xfce desktop.

You can install the Linux Mint version of Xfce as the primary desktop using the Linux Mint Xfce live DVD. The Xfce live DVD is available in 32-bit and 64-bit versions such as **linuxmint-18.2-dvd-64bit.iso**. You can then burn the DVD and run it as a live DVD. Double-click the Install icon to install Xfce on your computer. Follow the same basic steps for installing Linux Mint Xfce as for the Linux Mint Cinnamon or Mate DVDs. Like Cinnamon and Mate, Xfce also uses the LightDM Display Manager (LightDM) for logging in.

Xfce desktop shows a single expanded panel at the bottom (see Figure 3-20). The desktop displays an icon for your Home directory (upper left). Xfce displays a bottom panel with a button for a Whisker applications menu at the left. From this menu, you can access any software applications, along with administration tools. You can configure the Whisker menu by right-clicking on its icon and choose Properties to open its configuration dialog. To the right of the menu are icons for Show Desktop, the Firefox Web browser, the terminal window, the file manager, and the taskbar, showing buttons for open windows. The right side of the panel shows the time and date, network connections (Network Manager), sound volume, and notifications. A helpful item to add to the panel is the Places menu, which shows entries for your home folder, recent documents, and bookmarked folders, such as Documents and Pictures, as well as for the File System, Desktop folder, and your attached storage devices.

You can add more items by clicking the panel and choosing the Panel menu, and then selecting the "Add New Items" entry. This opens a window with several applets, such as the clock, workspace switcher, applications menu, and launcher. The launcher applet lets you specify an application to start and choose an icon image for it. To move an applet, right-click it and choose Move from the pop-up menu. Then move the mouse to the new insertion location and click.

The top of the Whisker menu shows the username and a toolbar with buttons for Settings, Lock screen, user management, and the shutdown dialog (see Figure 3-21). At the bottom of the menu is a search box for locating applications. The left side of the menu lists the application categories, including Favorites, Recently Used, and All. The Settings entry lists your system administration tools.

Figure 3-21: Xfce Whisker menu

Xfce file manager is called Thunar. The file manager will open a side pane in the shortcuts view that lists entries not only for the home directory but also for your file system, desktop, and trash contents. The File menu lets you perform folder operations, such as creating new directories. From the Edit menu, you can perform tasks on a selected file, such as renaming the file or creating a link for it. You can change the side pane view to a tree view of your file system by selecting from the menu bar View | Side Pane | Tree (Ctrl+e). The Shortcuts entry changes the view back (Ctrl+b).

To configure the Xfce interface, you use the Xfce Settings Manager, accessible by clicking the system settings icon in the top bar of the Whisker applications menu. This opens the Settings window, which shows icons for your desktop, display, panel, and appearance, among others (see Figure 3-22). Use the Appearance tool to select themes, icons, and toolbar styles (Settings). The Panel tool lets you add new panels and control features, such as fixed for freely movable and horizontally or vertically positioned. To configure the desktop, select the Desktop icon in the Settings window to open the Desktop window where you can select the background image (Background tab), control menu behavior (Menus tab), and set icon sizes (Icons tab).

Note: You can also access applications and Desktop Settings by right clicking on the desktop background to display the desktop menu.

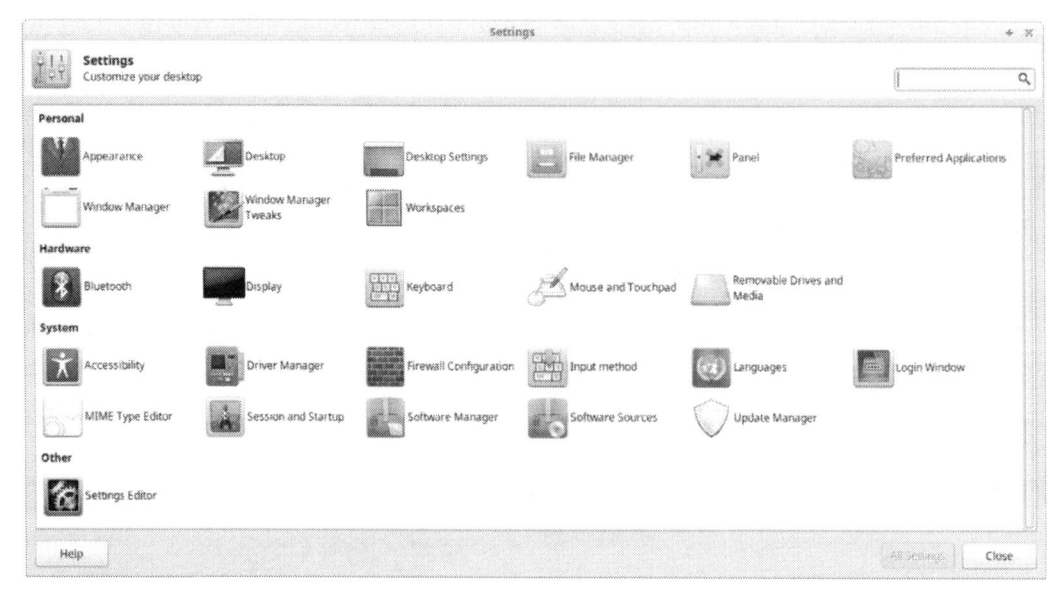

Figure 3-22: Xfce Settings Manager

Linux Mint Debian Edition (LMDE)

The Linux Mint Debian Edition, LMDE, installs the original Debian Linux distribution, instead of the Ubuntu. Debian upgrades packages as they are changed, instead of waiting for a release version as Ubuntu does. LMDE runs the latest version of Cinnamon and Mate. Major upgrades to both Debian packages and Cinnamon/Mate packages are installed as they become available. The install process is much the same as Linux Mint, with a few exceptions. You can choose the partition to install the GRUB bootloader on, and manual partitioning uses GParted and has an expert mode for complex installs. Also, LMDE, as does Debian, uses systemd for system startup and services.

Accessing File Systems and Devices

From the file manager, desktop, and panel you can access removable media and all your mounted file systems, remote and local, including any Windows shared directories accessible from Samba.

On Cinnamon, Mate, and KDE, you can access your file systems and removable media using any file manager window's sidebar or side pane, as shown here.

On Cinnamon and Mate, you can also access file systems and removable media by opening the Computer window (Go menu | Computer item), as shown here. The Computer window shows icons for all removable media (mounted CD/DVD-ROMs, USB drives, and so on), your local file system, additional partitions, and your network shared resources. Double-click any icon to open a file manager window displaying its contents. The File System icon will open a window showing the top-level directory for your file system. Access will be restricted for system directories (use the **sudo** command to perform any operations on system files).

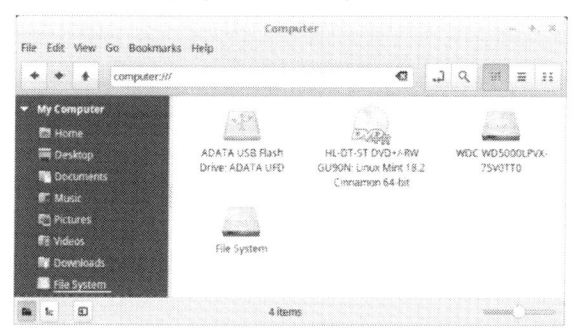

On Cinnamon and Mate, file systems on removable media and mounted file systems will also appear automatically as icons on the desktop, as shown here. A DVD/CD-ROM is automatically mounted when you insert it into your DVD/CD-ROM drive, displaying an icon for it with its label. The same kind of access is also provided for card readers, digital cameras, USB drives, and external USB/ESATA hard drives. When you attach an external USB/ESATA drive, it will be mounted automatically and opened in a file manager window. Be sure to unmount (Eject) the USB or external USB/ESATA drives before removing them so that data will be written.

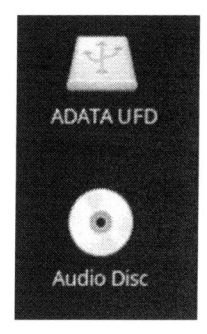

On Cinnamon and Mate, when removable drives are attached, a button for removable drives appears on the panel (the Removable drives applet). Clicking on the button opens a menu listing attached drives, with an eject button you can click to remove the drive, as shown here.

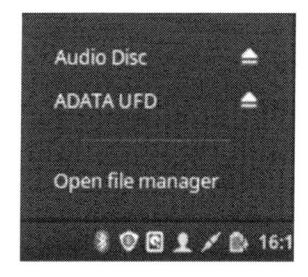

On Cinnamon, you can also access removable drives from the Mint menu under the Places submenu, as shown here.

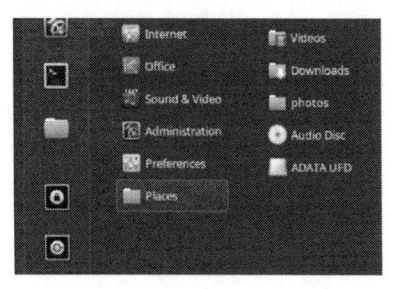

If you have already configured associated applications for audio and video CD/DVD discs, or discs with images, sound, or video files, the disc will be opened with the appropriate application; like Shotwell for images, Rhythmbox for audio, and Xplayer (Videos) for DVD/video.

You can access a DVD/CD-ROM disc or USB drive from the desktop by double-clicking its icon on the desktop, or from the Computer window by right clicking on the DVD/CD-ROM icon and selecting the Open entry, or from a file manager window's side pane. A file manager window opens to display the contents of the CD-ROM disc. To eject a CD-ROM, you right-click its icon and select Eject from the pop-up menu. The same procedure works for USB drives, using the USB drive icon.

To see network resources on the Cinnamon and Mate desktops, open the Network window by clicking the Network entry in any file manager window's sidebar or side pane. The network window will list your connected network computers. Opening these displays the shares they provide, such as shared directories that you have access to. Drag-and-drop operations are supported for all shared directories, letting you copy files and folders between a shared directory on another computer with a directory on your system. If you have a firewall active (Gufw), you first have to configure your firewall to accept Samba connections before you can browse Windows systems.

Accessing Archives from GNOME: Archive Mounter

Linux Mint supports the access of archives directly from GNOME using Archive Mounter. You can select the archive file, then right-click and select Archive Mounter to open the archive. The archive contents are listed in a Nemo file manager window. You can extract or display the contents.

You can also use Archive Mounter to mount CD/DVD disk ISO image files as archives. You can then browse and extract the contents of the CD/DVD. Right-click on a disk ISO image file (**.iso** extension) and select "Open with Archive Mounter." The image is automatically mounted as an archive. An entry for it appears on the file manager sidebar under Network. It will be read-only. The disc will also appear in the Computer folder as a valid disc. To unmount the disk image as an archive, click it's eject button, or right-click on the entry or icon and choose Unmount.

File Manager CD/DVD Creator interface

Using the GNOME file manager to burn data to a DVD or CD is a simple matter of dragging files to an open blank CD or DVD and clicking the Write To Disc button. When you insert and open a blank DVD/CD, a window will open labeled CD/DVD Creator. To burn files, just drag them to that window. Click the Write To Disc button when ready to burn a DVD/CD. Also, click the Properties button to open a dialog with burning options like the burn speed.

Burning ISO images from the file manager

The GNOME file manager also supports burning ISO images using Brasero. Just double-click the ISO image file or right-click the file and select Open with Brasero. This opens the Image Burning Setup dialog, which prompts you to burn the image. Be sure to insert a blank DVD into your CD/DVD burner. Brasero is no longer installed by default. Use Software Manager to install it.

Brasero Disc Burner application interface

You can perform disc copy, erasing, and checking using the Brasero CD/DVD burner. Choose Brasero Disc Burner from the menu. Brasero supports drag-and-drop operations for creating Audio CDs. In particular, it can handle CD/DVD read/write discs, and can erase discs. It also supports multi-session burns, adding data to DVD/CD disc. Initially, Brasero displays a dialog with buttons for the type of project you want to create. You can create a data or audio project, create a DVD/Video disc, copy a DVD/CD, or burn a DVD/CD image file.

For a Data project, the toolbar displays an Add button, which you use to select files and directories to be burned to your disc. You also can drag-and-drop files and folders to your data listing (right-pane). You can choose to display a side panel (View menu) which will let you select files and directories.

Laptop Power Management and Wireless Networks

For working on a laptop, you will need two important operations: power management, and support for multiple network connection, including wireless and LAN. Both are configured automatically. For power management, Linux Mint uses the Power dialog accessible from System Settings dialog. On a Laptop, the battery icon displayed on the panel will show how much power you have left, as well as when the battery becomes critical. It will indicate an AC connection, as well as when the battery is recharging.

For network connections, Linux Mint uses Network Manager. Network Manager will detect available network connections automatically. Click on the Network Manager icon in the panel. This displays a pop-up menu showing all possible wireless networks, as well as any wired networks. You can then choose the one you want to use. The name and strength of each wireless connection will be listed. When you try to connect to an encrypted wireless network, you will be prompted for the password. Wireless networks that you successfully connect to will be added to your Network Manager configuration. You also have the option to connect to a hidden wireless network.

On the Cinnamon desktop, you can also use the Networking tool, accessible from System Settings as Network and from the network menu on the panel as Network Settings, to quickly configure your wireless connection.

Network Connections

Network connections will be set up for you by Network Manager, which will detect your network connections automatically, both wired and wireless. Network Manager provides status information for your connection and allows you to switch easily from one configured connection to another as needed. For initial configuration, it detects as much information as possible about the new connection.

Wired connections will be started automatically. For wireless connections, when a user logs in, Network Manager selects the connection preferred by that user. The user can choose the wireless connection to use from a menu of detected wireless networks.

The network menu is displayed from the Network Manager applet on the bottom panel to the right. The Network Manager icon will vary according to the type of connection and your connection status. An Ethernet (wired) connection would display two diagonal plugs. A wireless connection will display a staggered wave graph as shown here.

If no connection is active (wireless or wired), an empty wave graph is displayed. When Network Manager makes a wired or wireless connection, it displays a pulsing staggered wave graph. If you have both a wired and wireless connection, and the wired connection is active, the wired connection image (plug) will be used.

Network Manager wired connections

For computers connected to a wired network, like an Ethernet connection, Network Manager will automatically detect the network connection and establish a connection. Most networks use DHCP to provide network information like an IP address and network DNS server automatically. With this kind of connection, Network Manager can connect automatically to your network whenever you start your system. The network connection would be labeled something like Wired connection 1. When you connect, a connection established message is displayed, as shown here. You do have the option to not display the connection message again.

The Network Manager panel icon will become solid. When not connected it becomes grayed out.

The Network Manager menu displays your wired connection as Wired, with a switch to turn it on or off (see Figure 3-23). To disconnect your wired connection, you can click the switch, turning it to the off position. Your Network Manager icon on the panel becomes grayed out. To reconnect later, click the switch again.

Figure 3-23: Network Manager connections menu

Network Manager wireless connections

With multiple wireless access points for Internet connections, a system could have several different network connections to choose from, instead of a single-line connection like DSL or cable. This is particularly true for notebook computers that could access different wireless connections at different locations. Instead of manually configuring a new connection each time one is encountered, the Network Manager tool can configure and select a connection to use automatically.

Network Manager will scan for wireless connections, checking for Extended Service Set Identifiers (ESSIDs). If an ESSID identifies a previously used connection, then it is selected by Network Manager. If several are found, then the recently used one is chosen. If only a new connection is available, then Network Manager waits for the user to choose one. A connection is selected only if the user is logged in.

Open the Network Manager menu to see a list of all possible network connections, including all available wireless connections (see Figure 3-24). Wireless entries display the name of the wireless network and a wave graph showing the strength of its signal. Computers with both wired and wireless devices show entries for both Wired Network and Wireless Networks. Computers with only a wireless device only show entries for Wireless Networks. You can disable the display of wireless networks by clicking the ON switch, turning it to OFF. To re-activate your wireless connections, click switch again.

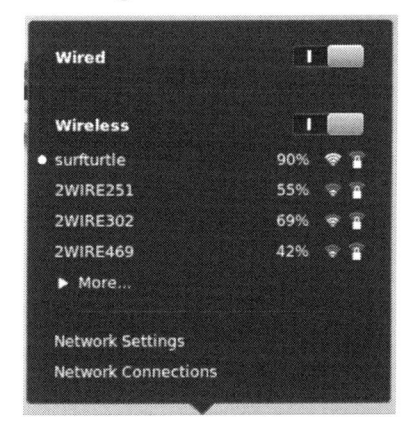

Figure 3-24: Network Manager connections menu: wired and wireless

To connect to a wireless network, find its network entry in the Network Manager menu and click on it. If this the first time you are trying to connect to that network, you will be prompted to enter connection information: the wireless security and passphrase. The type of wireless security used by the network will be detected. Figure 3-25 shows the prompt for the passphrase to a wireless network. A checkbox lets you see the passphrase should you need to check that you are entering it correctly. Click Connect to activate the connection.

Figure 3-25: Network Manager wireless authentication

Once connected a message is displayed indicating that the connection has been established, as shown here. You have the option to not show the connection message again.

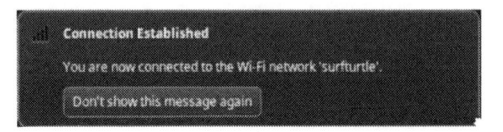

To disconnect from your wireless network, on the Network Manager menu click on the ON switch to turn it off.

When you connect to a wireless network for the first time, a configuration entry will be made for the wireless connection in the Wireless tab of the Network Connections dialog.

System Settings Network, Cinnamon (GNOME and proxies)

GNOME 3 provides a network dialog for basic information and network connection management, including proxy settings. It is designed to work with Network Manager. The dialog has been incorporated into the Cinnamon Desktop as Networking. To open the Networking dialog, choose Network Settings from the Network Manager applet menu, or click the Networking icon in the System Settings dialog, or choose Network in the Preferences menu (see Figure 3-26).

Figure 3-26: System Settings Networking wireless connections (Cinnamon)

Tabs for network connections are listed to the right. You should have entries for Wired, Wi-Fi, and Network proxy (Wireless is displayed on computers with wireless connections). The Wired tab lets you turn the wired connection on or off. The Wi-Fi tab lets you choose a wireless network and then prompts you to enter a passphrase. The connection and security type is automatically detected. Instead of using a wireless network, you can choose to connect to a local hidden network (Connect to a Hidden Network button). A switch at the top right lets you turn the wireless connection on or off.

Your current active connection will have a checkmark next to it, with gear and stop buttons to the right, as shown below. Click on the stop button to deactivate the connection. The button will change to a play button, which you can click to reconnect.

For quick access to networks you have already configured, you can click the Known Networks button to open the Know Networks dialog listing all your configured networks (see Figure 3-27). Use the play button to the right of the network name to start and stop the network. The configuration button opens that network's configuration dialog. To remove a network, click its checkbox, which activates the Forget button at the lower left, then click that button.

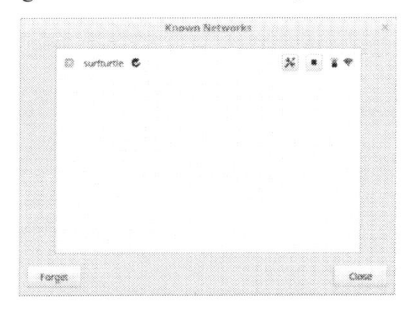

Figure 3-27: System Settings Networking wireless Known Networks (Cinnamon)

86 Part 1: Getting Started

Click on the wrench/screwdriver button to display a dialog with tabs for managing the connection. The Details tab provides information about the connection (see Figure 3-28). The Security, Identity, IPv4, and IPv6 tabs let you perform a detailed configuration of your connection, as described in Chapter 11. The settings are set to automatic by default. Should you make any changes, click on the Apply button to have them take effect. To remove a network's connection information, open the Reset tab and click the Forget button. The Reset button on the Reset tab lets you reset the settings. You can also remove a network using the Known Networks dialog (click the Known Networks button on the Networking dialog).

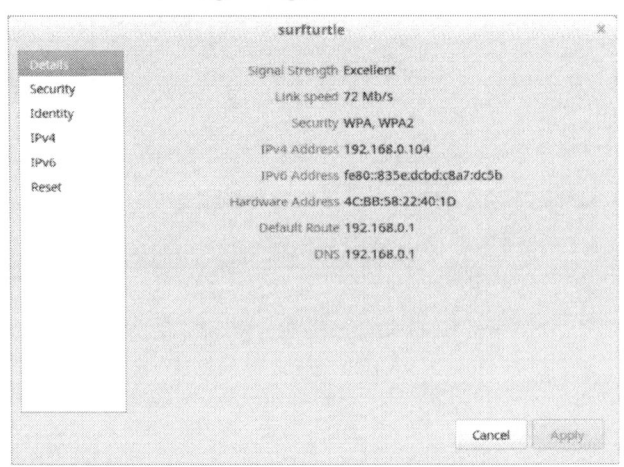

Figure 3-28: System Settings Networking wireless information (Cinnamon)

The Identity tab has options for connecting automatically and to make available to other users. These are set by default. Should you not want to connect to the wireless network automatically, be sure to un-check this option.

On the Networking dialog, the Wired tab shows basic information about the wired connection, including the IP addresses and DNS server. A switch at the top right corner allows you to disconnect the wired connection, letting you effectively work offline. The wrench/screwdriver button at the lower right opens a configuration dialog similar to the wireless configuration dialog, with tabs for Details, Security, Identity, IPv4, IPv6, and Reset. The Profile button to the left lets you add a different set of wired connection information (security, IPv protocols, and identity), should you connect to a different wired network.

The Proxy tab provides a Method menu with None, Manual, and Automatic options (see Figure 3-29). The Manual options let you enter address and port information. For the Automatic option, you enter a configuration address.

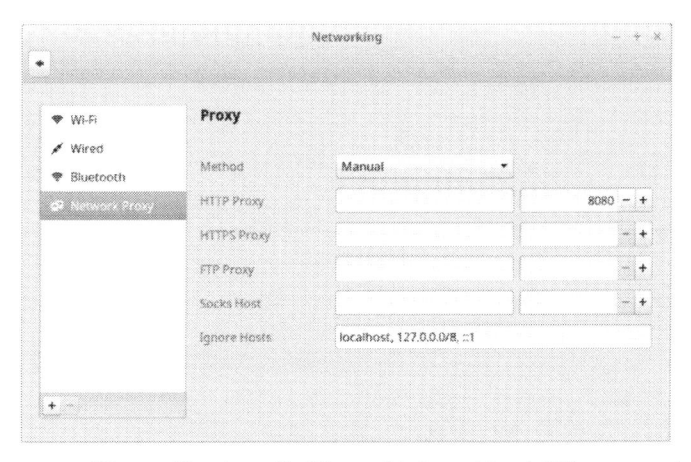

Figure 3-29: Proxy settings (System Settings Networking) (Cinnamon)

To add a new connection, such as a VPN connection, click the plus button (+) below the network devices listing. You are prompted to choose the interface types. The NetworkManager configuration dialogs will then start up to let you enter configuration information.

Figure 3-30: Connect to a Hidden Wireless Network

Wireless connections can also be hidden. These are wireless connections that do not broadcast an SSID, making them undetectable by an automatic scan. To connect to a hidden wireless network, you select "Connect to hidden network" on the Networking dialog Wi-Fi tab (see Figure 3-30). The Connection drop-down menu will select the New entry. If you have set up any hidden connections previously, they also are listed in the Connection drop-down menu. For a New connection, enter the wireless network name and select a security method. You are prompted in either case for your network keyring password.

Display Configuration and Device Drivers

The graphics interface for your desktop display is implemented by the X Window System. The version used on Linux Mint is X.org (**x.org**). X.org provides its own drivers for various graphics cards and monitors. You can find out more about X.org at **https://www.x.org**. X.org will automatically detect most hardware.

Device Drivers

Your display is detected automatically, configuring both your graphics card and monitor. Normally you should not need to perform any configuration yourself. However, if you have a graphics card that uses Graphics processors from a major Graphics vendor like AMD or Nvidia, you have the option of using their driver, instead of the open source X drivers installed with Linux Mint. Some graphics cards may work better with the vendor driver, and provide access to more of the card's features like 3D support. The open source AMD driver is **xserver-xorg-video-radeon**, and the open source NVidia driver is **xserver-xorg-video-nouveau**. When you install a new kernel, compatible kernel drivers for your proprietary graphics driver are generated automatically for you by the DKMS (Dynamic Kernel Module Support) utility.

If available, you can select proprietary drivers to use instead, such as the Nvidia driver. Open the Driver Manager application from System Setting (Administration | Driver Manager), or from the Administration menu | Driver Manager (see Figure 3-31). Select the driver entry you want and then click on the Apply Changes button to use download and install the driver. The drivers are part of the restricted repository, supported by the vendor but not by Linux Mint. They are not open source, but proprietary.

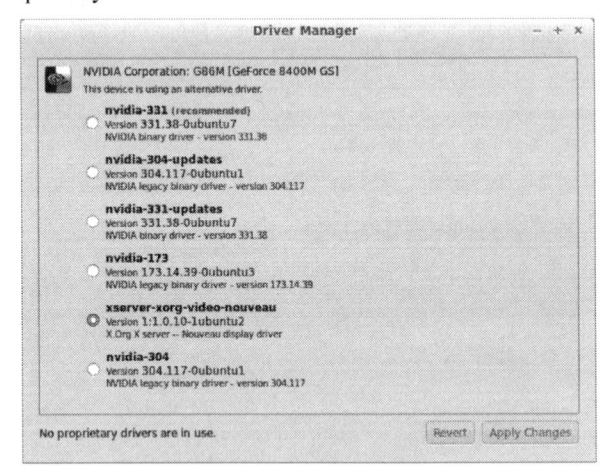

Figure 3-31: Hardware Drivers: Driver Manager

Once installed, an examination of the Device Drivers application will show the selected driver in use (see Figure 3-32). Should you want to use the original driver, click the Revert button. The open source Xorg driver will be automatically selected and used. For Nvidia cards, the Nouveau open source drivers are used, which provides some acceleration support. You can switch to another driver by selecting it and clicking the Apply Changes button.

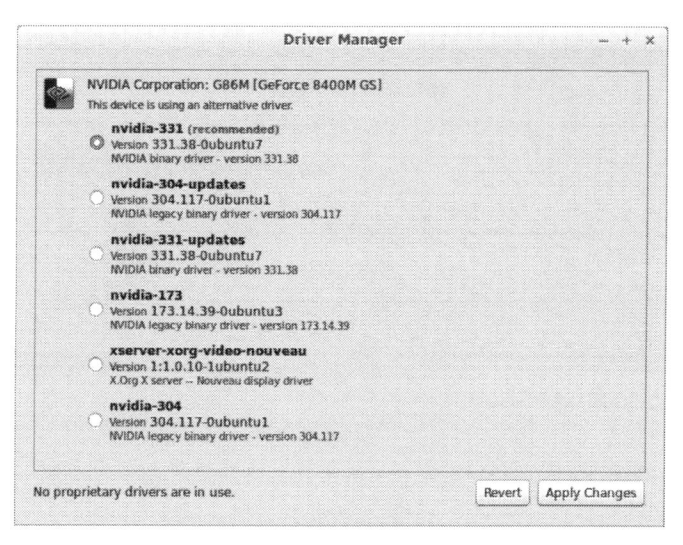

Figure 3-32: Proprietary video driver: Software Sources, Device Drivers tab

The graphic vendors also have their own Linux-based configuration tools, which are installed with the driver. The Nvidia configuration tool is in the **nvidia-settings** package. This interface provides Nvidia vendor access to many of the features of Nvidia graphics cards like color corrections, video brightness and contrast, and thermal monitoring. You can also set the screen resolution and color depth.

For AMD you would use the open source drivers, amdgpu or Xorg radeon. The **fglrx** driver (Catalyst proprietary driver) has been deprecated and is no longer supported by Ubuntu/Linux Mint. It is no longer available in any form for Ubuntu Linux 16.04 and later, and thereby not for Linux Mint 18.2. Much of the AMD video drivers have now become open source. For AMD video cards with GCN 1.2 capability and above (series 300 and above), it is recommended that you use the amdgpu AMD open source driver.

If you have problems with the vendor driver, you can always switch back to the original (Revert button). Your original Xorg open source driver will be used instead. The changeover will be automatic.

If the problem is more severe, with the display not working, you can use the GRUB menu on startup to select the recovery kernel. Your system will be started without the vendor graphics driver. You can use the "drop to shell" to enter the command line mode. From there you can use **apt-get** command line APT tool to remove the graphics driver. The Nvidia drivers have the prefix **nvidia**. In the following example, the asterisk will match on all the **nvidia** packages.

```
sudo apt-get remove nvidia*
```

Display (resolution and rotation)

Any user can specify their own resolution or orientation without affecting the settings of other users. The System Settings Displays dialog (Hardware section) provides a simple interface for setting rotation, resolution and selecting added monitors, allowing for cloned or extended displays across several connected monitors (see Figure 3-33).

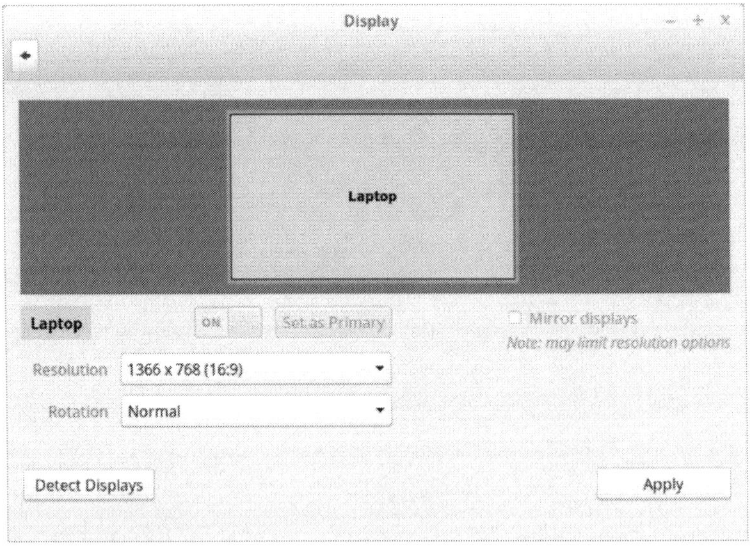

Figure 3-33: Displays

From the drop-down menus, you can set the resolution and rotation. After you select a resolution, click Apply. The new resolution is displayed with a dialog, with buttons that ask you whether to keep the new resolution or return to the previous one. You can use the Detect Displays button to detect any other monitors connected to your system. With multiple displays, you can turn a monitor off or mirror displays.

Hi-DPI

For smaller screens with very high resolutions (High Dots Per Inch), icons, windows, and fonts should be scaled to display them at a usable size. Cinnamon does this automatically in most cases. Should you need to manually configure HiDPI support, open the System Settings General dialog and, in the Desktop Scaling section set the "User interface scaling" option to Double (Hi-DPI).

On Mate, you can install the dconf editor. Open it and choose **org.gnome.desktop.interface**, then double click on that entry to change the 0 value to 2. You could also use the following command in a terminal window.

```
gsettings set org.gnome.desktop.interface scaling-factor 2
```

On KDE you can set the dpi for icons and fonts to 100 or more on their respective tabs in the System Settings Application Appearance dialog.

Color Profiles

You can manage the color for different devices using color profiles specified with the Color dialog accessible from System Settings (Hardware section). The Color dialog lists devices for which you can set color profiles. Click on a device to display buttons at the bottom of the screen to Add profile, Calibrate, Remove profile, and View details. Your monitor will have a profile set up automatically. Click View Details for the color profile information (see Figure 3-34).

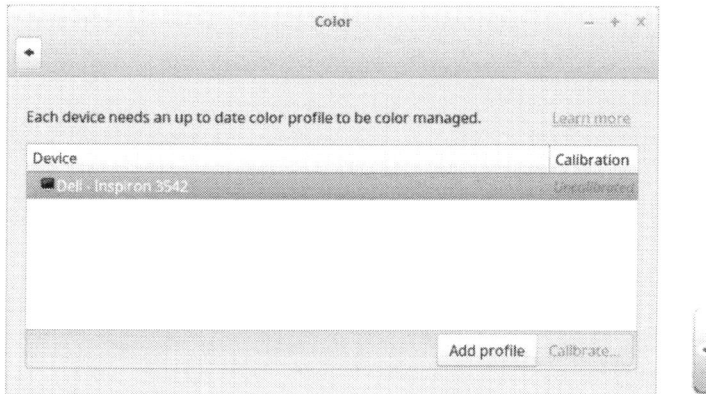

Figure 3-34: Color Management dialog

Click the Add Profile button to open a dialog with an Automatic Profiles menu from which you can choose a color profile to use. Click the Add button to add the Profile. Available profiles include Adobe RGB, sRGB, and Kodak ProPhoto RGB. You can also import a profile from an ICC profile file of your own.

Private Encrypted Directories (ecryptfs)

Linux Mint provides each user with the capability of setting up a private encrypted directory. Encryption adds a further level of security. Should others gain access to your home directory, they still would not be able to read any information in your private encrypted directory.

Private directory encryption is implemented using the **ecryptfs** utilities, **ecryptfs-utils** on the Linux Mint main repository. You use the **ecryptfs-setup-private** command to set up an encrypted private directory. During setup, an **.ecryptfs** directory is created which holds your encryption keys and manages access.

```
encrypts-setup-private
```

You are prompted to enter your user password, and then your mount password. The mount password is the password used to recover your private directory manually. Leave blank to have one generated automatically. A directory named **.Private** is set up which is the actual encrypted directory, holding the encrypted data files. This is a dot file, with a period preceding the name. Then a directory is set up named **Private**, which will serve as a mount point for the **.Private** directory. For security purposes, your encrypted private directory (**.Private**) remains unmounted until you decide to access it.

The **Private** directory is located in your home directory. You can open your file browser to the home directory where you will find an icon for the Private folder. When you start up your computer and first login, the Private folder will be unmounted (lock emblem). Open the folder to display a file named "Access Your Private Data." Click on it to mount the **.Private** folder. The contents of your Private directory are then displayed. You can double-click on this icon to mount and access your Private directory contents. You will be prompted to enter your login password.

The first time you try to run the "Access Your Private Data" file, you will receive a message saying that there is no application for it. The execute permission needs to be set to allow you to run it. Ownership is set originally to the root user. Use the following command in a terminal window to change ownership. For *user*, use your username.

```
sudo chown user Access-Your-Private-Data.desktop
```

You can then right click on the file, select Properties to open the Properties dialog, and on the Permissions tab, you can click the Execute checkbox.

If you are working from the command line interface, you can mount the **.Private** directory with the **ecryptfs-mount-private** command. Do not try to run this command from within the **Private** directory.

```
mount.ecryptfs_private
```

You can later unmount it with the **ecryptfs-umount-private** command.

To create a passphrase for your private directory, you use the **ecryptfs-manager** command. This displays a simple menu for creating passphrases.

Help Resources

A great deal of support documentation is already installed on your system and is accessible from online sources. The Linux Mint User Guide is available as a browser application on your desktop. As Linux Mint is based on Ubuntu, the help sites listed in Table 1-4 may prove helpful. Both the GNOME and KDE desktops feature Help systems that use a browser-like interface to display help files.

Linux Mint User Guide

To start the Linux Mint User Guide, choose Help from the Accessories menu. The User Guide displays several links covering Linux Mint topics (see Figure 3-35). Topics covered include the installation, the desktop, and software management.

You can use the right and left arrows to move through previous documentation you displayed. A menu on the toolbar lets you access previously viewed pages during a session. You can always return to the top page by choosing "Linux Mint 18.2" from the menu. You can also search for topics. Click on the topic menu on the toolbar to open a search box. As you enter a search term possible results are displayed.

You can add bookmarks for a page by clicking the star button on the right side of the menu, or by opening the bookmark menu and selecting the "Add Bookmark" entry. The star for bookmarked pages will be dark. You can access bookmarks from the bookmark menu. To remove a bookmark, open the bookmarked page and click the star to turn it clear, or click the "Remove Bookmark" entry in the Bookmarks menu.

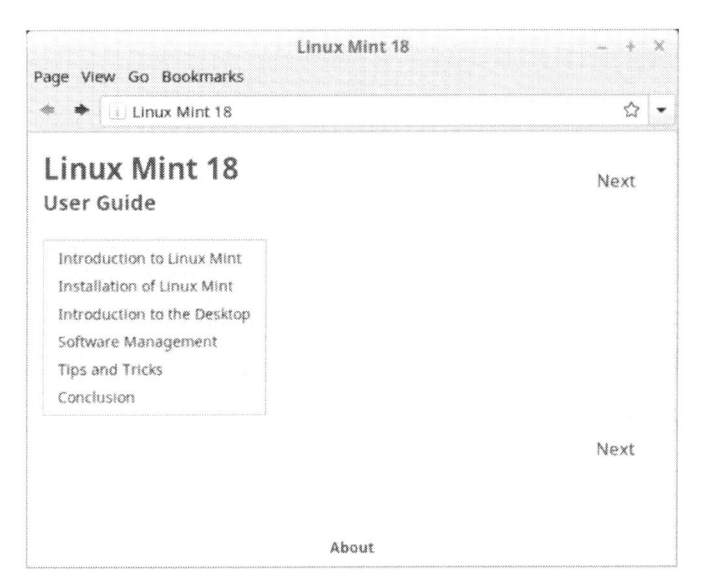

Figure 3-35: Linux Mint User Guide

Pages display a Next and Previous buttons, which you can use to move through the entire User Guide (see Figure 3-36). Some pages have links to other sections in a topic.

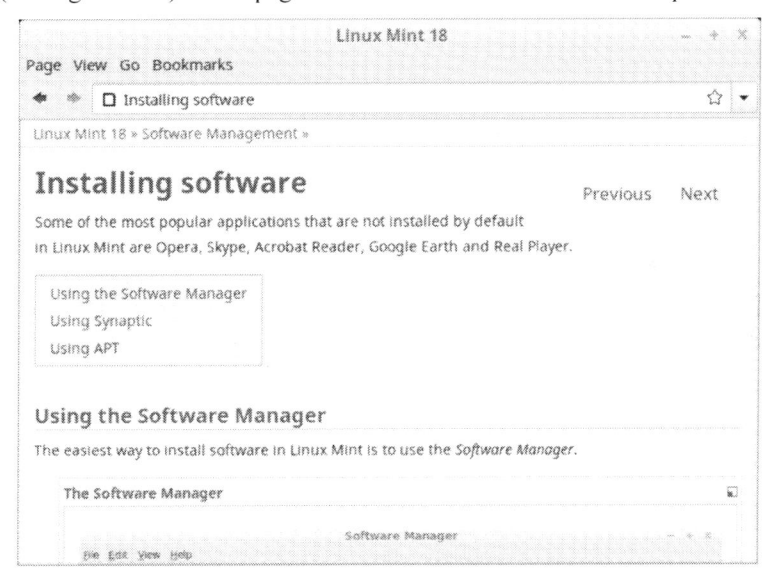

Figure 3-36: Linux Mint User Guide Topic

If you want to see available Cinnamon, Mate, and selected GNOME application help documents, choose All Documents from the Go menu. You will see application manuals installed applications such as the LightDM Display Manager (LightDM), Movie Player (Xplayer), Log Viewer (GNOME Log File Viewer), and Mate Power Manager (see Figure 3-37). Help documentation includes the X-Apps: Xed (Text Editor), Xplayer (Movie Player), Xreader, Pix, and Xviewer. . . . In this list, the "Desktop User Guide" is a guide to the Mate desktop.

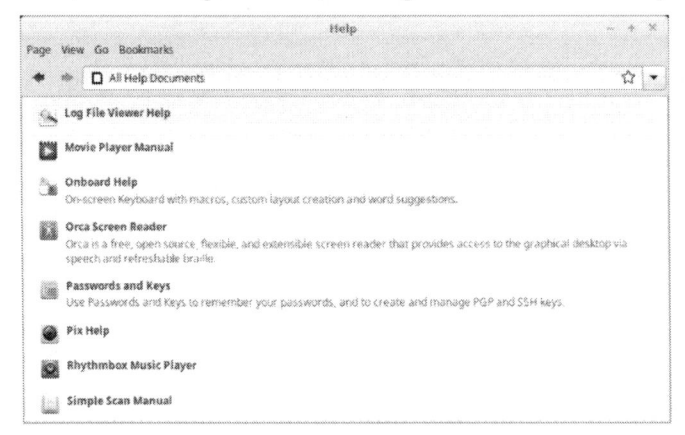

Figure 3-37: Linux Mint User Guide: All Documents

Application Documentation

On your system, the **/usr/share/doc** directory contains documentation files installed by each application. Within each directory, you can usually find HOW-TO, README, and INSTALL documents for that application.

The Man Pages

You can also access the Man pages, which are manuals for Linux commands available from the command line interface, using the **man** command. Enter **man** along with the command on which you want information. The following example asks for information on the **ls** command:

```
$ man ls
```

Pressing the SPACEBAR key advances you to the next page. Pressing the **b** key moves you back a page. When you finish, press the **q** key to quit the Man utility and return to the command line. You activate a search by pressing either the slash (/) or question mark (?) keys. The / key searches forward and the ? key searches backward. When you press the / key, a line opens at the bottom of your screen, where you can enter a word to search for. Press ENTER to activate the search. You can repeat the same search by pressing the **n** key. You need not re-enter the pattern.

The Info Pages

Documentation for GNU applications, such as the gcc compiler and the Emacs editor, also exist as info pages accessible from the GNOME and KDE Help Centers. You can also access this documentation by entering the command **info** in a terminal window. This brings up a special screen listing different GNU applications. The info interface has its own set of commands. You can learn more about it by entering **info info** at the command prompt. Typing **m** opens a line at the bottom of the screen where you can enter the first few letters of the application. Pressing ENTER brings up the info file on that application.

Terminal Window

The Terminal window allows you to enter Linux commands on a command line, accessible as Terminal from the Administration menu, and from the Cinnamon and Mate panels. It also provides you with a shell interface for using shell commands instead of your desktop. The command line is editable, allowing you to use the backspace key to erase characters on the line. Pressing a key will insert that character. You can use the left and right arrow keys to move anywhere on the line, and then press keys to insert characters, or use backspace to delete characters (see Figure 3-32). Folders, files, and executable files are color-coded: white for files, blue for folders, green for executable files, and aqua for links. Shared folders are displayed with a green background.

The terminal window will remember the previous commands you entered. Use the up and down arrows to have those commands displayed in turn on the command line. Press the ENTER key to re-execute the currently displayed command. You can even edit a previous command before running it, allowing you to execute a modified version of a previous command. This can be helpful if you need to re-execute a complex command with a different argument, or if you mistyped a complex command and want to correct it without having to re-type the entire command. The terminal window will display all your previous interactions and commands for that session. Use the scrollbar to see any previous commands you ran and their displayed results.

The menubar provides a full set options for your terminal window including search, help, zoom, and edit operations (see Figure 3-38). You can also access several common terminal operations such as opening a tab and accessing Profiles configurations from a pop-up menu accessible by right-clicking anywhere on the terminal window.

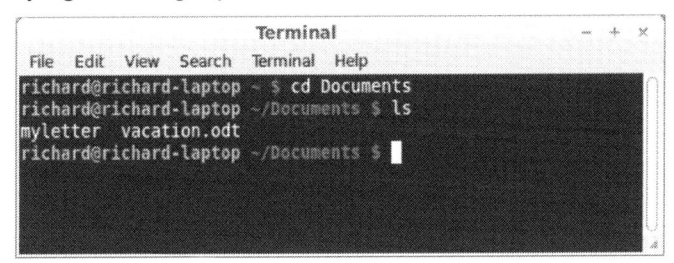

Figure 3-38: Terminal Window

You have the option to hide the menubar. Click the "Show Menubar" entry in the View menu. To re-display the menubar on the terminal window, choose the "Show Menubar" entry from the terminal pop-up menu. (see Figure 3-39).

You can open as many terminal windows as you want, each working in its own shell. Instead of opening a separate window for each new shell, you can open several shells in the same window, using tabs. Select Open Tab from the File menu to open a new tab (**Shift-Ctrl-t**) or from the pop-up menu. Each tab runs a separate shell, letting you enter different commands in each. You can use the Tabs menu to move to different tabs, or just click on its tab to select it. The Tab menu is displayed on the toolbar only if multiple tabs are open. For a single window, the Tab menu is not shown.

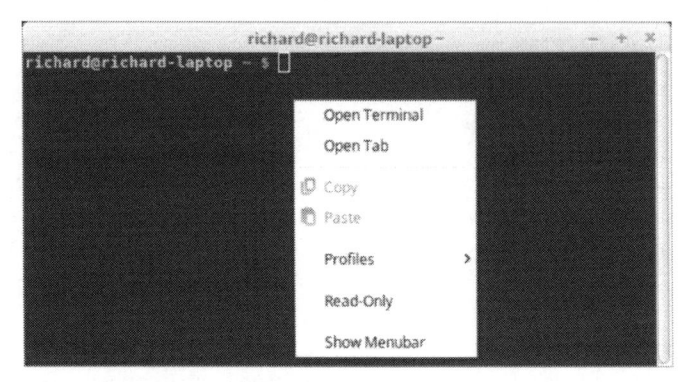

Figure 3-39: Terminal Window without menubar

       The terminal window also supports desktop cut/copy and paste operations. You can copy a line from a Web page and then paste it to the terminal window (you can use the Paste entry on the Terminal window's Edit menu or pop-up menu, or press **Shift-Ctrl-v**). The command will appear and then you can press ENTER to execute the command. This is useful for command line operations displayed on an instructional Web page. Instead of typing in a complex command yourself, just select and copy from the Web page directly, and then paste to the Terminal window. You can also perform any edits on the command, if needed, before executing it.

       You can customize terminal windows using profiles. A default profile is set up already. You can create new ones with customized preferences. Use the Change Profile submenu on the Terminal menu to change profiles. To customize your terminal window, select Profile Preferences from the Edit menu. This opens a window for setting your default profile options with tabs for General, Command, Colors, Scrolling, and Compatibility (see Figure 3-40).

Figure 3-40: Terminal Window Profile configuration

On the General tab, you can select the default size of a terminal window in text rows and columns.

The Scrolling tab specifies the number of command lines your terminal history will keep. These are the lines you can move back through and select to re-execute. You can set this to unlimited to keep all the commands.

Your terminal window will be set up to use a dark background with white text. To change this, you can edit the profile to change the background and text colors on the Colors tab. De-select the "Use colors from system theme" entry. This enables the "Built-in schemes" menu from which you can select a "Black on white" display. Other color combinations are also listed, such as "Black on light yellow" and "Green on black." The Custom option lets you choose your own text and background colors. The colors on your open terminal window will change according to your selection, allowing you to see how the color choices will look. For a transparent background, choose the "Use transparent background" entry and then set the amount of shading (none is completely transparent and full shows no transparency). You can also choose to use the transparency setting from the system theme instead.

To create a new profile, choose New Profile from the File menu to open the New Profile window where you can enter the profile name and select any profile to base it on. The default profile is chosen initially.

To edit an existing profile, select Preferences from the Edit menu to open the Preferences window, and then click on the Profiles tab to list your profiles. Choose the one you want to edit and then click the Edit button to open the Editing Profile window for that profile. You can also create new profiles, or delete existing ones. Use the selection menu to at the bottom of the tab to choose which dialog to use.

Command Line Interface

When using the command line interface, you are given a simple prompt at which you type in a command. Even when you are using a desktop like GNOME, you sometimes need to execute commands on a command line. You can do so in a terminal window, which is accessed from the Administration menu as Terminal, and from the Cinnamon and Mate panel. You could also enter the command line interface with a Ctrl-Alt-F1 key (F1 through F6). Use the Ctrl-Alt-F8 keys to return to the graphic interface. Linux commands make extensive use of options and arguments. Be careful to place your arguments and options in their correct order on the command line. The format for a Linux command is the command name followed by options, and then by arguments, as shown here:

```
$ command-name options arguments
```

An *option* is a one-letter code preceded by one or two hyphens, which modifies the type of action the command takes. Options and arguments may or may not be optional, depending on the command. For example, the `ls` command can take an option, `-s`. The `ls` command displays a listing of files in your directory, and the `-s` option adds the size of each file in blocks. You enter the command and its option on the command line as follows:

```
$ ls -s
```

If you are uncertain what format and options a command uses, you can check the command syntax quickly by displaying its man page. Most commands have a man page. Just enter the **man** command with the command name as an argument.

```
$ man ls
```

An argument is data the command may need to execute its task. In many cases, this is a filename. An argument is entered as a word on the command line that appears after any options. For example, to display the contents of a file, you can use the `more` command with the file's name as its argument. The `less` or `more` command used with the filename **mydata** would be entered on the command line as follows:

```
$ less mydata
```

The command line is actually a buffer of text you can edit. Before you press ENTER to execute the command, you can edit the command on the command line. The editing capabilities provide a way to correct mistakes you may make when typing a command and its options. The **Backspace** key lets you erase the character you just typed (the one to the left of the cursor) and the **Del** key lets you erase the character the cursor is on. With this character-erasing capability, you can backspace over the entire line if you want, erasing what you entered. **Ctrl-u** erases the whole command line and lets you start over again at the prompt. You can use the right and left arrow keys to move within a line, erasing and adding characters where you are positioned.

You can use the **Up Arrow** key to redisplay your last executed command. You can then re-execute that command, or you can edit it and execute the modified command. This is helpful when you have to repeat certain operations, such as editing the same file. This is also helpful when you have already executed a command you entered incorrectly.

4. Installing and Updating Software

Installing Software Packages

Linux Mint Package Management Software

Linux Mint Software Repositories

Updating Linux Mint with Update Manager

Managing Packages with Software Manager

Synaptic Package Manager

Source code files

DEB Software Packages

Managing software with apt-get

Managing non-repository packages with dpkg

Using packages with other software formats

Linux Mint software distribution is implemented using the online software repositories, which contain an extensive collection of Linux Mint-compliant software. With the integration of repository access into your Linux system, you can think of that software as an easily installed extension of your current collection. You can add software to your system by accessing software repositories that support Debian packages (DEB) and the Advanced Package Tool (APT). Software is packaged into DEB software package files. These files are, in turn, installed and managed by APT. Software Manager provides an easy-to-use front end for installing software with just a click, accessible from the Administration and System Tools menus, and, on Cinnamon, from the Favorites icon bar on the Cinnamon menu.

The software repositories used by Linux Mint are based on the Ubuntu software repositories, which are organized into sections, depending on how the software is supported. Software supported directly is located in the main Linux Mint repository section. Other Linux software that is most likely compatible is placed in the Universe repository section. Many software applications, particularly multimedia applications, have potential licensing conflicts. Such applications are placed in the Multiverse repository section, which is not maintained directly by Ubuntu. Many of the popular multimedia drivers and applications, such as video and digital music, support can be obtained from the Multiverse sections using the same simple APT commands you use for Linux Mint-supported software. Software from the Multiverse and Universe sections are integrated into Software Manager, and can be installed just as easily as Linux Mint main section software.

You can also download source code versions of applications, then compile, and install them on your system. Where this process once was complex, it has been streamlined significantly with the use of configure scripts. Most current source code, including GNU software, is distributed with a configure script, which automatically detects your system configuration and creates a binary file that is compatible with your system.

You can download Linux software from many online sources directly, but it is always advised that you use the Linux Mint/Ubuntu prepared package versions if available. Most software for GNOME and KDE have corresponding Linux Mint and Ubuntu compliant packages in the Ubuntu Universe and Multiverse repository sections.

Installing Software Packages

Installing software is an administrative function performed by a user with administrative access. During the Linux Mint installation, only some of the many applications and utilities available for users on Linux were installed on your system. On Linux Mint, you can install or remove software from your system with the Linux Mint Software Manager, the Synaptic Package Manager, or the **apt-get** command. Alternatively, you could install software as separate DEB files, or by downloading and compiling its source code.

APT (Advanced Package Tool) is integrated as the primary tool for installing packages. When you install a package with the Software Manager or with the Synaptic Package Manager, APT will be invoked and will select and download the package automatically from the appropriate online repository. This will include the entire Linux Mint online repository.

A DEB software package includes all the files needed for a software application. A Linux software application often consists of several files that must be installed in different directories. The application program itself is placed in a system directory such as **/usr/bin**, online manual files go in another directory, and library files go in yet another directory. When you select an application for installation, APT will install any additional dependent (required) packages. APT also will install all recommended packages by default. Many software applications have additional features that rely on recommended packages.

Linux Mint Package Management Software

Although all Linux Mint software packages have the same DEB format, they can be managed and installed using different package management software tools. The underlying software management tool is APT.

Software Manager (mintinstall) is the primary interface for locating and installing Linux Mint software, repository files at **/var/apt**. Designed as a central software management application for handling all Linux Mint packages.

APT (Advanced Package Tool) performs the actual software management operations for all applications installed from a repository. Software Manager, the Synaptic Package Manager, update-manager, dpkg, and apt-get are all front-ends for APT, repository files at **/var/apt**.

Synaptic Package Manager is a Graphical front end for APT that manages packages; repository files are located at **/var/apt**.

Update Manager is the Linux Mint graphical front end for updating installed software using APT.

tasksel is a cursor-based screen for selecting package groups and particular servers (front-end for APT). This tool will work on the command-line interface installed by the Linux Mint Server CD. You can also run it in a terminal window on a desktop (**sudo tasksel**). Use arrow keys to move to an entry, the spacebar to select, the tab key to move to the OK button. Press ENTER on the OK button to perform your installs.

dpkg is the older command line tool used to install, update, remove, and query software packages; uses its own database, **/var/lib/dpkg**; repository files are kept at **/var/cache/apt**, the same as APT.

apt-get is the primary command line tool for APT to install, update, and remove software; uses its own database, **/var/lib/apt/**.

aptitude is a cursor based front end for **dpkg** and **apt-get**, which uses its own database, **/var/lib/aptitude**.

Linux Mint Software Repositories

Linux Mint is derived from the Ubuntu Linux distribution and is configured to directly access the Ubuntu software repository. Five main components or sections make up the Linux Mint repository: main, upstream, import, backports, and romeo.

To see a listing of all packages in the Linux Mint repository see:

```
http://packages.linuxmint.com
```

To see the packages in the Linux Mint repositories, click on the Linux Mint link for your release. Linux Mint supported packages are listed, separated into sections for their repositories.

Unlike the Cinnamon, Mate, and Xfce editions, the Linux Mint KDE edition uses the Kubuntu repositories directly, not the Linux Mint repositories.

Repository Components

The following repository components are included in the Linux Mint repository:

main: Officially supported Linux Mint software, includes Cinnamon desktop packages, the Nemo file manager, and the LightDM display manager, along with administration tools including Software Manager, Software Updater, and the Linux Mint Software Sources.

upstream: Linux Mint compliant software, such as Rhythmbox, gedit, and tomboy notes.

import: Mostly imported Mate desktop software, including the Caja file manager. Also includes third-party software such as skype, opera, and the Linux Mint flash plugin.

backports: Software under development for the next Linux Mint release, but packaged for use in the current one. Not guaranteed or fully tested. Backports access is enabled by default.

Ubuntu Software Repositories

Linux Mint is derived from the Ubuntu Linux distribution and is configured to directly access the Ubuntu software repository. Four main components or sections make up the Ubuntu repository: main, restricted, universe, and multiverse. These components are described in detail at:

`https://help.ubuntu.com/community/Repositories`

To see a listing of all packages in the Ubuntu repository see:

`https://packages.ubuntu.com`

Repository Components

The following repository components are included in the Ubuntu repository:

main: Officially supported Ubuntu software (canonical), includes GStreamer Good plug-ins.

restricted: Software commonly used and required for many applications, but not open source or freely licensed, like the proprietary graphics card drivers from Nvidia and AMD needed for hardware support. Because they are not open source, they are not guaranteed to work.

universe: All open source Linux software not directly supported by Ubuntu includes GStreamer Bad plug-ins.

multiverse: Linux software that does not meet licensing requirements and is not considered essential. It is not guaranteed to work. For example, the GStreamer ugly package is in this repository. Check **https://www.ubuntu.com/about/about-ubuntu/licensing**.

Repositories

In addition to the Ubuntu repository, Ubuntu maintains several other repositories used primarily for maintenance and support for existing packages. The updates repository holds updated packages for a release. The security updates repository contains critical security package updates every system will need.

Ubuntu main repository: Collection of Ubuntu-compliant software packages for releases organized into main, universe, multiverse, and restricted sections.

Updates: Updates for packages in the main repository, both main and restricted sections.

Backports: Software under development for the next Ubuntu release, but packaged for use in the current one. Not guaranteed or fully tested. Backports access is now enabled by default.

Security updates: Critical security fixes for main repository software.

Partner: Third party proprietary software tested to work on Ubuntu. You need to authorize access manually.

The Backports repository provides un-finalized or development versions for new and current software. They are not guaranteed to work, but may provide needed features.

Note: Though it is possible to add the Debian Linux distribution repository, it is not advisable. Packages are designed for specific distributions. Combining them can lead to irresolvable conflicts.

Linux Mint Repository Configuration file: sources.list.d/ official-package-repositories.list

Repository configuration is managed by APT using configuration files in the **/etc/apt** directory. The **/etc/apt/sources.list** file traditionally holds repository entries. However, on Linux Mint, the main repository file is located in the in the **/etc/apt/sources.list.d** directory, and is named **official-package-repositories.list**. APT reads any text files in the **/etc/apt/sources.list.d** directory as part of the **sources.list** file.

```
/etc/apt/sources.list.d/official-package-repositories.list
```

A repository entry in the file consists of a single line with the following format:

```
format   URI   release   section
```

The format is normally **deb**, for Debian package format. The URI (universal resource identifier) provides the location of the repository, such as an FTP or Web URL. The release name is the official name of a particular Linux Mint distribution like petra or sonya. Linux Mint 18.2 has the name **sonya**. The section can be one or more terms that identify a section in that release's repository. There can be more than one term used to specify a section like **main** and **upstream**. You can also list individual packages if you want. Linux Mint has two entries, one for the Linux Mint set of packages, and the other for extra packages. All packages from the main repository, as well as any updated and advanced packages from the upstream, import, and backport are accessed.

```
deb http://packages.linuxmint.com/ sonya   main upstream import backport
```

In addition, all the Ubuntu repositories are activated, including the packages (trusty), package updates (trusty-updates, and security updates (trusty-security). The entry for the Ubuntu Xenial (Ubuntu 16.04) repositories is shown here.

```
deb http://archive.ubuntu.com/ubuntu/ xenial  main restricted universe multiverse
```

The Multiverse and Universe sections can be specified by single terms: **universe** and **multiverse**. On Linux Mint, the Ubuntu restricted, universe, and multiverse repositories are added, enabling all.

The update repository for a section is referenced by the **-updates** suffix, as in **xenial-updates**.

```
deb http://archive.ubuntu.com/ubuntu/ xenial-updates  main restricted universe multiverse
```

The security repository for a section is referenced with the suffix **-security**, as **xenial-security**.

```
deb http://archive.ubuntu.com/ubuntu/ xenial-security  main restricted universe multiverse
```

An activated entry is included for the Canonical partners repository. Partners include companies like Adobe.

```
deb http://archive.canonical.com/ubuntu/  xenial  partner
```

You could also add corresponding source code repositories, which use a **deb-src** format.

```
deb-src http://archive.ubuntu.com/ubuntu/ xenial main restricted universe multiverse
```

Comments begin with a # mark. You can add comments of your own if you wish. Commenting an entry effectively disables that component of a repository. Placing a # mark before a repository entry will effectively disable it.

Most entries, including third-party entries for Linux Mint partners, can be managed using Software Sources. Entries can also be managed by editing the **official-package-repositories.list** file with the following command, though it is recommended that you use Software Sources instead.

```
sudo xed /etc/apt/sources.list.d/official-package-repositories.list
```

You could add or remove the # at the beginning of the line to deactivate or activate a repository such as partners.

```
# deb http://archive.canonical.com/ubuntu/ xenial partner
```

Software Sources managed from Linux Mint

You can manage your repositories with the Software Sources dialog allowing you to enable or disable repository sections, as well as add new entries. This dialog edits the **official-package-repositories.list** file directly. You can access Software Sources from the System Settings, or from the Administration menu. You can also access it on Software Manager from the Edit menu, and on the Synaptic Package Manager from the Settings menu as the Repositories entry. The Software Sources dialog displays five tabs: Official repositories, PPAs, Additional repositories, Authentication keys, and Maintenance (see Figure 4-1). The Official repositories tab lists the Linux

Mint and Ubuntu repository locations. There are options to include backports and source code repositories, as well as unstable (testing) software. On this tab, you could change to a different repository mirror, should you find that the current ones are slow.

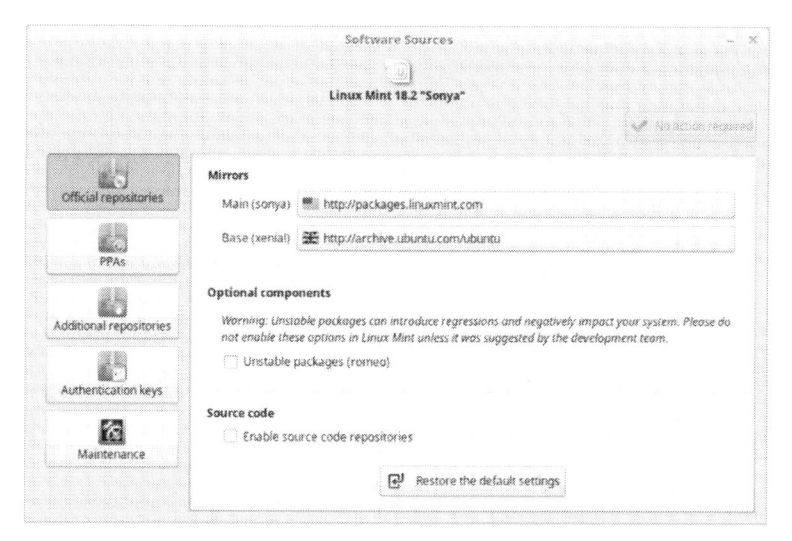

Figure 4-1: Software Sources Linux Mint Official Repositories.

Repository locations are specified in the Mirrors section. The "Main (sonya)" mirror is set to the main Linux Mint website. You can choose another mirror that may be closer and faster. Click on the "Main (sonya)" button to open the "Select a mirror" dialog with a list of current mirrors, with flags denoting the country they are in (see Figure 4-2). You can do the same with the "Base (xenial)" mirror.

Figure 4-2: Software Sources Mirrors

On the "Additional repositories" tab, you can add repositories for third-party software (see Figure 4-3). The repository for "CD-ROM (Installation Disc)" will already be listed, but not checked. To add a repository, click the "Add a new repository" button to open a dialog where you enter the complete APT entry, starting with the **deb** keyword, followed by the URL, release, and sections or packages. This is the line as it will appear in the sources file. Once entered, click the OK button. Use the "Edit URL" button to change an entry, and the "Remove" button to remove one.

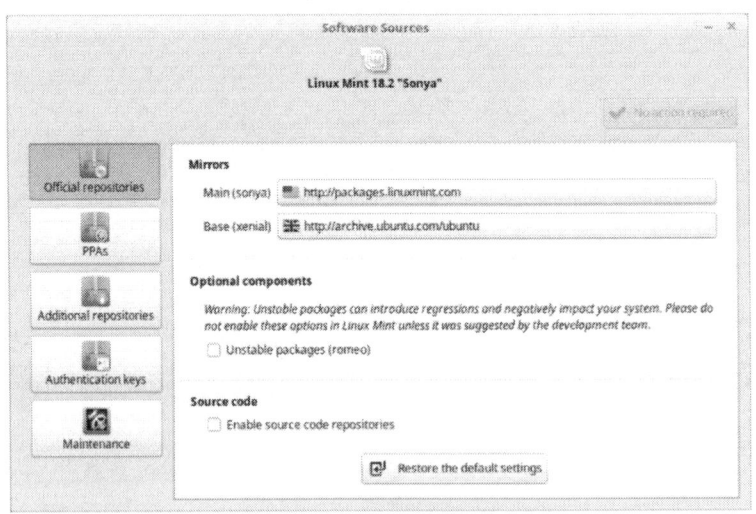

Figure 4-3: Software Sources Additional Repositories

      The PPAs tab lets you add Personal Package Archive repositories (see Figure 4-4). These are often repositories for specialized drivers or custom software. Click the "Add a new PPA" button to open a dialog where you can enter the PPA's URL and repository. Once installed, you can select the PPA and click the "Open PPA" button to open a dialog listing the PPA's packages. You can then choose the ones you want to install. The packages are installed directly from Software Sources.

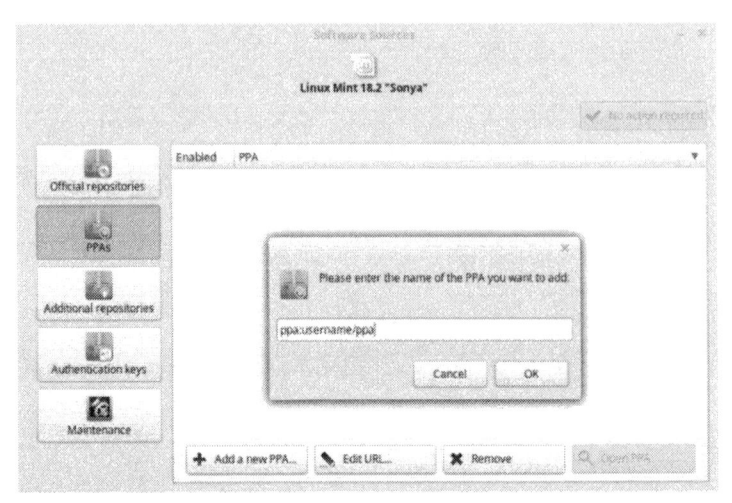

Figure 4-4: Software Sources PPA

The Authentication tab shows additional repository software signature keys that are installed on your system (see Figure 4-5). Most other third party or customized repositories will provide a signature key file for you to download and import. You can add such keys manually from the Authentication tab. Click the Import Key File to open a file browser where you can select the downloaded key file. This procedure is the same as the **apt-key add** operation. Both add keys that APT then uses to verify DEB software packages downloaded from repositories before it installs them.

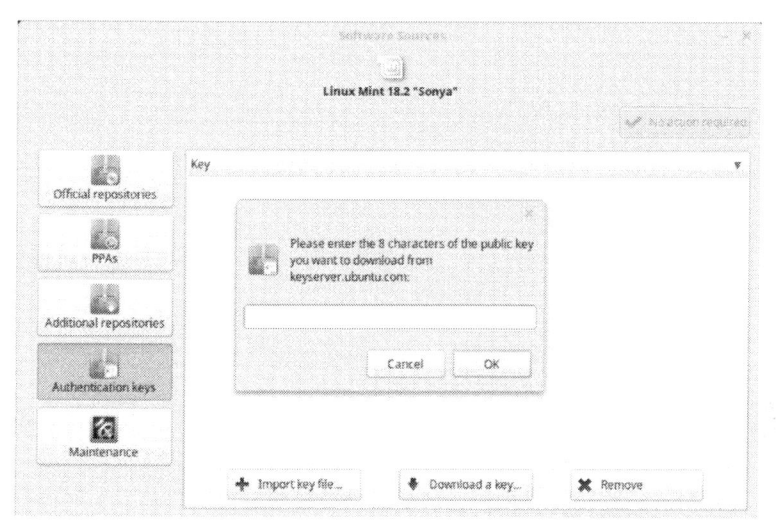

Figure 4-5: Software Sources Authentication Keys

The Maintenance tab lets you fix update issues such as mergelist problems and residual configuration (dependent files left over from removed applications).

After you have made changes and click the "Update the cache" button in the upper right corner to make the new repositories or components available on your package managers like Software Manager and the Synaptic Package Manager. The "Downloading package information" dialog opens and downloads the latest software listings from your repositories. You also can update your repository configuration by running **apt-get update**, or clicking the Reload button on the Synaptic Package Manager.

Codec packages on Linux Mint (mint-meta-codecs)

Applications and codecs with licensing issues, like the DVD Video commercial decoder (**libdvdcss2**), are installed by the mint-meta-codec package. This package accesses codecs from the Ubuntu universe and multiverse repositories. The **mint-meta-codecs-kde** package installs the KDE versions. The mint-meta-codecs package also installs the Gstreamer bad, ugly, ffmpeg packages, as well as the **unrar** archiver and the Linux Mint Flash plugin.

Updating Linux Mint with Update Manager

New updates are continually being prepared for particular software packages as well as system components. These are posted as updates you can download from software repositories and install on your system. These include new versions of applications, servers, and even the kernel. Such updates may range from single software packages to whole components. Updating your Linux Mint system is a very simple procedure, using Update Manager, a graphical update interface for APT.

The first time you start the Update Manager, the Updates Policy page is displayed, which gives you three options for selecting updates based on their stability (see Figure 4-6). In effect, you can configure a policy for managing your updates. You can choose to updates only known safe packages, security and kernel updates in addition to the safe updates, or all possible updates regardless of their potential stability. You can change to another policy by displaying the Update Policy page again (Edit | Updates policy).

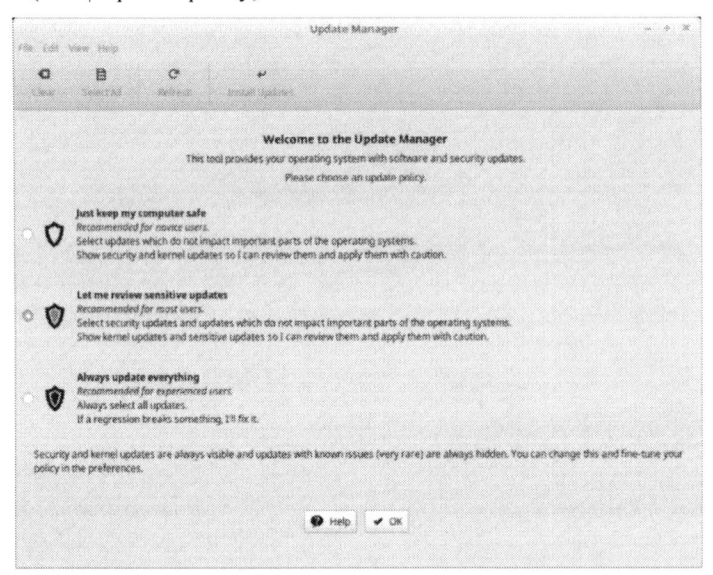

Figure 4-6: Update Policy

When updates are available, the Update Manager icon on the panel displays a blue color and the number 1 (see Figure 4-7). You can start the Update Manager clicking the Update Manager icon, or by selecting it from the Administration menu. To ensure that the update is current, you can click the Refresh button to download an updated listing of your packages from all your active repositories, detecting the modified packages (see Figure 4-6).

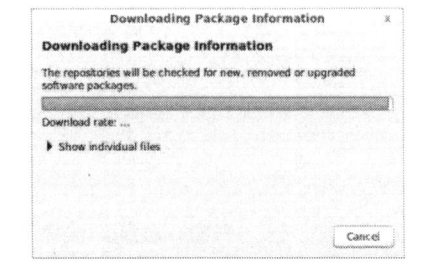

Figure 4-7: Update Manager update icon and package information dialog

The Update Manager dialog shows a listing of packages to be updated (see Figure 4-8). The checkboxes for each entry lets you de-select any packages you do not want to update. Package names may be aliased, displaying a more descriptive name than the original, such as **cinnamon-cjs** instead of just **cjs**. Packages are organized into levels, depending on the impact they have on the operating system. The first two are have minimal or no impact and your Update Manager is configured to display only packages in those levels. These are automatically selected. The first level has no impact on your system. Updates are level 2, which, of course, will have some impact. Level 3 are packages that impact several applications such as libraries, desktops, and toolkits. Kernels and sensitive updates are level 4. Level 3 and 4 are visible but not selected. Level 5 is almost never used and references broken or know dangerous updates. These are not shown default.

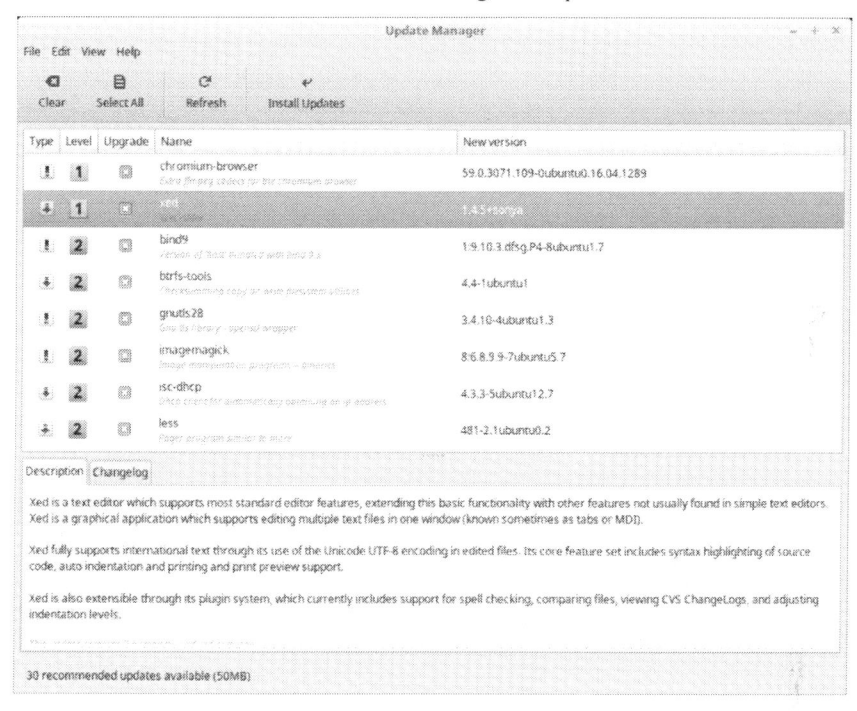

Figure 4-8: Update Manager with selected packages

The first column indicates the update type, whether it is a normal update, security update (exclamation icon), backports (new/unstable Ubuntu packages), and romeo (new/unstable Linux Mint packages). The "New version" column displays the version number of the package. To also display the version of the currently installed package, click the "Old column" entry in the View | Visible columns menu.

To see a detailed description of a particular update, select the update to display the description in the section at the bottom of the screen. Two tabs are displayed in this section: Description and Changelog. The Changelog tab lists detailed update information, and Description tab provides information about the software.

All updates are selected automatically. You can use the checkboxes in the Upgrade column to select or de-select a package. On the toolbar, you can click the Clear button to deselect

110 *Part 1: Getting Started*

all selected updates, and the Select All button to select them all. The Refresh button downloads the latest listing of packages from your repositories again.

Click the Install Updates button on the toolbar to start updating. The packages will be downloaded from their appropriate repository. Once downloaded, the packages are updated. When downloading and installing, a dialog appears showing the download and install progress (see Figure 4-9). Click the Details arrow to see install messages for particular software packages. A window will open up that lists each file and its progress. Once downloaded, the updates are installed. When the update completes, Update Manager will display a message saying that your system is up-to-date.

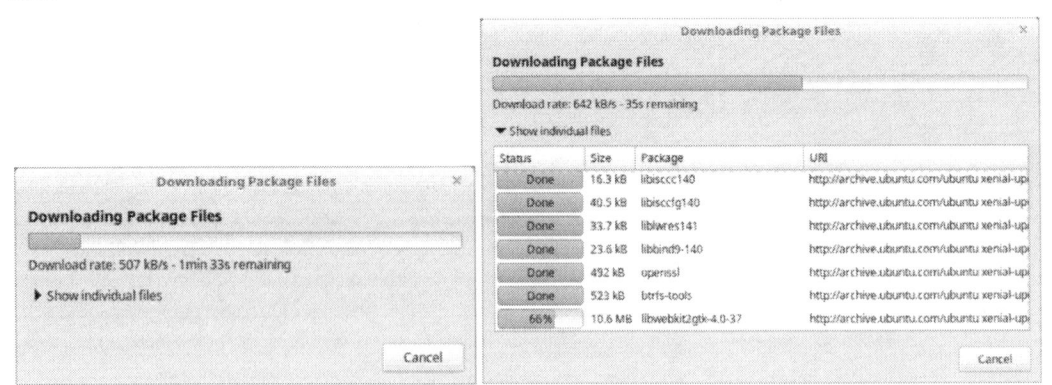

Figure 4-9: Update download and install

Update Manager notifies you of any issues with accessing your repositories. It warns you if the mirror you are using is not up to date, if it is corrupted, or if a faster one is available. When you first use Update Manager, you will likely be prompted to use a local mirror for faster access, as shown here. Clicking on the OK button opens the Software Sources dialog at the "Official repositories" tab, where you can change to a different mirror.

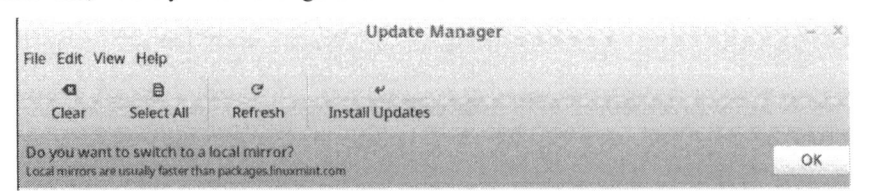

You can configure the Update Manager using the Update Manager's Preferences dialog accessible from the Update Manager's Edit menu (see Figure 4-10). The Update Manager Preferences dialog has four tabs: Options, Levels, Auto-Refresh, and Blacklisted. On the Levels tab, you can choose to update according to the impact the packages have on your system: minimal, normal, large, sensitive, and dangerous. The low impact packages (levels 1 and 2) are already marked as selected and visible to Update Manager. These are packages that are maintained by Linux Mint (level 1), recommended and also tested by Linux Mint (level 2). Also, visible but not selected are the large and sensitive levels. Level 3 are packages that impact several applications such as libraries, desktops, and toolkits. Kernels and sensitive updates are level 4. In addition, you could add known unstable and possibly dangerous packages (level 5).

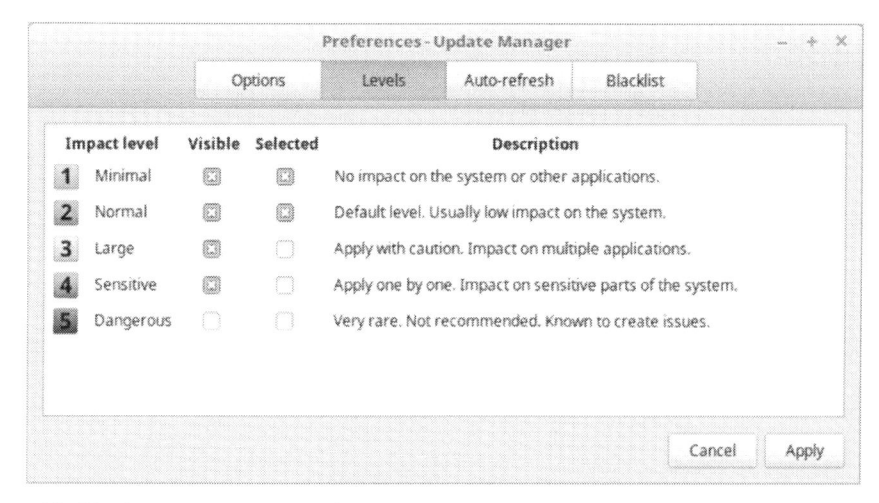

Figure 4-10: Update Manager Preferences

On the Options tab, you can choose to show and select security updates, and whether to update packages that have dependent packages (new packages that also have to be installed or removed to make a package work). The Auto-Refresh tab lets you specify how often updates are checked. On the "Blacklist " tab you can specify packages that you would not want to be updated.

The Linux Kernels dialog (View | Linux kernels) lists the available Linux kernels, showing what they fix and what changes they make. It also shows which one is currently loaded and allows you to install new ones.

Managing Packages with Software Manager (mintinstall)

To perform simple installation and removal of software, you can use Software Manager (mintinstall), which is the primary supported package manager for Linux Mint. Software Manager is designed to be the centralized utility for managing all your software. Software Manager is a front end for the APT package manager. When you install a package with Software Manager, APT is invoked and automatically selects and downloads the package from the appropriate online repository.

Software Manager displays a dialog of category icons you can click to list packages in that category (see Figure 4-11). You can return to the Categories dialog at any time by clicking the Categories button in the upper right corner. Many categories will have subcategories, such as Graphics, which has subcategories for Drawing, Photography, and Publishing (see Figure 4-12). These are listed at the top of the dialog, with a full software listing below. As you progress through categories and their subcategories, buttons appear next to the Categories button, letting you move back to a previous subcategory (see Figure 4-13).

Figure 4-11: Software Manager

Figure 4-12: Software Manager sub-categories

  Instead of scrolling through category listings, you can use the search box to search directly for a package. You can set search preferences on the Edit menu Preferences submenu, such as whether to search summaries or descriptions or perform dynamic searches (search while typing).

  On the menu bar, the View menu lets you limit packages displayed to Available, Installed, or both. The "Account information" entry opens a dialog where you can log in to your account on **community.linuxmint.com**, which allows you to submit software reviews.

A status box at the bottom displays ongoing tasks, such as package installs and removals. Click on the status button, displays a detailed list of all tasks showing their name, status, and progress. The status button is the long buttons at the bottom of the Software Manager dialog with a gear icon on the left side with either an "ongoing actions" or a "No ongoing actions" label. Click the Categories button to return to the Categories dialog.

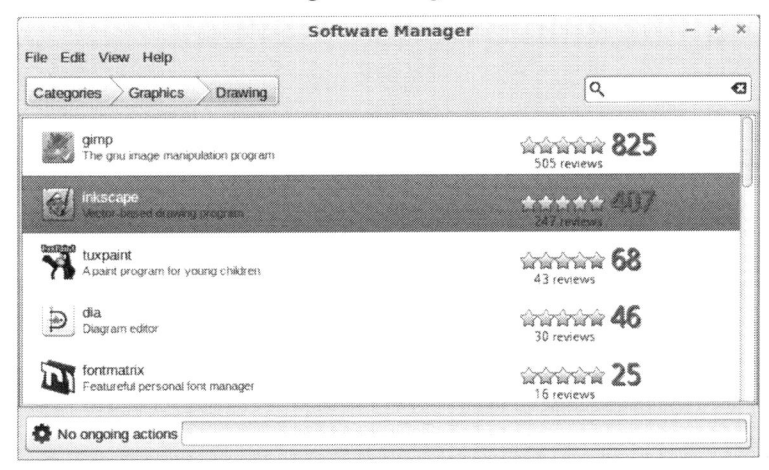

Figure 4-13: Software Manager package listing

To install a package, first, locate it (see Figure 4-13). Then double-click it to open the application page (see Figure 4-14). The application page for an uninstalled package will have an Install button at the upper right and a "Not installed" notice. To install the application, click the Install button.

During the install, a progress icon appears in the bottom status bar. You can click on the "ongoing actions" button to open the Active Tasks page, which displays a progress bar showing the download and install progress (see Figure 4-15). You can switch back to the application page by clicking its button at the top of the Software Manager dialog.

When finished, the application page displays a Remove button and an Installed notice with a green checkmark on the application icon (see Figure 4-14). The entry in the list of applications also will have a green checkmark emblem on its icon indicating that the application is installed.

The application page displays a detailed description of the application, install details, and reviews (see Figure 4-14). You can click the website link at the end of the description to access the application's website, which may provide detailed documentation. If an application thumbnail is displayed, you can click on it to display the full image. You can also write and submit a review. The software package's score and number of reviews are displayed in the upper right corner.

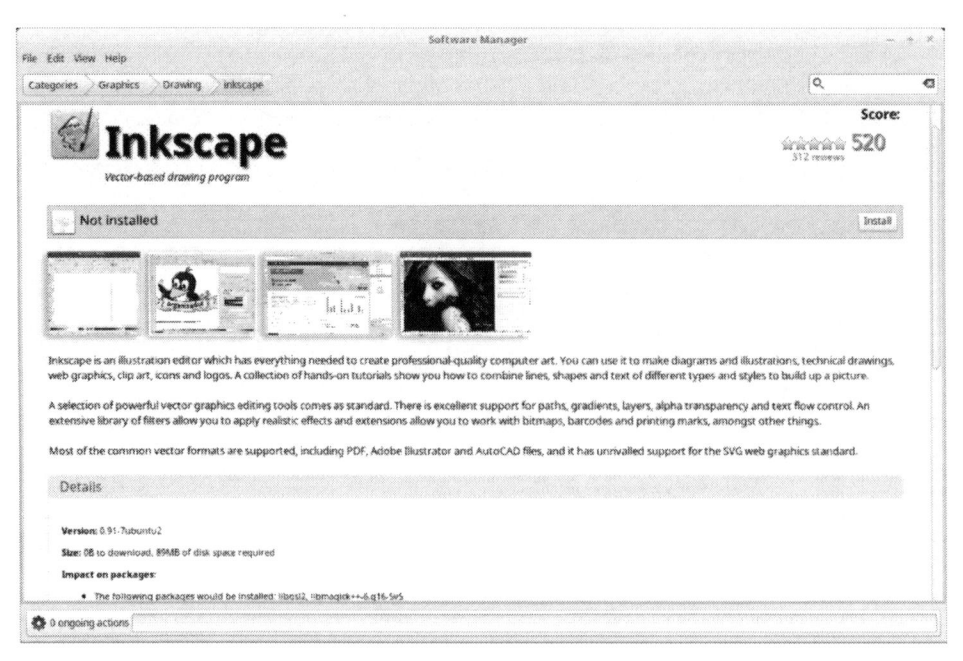

Figure 4-14: Software Manager application

Version, License, size, and update information is listed in the Details section. The update information shows the impact on packages, listing associated packages that will be installed or removed.

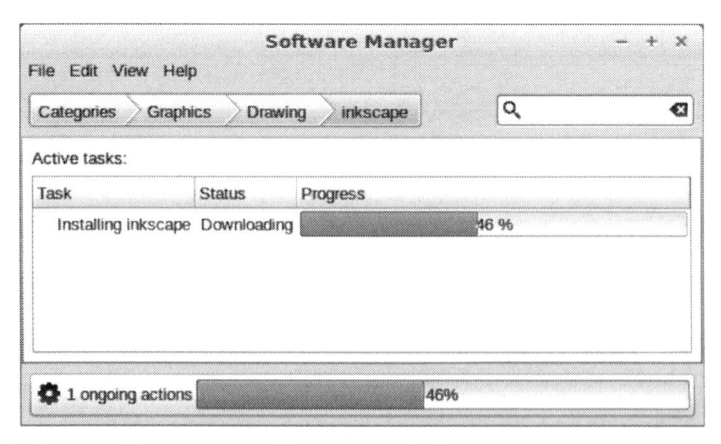

Figure 4-15: Software Manager and Launcher item download and install progress

When finished, the application page displays a Remove button and a green check mark with the installed label and the date (see Figure 4-16). The entry in the list of applications also will have a green checkmark emblem indicating that the application is installed.

To remove a package, first, locate it in the package lists, click on it to open its application Info page, and click the Remove button.

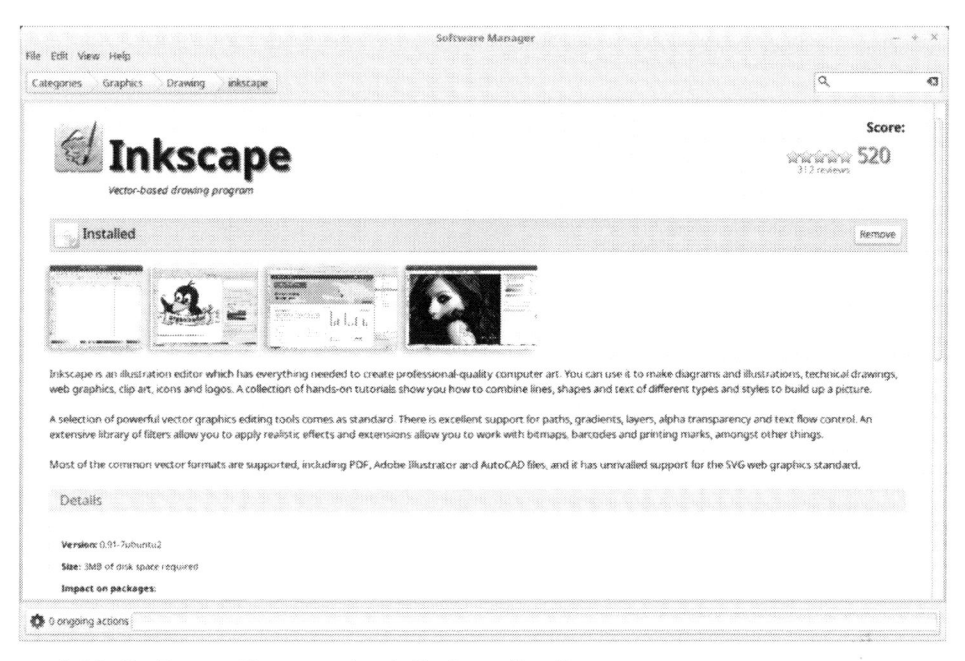

Figure 4-16: Software Manager installed application

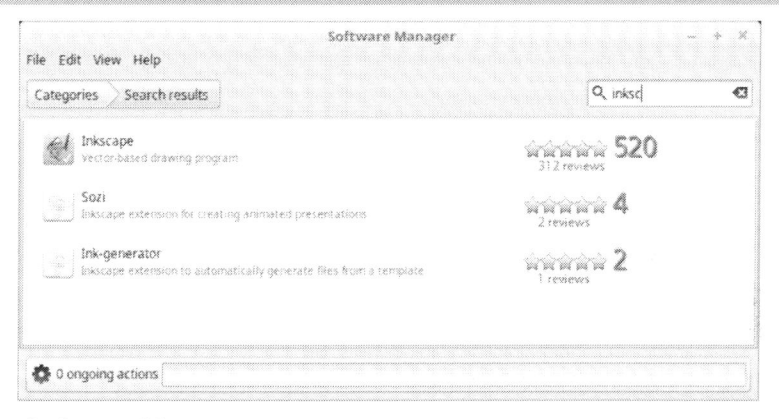

Figure 4-17: Software Manager search

You can perform a search using the Search box. The search is performed on the description and the package name. Searches are performed globally at the top category, or within the current category. The results are listed in a Search Results page (see Figure 4-17). You can double-click on an entry to open an application page. Click the Search Results button to return to the list of applications.

Synaptic Package Manager

The Synaptic Package Manager has been replaced by Software Manager as the primary package manager, though it is installed by default. Packages are listed by name and include

Part 1: *Getting Started*

supporting packages like libraries and system critical packages. You can access the Synaptic Package Manager from the Administration menu.

The Synaptic Package Manager displays three panes: a side pane for listing software categories and buttons, a top pane for listing software packages, and a bottom pane for displaying a selected package's description. When a package is selected, the description pane also displays a Get Screenshot button. Clicking this button will download and display an image of the application if there is one. Click the Get Changelog button to display a window listing the application changes.

Buttons at the lower left of the Synaptic Package Manager window provide options for organizing and refining the list of packages shown (see Figure 4-18). Five options are available: Sections, Status, Origin, Custom Filters, and Search results. The dialog pane above the buttons changes depending on which option you choose. Clicking the Sections button will list section categories for your software such as Graphics, Communications, and Development. The Status button will list options for installed and not installed software. The Origin button shows entries for different repositories and their sections, as well as those locally installed (manual or disc-based installations). Custom filters let you choose a filter to use for listing packages. You can create your own filter and use it to display selected packages. Search results will list your current and previous searches, letting you move from one to the other.

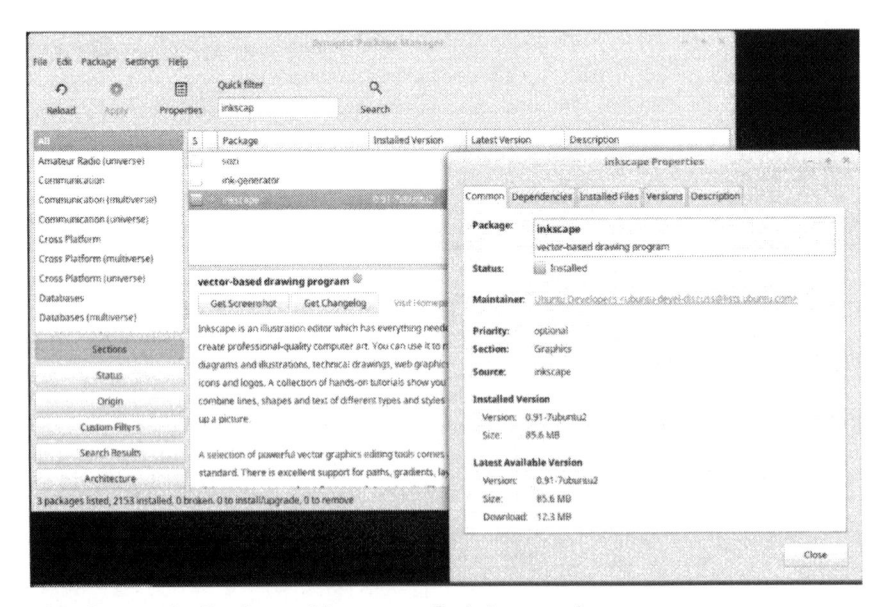

Figure 4-18: Synaptic Package Manager: Quick search

The Sections option is selected by default (see Figure 4-19). You can choose to list all packages, or refine your listing using categories provided in the pane. The All entry in this pane will list all available packages. Packages are organized into categories such as Cross Platform, Communications, and Editors. Each category is, in turn, subdivided by multiverse, universe, and restricted software.

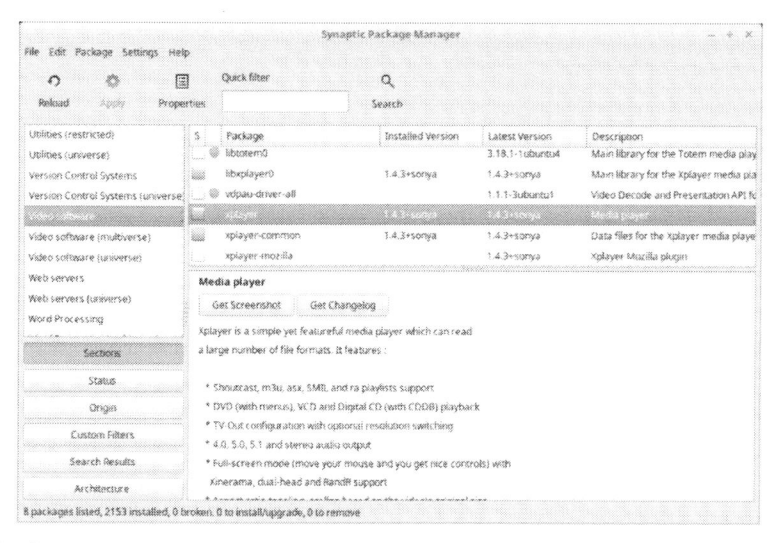

Figure 4-19: Synaptic Package Manager: Sections

To perform a quick search, enter the pattern to be searched for in the "Quick search" box and the results will appear. In Figure 4-18 the *inkscape* pattern is used to locate the Inkscape graphics software. Quick searches will be performed within selected sections. Selecting different sections applies your quick search pattern to the packages in that section. Clicking on the Editors section with an Inkscape search pattern would give no results since Inkscape is not an editor package.

Status entries further refine installed software as manual or as upgradeable (see Figure 4-20). Local software consists of packages you download and install manually.

With the Origin options, Ubuntu and Linux Mint compliant repositories may further refine access according to mint, multiverse, universe, and restricted software. The main section selects Ubuntu and Linux Mint supported software. The Architecture options let you select software compatible with a specified architecture, such as 64-bit or 32-bit.

To perform more detailed searches, you can use the Search tool. Click the Search button on the toolbar to open a Search dialog with a text box where you can enter search terms. A pop-up menu lets you specify what features of a package to search such as the "Description and Name" feature. You can search other package features like the Name, the maintainer name (Maintainer), the package version (Version), packages it may depend on (Dependencies), or associated packages (Provided Packages). A list of searches will be displayed in Search Results. You can move back and forth between search results by clicking on the search entries in this listing.

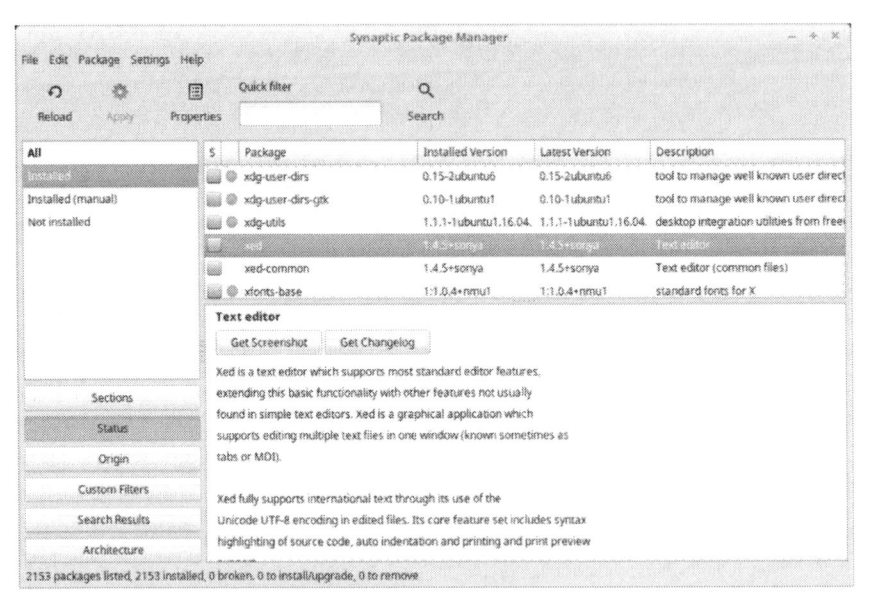

Figure 4-20: Synaptic Package Manager: Status

Properties

To find out information about a package, select the package and click the Properties button. This opens a window with Common, Dependencies, Installed Files, Versions, and Description tabs (see Figure 4-18). The Common tab provides section, versions, and maintainer information. The Installed Files tab show you exactly what files are installed, which is useful for finding the exact location, and names for configuration files, as well as commands. The Description tab displays detailed information about the software. The Dependencies tab shows all dependent software packages needed by this software, usually libraries.

Installing packages

Before installing software, you should press the Reload button to load the most recent package lists from the active repositories

To install a package, right-click on its name to display a pop-up menu and select the Mark for installation entry. Should any dependent packages exist, a dialog opens listing those packages. Click the Mark button in the dialog to mark those packages for installation. The package entry's checkbox will then be marked in the Synaptic Package Manager window.

Once you have selected the packages you want to install, click the Apply button on the toolbar to begin the installation process. A Summary dialog opens showing all the packages to be installed. You have the option to download the package files. The number of packages to be installed is listed, along with the size of the download and the amount of disk space used. Click the Apply button on the Summary dialog to download and install the packages. A download window will then appear showing the progress of your package installations. You can choose to show the progress of individual packages, which opens a terminal window listing each package as it is downloaded and installed.

Once downloaded, the dialog name changes to Installing Software. You can choose to have the dialog close automatically when finished. Sometimes installation requires user input to configure the software. You will be prompted to enter the information if necessary.

When you right-click a package name, you also see options for Mark Suggested for Installation or Mark Recommended for Installation. These will mark applications that can enhance your selected software, though they are not essential. If there are no suggested or recommended packages for that application, then these entries will be grayed out.

Certain software, like desktops or office suites that require a significant number of packages, can be selected all at once using metapackages. A metapackage has configuration files that select, download, and configure the range of packages needed for such complex software. Linux Mint metapackages begin with the term mint-meta, such as those for Linux Mint desktops and codecs like **mint.meta.kde**, **mint meta-xfce**, **mint-meta-mate**, and **mint-meta-codecs**.

Removing packages

To remove a package, first, locate it. Then right-click it and select the "Mark package for removal" entry. This will leave configuration files untouched. Alternatively, you can mark a package for complete removal, which will also remove any configuration files, "Mark for Complete Removal." Dependent packages will not be removed.

Once you have marked packages for removal, click the Apply button. A summary dialog displays the packages that will be removed. Click Apply to remove them.

The Synaptic Package Manager may not remove dependent packages, especially shared libraries that might be used by other applications. This means that your system could have installed packages that are never being used.

Search filters

You can further refine your search for packages by creating search filters. Select the Settings | Filters menu entry to open the Filters window. The Filters window shows two panes, a filter list on the left, and three tabs on the right: Status, Section, and Properties. To create a new filter, click the New button located just below the filter listing. Click the New Filter 1 entry in the filter list on the left pane. On the Status tab, you can refine your search criteria according to a package's status. You can search only uninstalled packages, include installed packages, include or exclude packages marked for removal, or search or those that are new in the repository. Initially, all criteria are selected. Uncheck those you do not want included in your search. The Section tab lets you include or exclude different repository sections like games, documentation, or administration. If you are looking for a game, you could choose to include just the game section, excluding everything else. On the Properties tab, you can specify patterns to search on package information such as package names, using Boolean operators to refine your search criteria. Package search criteria are entered using the two pop-up menus and the text box at the bottom of the tab, along with AND or OR Boolean operators.

Software Manager for separate DEB packages

You can also use Software Manager to perform an installation of a single DEB software package. Usually, these packages are downloaded directly from a website and have few or no dependent packages. When you use your browser to download a particular package, you will be prompted to open it with Software Manager. Software Manager opens to an install page for that software package, displaying information about the package and checking to see if it is compatible with your system. Click the Install button to download and install the package. It is advisable to use Software Manager to install a manually downloaded package.

You could also first download the package, and then later select it from your file manager window (usually the Downloads folder). Double clicking should open the package with Software Manager. You can also right-click and choose to open it with Software Manager.

Installing and Running Windows Software on Linux: Wine

Wine is a Windows compatibility layer that will allow you to run many Windows applications natively on Linux. The actual Windows operating system is not required. Windows applications will run as if they were Linux applications, able to access the entire Linux file system and use Linux-connected devices. Applications that are heavily driver-dependent, like graphic intensive games, may not run. Others that do not rely on any specialized drivers, may run very well, including Photoshop, Microsoft Office, and newsreaders like Newsbin. For some applications, you may also need to copy over specific Windows dynamic link libraries (DLLs) from a working Windows system to your Wine Windows system32 or system directory.

You can install Wine on your system from Software Manager | System tools | Wine Microsoft Windows Compatibility Layer. The **ttf-mscorefonts-installer** for the Microsoft core fonts will also be installed. You will be prompted to accept the Microsoft end user agreement for using those fonts.

Once installed, you can access Wine applications from the Applications menu. The Wine applications include Wine configuration, the Wine software uninstaller, and Wine file browser, as well as Winetricks and notepad.

To set up Wine, start the Wine Configuration tool ("Configure Wine") to open a window with tabs for Applications, Libraries (DLL selection), Audio (sound drivers), Drives, Desktop Integration, and Graphics. On the Applications tab, you can select the version of Windows an application is designed for. The Drives tab lists your detected partitions, as well as your Windows-emulated drives, such as drive C. The C: drive is actually just a directory, **.wine/drive_c**, not a partition of a fixed size. Your actual Linux file system will be listed as the Z drive.

Once configured, Wine will set up a **.wine** directory on the user's home directory (the directory is hidden, enable Show Hidden Files in the file manager View menu to display it). Within that directory will be the **drive_c** directory, which functions as the C: drive that holds your Windows system files and program files in the Windows and Program File subdirectories. The System and System32 directories are located in the Windows directory. This is where you would place any needed DLL files. The Program Files directory holds your installed Windows programs, just as they would be installed on a Windows Program Files directory.

To install a Windows application with Wine, you right-click on the application icon in the file manager window, and then choose "Open With Wine Windows Program Loader." Alternatively, you can open a terminal window and run the `wine` command with the Windows application as an argument.

```
$ wine winprogram.exe
```

Icons for installed Windows software will appear on your desktop. Just double-click an icon to start up an application. It will run normally within a Linux window, as would any Linux application.

Installing Windows fonts on Wine is a simple matter of copying fonts from a Windows font directory to your Wine **.wine/drive_c/Windows/fonts** directory. You can copy any Windows **.ttf** file to this directory to install a font.

Wine should work on both **.exe** and **.msi** files. You may have to make them executable by checking the file's Properties dialog Permissions tab's Execute checkbox. If an **.msi** file cannot be run, you may have to use the **msiexec** command with the **/a** option.

```
msiexec /a winprogram.msi
```

Alternatively, you can use the commercial Windows compatibility layer called Crossover Office. This is a commercial product tested to run certain applications like Microsoft Office. Check **https://www.codeweavers.com** for more details. Crossover Office is based on Wine, which CodeWeavers supports directly.

Source code files

You can install source code files using **apt-get**. Specify the **source** operation with the package name. Packages will be downloaded and extracted.

```
sudo apt-get source mplayer
```

The **--download** option lets you just download the source package without extracting it. The **--compile** option will download, extract, compile, and package the source code into a Debian binary package, ready for installation.

With the **source** operation, no dependent packages will be downloaded. If a software package requires any dependent packages to run, you would have to download and compile those. To obtain needed dependent files, you use the **build-dep** option. All your dependent files will be located and downloaded for you automatically.

```
sudo apt-get build-dep mplayer
```

Installing from source code requires that supporting development libraries and source code header files be installed. You can do this separately for each major development platform like GNOME, KDE, or the kernel. Alternatively, you can run the APT meta-package **build-essential** for all the Linux Mint development packages. You will have to do this only once.

```
sudo apt-get install build-essential
```

Software Package Types

Linux Mint uses Debian-compliant software packages (DEB) whose filenames have a **.deb** extension. Other packages, such as those in the form of source code that you need to compile, may come in a variety of compressed archives. These commonly have the extension **.tar.gz**, **.tgz**, or **.tar.bz2**. Packages with the **.rpm** extension are Red Hat Package software packages used on Red Hat, Fedora, SuSE and other Linux distributions that use RPM packages. They are not compatible directly with Linux Mint. You can use the **alien** utility to convert most RPM packages to DEB packages that you can then install on Linux Mint. Table 4-1 lists several common file extensions that you will find for the great variety of Linux software packages available. You can download any Linux Mint-compliant deb package as well as the original source code package, as single files, directly from **http://packages.linuxmint.com**.

Extension	File
.deb	A Debian/Linux Mint Linux package
.gz	A **gzip**-compressed file (use **gunzip** to decompress)
.bz2	A **bzip2**-compressed file (use **bunzip2** to decompress; also use the **j** option with **tar**, as in **xvjf**)
.tar	A tar archive file (use **tar** with **xvf** to extract)
.tar.gz	A **gzip**-compressed **tar** archive file (use **gunzip** to decompress and **tar** to extract; use the **z** option with **tar**, as in **xvzf**, to both decompress and extract in one step)
.tar.bz2	A **bzip2**-compressed **tar** archive file (extract with **tar -xvzj**)
.tz	A **tar** archive file compressed with the **compress** command
.Z	A file compressed with the **compress** command (use the **decompress** command to decompress)
.bin	A self-extracting software file
.rpm	A software package created with the Red Hat Software Package Manager used on Fedora, Red Hat, Centos, and SuSE distributions

Table 4-1: Linux Software Package File Extensions

DEB Software Packages

A Debian package will automatically resolve dependencies, installing any other needed packages instead of simply reporting their absence. Packages are named with the software name, the version number, and the **.deb** extension. Check **https://www.debian.org/doc** for more information. Filename format is as follows:

the package name

version number

distribution label and build number. Packages created specifically for Linux Mint have the Linux Mint label here. Attached to it is the build number, the number of times the package was built for Linux Mint.

architecture   The type of system on which the package runs, like i386 for Intel 32-bit x86 systems, or amd64 for both Intel and AMD 64-bit systems, x86_64.

package format. This is always **deb**

For example, the package name for 3dchess is 3dchess, with a version and build number 0.8.1-17, and an architecture amd64 for a 64-bit system.

```
3dchess_0.8.1-17_amd64.deb
```

The following package has an ubuntu label, a package specifically created for Ubuntu. The version and build number is 3.6.0.2, with the Ubuntu label ubuntu1. The architecture is i386 for a 32-bit system.

```
gnome-mahjongg_3.6.0.2-0ubuntu1_i386.deb
```

Managing software with apt-get

APT is designed to work with repositories, and will handle any dependencies for you. It uses **dpkg** to install and remove individual packages, but can also determine what dependent packages need to be installed, as well as query and download packages from repositories. Several popular tools for APT let you manage your software easily, like the Synaptic Package Manager, Software Manager, and aptitude. Software Manager and the Synaptic Package Manager rely on a desktop interface like GNOME. If you are using the command line interface, you can use **apt-get** to manage packages. Using the **apt-get** command on the command line you can install, update, and remove packages. Check the **apt-get** man page for a detailed listing of **apt-get** commands (see Table 4-2).

```
apt-get  command  package
```

Command	Description
update	Download and resynchronize the package listing of available and updated packages for APT supported repositories. APT repositories updated for Linux Mint are those specified in **/etc/apt/sources.list.d/official-package-repositories.list**
upgrade	Update packages, install new versions of installed packages if available.
dist-upgrade	Update (upgrade) all your installed packages to a new release
install	Install a specific package, using its package name, not full package file name.
remove	Remove a software package from your system.
source	Download and extract a source code package
check	Check for broken dependencies
clean	Removes the downloaded packages held in the repository cache on your system. Used to free up disk space.

Table 4-2: apt-get commands

The **apt-get** command takes two arguments: the command to perform and the name of the package. Other APT package tools follow the same format. The command is a term such as **install** for installing packages or **remove** to uninstall a package. Use the **install**, **remove**, or **update** commands respectively. You only need to specify the software name, not the package's full filename. APT will determine that. You need administrative access to perform and apt-get command, so be sure to precede it with the **sudo** command. You will be prompted for your password. To install the Shotwell package you would use:

```
sudo apt-get install shotwell
```

To make sure that **apt-get** has current repository information, use the **apt-get update** command.

```
sudo apt-get update
```
To remove packages, you use the **remove** command.
```
sudo apt-get remove shotwell
```
You can use the **-s** option to check the remove or install first, especially to check whether any dependency problems exist. For remove operations, you can use **-s** to find out first what dependent packages will also be removed.
```
sudo apt-get remove -s shotwell
```
The **apt-get** command can be very helpful if your X Windows System server ever fails (your display driver). For example, if you installed a restricted vendor display driver, and then your desktop fails to start, you can start up in the recovery mode, start the root shell, and use **apt-get** to remove the restricted display driver. Your former X open source display drivers would be restored automatically. The following would remove the Nvidia restricted display driver.
```
sudo apt-get remove nvidia*
```
A complete log of all install, remove, and update operations are kept in the **/var/log/dpkg.log** file. You can consult this file to find out exactly what files were installed or removed.

Configuration for APT is held in the **/etc/apt** directory. Officially the **/etc/apt/sources.list** file is supposed to list the distribution repositories from where packages are installed. Source lists for additional third-party repositories are kept in the **/etc/apt/sources.list.d** directory. However, on Linux Mint, the list of distribution repositories is kept in the **/etc/apt/sources.list.d/official-package-repositories.list** fie. GPG (GNU Privacy Guard) database files hold validation keys for those repositories. Specific options for **apt-get** are can be found in an **/etc/apt.conf** file or in various files located in the **/etc/apt.conf.d** directory.

Updating packages (Upgrading) with apt-get

The **apt-get** tool also lets you easily update your entire system at once. The terms update and upgrade are used differently from other software tools. In **apt-get**, the **update** command just updates your package listing, checking for packages that may need to install newer versions, but not installing those versions. Technically, it updates the package list that APT uses to determine what packages need to be updated. The term upgrade is used to denote the actual update of a software package; a new version is downloaded and installed. What is referred to as updating by **apt-get**, other package managers refer to a obtaining the list of software packages to be updated (the reload operation). In **apt-get**, upgrading is what other package managers refer to as performing updates.

> **TIP:** The terms update and upgrade can be confusing when used with apt-get. The update operation updates the Apt package list only, whereas an upgrade actually downloads and installs updated packages.

Upgrading is a simple matter of using the **upgrade** command. With no package specified, using **apt-get** with the **upgrade** command will upgrade your entire system. Add the **-u** option to list packages as they are upgraded. First, make sure your repository information (package list) is up to date with the **update** command, then issue the **upgrade** command.
```
sudo apt-get update
sudo apt-get -u upgrade
```

Command Line Search and Information: dpkg-query and apt-cache tools

The **dpkg-query** command lets you list detailed information about your packages. It operates on the command line (terminal window). Use **dpkg-query** with the **-l** option to list all your packages.

```
dpkg-query -l
```

The **dpkg** command can operate as a front end for **dpkg-query**, detecting its options to perform the appropriate task. The preceding command could also be run as:

```
dpkg -l
```

Listing a particular package requires and exact match on the package name unless you use pattern-matching operators. The following command lists the **wine** package (Windows Compatibility Layer).

```
dpkg-query -l wine
```

A pattern matching operator, such as *, placed after a pattern will display any packages beginning with the specified pattern. The pattern with its operators needs to be placed in single quotation marks to prevent an attempt by the shell to use the pattern to match on filenames in your current directory. The following example finds all packages beginning with the pattern "wine". This would include packages with names such as **wine-doc** and **wine-utils**.

```
dpkg-query -l 'wine*'
```

You can further refine the results by using **grep** to perform an additional search. The following operation first outputs all packages beginning with **wine**, and from those results, the **grep** operations lists only those with the pattern *utils* in their name, such as **wine-utils**.

```
dpkg -l 'wine*' | grep 'utils'
```

Use the **-L** option to list the files that a package has installed.

```
dpkg-query -L wine
```

To see the status information about a package, including its dependencies and configuration files, use the **-s** option. Fields will include Status, Section, Architecture, Version, Depends (dependent packages), Suggests, Conflicts (conflicting packages), and Conffiles (configuration files).

```
dpkg-query -s wine
```

The status information will also provide suggested dependencies. These are packages not installed, but likely to be used. For the wine package, the **ttf-mscorefonts** Windows font package is suggested.

```
dpkg-query -s wine | grep Suggests
```

Use the **-S** option to determine to which package a particular file belongs to.

```
dpkg-query -S filename
```

You can also obtain information with the **apt-cache** tool. Use the search command with **apt-cache** to perform a search.

```
apt-cache search wine
```

To find dependencies for a particular package, use the **depends** command.

```
apt-cache depends wine
```

To display just the package description, use the **show** command.

```
apt-cache show wine
```

Note: If you have installed Aptitude software manager, you can use the aptitude command with the search and show options to find and display information about packages.

Managing non-repository packages with dpkg

You can use **dpkg** to install a software package you have already downloaded directly, not with an APT enabled software tool such as **apt-get**, Software Manager, or the Synaptic Package Manager. In this case, you are not installing from a repository. Instead, you have manually downloaded the package file from a Web or FTP site to a folder on your system. Such a situation would be rare, reserved for software not available on the Linux Mint repository or any APT enabled repository. Keep in mind that most software is already on your Linux Mint or APT enabled repositories. Check there first for the software package before performing a direct download and install with **dpkg**. The **dpkg** configuration files are located in the **/etc/dpkg** directory. Configuration is held in the **dpkg.cfg** file. See the **dpkg** man page for a detailed listing of options.

One situation, for which you would use **dpkg**, is for packages you have built yourself, like packages you created when converting a package in another format to a Debian package (DEB). This is the case when converting an RPM package (Red Hat Package Manager) to a Debian package format.

For **dpkg**, you use the **-i** option to install a package and **-r** to remove it.

```
sudo dpkg -i package.deb
```

The major failing for **dpkg** is that it provides no dependency support. It will inform you of needed dependencies, but you will have to install them separately. **dpkg** installs only the specified package. It is useful for packages that have no dependencies.

You use the **-I** option to obtain package information directly from the DEB package file.

```
sudo dpkg -I package.deb
```

To remove a package, you use the **-r** option with the package software name. You do not need version or extension information like **.386** or **.deb**. With **dpkg**, when removing a package with dependencies, you first have to remove all its dependencies manually. You will not be able to uninstall the package until you do this. Configuration files are not removed.

```
sudo dpkg -r packagename
```

If you install a package that requires dependencies, and then fail to install these dependencies, your install database will be marked as having broken packages. In this case, APT will not allow new packages to be installed until the broken packages are fixed. You can enter the **apt-get** command with the **-f** and install options to fix all broken packages at once.

```
sudo apt-get -f install
```

Using packages with other software formats

You can convert software packages in other software formats into DEB packages that can then be installed on Linux Mint. To do this you use the **alien** tool, which can convert several different kinds of formats such as RPM and even TGZ (**.tgz**). You use the **--to-deb** option to convert to a DEB package format that Linux Mint can then install. The **--scripts** option attempts also to convert any pre or post install configuration scripts. Once you have generated the **.deb** package, you can use **dpkg** or Software Manager to install it.

```
alien  --scripts  --to-deb   package.rpm
```

5. Applications

X-Apps
Office
Mail
Graphics
Multimedia
Internet
Social Networking

All Linux software for Linux Mint is currently available from online repositories. You can download applications for desktops, Internet servers, office suites, and programming packages, among others. Software packages are distributed primarily through the official Linux Mint and Ubuntu repositories. Downloads and updates are handled automatically by your desktop software manager and updater. Many popular applications are included in separate sections of the repository. During installation, your system is configured to access Linux Mint repositories. You can update to the latest software from the Linux Mint repository using the Update Manager.

The listing of Linux Mint software packages for a release is provided for at:

`http://packages.linuxmint.com`

A more descriptive listing is kept at Linux Mint Community site at:

`https://community.linuxmint.com/software`

Linux Mint is based on Ubuntu. A listing of the software packages for the Ubuntu distribution is located at:

`http://packages.ubuntu.com`

All software packages in the Linux Mint and Ubuntu repositories are accessible directly with Software Manager and the Synaptic Package Manager, which provide easy software installation, removal, and searching.

Due to licensing restrictions, multimedia support for popular operations like MP3, DVD, and DivX are installed separately by the **mint-meta-codecs** package. If not already installed, choose "Install Multimedia Codecs" from the Sound & Video menu, or click the "Multimedia codecs" icon on the Welcome screen.

In addition, you could download from third-party sources software that is in the form of compressed archives or in DEB packages. DEB packages are archived using the Debian Package Manager and have the extension **.deb**. Compressed archives have an extension such as **.tar.gz**. You also can download the source version and compile it directly on your system. This has become a simple process, almost as simple as installing the compiled DEB versions.

X-Apps

The X-Apps project provides generic applications for traditional GTK (GNOME) desktops, such as Mate, Cinnamon, and Xfce. X-Apps are not supported for Linux Mint KDE. Improvements to an X-App would work automatically on all the desktops that X-Apps supports. X-Apps installed by Linux Mint desktops include Xed (text editor), Xplayer (video player), Xviewer (image viewer), and Xreader (document viewer). Though many GNOME applications may change with different releases, X-Apps remains the same, and will always work. You can still install and use the corresponding GNOME applications, such as Gedit, Totem, and Eye of GNOME, but X-Apps will integrate more easily. Available X-Apps are listed in Table 5-1. Most options for an X-App can be set by the Preferences dialog. Options can also be set using the dconf editor (**org.x**), which can also set options such as the default display configuration.

Application	Description
Xed	Text Editor (based on Pluma)
Xplayer	Video player (based on Videos/Totem)
Xviewer	Image viewer (based on Eye of GNOME)
Pix	Photo organizer (base on Gthumb)
Xreader	PDF reader (based on Atril)

Table 5-1: X-App Applications

Office Applications

Several office suites are now available for Linux. These include professional-level word processors, presentation managers, drawing tools, and spreadsheets. The freely available versions are described in this chapter. All the software are Ubuntu packages. LibreOffice is currently the primary office suite supported by Linux Mint. Calligra is an office suite designed for use with KDE. The GNOME Office suite integrates GNOME applications into a productivity suite. You can also purchase commercial office suites such as Oracle Open Office from Oracle.

Several database management systems are also available for Linux, which includes high-powered, commercial-level database management systems. Most of the database management systems available for Linux are designed to support large relational databases. Linux Mint includes both MySQL, MariaDB, and PostgreSQL open source databases in its distribution, which can support smaller databases.

Linux also provides several text editors that range from simple text editors for simple notes to editors with more complex features such as spell-checkers, buffers, or complex pattern matching. All generate character text files and can be used to edit any Linux text files. Text editors are often used in system administration tasks to change or add entries in Linux configuration files found in the **/etc** directory or a user's initialization or application configuration files located in a user's home directory (dot files). You can also use a text editor to work on source code files for any of the programming languages or shell program scripts.

Linux Mint also supports several Ebook readers. Some such as Calibre and FBReader run natively on Linux.

LibreOffice

LibreOffice is a fully integrated suite of office applications developed as an open source project and freely distributed to all. It is the primary office suite for Linux. LibreOffice applications are accessible from the Office menu. There are also default Launcher items for three commonly used LibreOffice applications (Writer, Calc, and Impress). LibreOffice is the open source and freely available office suite derived originally from OpenOffice. LibreOffice is supported by the Document Foundation, which was established after Oracle's acquisition of Sun, the main developer for Open Office. LibreOffice is now the primary open source office software for Linux. Oracle retains control of all the original OpenOffice software and does not cooperate with any LibreOffice development. LibreOffice has replaced OpenOffice as the default Office software for most Linux distributions.

LibreOffice includes word processing, spreadsheet, presentation, and drawing applications (see Table 5-2). Versions of LibreOffice exist for Linux, Windows, and Mac OS. You can obtain information such as online manuals and FAQs as well as current versions from the LibreOffice website at **http://www.libreoffice.org**.

Application	Description
Calc (Spreadsheet)	LibreOffice spreadsheet
Draw (Drawing)	LibreOffice drawing application
Writer (Word Processing)	LibreOffice word processor
Math (Formula)	LibreOffice mathematical formula composer
Impress (Presentation)	LibreOffice presentation manager
Base (Database)	Database front end for accessing and managing a variety of different databases.

Table 5-2: LibreOffice Applications

Calligra

Calligra is an integrated office suite for the K Desktop Environment (KDE) consisting of several office applications, including a word processor, a spreadsheet, and graphics applications (see Table 5-3). You can download it from the Universe repository, using Software Manager or the Synaptic Package Manager. Calligra allows components from any one application to be used in another, letting you embed a spreadsheet from Calligra Sheets or diagrams from Karbon in a Calligra Words document. It also uses the open document format (ODF) for its files, providing cross-application standardization. There is also a Windows version available. You can obtain more information about Calligra from **https://www.calligra.org**.

Application	Description
Braindump	Whiteboards for notes, images, and charts
Calligra Flow	Flow chart applications
Calligra Stage	Presentation application
Calligra Words	Word processor (desktop publisher)
Calligra Sheets	Spreadsheet
Karbon	Vector graphics program
Kexi	Database integration
Plan	Project management and planning
Krita	Paint and image manipulation program
Kontact (separate project)	Contact application including mail, address book, and organizer

Table 5-3: Calligra Applications

GNOME Office Applications

There are several GNOME Office applications available including AbiWord, Gnumeric, Evince, and Evolution. You can find out more about the GNOME Office applications at **https://wiki.gnome.org/action/show/Projects/GnomeOffice**. A current listing of common GNOME Office applications is shown in Table 5-4. All implement the support for embedding components, ensuring drag-and-drop capability throughout the GNOME interface.

Application	Description
AbiWord	Cross-platform word processor
Gnumeric	Spreadsheet
Evince	Document Viewer
Evolution	Integrated email, calendar, and personal organizer
Dia	Diagram and flow chart editor
GnuCash	Personal finance manager
Glom	Database front end for PostgreSQL database
Planner	Project planner

Table 5-4: GNOME Office and Other Office Applications for GNOME

Document Viewers, and DVI)

Xreader is the default document viewer for Linux Mint. It is started automatically whenever you double-click a PDF file on the desktop (see Figure 5-1). Its menu entry is Document Viewer in the Office menu. Xreader is an X-App based on Atril, the MATE document viewer. Evince is the GNOME document viewer. Okular is the document viewer for KDE. The PDF viewers include many of the standard Adobe reader features such as zoom, two-page display, and full-screen mode. Alternatively, you can use Acrobat reader from Adobe (Partner repository) to display PDF files. Evince (PostScript, PDF and Okular can display both PostScript (**.ps**) and PDF (**.pdf**) files.

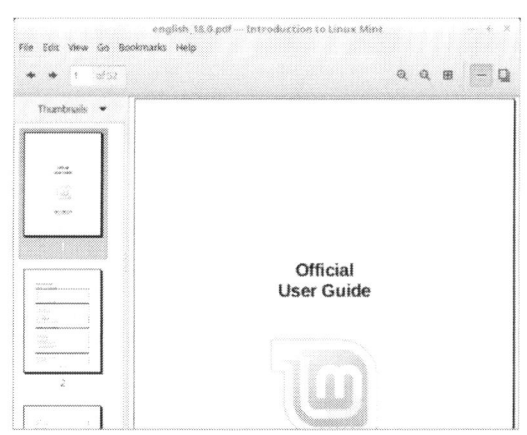

Figure 5-1: Xreader X-App Document Viewer

Viewer	Description
Xreader	X-App Document Viewer, the default (based on Atril)
Atril	MATE Document Viewer for PostScript, DVI, and PDF files
Evince	GNOME Document Viewer for PostScript, DVI, and PDF files
Okular	KDE4 tool for displaying PDF, DVI, and postscript files
xpdf	X Window System tool for displaying PDF files only
Acrobat Reader for Linux	Adobe PDF viewer and Ebook reader
Scribus	Desktop publisher for generating PDF documents
pdfedit	Edit PDF documents
Simple Scan	GNOME Scanner interface for scanners

Table 5-5: PostScript, PDF, and DVI viewers

Ebook Readers: FBReader and Calibre

On Linux, for Ebooks, you can use Calibre and FBReader (see Table 5-6). FBReader is an open source reader that can read non-DRM ebooks, including mobipocket, html, palmdoc, chm, EPUB, text, and rtf.

Viewer	Description
Calibre	Ebook reader and library, also converts various inputs to EPUB ebooks.
E-book reader	FBReader Ebook reader

Table 5-6: Ebook Readers

Editors

The Linux desktops (GNOME and KDE) support powerful text editors with full mouse support, scroll bars, and menus. These include basic text editors, such as Xed, Gedit, Pluma, and Kate, as well as word processors, such as LibreOffice Word, AbiWord, and Calligra Words. Xed is the default text editor (see Figure 5-2), an X-App designed to work on all Linux Mint desktops. It features a toolbar and search bar. Linux also provides the cursor-based editors Nano, Vim, and Emacs. Nano is the default cursor-based editor with an easy-to-use interface supporting menus and mouse selection (if run from a terminal window). Vim is an enhanced version of the Vi text editor used on the Unix system. These editors use simple, cursor-based operations to give you a full-screen format. Table 5-7 lists several desktop editors for Linux. Vi and Emacs have powerful editing features that have been refined over the years. Emacs, in particular, is extensible to a full-development environment for programming new applications. Later versions of Emacs and Vim, such as GNU Emacs, XEmacs, and Gvim provide support for mouse, menu, and window operations.

Note: Three helpful tools are the GNOME clocks, calendar, and weather applications. Clocks provided the time for global locations. Calendar provides an online calendar. Weather provides the weather, also for global locations.

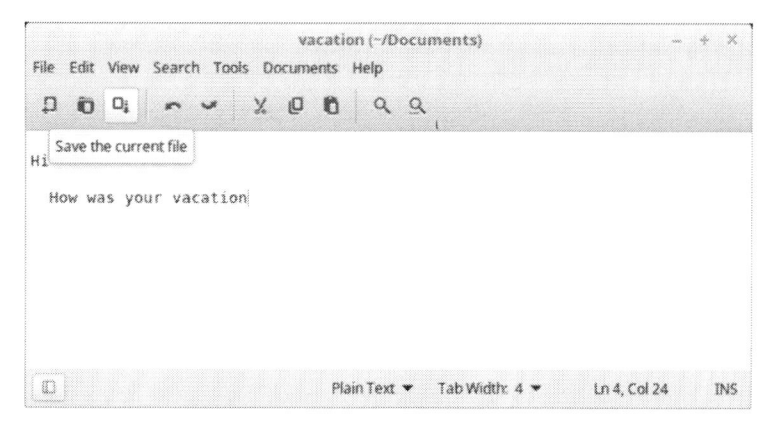

Figure 5-2: Xed X-App editor

Application	Description
Xed	X-App Text editor (based on Pluma)
Kate	Text and program editor
Calligra Words	Desktop publisher, part of Calligra Suite
Gedit	Text editor
AbiWord	Word processor
OpenWriter	LibreOffice word processor that can edit text files
nano	Easy to use screen-based editor, installed by default
GNU Emacs	Emacs editor with X Window System support
XEmacs	X Window System version of Emacs editor
gvim	Vim version with X Window System support
Pluma	MATE text editor

Table 5-7: Desktop Editors

Database Management Systems

Several database systems are provided for Ubuntu, including LibreOffice Base, MySQL, SQLite, and PostgreSQL. Ubuntu continues to provide the original MySQL database. In addition, commercial SQL database software is also compatible with Ubuntu. SQLite is a simple and fast database server requiring no configuration and implementing the database on a single disk file. In addition, Ubuntu also supports document-based non-SQL databases such as MongoDB. MongoDB is a document-based database that can be quickly searched. Table 5-8 lists database management systems currently available for Linux.

System	Site
LibreOffice	LibreOffice database: **www.libreoffice.org**
PostgreSQL	The PostgreSQL database: **www.postgresql.org**
MySQL	MySQL database: **www.mysql.com**
MariaDB	MariaDB database, based on MySQL: **https://mariadb.org/**
MongoDB	Document-based database: **www.mongodb.org**

Table 5-8: Database Management Systems for Linux

SQL Databases (RDBMS)

SQL databases are relational database management systems (RDBMSs) designed for extensive database management tasks. Many of the major SQL databases now have Linux versions, including Oracle and IBM. These are commercial and professional database management systems. Linux has proved itself capable of supporting complex and demanding database management tasks. In addition, many free SQL databases are available for Linux that offers much the same functionality. Most commercial databases also provide free personal versions.

LibreOffice Base

LibreOffice provides a basic database application, LibreOffice Base that can access many database files. You can set up and operate a simple database, as well as access and manage files from other database applications. When you start up LibreOffice Base, you will be prompted either to start a new database or connect to an existing one. File types supported include ODBC (Open Database Connectivity), JDBC (Java), MySQL, PostgreSQL, and MDB (Microsoft Access) database files (install the **unixodbc** and **java-libmysql** packages). You can also create your own simple databases. Check the LibreOffice Base page (**http://www.libreoffice.org/discover/base/**) for detailed information on drivers and supported databases.

PostgreSQL

PostgreSQL is based on the POSTURES database management system, though it uses SQL as its query language. POSTGRESQL is a next-generation research prototype developed at the University of California, Berkeley. Linux versions of PostgreSQL are included in most distributions, including the Red Hat, Fedora, Debian, and Ubuntu. You can find more information on it from the PostgreSQL website at **https://www.postgresql.org**. PostgreSQL is an open source project, developed under the GPL license.

MySQL

MySQL is a true multi-user, multithreaded SQL database server, supported by MySQL AB. MySQL is an open source product available free under the GPL license. You can obtain current information on it from its website, **https://www.mysql.com**. The site includes detailed documentation, including manuals and FAQs.

MariaDB

MariaDB is a fully open source derivative of MySQL, developed after MySQL was acquired by Oracle. It is designed to be fully compatible with MySQL databases. Like MySQL,

MariaDB is structured on a client/server model with a server daemon filling requests from client programs. MariaDB is designed for speed, reliability, and ease of use. It is meant to be a fast database management system for large databases and, at the same time, a reliable one, suitable for intensive use. To create databases, you use the standard SQL language. Packages to install are **mariadb-client** and **mariadb-server**.

Mail (email) and News

Linux supports a wide range of both electronic mail and news clients. Mail clients let you send and receive messages to and from other users on your system or users accessible from your network. News clients let you read articles and messages posted in newsgroups, which are open to access by all users.

Mail Clients

You can send and receive email messages in a variety of ways, depending on the type of mail client you use. Although all email utilities perform the same basic tasks of receiving and sending messages, they tend to use different interfaces. Some mail clients are designed to operate on a specific desktop interface such as KDE and GNOME. Several older mail clients use a screen-based interface and can be started only from the command line. For Web-based Internet mail services, such as Gmail and Yahoo, you use a Web browser instead of a mail client to access mail accounts provided by those services. Table 5-9 lists several popular Linux mail clients. Mail is transported to and from destinations using mail transport agents like Sendmail, Exim, and Postfix. To send mail over the Internet, Simple Mail Transport Protocol (SMTP) is used.

Mail Client	Description
Kontact (KMail, KAddressbook, KOrganizer)	Includes the K Desktop mail client, KMail; integrated mail, address book, and scheduler
Evolution	Email client, https://projects.gnome.org/evolution/
Thunderbird	Mozilla mail client and newsreader
Sylpheed	Gtk mail and news client
Claws-mail	Extended version of sylpheed Email client
GNUEmacs and XEmacs	Emacs mail clients
Mutt	Screen-based mail client
Mail	Original Unix-based command line mail client
Squirrel Mail	Web-based mail client
gnubiff	Email checker and notification tool
Mail Notification	Email checker and notification that works with numerous mail clients, including MH, Sylpheed, Gmail, Evolution, and Mail

Table 5-9: Linux Mail Clients

Usenet News

Usenet is an open mail system on which users post messages that include news, discussions, and opinions. It operates like a mailbox to which any user on your Linux system can read or send messages. Users' messages are incorporated into Usenet files, which are distributed to any system signed up to receive them. Certain Usenet sites perform organizational and distribution operations for Usenet, receiving messages from other sites and organizing them into Usenet files, which are then broadcast to many other sites. Such sites are called backbone sites, and they operate like publishers, receiving articles and organizing them into different groups.

To access Usenet news, you need access to a news server, which receives the daily Usenet newsfeeds and makes them accessible to other systems. Your network may have a system that operates as a news server. If you are using an Internet service provider (ISP), a news server is probably maintained by your ISP for your use. To read Usenet articles, you use a newsreader, a client program that connects to a news server and accesses the articles. On the Internet and in TCP/IP networks, news servers communicate with newsreaders using the Network News Transfer Protocol (NNTP) and are often referred to as NNTP news servers. You can also create your own news server on your Linux system to run a local Usenet news service or to download and maintain the full set of Usenet articles. News transport agent applications can be set up to create such a server.

You read Usenet articles with a newsreader, such as Pan or tin, which enable you to select a specific newsgroup and then read the articles in it. A newsreader operates like a user interface, letting you browse through and select available articles for reading, saving, or printing. Most newsreaders employ a retrieval feature called threads that pulls together articles on the same discussion or topic. Several popular newsreaders are listed in Table 5-10.

Most newsreaders can read Usenet news provided on remote news servers that use the NNTP. Desktop newsreaders have you specify the Internet address for the remote news server in their own configuration settings. Shell-based newsreaders such as **tin**, obtain the news server's Internet address from the NNTPSERVER shell variable, configured in the **.profile** file.

```
NNTPSERVER=news.domain.com
export NNTPSERVER
```

A binary newsreader can convert text messages to binary equivalents, like those found in **alt.binaries** newsgroups. There are some news grabbers, applications designed only to download binaries. The binaries are normally encoded with RAR compression, which has an **.rar** extension. To decode them you first have to install the **unrar-free** package. Binaries normally consist of several rar archive files, some of which may be incomplete. To repair them you can use Par2 recovery program. Install the **par2** and **pypar2** packages. A binary should have its own set of par2 files also listed on the news server that you can download and use to repair any incomplete **rar** files. The principle works much the same as RAID arrays using parity information to reconstruct damaged data. You can use the PyPar2 application to manually repair rar archive files, accessible from the Accessories menu.

Newsreader	Description
Pan	GNOME Desktop newsreader
Thunderbird	Mail client with newsreader capabilities (X based)
Sylpheed	GNOME Windows-like newsreader
Slrn	Newsreader (cursor based)
Emacs	Emacs editor, mail client, and newsreader (cursor based)
tin	Newsreader (command line interface)
trn4	Newsreader (command line interface)
Newsbin	Newsreader (Windows version works under Wine)
Knews	KDE news reader
xpn	Desktop newsreader
nzb	Binary only NZB based news grabber

Table 5-10: Linux Newsreaders

Graphics Applications

The GNOME and KDE desktops support an impressive number of graphics applications, including image viewers, window grabbers, image editors, and paint tools. These tools can be found on the Graphics menu. Xviewer is the default image viewer (an X-App) and is accessible as "Image Viewer" from the Graphics menu (see Figure 5-3) . It is based on GNOME's Eye of GNOME image viewer. Shotwell provides an easy and powerful way to manage, display, and import, and publish your photos and images. GNOME Photos is a simple image viewer and organizer for the images in your Pictures folder. The Eye of GNOME is the GNOME image viewer. Gthumb is an image viewer, organizer, and simple editor (see Figure 5-4). Pix is the X-App version of Gthumb and is installed by default. GIMP is the GNU Image Manipulation Program, a sophisticated image application much like Adobe Photoshop. Inkscape is a Gnome based vector graphics application for SVG (Scalable Vector Graphics) images. Only Xviewer and Pix are installed by default, the others can be installed with the Linux Mint Software Manager. The KDE desktop features the same variety of graphics applications found on the GNOME desktop. Older X Window System-based applications run directly on the underlying X Window System, such as Xpaint and Xfig (not to be confused with X-Apps).

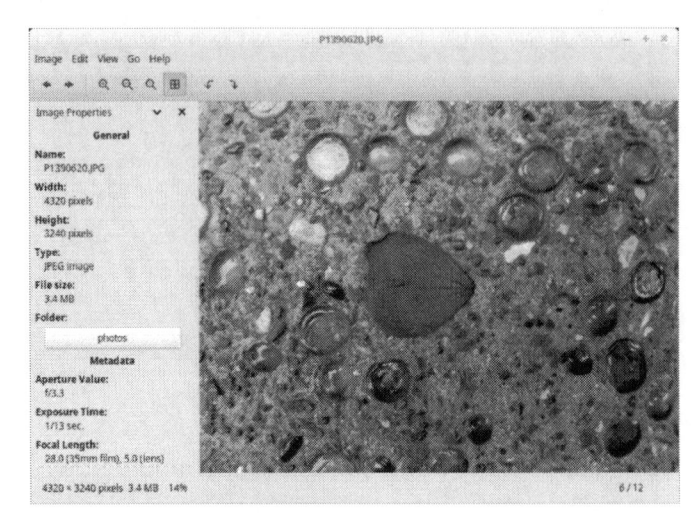

Figure 5-3: Xviewer X-App Image Viewer

Figure 5-4: Pix X-App Image Viewer, Organizer, and Editor

Tools	Description
Shotwell	GNOME digital camera application and image and video library manager (**https://wiki.gnome.org/Apps/Shotwell**)
Cheese	GNOME Webcam application for taking pictures and videos
Photos	GNOME photo viewer and organizer
Digikam	Digital photo management tool, works with both GNOME and KDE
KDE	
Gwenview	Image browser and viewer (default for KDE)
ShowFoto	Simple image viewer, works with digiKam (**https://www.digikam.org**)
KSnapshot	Screen grabber
KolourPaint	Paint program
Krita	Image editor (**https://www.calligra.org/krita/**)
GNOME	
Xviewer	X-App Image Viewer (based on Eye of GNOME)
Pix	X-App Image viewer, organizer, and editor (based on Gthumb)
Gthumb	GNOME image viewer, organizer, and editor
Eye of Gnome	GNOME Image Viewer
GIMP	GNU Image Manipulation Program (**https://www.gimp.org**)
Inkscape	GNOME Vector graphics application (**https://www.inkscape.org**)
gpaint	GNOME paint program
Blender	3d modeling, rendering, and animation
LibreOffice Draw	LibreOffice Draw program
X Window System	
Xpaint	Paint program
Xfig	Drawing program
ImageMagick	Image format conversion and editing tool

Table 5-11: Graphics Tools for Linux

Multimedia

Many applications are available for both video and sound, including sound editors, music players, and video players (see Tables 6-5 and 6-6). Linux sound applications include mixers, digital audio tools, CD audio writers, MP3 players, and network audio support.

Multimedia support

Linux Mint/Ubuntu provides a codec wizard that automatically detects whenever you need to install additional multimedia codecs. If you try to run a media file for which you do not have the proper codec, the codec wizard will appear, listing the codecs you need to download and install. This wizard will appear if, during installation, you did not click the "Install third party software" checkbox on the second screen, which installs the **mint-meta-codecs** package, or if you have already installed the **mint-meta-codecs** package.

Often there are several choices (see Figure 5-5). The codec wizard will select and install these packages for you, simplifying the process of installing the various multimedia codecs available for Linux.

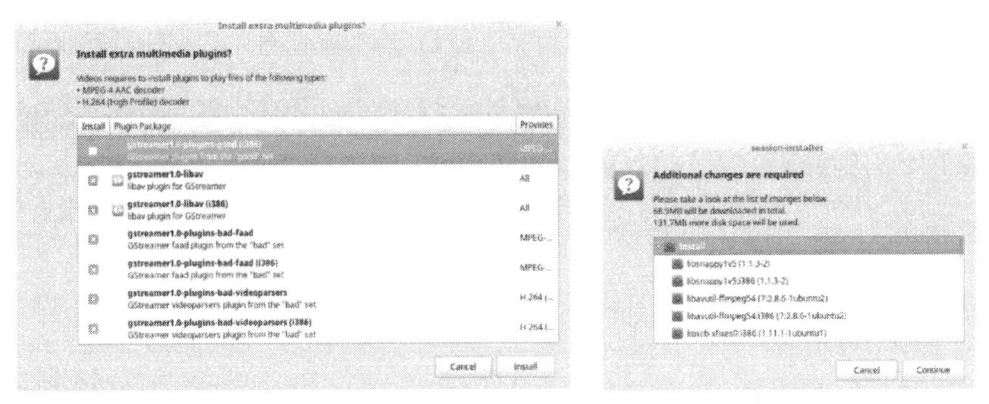

Figure 5-5: Linux Mint codec wizard selection

To install support for most of the commonly used codecs, if not already installed, you can install the **mint-meta-codecs** package. There are several ways to do this. On the Welcome screen, you can simply click on the "Multimedia codecs" icon. On the Cinnamon menu, on the Sound & Video submenu, you can select the "Install Multimedia Codecs" item. You could also just use the Software Manager or the Synaptic Package Manager to install the **mint-meta-codecs** package.

For KDE application, install the **mint-meta-codecs-kde** package. The **mint-meta-codecs** package installs Xplayer plugins and the **mint-meta-codecs-core** package, which, in turn, installs the third-party codecs, including libdvdcss2, ffmpeg, vlc, and unrar. The codecs provide support for DVD, MP3, MPEG4, DivX, and AC3, as well as Adobe Flash. For GStreamer supported applications like the X-player movie player, the gstreamer-bad and gstreamer-ugly plugins are installed.

```
mint-meta-codecs
mint-meta-codecs-kde
```

GStreamer

Many GNOME-based applications make use of GStreamer, a streaming media framework based on graphs and filters (**https://gstreamer.freedesktop.org**). Using a plug-in structure, GStreamer applications can accommodate a wide variety of media types:

The Videos (Totem and Xplayer) video player uses GStreamer to play DVDs, VCDs, and MPEG media.

Rhythmbox provides integrated music management.

Sound Juicer is an audio CD ripper.

GStreamer can be configured to use different input and output sound and video drivers and servers, using the GStreamer properties tool, the Multimedia System Selector. You can access it on the Multimedia dash. It is not displayed by default; use Main Menu to have it listed.

GStreamer Plug-ins: the Good, the Bad, and the Ugly

Many GNOME multimedia applications like Videos use GStreamer to provide multimedia support. To use such features as DVD Video and MP3, you have to install GStreamer extra plug-ins. You can find more information about GStreamer and its supporting packages at **https://gstreamer.freedesktop.org**.

GStreamer has four different support packages called the base, the good, the bad, and the ugly. The base package is a set of useful and reliable plug-ins. These are in the main repository. The good package is a set of supported and tested plug-ins that meets all licensing requirements. This is also part of the main repository. The bad package is a set of unsupported plug-ins whose performance is not guaranteed and may crash, but still meet licensing requirements. The ugly package contains plug-ins that work fine, but may not meet licensing requirements, like DVD support.

The base Reliable commonly used plug-ins

The good Reliable additional and useful plug-ins

The ugly Reliable but not fully licensed plug-ins (DVD/MP3 support)

The bad Possibly unreliable but useful plug-ins (possible crashes)

Music Applications

Many music applications are currently available for GNOME, including sound editors, MP3 players, and audio players (see Table 5-12). You can use Rhythmbox, and Sound Juicer to play music from different sources, and the GNOME Sound Recorder to record sound sources. GNOME Music is the new GNOME Music player with tabs for Albums, Artists, Songs, and Playlists. Several applications are also available for KDE, including the media players Amarok and Juk, a mixer (KMix), and a CD player (Kscd). For sound and music editing you can use Jokosher.

Video Applications

Several projects provide TV, video, DivX, DVD, and DVB support for Linux (see Table 5-13). Aside from GStreamer applications, there are also several third-party multimedia applications you may want, including MPlayer and VideoLan. The default video player is Xplayer, an X-App based on Totem and installed by default (see Figure 5-6).

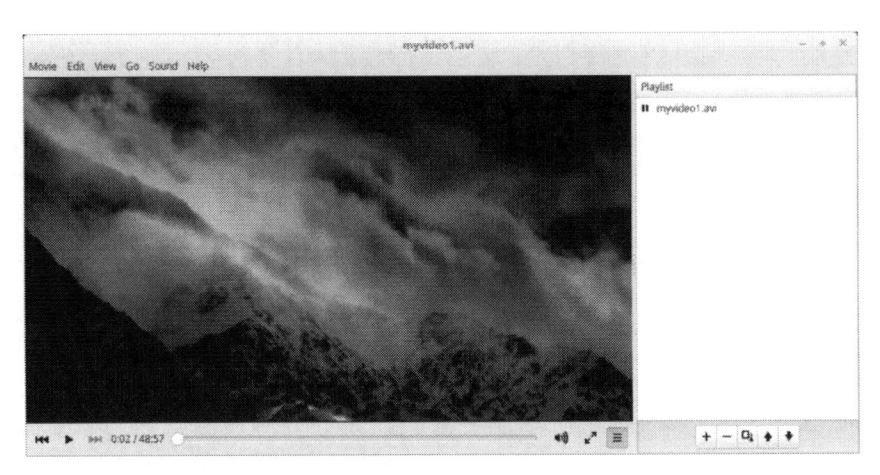

Figure 5-6: Xplayer X-App Video Player

Application	Description
Rhythmbox	Music management (GStreamer), default Music player with iPod support
Sound Juicer	GNOME CD audio ripper (GStreamer)
Amarok	KDE4 multimedia audio player
Audacious	Multimedia player
Kscd	Music CD player
JuK	KDE4 Music player (jukebox) for managing music collections
GNOME CD Player	CD player
GNOME Sound Recorder	Sound recorder
GNOME Music	GNOME Music player
XMMS	CD player
Tomahawk	Music player for online music (KDE).
ubuntustudio-audio	Ubuntu Studio metapackage (Meta Packages (universe)), includes a collection of audio applications. Use Synaptic Package Manager
Audex	KDE CD audio ripper
Specimen	MIDI controlled sampler
QMidiRoute	MIDI event router and filter

Table 5-12: Music players, editors, and rippers

Video and DVD Players

Most current DVD and media players are provided on the Linux Mint/Ubuntu repositories.

Xplayer is the X-App video player, based on Totem (see Figure 5-6). It is installed by default and is accessible from the Sound & Video menu as Videos . To expand Xplayer capabilities, you need to install added GStreamer plug-ins, as discussed previously. The codec wizard will prompt you to install any needed media codecs and plugins. You can use the dconf editor to modify default settings (org.x.player) (**xplayer** package).

Totem is the GNOME movie player that uses GStreamer, labeled with the name Videos. You can use the dconf editor to modify default settings (org.gnome.totem) (**totem** package).

The **VideoLAN** project (**http://www.videolan.org**) offers network streaming support for most media formats, including MPEG-4 and MPEG-2. It includes a multimedia player, VLC, which can work on any kind of system (**vlc** package, Universe repository). VLC supports high-def hardware decoding.

Dragon Player is a KDE multimedia player, installed with KDE desktop but will play on the GNOME desktop.

GNOME Media Player provides a simple interface for playing media files using the xine, vlc, or Gstreamer engines.

Kaffeine is a KDE multimedia player (video and dvb) (**kaffeine** package).

MPlayer is one of the most popular and capable multimedia/DVD players in use. It is a cross-platform open source alternative to RealPlayer and Windows Media Player (**www.mplayerhq.hu**). MPlayer uses an extensive set of supporting libraries and applications like **lirc**, **lame**, **lzo**, and **aalib**. If you have trouble displaying video, be sure to check the preferences for different video devices and select one that works best (**mplayer** package).

Videos Plugins (Xplayer and Totem)

The Videos movie player uses plugins to add capabilities like Internet video streaming. Select Edit | Preferences and click on the Plugins button to open the Configure Plugins window. Choose the plugins you want. For added support, install the **xplayer-plugins-extra** package. This provides the Gromit annotation tool. The default video player is Xplayer. The Totem video player also provides the plugin support (**totem-plugins-extra**).

PiTiVi Video editor

The PiTiVi Video editor is an open source application that lets you edit your videos. Check the PiTiVi website for more details (**http://www.pitivi.org**). You can download a quick-start manual from the Documentation page. Pitivi is a GStreamer application and can work with any video file supported by an installed GStreamer plugin. However, third-party playback plugins designed to be licensed officially such as Fluendo MP3 and MPEG plugins, may not be compatible. These plugins are designed to be playback only and do not provide full codec support. You should use the GStreamer Ugly plugins instead.

Projects and Players	Sites
Xplayer	X-App video player (based on Totem)
Totem	Totem video and DVD player for GNOME using GStreamer, includes plugins for DVB, YouTube, and MythTV
Dragon Player	Dragon Player video and DVD player for KDE4
VLC Media Player (vlc)	Network multimedia streaming. www.videolan.org
MPlayer	MPlayer DVD/multimedia player www.mplayerhq.hu
me-tv	TV viewer featuring DVB support
tvtime	TV viewer, http://tvtime.sourceforge.net
XviD	Open Source DivX, https://www.xvid.com/
Kaffeine	KDE media player, including HDTV, DVB, DVD, CD, and network streams
PiTiVi	Video editor
GNOME Media Player	Basic media player using GStreamer, vlc, or xine engines

Table 5-13: Video and DVD Projects and Applications

TV Players

The following TV players are provided on Linux Mint/Ubuntu repositories:

TV player **tvtime** works with many common video capture cards, relying on drivers developed for TV tuner chips. It can only display a TV image. It has no recording or file playback capabilities. Check **http://tvtime.sourceforge.net** for more information.

MythTV is a popular video recording and playback application on Linux systems. (Mythbuntu release, multiverse repository). See **www.mythbuntu.org** for more information.

me-tv is a DVB and HDTV video recording and playback application for Linux systems.

Kaffeine is a popular KDE video recording and playback application on Linux systems. It can also play ATSC over the air digital broadcasts.

Note: To play DivX media on Linux Mint you use the Xvid OpenDivX codec, xvidcore.

DVB and HDTV support

For DVB and HDTV reception, you can use most DVB cards as well as many HDTV cards. The DVB kernel driver is loaded automatically. You can use the **lsmod** command to see if your DVB module is loaded. The VideoLan (VLC) player can run HD media (x264) using your display card's native high definition decoder (hardware decoding instead of software decoding), check Tools | Preferences | Codecs | Use GPU acceleration.

Kaffeine DVB and ATSC tuning

The Kaffeine KDE media player can scan for both DVB and ATSC channels. You will need to have a DVB or ATSC tuner installed on your system. On Kaffeine, from the Television menu choose Configure Television, and on the device tab choose the source such as ATSC. Then from the Television menu, select Channels to open a Channel dialog. Your tuner device is selected on the Search on menu. Click on the Start scan button to begin scanning. Detected channels are listed on the "Scan results" scroll box. Select the ones you want and click Add Selected to place them in the Channels scroll box. Be sure to add the channel you want to watch on the Channel list.

Xvid (DivX) and Matroska (mkv) on Linux

MPEG-4 compressed files provide DVD-quality video with relatively small file sizes. They have become popular for distributing high-quality video files over the Internet. When you first try to play an MPEG-4, the codec wizard will prompt you to install the needed codec packages to play it. Many multimedia applications like VLC already support MPEG-4 files.

MPEG-4 files using the Matroska wrapper, also known by their file extension **mkv**, can be played on most video players including the VideoLan vlc player, Totem, Dragon Player, and Kaffeine. You will need HDTV codecs, like MPEG4 AAC sound codec, installed to play the high definition **mkv** file files. If needed, the codec wizard will prompt you to install them. To manage and create MKV files you can use the **mkvtoolnix-gui** tools.

You use the open source version of DivX known as Xvid to play DivX video (**libxvidcore** package. Most DivX files can be run using XviD. XviD is an entirely independent open source project, but it is compatible with DivX files. You can also download the XviD source code from **https://www.xvid.com/**.

CD/DVD Burners

Several CD/DVD ripper and writer programs can be used for CD music and MP3 writing (burners and rippers). These include Sound Juicer, Brasero (see Chapter 3), and K3b (See Table 5-14). GNOME features the CD audio ripper Sound Juicer. You can also use Serpentine to create audio CDs. For burning DVD/CD music and data discs, you can use Brasero CD/DVD burner. For KDE you can use K3b.

Application	Description
Brasero	Full service CD/DVD burner, for music, video, and data discs (no longer installed by default)
Sound Juicer (Audio CD Extractor)	GNOME music player and CD burner and ripper
Serpentine	GNOME music CD burner and ripper
ogmrip	DVD ripping and encoding with DivX support
K3b	KDE CD writing interface

Table 5-14: CD/DVD Burners

Brasero, K3b, and dvdauthor can all be used to create DVD Video discs. All use mkisofs, cdrecord, and cdda2wav DVD/CD writing programs installed as part of your desktop. OGMrip can rip and encode DVD video. DVD-Video and CD music rippers may require addition codecs installed, for which the codec wizard will prompt you.

Internet Applications

Linux provides powerful Web and FTP clients for accessing the Internet. Some of these applications are installed automatically and are ready to use when you first start up your system. Linux also includes full Java development support, letting you run and construct Java applets. Web and FTP clients connect to sites that run servers, using Web pages and FTP files to provide services to users.

You can choose from several Web browsers, including Firefox, Rekonq, Epiphany, Chromium, and Lynx. Firefox, Rekonq, Chromium, and Epiphany are desktop browsers that provide full picture, sound, and video display capabilities. The Lynx browser is a line-mode browser that displays only lines of text.

Web browsers and FTP clients are commonly used to conduct secure transactions, such as logging into remote sites, ordering items, or transferring files. Such operations are currently secured by encryption methods provided by the Secure Sockets Layer (SSL). If you use a browser for secure transactions, it should be SSL enabled. Most browsers include SSL support. Linux distributions include SSL (OpenSSL) as part of a standard installation.

Web Browsers

Popular browsers for Linux Mint include Firefox (Mozilla), Rekonq, Chromium (Google), Web (Epiphany), and Lynx (see Table 5-15). Firefox is the default Web browser used on most Linux distributions. Rekonq is the KDE Web browser, accessible from the KDE desktop, and Web is the GNOME Web browser (formerly known as Epiphany). Chromium is the open source version of the Google Web browser. Lynx and ELinks are command line-based browsers with no graphics capabilities, but in every other respect, they are fully functional Web browsers.

Web Site	Description
Firefox	The Mozilla project Firefox Web browser, desktop default browser https://www.mozilla.org
Rekonq	KDE desktop Web browser https://rekonq.kde.org/
Web	GNOME Web browser https://wiki.gnome.org/Apps/Web
Chromium	Open source version of Google Chrome Web browser http://www.chromium.org
lynx	Text-based command-line Web browser http://lynx.browser.org/
elinks	Text-based command-line Web browser http://elinks.or.cz

Table 5-15: Web browsers

Java for Linux

To develop Java applications, use Java tools, and run many Java products, you use the Java Software Development Kit (SDK) and the Java Runtime Environment (JRE). The SDK is a superset of the JRE, adding development tools like compilers and debuggers. Sun (now owned by Oracle) has open sourced Java as the OpenJDK project and supports and distributes Linux versions. The JRE subset can be installed as OpenJRE. The **openjdk-8-jre** package installs the Java runtime environment, and **openjdk-8-jdk** installs both the JRE and the Java development tools. Java packages and applications are listed in Table 5-16.

Several compatible GNU packages (Java-like) are provided that allow you to run Java applets using GNU free Java support. These include GNU Java compiler (**gcj**) and the Eclipse Java compiler (**ecj**).

Application	Description
Java Development Kit, OpenJDK	An open source Java development environment with a compiler, interpreters, debugger, and more (include the JRE), **http://openjdk.java.net**, **openjdk-7-jdk**
Java Runtime Environment, OpenJRE	An open source Java runtime environment, including the Java virtual machine, **openjdk-7-jre**. **http://openjdk.java.net**
Java Platform Standard Edition (JSE)	Complete Java collection, including JRE, JDK, and API, **http://java.sun.com/javase**
GNU Java Compiler	GNU Public Licensed Java Compiler (GCJ) to compile Java programs, **https://gcc.gnu.org/java**., **gcj**

Table 5-16: Java Packages and Java Web Applications

BitTorrent Clients (transmission)

GNOME and KDE provide very effective BitTorrent clients. With BitTorrent, you can download very large files quickly in a shared distributed download operation where several users participate in downloading different parts of a file, sending their parts of the download to other participants, known as peers. Instead of everyone trying to access a few central servers, all peers participating in the BitTorrent operation become sources for the file being downloaded. Certain peers function as seeders, those who have already downloaded the file, but continue to send parts to those who need them.

Linux Mint will install and use the GNOME BitTorrent client, Transmission, accessible from the Internet menu. For KDE you can use the Ktorrent BitTorrent client. To perform a BitTorrent download you need the BitTorrent file for the file you want to download.

FTP Clients

With File Transfer Protocol (FTP) clients, you can connect to a corresponding FTP site and download files from it. These sites feature anonymous logins that let any user access their files. Basic FTP client capabilities are incorporated into the Dolphin (KDE), Nemo (Cinnamon), and Caja (Mate) file managers. You can use a file manager window to access an FTP site and drag files to local directories to download them. Effective FTP clients are also now incorporated into most

Web browsers, making Web browsers the primary downloading tool. Firefox, in particular, has strong FTP download capabilities.

Although file managers and Web browsers provide effective access to public (anonymous login) sites, to access private sites, you may need a stand-alone FTP client like curl, wget, Filezilla, gFTP, lftp, or **ftp**. These clients let you enter usernames and passwords with which you can access a private FTP site. The stand-alone clients are also useful for large downloads from public FTP sites, especially those with little or no Web display support. Popular Linux FTP clients are listed in Table 5-17.

FTP Clients	Description
Dolphin	KDE file manager
Nemo	GNOME file manager
gFTP	GNOME FTP client, **gftp-gtk**
ftp	Command line FTP client
lftp	Command line FTP client capable of multiple connections
curl	Internet transfer client (FTP and HTTP)
Filezilla	Linux version of the open source Filezilla ftp client (Universe repository)

Table 5-17: Linux FTP Clients

Network File Transfer: FTP

With File Transfer Protocol (FTP) clients, you can transfer extremely large files directly from one site to another (see Table 5-4). FTP can handle both text and binary files. FTP performs a remote login to another account on another system connected to you on a network. Once logged into that other system, you can transfer files to and from it. To log in, you need to know the login name and password for the account on the remote system. Many sites on the Internet allow public access using FTP, however. Such sites serve as depositories for large files anyone can access and download. These sites are often referred to as FTP sites, and in many cases, their Internet addresses begin with the term ftp, such as **ftp.gnome.org**. These public sites allow anonymous FTP login from any user. For the login name, you use the word "anonymous," and for the password, you use your email address. You can then transfer files from that site to your own system.

Several FTP protocol are available for accessing sites that support them. The original FTP protocol is used for most anonymous sites. FTP transmissions can also be encrypted using SSH2, the SFTP protocol. More secure connections may use FTPS for TLS/SSL encryption. Some sites support a simplified version of FTP called File Service Protocol, FSP. FTP clients may support different protocols like gFTP for FSP and Filezilla for TLS/SSL. Most clients support both FTP and SSH2.

Web Browser–Based FTP

You can access an FTP site and download files from it with any Web browser. Browsers are useful for locating individual files, though not for downloading a large set of files. A Web browser is effective for checking out an FTP site to see what files are listed there. When you access an FTP site with a Web browser, the entire list of files in a directory is listed as a Web page. You can move to a subdirectory by clicking its entry. You can easily browse through an FTP site to download files. To download a file, click the download link. This will start the transfer operation, opening a dialog for selecting your local directory and the name of the file. The default name is the same as on the remote system. On many browsers, you can manage your downloads with a download manager, which will let you cancel a download operation in progress or remove other downloads. The manager will show the time remaining, the speed, and the amount transferred for the current download.

GNOME Desktop FTP: Connect to Server

The easiest way to download files is to use the built-in FTP capabilities of the GNOME file managers, Nemo and Caja. On GNOME, the desktop file manager has a built-in FTP capability much like the KDE file manager. The FTP operation has been seamlessly integrated into standard desktop file operations. Downloading files from an FTP site is as simple as dragging files from one directory window to another, where one of the directories happens to be located on a remote FTP site. Use the file manager to access a remote FTP site, listing files in the remote directory, just as local files are. In a file manager's Location bar (**Ctrl-l** or Location button), enter the FTP site's URL following the prefix **ftp://** and press ENTER. A dialog opens prompting you to specify how you want to connect. You can connect anonymously for a public FTP site, or connect as a user supplying your username and password (private site). You can also choose to remember the password.

For more access options such as a secure SSH connection, windows share, and Secure Web (HTTPS), you can use the Connect to Server dialog (see Figure 5-7). To open the Connect to Server dialog, choose File | Connect to Server menu item on any file manager window, or on the Desktop applications menu. From the Type menu, you can select the service type. Entry options change accordingly, with the "FTP (with login)" adding an entry for the username. Click the Connect button to access the site.

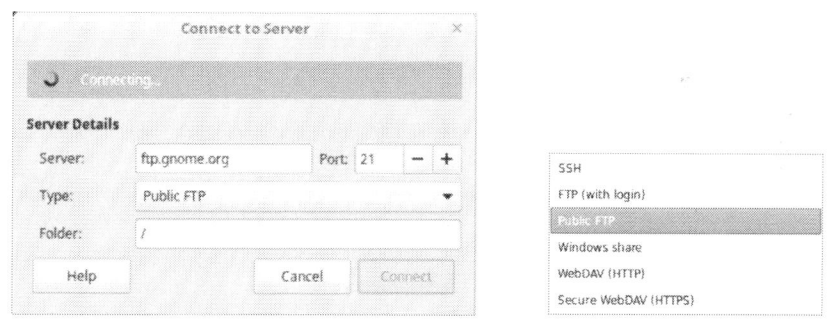

Figure 5-7: GNOME FTP access Connect to Server dialog

The top directory of the remote FTP site will be displayed in a file manager window (see Figure 5-8. Use the file manager to progress through the remote FTP site's directory tree until you find the file you want. Then, open another window for the local directory to which you want the remote files copied. In the window showing the FTP files, select those you want to download. Then click and drag those files to the window for the local directory. As files are downloaded, a dialog appears showing the progress.

152 Part 1: Getting Started

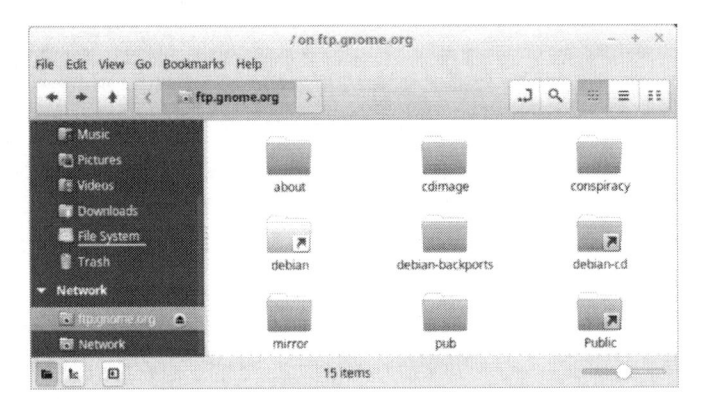

Figure 5-8: GNOME FTP access with Connect to Server and the file manager

The file manager window's sidebar (Network section) will list an entry for the FTP site accessed. An eject button is shown to the right of the FTP site's name. To disconnect from the site, click this button. The FTP entry will disappear along with the FTP sites icons and file listings.

Social Networking

Linux provides integrated social networking support for IM (Instant Messenger) and VoIP (Voice over Internet). Users can communicate directly with other users on your network (see Table 5-18). These applications are installed automatically and are ready to use when you first start up your system. Instant messenger (IM) clients allow users on the same IM system to communicate anywhere across the Internet. With Voice over the Internet Protocol applications, you can speak over Internet connections.

Clients	Description
Ekiga	VoIP application
Skype	VoIP application (Partner repository)
empathy	GNOME instant messenger
KDE empathy	KDE instant messenger client
Pidgin	Older instant messenger client
Jabber	Jabber IM service (gajim, psi, emacs, empathy)
Finch	Command line cursor-based IM client
Hexchat	IRC client

Table 5-18: Instant Messenger, Talk, and VoIP Clients

Skype can be installed with Software Manager. Once installed, you can access Skype from the Internet menu. When you first start Skype, you are asked to accept a user agreement. The interface is similar to the Windows version. A Skype panel icon will appear on the panel, once you start Skype. You can use it to access Skype throughout your session. Click to open Skype and right-click to display a menu from which you can change your status, sign out, access options, list contact groups, and start a conference call. The panel icon changes according to your status.

Part 2: Desktops

Cinnamon
Mate
KDE

6. Cinnamon Desktop

Cinnamon
Desklets
Windows
Cinnamon Menu
Panel
Applets
Workspaces
The Nemo File Manager
System Settings

Linux Mint features the Cinnamon desktop as its advanced desktop. Though Cinnamon was originally derived from GNOME 3, its interface is similar to GNOME 2, using a simple panel with applets. Linux Mint uses the Nemo file manager for Cinnamon, as well as some of GNOME 3 desktop configuration tools. You can find out more about Cinnamon at **http://developer.linuxmint.com**.

The Cinnamon desktop is designed to be easily extensible).. You can add themes, applets, desklets and extensions from certified third-party developers and artists. These addons are called Spices and they are available from the Cinnmon Spices website at **https://cinnamon-spices.linuxmint.com/,** which is the official Cinnmon addons repository.

Cinnamon Desktop

The Cinnamon desktop is designed for ease of use on desktop systems, using a traditional panel with applets for most desktop tasks. Applets for Network Manager, sound volume, updates, and time and date are placed on the right side of the panel (see Figure 6-1). The left side of the panel is the Cinnamon menu, the panel launchers applet to quick start applications, and the Windows List applet for open windows. You can easily add and remove applets using the System Settings Applets dialog, accessible from the Panel applet. The Panel Edit mode (right-click on the panel) lets you reposition and remove applets. System supported folders, such as Computer and Home, are displayed on the desktop. You can restart the Cinnamon desktop without restarting the system, by pressing CTRL-ALT-ESC.

Figure 6-1: Cinnamon desktop

The Cinnamon desktop features a Cinnamon menu for applications, places, and tasks, with a Favorites icon bar for the commonly used applications and tasks (see Figure 6-2). The Favorites icon bar shows icons for the Firefox browser, the Software Manager, System Settings, the terminal window, and the Nemo file manager. There are also icons for lock, logout, and shut down operations.

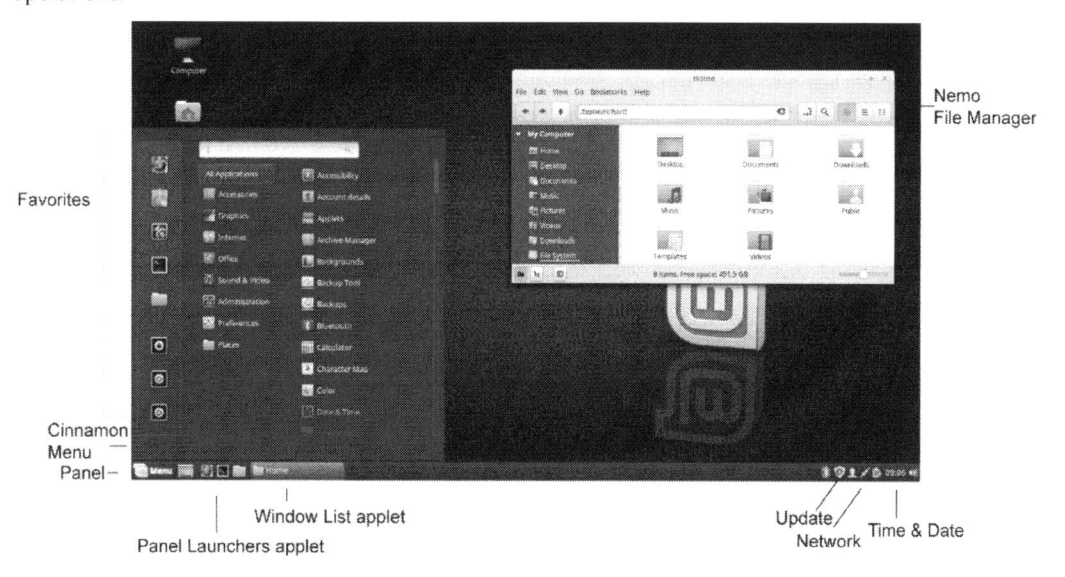

Figure 6-2: Cinnamon desktop with Cinnamon Menu and Nemo file manager

Right-clicking anywhere on the desktop displays the desktop menu, from which you can add new folders to the desktop, open the file manager with administrative (root) access, open a terminal window, change the background, access desktop settings, and add desklets. The Desktop submenu lets you control the display of your desktop icons. You can change the size (small, normal. and large), display them in a grid (Auto-arrange), display icons vertically (columns) or horizontally (lines), sort by name, size, date, and type, or deselect the Auto-arrange option to place icons anywhere. The desktop menu is shown here.

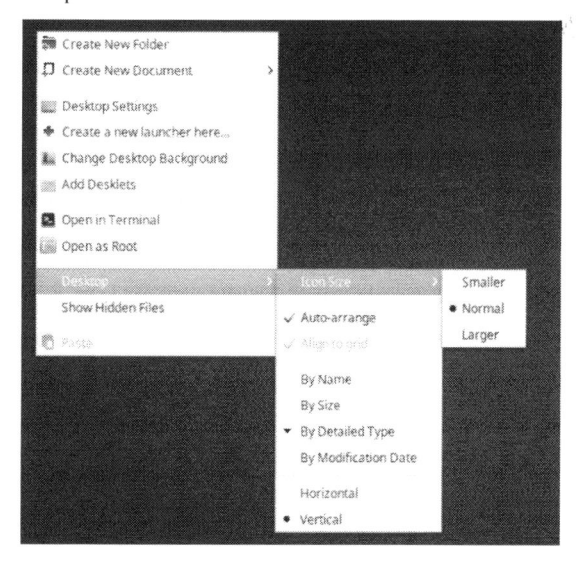

On the System Settings Desktop dialog, you can specify the icons to be displayed on the desktop (see Figure 6-3). By default, the computer and home icons are shown, along with icons for any file systems and devices that you mount, such as a USB drive or DVD disc. You can also choose to display the file manager's network folder (network servers) and the trash. The "Desktop layout" option lets you choose whether to show desktop icons, on all attached monitors, or just primary monitors. If an additional monitor is missing, you can choose to still display its icons.

You can search for desktop items quickly by clicking and holding down the meta key when entering the first character of a pattern. This opens a text box in which you enter a search pattern. It highlights the icon for the best first match.

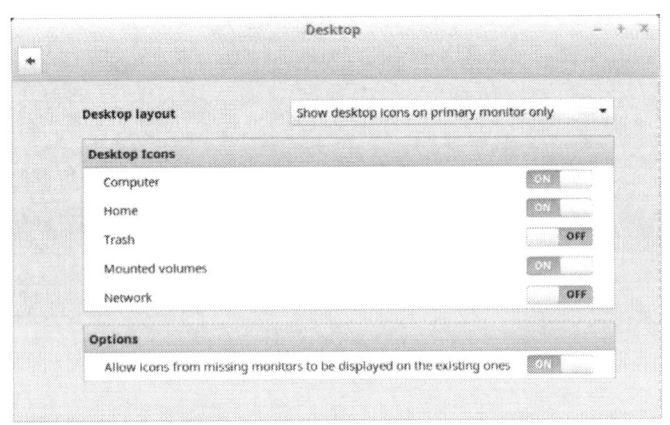

Figure 6-3: System Settings Desktop

Desklets

A desklet works much like an applet, but for the desktop instead of the panel (see Figure 6-4). It is very similar to a plasmoid on the KDE desktop. You can use the "Show desktop" icon on the panel to display only your desklets and desktop icons, hiding your open windows.

Figure 6-4: Desklets on the desktop

Three desklets are installed (but not activated) by default: clock, photo, and launcher. The Clock desklet displays a digital clock. The Digital photo frame desklet displays a small dialog that performs a slide show of the images in your Pictures folder. The Launcher desklet can be configured to launch an application. A listing of available applets can be found at **https://cinnamon-spices.linuxmint.com/desklets**.

You can add desklets to the desktop (activate) using the System Settings Desklets dialog. Like the Applets dialog, Desklets has "Installed desklets" and "Available desklets (online)" tabs (see Figure 6-5). The "Installed desklets" tab lists desklets that have been installed your computer.

The Show menu can list all, active, or inactive desklets. You can also search for desklets using the search box. To activate a desklet, click on its entry and click the "Add to desktop" button, or right-click on the entry and choose "Add to desktop." To remove a desklet from the desktop, right-click on its entry in the Desklets dialog and choose "Remove from desktop" from the pop-up menu.

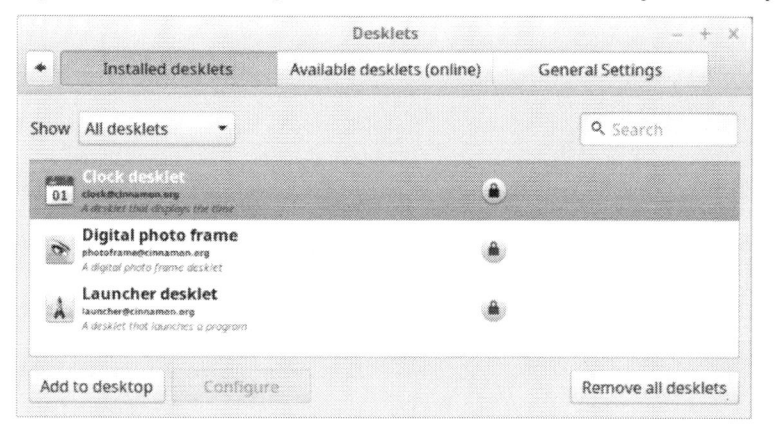

Figure 6-5: Desklets Installed tab

You can download and install addition desklets from the Linux Mint repository by clicking on the "Available desklets (online)" tab (see figure 6-6). The "Sort by" menu lets you sort by name, popularity, and date (latest). Only are few desklets are currently available, such as an analog clock. To see more information about a desklet, click the "More info" link to open its Web page. To install a desklet, click on the desklet's checkbox, and click the "Install or update selected" button. A check mark icon then appears in the desklet entry. You will then see it listed on the Installed tab. From there you can activate it to add it to the desktop.

The "General Desklets Settings" tab lets you determine how desklets are displayed. You can show a border around them, no border, or both the border and desklet title (header). You can snap desklets to a grid, or allow a free placement.

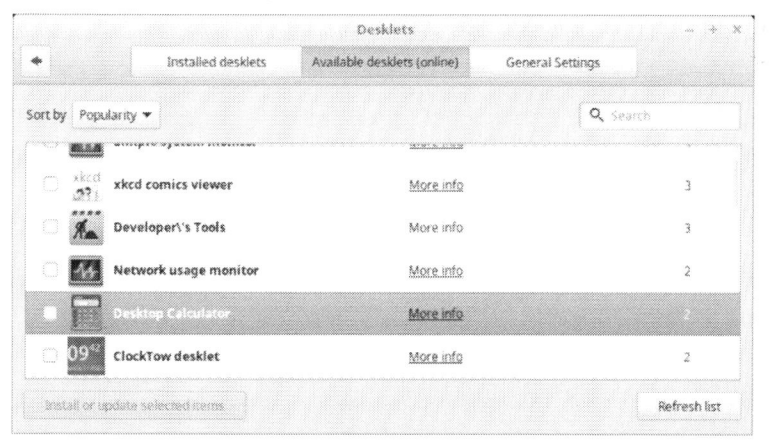

Figure 6-6: Desklets "Get more online" tab

Hot Corners

Hot Corners allows you to configure the corners of your screen to run the Expo workspace switcher, the Scale windows switcher, the show desktop function, or a program of your choosing (command). You can activate the operations by hovering the mouse in a corner. Moving the mouse to the corner and holding it there, runs the operation.

You configure Hot Corners using the System Settings Hot Corners dialog. On the dialog, each corner has a menu from which to choose an application: Show all workspaces (Expo), Show all windows (Scale), Show the desktop, and Run a command (custom). The "Show all workspaces" option runs the Expo workspace configuration and switcher, and the "Show all windows" option runs the Scale screen-based window switcher, which scales windows to a grid. The corners are disabled by default, showing a light red color for each corner. To turn a corner on, click the "Hover enabled" checkbox, which then shows a solid green color. You move the mouse to the corner for a moment to activate the setting. The "Hover delay" option lets you set the speed at which the corner is activated, letting you set a delay if you want. In Figure 6-7, as an example, the top left corner is configured to run the Expo workspace switcher using a mouse hover on that corner with no delay. The right corner is configured to run the Scale window switcher with a short delay. Either will work. The bottom left corner is disabled, which shows a light red color for the corner.

The "Show desktop" option toggles the minimizing of your open windows on the desktop. If displayed, all windows are minimized to the window list applet on the panel. If all are minimized, they are then all displayed on the desktop.

The "Run a command" option opens a text box in which you can enter an application name. In Figure 6-7, the bottom right corner is configured to run the Nemo file manager using a text box. With this setting, the Nemo file manager would open a window with your home folder each time you move the mouse to that corner after a delay.

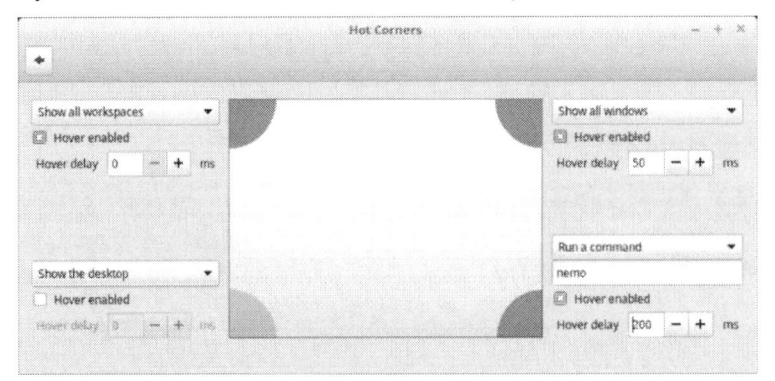

Figure 6-7: System Settings Hot Corners

Keyboard and Mouse Shortcuts

Keyboard shortcuts can be configured on the System Settings Keyboard dialog's Shortcuts tab (see Figure 6-8). There are shortcuts for the general, windows, workspaces, system, launchers, sound and media should your keyboard support those keys, and universal access. Categories are listed to the left, with additional expanded entries for specific operations, such a positioning of windows. Within a category, you can choose a shortcut task, for which the key is displayed in the

Keyboard binding section below. To change or add a key click on its string in the Keyboard bindings section to open a window where you can type in the new key or key combinations. A listing of common shortcuts is provided in Table 6-1.

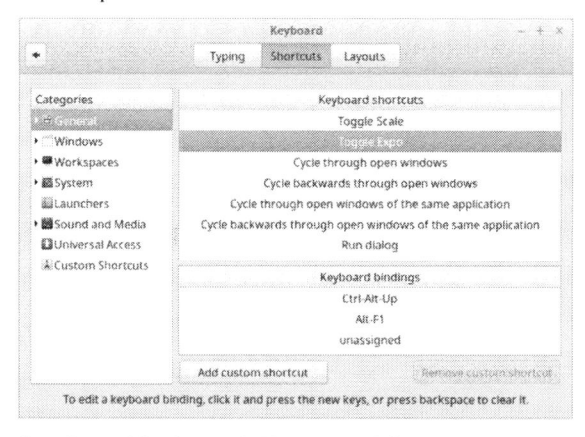

Figure 6-8: System Settings Keyboard, Keyboard Shortcuts

Keys	Description
Cinnamon	
Atl-F2	Run a command from a command line
Meta	Displays the Cinnamon menu (Windows key)
Meta with character	Opens a desktop search box for desktop icons
Ctrl-Alt-t	Opens a terminal window
Ctrl-Alt-Escape	Restart the Cinnamon desktop only
Workspaces	
Alt-F1	Toggle the Expo workspace switcher
Ctrl-Alt-*uparrow*	Toggle the Expo workspace switcher
Ctrl-Alt-*leftarrow*	Move to left workspace
Ctrl-Alt-*rightarrow*	Move to right workspace
Ctrl-Alt-Shift-*arrows*	Use left or right arrows to move a window to a new workspace
Panel	
Ctrl-Alt-L	Lock the screen
Ctrl-Alt-Delete	Log out
Windows	
Ctrl-Alt-*downarrow*	Toggle the scale window switcher
Alt-Tab	Switch between windows
Alt-Shift-Tab	Switch between windows, backwards

162 Part 2: Desktops

Alt-~	Switch between windows for the same application
Alt-F5	Unmaximize the current window
Alt-F4	Close the current window
Meta -*leftarrow*	Tile current window to left side of screen
Meta-*rightarrow*	Tile current window to right side of screen
Meta-*uparrow*	Tile current window to the top
Meta-*downarrow*	Tile current window to the bottom
Ctrl-Alt-Numpad 0	Maximize window
Ctrl-Alt-Numpad 5	Center/Maximize the window in the middle of the screen

Table 6-1: Cinnamon Keyboard Shortcuts

Menu

The Cinnamon menu consists of a Favorites icon bar for frequently used applications and operations, menus based on application categories, and a search box for locating applications (see Figure 6-9). In addition, the menu also displays folder bookmarks (Places) and recently accessed files. The Cinnamon menu is a panel applet located on the left side of the panel.

Figure 6-9: Cinnamon menu

On the Menu, favorites are displayed on the left. To the right is a category menu and a menu of items in a selected category. If all the items cannot be displayed, then the menu list becomes a scroll box, letting you scroll through items. The All Applications entry on the category list displays all applications. Items not assigned to a particular category can be located in this category. The Places category lists your folder bookmarks, and Recent Files lists recently accessed files. The search box at the top lets you search quickly for applications using patterns (see Figure 6-10).

Figure 6-10: Cinnamon menu search

The favorites icon bar shows applications in the upper part, and system shutdown, logout, and lock tasks in the lower part (see Figure 6-11). The parts are separated by a blank space. When you move your mouse over an icon, its name and description appear in the lower right corner of the menu. Clicking on an application icon opens that application. Clicking on any of the shutdown, logout, and lock icons open their respective dialogs and lets you perform the task.

Figure 6-11: Cinnamon menu favorites

Application favorites can be easily added or removed using an item's pop-up menu. Right-click on an item to display a menu with options to add the item to the panel, desktop, and favorites (see Figure 6-12). If you add an item to Favorites, then the item's pop-up menu will display a "Remove from favorites" entry, which you can use to remove it from the Favorites icon bar. As you add items to Favorites bar, they become smaller and smaller to fit. To remove an item from Favorites, you can display its name in the lower right corner by passing the mouse over it and then use that name in the search box to locate the menu item. Right-click on the menu item and choose "Remove from favorites."

164 Part 2: Desktops

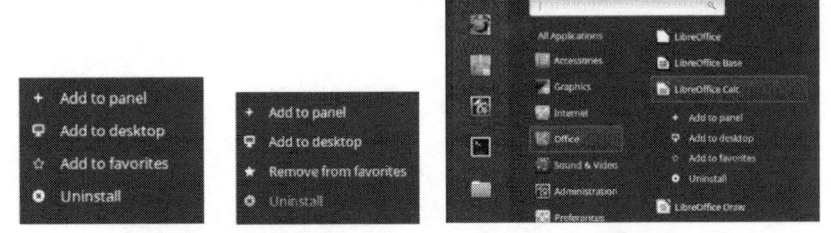

Figure 6-12: Cinnamon menu

Right clicking on the menu panel applet opens a menu with options to remove the menu or to configure the menu, as shown here. The "Remove this applet" entry removes the menu applet from the panel. Choosing the configure option opens the System Settings Menu dialog.

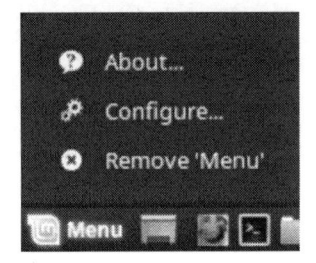

The Menu configuration dialog's Panel tab lets you choose a panel icon and the text displayed for the Cinnamon menu (see Figure 6-13). Instead of clicking on the menu applet to open the menu, you can choose to simply move the mouse over it, along with specifying a hover delay. The keyboard shortcut keys to open and close the menu can also be set here. On the Menu tab, you can set display features such as to show bookmarks and places, application and category icons, and favorites (Layout and content section). You can also enable auto-scrolling in the application list, and for searches, you can use full pathnames for applications (Behavior section).

The menu button (right-most button) list a menu with options to reset defaults and to save or import your menu items.

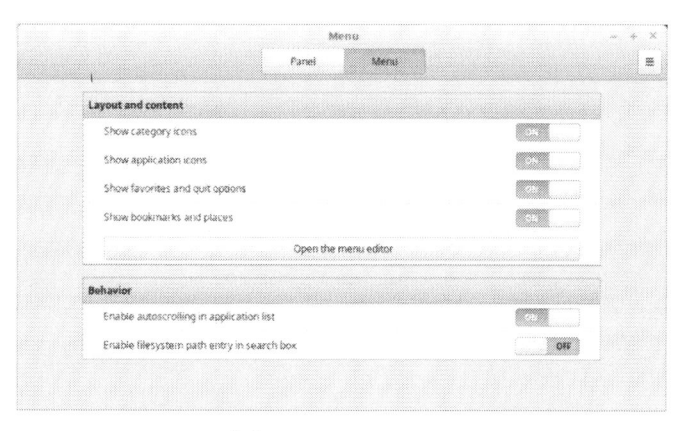

Figure 6-13: Cinnamon menu applet menu

Figure 6-14: Cinnamon menu Main Menu editor

To edit the items on the menu, click on the "Open the menu editor" button on the Menu tab of the Settings Menu dialog. This opens the Main Menu editor, where you can choose applications to be displayed on the menu (see Figure 6-14). Menu categories are listed in the left scroll box, and application items are shown in the right scroll box. To hide an item, deselect its checkbox. To remove an item permanently, select it and click the Delete button. To move an item to a different category, select it, click the Cut button, then click on the category you want it moved to, and then click the Paste button. Categories can be re-positioned, moving them up or down. To restore the original set of categories, applications, and their positions, you click the "Restore System Configuration" button.

The New Menu button lets you create new category menus. You enter a name and choose the icon to use. The New Item button lets you add a menu item, which can be an application, application in a terminal window (shell script), or location (folder). You will have to manually specify the name and the command.

Windows

Windows on Linux Mint operate much as they do on other Linux distributions, with similar maximizing, minimizing, and workspace operations. You use the window buttons on the right side of the window title bar to minimize (minus), maximize (plus), and close (x) a window.

Preferences for windows, such as the effect of double clicking the title bar, the title bar font, and the button order, can be set using the System Settings Windows dialog (see Figure 6-15). The dialog has three tabs: Titlebar, Behavior, and Alt-Tab. The Titlebar tab has a Buttons section where you can position window buttons and a Titlebar section for choosing actions that can be performed on the titlebar. In the Buttons section, the title bar buttons are already ordered for the right side. You could add another button for the window menu. You could also move them to the left side, by choosing the empty menu option for the right side buttons and selecting the Minimize, Maximize, and Close entries for the left side buttons.

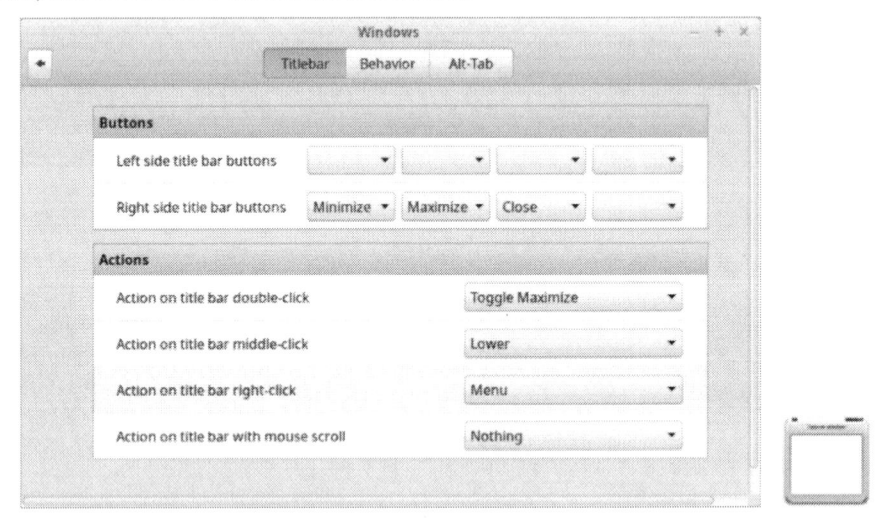

Figure 6-15: Windows Settings: Titlebar tab

In the Actions section, the action-double-click-titlebar key is set to toggle-maximize (maximize the window), but a menu lets you choose options such as toggle-shade, which rolls up the window instead of maximizing it. There are also menus for the middle-click and right-click operations (by default set to Menu - the window menu). The "Action on the title bar with mouse scroll" menu lets you change the opacity of a window by scrolling on the title bar, making it transparent so you can see windows or icons underneath it.

The Behavior tab lets you modify window movement and display (see Figure 6-16). It has two sections: "Windows Focus" and "Moving and Resizing Windows." In the Windows Focus section, you can set the focus mode (click, mouse, or sloppy). The "Attach dialog window to their parent window's titlebar" option will display a dialog opened by an application window as an overlay of the application window. In the "Moving and Resizing Windows" section you can determine the initial placement of new windows, choose a key to resize or move windows (Alt, Meta, Super, or Control). Alt is already selected.

Figure 6-16: Windows Settings: Behavior tab

The Alt-Tab tab lets you configure the window switcher display (see Figure 6-17). You can choose a style for the menu such as icons only, thumbnails only, icons and window preview, and icons and thumbnails (the default). For accelerated supported graphics (3D), you can also choose coverflow and timeline. Most computers now support accelerated graphics.

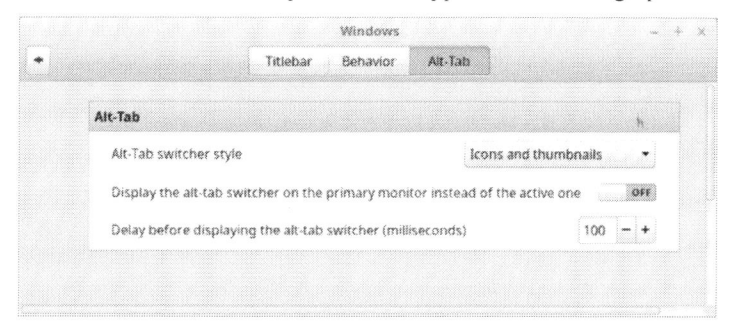

Figure 6-17: Windows Settings: Alt-tab tab

To manage window tiling and edge flipping you use the Window Tiling dialog on System Settings. The "Enable Window Tiling and Snapping" option enables window tiling and snapping when you move a window to the edge of the screen (see Figure 6-18). It is turned on by default. You can also select a key to toggle between snap and tile mode. When moving a window to the top edge of the screen it is set to tile, covering the top part of the screen. You can change this to maximize by turning on the "Maximize, instead of tile, when dragging a window to the top edge" option.

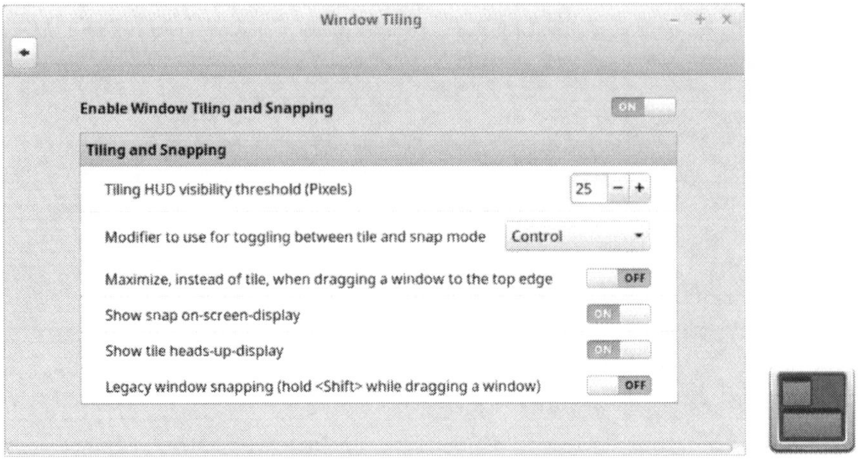

Figure 6-18: Window Tiling and Edge Flip

Minimizing, Maximizing, and Closing Windows

To maximize a window, you can double-click on the title bar, click and drag the title bar to the top of the screen, or click on its maximize button (plus image) on the right side of the title bar. You can also right-click on the title bar and choose the Maximize entry from the pop-up menu or press the Ctrl-Alt-5 keys.

To unmaximize a window, drag its title bar down and away from the top of the screen, or click on it's maximize button on the left side of the title bar (plus image).

To move a window, click and drag on its title bar. As you move, your mouse pointer changes to a hand. You can also press the Alt key with a mouse click, and drag to move a window, or you can right-click on the title bar and choose the Move entry from the pop-up menu.

From the keyboard, you can press the Alt-space keys to display the window menu for that window, and use the arrow key to move to the Move entry. You can also press the Alt-F7 keys.

To minimize a window, you can click the window's minimize button (minus sign) on the right side of the title bar. Minimized windows are reduced to buttons on the window list applet on the panel. To restore a minimized window, click on its button. If the window is not maximized, you can also right-click on the title bar and choose the Minimize entry from the pop-up menu, or press the Ctrl-Alt-0 keys.

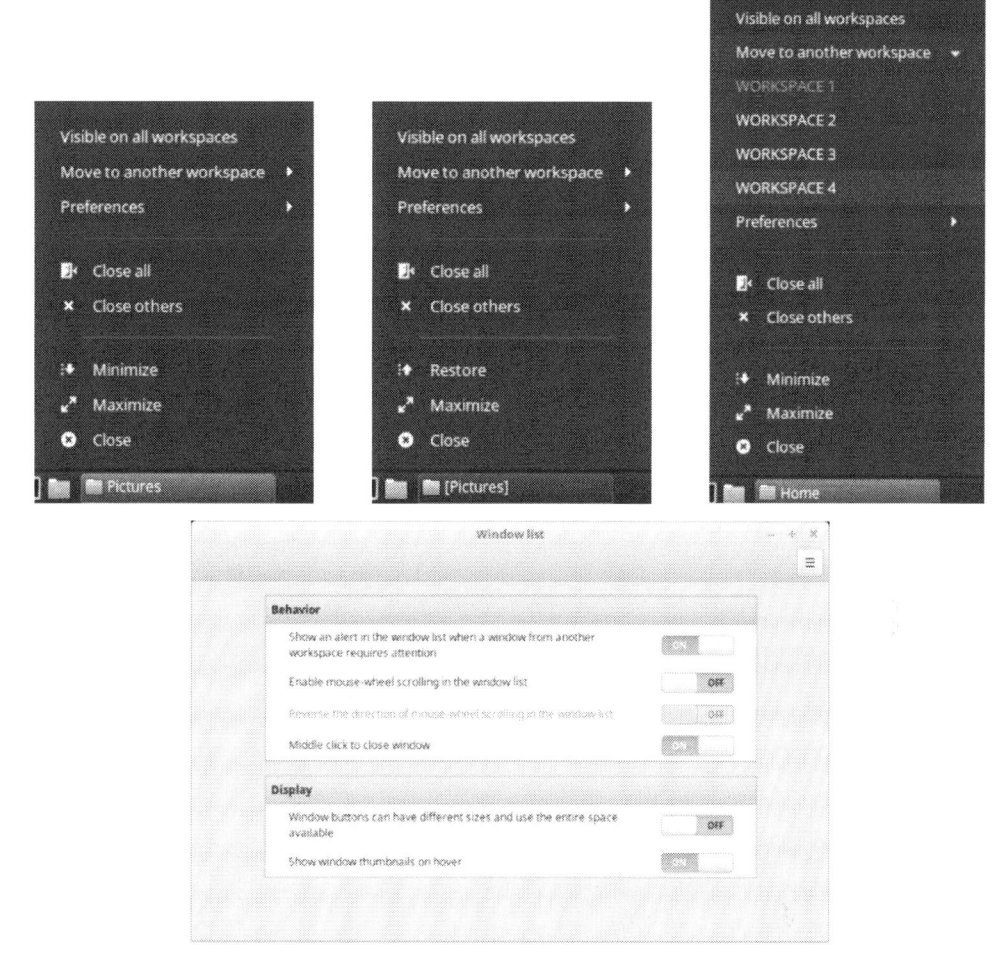

Figure 6-19: Window List menus and configuration

To close a window, click the window close button (the x character) on the right side of the title bar. You can also right-click on the title bar and choose the Close entry from the pop-up menu. From the keyboard, you can press Alt+F4, or press Alt+space to display the window menu and then press c to choose the Close entry.

Each open window has a corresponding button on the window list applet on the bottom panel. Clicking on it toggles the window between minimize and display. A minimized window will have brackets encasing the window name on its window list button. You can right-click on a window list button to open a pop-up menu, which provides options to maximize, close, and move the window to another workspace (see Figure 6-19). A minimized window has the option to restore the window, instead of minimize. You can also close all windows, or just close all other windows. To move a window to another workspace, click on the "Move to another workspace" entry to expand the menu to a list of your workspaces. To configure the window list, right click on a button on the panel for an open window and choose Preferences to expand the menu to show a Configure entry. This opens the Window List configuration dialog (see Figure 6-19), where you can set the behavior and display of the window list buttons such as enabling mouse wheel scrolling and showing window thumbnails on a mouse hover. From the menu in the upper right you can save and import window list configuration settings.

Resize and tiling Windows

You can resize a window vertically, horizontally, or both at the same time. To resize in both directions at once, move the mouse to any corner of the window until it becomes a corner-pointer, an arrow with a right-angle pointer image. You can then click-and-drag to the size you want. For side changes, move the mouse to the left or right side edge of the window until it changes to a side-pointer, an arrow with a line image. The same operation works for changes at the top or bottom of the window.

Linux Mint supports window snapping (tiling). Moving the window to the right or left edge of the screen (when the mouse reaches the edge) expands the window to take up that side of the screen. Moving the window to the top of the screen maximizes the window to use the full screen, with the window menu bar and buttons across the top.

You can also tile two windows so that one takes up one-half the screen, and the other uses the other half. Drag a window to left side (click and drag the title bar, or Alt-click on the window). When your mouse pointer meets the edge of your screen, the entire left side of the screen is highlighted. When you release your mouse, the window snaps to display on the entire left side of the screen. The same operation works for the right side. To restore the window to its previous size, simply drag it down and away from the edge.

Switching Windows with the Windows QuickList

You can also switch windows using the windows quicklist, which you can add to the panel. The windows quicklist lists all your open windows, organized by workspace (see Figure 6-20).

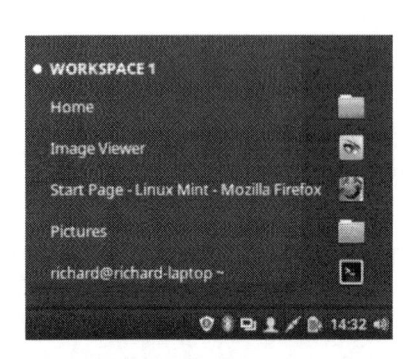

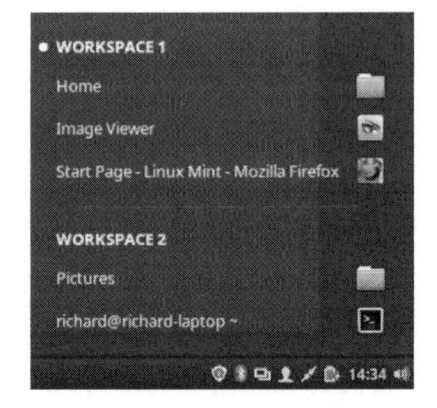

Figure 6-20: Windows QuickList menu

Switching Windows with the Scale Screen and Alt-Tab

You can switch between open windows using the Scale screen, which displays your open windows in a grid (see Figure 6-21). The window title and application icon is displayed below each window. Clicking on a window returns you to the desktop, with the selected window now the active window. You can also press the Esc key to return to the desktop. On the Scale screen, you can close windows. When you pass your mouse over a window, a close button appears in the upper right corner, which you can click to close the window.

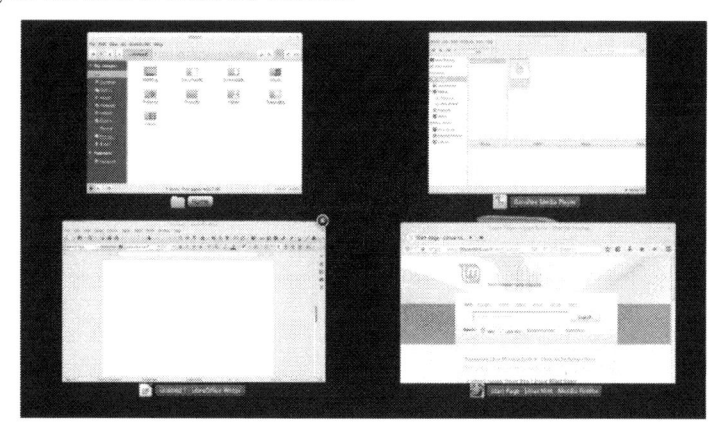

Figure 6-21: Scale: zoomed windows to switch windows (Hot corners, Show all windows)

You can access the Scale screen by pressing the Ctrl-Alt-downarrow key. You can also use a hot corner configured for Scale, or by using the Scale applet (shown here). For hot corners, use the System Settings Hot Corners dialog to enable "Show all windows" at a corner and choose Hover enabled. The upper right corner already has "Show all windows" selected. When you move your mouse to that corner, the Scale screen is displayed. For the Scale applet, first, install it, then click the Scale applet button on the panel to display the Scale screen.

You can also switch between windows using the Alt-Tab keys to display the window switcher (see Figure 6-22). Open windows are displayed using their application icons in the center of the screen. Use the Alt-Tab key to select the one you want. As you move through the row of icons, a thumbnail of the currently selected window is displayed below the icon. The Alt-Shift-Tab keys move backward through the windows, and the Alt-~ keys move through windows of the same application.

172 Part 2: Desktops

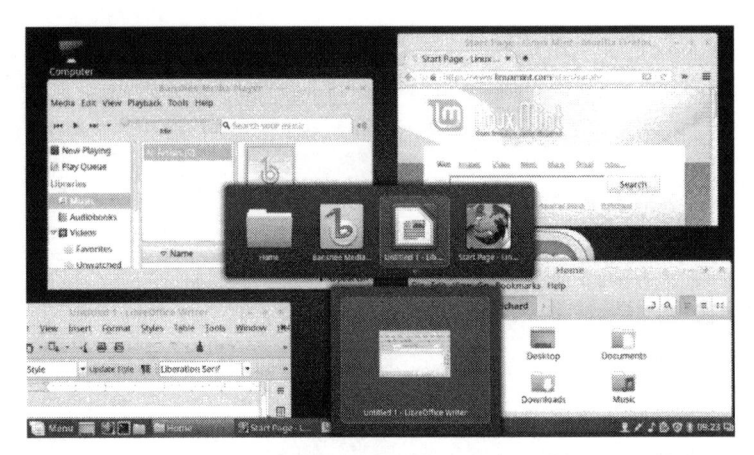

Figure 6-22: Window switching with Alt-Tab (Icons and Thumbnails)

The window switcher can be configured on the System Settings Windows dialog, Alt-Tab tab. The "Alt-tab switcher style" menu lets you choose what the window switcher displays. The default is "Icons and thumbnails", but you can set it to just icons or use window previews instead of icons or thumbnails. The window preview blanks out the screen except for the selected window.

You can also use a 3D window switcher similar to those used in the previous 3D enabled GNOME releases. The Coverflow (3D) option displays the non-selected windows on either side of the selected window (see Figure 6-23). Timeline 3D displays a single stack of non-selected windows to the side.

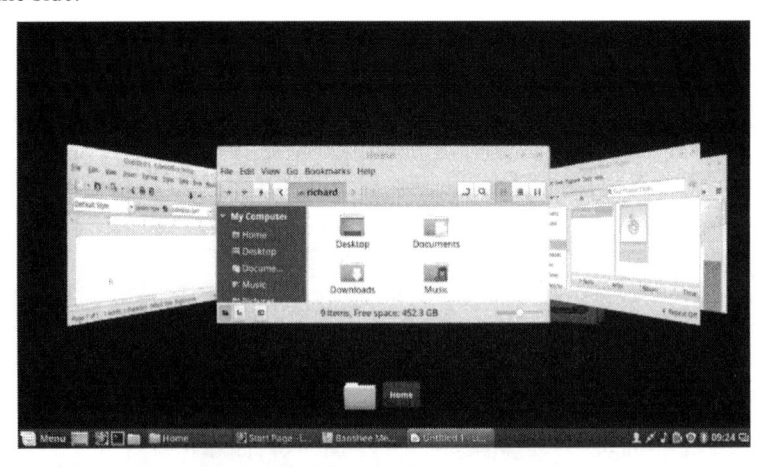

Figure 6-23: Window switching with Alt-Tab (Coverflow 3D)

Effects

The Effects dialog lets you enable desktop effects for windows, dialogs, and scroll boxes (see Figure 6-24). The Effect dialog has two tabs: "Enable effects" and Customize. On the "Enable effects" tab you can turn window effect on or off, enable effects for dialogs, and choose an effects style such as Cinnamon (the default), Scale, Fade, or Blend. On the Customize tab, you can choose effects for specific window tasks, such as scale, fade, or none for window minimize and close operations (see Figure 6-25). For maximize tasks you can choose scale or none. You can also choose the shape of the effect.

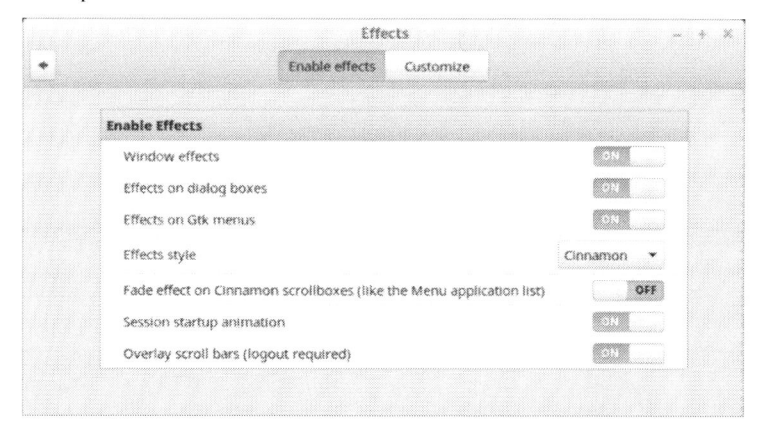

Figure 6-24: System Settings Effects: Enable effects tab

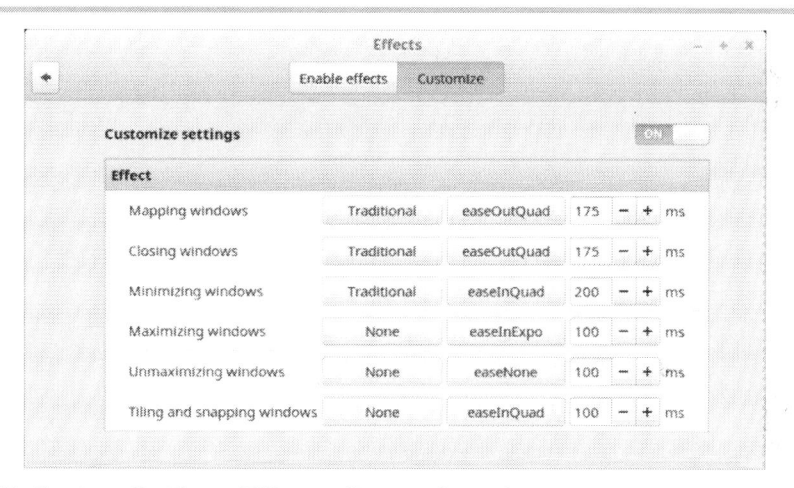

Figure 6-25: System Settings Effects: Customize tab

Workspace Selection with Hot Corners (expo) and expo applet

Linux Mint supports workspaces, with two enabled by default. You can set up several workspaces, each with open windows. You can switch workspaces directly or through the Expo screen. To switch directly you have to add the workspace switcher applet to the panel or use the Ctrl-Alt-arrow keys to move to a workspace. Workspaces are arranged in a row. Initially, with four workspaces, you have a single row of four workspaces. Use the Ctrl-Alt-right-arrow to move to the next workspace, and Ctrl-Alt-left-arrow to move back. On the System Settings Workspaces dialog, you can enable the "Allow cycling through workspaces" option to cycle back to the first workspace by continually using the Ctrl-Alt-right-arrow key. Should you want to display the workspace name on your desktop briefly as you move to it, you can enable the "Enable workspace OSD" option on the System Settings Workspace dialog.

The Workspace switcher panel applet displays button for your workspaces on the panel, just as with GNOME 2 versions (see Figure 6-26). Click on the workspace button to switch to that workspace. The current workspace is highlighted. As you add workspaces, they are numbered and added to the row.

Figure 6-26: Workspace Switcher applet

Workspaces are managed using Expo. With Expo, you can add or remove workspaces, as well as change their names and move open windows directly from one workspace to another. You can access Expo in several ways. From the keyboard, you can press the Atl-F1 or the Ctrl-Alt-uparrow keys to toggle the Expo screen. You can also configure a hot corner to open the Expo screen, or install the Expo applet. The Expo applet (shown here) places an Expo button on the panel, which opens the Expo screen.

The hot corner Expo screen access is configured with the System Setting Hot Corners dialog (see Figure 6-27). Each corner of your screen can be enabled as a hot corner. Each corner has a menu with options for Show all workspaces (Expo), Show all windows (Scale), Show the desktop, and Run a command. The "Show all workspaces" option opens the Expo screen, whereas "Show all windows" opens a window switcher screen. A corner is not enabled until you click the "Hover enabled" option. The corner in the center image then turns solid green. Un-enabled corners are faded pink. The defaults are shown in Figure 6-24, along with the upper left and right corners enabled. The upper left shows workspaces, the lower left and upper right show windows, and the lower right shows the desktop.

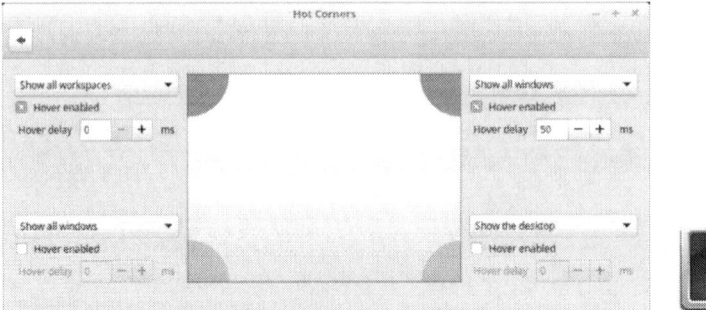

Figure 6-27: Hot Corner with Expo enabled

The Expo screen (Show all workspaces) displays your current workspaces, along with their names and plus button on the right side of the screen, which you use to add workspaces (see Figure 6-28). Moving your mouse over a workspace, highlights it and displays a close box in the upper right corner, which allows you to delete a workspace. It also scales your windows into a square grid. Clicking the plus buttons add a workspace. By default, these are added as part of a square grid. To leave the Expo screen, click on a particular workspace or press the Esc key.

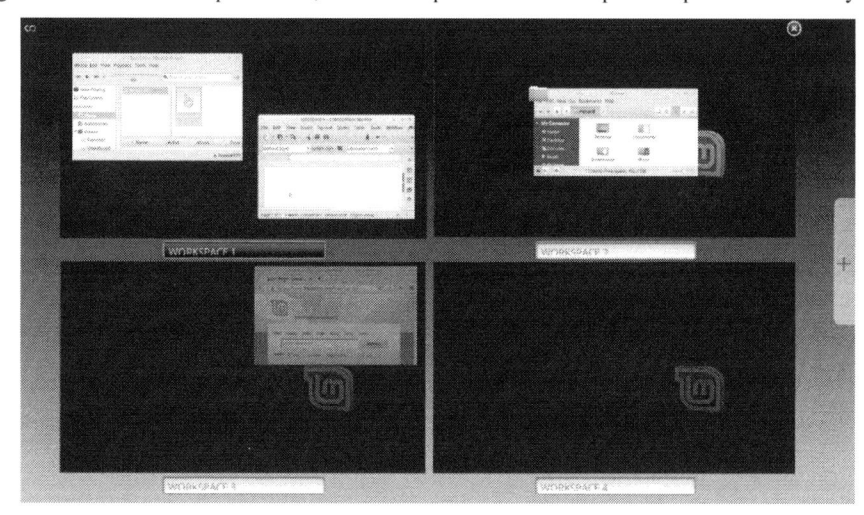

Figure 6-28: Expo workspace configuration (square grid)

You can use the System Setting Workspaces dialog to display the workspaces in the Expo screen as a row instead a grid (see Figure 6-29). Turn the "Display Expo view as a grid" switch to off. You can also change the workspace names. Each workspace has a textbox below it with its name. Click on it to edit the name.

Figure 6-29: Expo workspace configuration (no grid)

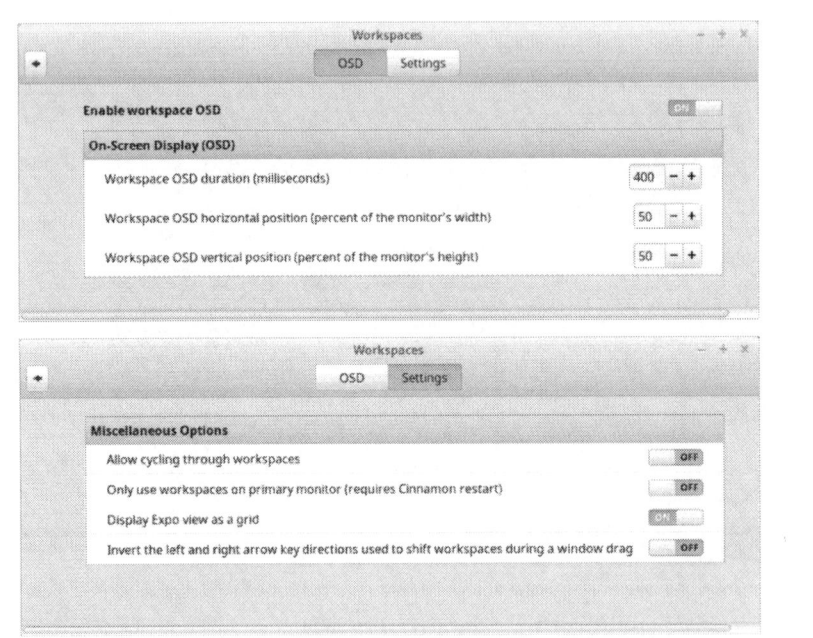

Figure 6-30: System Settings Workspaces: OSD and Settings tabs

To move a window to a different workspace, simply click and drag that window to a different workspace. When you pass your mouse over a window in a workspace, the windows are scaled to a grid, letting you easily select a window to move. You can also move windows to other workspaces directly from your desktop. To quickly move a window to another workspace, select the window, and then use **Ctrl+Alt+Shift**+arrow keys, with the left, right arrow keys moving the window to the next workspace. You can also right-click on the title bar and choose one of the Move to Workspace entries. The "Move to Another Workspace" entry displays a submenu listing all workspaces.

The System Setting Workspace dialog shows a few basic options for displaying your workspaces (see Figure 6-30). On the OSD tab, you can enable the workspace switching OSD with duration and position options. On the Settings tab, you can set additional workspace options such as enabling workspace cycling, displaying the Expo view as a grid, and restricting workspace use to the primary monitor.

The Linux Mint Panel

With the panel, you can access menus, run applets, and start applications (see Figures 6-31). The panel is based on the GNOME 2 panel and provides a simple and effective use of applets for the desktop. The left side of the panel features the Cinnamon menu, application buttons, and minimized windows. The right side features applets, such as the time, window menu, battery, Network Manager, and sound. You can customize a panel to fit your own needs, holding applets and menus of your own selection. You may add new panels, add applications to the panel, and add various applets.

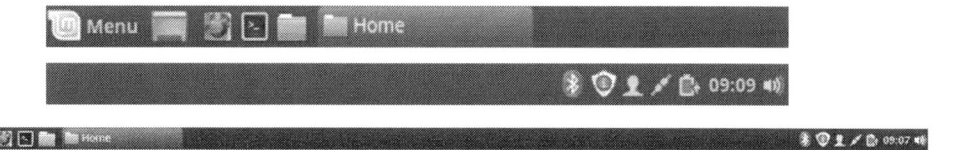

Figure 6-31: The Linux Mint panel with menu, window list, and applets, at the bottom of Linux Mint desktop

Should you remove a key applet, such as the network or sound applets, these applets are automatically displayed in the system tray when action needs to be taken on them. Currently, only the update notification applet is part of the system tray and appears only when updates occur.

Panel configuration tasks such as adding applications, selecting applets, setting up menus, and creating new panels are handled from the Panel pop-up menu. Just right-click on the empty space on your panel (the middle) to display a menu with entries for "Add applets to the panel", Panel settings, Themes, All Settings, Troubleshoot, Panel Edit mode (see Figure 6-32).

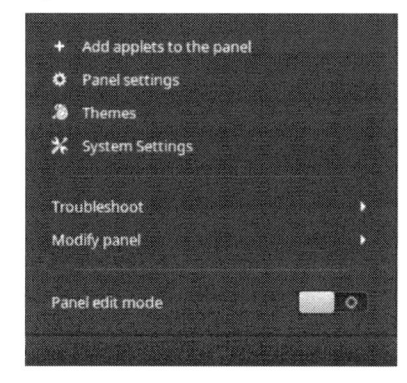

Figure 6-32: The panel pop-up menu (right-click on middle) and panel applet menu

The first four entries display System Settings configuration dialogs: Themes, Applets, Panel, and System Settings. The Troubleshoot entry displays a submenu listing items to restart the desktop (Restart Cinnamon), restore desktop defaults (Restore all settings to default), and to start a scan for errors (Looking Glass) (see Figure 6-33).

The "Modify panel" entry displays a submenu with options to remove or move the panel, add another panel, and to clear all applets from the panel leaving you with an empty panel. The move option displays the four edges of your screen an allows you to move the panel to any edge, including the sides. Click the edge you want to move the panel to. The copy and paste configuration lets you to add a set of applets to a new panel that are already present in another. Use the "Copy applet configuration" entry to make a copy of the current panel's applet set, and then select another panel to which you can paste (add) that set of applets. The paste operation to a panel will remove any applets already in that panel. Some applets cannot be present in multiple panels, such as the network and sound applets.

178 Part 2: Desktops

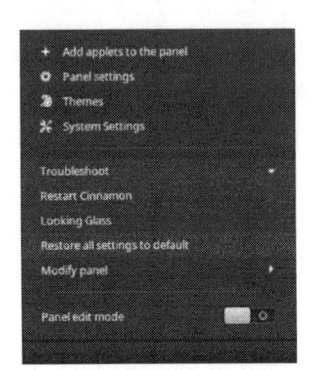

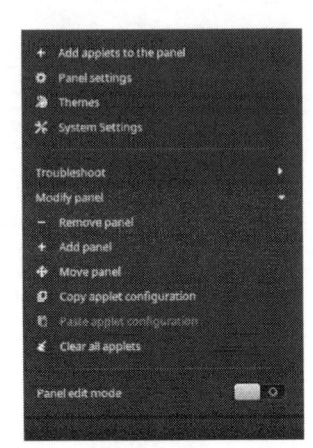

Figure 6-33: The panel menu Troubleshoot and Modify submenus

The "Panel Edit mode" switch allows you move or remove applets on the panel. The switch should remain off when the panel is in use. To edit the panel, click the switch to turn it on. The background for different sections will have colors, such as red for the application applets on the left side, green for empty parts of the panel (the middle), and blue for the applets on the right side (see Figure 6-34). To move an item, click and drag it. Your pointer image changes to a hand as you move the item. To remove an item, right-click on it to display a menu with a "Remove this applet" entry. When you are finished editing your menu, open the panel menu again and click on the "Panel Edit mode" switch to turn it off.

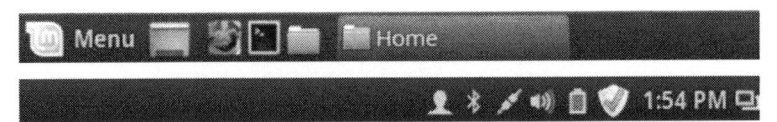

Figure 6-34: The Linux Mint panel in edit mode

The "Panel settings" entry opens the System Settings Panel dialog, letting you configure your panel (see Figure 6-35). You can add new panels, set the size, and auto-hide panels. In the Settings section, if you choose auto hide from the Auto-hide panel menu, your panel is hidden until you move your mouse to the bottom of the screen. If you turn on the custom panel size option, a scale is displayed where you can change the panel height. You can also choose to adjust the scale automatically. In the General Panel Options section, you can add a new panel. The "Panel edit mode" button is an easy way to turn on the panel edit mode.

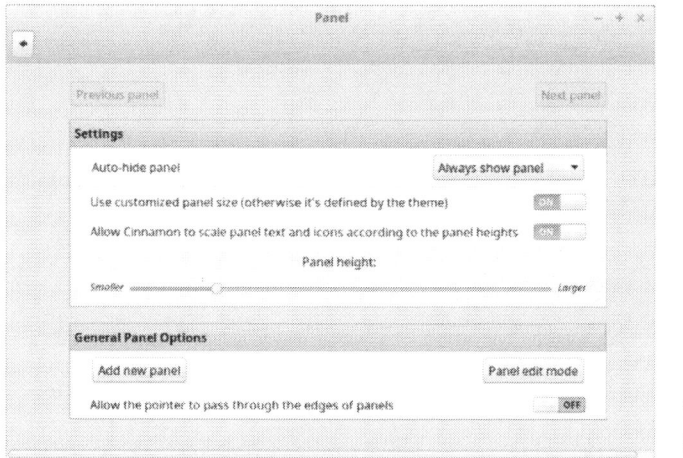

Figure 6-35: The panel settings dialog

Linux Mint Applets

Applets are small programs that perform tasks within the panel. A listing of available applets can be found at **https://cinnamon-spices.linuxmint.com/applets**. To add applets to the panel, open the System Settings Applets dialog, which you can open from System Settings or from the panel pop-up menu. On the "Installed applets" tab, the Applets dialog lists applets already available on your system. Those that are active and on the panel have a green dot icon (see Figure 6-36). If an applet cannot be modified (read-only) it has a lock icon. Linux Mint supplied applets are read only. From the Show menu, you can display all applets, only active applets, or inactive applets. The inactive option will show applets you can add, and the active option lists applets already on the panel.

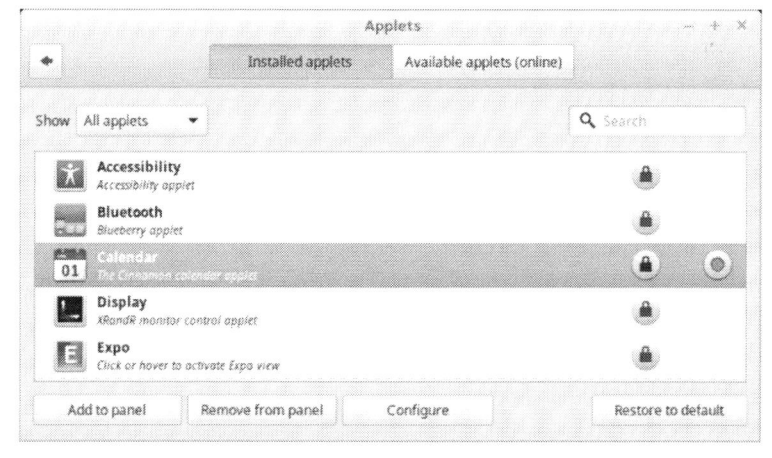

Figure 6-36: The Applets Dialog Installed tab

To add an applet to the panel, click on it to display an "Add to panel" button on the lower left corner. Click on the button. You can also right-click on the applet entry to display a pop-up menu with and "Add to panel" entry. When you add the applet, the green active dot icon appears for it on the Applets dialog, and the applet appears on the panel.

To remove an applet from the panel, you can select the applet and click the "Remove from panel" button, or right-click on its entry and choose "Remove from panel" from the pop-up menu.

A large number of additional applets can be added that are supported by third-party developers. These are listed on the "Available applets (online)" tab (see Figure 6-37). The Sort by menu lets you sort the listing by name, score (popularity), and date. The Refresh list button at the bottom right updates the listing. An applet entry has a "More info" link, which opens your Web browser to the Linux Mint page describing the applets and comments by users about it. The entry also lists a numeric score for the applet. To install the applet, click its checkbox. The "Install or update selected" button at the bottom of the dialog becomes active. You can select several applets, clicking their checkboxes. Click on the install button to perform the download and install of all selected applets. You will be prompted to enter your administrative password. A checkmark icon then appears on the installed applets entry. The applets also appear on the Installed tab. You can then select them and add them to the panel. Some third-party applets may require additional software installed. When you try to add them to the panel, you are notified of the packages that need to be installed. Linux Mint features a number of helpful third-party applets.

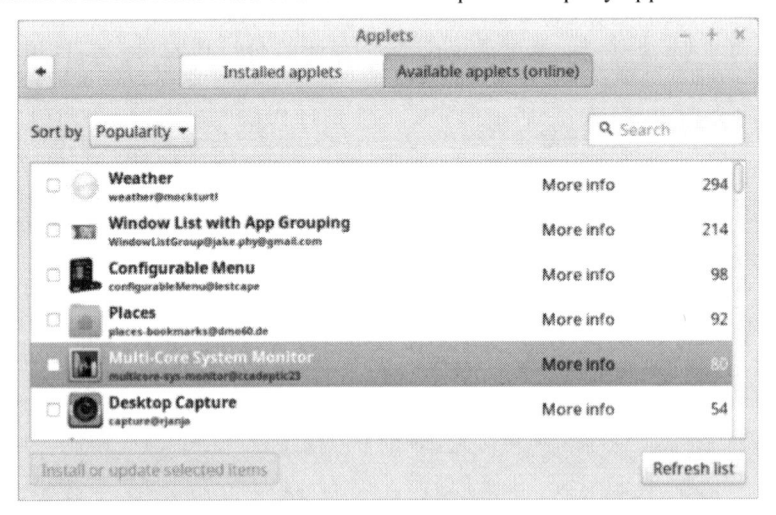

Figure 6-37: The Applets dialog "Available applets (online)" tab

Panel Launchers Applet

The panel launcher applet lets you launch applications from the panel. A panel launcher applet is already installed at the left side of the Linux Mint panel and lists the Firefox Web browser, the terminal, and Files (Nemo file manager, home folder). Click on an application icon to start it. Moving your mouse over the icon displays its name. To display a menu of actions you can perform on an application icon, right click on any icon in the panel launcher applet (see Figure 6-38). The menu has entries for Launch, Add, Edit, and Remove. The Add and Edit entries open a dialog where you can manually enter or edit the application name and launch options. The Remove entry removes the application icon from the panel launcher applet. Additional entries are tailored to the application. The Firefox Web browser has entries to open in a new window or in a private window. The terminal has an entry to open a new terminal window. The file manager has entries for the home, computer and trash folders, with the home folder as the default.

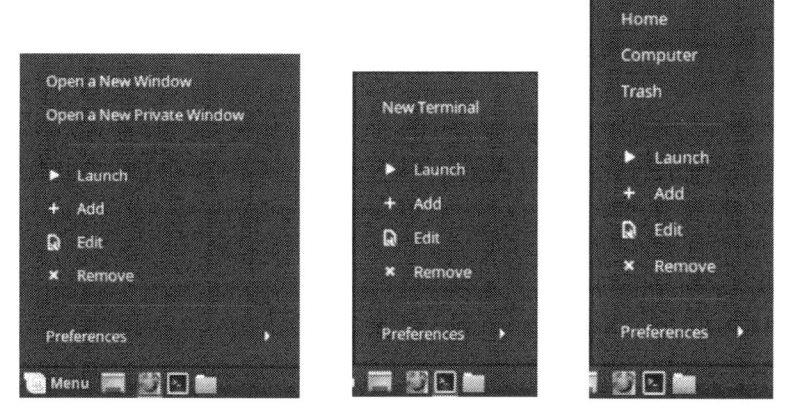

Figure 6-38: Panel Launchers applet

All the entries in the Applications menu are application launchers. For any menu item, you can click-and-drag a menu item from the menu to the panel launcher applet. An application launcher for that application is added to the panel launcher applet on the panel. For example, if you use Xed frequently and want to add its icon to the panel, click-and-drag the "Text Editor" menu entry in the Accessories menu to a panel launcher applet. The Xed icon appears in your panel. Instead of performing a click-and-drag operation, you can right-click on a menu entry and select the "Add to panel" option.

Nemo File Manager

The Nemo file manager supports the standard features for copying, removing, and deleting items as well as setting permissions and displaying items. The name used for the file manager is Files, but the actual program name is still **nemo**.

Home Folder Sub-folders and Bookmarks

Like Ubuntu, Linux Mint uses the Common User Directory Structure (xdg-user-dirs at **https://freedesktop.org**) to set up sub-folders in the user home directory. Folders will include **Documents**, **Music**, **Pictures**, **Downloads**, and **Videos**. These localized user folders are used as defaults by many desktop applications. Users can change their folder names or place them within each other using the file browser. For example, Music can be moved into **Documents**, **Documents/Music**. Local configuration is held in the **.config/user-dirs.dirs** file. System-wide defaults are set up in the **/etc/xdg/user-dirs.defaults** file. The icons for these folders are displayed in Figure 6-39.

182 Part 2: Desktops

Documents   Downloads   Music   Pictures   Public   Videos

Figure 6-39: Nemo file manager home folders

The folders are also default bookmarks. You can access a bookmarked folder directly from the either the Nemo window sidebar or from the Bookmarks menu. You can also add your own bookmarks for folders by opening the folder and choosing "Add Bookmarks" from the Bookmarks menu. Your folder will appear in the Bookmarks section of the Nemo sidebar and on the Bookmarks menu. You can manage bookmarks using the file manager Bookmarks dialog, accessible from the Bookmarks menu as Edit Bookmarks. Here you can remove a bookmark or change is name and location.

You use Desktop dialog in System Settings to display basic folders such as the home, network, and trash folders on the desktop area.

File Manager Windows

When you click the Home folder icon on the desktop, the folder icon on the Panel Launcher applet or the Home folder icon on the Cinnamon menu favorites icon bar, a file manager window opens showing your home folder. The file manager window displays several components, including a menubar, a main toolbar, and a sidebar (see Figure 6-40).

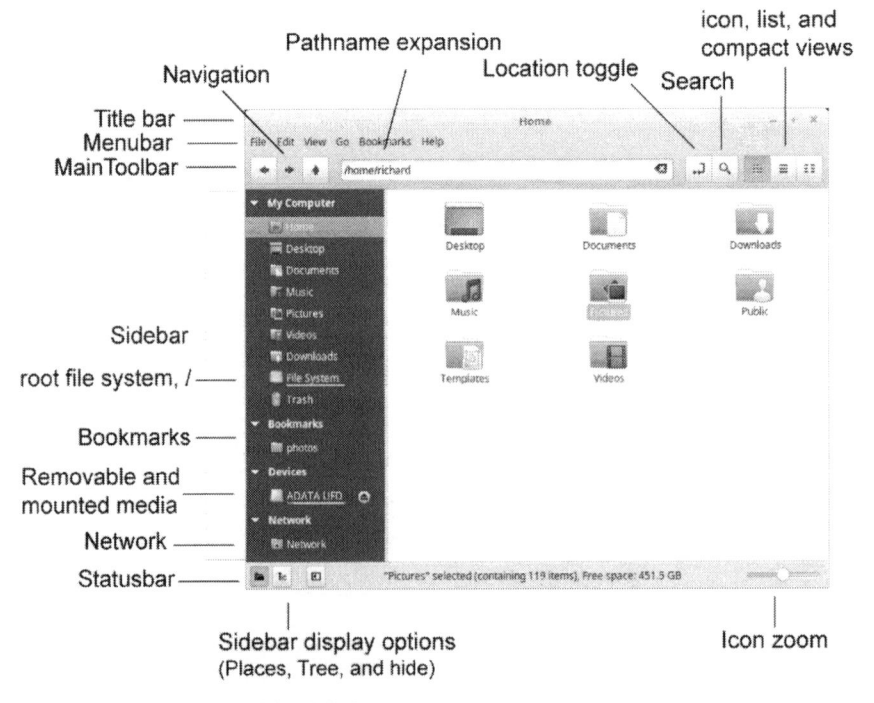

Figure 6-40: File manager with sidebar

The sidebar displays sections for My Computer, Bookmarks, Devices, and Network items showing your file systems and default home folder sub-folders. The Bookmarks and Devices items only appear if bookmarks exist or devices are attached. You can choose to display or hide the sidebar by selecting the "Show Sidebar" entry in the View menu's Sidebar submenu, or by clicking the hide button on the status bar below the sidebar. The main pane (to the right) displays the file and folder icons or listing of files and folders in the current working folder. When you select a file or folder, the status bar at the bottom of the window displays the name of the file or folder selected, and for files the size, and for folders the number of items contained. The status bar also displays the remaining free space on the selected file system.

Note: Nemo works as an operational FTP browser. You can use the Connect to Server entry on the Files top bar applications menu to open a "Connect to Server" dialog, where you can enter the URL for the FTP site.

The File menu has entries for opening a new tab (Ctrl-t), opening a new file manager window (Ctrl-n), creating a new folder (Shift-Ctrl-n), connecting to a remote FTP server, and displaying the properties of the current folder (Alt-Return). Most have corresponding keys (see Figure 6-45).

File Manager Sidebar and Bookmarks

The file manager sidebar shows file system locations that you would normally access: computer folders (My Computer), devices (Devices), and network folders (Network) (see Figure 6-41). Selecting the File System entry places you at the top of the file system, letting you move to any accessible part of it. In the My Computer section, you can search your default folders, such as Documents and Pictures. Should you bookmark a folder (Bookmarks menu, "Add Bookmark" entry (Ctrl-d)), the bookmark will appear on the sidebar in the Bookmarks section. To remove or rename a bookmark, right-click on its entry on the sidebar and choose Remove or Rename from the pop-up menu. The bookmark name changes, but not the original folder name.

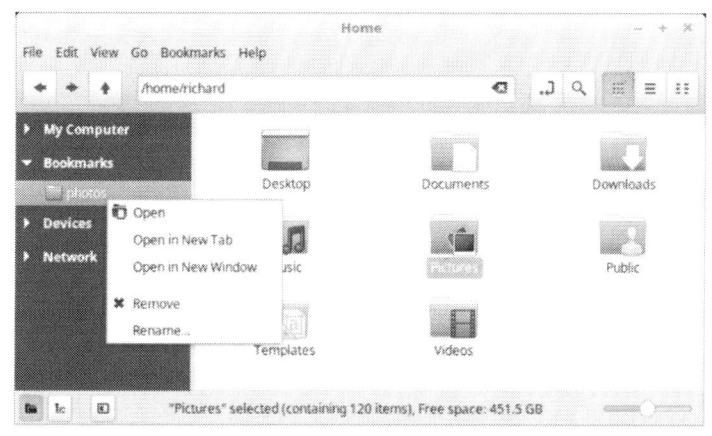

Figure 6-41: File manager sidebar with bookmarks menu

The sidebar has two menu views: places and treeview. You can switch between the two using the buttons on the lower button bar, as shown here. The third button will hide the sidebar.

The places menu has expandable menus (see Figure 6-42). The My Computer menu expands to your home folder, default bookmarks, root folder (File System), and trash. When you create a bookmark, it is listed in the Bookmarks menu. When you attach a device, a Devices submenu appears which expands to show the attached devices. The devices have eject buttons, which you can use to remove the device. You can collapse all the menus to just the menu titles.

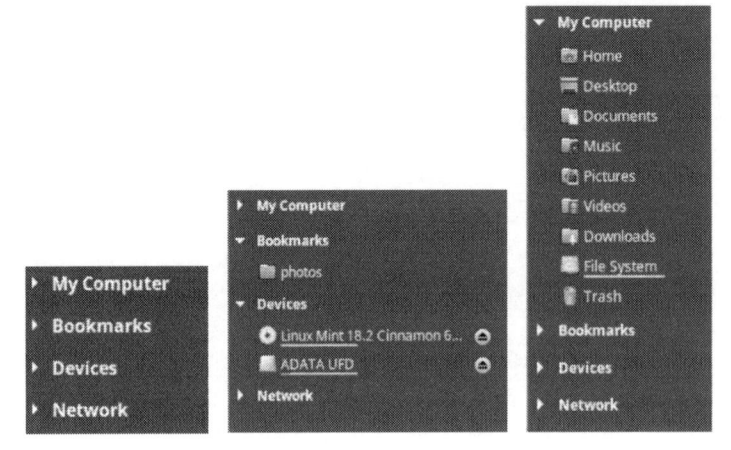

Figure 6-42: File manager sidebar Places menus, expanded and unexpanded

The treeview shows expandable menus for both the home folder and the file systems (see Figure 6-43). You can collapse them, showing just one or the other.

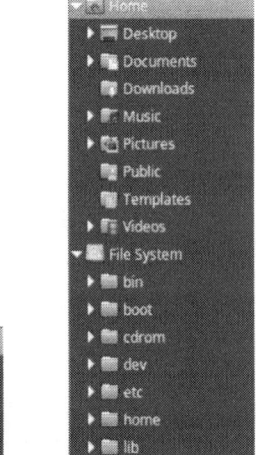

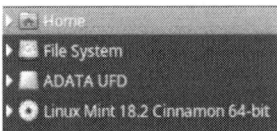

Figure 6-43: File manager sidebar Treeview menus, expanded and unexpanded

Tabs

The Nemo file manager supports tabs with which you can open up several folders in the same file manager window. To open a tab, select New Tab from the Files menu (see Figure 6-44) or press **Ctrl-t**. A tab bar appears with tab icons for each tab, displaying the name of the folder open, and an **x** close button. You can re-arrange tabs by clicking and dragging their tab icons to the right or left. You can also use the Ctrl-PageUp and Ctrl-PageDown keys to move from one tab to another. Use the Shift-Ctrl-PageUp and Shift-Ctrl-PageDown keys to rearrange the tabs. To close a tab, click its close **x** button on the right side of the tab. Tabs are detachable. You can drag a tab out to its own window, opening it in a new window.

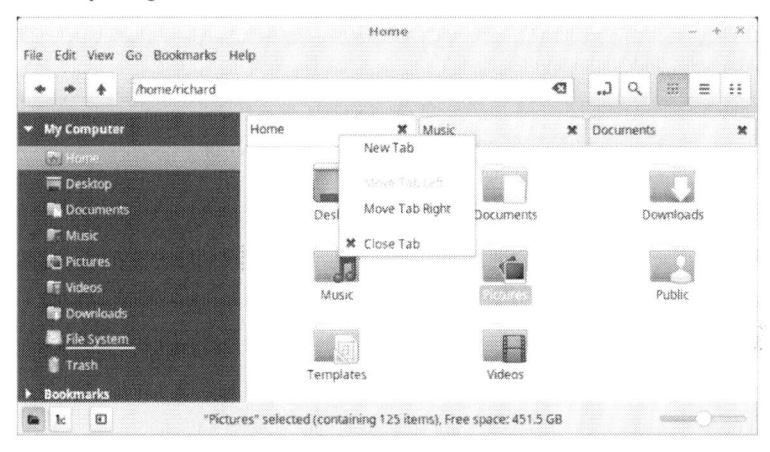

Figure 6-44: File manager window with tabs

Displaying Files and Folders

You can view a directory's contents as icons, a compact list, or as a detailed list, which you can choose from the View icons on the right side of the main toolbar: icon, list, and compact, as shown here.

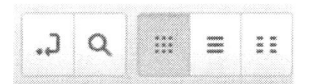

Use the control keys to change views quickly: **Ctrl-1** for Icons, **Ctrl-2** for list, and **Ctrl-3** for the compact view. The List view provides the name, size, type, and date. Buttons are displayed for each field across the top of the main pane. You can use these buttons to sort the list according to that field. For example, to sort the files by date, click the Date Modified button; to sort by size, click Size button. Click again to alternate between ascending and descending order.

Certain types of file icons will display previews of their contents. For example, the icons for image files will display a thumbnail of the image. A text file will display in its icon the first few words of its text.

The View menu has entries for managing and arranging your file manager icons (see Table 6-2) (see Figure 6-45). You can choose Icons, List, and Compact views. In the Icon view, the

"Arrange items" submenu appears, which provides entries for sorting icons by name, size, type, and modification date. You can also simply reverse the order, or position icons manually.

Menu Item	Description
Stop	Stop current task
Reload	Refresh file and directory list
Sidebar | Places, Tree	Displays sidebar in Places view or Tree view.
Sidebar | Show Sidebar	*Displays sidebar with Devices, Network, and Bookmark items.*
Main Toolbar	Displays main toolbar
Menubar	Displays menu bar
Status bar	Displays status bar at bottom of folder window
Extra Pane	Open dual panes in the file manager window, with different folders in each.
Location	Open the location box for folder path names
Reset View to Defaults	Default view and sorting
Show Hidden Files	Show administrative dot files.
Arrange Items: By Name, Size, Type, and Modification Date	Arrange files and directory by specified criteria
Organize by Name	In Icon View, order icons by name
Reversed Order	In List view, reverse order of file list
Zoom In	Provides a close-up view of icons, making them appear larger.
Zoom Out	Provides a distant view of icons, making them appear smaller.
Normal Size	Restores view of icons to standard size.
Icons	Displays icons
List	Displays file list with name, size, type, and date. Folders are expandable.
Compact	Displays compact file list using only the name and small icons

Table 6-2: File Manager View Menu

Figure 6-45: File manager File, View, and Edit menus

The Zoom In entry enlarges your view of the window, making icons bigger, and Zoom Out reduces your view, making them smaller. Normal Size restores them to the standard size. You can also use the **Ctrl-+** and **Ctrl--** keys to zoom in and out.

File manager menus and tools

From the File menu, you can perform key file manager tasks, such as creating a new folder, displaying a new tab, opening the file manager in a new window, connecting to a remote server (FTP), and opening the file manager properties dialog (see Table 6-3 and Figure 6-45).

Menu Item	Description
New Tab	Creates a new tab.
New Window	Open a new file manager window
Create New Folder	Creates a new subdirectory in the directory.
Create New Document	Creates a text document.
Connect to server	Connect to an FTP server using the file manager
Properties	Properties for the currently open folder
Close All Windows	Close all file manage windows
Close	Close the file manager window.

Table 6-3: File Manager File Menu

From the Edit menu, you can paste files you have cut or copied to move or copy them between folders, or make duplicates (see Table 6-4 and see Figure 6-45). The selection menu items let you select all files and folders, those matching a simple regular expression, and to invert a selection, choosing all those not selected. You can also bookmark the folder, restore missing files, and close the file manager window. Properties opens the folder properties dialog with Basic and Permissions tabs. If a folder is selected, you can also change the folder icon's color.

Menu Item	Description
Undo, Redo	Undo or Redo a paste operation
Cut, Copy	Move or copy a file or directory
Paste	Paste files that you have copied or cut, letting you move or copy files between folders, or make duplicates.
Select All	Select all files and folders in this folder
Select Items Matching	Quick search for files using basic pattern matching.
Invert Selection	Select all other files and folders not selected, deselecting the current selection.
Duplicate	Make a copy of a selected file
Make Links	Make a link to a file or folder
Rename	Rename a selected file or folder
Copy to	Copy a file or folder to one of the default bookmarks
Move to	Move a file or folder to one of the default bookmarks
Move To Trash	Move a file for folder to the trash folder for later deletion
Delete	Delete a file or folder immediately.
Compress	Compress selected files and folders to a compressed archive file such as a tar, cpio, lmza, or zip file. The archive file can be password protected
Sharing Options	Active when a folder is selected. You can choose to share the folder on your network.
Preferences	The Nemo File Manager preferences for your account.

Table 6-4: File Manager Edit Menu

In the icon view, you can click anywhere on the empty space on the main pane of a file manager window to display a pop-up menu with entries to create a new folder, arrange icons, zoom icons, show hidden files, and open the folder properties dialog (see Table 6-5).

Menu Item	Description
Create New Folder	Creates a new subdirectory in the directory.
Create New Document	Creates a text document.
Create New Launcher	Create launcher icon for an application
Open in Terminal	Open the current folder in a terminal window
Show Hidden Files	Show administrative dot files.
Paste	Paste files that you have copied or cut.
Zoom In	Provides a close-up view of icons, making them appear larger.
Zoom Out	Provides a distant view of icons, making them appear smaller.
Properties	Opens the Properties dialog for the directory
Normal Size	Restores view of icons to standard size.

Table 6-5: File Manager Pop-up Menu

Navigating in the file manager

The file manager operates similarly to a Web browser, using the same window to display open folders. It maintains a list of previously viewed folders, and you can move back and forth through that list using the toolbar navigation buttons (left side) (see Figure 6-46) The left arrow button moves you to the previously displayed folder, the right arrow button moves you to the next displayed folder, and the up arrow moves to the parent folder. From the Go menu, you can perform the same navigation operation, as well as access the Home, Computer, Network and Trash folders (see Table 6-6).

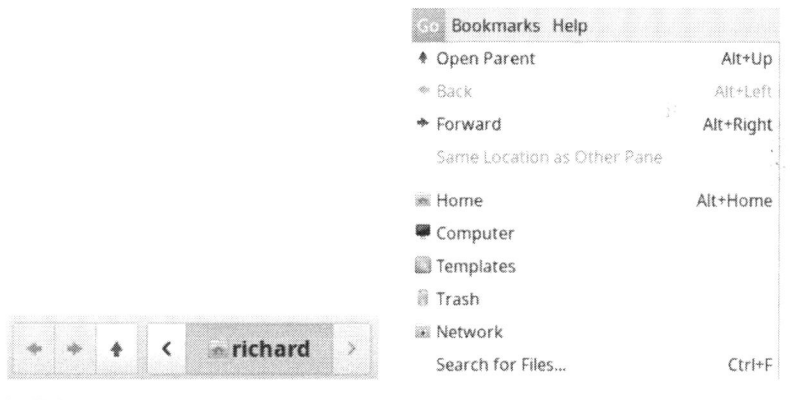

Figure 6-46: File manager navigation

When you open a new folder, the same window is used to display it, and you can use the Forward and Back arrows to move through previously opened folders (top left on the main toolbar). As you open sub-folders, the main toolbar displays buttons for your current folder and its parent folders (see Figure 6-47). You can click on a folder button to move to it directly. Clicking on the arrow to the left of the home folder button expands the list to the root directory, shown as a button with a hard drive icon.

Menu Item	Description
Open Parent	Move to the parent folder
Back	Move to the previous folder viewed in the file manager window
Forward	Move to the next folder viewed in the file manager window
Paste	Paste files that you have copied or cut, letting you move or copy files between folders, or make duplicates.
Same Location as Other Pane	If you have two panes open on the window, you can make both panes view the same folder
Home	Move to the Home folder
Computer	Move to the Computer folder, showing icons for your devices
Templates	Move to the Templates folder
Trash	Open the trash folder to see deleted files and folders, which can be restored.
Network	Move to the network folder showing connected systems on your network and open remote folders.
Search for Files	Search for files and folders using the file manager window

Table 6-6: File Manager Go Menu

You can also display a location URL text box instead of buttons, where you can enter the location of a folder, either on your system or on a remote system (see Figure 6-47). To display the location text box, press **Ctrl-l** or click the Location toggle at the end of the location path on the main toolbar. You can also press F9 or choose Location on the View menu (View | Location). These access methods operate as toggles that move you a back and forth from the location text box to the button path.

Figure 6-47: Expanded and unexpanded paths and location

Use the sidebar's Places view to access your bookmarked folders, storage devices (USB, CD/DVD disc, and attached hard drives), and mounted network folders. On the "My Computer" section of the sidebar, you can access your home folders, trash, the file system (root directory), and additional bookmarks you created.

To open a subdirectory, you can double-click its icon or right-click the icon and select Open from the menu. To open the folder in a new tab, select "Open in New Tab." You can also click on the folder to select it, and then choose Open from the File menu (File | Open).

You can open any folder or file system listed in the sidebar by clicking on its bookmark. You can also right-click on a bookmark to display a menu with entries to Open, "Open in a New

Tab", and "Open in a New Window" (see Table 6-7). The "Open in a New Window" item is an easy way to access devices from the file manager. The menu for the Trash entry lets you empty the trash. For any folder bookmark, you can also remove and rename the entry. Entries for removable devices in the sidebar such as USB drives also have menu items for Eject and Safely Remove Drive. Internal hard drives have an Unmount entry instead.

Menu Item	Description
Open	Opens the file with its associated application. Directories are opened in the file manager. Associated applications are listed.
Open In A New Tab	Opens a directory in a new tab in the same window.
Open In A New Window	Opens a directory in a separate window, accessible from the toolbar, right-click.
Remove	Remove bookmark from the sidebar.
Rename	Rename a bookmark.

Table 6-7: The File Manager Sidebar Pop-Up Menu

Nemo File Manager Search

The Nemo file manager provides a search tool, which you can access either from the desktop menu or from any file manager window. From a file manager window, click the Search button on the toolbar (Looking glass at right), or select Go | Search for Files, to open a Search box below the toolbar. Enter the pattern to search and press ENTER. The results are displayed (see Figure 6-48).

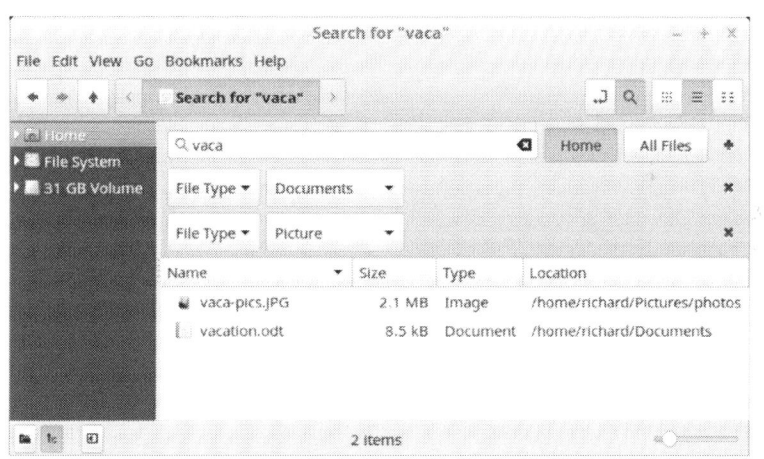

Figure 6-48: Nemo File Manager Search

Drop-down menus for file type will appear in the folder window, with + and - buttons for adding or removing file type search parameters. Click the plus + button to add file type search parameters. Click the Home button to search from your home folder, and click the All Files button to search the entire system.

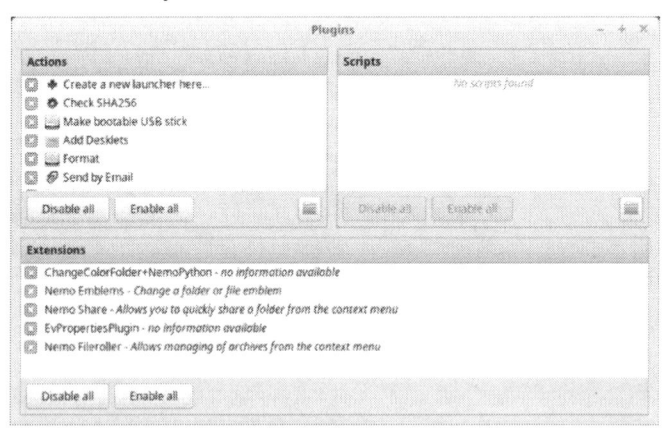

Nemo Plugins and Extensions

You can enhance Nemo using plugins and extensions such as NemoShare for folder sharing options, and "Nemo Fileroller" that allows you to create (compress) and extract archives. Several plugins and extensions are already installed are enabled by default, and will display entries in appropriate menus. To add more extension, use the Software Manager to install the nemo extension and plugin packages. Extension and plugin packages have the prefix **nemo-**, such as **nemo-share** and **nemo-fileroller**.

Plugins and Extensions are enabled on the Plugins dialog, accessible from the Edit menu (Edit | Plugins), also with the Alt+p key (see Figure 6-49). Actions are tasks that can be taken from the desktop menu (right-click on any empty area on the desktop) and from other pop-up file and folder menus. Enabling an action lists it in the menu. Disabling it will remove it from that menu. For example, enabling the "Set as Wallpaper" action places a "Set as Wallpaper" entry in the pop-up menu for an image file (right-click on an image file). Enabling the "Add Desklets" action adds an "Add Desklets" entry in the desktop pop-up menu. The Extensions section list the installed extensions, such as NemoShare and Nemo Fileroller. Those that are enabled have their checkbox checked. Click on a checkbox to toggle enabling and disabling an extension. If you disable or enable an extension, you have to restart Nemo to have the changes take effect. When you make a change, a button appears "Extension changed. Restart required." Click the button to restart Nemo. There are also buttons that allow you to disable or enable actions and extensions all at once.

Figure 6-49: Nemo Plugins and Extensions

You can also add your own action and script files to the actions and scripts folders in your **.local/share/nemo/** folder. Click on the folder icons in the actions and scripts sections to open these folders. Scripts allow you to add executable files of your own.

Managing Files and Folders

As a GNOME-compliant file manager, Nemo supports desktop drag-and-drop operations for copying and moving files. To move a file or directory, drag-and-drop from one directory to another as you would on Windows or Mac interfaces. The move operation is the default drag-and-drop operation in GNOME. To copy a file to a new location, press the Ctrl key as you drag-and-drop.

Menu Item	Description
Open	Opens the file with its associated application. Directories are opened in the file manager. Associated applications are listed.
Open In A New Tab	Opens a folder in a new tab in the same window.
Open In A New Window	Opens a folder in a new window
Open With	Selects an application with which to open this file. An Open With dialog opens listing possible applications.
Cut Copy	Entries to cut and copy the selected file.
Make Link	Creates a link to that file in the same directory.
Rename (F2)	Renames the file.
Copy To	Copy a file to the Home Folder, Desktop, or to a folder displayed in another pane in the file manager window.
Move To	Move a file to the Home Folder, Desktop, or to a folder displayed in another pane in the file manager window.
Move To Trash	Moves a file to the Trash directory, where you can later delete it.
Delete	Delete the file or folder permanently
Send	Email the file using default mail application
Compress	Archives file using File Roller.
Sharing Options	Displays the Folder Sharing dialog (Samba and NFS).
Properties	Displays the Properties dialog.
Open in Terminal	Open the current directory in a terminal window
Open as Root	Open a terminal window as the administrative user

Table 6-8: The File and Directory Pop-Up Menu

Using a file's pop-up menu

You can also perform remove, rename, and link creation operations on a file by right-clicking its icon and selecting the action you want from the pop-up menu that appears (see Table 6-8). For example, to remove an item, right-click it and select the Move To Trash entry from the pop-up menu. This places it in the Trash directory, where you can later delete it. To create a link, right-click the file and select Make Link from the menu. This creates a new link file that begins with the term "Link."

Renaming Files

To rename a file, you can either right-click the file's icon and select the Rename entry from the pop-up menu or click its icon and press the F2 function key. The name of the icon will be bordered, encased in a small text box. You can overwrite the old one, or edit the current name by clicking a position in the name to insert text, as well as use the backspace key to delete characters. You can also rename a file by entering a new name in its Properties dialog box (Basic tab). Cinnamon also supports Quick-Rename, though this feature is not enabled by default. With Quick-

Rename you can click the filename below the icon twice with an intervening pause to activate the renaming process. To turn on this feature, open the file manager Preferences dialog (Edit | Preferences) and select the Behavior tab. In the Behavior section, click on the checkbox for the entry "Click twice with a pause in between to rename items."

Grouping Files

You can select a group of files and folders by clicking the first item and then hold down the SHIFT key while clicking the last item, or by clicking and dragging the mouse across items you want to select. To select separated items, hold the CTRL key down as you click the individual icons. If you want to select all the items in the directory, choose the Select All entry in the Edit menu (Edit | Select All) (**Ctrl-a**). You can then copy, move, or even delete several files at once. To select items that have a certain pattern in their name, choose Select Items Matching from the tools menu to open a search box where you can enter the pattern (**Ctrl-s**). Use the * character to match partial patterns, as in *let* to match on all filenames with the pattern "let" in them. The pattern **my*** would match on filenames beginning with the "my" pattern, and *.png would match on all PNG image files (the period indicates a filename extension).

Opening Applications and Files MIME Types

You can start any application in the file manager by double-clicking either the application itself or a data file used for that application. If you want to open the file with a specific application, you can right-click the file and select one of the Open With entries. One or more Open with entries will be displayed for default and possible application, like "Open with xed" for a text file. If the application you want is not listed, you can select Open with | Other Application to open a dialog listing available applications. Drag-and-drop operations are also supported for applications. You can drag a data file to its associated application icon (say, on the desktop); the application then starts up using that data file.

To change or set the default application to use for a certain type of file, you open a file's Properties dialog and select the Open With tab. Here you can choose the default application to use for that kind of file. Possible applications will be listed, organized as the default, recommended, related, and other categories. Click on the one you want to change to the default and click the "set as default" button. Once you choose the default, it will appear in the Open With list for this file.

If you want to add an application to the Open With menu, click the "Show other applications" button to list possible applications. Select the one you want and click the Add button. If there is an application on the Open With tab you do not want listed in the Open With menu items, right-click on it, and choose **Forget association**.

File and Directory Properties

In a file's Properties dialog, you can view detailed information on a file and set options and permissions (see Figure 6-50). A file's Properties dialog has three tabs: Basic, Permissions, and Open With. Folders will have an additional share tab. The Basic tab shows detailed information such as type, size, location, and date modified. The type is a MIME type, indicating the type of application associated with it. The file's icon is displayed at the top with a text box showing the file's name. You can edit the filename in the Name text box, changing that name. If you want to change the icon image used for the file or folder, click the icon image (next to the name) to open a Select Custom Icon dialog to browse for the one you want. The **/usr/share/pixmaps** directory holds the set of current default images, though you can select your own images (click **pixmaps** entry in the Places sidebar). Click an image file to see its icon displayed in the right pane. Double-click to change the icon image.

The Permissions tab for files shows the read, write, and execute permissions for owner, group, and others, as set for this file. You can change any of the permissions here, provided the file belongs to you. You configure access for the owner, the group, and others, using drop-down menus. You can set owner permissions as Read Only or Read And Write. For group and others, you can also set the None option, denying access. Clicking on the group name displays a menu listing different groups, allowing you to select one to change the file's group. If you want to execute this as an application, you check the "Allow executing file as program" entry. This has the effect of setting the execute permission.

The Open With tab for files lists all the applications associated with this kind of file. You can select the one you want to use as the default. This can be particularly useful for media files, where you may prefer a specific player for a certain file or a particular image viewer for pictures.

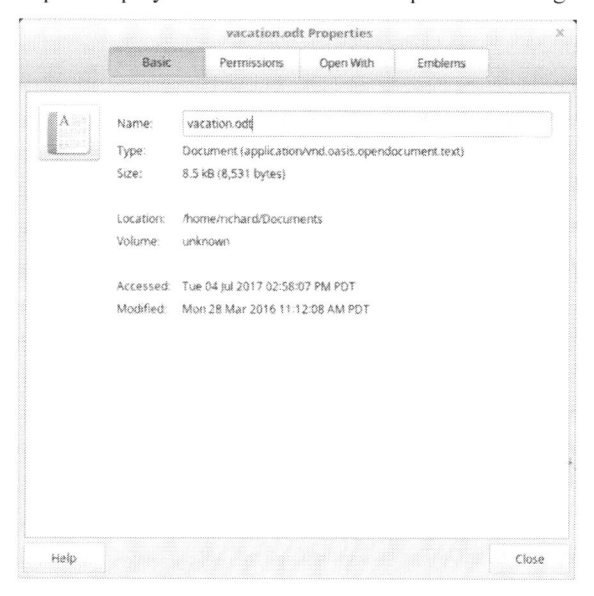

Figure 6-50: File properties on Nemo

Certain kinds of files will have additional tabs, providing information about the file. For example, an audio file will have an Audio tab listing the type of audio file and any other information like a song title or compression method used. An image file will have an Image tab listing the resolution and type of image.

The Permissions tab for folders operates much the same way, but it includes two access entries: Folder Access and File Access. The Folder Access entry controls access to the folder with options for None, List Files Only, Access Files, and Create And Delete Files. These correspond to read, read and execute permissions given to directories. The File Access entry lets you set permissions for all those files in the directory. They are the same as for files: for the owner, Read or Read and Write; for the group and others, the entry adds a None option to deny access. To set the permissions for all the files in the directory accordingly (not just the folder), you click the "Apply Permissions To Enclosed Files" button.

The Share tab for folders allows you to share folders as network shares. If you have Samba or NFS, these will allow your folders and files to be shared with users on other systems. You have the option to specify whether the shared folder or file will be read-only or allow write access. To allow write access check the "Allow other to create and delete files in this folder" entry. To open access to all users, check the Guest access entry.

Nemo Preferences

You can set preferences for your Nemo file manager in the Preferences dialog, accessible by selecting the Preferences item in any Nemo file manager window's Edit menu (Edit | Preferences).

> The Views tab allows you to select how files are displayed by default, such as the list, icon, or compact view. You also can set default zoom levels for icon, compact, and list views.
>
> Behavior lets you choose how to select files, manage the trash, and handle scripts.
>
> Display lets you choose what added information you want displayed in an icon caption, like the size or date.
>
> The List Columns tab lets you choose both the features to display in the detailed list and the order in which to display them. In addition to the already-selected Name, Size, Date, and Type, you can add permissions, group, MIME type, and owner.
>
> The Preview tab lets you choose whether you want small preview content displayed in the icons, like beginning text for text files.
>
> The Toolbar tab lets you choose some of the icons to display on the toolbar, such as search, up, refresh, computer, and home.

System Settings

You can configure desktop settings and perform most administrative tasks using the administration tools listed in the System Settings dialog, accessible from the System Tools menu and from the menu Favorites icon bar. System Settings organizes tools into Appearance, Preferences, Hardware, and Administration categories (see Figure 6-51 and see Figure 6-52). Some invoke the Ubuntu supported system tools available from previous releases such as Sound (PulseAudio) and Printers (system-config-printer). Others use the GNOME 3 configuration and administrative tools such as Networking and Power Management.

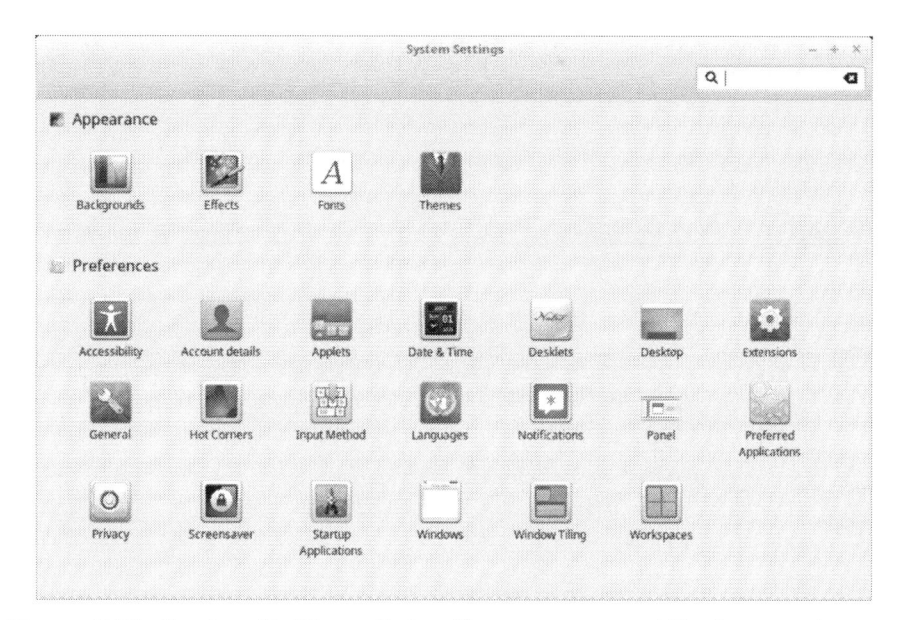

Figure 6-51: System Settings dialog (Appearance and Preferences)

System Settings tools will open with a back arrow button at the top, which you can click to return to the System Settings dialog. Table 6-9 lists the System Settings tools.

Figure 6-52: System Settings dialog (Hardware and Administration)

Setting	Icon	Description
Appearance section		
Backgrounds		Selects Backgrounds with options for aspect, gradient, and colors.
Themes		Install themes and choose select styles for icons, controls, window borders, pointers, and key bindings (Other Settings tab).
Fonts		Select default, window title, and document fonts with options for scaling, anti-aliasing, and hinting.
Effects		Fade and Scale effects for closing, opening, and maximize/minimizing windows and dialogs.
Preferences section		**(desktop configuration)**
Applets		Add applets to the panel
Desklets		Add desklets to the desktop
Desktop		Choose icons to display on the desktop for the home folder, computer, and trash, as well as mounted volumes and network servers. The default is computer, home, and mounted volumes.
Hot Corners		Corner that when clicked can display the workspace selection screen (Show all workspaces option), scaled open windows (Show all windows option), show the desktop, or run a selected application.
Input Method		The Input Method tab of the Language Settings dialog
Preferred Applications		Set default applications and defaults for removable media.
Panel		Set panel default and features such as panel size. Panel layout can be traditional (one bottom panel, default), flipped (panel at the top), and classic (two panels, one on the top and one on the bottom).
Windows		Set window display options such as click actions on the title bar, focus mode, the title bar buttons to be displayed. You can also configure the open window switcher (Alt-tab).
Window Tiling and Edge Flip		Set window display options for window tiling, snapping, and edge flipping.
Workspaces		Configure workspace display
Extensions		Add desktop extensions, such as desktop cube, scroller, and dock.

Notifications		Configure display of desktop notification
Privacy		Enable remembering of recently accessed files
Preferences section		**(system configuration)**
Account Details		Set your password, picture, and full name.
Date & Time		Set the time and date manually or with network time, with options that let you set the time format.
Screensaver		Screensaver and screen locker options, set the inactivity time to dim or lock the screen.
General		Set message display.
Universal Access		Enables features like accessible login and keyboard screen
Languages		Language selection
Startup Programs		Open the Startup Applications Preferences dialog to choose applications to start on startup.
Hardware section		
System Info		System and hardware information
Keyboard		Configure repeat key sensitivity and keys for special tasks.
Mouse and Touchpad		Mouse and touchpad configuration: select hand orientation, speed, and accessibility
Networking		Lets you turn wired and wireless networks on and off. You can access an available wireless network and proxy configuration.
Bluetooth		Bluetooth detection and configuration
Display		Change your screen resolution, refresh rate, and screen orientation.
Power Management		Set the power options for laptop inactivity

Sound		Configure sound effects, output volume, sound device options, input volume, and sound application settings
Color		Set the color profile for a device.
Graphics Table		Configure a graphics tablet
Printers		Printer configuration with system-config-printer
Administration section		
Firewall		Open the Gufw dialog for managing the ufw firewall. Gufw needs to be installed.
Login Screen		Open the Login Window Preferences dialog for configuring the Linux LightDM display manager (LightDM).
Device Drivers		Select device drivers for cards such as graphics cards.
Software Sources		Open the Linux Mint Software Sources selection dialog to activate and deactivate software repositories.
Users and Groups		Manage users

Table 6-9: Desktop System Settings

Appearance

The Appearance section on System Settings provides four dialogs to configure backgrounds, themes, fonts, and desktop effects.

Backgrounds

The Backgrounds dialog lists backgrounds you can choose from (see Figure 6-53). On the Images tab, a scrollbox to the left lists installed background collections. You can choose a custom image from a local folder by clicking on the plus button in the lower left corner of the scrollbox. This opens an "Add folder" dialog, allowing you to choose a folder of images. You can remove the folder using the minus button at the bottom left of the scrollbox.

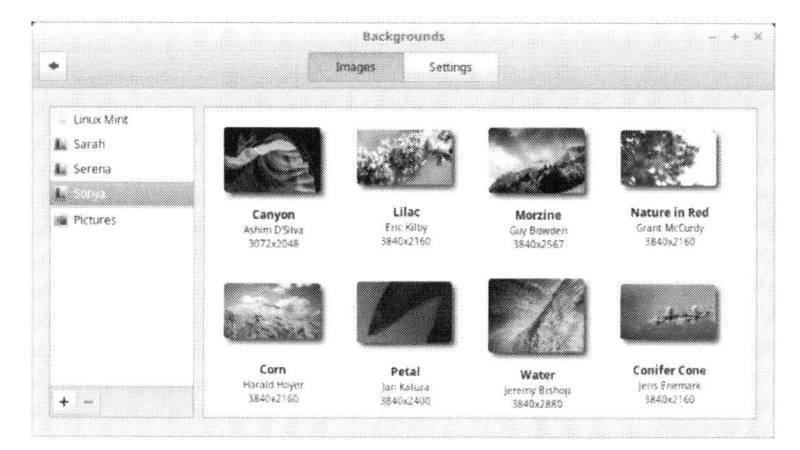

Figure 6-53: Backgrounds: Images tab

On the Settings, you can choose to run a slideshow from the selected folder, with options for random order and the time interval (see Figure 6-54). From the Picture aspect menu, you can choose display options such as Zoom, Centered, Scaled, Mosaic, Stretched, Spanned or No picture. A centered or scaled image will preserve the image proportions. Stretched and Spanned may distort it. Any space not filled, such as with a centered or scaled images, will be filled in with the desktop color.

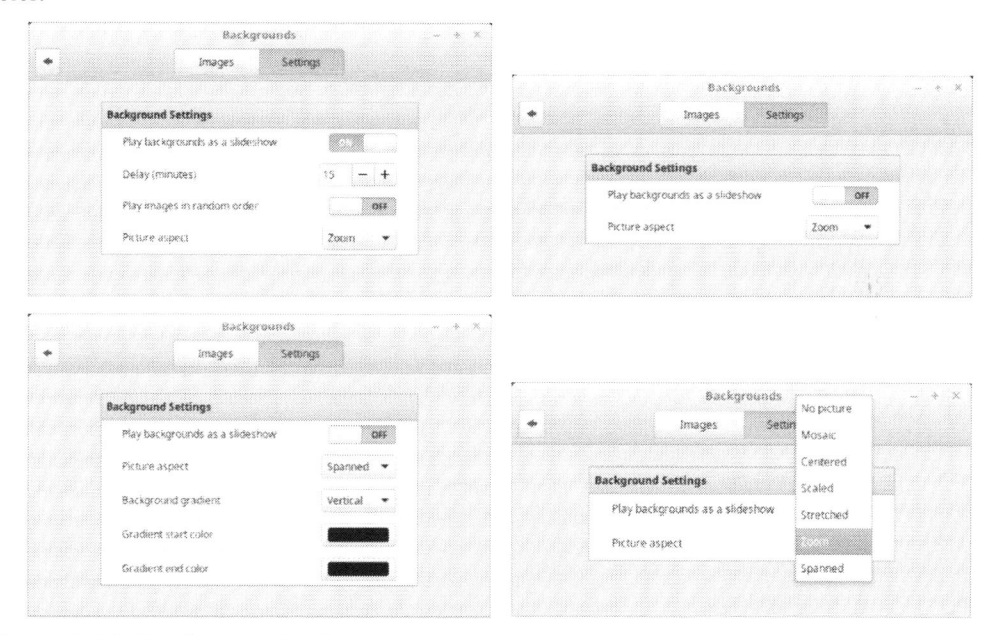

Figure 6-54: Backgrounds: Settings tab

The Centered, Scaled, and Spanned options also show gradient options. For gradients, use the Gradient color buttons for selecting a color at each end of the gradient. From the Background gradient menu, you can choose a vertical or horizontal gradient. Click on the color button to open a

"Pick a Color" dialog where you can select a color. Click the plus button on this dialog to open a color selector where you can enter a color hex number or choose one from a sliding scale, and then adjust its shade.

Initially, only the Linux Mint backgrounds are listed, including backgrounds from previous Linux Mint releases). Install the **gnome-backgrounds** package to add a collection of GNOME backgrounds. You can also add backgrounds from previous Linux Mint releases, such as **mint-backgrounds-nadia**. You can download more GNOME backgrounds from **https://www.gnome-look.org/**.

Fonts

The Fonts dialog lets you set the default font for the desktop, documents, and the window title on window title bars, as well as anti-aliasing, hinting, and text scaling features. It also sets the monospace font (see Figure 6-55).

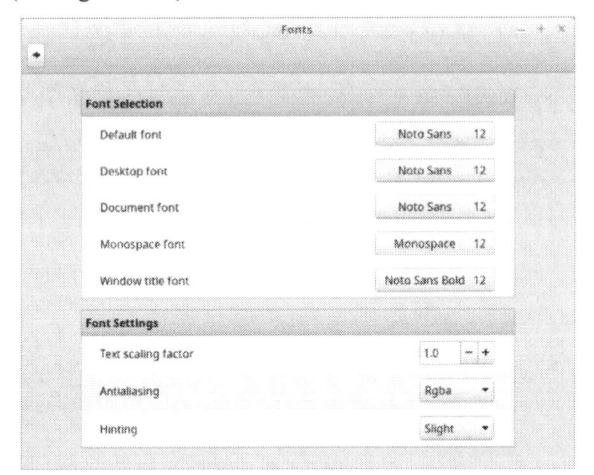

Figure 6-55: Fonts

Themes

The Themes dialog shows the components of the currently selected theme (see Figure 6-56). In the Themes section, you can customize your desktop by choosing different icon sets, different controls, window border, and mouse styles. Clicking on the icon for an item opens an icon menu from which to can choose other sets. On the Settings tab, you can set options for showing icons in menus and buttons.

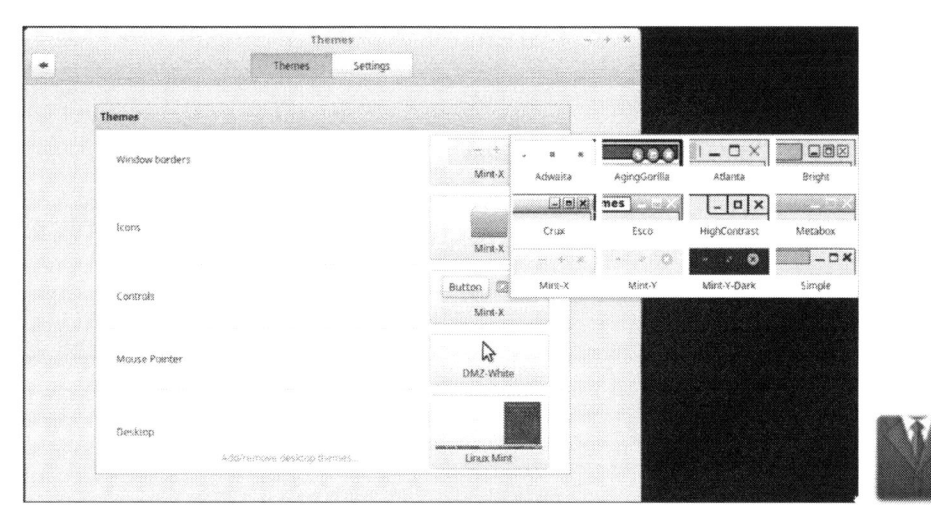

Figure 6-56: Themes

To choose another installed theme, or to download other themes, you click on the "Add/remove desktop themes" link at the bottom the Themes tab, in the Desktop section. This opens a "Desktop themes" dialog with "Installed themes" and "Available themes (online)" tabs (see Figure 6-57). The "Installed themes" tab list all your installed themes. The current theme has a checkmark icon. Themes that are read-only and cannot be uninstalled have a lock icon. From the search box, you can search for themes. To choose a new theme, select the theme and then click the "Apply theme" button. Linux Mint uses the Mint-X theme. Also available are the new Mint-Y themes (light, dark, and darker).

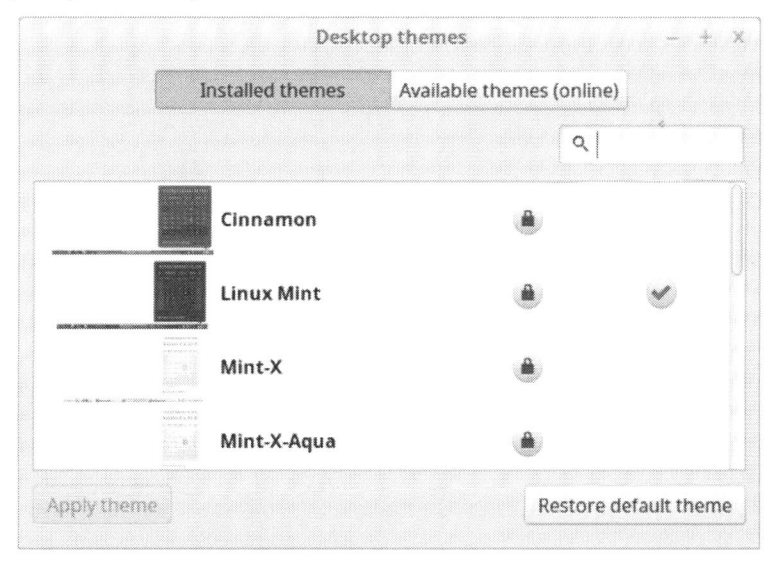

Figure 6-57: Themes (Installed Themes)

204 Part 2: Desktops

On the "Available themes (online)" tab you can download the lists of available themes (see Figure 6-58). The "Sort by" menu lets you sort them by popularity, name, or date. Click the "Refresh list" button on the lower right to update the list. Click the checkboxes of the themes you want to install, and then click the "Install or update selected items" button (lower left). A list of available applets can be found at **https://cinnamon-spices.linuxmint.com/themes**.

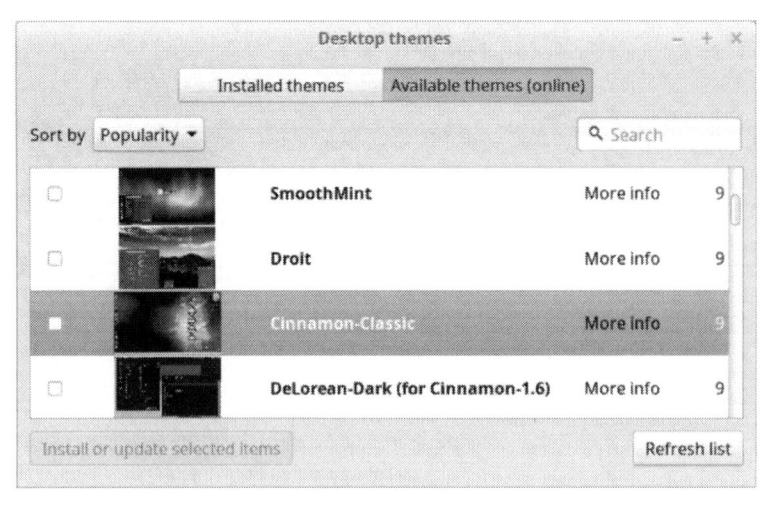

Figure 6-58: Themes (Online Themes)

On the Themes dialog, clicking on the Settings tab displays options to show icons on desktop menus and on desktop buttons, such as close buttons (see Figure 6-59).

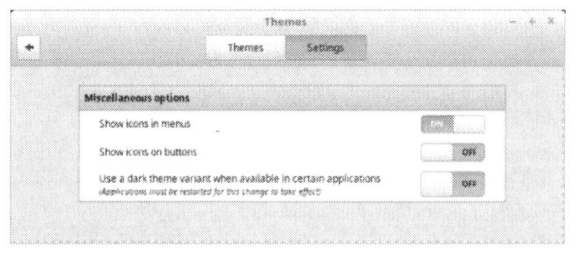

Figure 6-59: Themes (Settings tab)

Preferences

In the System Settings Preferences section, dialogs, such as Applets and Menu, let you configure your desktop. Preference dialogs common to both Cinnamon and Mate and are discussed in Chapter 3. Preferences that differ for Cinnamon, such as the time settings (calendar) and application defaults (Applications & Removable media), are discussed here. Some are GNOME 3 dialogs and are similar to those found on current Ubuntu and Fedora releases. Preferences that deal with major administrative task such as Users and Groups, software sources, and firewalls, are discussed in the chapters dealing with those topics.

Preferred Applications and Removable Media

The Preferred Applications dialog lets you set default applications for tasks and media. On the "Preferred applications" tab you set default applications for basic types of files: Web, Mail, Documents, Text editor, Music, Video, Photos, Source Code, and Terminal (see Figure 6-60). Use the drop-down menus to choose installed alternatives, such as Thunderbird instead of Evolution for Mail, or Image Viewer instead of Shotwell for Photos.

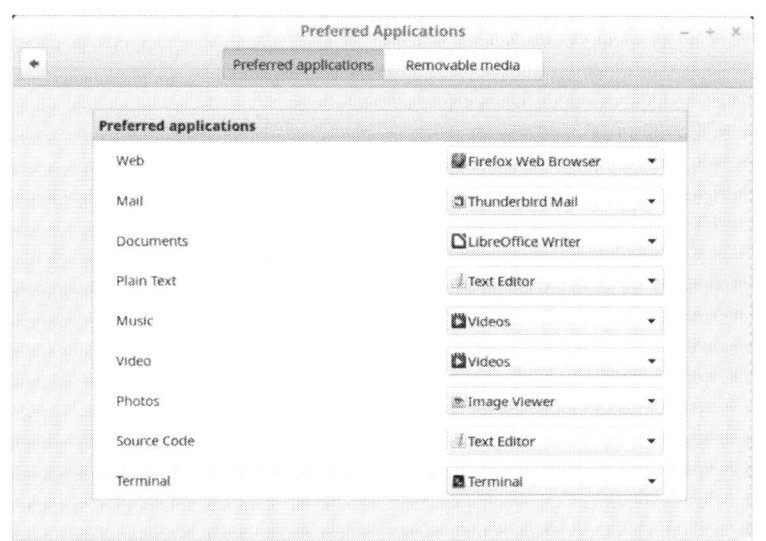

Figure 6-60: Preferred Applications

On the "Removable media" tab you can specify default actions for different kinds of media: CD Audio, DVD Video, Music Player, Photos, and Software media. You can turn off this function by switching off the "Prompt or start programs on media insertion" option. You can select the application to use for the different media from the menus (see Figure 6-61). These menus also include options for Ask What To Do, Do Nothing, and Open Folder. The Open Folder option will open a window displaying the files on the disc. A button labeled "Other Media" opens a dialog that lets you set up an association for less used media like Blu-Ray discs and Audio DVD. Initially, the "Ask what to do" option is set for all entries. Possible options are listed for the appropriate media, like Rhythmbox Media Player for CD Audio discs and Movie Player (Totem) for DVD-Video. Photos can be opened with the Shotwell Photo-manager.

Figure 6-61: Preferred Applications: Removable media

When you insert removable media, such as a CD audio disc, its associated application is automatically started, unless you change that preference. If you want to turn off this feature for a particular kind of media, you can select the Do Nothing entry from its application menu. If you want to be prompted for options, use the "Ask what to do" entry. Then, when you insert a disc, a dialog with a drop-down menu for possible actions is displayed. From this menu, you can select another application or select the Do Nothing or Open Folder options.

Time & Date Settings (Calendar applet)

The Calendar applet is located on the bottom panel to the right (see Figure 6-62). The calendar shows the current date, but you can move to different months and years using the month and year scroll arrows at the top of the calendar.

Figure 6-62: Calendar applet

Date & Time options are set using the System Settings Date & Time dialog, which opens by choosing "Date and Time Settings" in the Calendar menu, or by clicking the Date & Time icon in the System Settings Preferences section (see Figure 6-63).

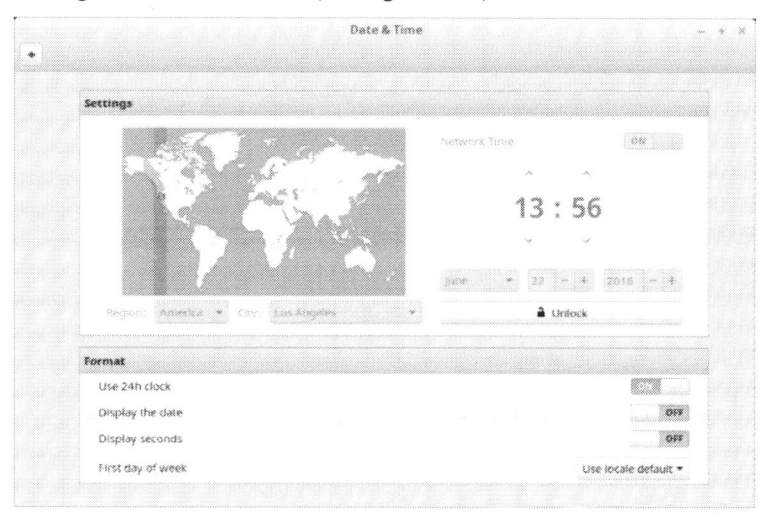

Figure 6-63: Time & Date settings, network time

You set the time zone using the map to the left or by selection a region or city from the Region or City menus. You can also specify the time format, using a 24-hour clock, displaying the date, and also the seconds. The time and date can be set manually or automatically from a timeserver (the Network Time switch). For manual changes, you can set the time and date directly by turning off the Network Time switch.

Configuring the Calendar applet from the Applet dialog (or right-click on the date applet on the panel and choose Configure), displays options for specifying the date display format for the panel and the applet (see Figure 6-64). The format uses format specifiers for different date elements, such as **%a** for the day of the week, **%l** for the hour, and **%y** for the year. You can click on the "Show information on date format syntax" button to open a website where you can learn about formats.

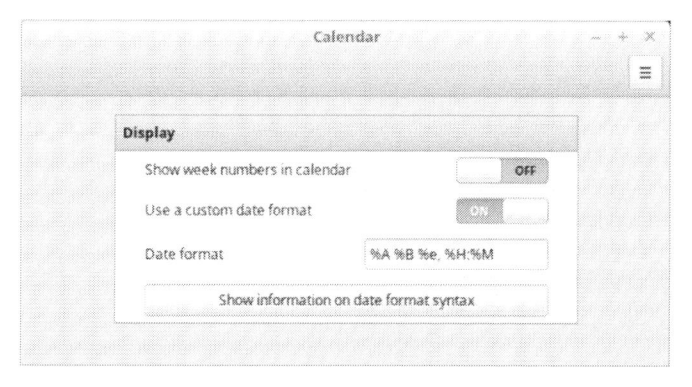

Figure 6-64: Calendar applet

Alternatively, you can manage the system time and date using the **timedatectl** command. The date and time on Linux Mint are implemented using the timedated daemon, a systemd daemon. The **timedatectl** command takes several options: **set-time** to set the time, **set-timezone** for the time zone, and **set-ntp** turns on NTP network time. The **status** option displays the current settings. See the **timedatectl** man page for a detailed listing of options and examples. Use dashes for the date and colons for the time. If you set both the date and time at the same time, enclose them in quotes. The following sets the date and time June 21, 2016 at 3:40 PM, ten seconds.

```
sudo timedatectl set-time "2016-6-21 15:40:10"
timedatectl status
```

Screensaver

The System Settings Screensaver dialog incorporates the screen lock options from previous releases and lets you choose screensaver images. On the Screensaver tab, you can choose the screensaver to use when the system is locked (see Figure 6-65). Screen locker is the default, which simply shows the date and the background image. Other screensavers include Rocks and Abstractile.

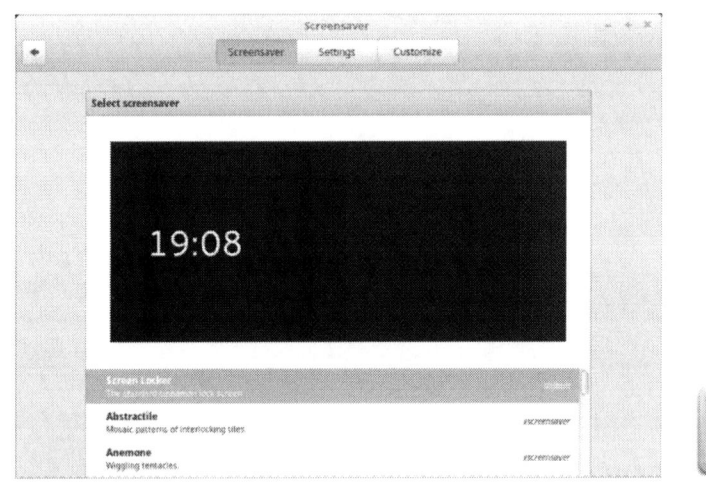

Figure 6-65: Screensaver

On the Screensaver Settings tab, you can specify the idle time for the screen, having it turn off when not in use. You can also control whether to lock the screen or not. You can set the lock to a specific time, or to when the screen turns off (see Figure 6-66).

On the Customize tab, you can set up an away message to be displayed when you lock the screen, customize the size and font of the time displayed, and enable additional options such as allowing keyboard shortcuts and a floating clock.

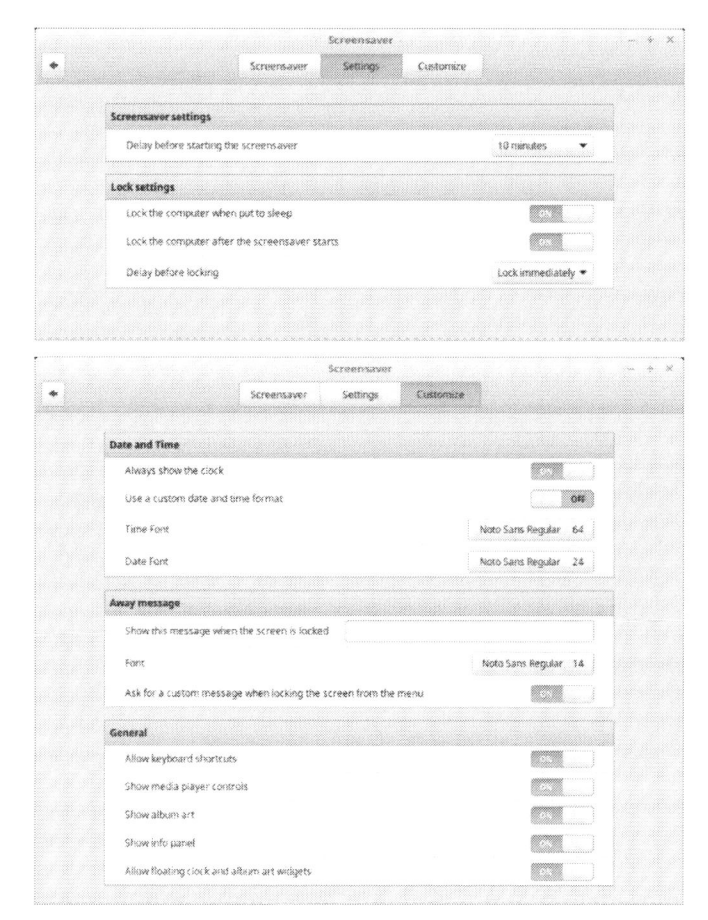

Figure 6-66: Screensaver: Settings tab

Languages

On the Language Settings, dialog you can choose the language for your menus and windows (see Figure 6-67). The currently selected language is displayed on the Language tab. Click on the icon for the language and region to display an icon menu for language variations, such as "English, Ireland" or "English, India." The Region option adjusts for features such as currency, numbering, and measurement, for example, "English, United Kingdom or "English Hong Kong." Click the "Apply System-Wide" button to apply the language for your entire system. Use the "Install/Remove Languages" button to open the "Install/Remove Languages" dialog, where you can add a new language or remove installed ones. Click the Add button on this dialog to add a new language. On the "Input Method" tab, you can add support for various input methods such as IBus and SCIM. You can install several and choose the one to use from the "Input method" menu.

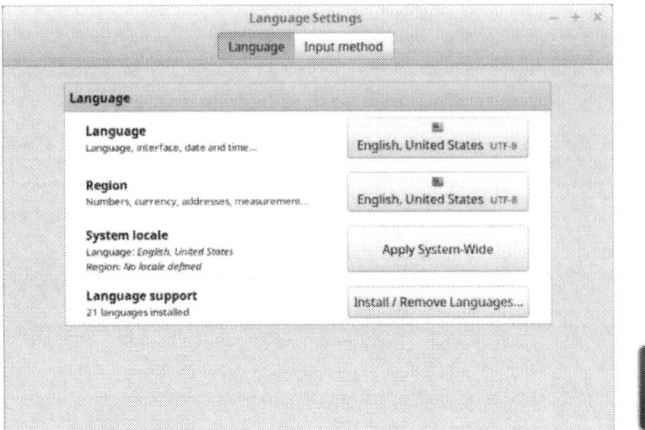

Figure 6-67: Languages

Accessibility

The Accessibility dialog in System Settings lets you configure alternative access to your interface for your keyboard and mouse actions. Four tabs set the display, keyboard properties, typing, and mouse features. Visual lets you adjust the contrast and text size, and whether to allow use of screen reader (see Figure 6-68). Keyboard displays a screen keyboard and uses visual cues for alert sounds. "Typing assistance" adjusts key presses. Mouse lets you use the keyboard for mouse operations.

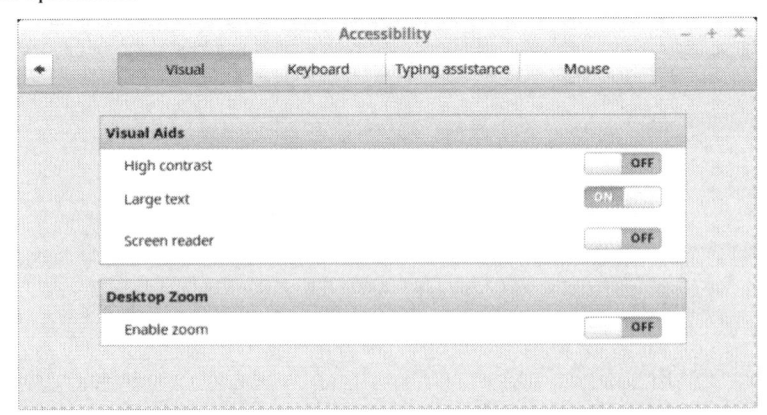

Figure 6-68: Accessibility

Startup Applications

On the Startup Applications dialog, you can select additional programs you want to be started automatically. Some are turned on automatically (see Figure 6-69). Turn off an entry if you no longer want it to start up automatically. To add an application not listed, click the Add button and choose either "Custom command" or "Choose application." The "Choose application" entry open an Applications dialog listing possible application. The "Custom command" entry opens a dialog where you can type in the application name and program (use Browse to select a program, usually in **/usr/bin**).

Figure 6-69: Startup Applications Preferences

Hardware

Several hardware-based tasks such as configuring your mouse, keyboard, and power management are discussed here. Some are GNOME 3 dialogs, similar to those available on Ubuntu and Fedora releases.

System Info

The System Info dialog shows system information, such as your hardware specifications (memory, processor, graphics card, and disk size), the distribution (64 or 32-bit system), and the Cinnamon version (see Figure 6-70).

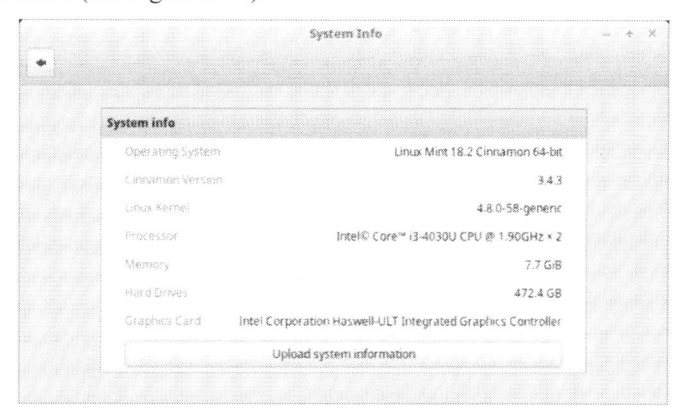

Figure 6-70: System Info

Mouse and Touchpad

The System Settings Mouse and Touchpad dialog is the primary tool for configuring your mouse and touchpad (see Figure 6-71). On the Mouse tab, you can choose the mouse speed and size, hand orientation, double-click times, and "Drag and drop" thresholds, as well as the double-click times. For laptops, you can configure your touchpad on the Touchpad tab, enabling touchpad clicks and edge scrolling (left side).

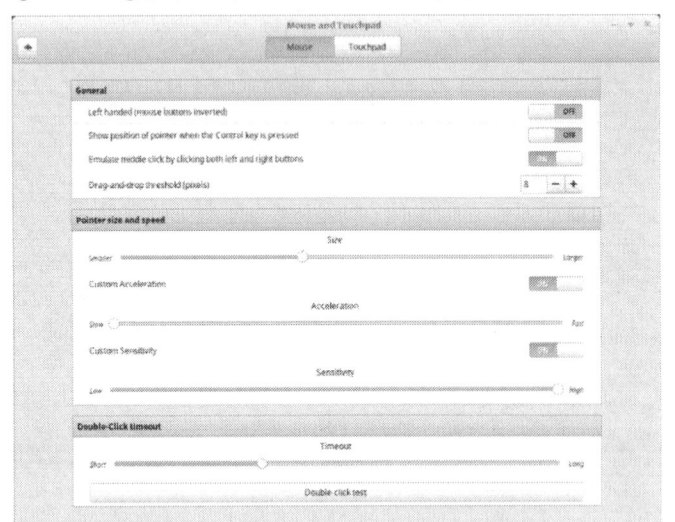

Figure 6-71: System Settings, Mouse and Touchpad

Power Management

For power management, Linux Mint uses the GNOME Power Manager, which makes use of Advanced Configuration and Power Interface (ACPI) support provided by a computer to manage power use. The GNOME Power Manager displays an icon on the panel showing the current power source, a battery (laptop) or lightning (desktop). Clicking on the battery icon displays a menu showing the power charge of your wireless devices, including your laptop and any other wireless devices like a wireless mouse (see Figure 6-72). The device entries include the device product and model names. You can right-click on the power manager panel icon to display a menu with a Configure entry. Click on it to display the Power Manager applet configuration dialog, which lists display options for the applet (see Figure 6-72). Should you want the percentage of battery power left displayed on the panel with the battery icon, you can select the "Show percentage" option.

You can also quickly turn off power management from the panel with the Inhibit applet (add it to the panel with Applets).

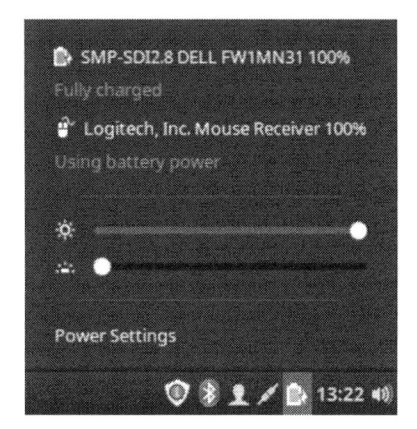

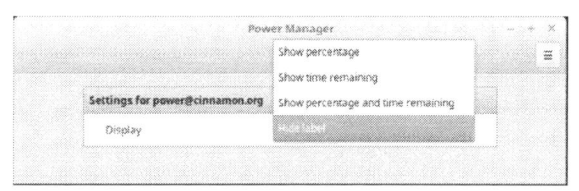

Figure 6-72: GNOME Power Manager menu and applet configuration

The GNOME Power manager is configured with the Power dialog, accessible as Power from System Settings. On the Power tab, you have the options to set the suspension time out, and what action to take when the lid is closed or the power is low (see Figure 6-73). If present, battery levels for your laptop and wireless mouse are displayed on the Batteries tab.

On the Brightness tab, you can set the screen brightness, as well as dimming options for when the system is inactive (see Figure 74).

To see how your laptop or desktop is performing with power, you can use Power statistics, accessible from the System Tools menu. The Power Statistics window displays a sidebar listing your different power devices. A right pane will show tabs with power use information for a selected device. The Laptop battery device will display three tabs: Details, History, and Statistics. The History tab will show your recent use, with graph options for Time to empty (time left), Time to full (recharging), Charge, and Rate. The Statistics tab can show charge and discharge graphs.

Figure 6-73: GNOME Power Manager

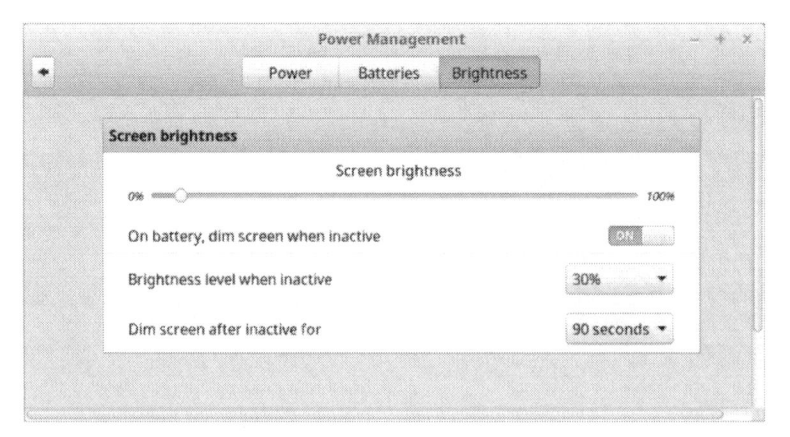

Figure 6-74: GNOME Power Manager: Brightness tab

Keyboard Settings

The System Settings Keyboard dialog shows tabs for typing, shortcuts, and layouts. The Typing tab adjusts repeat keys and cursor blinking (see Figure 6-75). The Shortcuts tab lets you assign keys to perform tasks such as starting the Web browser or mapping multimedia keys on a keyboard to media tasks, like play and pause. Just select the task and then press the key. There are tasks for the desktop (Cinnamon), multimedia (Sound and Media), window management, and workspace management. With workspace management, you can also map keys to perform workspace switching. Keys that are already assigned will be shown.

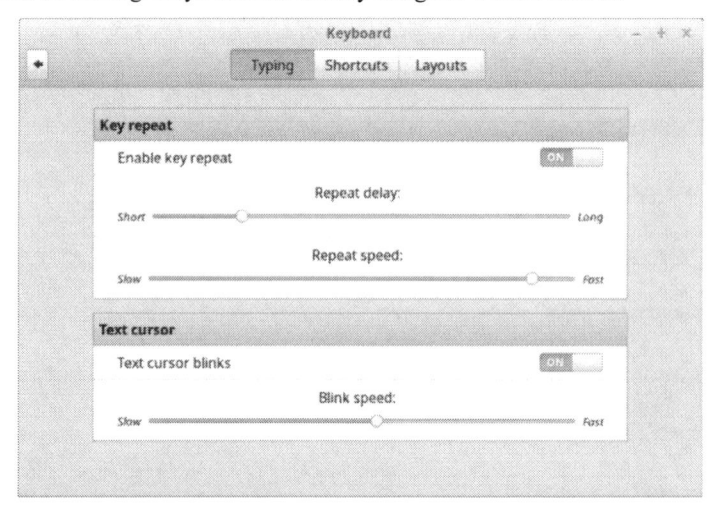

Figure 6-75: Keyboard Typing

The Layouts tab lets you choose a language (see Figure 6-76). The current input language source is listed and selected. Click the plus button to open a dialog listing other language sources, which you can add. Click the keyboard button to see the keyboard layout of your currently selected input source. You can also allow different language layouts for different windows.

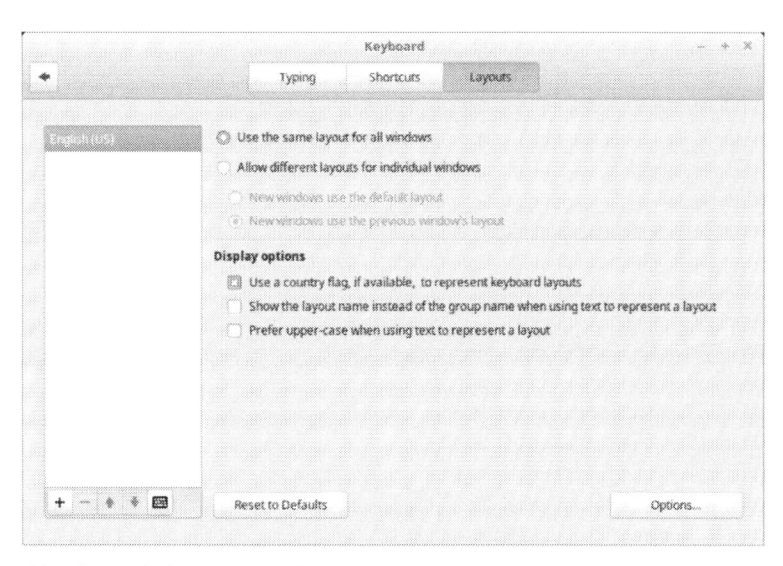

Figure 6-76: Keyboard: Layouts tab

For specialized keyboard options, click the Options button to list options such as enabling the key sequence to kill the X server (see Figure 6-77).

The system location and keyboard layout settings can also be set using the **localectl** command in a terminal window. Check the **localectl** man page for a detailed listing of options. The **status** option displays the current locale and keyboard layout. The **set-locale** option changes the location and **list-locale** lists available locations. The **set-keymap** option sets the keyboard layout and the **list-keymaps** option lists possible layouts.

```
localectl status
```

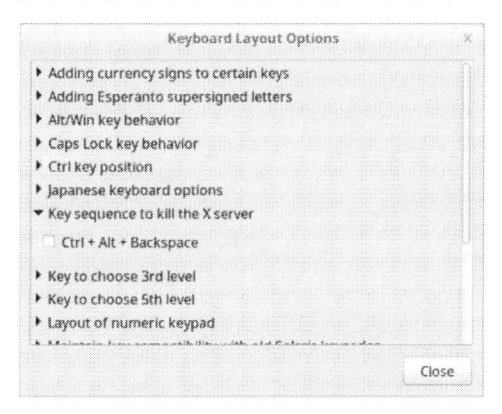

Figure 6-77: Keyboard Layout Options

Notifications

The System Settings Notifications dialog lets you configure your desktop notifications (see Figure 6-78). There are switches to enable notifications, remove them after a timeout, and fade them when hovering over them. If the fade out options is on, then you also have the option to set the opacity for your notification. The "Display a test notification" will show a sample of a notification, using your current settings. On this dialog, you can also set the size of the OSD media keys.

You can also quickly turn off notifications from the panel with the Inhibit applet (add it to the panel with Applets).

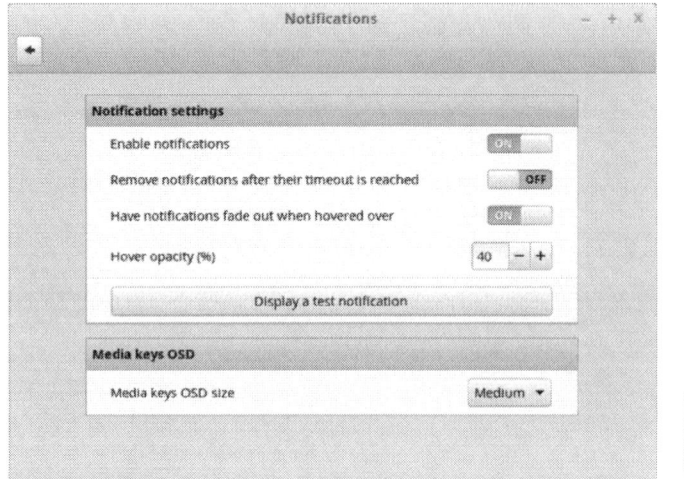

Figure 6-78: Notifications

Privacy

The System Settings Privacy dialog lets you decide if you want to remember recent files (see Figure 6-79). If you choose to remember recent files, you have the options to never forget them.

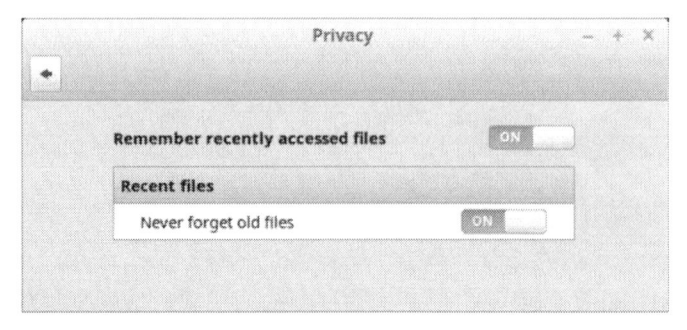

Figure 6-79: Privacy

7. Mate Desktop

- Mate Desktop
- Windows
- Workspaces
- Linux Mint Menu (Mate)
- Mate Panel
- Applets
- The Caja File Manager
- Preferences (desktop configuration)

The Mate desktop is a simplified and easy-to-use version of the GNOME 2 desktop. Mate's official file manager is Caja. Those familiar with GNOME 2 will find most of the same features, with a few changes. Mate has only one panel by default, though you can add more. The workspace switcher is not installed by default but works that same way as in GNOME 2. The menu used for the Linux Mint version of Mate is the Linux Mint menu.

The GNU Network Object Model Environment, also known as GNOME, is a powerful and easy-to-use environment consisting primarily of a panel, a desktop, and a set of desktop tools with which program interfaces can be constructed. GNOME is designed to provide a flexible platform for the development of powerful applications.

The Mate Desktop

The Mate desktop is designed to be very simple, with a single panel and desktop icons (see Figure 7-1). The panel appears as a long bar across the bottom of the screen. It holds menus, program launchers, and applet icons (an *applet* is a small program designed to be run within the panel). You can display the panel horizontally or vertically, and have it automatically hide to show you a full screen.

Figure 7-1: Mate desktop and panel

On the left side of the panel is the button for the Linux Mint menu. With this menu, you can access places and applications. Next to the menu are application buttons, followed by the Window List applet, which shows buttons for open windows. To the right of the panel are system tools such as icons for the Network Manager, Update Manager, Power, sound volume, and the clock.

The remainder of the screen is the desktop, where you can place folders, files, and application launchers. You can use a click-and-drag operation to move a file from one window to another or to the desktop. A drag-and-drop with the CTRL key held down will copy a file. A drag-and-drop operation with both the CTRL and SHIFT keys held down (Ctrl-Shift) creates a link on the desktop to that folder or file. Your home directory is accessed from the Home Folder icon on the desktop. Double clicking it opens a file manager window for your home directory. A right-click anywhere on the desktop displays a desktop menu with which you can align your desktop icons and create new folders.

To quit the desktop, you use the Quit entry in the menu. Clicking on it opens a menu with options to Suspend, Hibernate, Restart, and Shut Down.

Mate Components

From a user's point of view, the desktop interface has four components: the desktop, the panels, the main menu, and the file manager (see Figure 7-2). You have a single panel displayed, used for menus, application icons, and managing your windows. When you open a window, a corresponding button for it will be displayed in the lower panel, which you can use to minimize and restore the window.

To start a program, you can select its entry from the Linux Mint menu. You can also click its application icon in the panel (if one appears) or drag-and-drop data files to its icon. To add an icon for an application to the desktop, right-click on its entry in the Linux Mint menu and select "Add to desktop."

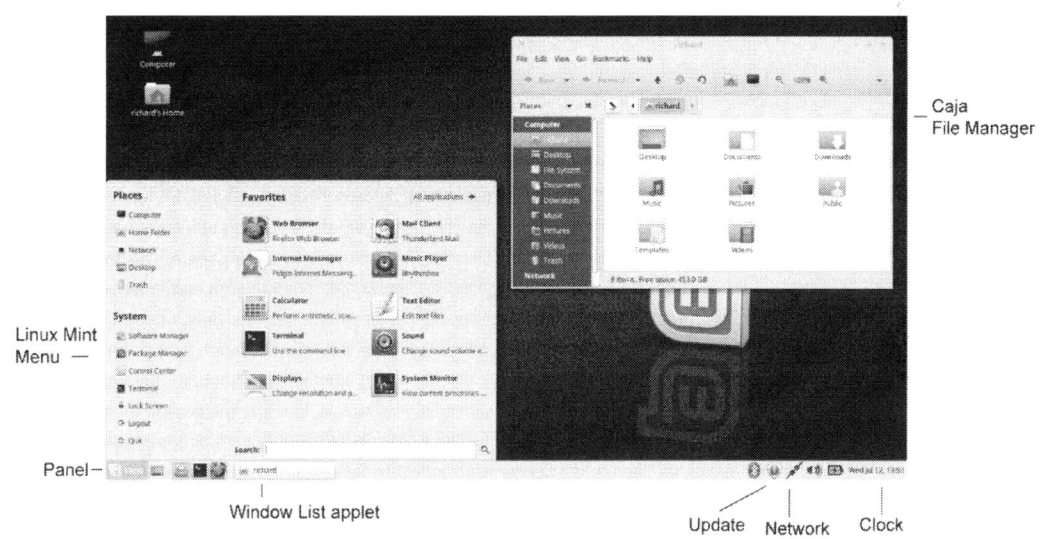

Figure 7-2: Mate with Linux Mint menu and Caja file manager

Drag-and-Drop Files to the Desktop

Any icon for an item that you drag-and-drop from a file manager window to the desktop also appears on the desktop. The default drag-and-drop operation is a move operation. If you select a file in your file manager window and drag it to the desktop, you are actually moving the file from its current directory to the desktop folder, which is located in your home folder and holds all items on the desktop. The desktop folder is **Desktop**. In the case of dragging folders to the desktop, the entire folder and its subfolders will be moved to the desktop folder.

To remove an icon from the desktop, you right-click and choose "Move to Trash." If you choose to display the trash icon on the desktop, you can simply drag-and-drop it in the trash.

You can copy a file to your desktop by pressing the CTRL key and then clicking and dragging it from a file manager window to your desktop. You will see the mouse icon change to hand with a small + symbol, indicating that you are creating a copy, instead of moving the original.

You can also create a link on the desktop to any file. This is useful if you want to keep a single version in a folder and just be able to access it from the desktop. You could also use links for customized programs that you may not want to appear on the menu or panel. There are two ways to create a link. While holding down the Ctrl and Shift keys, CTRL-SHIFT, drag the file to where you want the link created. A copy of the icon then appears with a small arrow in the right corner indicating it is a link. You can click this link to start the program, open the file, or open the folder, depending on the type of file to which you linked. Alternatively, first click and drag the file out of the window, and after moving the file but before releasing the mouse button, press the ALT key. This will display a pop-up menu with selections for Move Here, Copy Here, and Link Here. Select the Link Here option to create a link.

The drag-and-drop file operation works on virtual desktops provided by the Workspace Switcher. The Workspace Switcher creates icons for each virtual desktop in the panel, along with buttons for any window open on them. The Workspace Switcher is not added by default. You will have to add it to the panel.

Desktop Settings

You can configure desktop and window display settings using the Desktop Settings dialog, which you can access from the Preferences menu, or from the Control Center (see Figure 7-3). The Desktop Settings dialog has four tabs: Desktop, Windows, Interface, and Terminal. The Desktop tab lets you choose which system icons to display on the desktop. The Computer and Home folder icons are initially selected, along with Mounted volumes for external file systems such as USB drives and DVDs that you insert. You can also choose to display the Network and Trash icons.

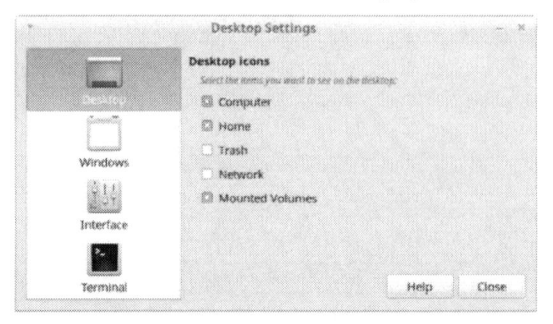

Figure 7-3: Mate Desktop Settings

On Windows tab, you can turn off compositing and change the location of the minimize, maximize, and close buttons from the right side of the title bar to the left side.

The Interface tab lets you choose whether to show icons on menus, buttons, and toolbars.

Applications on the Desktop

In some cases, you will want to create another way on the desktop to access a file without moving it from its original folder. You can do this either by using an application launcher icon or by creating a link to the original program. Application launcher icons are the components used in menus and panels to display and access applications. To place an application icon on your desktop for an entry in the menus, you can simply drag-and-drop the application entry from the menu to the desktop, or right-click and select "Add to desktop."

For applications that are not on a menu, you can either create an application launcher button or create a direct link for it. To create an application launcher, right-click the desktop background to display the desktop menu, and then select the "Create Launcher" entry. To create a simple link, click-and-drag a program's icon while holding the Ctrl-Shift keys down to the desktop.

The Desktop Menu

You can right-click anywhere on the empty desktop to display the desktop menu that includes entries for common tasks, such as creating an application launcher, creating a new folder, or organizing the icon display. Keep in mind that the New Folder entry creates a new folder on your desktop, specifically in your desktop folder (**DESKTOP**), not your home folder. The entries for this menu are listed in Table 7-1.

Menu Item	Description
Create Folder	Creates a new directory on your desktop, within your DESKTOP directory.
Create Launcher	Creates a new desktop icon for an application.
Create Document	Creates files using installed templates
Organize Desktop by Name	Arranges your desktop icons.
Keep Aligned	Aligns your desktop icons.
Cut, Copy, Paste	Cuts, copies, or pastes files, letting you move or copy files between folders.
Change Desktop Background	Opens a Background Preferences dialog to let you select a new background for your desktop.

Table 7-1: The Desktop Menu

Windows

You can resize a window by clicking any of its sides or corners and dragging. You can move the window with a click-and-drag operation on its title bar. You can also ALT-click and drag anywhere on the window. The upper-right corner of a window shows the Minimize, Maximize, and Close buttons (minus, plus, and x buttons) (see Figure 7-4). Clicking the Minimize button no longer displays the window on the desktop. A button for it remains on the bottom panel (the Window list applet) that you can click to restore it. The panel button for a window works like a display toggle. If the window is displayed when you click the panel button, it will no longer be shown. If not displayed, it will then be shown. On the left side of the title bar is a drop-down menu that displays a window menu with entries for window operations (you can also right-click anywhere on the title bar to display the menu) (see Figure 7-4). The options include workspace entries to move the window to another workspace (virtual desktop) or make visible on all workspaces, which displays the window no matter to what workspace you move.

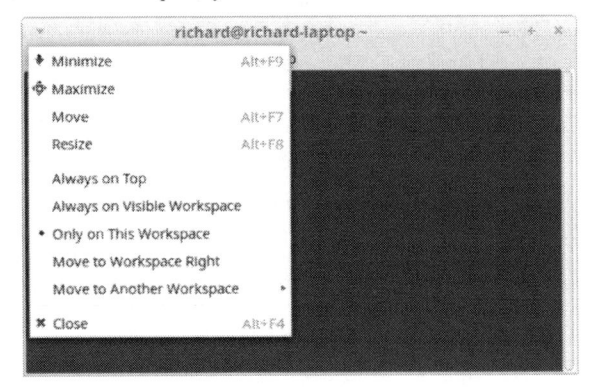

Figure 7-4: Mate window

You can quickly move between windows by pressing the Alt-Tab keys. A window switcher bar opens displaying thumbnails of open windows (see Figure 7-5). Continue pressing the Alt-Tab keys to move through them. You can use the Windows Preferences dialog's General tab (Control Center) to enable or disable thumbnails. The Compositing Window Manager enables them. If you disable thumbnails for the switcher, only small icons are displayed for the open windows.

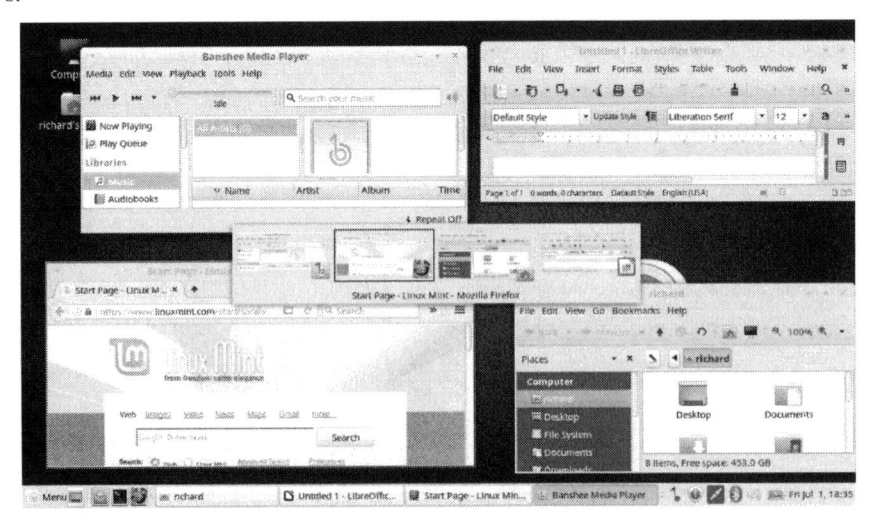

Figure 7-5: Switching Windows with thumbnails

You can configure window behavior using the Window Preferences dialog's Behavior tab accessible as Windows from the Preferences menu and the Control Center. You choose features such as compositing, select windows by moving the mouse over them and use the meta key instead of the Alt key to move a window. From a menu, you can choose the action to perform when the title bar is double-clicked. The default is maximize, but other options include to roll up the window and minimize it.

Window List

The Window List applet shows currently opened windows (see Figure 7-6). The Window List arranges opened windows in a series of buttons, one for each window. A window can include applications such as a Web browser or a file manager window displaying a folder. You can move from one window to another by clicking its button. When you minimize a window, you can later restore it by clicking its entry in the Window List.

Right clicking a window's Window List button opens a menu that lets you Minimize or Unminimize, Move, Resize, Maximize, or Close the window, and move the window to another workspace. The Minimize operation will reduce the window to its Window List entry. Right clicking the entry will display the menu with an Unminimize option instead of a Minimize one, which you can then use to redisplay the window. The Close entry will close the window, ending its application. There are also entries for moving the window to an adjacent workspace, or to a specific one.

Figure 7-6: Window List applet

The Window List applet is represented by a small serrated bar at the beginning of the window list applet (see Figure 7-6). To configure the Window List applet, right-click on this bar and select the Preferences entry to open the Window List Preferences dialog (see Figure 7-7). Here, you can set features such as whether to group windows on the panel, whether to show all open windows or those from just the current workspace or which workspace to restore windows to.

Figure 7-7: Window List Preferences

If you choose to group windows, then common windows are grouped under a button that will expand like a menu, listing each window in that group. For example, all open terminal windows would be grouped under a single button, which when clicked would pop up a list of their buttons. The button shows the number of open windows. You can also choose to group only if there is not enough space on the Window List applet to display a separate button for each window,

Workspace Switcher

The Workspace Switcher applet lets you switch to different virtual desktops (see Figure 7-8). You can add the Workspace Switcher to any panel by selecting it from that panel's "Add to Panel" box. It is not added by default. The Workspace Switcher shows your entire virtual desktop as separate rectangles listed next to each other. Open windows show up as small colored rectangles in these squares. You can move any window from one virtual desktop to another by clicking and dragging its image in the Workspace Switcher from one workspace to another.

Figure 7-8: Workspace switcher, one row and two rows

In addition to the Workspace Switcher, you can use the scroll button on your mouse, or the Ctrl-Alt-arrow keys to move from one workspace to another. When you use the Ctrl-Alt-arrow keys, the right and left arrows move you through a row, and the up and down keys move you from one row to another. A small workspace bar appears at the center of the screen, highlighting the current workspace and displaying its name (see Figure 7-9).

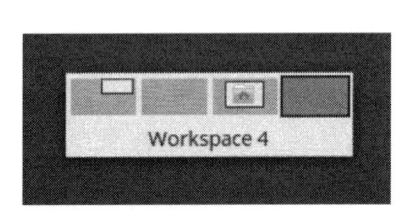

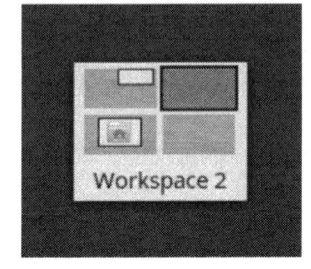

Figure 7-9: Switching workspaces, Ctrl-Alt-*arrow*

To configure the Workspace Switcher, right-click on the applet to display a menu, and then select Preferences to display the Workspace Switcher Preferences dialog box (see Figure 7-10). Here, you can select the number of workspaces and name them. The default is four. You can also choose the number of rows for the workspace.

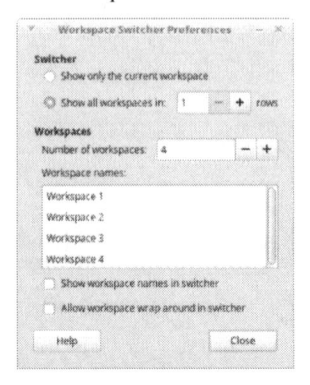

Figure 7-10: Workspace Switcher Preferences

Linux Mint Menu for Mate

Linux Mint provides its own menu for the Mate interface called the Linux Mint Menu. It is derived from the SUSE Slab menu. The Linux Mint Menu is located on the left side of the panel. You can also open it with the Ctrl-meta keys.

The Linux Mint Menu has three sections: Places, System, and Favorites/Applications (see Figure 7-11). The Places section displays buttons for accessing commonly used locations: the computer window for your devices and mounted folder, your home folder, the network window for shared devices and folders, your trash folder, and the Desktop configuration dialog for Linux Mint Mate.

The System section has buttons for software management, the Control Center, a terminal window, and for the lock, logout, and shut down operation. Software Manager opens the Linux Mint Software Manager, letting you install software from Linux Mint and Ubuntu repositories. The Package Manager button opens the older Synaptic Package Manager, with the same repository access.

Control Center opens a dialog similar to System Settings in the Cinnamon desktop, which shows icons for system and desktop configuration, and for administration. Many of the administrative tools are the same as those used for Cinnamon and are supported by Ubuntu. The Logout button logs you out to the login screen. The Quit button opens the shutdown dialog with options to suspend, hibernate, restart, and shut down.

The Applications/Favorites section is a toggle showing either your favorite applications or all installed applications. You can toggle between the two using the button on the upper right side of the menu. The Applications view is organized into two scroll boxes, one for software categories and the other for applications in those categories. You can use the scroll wheel on your mouse to scroll through the larger listings. In Figure 7-11, the applications in the Graphics category are listed. In the category list, the Preferences, Administration, and System Tools menus list the administration and configuration applications, such as Software Manager in System Tools.

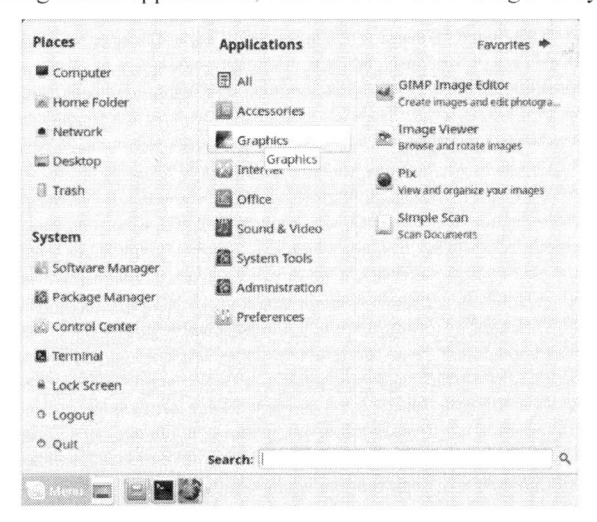

Figure 7-11: Linux Mint Menu for Mate

226 Part 3: Desktops

The Linux Mint Menu supports a search operation, using the Search text box in the bottom right corner. When you click on the Search text box, the All category is selected. As you type, matching applications are displayed in the Applications section of the menu. If there are no matches, then un-installed applications are searched for, with buttons displayed that let you install the matching applications (see Figure 7-12). In addition, there are entries to search Google, Wikipedia, your dictionary, and your computer for that term.

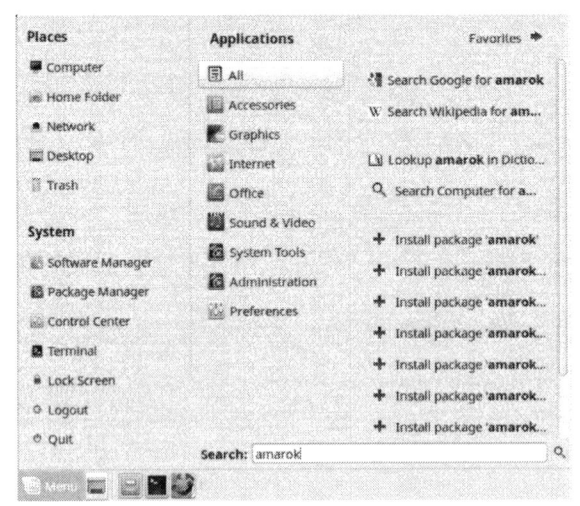

Figure 7-12: Linux Mint Menu search

Several actions can be performed on a menu application item using its pop-up menu. Right-click on the item to display the menu (see Figure 7-13).

Figure 7-13: Linux Mint Menu Applications pop-up menu.

You can add an application launcher to the panel or the desktop by dragging its icon from the menu to the desktop or panel. You can also right-click on the application icon and choose "Add to desktop" or "Add to panel" (see Figure 7-13).

Should you want an application to start up when you log in, you right-click on it on the menu and choose "Launch when I log in." From the pop-up menu, you can also directly uninstall an application, and open the application's properties dialog.

The Favorites section lists default favorites you may want. Click on the Favorites button in the top right corner to display your favorites. You can add any application to the favorites list by right-clicking on its entry and choosing "Show in my favorites" (see Figure 7-14). You can reorder favorites on the menu by simply clicking and dragging them to new locations. To remove a favorite, right-click and choose Remove.

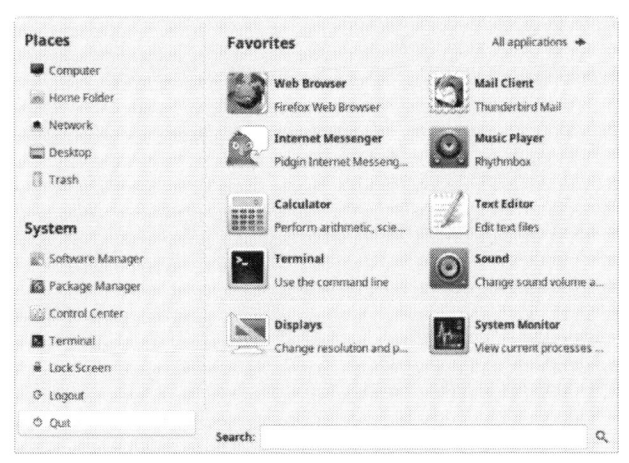

Figure 7-14: Linux Mint Menu Favorites

Linux Mint Menu Preferences dialog

You can configure the menu using the Menu preferences dialog, which you can access by right-clicking on the Menu button on the panel and choosing "Preferences" from the pop-up menu. Menu Preferences has seven tabs: Main button, Plugins, Theme, Applications, Favorites, Places, and System (see Figure 7-15). On the "Main button" tab you can specify the Linux Mint Menu applet's name (text) and whether to show an icon. You can choose a different icon, and specify the keyboard command to use to display the menu.

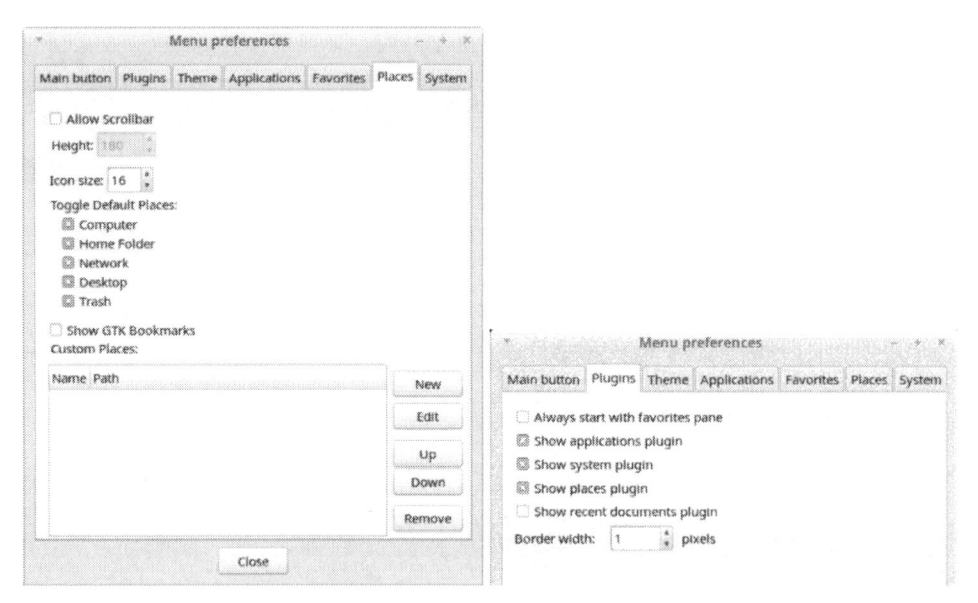

Figure 7-15: Linux Mint Menu Preferences dialog

The Linux Mint Menu is enhanced by plugins, of which three are active by default. You can specify the plugins to use on the Plugins tab. The "Show Recent Documents" entry lets you activate an added pane in the Linux Mint Menu for recent documents (see Figure 7-16). The "Always start with favorites pane" will display the Favorites pane instead of the Applications pane, when you first display the menu.

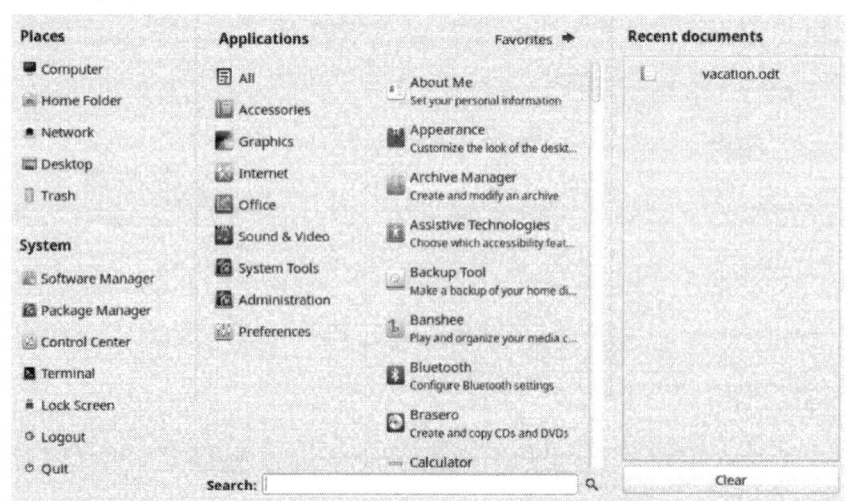

Figure 7-16: Linux Mint Menu with Recent Documents plugin

The Theme tab lets you choose custom colors for headings, borders, and background. You can also choose a theme.

On the Applications tab, you can configure the Applications pane, choosing to display category icons, show application comments in pop-up notes, and to let mouse hovering select an entry. You can also configure the search function to search for uninstalled packages, and to remember the last search.

For Favorites, you can configure the number of columns and the icons size.

For Places, you can enable a scrollbar, set the icon size, choose which default items to display, and whether to display your bookmarks. You can also add custom places (folders) for the menu. Click the New button to open a dialog where you can enter the place's name and the path name of the folder.

On the System tab, you can choose to allow a scrollbar, set the icon size, and choose the default items to display.

Note: You can replace the Linux Mint Menu with the Mate Menu by removing the Linux Mint Menu from the panel, and then adding the "Main Menu" applet to the panel. The name of the Linux Mint Menu is mintMenu, should you want to add it again later.

Mate Panel

The panel is the main component of the Mate interface. Through it, you can start your applications, run applets, and access desktop areas. You can think of the Mate panel as a type of tool you can use on your desktop. You can have several Mate panels displayed on your desktop, each with applets and menus you have placed in them. In this respect, Mate is flexible, enabling you to configure your panels any way you want. The Mate panel works much the same as the GNOME 2 panel. You can easily add applets to the panel, along with application launchers. A default panel is set up for you at the bottom of the screen, with applets for the menu, Show Desktop, application launchers, the window list, and several system applets (see Figure 7-17). These include buttons for the Update Manager, volume control, Network Manager, the power manager, and the clock.

Figure 7-17: Mate Panel

Panel configuration tasks such as adding applications, selecting applets, setting up menus, and creating new panels are handled from the Panel pop-up menu (see Figure 7-17). Just right-click anywhere on an empty space in your panel to display a menu with entries for Properties, New Panel, Add to Panel, and Delete This Panel, along with Help and About entries. New Panel lets you create other panels; Add to Panel lets you add items to the panel such as application launchers, applets for simple tasks like the Workspace Switcher, and menus like the Linux Mint menu. The Properties entry will display a dialog for configuring the panel, like setting the position of the panel and its hiding capabilities.

To add a new panel, select the New Panel entry in the Panel pop-up menu (see Figure 7-18). A new expanded panel is automatically created and displayed at the top of your screen. You can then use the panel's properties box to set different display and background features, as described in the following sections.

- Add to Panel...
- Properties
- Delete This Panel
- New Panel
- Help
- About Panels

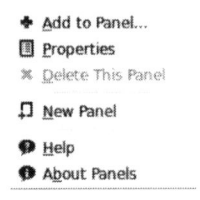

Figure 7-18: Mate Panel pop-up menu

Panel Properties

To configure individual panels, you use the Panel Properties dialog box (see Figure 7-19). To display this dialog box, you right-click a particular panel and select the Properties entry in the pop-up menu. For individual panels, you can set general configuration features and the background. The Panel Properties dialog box displays two tabs, General and Background.

Displaying Panels

On the General tab of a panel's properties box, you determine how you want the panel displayed. Here you have options for orientation, size, and whether to expand, auto-hide, or display hide buttons. The Orientation entry lets you select which side of the screen you want the panel placed on. You can then choose whether you want a panel expanded or not. An expanded panel will fill the edges of the screen, whereas a non-expanded panel is sized to the number of items in the panel and shows handles at each end. Expanded panels will remain fixed to the edge of the screen, whereas unexpanded panels can be moved.

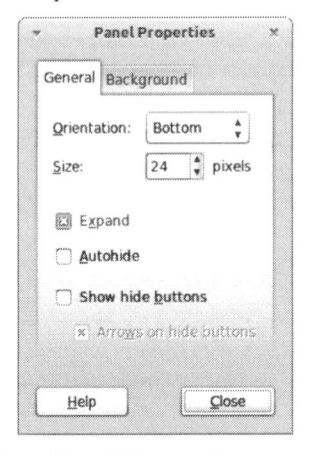

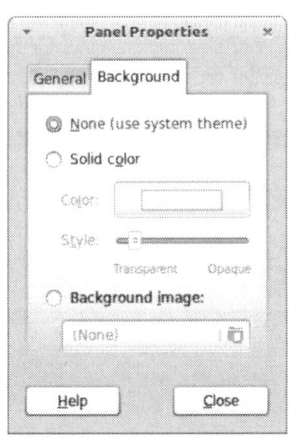

Figure 7-19: Mate Panel Properties

Moving and Hiding Expanded Panels

Expanded panels can be positioned at any edge of your screen. You can move expanded panels from one edge of a screen by selecting its orientation (side) on the Panel Properties General tab. If a panel is already there, the new one will stack on top of the current one. You cannot move unexpanded panels in this way. Bear in mind that if you place an expanded panel on the side edge, any menus titles will be displayed vertically. You can hide expanded panels either automatically or manually. These are features specified in the panel properties General box as Autohide and "Show hide buttons." To automatically hide panels, select the Autohide feature. To redisplay the panel, move your mouse to the edge where the panel is located. You can enable or disable the Autohide features in the panel's properties window.

If you want to be able to hide a panel manually, select the "Show hide buttons." Two hide buttons showing arrows are displayed at either end of the panel. You can further choose whether to have these buttons display arrows or not (displaying arrows is the default). You can then hide the panel at any time by clicking either of the hide buttons located on each end of the panel. The arrows show the direction in which the panel will hide.

Unexpanded Panels: Movable and Fixed

Whereas an expanded panel is always located at the edge of the screen, an unexpanded panel is movable. It can be located at the edge of a screen, working like a shrunken version of an expanded panel, or you can move it to any place on your desktop, just as you would an icon.

An unexpanded panel will shrink to the number of its components, showing handles at either end. You can then move the panel by dragging its handles. To access the panel menu with its properties entry, right-click either of its handles.

To fix an unexpanded panel at its current position, select the "Show hide buttons" feature on its properties box. This will replace the handles with Hide buttons and make the panel fixed. Clicking a Hide button will hide the panel to the edge of the screen, just as with expanded panels. If an expanded panel is already located on that edge, the button for a hidden unexpanded panel will be on top of it, just as with a hidden expanded panel. The Autohide feature will work for unexpanded panels placed at the edge of a screen.

If you want to fix an unexpanded panel to the edge of a screen, make sure it is placed at the edge you want, and then set its "Show hide buttons" feature.

Panel Background

With a panel's Background pane on its properties box, you can change the panel's background color or image. For a color background, you click the Color button to display a color selection window where you can choose a color from a color wheel or a list of color boxes, or you can enter its number. Once your color is selected, you can use the Style slide bar to make it more transparent or opaque. To use an image instead of a color, select the image entry and use the Browse button to locate the image file you want. For an image, you can also drag and drop an image file from the file manager to the panel; that image then becomes the background image for the panel.

Panel Objects

A panel can contain several different types of objects. These include menus, launchers, applets, drawers, and special objects.

Menus   A panel menu has launchers that are buttons used to start an application or execute a command.

Launchers   You can select any application entry in the Applications menu and create a launcher for it on the panel.

Applets   An applet is a small application designed to run within the panel. The Workspace Switcher showing the different desktops is an example of a GNOME applet.

Drawers   A drawer is an extension of the panel that can be opened or closed. You can think of a drawer as a shrinkable part of the panel. You can add anything to it that you can to a regular panel, including applets, menus, and even other drawers.

Special objects   These are used for special tasks not supported by other panel objects. For example, the Logout and Lock buttons are special objects.

Moving, Removing, and Locking Objects

To move any object within the panel, right-click it and choose the Move entry. You can move it either to a different place on the same panel or to a different panel. For launchers, you can just drag the object directly where you want it to be. To remove an object from the panel, right-click it to display a pop-up menu for it, and then choose the Remove From Panel entry. To prevent an object from being moved or removed, you set its lock feature (right-click the object and select the Lock To Panel entry). To later allow it to be moved, you first have to unlock the object (right-click it and select Unlock).

Adding Objects

To add an object to a panel, select the object from the panel's "Add to Panel" dialog (see Figure 7-20). To display the "Add to Panel" dialog, right-click on the panel and select the "Add to Panel' entry. This "Add to Panel" dialog displays a lengthy list of common objects, such as the mintMenu menu (Linux Mint Menu), Log Out, and Clock. For Application applets, you can click on the Applications Launcher entry and click the Forward button to list all your installed applications. Launchers can also be added to a panel by just dragging them directly. Launchers include applications, windows, and files. The Custom Application Launcher lets you create a custom launcher.

Application Launchers

To add an application that already has an application launcher to a panel is easy. You just have to drag the application launcher to the panel. This will automatically create a copy of the launcher for use on that panel. Launchers can be menu items or desktop icons. All the entries in the Linux Mint menu are application launchers. To add an application from the menu, just select it and drag it to the panel. You can also drag any desktop application icon to a panel to add a copy of it to that panel.

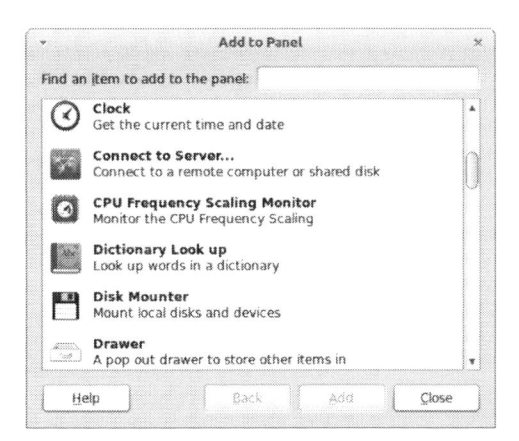

Figure 7-20: Mate Panel "Add to Panel" dialog for panel applets

For any menu item, you can also go to its entry and right-click it, and then select the "Add to panel" entry. An application launcher for that application is then added to the panel. Suppose you use the Xed text editor frequently and want to add its icon to the panel, instead of having to go through the Application menu all the time. Right-click the Text Editor menu entry in the Accessories menu, and select the "Add to panel" entry. The Xed text editor icon now appears in your panel.

Also, as previously noted, you can open the Add to Panel dialog, and then choose the Application Launcher entry and click the Forward button. This will display a dialog with a listing of all the Application menu entries along with Preferences and Administration menus, expandable to their items. Just find the application you want added, select it, and click the Add button.

Adding Drawers

You can also group applications under a Drawer icon. Clicking the Drawer icon displays a list of the different application icons you can then select. To add a drawer to your panel, right-click the panel and select the "Add to panel" entry to display the "Add to Panel" dialog. From that list select the Drawer entry. This will create a drawer on your panel. You can then drag any items from desktop, menus, or windows to the drawer icon on the panel to have them listed in the drawer.

You can also add applets and applications to a drawer using the Add to Drawer dialog. Right-click on the drawer and choose the Add to Drawer entry to open the dialog. Then click the applet you want added to the drawer. To add applications, select the Applications Launcher entry and click for Forward to list your application menu categories, which are expandable to list applications. You can add a menu to the drawer by choosing the application category and clicking the Add button.

Adding Menus

A menu differs from a drawer in that a drawer holds application icons instead of menu entries. You can add application menus to your panel, much as you add drawers. To add an application menu to your panel, open the Add to Panel dialog and select the Application Launcher entry, clicking Forward to open the list of Application categories. Select the category you want, and click the Add button. That menu category with all its application items is added to your panel as a menu.

Adding Folders and Files

You can also add directory folders to a panel. Click and drag the Folder icon from the file manager window to your panel. Whenever you click this Folder button, a file manager window opens, displaying that directory. You can also add directory folders to any drawer on your panel. To add a file, also drag it directly to the panel.

Adding Applets

Applets are small programs that perform tasks within the panel. To add an applet, right-click the panel and select Add To Panel from the pop-up menu. This displays the Add To box listing common applets along with other types of objects, such as launchers. Select the one you want. For example, to add the clock to your panel, select Clock from the panel's Add To box. Once added, the applet will show up in the panel. If you want to remove an applet, right-click it and select the Remove From Panel entry.

Mate features a number of helpful applets. Some applets monitor your system, such as the Battery Charge Monitor, which checks the battery in laptops, and System Monitor, which shows a graph indicating your current CPU and memory use.

Several helpful utility applets provide added functionality to your desktop. The Clock applet can display time in a 12 or 24 hour format. Right-click the Clock applet and select the Preferences entry to change its setup. The CPU Frequency Scaling Monitor displays CPU usage for CPUs.

Caja File Manager

The Caja file manager supports the standard features for copying, removing, and deleting items as well as setting permissions and displaying items. The program name for the file manager is **caja**. You can enhance Caja using extensions such as "Open terminal" to open the current folder in a new terminal window, and Engrampa that allows you to create (compress) and extract archives. Several extensions are already installed and enabled by default. They will display entries in appropriate menus. Extensions are enabled on the Extension tab of the File Management Preferences dialog (Edit | Preferences). To add more extension, use the Software Manager to install the caja extension packages. Extension packages have the prefix **caja-**, such as **caja-share**, **caja-dropbox**, and **caja-wallpaper**.

Home Folder Sub-folders and Bookmarks

Like Ubuntu, Linux Mint uses the Common User Directory Structure (xdg-user-dirs at **https://freedesktop.org**) to set up sub-folders in the user home directory. Folders will include **Documents**, **Music**, **Pictures**, **Downloads**, and **Videos**. These localized user folders are used as defaults by many desktop applications. Users can change their folder names or place them within each other using the file browser. For example, Music can be moved into **Documents**, **Documents/Music**. Local configuration is held in the **.config/user-dirs.dirs** file. System-wide defaults are set up in the **/etc/xdg/user-dirs.defaults** file. The icons for these folders are displayed in Figure 7-21.

Documents   Downloads   Music   Pictures   Public   Videos

Figure 7-21: Caja file manager home folders

The folders are also default bookmarks. You can access a bookmarked folder directly from the Caja window sidebar. You can also add your own bookmarks for folders by opening the folder and choosing "Add Bookmark" from the Bookmarks menu. Your folder will appear in the Bookmarks section of the Caja side pane Places menu and on the Bookmarks menu. Use the Edit Bookmarks dialog to remove bookmarks. Here you can remove a bookmark or change is name and location.

You use Desktop Settings to display basic folders such as the home, network, and trash folders on the desktop area.

File Manager Windows

When you click Home folder icon on the desktop or the Home folder entry on the Mate menu Places section, a file manager window opens showing your home folder. The file manager window displays several components, including a menubar, a main toolbar, and a side pane (see Figure 7-22). The side pane works like the sidebar in the Nemo and Nautilus file managers, but with a menu, like the file manager in GNOME 2. The file manager window's main pane (to the right) displays the icons or listing of files and sub-folders in the current working folder. When you select a file and folder, the status bar at the bottom of the window displays the name of the file or folder selected and for files the size, and for folders the number of items contained. The status bar also displays the remaining free space on the current file system.

236   Part 3: Desktops

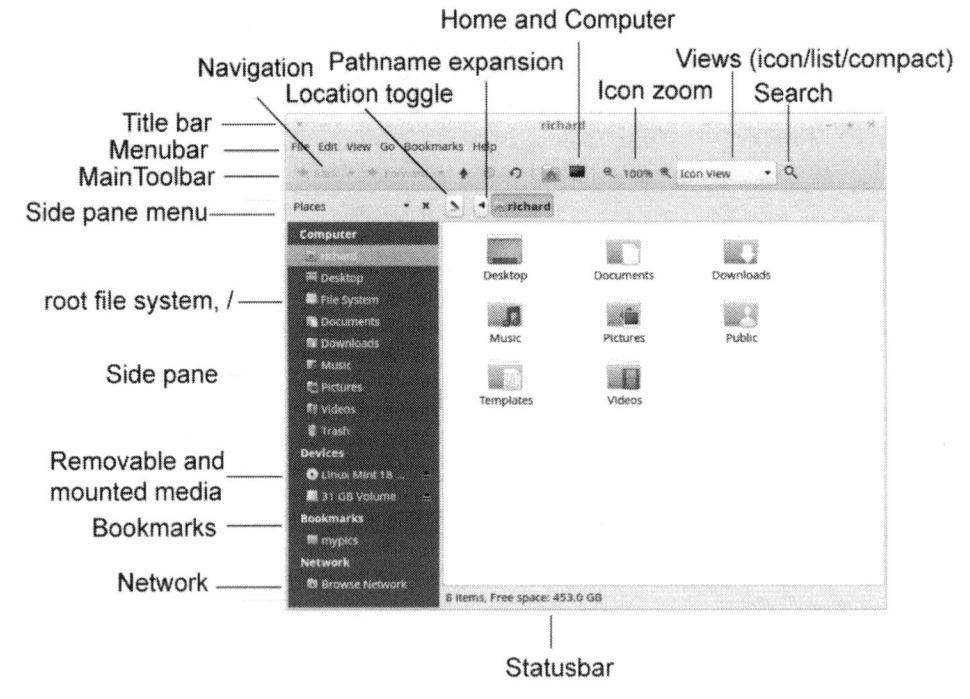

Figure 7-22: Caja file manager with sidebar

Note: Caja works as an operational FTP browser. You can use the Connect to Server entry on the Files top bar applications menu to open a "Connect to Server" dialog, where you can enter the URL for the FTP site.

When you open a new folder, the same window is used to display it, and you can use the Forward and Back buttons to move through previously opened folders (top left on the main toolbar) (see Figure 7-23). Down triangles to the right of the Back and Forward buttons display menus of previously accessed folders, which you can use to access a previous folder directly. There is also an up arrow to move to the parent directory, and a Home folder button to move directly to your home folder. The Computer button displays the computer window showing your file systems and attached devices. You can also access these operations from the file manager's Go menu (see Table 7-2).

Figure 7-23: Caja navigation buttons: back, forward, parent, home, computer

As you open sub-folders, the main toolbar displays buttons for your current folder and its parent folders (see Figure 7-24). You can click on a folder button to move to it directly. Initially, the button shows a path of subdirectories from your home folder. Clicking on the small triangle arrow to the left expands the path to the top level, from the root directory (the hard disk icon).

Chapter 7: Mate Desktop   237

Menu Item	Description
Open Parent	Move to the parent folder
Back	Move to the previous folder viewed in the file manager window
Forward	Move to the next folder viewed in the file manager window
Paste	Paste files that you have copied or cut, letting you move or copy files between folders, or make duplicates.
Same Location as Other Pane	If you have two panes open on the window, you can make both panes view the same folder
Home Folder	Move to the Home folder
Computer	Move to the Computer folder, showing icons for your devices
Templates	Move to the Templates folder
Trash	Open the trash folder to see deleted files and folders, which can be restored.
Network	Move to the network folder showing connected systems on your network and open remote folders.
Location	Open the location navigation box for entering the path name of a file or folder
Search for Files	Search for files and folders using the file manager window

Table 7-2: File Manager Go Menu

You can also display a location URL text box instead of buttons, where you can enter the location of a folder, either on your system or on a remote system. To display the location text box, press **Ctrl-l**, or from the Go menu select Location, or click the Location toggle at the beginning of the location path on the main toolbar (see Figure 7-24). These access methods operate as toggles that move you a back and forth from the location text box to the button path.

Figure 7-24: Caja locations: unexpanded, expanded, and location path

The File menu has entries for opening a new tab (Ctrl-t), opening a new file manager window (Ctrl-n), creating a new folder (Shift-Ctrl-n), connecting to a remote FTP server, and displaying the properties of the current folder (Alt-Return). Most have corresponding keys (see Table 7-3) (see Figure 7-28).

Part 3: Desktops

Menu Item	Description
New Tab	Creates a new tab.
New Window	Open a new file manager window
Create Folder	Creates a new subdirectory in the directory.
Create Document	Creates a text document.
Connect to server	Connect to an FTP server using the file manager
Open in Terminal	Open the current folder in a new terminal window (Open Terminal extension)
Properties	Properties for the current open folder
Empty Trash	Empty the trash folder
Close All Windows	Close all file manage windows
Close	Close the file manager window.
Open With	When a file is selected the Open With item is displayed showing possible applications to open the file with
Open	When a folder is selected the Open item is displayed showing also the "Open in New Tab" and "Open in New Window" items, along with the Open With submenu.

Table 7-3: File Manager File Menu

File Manager Side Pane

The file manager side pane has a menu from which you can choose to display places (Places), the tree view of the file system (Tree), information on the current or selected directory or file (Information), the history of previously opened folders for that login session (History), notes (Notes), and emblems you can place on a file or folder (Emblems).

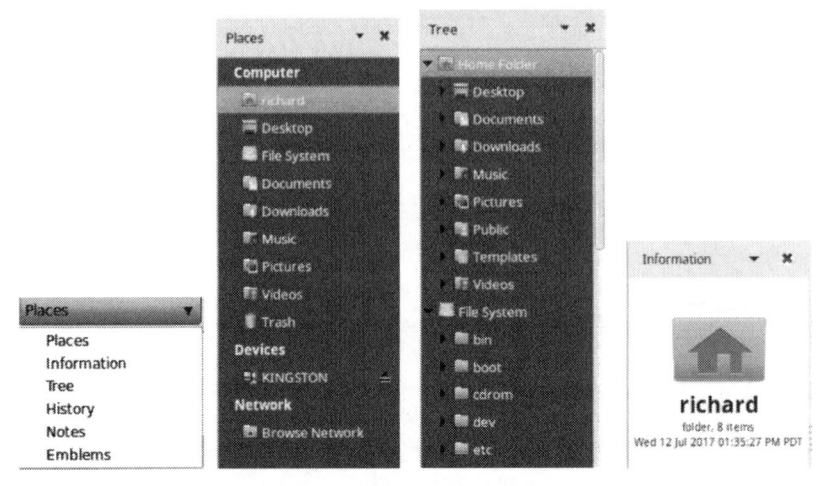

Figure 7-25: File manager side pane menu and views

The default for the side pane is the Places view, which displays sections for Computer, Devices, Bookmarks, and Network items showing your file systems and default home folder sub-folders (see Figure 7-25). You can choose to display or hide the side pane by selecting the "Side Pane" entry in the View menu, or by clicking the close button on the right side of the side pane menu. You can also use F9 to toggle the side pane on and off.

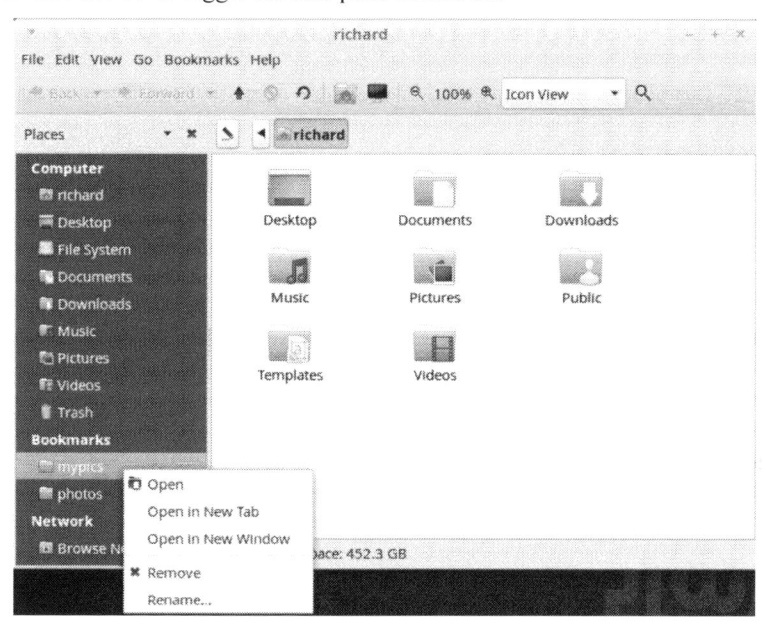

Figure 7-26: File manager side pane with bookmarks menu

Selecting the File System entry in the side pane places you at the top of the file system, letting you move to any accessible part of it. In the Computer section, you can search your default folders, such as Documents and Pictures. Should you bookmark a folder (Bookmarks menu, "Add Bookmark" entry (Ctrl-d)), a Bookmark section appears on the side pane with the bookmark. To remove or rename a bookmark, right-click on its entry in the side pane and choose Remove or Rename from the pop-up menu (see Figure 7-26). The bookmark name changes, but not the original folder name.

Tabs

The Caja file manager supports tabs with which you can open up several folders in the same file manager window. To open a tab, select New Tab from the File menu or press **Ctrl-t**. A tab bar appears with tab icons for each tab, displaying the name of the folder open, and an **x** close button (see Figure 7-27). You can re-arrange tabs by clicking and dragging their tab icons to the right or left. You can also use the Ctrl-PageUp and Ctrl-PageDown keys to move from one tab to another. Use the Shift-Ctrl-PageUp and Shift-Ctrl-PageDown keys to rearrange the tabs. To close a tab, click its close **x** button on the right side of the tab.

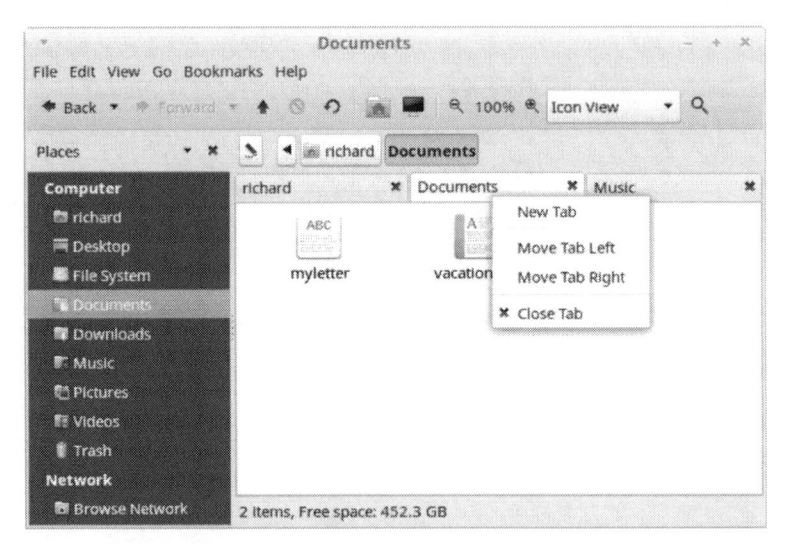

Figure 7-27: File manager window with tabs

Displaying Files and Folders

You can view a directory's contents as icons, a compact list, or as a detailed list, which you can choose from the View menu on the right side of the main toolbar: icon, list, and compact views, as shown here.

Use the control keys to change views quickly: **Ctrl-1** for Icons, **Ctrl-2** for list, and **Ctrl-3** for the compact view. The List view provides the name, size, type, and date. Buttons are displayed for each field across the top of the main pane. You can use these buttons to sort the list according to that field. For example, to sort the files by date, click the Date Modified button; to sort by size, click Size button. Click again to alternate between ascending and descending order.

Certain types of file icons will display previews of their contents. For example, the icons for image files will display a thumbnail of the image. A text file will display in its icon the first few words of its text.

The View menu has entries for managing and arranging your file manager icons (see Table 7-4) (see Figure 7-28). You can choose Icons, List, and Compact views. In the Icon view, the "Arrange items" submenu appears, which provides entries for sorting icons by name, size, type, emblem, and modification date. You can also simply reverse the order, or position icons manually.

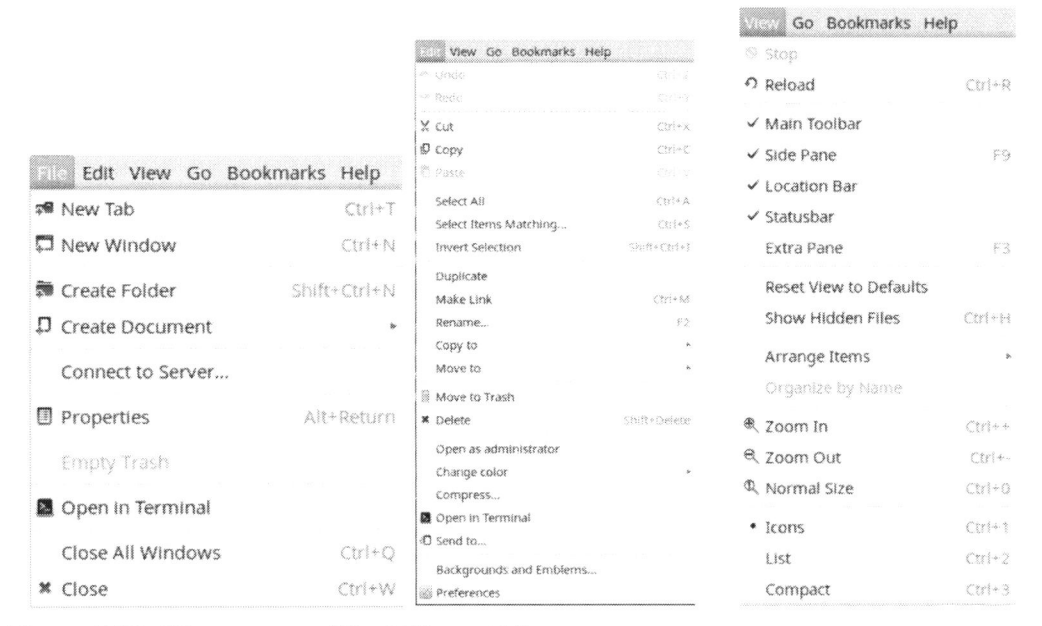

Figure 7-28: File manager File, Edit, and View menus

The View | Zoom In entry enlarges your view of the window, making icons bigger, and Zoom Out reduces your view, making them smaller. Normal Size restores icons to the standard size. You can also use the **Ctrl-+** and **Ctrl--** keys to zoom in and out.

File manager tools and menus

From the Edit menu, you can paste files you have cut or copied to move or copy them between folders, or make duplicates (see Table 7-5 and see Figure 7-28). The selection menu items let you select all files and folders, those matching a simple regular expression, and to invert a selection, choosing all those not selected. On the Files menu, the Properties entry opens the folder properties dialog with Basic and Permissions tabs.

In the icon view, you can click anywhere on the empty space on the main pane of a file manager window to display a pop-up menu with entries to create a new folder, arrange icons, zoom icons, and open the folder properties dialog (see Table 7-4).

Navigating in the file manager

The file manager operates similarly to a Web browser, using the same window to display opened directories. It maintains a list of previously viewed directories, and you can move back and forth through that list using the toolbar navigation buttons (left side). The left arrow button moves you to the previously displayed directory, the right arrow button moves you to the next displayed directory, and the up arrow moves to the parent directory. The home icon opens your home directory, and the computer icon (monitor) opens the Computer window, which lists icons for your file system and removable devices.

Menu Item	Description
Stop	Stop current task
Reload	Refresh file and directory list
Main Toolbar	Displays main toolbar
Side Pane	Displays side pane
Location Bar	Displays location bar
Statusbar	Displays status bar at bottom of folder window
Extra Pane	Display dual panes for file manager window, with separate folders open in each
Reset View to Defaults	Displays files and folders in default view
Show Hidden Files	Show administrative dot files.
Arrange Items: By Name, Size, Type, Modification Date, and Emblems	Arrange files and directory by specified criteria
Organize by Name	Sort icons in Icon view by name
Zoom In	Provides a close-up view of icons, making them appear larger.
Zoom Out	Provides a distant view of icons, making them appear smaller.
Normal Size	Restores view of icons to standard size.
Icons	Displays icons
List	Displays file list with name, size, type, and date. Folders are expandable.
Compact	Displays compact file list using only the name and small icons

Table 7-4: File Manager View Menu

Use the side pane's Places view to access your bookmarked folders, storage devices (USB, CD/DVD disc, and attached hard drives), and mounted network folders. On the Computer section of the side pane, you can access your home folders, trash, the file system (root directory). On the Bookmarks section, you can access any additional bookmarks you created.

To open a subdirectory, you can double-click its icon or right-click the icon and select Open from the menu. You can also open the folder in a new tab or a new window. The Open With submenu lists other possible file managers and applications to open the folder with such as Files (Caja) and Dolphin (KDE). You can also click on the folder to select it, and then choose Open from the File menu (File | Open). The tab, new window, and open with items are also listed when a folder is selected. Figure 7-29 shows the File menu with the different Open items for a folder and the Open With submenu for a file. Table 7-3 lists the File menu options.

Chapter 7: Mate Desktop 243

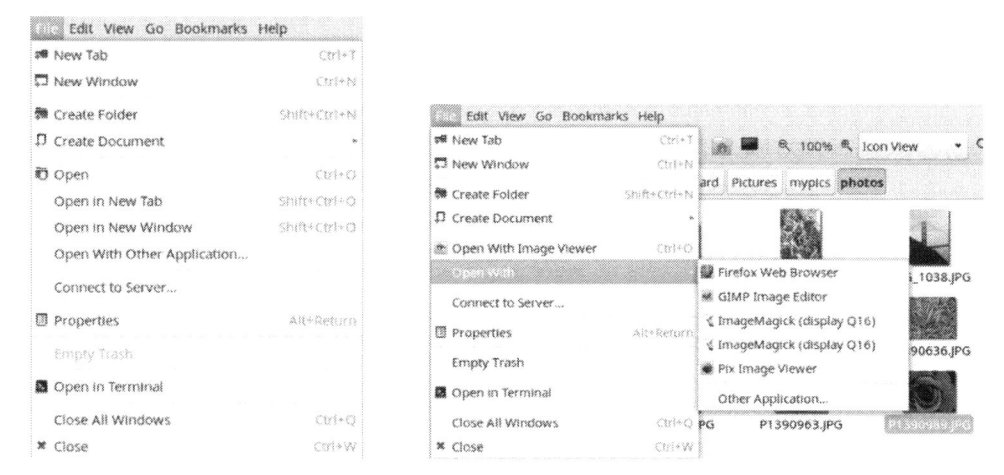

Figure 7-29: File manager File | Open with submenu for folders and files

Menu Item	Description
Cut, Copy	Move or copy a file or directory
Paste	Paste files that you have copied or cut, letting you move or copy files between folders, or make duplicates.
Undo, Redo	Undo or Redo a paste operation
Select All	Select all files and folders in this folder
Select Items Matching	Quick search for files using basic pattern matching.
Invert Selection	Select all other files and folders not selected, deselecting the current selection.
Duplicate	Make a copy of a selected file
Make Link	Make a link to a file or folder
Rename	Rename a selected file or folder
Copy to	Copy a file or folder to one of the default bookmarks
Move to	Move a file or folder to one of the default bookmarks
Move To Trash	Move a file for folder to the trash folder for later deletion
Delete	Delete a file or folder immediately.
Compress	Compress selected files and folders to a compressed archive file such as a tar, cpio, or zip file (Engrampa extension).
Backgrounds and Emblems	Choose a background for the file manager windows. Add emblems to any folder or file in the file manager window.
Preferences	The Caja File Manager preferences for your account.

Table 7-5: File Manager Edit Menu

244 Part 3: Desktops

You can open any folder or file system listed in the side pane Places view by clicking on its folder or bookmark. You can also right-click on a bookmark or folder to display a menu with entries to Open, "Open in a New Tab", and "Open in a New Window" (see Table 7-7). The "Open in a New Window" item is an easy way to access devices from the file manager. The menu for the Trash entry lets you empty the trash. For any bookmark, you can also remove and rename the entry. Entries for removable devices in the sidebar such as USB drives also have menu items for Eject and Safely Remove Drive. Internal hard drives have an Unmount entry instead.

Menu Item	Description
Create Folder	Creates a new subdirectory in the directory.
Create Document	Creates a text document.
Arrange Items: By Name, Size, Type, Modification Date, and Emblems	Arrange files and directory by specified criteria
Organize by Name	Sort icons in Icon view by name
Open in Terminal	Open a terminal window at that folder (Open terminal extension)
Zoom In	Provides a close-up view of icons, making them appear larger.
Zoom Out	Provides a distant view of icons, making them appear smaller.
Normal Size	Restores view of icons to standard size.
Properties	Opens the Properties dialog for the directory

Table 7-6: File Manager Pop-up Menu

Menu Item	Description
Open	Opens the file with its associated application. Directories are opened in the file manager. Associated applications are listed.
Open In A New Tab	Opens a directory in a new tab in the same window.
Open In A New Window	Opens a directory in a separate window, accessible from the toolbar, right-click.
Remove	Remove bookmark from the sidebar.
Rename	Rename a bookmark.

Table 7-7: The File Manager Side Pane Pop-Up Menu

Caja File Manager Search

The Caja file manager provides a search tool that operates the same as the Nemo file manager search. From a file manager window, click the Search button on the toolbar (Looking glass at right), or select Go | Search for Files, to open a Search box below the toolbar. Enter the pattern to search and press ENTER or click the looking glass button on the right side of the text box. The results are displayed.

Drop-down menus for location and file type will appear in the folder window, with + and - buttons for adding or removing location and file type search parameters. Click the plus + button to add more location and file type search parameters. The search begins from the folder opened, but you can specify another folder to search (a Location menu). To search multiple folders at once, click the + button to add a Location menu for each folder, and specify that folder. You can do the same for multiple file types, specifying only files with certain types.

Managing Files and Folders

As a GNOME-compliant file manager, Caja supports desktop drag-and-drop operations for copying and moving files. To move a file or directory, drag-and-drop from one directory to another. The move operation is the default drag-and-drop operation in GNOME. To copy a file to a new location, press the Ctrl key as you drag.

Using a file's pop-up menu

You can also perform remove, rename, and link creation operations on a file by right-clicking its icon and selecting the action you want from the pop-up menu that appears (see Table 7-8). For example, to remove an item, right-click it and select the Move To Trash entry from the pop-up menu. This places it in the Trash directory, where you can later delete it. To create a link, right-click the file and select Make Link from the pop-up menu. This creates a new link file that begins with the term "Link." If you select an archive file, the pop-up menu also displays entries to "Extract Here" and "Extract to" (Engrampa extension).

Renaming Files

To rename a file, you can either right-click the file's icon and select the Rename entry from the pop-up menu or click its icon and press the F2 function key. The name of the icon will be bordered, encased in a small text box. You can overwrite the old one, or edit the current name by clicking a position in the name to insert text, as well as use the backspace key to delete characters. You can also rename a file by entering a new name in its Properties dialog box (Basic tab).

Grouping Files

You can select a group of files and folders by clicking the first item and then hold down the SHIFT key while clicking the last item, or by clicking and dragging the mouse across items you want to select. To select separated items, hold the CTRL key down as you click the individual icons. If you want to select all the items in the directory, choose the Select All entry in the Edit menu (Edit | Select All) (**Ctrl-a**). You can then copy, move, or even delete several files at once. To select items that have a certain pattern in their name, choose Select Items Matching from the tools menu to open a search box where you can enter the pattern (**Ctrl-s**). Use the * character to match partial patterns, as in *let* to match on all filenames with the pattern "let" in them. The pattern **my*** would match on filenames beginning with the "my" pattern, and ***.png** would match on all PNG image files (the period indicates a filename extension).

Opening Applications and Files MIME Types

You can start any application in the file manager by double-clicking either the application itself or a data file used for that application. If you want to open the file with a specific application, you can right-click the file and select one of the Open With entries. One or more Open with entries will be displayed for default and possible application, like "Open with Text Editor" for a text file. If the application you want is not listed, you can select Open with | Other Application to open a dialog listing available applications. Drag-and-drop operations are also supported for applications. You can drag a data file to its associated application icon (say, on the desktop); the application then starts up using that data file.

Menu Item	Description
Open	Opens the file with its associated application. Directories are opened in the file manager. Associated applications are listed.
Open In A New Tab	Opens a folder in a new tab in the same window.
Open In A New Window	Opens a folder in a new window
Open With	Selects an application with which to open the file, or a file manager to use to open a folder.
Cut Copy	Entries to cut and copy the selected file.
Paste into Folder	Paste the selected folder
Make Link	Creates a link to that file in the same directory.
Rename (F2)	Renames the file.
Copy To	Copy a file to the Home Folder, Desktop, or to a folder displayed in another pane in the file manager window.
Move To	Move a file to the Home Folder, Desktop, or to a folder displayed in another pane in the file manager window.
Move To Trash	Moves a file to the Trash directory, where you can later delete it.
Delete	Delete the file or folder permanently
Compress	Archives files (Engrampa extension).
Extract Here Extract To	When an archive is selected, these entries appear (Engrampa extension).
Properties	Displays the Properties dialog.

Table 7-8: The File and Directory Pop-Up Menu

Folders also have an Open With submenu, listing alternative file managers you can use to open the folder, such as Files (Caja) and Dolphin (KDE). Applications that work on folders are also listed such as the Gwenview image manager and the Disk Usage Analyzer.

To change or set the default application to use for a certain type of file, you open a file's Properties dialog and select the Open With tab. Here you can choose the default application to use for that kind of file. Possible applications will be listed with a radio button next to each entry. The default has its radio button turned on. Click the radio button of the one you want to change to the default. Once you choose the default, it will appear in the Open With item for this type of file. If there is an application on the Open With tab you do not want listed in the Open With menu, select it and click the Remove button.

If you want to add an application to the Open With menu, click the "Add" button to open the Add Application dialog, which lists possible applications. Select the one you want and click the Add button. You can use the "Use a custom command" text box to enter a command. The Browse button lets you locate a command.

File and Directory Properties

In a file's Properties dialog, you can view detailed information on a file and set options and permissions (see Figure 7-30). A file's Properties dialog has five tabs: Basic, Emblems, Permissions, Open With, and Notes. Folders do not have an Open With tab. The Basic tab shows detailed information such as type, size, location, and date modified. The type is a MIME type, indicating the type of application associated with it. The file's icon is displayed at the top with a text box showing the file's name. You can edit the filename in the Name text box, changing that name.

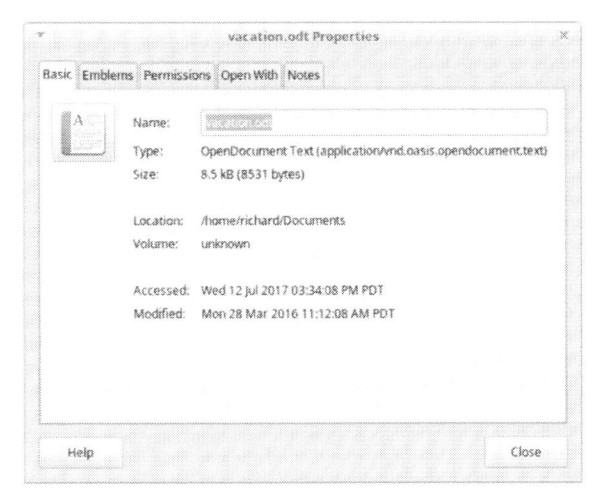

Figure 7-30: File properties on Caja

If you want to change the icon image used for the file or folder, click the icon image (next to the name) to open a Select Custom Icon dialog to browse for the one you want. The **/usr/share/pixmaps** directory holds the set of current default images, though you can select your own images (click **pixmaps** entry in the Places side pane). Click an image file to see its icon displayed in the right pane. Double-click to change the icon image.

The Permissions tab for files shows the read, write, and execute permissions for owner, group, and others, as set for this file. You can change any of the permissions here, provided the file belongs to you. You configure access for the owner, the group, and others, using drop-down menus. You can set owner permissions as Read Only or Read And Write. For group and others, you can also set the None option, denying access. Clicking on the group name displays a menu listing different groups, allowing you to select one to change the file's group. If you want to execute this as an application, you check the "Allow executing file as program" entry. This has the effect of setting the execute permission.

The Open With tab for files lists all the applications associated with this kind of file. You can select the one you want to use as the default. This can be particularly useful for media files, where you may prefer a specific player for a certain file or a particular image viewer for pictures.

Certain kinds of files will have additional tabs, providing information about the file. For example, an audio file will have an Audio tab listing the type of audio file and any other information like a song title or compression method used. An image file will have an Image tab listing the resolution and type of image.

The Permissions tab for folders operates much the same way, but it includes two access entries: Folder Access and File Access. The Folder Access entry controls access to the folder with options for None, List Files Only, Access Files, and Create And Delete Files. These correspond to read, read and execute permissions given to directories. The File Access entry lets you set permissions for all those files in the directory. They are the same as for files: for the owner, Read or Read and Write; for the group and others, the entry adds a None option to deny access. To set the permissions for all the files in the directory accordingly (not just the folder), you click the "Apply Permissions To Enclosed Files" button.

The Share tab for folders allows you to share folders as network shares. If you have Samba or NFS, these will allow your folders and files to be shared with users on other systems. You have the option to specify whether the shared folder or file will be read-only or allow write access. To allow write access check the "Allow other to create and delete files in this folder" entry. To open access to all users, check the Guest access entry.

Caja Preferences

You can set preferences for your Caja file manager in the Preferences dialog, accessible by selecting the Preferences item in any Caja file manager window's Edit menu (Edit | Preferences).

- The Views tab allows you to select how files are displayed by default, such as the list, icon, or compact view. You can set default zoom levels for icon, compact, and list views.

- Behavior lets you choose how to select files, manage the trash, and handle scripts.

- Display lets you choose what added information you want displayed in an icon caption, like the size or date.

- The List Columns tab lets you choose both the features to display in the list view and the order in which to display them. In addition to the already-selected Name, Size, Date, and Type, you can add features such as permissions, group, MIME type, and owner.

- The Preview tab lets you choose whether you want small preview content displayed in the icons, like beginning text for text files.

- The Media tab lets you choose what applications to run for certain media, such as run the VLC media player for DVD videos, or Rhythmbox for audio files.

- Extensions lists extensions installed for Caja.

Control Center

Both Preference and Administration tools can be accessed either from the Linux Mint menu or from the Control Center (see Figure 7-31). You can access the Control Center from the System section on the Linux Mint menu. The Control Center opens a window listing the different applications by section: Administration, Hardware, Internet and Network, Look and Feel, Personal, and Other. Icons for the tools are displayed. Single-click on an icon to open it. The Control Center also has a dynamic search capability. A side pane holds a filter search box and links for the groups.

As you enter a pattern in the Filter search box, matching applications appear at the right. Commonly used applications can be listed under Common Tasks. If you want an application to be started when your system starts, you can right-click on its icon and choose "Add to Startup Programs" to add it directly to the Startup Applications dialog. Several of the tools are administration applications such as Software Manager, Backup Tool, Users and Groups, and Printers. Others are GNOME preferences used for Mate, such as Appearance, About Me, Screensaver, and Keyboard. Others are the same as Cinnamon tools, such as Login Window and Languages.

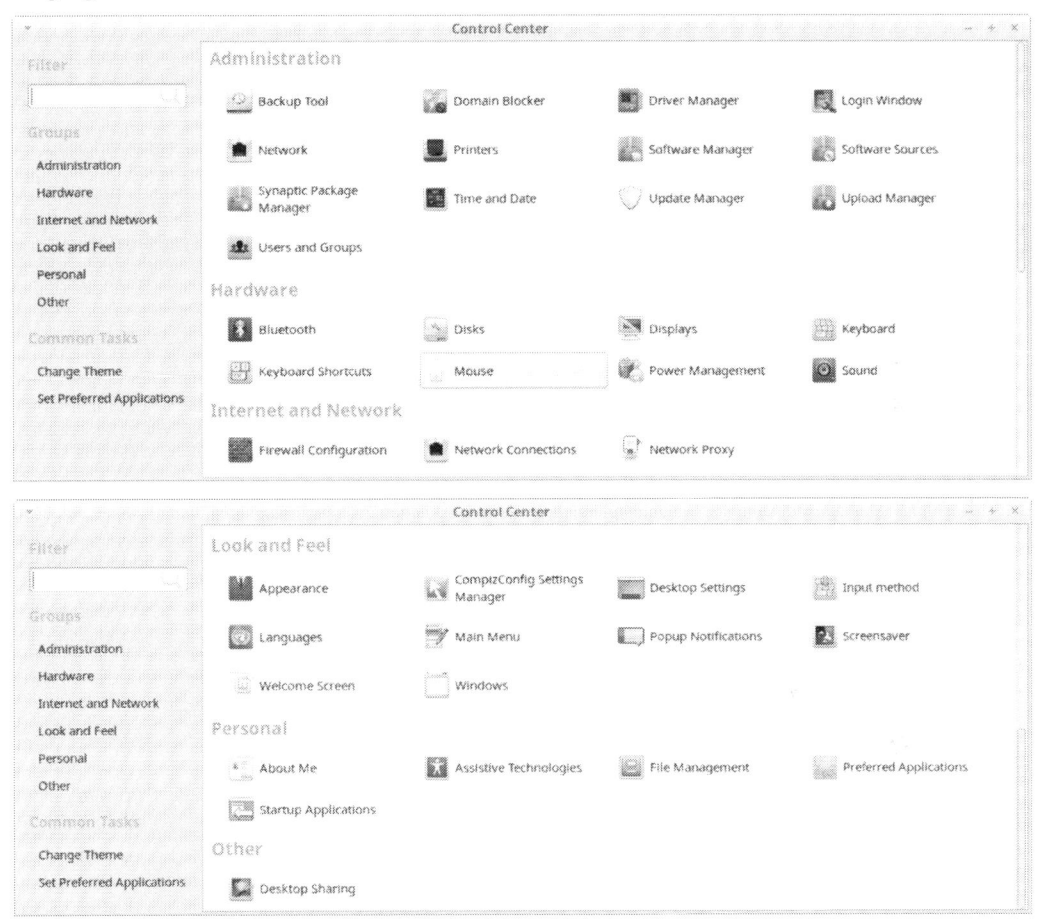

Figure 7-31: GNOME Control Center

Mate Preferences

You can configure different parts of your Mate interface using tools listed in the Preferences menu on the Linux Mint menu, and from the Control Center. Linux Mint provides several tools for configuring your Mate desktop. The Mate preferences are listed in Table 7-9. On some preferences tools, a Help button displays detailed descriptions and examples. Some of the more important tools are discussed here.

The keyboard shortcuts configuration (Keyboard Shortcuts) lets you map keys to certain tasks, like mapping multimedia keys on a keyboard to media tasks like play and pause. Just select the task and then press the key. There are tasks for the desktop, multimedia, and window management. With window management, you can also map keys to perform workspace switching. Keys that are already assigned will be shown.

The Windows configuration (Windows) is where you can enable features like window roll-up (Titlebar Action), window movement key, and mouse window selection.

Preferences	Description
About Me	Personal information like image, addresses, and password.
Assistive Technologies	Enables features like accessible login and keyboard screen.
Appearance	Desktop Appearance configuration: Themes, Fonts, Backgrounds, and Visual Effects.
CompizConfig Settings Manager	Advanced configuration dialog for the GNOME enhanced graphics features, such as 3D windows, animations, and desktop cube workspace switching.
Desktop Settings	Basic settings such as the display of home and computer icons on the desktop, button layout on windows, and showing icons in menus.
Desktop Sharing	Configure access by others to your desktop.
Disk	Opens the GNOME Disks utility.
Displays	Opens the GNOME Monitor Preferences dialog for detecting monitors and setting resolution.
Domain Blocker	Blocks specified domains.
File Management	File Manager options including media handling applications, icon captions, and the default view (also accessible from file manager window, Edit | Preferences).
Keyboard	Configure your keyboard: selecting options, models, and typing breaks, as well as accessibility features like slow, bounce, and sticky keys.
Keyboard Shortcuts	Configure keys for special tasks, like multimedia operations.
Languages	Specify a language, same as Cinnamon.
Login Window	Configure the Login Window for the LightDM display manager, same as Cinnamon.
Main Menu	Add or remove categories and menu items for the Applications, Preferences, and System menus.
Displays	Change your screen resolution, refresh rate, and screen orientation.
Mouse	Mouse and touchpad configuration: select hand orientation, speed, and accessibility.
Network Proxy	Specify proxy configuration if needed: manual or automatic

Monitors	Change your screen resolution, refresh rate, and screen orientation.
Popup Notifications	Placement and display theme for notifications.
Power Management	The GNOME power manager for configuring display, suspend, and shutdown options.
Preferred Applications	Set default Web browser, mail application, music player, and terminal window.
Remote Desktop	Allow remote users to view or control your desktop. Can control access with a password.
Screensaver	Select and manage your screen saver, including the activation time.
Startup Applications	Manage your session with startup programs and save options.
Sound	Configure sound effects, output volume, sound device options, input volume, and sound application settings (Pulseaudio).
Time and Date	Set the time, date, and time zone.
Welcome Screen	Displays the Linux Mint welcome screen with links to the user guide, tutorial, and software manager.
Windows	Enable window abilities like roll up on the title bar, movement key, window selection.

Table 7-9: The Mate Preferences

Mouse and Keyboard Preferences

The Mouse and Keyboard preferences are the primary tools for configuring your mouse and keyboard. Mouse preferences lets you choose its speed, hand orientation, and double-click times. For laptops, you can configure your touchpad, enabling touchpad clicks and edge scrolling (left side). Keyboard preferences shows several tabs for selecting your keyboard model (Layouts), configuring keys (Layouts tab, Options button), repeat delay (General tab), and enforcing breaks from power typing as a health precaution (Typing Break) (see Figure 7-32).

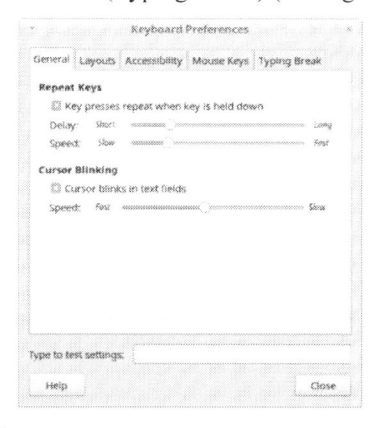

Figure 7-32: Keyboard Preferences

To configure your sound devices you use the Sound Preferences tool (Sound), see Chapter 9. Mate uses sound themes to specify an entire set of sounds for different effects and alerts.

Configuring your personal information

To set up personal information, including the icon to be used for your graphical login, you use the About Me preferences tool. You can access it from the Linux Mint menu Preferences menu (Preferences | About Me) and from the GNOME Control Center. The About Me preferences dialog lets you change your password (see Figure 7-33) and the icon or image used to represent the user. Should you want to change your password, you can click on the Change Password button to open a change password dialog.

Clicking on the image icon opens a browser window where you can select a personal image. The **faces** directory is selected by default, which displays several images. The selected image displays at the right on the browser window. For a personal photograph, you can select the Picture folder. This is the Pictures folder on your home directory. Should you place a photograph or image there, you could then select if for your personal image. The image will be used in the login screen when showing your user entry.

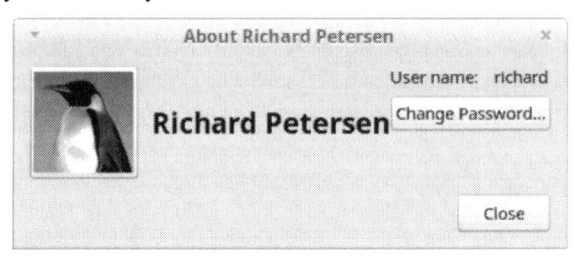

Figure 7-33: About Me information: Preferences | About Me

Appearance

Several appearance-related configuration tasks are combined into the Appearance Preferences dialog (Preferences | Appearance, or Appearance icon on the Control Center's Personal section). You can change your theme, background image, or configure your fonts. The Appearance dialog shows four tabs: Theme, Background, Fonts, and Interface (see Figure 7-11). On the Interface tab, you can choose to show icons in menus and labels on toolbar buttons.

Desktop Themes

You use the Themes tab on the Appearance Preferences dialog to select or customize a theme. Themes control your desktop appearance. The Themes tab will list icons for currently installed themes (see Figure 7-34). The icons show key aspects or each theme such as window, folder, and button images, in effect previewing the theme for you.

The Linux Mint custom theme is initially selected. You can move through the icons to select a different theme if you wish. If you have downloaded additional themes from **https://www.gnome-look.org/**, you can click the install button to locate and install them. Once installed, the additional themes will also be displayed in the Theme tab. If you download and install a theme or icon set from the Linux Mint repository, it will be automatically installed for you.

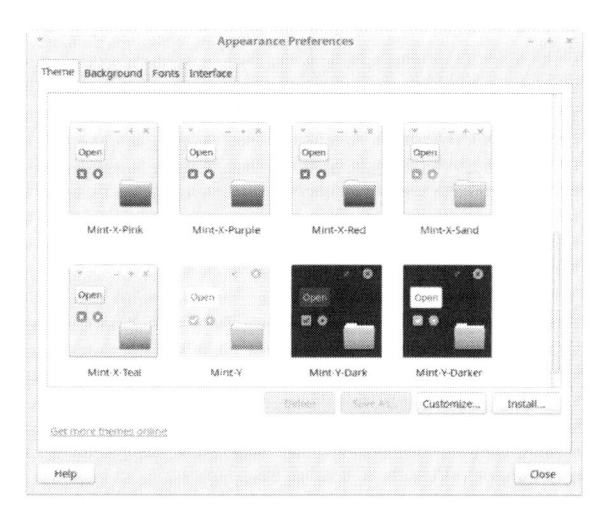

Figure 7-34: Selecting GNOME themes

The true power of Themes is shown its ability to let users customize any given theme. Themes are organized into five components: controls, colors, window border, icons, and pointer. Controls covers the appearance of window and dialog controls like buttons and slider bars. Window border lets you choose title bars, borders, window buttons sets. Icons lets you choose different icon sets. Pointers provides different pointer sets to use. Colors lets you choose the background and text color for windows, input boxes, selections, and tool tips. You can even download and install separate components like specific icon sets, which you can then use in a customized theme.

Clicking the Customize button opens a Customize Theme dialog with tabs for different theme components. The components used for the current theme are selected by default. The Colors tab lets you set the background and text colors for windows, input boxes, and selected items. In the Controls, Window Border, and Icons tabs you will see listings of the different themes. You can then mix and match different components from those themes, creating your own customized theme, using window borders from one theme and icons from another. Upon selecting a component, your desktop changes automatically showing you how it looks. If you have added a component, like a new icon set, it also is shown.

Once you have created a new customized theme, a Custom Theme icon appears in the list on the Theme tab. To save the customized theme, click the Save As button. This opens a dialog where you can enter the theme name, any notes, and specify whether you also want to keep the theme background.

Customized themes and themes installed directly by a user are placed in the **.themes** directory in the user's home directory. Should you want these themes made available for all users, you can move them from the **.themes** directory to the **/usr/share/themes** directory. In a terminal window run a **cp** command as shown here for the **mytheme** theme. The operation requires administrative access (**sudo**).

```
sudo cp -r .themes/mytheme  /usr/share/themes
```

You can do the same for icon sets you have downloaded. Such sets will be installed in the user's **.icons** directory. You can then copy them to the **/usr/share/icons** directory to make them available to all users.

Desktop Background

You use the Background tab on the Appearance Preferences tool to select or customize your desktop background image (see Figure 7-35). You can also access the Background tab by clicking the desktop background and select Change Desktop Background from the desktop menu. Installed backgrounds are listed here, with the current background selected. To add your own image, either drag-and-drop the image file to the Background tab or click on the Add button to locate and select the image file. To remove an image, select it and click the Remove button.

From the Style drop-down menu, you can choose display options such as Zoom, Centered, Scaled, Tiled, or Fill Screen. A centered or scaled image will preserve the image proportions. Fill screen may distort it. Any space not filled, such as with a centered or scaled images, will be filled in with the desktop color. From the Colors drop-down menu, you can set the desktop color to a solid color, horizontal gradient, or vertical gradient. Click on the color button next to the Colors drop-down menu to open a "Pick a Color" dialog where you can select a color from a color wheel. For gradients, two color buttons are displayed for selecting a color at each end of the gradient.

Initially, only the Linux Mint/Ubuntu backgrounds are listed. Install the **gnome-background** package to add a collection of GNOME backgrounds. To download more backgrounds, click the "Get more backgrounds online" link.

Figure 7-35: Choosing a desktop background, System | Preferences | Appearance

Fonts

On the Font tab, you can change font sizes, select fonts, and configure rendering options (see Figure 7-36). Fonts are listed for Applications, Documents, Desktop, Window title, and Fixed width. Click on a font button to open a "Pick a Font" dialog where you can select a font, choose its style (regular, italic, or bold), and change its size. You can further refine your font display by clicking the Details button to open a window where you can set features like the dots-per-inch, hinting, and smoothing.

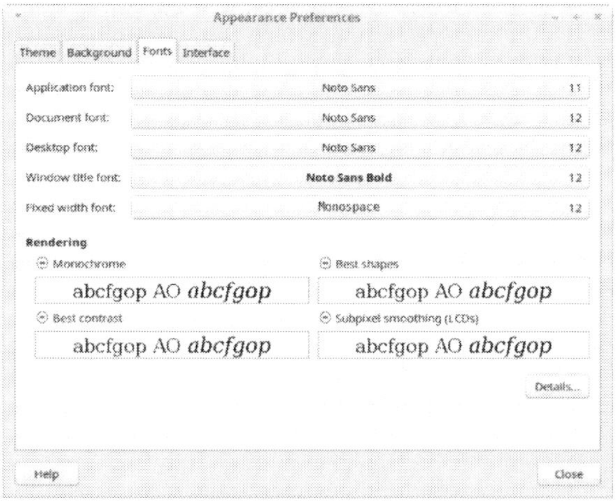

Figure 7-36: Fonts

With very large monitors and their high resolutions becoming more common, one feature users find helpful is the ability to increase the desktop font sizes. On a large widescreen monitor, resolutions less than the native one tend not to scale well. A monitor always looks best in its native resolution. With a large native resolution text sizes become so small they are hard to read. You can overcome this issue by increasing the font size. The default size is 10; increasing it to 12 makes text in all desktop features like windows and menus much more readable.

Configuring Fonts

To refine your font display, you can use the font rendering features. Open the Fonts tab on the Appearance tool. In the Font Rendering section are basic font rendering features like Monochrome, Best contrast, Best shapes, and Subpixel smoothing. Choose the one that works best. For LCD monitors choose subpixel smoothing. For detailed configuration, click the Details button. Here you can set Smoothing, Hinting (anti-aliasing), and Subpixel color order features. The Subpixel color order is hardware dependent.

On Mate, clicking on a font button in the Fonts Preferences tool will open a "Pick a Font" dialog that lists all available fonts. You can also generate a listing by using the **fc-list** command. The list will be unsorted, so you should pipe it first to the sort command. You can use **fc-list** with any font name or name pattern to search for fonts, with options to search by language, family, or styles.

```
fc-list | sort
```

Adding Fonts

Numerous font packages are available on the Linux repositories. When you install the font packages, the fonts are installed automatically on your system and ready for use. True type font packages begin with **ttf-** prefix. Microsoft true type fonts are available from the **ttf-mscorefonts-installer** package. Fonts are installed in the **/usr/share/fonts** directory. This directory will have subdirectories for different font collections like **truetype** and **X11**. You can install fonts manually yourself by copying fonts to the **/user/share/fonts** directory (use the **sudo** command). For dual-boot systems, where Windows is installed as one of the operating systems, you can copy fonts directly from the Windows font directory on the Windows partition (which is mounted in **/media**) to **/usr/share/fonts**.

Mate Power Management

For power management, Mate uses the Mate Power Manager, **mate-power-manager**, which makes use of Advanced Configuration and Power Interface (ACPI) support provided by a computer to manage power use. The Mate Power Manager can display an icon on the panel showing the current power source, a battery or plugin (lightning). Clicking on the battery icon displays a menu showing the power charge of your wireless devices, both your laptop and any other wireless devices like a wireless mouse.

The Mate Power manager is configured with Power Management Preferences (**mate-power-preferences**), accessible from Preferences | Power Management, and by right clicking on the Mate Power Management panel icon and selecting Preferences from the pop-up menu (also on the GNOME Control Center | Hardware section). Power Manager preferences can be used to configure both a desktop and a laptop.

For a desktop, two tabs appear on the Power Management Preferences window, On AC Power and General. The AC Power tab offers two sleep options, one for the computer and one for the display screen. You can put each to sleep after a specified interval of inactivity. On the General tab, you set desktop features like actions to take when you press the power button or whether to display the power icon.

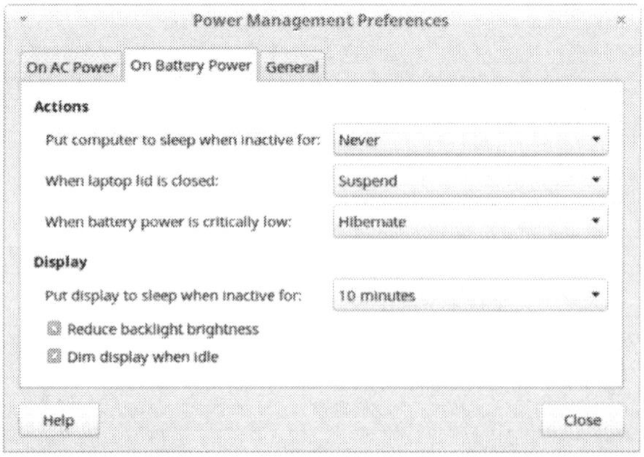

Figure 7-37: Mate Power Manager

Display of the Power Management icon on the panel is configured on the General tab. In the Notification Area section, you can set options to never display, always display the icon, displaying the icon when the battery is low, or when it is charging or discharging, or only if there is a battery. The default is to display the icon only when a battery is present.

Note: The Mate Power Manager will not only check the power level of a laptop battery, but also the power level of other battery wireless devices, like the battery of a wireless mouse or keyboard.

A laptop will also have an On Battery Power tab where you can set additional options for the battery and display, such as shutting down if the battery is too low, or dimming the display when the system is idle (see Figure7-37). The laptop On AC Power tab will also have an Actions option for actions to take when the laptop lid is closed, like suspend, hibernate, and shutdown.

To see how your laptop or desktop is performing with power, you can use Power statistics. This is accessible from the System Tool menus as Power Statistics. The Power Statistics window will display a sidebar listing your different power devices. A right pane will show tabs with power use information for a selected device. The Laptop battery device will display three tabs: Details, History, and Statistics. The History tab will show your recent use, with graph options for Time to empty (time left), Time to full (recharging), Charge, and Rate. The Statistics tab can show charge and discharge graphs.

Preferred Applications for Web, Mail, Accessibility, and terminal windows

Certain types of files will have default applications already associated with them. For example, double-clicking a Web page file will open the file in the Firefox Web browser. If you prefer to set a different default application, you can use the Preferred Applications tool (see Figure 7-38). You access the Preferred Applications tool from the Preferences menu (Preferences | Preferred Applications), and from the GNOME Control Center (Personal section). This tool will let you set default applications for Web pages, mail readers, accessibility tools, multimedia and office applications, and the system-level tools. Available applications are listed in popup menus. In Figure 7-38 the default mail reader is Thunderbird, and the default Web browser is Firefox. To make another application the default, click on the menu button to display a list of other possible installed applications. The Preferred applications tool has tabs for Internet, Multimedia, System, Office, and Accessibility. On the Multimedia tab, you can select default image viewer, video player, and multimedia player. On the Office tab, you can specify the default document viewer, word processor, and spreadsheet applications. On the System tab, you can choose the default text editor, terminal window application, and file manager. The Accessibility panel has options for selecting a magnifier.

Figure 7-38: Preferred Applications tool

Default Applications for Media

Caja directly handles preferences for media operations. You set the preferences using the File Management Preferences dialog. It is accessible from the Edit | Preferences menu item on any Caja file manager window, from the Linux Mint menu Preferences menu as File Management, or from the Control Center as File Management (in the Personal section).

The Media tab of the File Management Preferences dialog lists entries for Cd Audio, DVD Video, Music Player, Photos, and Software. Pop-up menus let you select the application to use for the different media (see Figure 7-39). You also have options for Ask what to do, Do Nothing, and Open folder. The Open Folder options will just open a window displaying the files on the disc. A segment labeled "Other media" lets you set up an association for less used media like Blu-Ray discs. Initially, the "Ask what to do" option will be set for all entries. Possible options are listed for each drop down menu, like Rhythmbox Music Player for Cd Audio discs and Movie Player (Totem) for DVD Video. Photos can be opened with the Pix Photo-manager. Once you select an option, when you insert removable media, like a CD Audio discs, its associated application is automatically started.

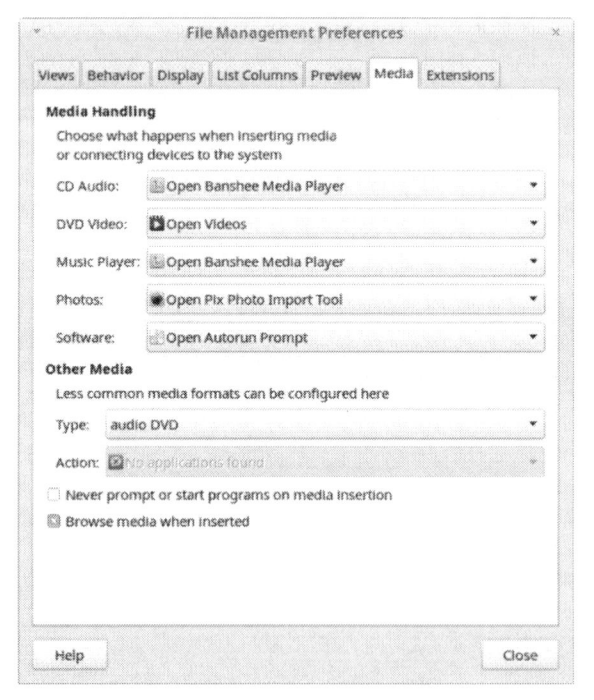

Figure 7-39: File Management Preferences for Media

If you just want to turn off the startup for a particular kind of media, you can select the Do Nothing entry from its application pop-up menu. If you want to be prompted for options, then set the "Ask what to do" entry in the Media tab's pop-up menu. When you insert a disc, a dialog with a pop-up menu for possible actions is displayed. The default application is already selected. You can select another application or select the Do Nothing or Open Folder options.

You can turn the automatic startup off for all media by checking the box for "Never prompt or start programs on media insertion" at the bottom of the Media panel. You can also enable the option "browse media when inserted" to just open a folder showing its files.

Screen Saver and Lock

With the Screensaver Preferences, you can control when the computer is considered idle and what screen saver to use if any (see Figure 7-40). You can access the Screensaver Preferences dialog from the Linux Mint menu Preferences menu as Screensaver, or from the Control Center in the Personal section. You can choose from various screen savers, using the scroll box to the left, with a preview displayed at the right. You can also control whether to lock the screen or not, when idle and for how long. You can turn off the Screensaver by unchecking the "Activate screensaver when computer is idle" box.

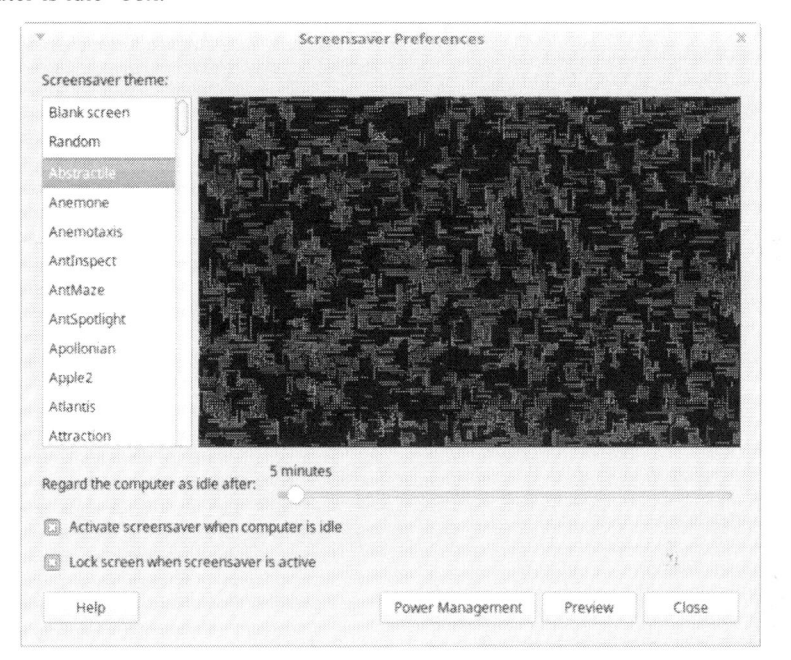

Figure 7-40: Screensaver Preferences

Assistive Technologies

On Mate, the Assistive Technologies dialog is a simple set of buttons for accessing accessibility tabs for other tools (see Figure 7-41). In the Assistive Technologies section, use the "Enable assistive technologies" checkbox to turn assistive technologies on and off. The Preferred Applications button opens the Accessibility tab on the Preferred Applications dialog.

In the Preferences section, there are buttons to open the accessibility tabs for the keyboard and mouse preferences dialogs. On the keyboard accessibility tab, you can configure features such as sticky, slow, and bound keys. The mouse button simply opens the mouse preferences dialog.

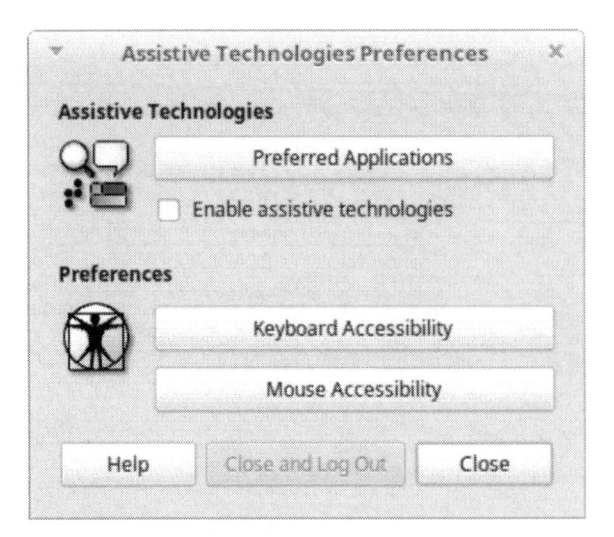

Figure 7-41: Assistive Technologies Preferences

8. KDE Linux Mint (KDE)

The KDE Desktop

Kickoff menu

KDE Network Manager

Plasma

Dashboard

Activities

KWin: Desktop Effects

KDE File Manager: Dolphin

KDE System Settings

KDE Directories and Files

The K Desktop Environment (KDE) includes the standard desktop features, such as a window manager and a file manager, as well as an extensive set of applications that cover most Linux tasks. The KDE version of Linux Mint is called Linux Mint KDE and is available as a separate Desktop DVD, and as the **mint-meta-kde** meta-package on Software Manager and the Synaptic Package Manager. The KDE desktop is developed and distributed by the KDE Project. KDE is open source software provided under a GNU Public License and is available free of charge along with its source code. KDE development is managed by the KDE Core Team.

Numerous applications written specifically for KDE are accessible from the desktop. These include editors, photo and image applications, sound and video players, and office applications. Such applications usually have the letter *K* as part of their name, for example, KMail. On a system administration level, KDE provides several tools for managing your system, such as Discover Software and the Muon Package Manager, and the KDE system monitor. KDE applications also feature a built-in Help application.

Web Site	Description
https://www.kde.org	KDE website
https://www.linux-apps.com	KDE software repository
https://docs.kde.org	KDE documentation site
https://www.qt.io/	Site for the Qt company
http://store.kde.org	KDE desktop themes, select KDE entry
https://mail.kde.org/mailman/listinfo/	KDE mailing lists

Table 8-1: KDE Websites

KDE, initiated by Matthias Ettrich in October 1996, is designed to run on any Unix implementation, including Linux, Solaris, HP-UX, and FreeBSD. The official KDE website is **https://www.kde.org**, which provides news updates, download links, and documentation. Several KDE mailing lists are available for users and developers, including announcements, administration, and other topics. Detailed documentation for the KDE desktop and its applications is available at **https://docs.kde.org**. A great many additional applications are currently available for KDE at **https://www.linux-apps.com**. Development support can be obtained at the KDE Techbase site at **https://techbase.kde.org**. Most applications are available on the Mint/Ubuntu repositories and can be installed directly from Discover Software, the Muon Package Manager, the Synaptic Package Manager, and GNOME Software. Various KDE websites are listed in Table 8-1. KDE uses as its library of GUI tools the Qt library, currently developed and supported by the QT company, owned by Digia (**https://www.qt.io**). It provides the Qt libraries as Open Source software that is freely distributable, though a commercial license is also available.

KDE Plasma 5

The KDE Plasma 5 release is a major reworking of the KDE desktop. KDE Plasma 5.8 is included with the Linux Mint 18.2 distribution. Check the Linux Mint and KDE sites for detailed information on KDE 5.

https://www.kde.org/announcements/plasma5.0/

For features added with KDE Plasma 5.5, check:

https://www.kde.org/announcements/plasma-5.5.0.php

For features added with KDE Plasma 5.6 (current Linux Mint KDE edition), check:

https://www.kde.org/announcements/plasma-5.8.0.php/

KDE development is organized into a plasma and applications releases. The plasma release covers the desktop interface (the Plasma desktop shell), and the applications release covers KDE applications. Plasma has containments and plasmoids (also called widgets). Plasmoids operate similarly to applets, small applications running on the desktop or panel. Plasmoids operate within containments. On KDE 5, there are two Plasma containments, the panel and the desktop. In this sense, the desktop and the panel are features of an underlying Plasma operation. They are not separate programs. Each has their own set of plasmoids.

Each containment has a toolbox for configuration. The desktop has a toolbox at the top left corner, and panels will have a toolbox on the right side. The panel toolbox includes configuration tools for sizing and positioning the panel. KDE also supports Activities, multiple plasma desktop containments, each with their own set of active plasmoids (widgets) and open windows.

KDE Linux Mint 18.2

The KDE Linux Mint edition of Linux Mint installs KDE as the primary desktop from the KDE Linux Mint install disc. KDE Linux Mint 18.2 officially supports and installs KDE Plasma 5.8. The latest features included with KDE Linux Mint 18.2 are discussed at:

https://www.linuxmint.com/rel_sonya_kde_whatsnew.php

For repository configuration, Linux Mint KDE adds an **ubuntu-defaults.list** file in the **/etc/apt/sources.list.d** directory which accesses the Kubuntu backports repository. Kubuntu is the Ubuntu version of KDE. The latest upgrades to Kubuntu applications and libraries are installed directly from this backports repository.

Installing KDE Linux Mint

You can download the KDE Linux Mint discs from the KDE Linux Mint site at:

https://www.linuxmint.com/download.php

You can also add KDE Linux Mint as a desktop to a Linux Mint installation. KDE includes numerous packages. Instead of trying to install each one, you should install KDE using its metapackage on Software Manager: **mint-meta-kde**.

You will be prompted to keep the LightDM display manager for logins, though you can change to SDDM the Simple Desktop Display Manager. Once installed, KDE will then become an option you can select from the Sessions menu on the Login screen as "KDE Plasma Workspace."

If you are installing KDE Linux Mint from the KDE Linux Mint DVD, you will follow the same steps as those used for the Linux Mint DVD: language, keyboard, partition (Disk Setup), time zone, user and hostname (User Info). Installation will begin as soon as you choose the partition configuration. The artwork will be different, but the tasks will be the same. The "Installation type" screen (partitioning) lets you choose a default general, LVM, disk encryption, or manual partitioning. The initial install screen has options for Start KDE Linux Mint, Check disc for defects, Test memory, and boot from first hard disk.

Note: KDE Linux Mint has its own multimedia package, mint-meta-codecs-kde, for multimedia codecs.

SDDM

KDE Linux Mint uses the Simple Desktop Display Manager (SDDM) to manage logins. A login greeter is displayed at the center of the screen where you can select a user icon and enter a password (see Figure 8-1). Suspend, Restart, Shutdown, and Different User buttons are displayed below the login button. Use the Different User button to login as a user not displayed in the user list.

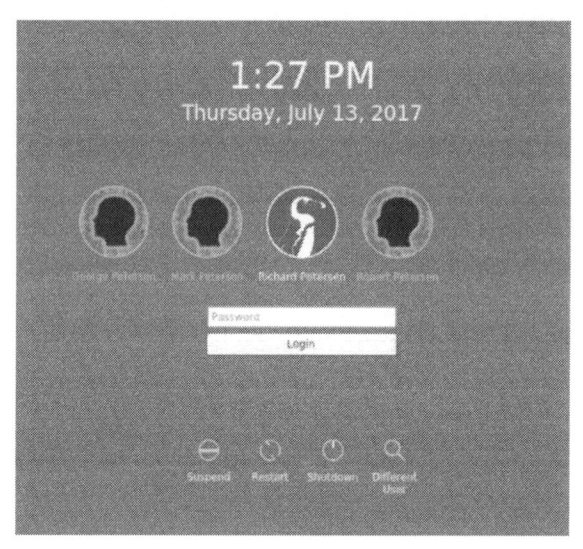

Figure 8-1: SDDM Display Manager, login screen

Upon choosing a user icon and entering the password, press ENTER or clicking the login button at the right end of the password text box. Your KDE session then starts up.

If you have more than one desktop installed on your system, such as Cinnamon, Mate, or Xfce, then a "Desktop Session Plasma" menu is displayed on the lower left corner of the screen. Use this menu to choose a different desktop to login to. The KDE desktop is called Plasma.

You can change the theme of the login greeter using the Login Screen (SDDM) tab in the Startup and Shutdown dialog (System Settings | Startup and Shutdown in the Workspace section). The theme section lists available theme. Currently, only Breeze is listed. To change the background image, click on a theme to display it in the Customize section to the right. Then click on the Background icon and choose the "Load from file" option from the pop-up menu. On the Advanced tab, you can choose the default user, the desktop for your session, and whether to automatically log in. You can also choose a cursor theme and an alternative desktop (session). You can also manually configure SDDM using the **/etc/sddm.conf** file.

The KDE Desktop

One of KDE's aims is to provide users with a consistent integrated desktop (see Figure 8-2). KDE provides its own window manager (KWM), file manager (Dolphin), program manager, and desktop and panel (Plasma). You can run any other X Window System–compliant application, such as Firefox, in KDE, as well as any GNOME application. In turn, you can also run any KDE application, including the Dolphin file manager in GNOME. The KDE 5 desktop features the Plasma desktop shell with new panel, menu, widgets, and activities. Keyboard shortcuts are provided for many desktop operations, as well as plasmoid (widget) tasks (see Table 8-2).

Keys	Description
Alt-F1	Kickoff menu
Alt-F2	Krunner, command execution, entry can be any search string for a relevant operation, including bookmarks and contacts, not just applications.
up/down arrows	Move among entries in menus, including Kickoff and menus
left/right arrows	Move to submenus menus, including Kickoff and Quick Access submenus menus
ENTER	Select a menu entry, including a Kickoff or QuickAccess
PageUp, PageDown	Scroll up fast
Alt-F4	Close current window
Alt-F3	Window menu for current window
Ctrl-Alt -F6	Command Line Interface
Ctrl-Alt -F8	Return to desktop from command line interface
Ctrl-r	Remove a selected widget
Ctrl-s	Open a selected widget configuration's settings
Ctrl-a	Open the Add Widgets window to add a widget to the desktop
Ctrl-l	Lock your widgets to prevent removal, adding new ones or changing settings
Alt-Tab	Cover Switch or Box Switch for open windows
Ctrl-F8	Desktop Grid
Ctrl-F9	Present Windows Current Desktop
Ctrl-F10	Present Windows All Desktops
Ctrl-F11	Desktop Cube for switching desktops

Table 8-2: Desktop, Plasma, and KWin Keyboard Shortcuts

To configure your desktop, you use the System Settings dialog (Computer| System Settings), which lists icons for dialogs such as Workspace Theme, Font, Icons, Applications Style Desktop Behavior, Search, Application Style, Window Management, Driver Manager, and

Bluetooth. Workspace Theme lets you choose desktop, cursor, and splash themes. Desktop Behavior is where you can set desktop effects and virtual desktops. Windows Management controls window display features like window switchers, title bar actions, and screen edge actions.

The desktop supports drag-and-drop and copy-and-paste operations. With the copy-and-paste operation, you can copy text from one application to another. You can even copy and paste from a Konsole terminal window.

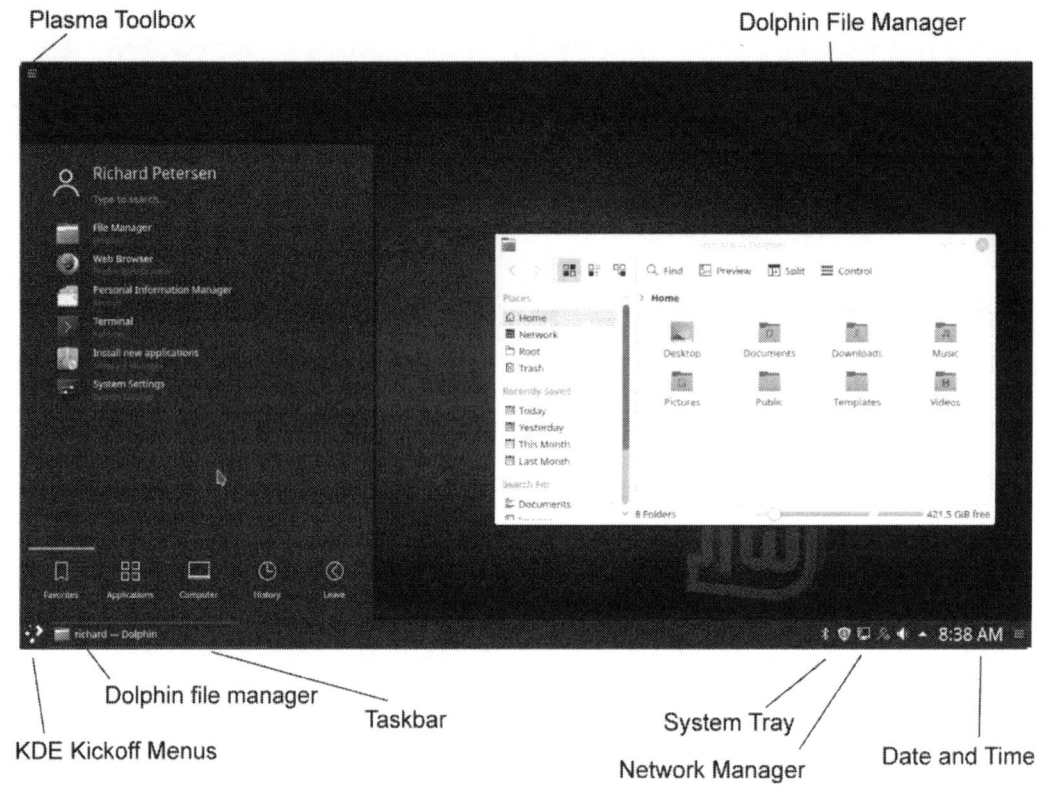

Figure 8-2: The KDE desktop

The KDE Help Center

The KDE Help Center provides a browser-like interface for accessing and displaying both KDE Help files and Linux Man and info files (see Figure 8-3). It may not be installed by default. Install the **khelpcenter** package. The same documentation is available at **https://docs.kde.org**. You can start the Help Center by searching for "help" in the search box of the Kickoff Applications menu. The Help window displays a sidebar that holds two tabs, one listing contents and one providing a glossary. The main pane displays currently selected document. A help tree on the contents tab in the sidebar lets you choose the kind of Help documents you want to access. Here you can choose KDE manuals, Man pages (UNIX manual pages), or info documents (Browse info Pages), or even application manuals (Application Manuals). Online Help provides links to KDE websites such as the KDE user forum and the KDE tech base sites. Click the "Table of Contents" button to open a listing of all KDE help documents, which you can browse through and click on to open.

A navigation toolbar enables you to move through previously viewed documents. KDE Help documents contain links you can click to access other documents. The Back and Forward buttons move you through the list of previously viewed documents. The KDE Help system provides an effective search tool for searching for patterns in Help documents, including Man and info pages. Click the Find button on the toolbar or choose the Find entry from the Edit menu, to open a search box at the bottom of the Help window where you can enter a pattern to search on the current open help document. The Options menu lets you refine your search with regular expressions, case sensitive queries, and whole words-only matches.

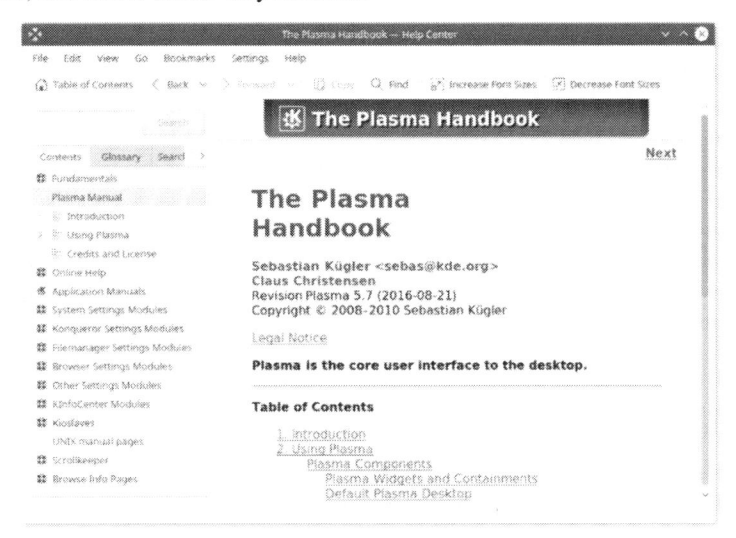

Figure 8-3: KDE Help Center

Desktop Backgrounds (Wallpaper)

The background (wallpaper) is set from the desktop menu directly. Right-click on the desktop to display the desktop menu and then select Desktop Settings to open the Desktop Settings dialog (see Figure 8-4).

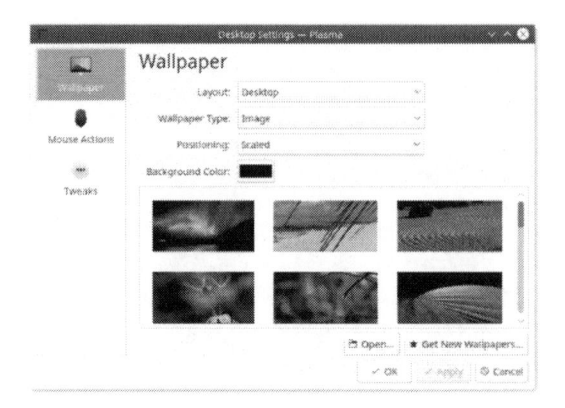

Figure 8-4: Default Desktop Settings, wallpaper

You can also select Desktop Settings from the activities menu in the upper left corner of the desktop. The background is called wallpaper in KDE and can be changed in the Wallpaper tab. You can select other wallpapers from the wallpaper icons listed or select your own image by clicking the Open button.

You can add more wallpaper by clicking the "Get New Wallpaper" button to open a "Get Hot New Stuff" dialog, which lists and downloads wallpaper posted on the **www.kde-look.org** site (see Figure 8-5). Each wallpaper entry shows an image, description, and rating. Buttons at the upper right of the dialog let you view the entries in details (list) or icon mode. You can refine the wallpaper listing by size (category), newest, rating, and popularity (most downloads). Click the Install button to download the wallpaper and add it to your Desktop Setting's Wallpaper tab. The wallpaper is downloaded and the Install button changes to Uninstall. To remove a wallpaper, you can select installed wallpapers to find the entry quickly. You can also search by pattern for a wallpaper.

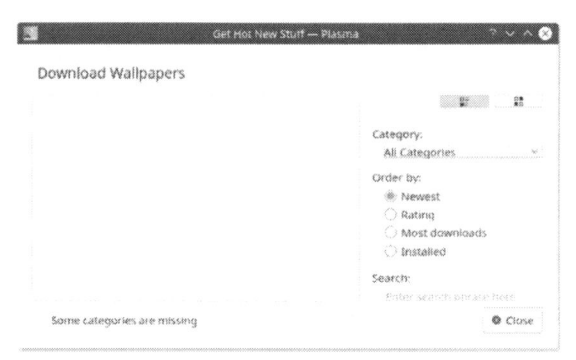

Figure 8-5: Default Desktop Settings, Get New Wallpapers

Themes

For your desktop, you can also select a variety of different themes, icons, and window decorations. A theme changes the entire look and feel of your desktop, affecting the appearance of desktop elements, such as scrollbars, buttons, and icons. Themes and window decorations are provided for workspaces. Access the System Settings dialog from the KDE Kickoff Computer menu or the Applications | Settings menu. On the System Settings dialog, click the Workspace Theme icon in the "Appearance" section. The Workspace Theme dialog lets you choose overall look and feel, cursor themes, desktop themes, and a splash screen (startup) themes. The Desktop Themes tab lists installed themes, letting you choose the one you want. Click the Get New Themes button to open a Get Hot New Stuff dialog, listing desktop themes from **https://store.kde.org** (see Figure 8-6). Click a theme's Install button to download and install the theme.

For window decorations, you use the Application Style dialog, Window Decorations tab, where you can select window decoration themes. Click the Get New Decorations button to download new decorations. Icons styles are chosen using the Icons dialog, Icons tab, where you can choose the icon set to use, and even download new sets (Get New Themes).

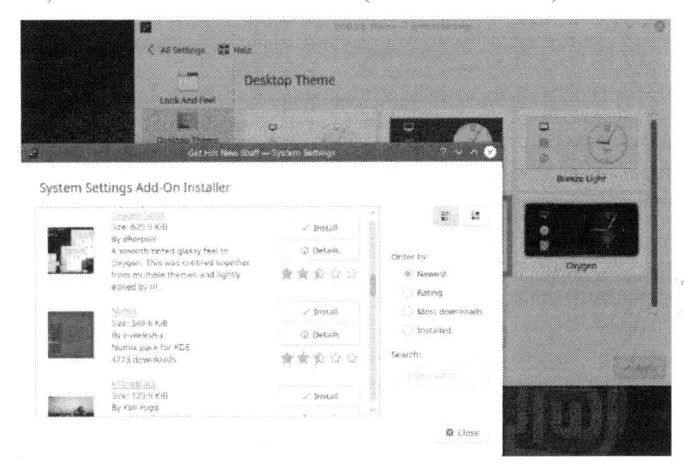

Figure 8-6: System Settings | Workspace Theme | Desktop Theme, Get New Themes

Leave KDE

To leave KDE, click the Leave tab on the KDE Kickoff menu (see Figure 8-7). Here you will find options to log out, lock, switch user, suspend, shutdown, and restart. There are Session and System sections. The Session section has entries for Logout, Lock, and Switch User. The System section lists the system-wide operations: Shut Down, Reboot, Hibernate, and Suspend. When you select a leave entry, a dialog for that action appears on the desktop, which you then click. The Shut Down entry will display the Shutdown and Logout dialog with the Shutdown button selected (see Figure 8-8). The Logout option displays the same dialog with the Logout button selected. The Switch User option displays a dialog with the currently logged in users to choose from, along with a plus button for a new login.

270   Part 3: Desktops

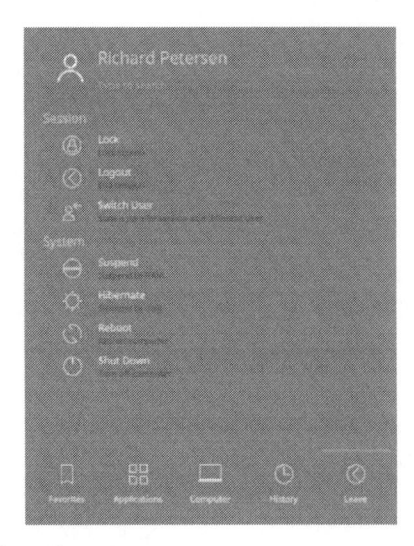

Figure 8-7: The Kickoff Menu Leave

The Lock, and Switch User display manager (SSDM) screens display both a button for the current user and a plus button for starting a new session (Switch User shows the icon for the user you selected). The new session button displays the login screen with its list of users to log in as.

If you logout and more than one user is logged in from a prevous Swith User operation, then the Log Out display manager screen will show a logged in user button and a plus button. Use the plus button to display the main login screen.

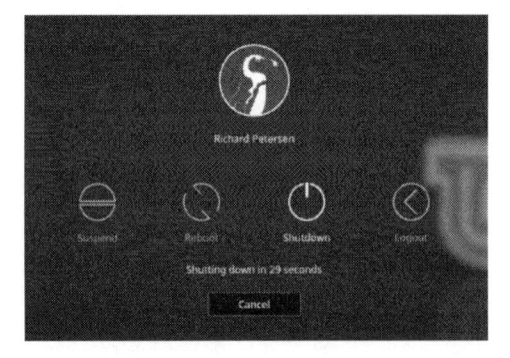

Figure 8-8: Shutdown and Logout dialog

If you have installed the Application Dashboard widget, you can click the logout, shutdown, and restart button on the lower left. For a complete selection choose the Power/Session category on the right (see Figure 8-9).

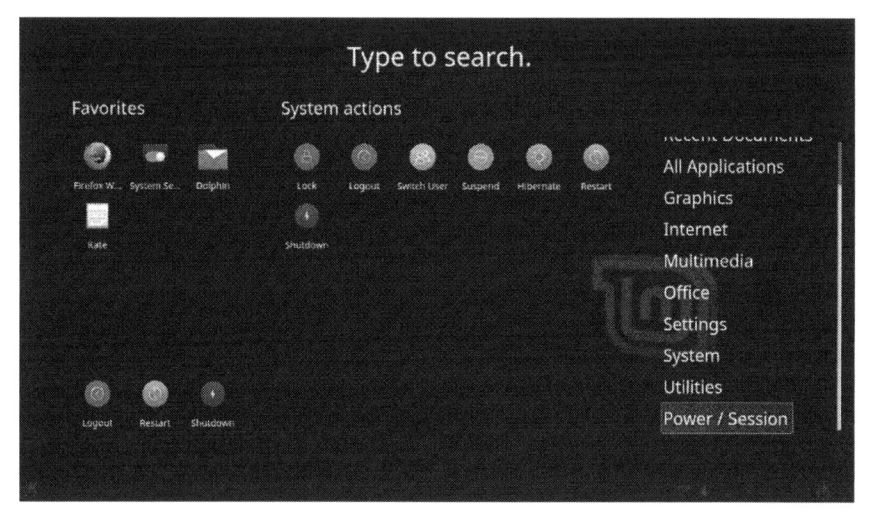

Figure 8-9: The Application Dashboard Menu Power/Session

You can also either press your computer's power button or right-click anywhere on the desktop and select the Leave entry from the pop-up menu, to open a leave dialog with the Logout button selected, as shown here. Buttons to the left let you choose between the suspend, resboot, and shutdown operations.s

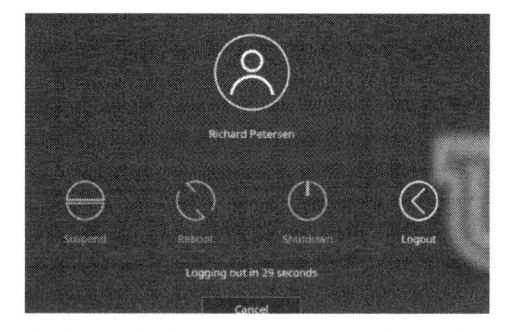

If you just want to lock your desktop, you can select the Lock Screen entry (Lock on the Kickoff and Application Dashboard menus), and your screen saver will appear. To access a locked desktop, click on the screen and a box appears prompting you for your login password. When you enter the password, your desktop re-appears.

KDE Kickoff menus

The Kickoff application launcher (see Figure 8-10) organizes menu entries into tabs that are accessed by icons at the bottom of the Kickoff menu. There are tabs for Favorites, Applications, Computer, History, and Leave. You can add an application to the Favorites tab by right-clicking on the application's Kickoff entry and selecting Add to Favorites. To remove an application from the Favorites menu, right-click on it and select Remove from Favorites. The Applications tab shows application categories. Click the Computer tab to list all your fixed and removable storage. The History tab shows previously accessed documents and applications. Kickoff also provides a Search box where you can search for a particular application instead of paging through menus. As you move through sub-tabs, they are listed at the top of the Kickoff menu, below the search box, allowing you to move back to a previous tab quickly. Click on a tab name to move directly to that tab.

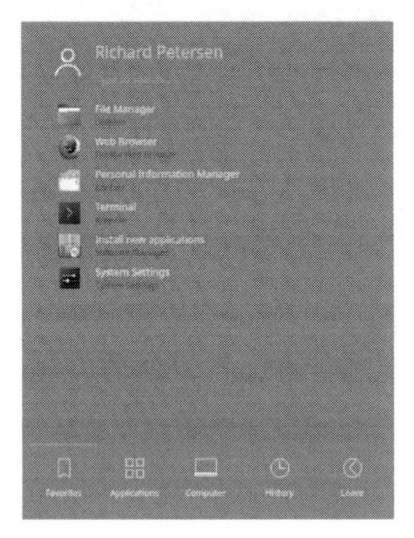

Figure 8-10: The Kickoff Menu Favorites

The Computer menu has Applications, Places, and Removable Storage sections (see Figure 8-11). The Applications section has an entry for System Settings and Run Command (Krunner). The Places section is similar to the Places menu in GNOME, with entries for your home folder, root folder, network, and the trash. The root folder is the same as the system folder on GNOME, the top level directory in the Linux file system. The Removable Storage section shows removable devices like USB drives and DVD/CD discs.

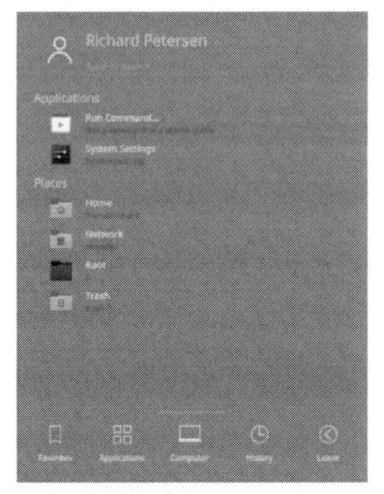

Figure 8-11: The Kickoff Menu Computer

The Applications menu has most of the same entries as those found on GNOME (see Figure 8-12). You can find entries for categories such as Internet, Graphics, and Office. These menus list both GNOME and KDE applications you can use. However, some of the KDE menus contain entries for alternate KDE applications, like KMail on the Internet menu. Other entries will invoke the KDE version of a tool, like the Terminal entry in the System menu, which will invoke the KDE terminal window, Konsole. There is no Preferences menu.

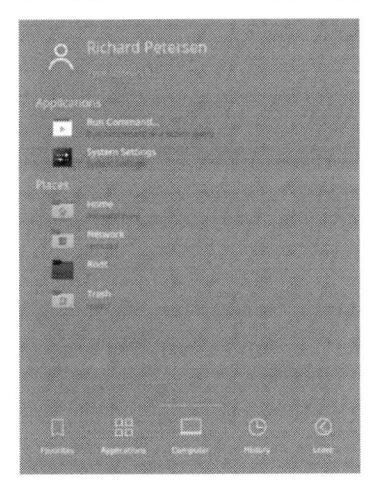

Figure 8-12: The Kickoff Menu Applications

KDE Application Dashboard menus

You can install the Application Dashboard as a desktop or panel widget. The Applications Dashboard menu launcher displays menu entries on a full-screen dashboard, showing sections for applications, favorites, logout/shutdown options, and categories (see Figure 8-13). Press the Esc key to leave the dashboard without making a selection. You can add an application to the Favorites section by right-clicking on the application's icon and selecting Add to Favorites. To remove an application from the Favorites section, right-click on it and select Remove from Favorites. The Applications section shows categories to the right. and the icons for a selected category to the left. There are also categories for recent applications and documents. The Power/Section category lists the complete set of leave options, including lock, suspend, and new session. The All Applications category lists all your applications under alphabetic headings (see Figure 8-14).

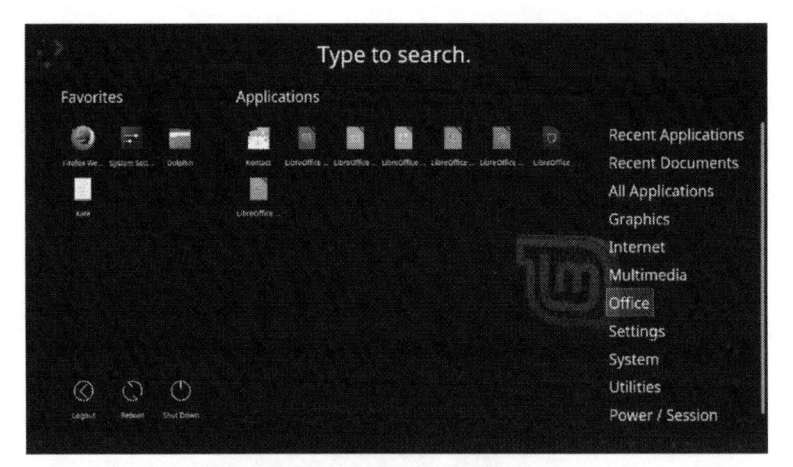

Figure 8-13: The Application Dashboard Menu: Office

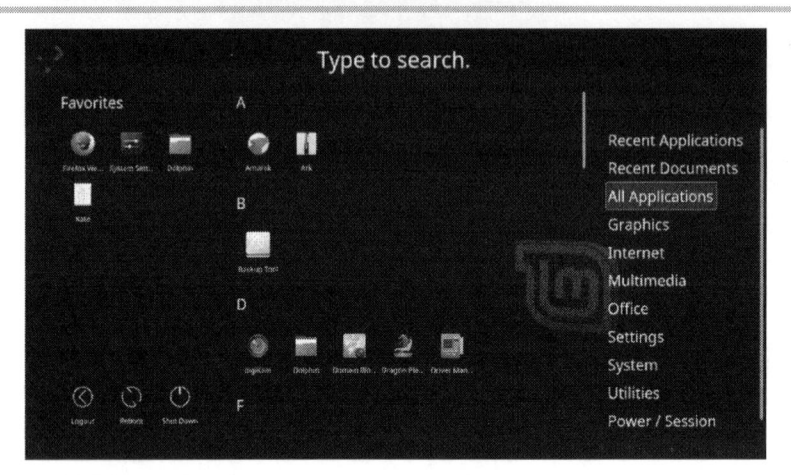

Figure 8-14: Application Dashboard Menu: All Applications

Krunner

For fast access to applications, bookmarks, contacts, and other desktop items, you can use Krunner. The Krunner widget operates as a search tool for applications and other items. To find an application, enter a search pattern and a listing of matching applications is displayed. Click on an application entry to start the application. You can also place an icon (application launcher) for an entry on the desktop by simply clicking and dragging its entry for the list to the desktop. For applications where you know the name, part of the name, or just its basic topic, Krunner is a very fast way to access the application. To start Krunner, press Alt-F2, Alt-space, or right-click on the desktop to display the desktop menu and select "Run Command." Enter the pattern for the application you want to search for and press enter. The pattern "software" or "package" would display both an entry for Discover Software and the Muon Package Manager (if installed). Entering the pattern "office" displays entries for all the LibreOffice applications (see Figure 8-15).

Clicking the settings button at the left opens the Configure Search dialog, which lists plugins for searching applications, widgets, and bookmarks, as well as providing capabilities such a running shell commands, opening files, and spell checking. The Clear History button deletes earlier search results. You can also configure Krunner search using the Plasma Search tab on System Settings Search (Workspace section).

Figure 8-15: Krunner application search

Removable Devices: Device Notifier

Installed on the system tray to the right is the Device Notifier. When you insert a removable device like a CD/DVD disc or a USB drive, the New Device Notifier briefly displays a dialog showing all your removable devices, including the new one. The Device Notifier icon is displayed on the system tray. You can click on the New Device Notifier any time to display this dialog. Figure 8-16 shows the New Device Notifier displayed on the panel and its panel icon. The New Device Notifier is displayed only if at least one removable device is attached.

Removable devices are not displayed as icons on your desktop. Instead, to open the devices, you use the New Device Notifier. Click on the Device Notifier icon in the panel to open its dialog. The device is unmounted initially with an unmount button displayed. Click on this button to mount the device. An eject button is then displayed which you can later use to unmount and eject the device. Opening the device with an application from its menu will mount the device automatically. Clicking on the eject button for a DVD/CD disc will physically eject it. For a USB drive, the drive will be unmounted and prepared for removal. You can then safely remove the USB drive.

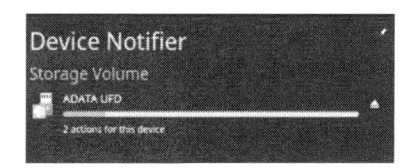

To open a device, click on its entry in the Device Notifier, like one for your DVD/CD disc or your USB drive (see Figure 8-16).

Removable media are also displayed on the File manager window's side pane. You can choose to eject removable media from the file manager instead of from the Device Notifier by right-clicking on the removable media entry, and select "Safely remove" from the popup menu.

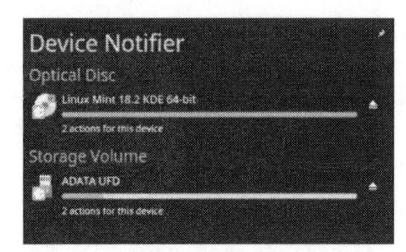

Figure 8-16: Device Notifier and its panel widget icon

KDE Network Connections: Network Manager

On KDE, the Network Manager plasma widget provides panel access for Network Manager. This is the same Network Manager application but adapted to the KDE interface. The widget icon image changes for wireless only and wired connections. Clicking on the widget icon in the panel opens a dialog listing your current available wireless and wired connections. When you pass the mouse over an active connection, a Disconnect buttons appear (see Figure 8-17). For entries not connected, Connect buttons are displayed. To rescan your available connections, click the rescan button (circle) located to the right of the "Available connections" heading. Clicking on a connected entry opens tabs for Speed and Details (see Figure 8-18).

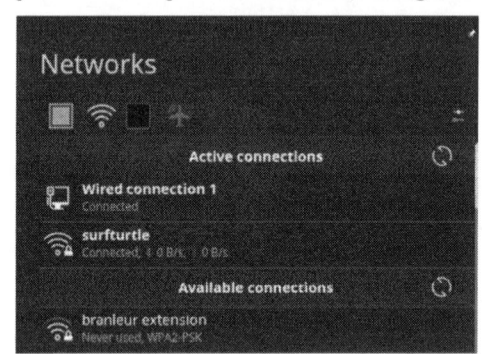

Figure 8-17: Network Manager connections and panel icons.

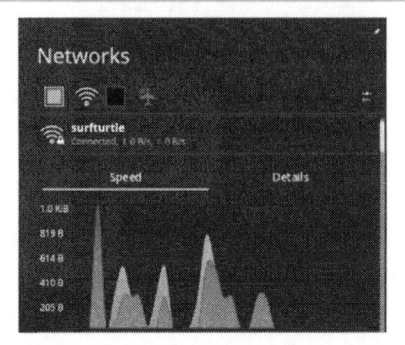

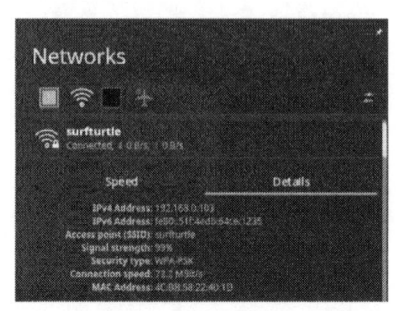

Figure 8-18: KDE Network Manager connection information: speed and details.

The toolbar at the top of the network plasma widget has buttons for wireless and airplane mode connections (shown below). Checkboxes next to each connection icon show if it is enabled. Clicking on the checkbox for a connection will enable or disable the connection. Disabled connections have an empty checkbox and a red icon.

You can use the "Connection editor" to configure your established connections. Either click the settings button on the right side of the toolbar at the top of the network dialog or right-click on the network dialog to display a menu where you can choose "Configure Network Connections." The Connection editor then opens, which lists your connections (see Figure 8-19). Select a connection and then click the Edit button on the toolbar to open the Network Manager editor for KDE, with the same General, Wired, Security, and IPv tabs for a wired or wireless connections as described in Chapter 15 (see Figure 8-17). To add a new connection manually, click the Add button on the Connection editor to display a menu for different connection types.

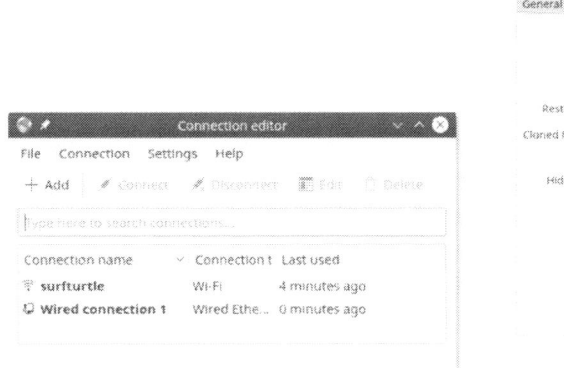

Figure 8-19: KDE connection editor and KDE Network Manager

Desktop Plasmoids (Widgets)

The KDE desktop features the Plasma desktop that supports plasmoids. Plasmoids are integrated into the desktop on the same level as windows and icons. Just as a desktop can display windows, it can also display plasmoids. Plasmoids can take on desktop operations, running essential operations, even replacing, to a limited extent, the need for file manager windows. The name for plasmoids used on the desktop is widgets. The tools and commands on the desktop that manage plasmoids, refer to them as widgets. For that reason, they will be referred to as widgets.

Managing desktop widgets

When you long click (click and hold for several seconds) your mouse on a widget, its sidebar is displayed with buttons for resizing, rotating, settings, and removing the widget (see

278 Part 3: Desktops

Figure 8-18). Click and drag the resize button to change the widget size. Clicking the settings button opens that widget's settings dialog (see Figure 8-20).

To move a widget, long click on it to display its sidebar and while holding the click, drag the icon to the position you want.

Figure 8-20: Clock Widget with task sidebar and configuration dialog

To add a widget (plasmoid) to the desktop, right-click anywhere on the desktop and select Add Widgets from the pop-up menu. This opens the Widgets dialog at the left side of the desktop that lists widgets you can add (see Figure 8-21). Clicking on the Categories button opens a pop-up menu with different widget categories like Date and Time, Online Services, and Graphics. Double-click or drag a widget to the desktop to add it to the desktop. You can enter a pattern to search for a widget using the search box located at the top of the dialog.

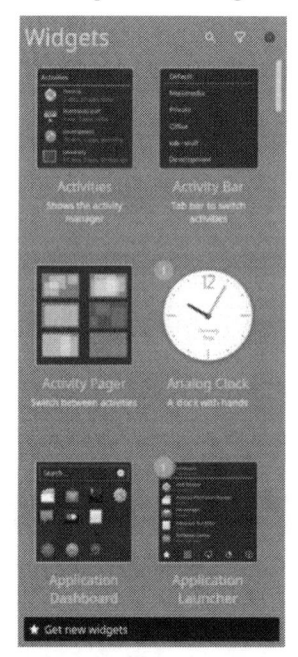

Figure 8-21: Adding a widget: Widgets dialog

To remove a widget, long click on the widget to display its toolbar, and then click on the red Remove button at the bottom of the toolbar. When you remove a widget, a notification message is displayed with an Undo button, as shown here. Clicking on the Undo button will restore the widget.

Figure 8-22 shows the folder, digital clock, notes, calculator, and cpu monitor widgets. The desktop folder widget is just a folder widget set initially to the desktop folder.

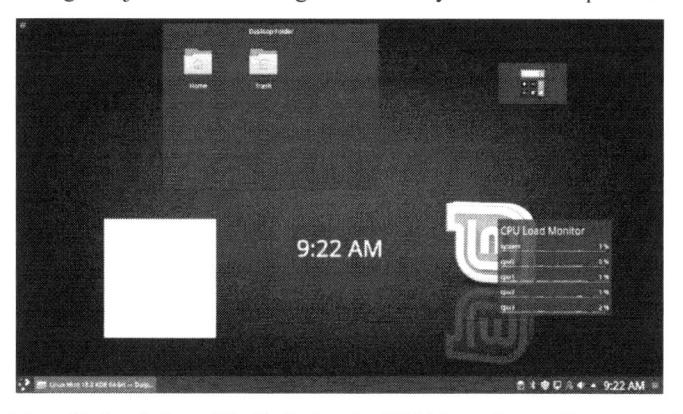

Figure 8-22: Folder, Calculator, Digital clock, CPU Load monitor, and Notes widgets.

Folder and Icon Widgets

You can place access to any folders on the desktop by simply dragging their icons from a file manager window to the desktop (see Figure 8-23). A small menu will appear that includes options for the Icon and Folder widgets. The Folder option sets up a Folder widget for the folder showing icons for subfolders and files. The Icon entry creates an Icon widget, as shown here.

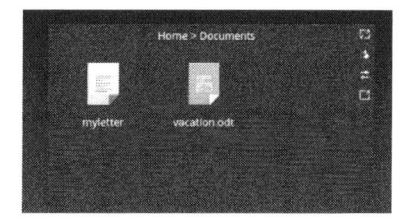

Figure 8-23: Folder and Icon widgets.

For any Folder widget, you can use that widget's settings dialog to change the folder it references. A Folder widget has options for showing the desktop folder, a folder on your Places list, or a specific folder. You can also specify a title. You can easily create a Folder widget for your home folder.

Activities

KDE is designed to support multiple activities. Activities are different plasma containments, each with its set of widgets. An activity is not the same as virtual desktop. Virtual desktops affect space, displaying additional desktops. An activity has its own set of widgets (widgets) and windows, displaying a different set of widgets and windows for each activity. In effect, each activity has a different desktop and set of virtual desktops. Technically, each activity is a Plasma containment that has its own collection of widgets and windows. You can switch to a different activity (containment) and display a different collection of widgets and windows on your desktop.

An activity if often tailored for a certain task. You could have one activity for office work, another for news, and yet another for media. Each activity could have its own set of appropriate widgets, like clock, calculator, notes, and folder widgets for an office activity. A media activity might have a Media Player widget and media applications open.

Multiple activities are managed using the Activities Manager, which is accessed through the Activities entry on the desktop toolbox menu or the Activities widget, which you can install on the panel or desktop. Both are shown here.

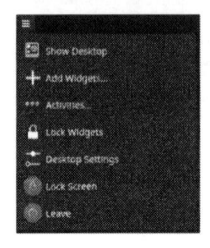

Files and folders can be attached to an activity, displaying them only on that activity. Right-click on the folder or file icon in the File Manager, and choose the Activities submenu to choose an activity. Windows are set by default to display on the activity they are opened on. The window switcher is configured to work only on the current activity. The setting is configured in the Window Management dialog (Workspace section of the System settings dialog). On the Task Switcher tab, the 'Filter windows by" section has Activities checked and Current activity selected.

To add an activity, click the "Activities" entry in the toolbox or desktop menus. If you have added and Activities widget to the panel, you can click the Activities button. The Activities Manager is displayed listing your activities on the left side of the screen (see Figure 8-24). A default activity icon for your desktop will already be displayed. Click the Create Activity button (plus button) to add a new activity. A "Create a new activity" window opens with entries for the name and description (see Figure 8-25). Click on the Icon image to open a dialog where you can choose an icon for your activity. On the Other tab, you can choose not track usage and to set up a keyboard shortcut for the activity. Click the Create button to add the new activity. An activity entry then appears on the Activity Manager. To switch to another activity, click its icon.

Note: If you cannot add activities, install the kactivitymanagerd package.

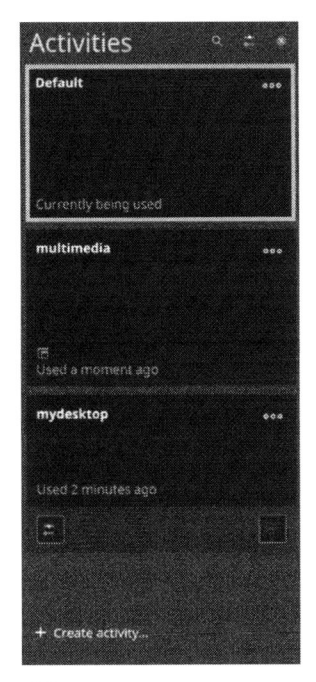

Figure 8-24: Activity toolbar and icons

Moving the mouse over an activity icon displays Configure and Stop buttons. The Configure button opens the "Activity settings" dialog for that activity, which is the same as the create dialog, with Name, description, and icon settings. The Stop button deactivates the activity and places it at the bottom of the Activity Manager under the "Stopped activities" heading. To start a stopped activity, simply click its icon in the "Stopped activities" list.

To remove an activity, first stop it, then move your mouse over the activity icon in the Stopped activities section (see Figure 8-26). A remove button appears to the right of the activity entry. Click it to remove the activity. You are prompted to confirm the deletion.

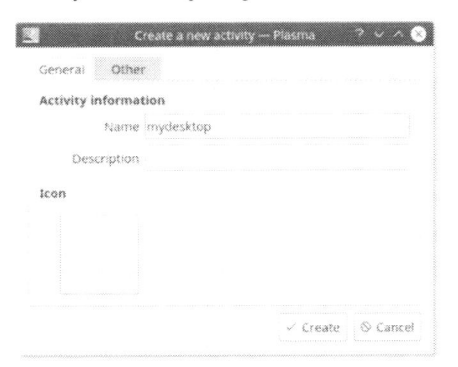

Figure 8-25: Create an activity

To add widgets to an activity, first, click the activity to make it the current activity, and then click the Add Widgets button to display the Widgets dialog. Widgets you add are placed in the current activity.

To switch from one activity to another, first, display the Activities Manager by choosing Activities from the desktop toolbox menu (right-click on desktop) or the Activates button on the panel (if installed). Then click on the activity icon you want. The new Activity becomes your desktop (see Figure 8-27). To change to another activity, open the Activities Manager again, and click the activity icon you want. Your original desktop is the first icon (Default).

Figure 8-26: stop Activity icons

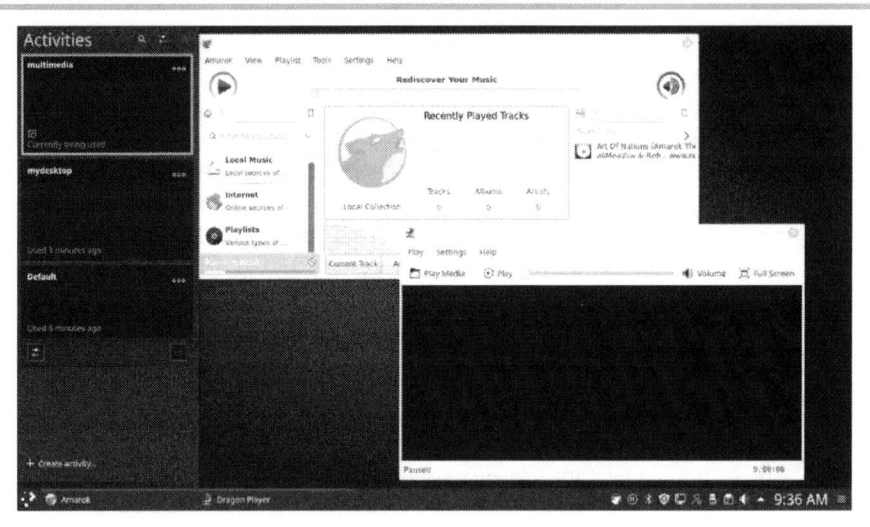

Figure 8-27: Activity Manager and screen of selected activity

To move easily between activities, you can add the Activity bar widget, either to the panel or to the desktop. On the panel, the Activity bar displays buttons for each activity. Click to move to a different activity. On the desktop, the Activity bar displays a dialog with an arrow button for moving from one activity to another.

KDE Windows

A KDE window has the same functionality you find in other window managers and desktops. You can re-size the window by clicking and dragging any of its corners or sides. A click-and-drag operation on a side extends the window in that dimension, whereas a corner extends both height and width at the same time. The top of the window has a title bar showing the name of the window, the program name in the case of applications, and the current directory name for the file manager windows. The active window has the title bar highlighted. To move the window, click the title bar and drag it where you want. Right-clicking the window title bar displays a pop-up menu with entries for window operations, such as minimize, maximize, and moving the window to a different desktop or activity. The More Actions submenu includes closing or resizing the window, the shade option to roll up the window to the title bar, and full screen. Within the window, menus, icons, and toolbars for the particular application are displayed.

You can configure the appearance and operation of a window by selecting the Window Manager Settings from the More Actions submenu in the Window menu (right-click the title bar). Here you can set appearance (Window Decoration), button and key operations (Actions), the focus policy, such as a mouse-click on the window or just passing the mouse over it (Focus), and how the window is displayed when moving it (Moving). All these features can be configured also using the System Setting's Window Behavior tool in the Workspace section.

Opened windows are shown as buttons on the KDE taskbar located on the panel. The taskbar shows buttons for the different programs you are running or windows you have open. This is essentially a docking mechanism that lets you change to a window or application by clicking its button. When you minimize a window, it is reduced to its taskbar button. You can then restore the window by clicking its taskbar button. A live thumbnail of a window on the taskbar is displayed as your mouse passes over its taskbar button, showing its name, desktop, and image.

Taskbar buttons also function as progress bars, showing the progress of copy and download operations. Music and video players also show basic multimedia controls, such as pause, start, next, and previous.

To the right of the title bar are three small buttons for minimizing, maximizing, or closing the window (down, up, and x symbols). You can switch to a window at any time by clicking its taskbar button. You can also maximize a window by dragging it to the top edge of the screen.

From the keyboard, you can use the ALT-TAB key combination to display a list of current open windows. Holding down the ALT key and sequentially pressing TAB moves you through the list.

A window can be displayed as a tile on one-half of the screen. Another tile can be set up for a different window on the other side of the screen, allowing you to display two windows side by side on the full screen (see Figure 8-28). You can tile a window by dragging it to the side of the screen (over the side edge to the middle of the window). A tile outline will appear. Add a second tile by moving a window to the other side edge. You can add more windows to a tile by moving them to that edge. Clicking on a window's taskbar button will display it on its tile.

The same process works for corners. You can tile a window to a corner by moving it to that corner. You can then have four tiled windows open at each corner. You could even have server windows open on the same corner, displaying the one you want by clicking its taskbar icon.

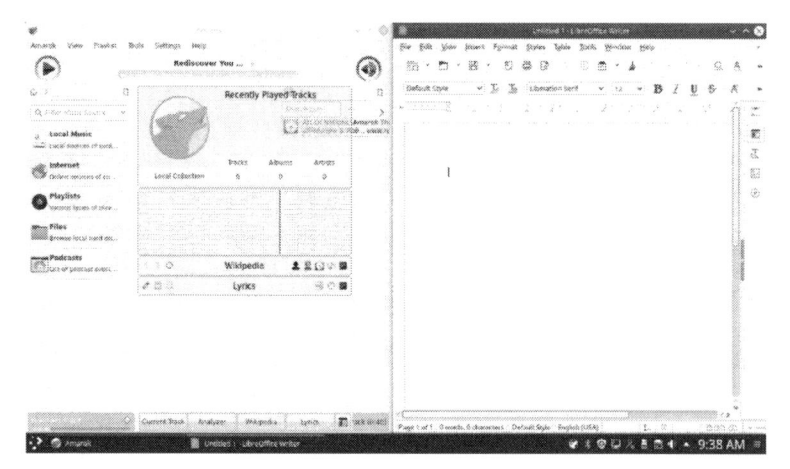

Figure 8-28: Window tiles

Applications

You can start an application in KDE in several ways. If an entry for it is in the Kickoff Applications menu or Application dashboard, you can select that entry to start the application. You can right-click on any application entry in the Applications menu to display a pop-up menu with "Add to Panel" and "Add to Desktop" entries. Select either to add a shortcut icon for the application to the desktop or the panel. You can then start an application by single-clicking its desktop or panel icon.

An application icon on the desktop is implemented as a desktop widget. Performing a long click on the application icon on the desktop displays a sidebar with the icon for the widget settings. This opens a Settings window that allows you to specify a keyboard shortcut.

You can also run an application by right-clicking on the desktop and selecting the Run Command (or press Alt-F2 or Alt-space) which will display the Krunner tool consisting of a box to enter a single command. Previous commands can be accessed from a pop-up menu. You need only enter a pattern to search for the application. Results will be displayed in the Krunner window. Choose the one you want.

Virtual Desktops: Pager

KDE supports virtual desktops, extending the desktop area on which you can work. You could have a Web browser running on one desktop and be using a text editor in another. KDE can support up to 16 virtual desktops. To use virtual desktops, add the Pager widget to your panel or desktop. On the panel, you can use the panel editor (toolbox, right side) to move it to the location you want on the panel. The panel and desktop pagers are shown here.

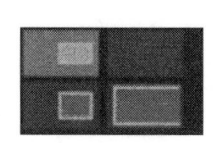

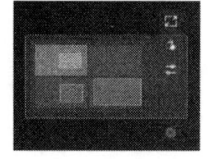

The Pager represents your virtual desktops as miniature screens showing small squares for each desktop. It works much like the GNOME Workspace Switcher. To move from one desktop to another, click the square for the destination desktop. The selected desktop will be highlighted. Just passing your mouse over a desktop image on the panel will open a message displaying the desktop number along with the windows open on that desktop.

If you want to move a window to a different desktop, first open the window's menu by right-clicking the window's title bar. Then select the To Desktop entry, which lists the available desktops. Choose the one you want.

You can also configure KDE so that if you move the mouse over the edge of a desktop screen, it automatically moves to the adjoining desktop. You need to imagine the desktops arranged next to each. You enable this feature by enabling the "Switch desktop on edge" feature in the System Settings | Desktop Behavior | Screen Edges tab. This feature will also allow you to move windows over the edge to an adjoining desktop.

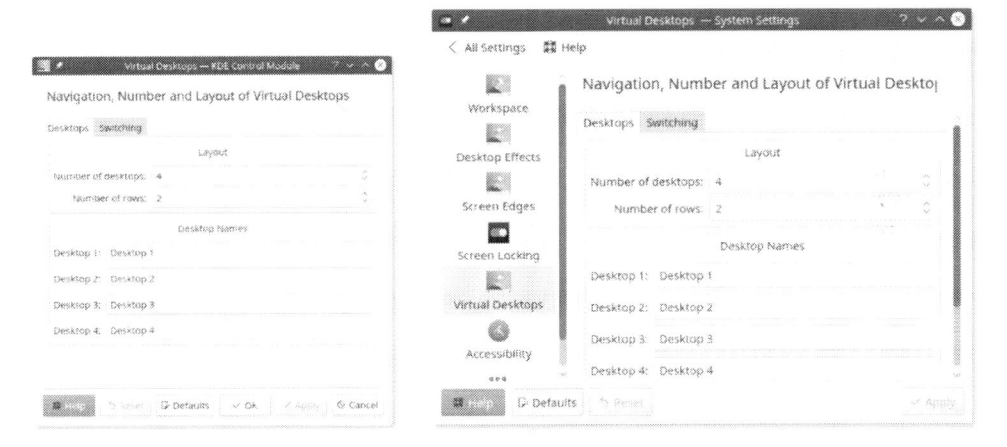

Figure 8-29: Virtual desktop configuration (Desktop Behavior) and Pager widget icon.

To change the number of virtual desktops, right-click on the Desktop Pager widget, select the Configure Desktops entry in the pop-up menu to open the Virtual Desktops dialog, and choose the Desktops tab, which displays entries for your active desktops. You can also access the Virtual Desktops dialog from System Settings | Desktop Behavior in the Workspace section (see Figure 8-29). The text box labeled "Number of Desktops" controls the number of active desktops. Use the arrows or enter a number to change the number of active desktops. You can change any of the desktop names by clicking an active name and entering a new one.

To change how the pager displays desktops on the pager, right-click on the pager and choose Pager Settings to open the Pager Settings dialog (see Figure 8-30). Here you can configure the pager to display numbers or names for desktops, or show icons of open windows.

Figure 8-30: Pager Settings.

Tip: Use CTRL key in combination with a function key to switch to a specific desktop: for example, CTRL-F1 switches to the first desktop and CTRL-F3 to the third desktop.

KDE Panel

The KDE panel, located at the bottom of the screen, provides access to most KDE functions (see Figure 8-31). The panel is a specially configured Plasma containment, just like the desktop. The panel can include icons for menus, folder windows, specific programs, and virtual desktops. These are widgets that are configured for use on the panel. At the left end of the panel is a button for the Kickoff menu, a KDE *K* icon.

To add an application to the panel, right-click on its entry in the Kickoff menu to open a pop-up menu and select Add to Panel.

Figure 8-31: KDE panel

To add a widget to the panel, right-click on any panel widget on the panel to open a pop-up menu, and select Panel Options submenu from which you can select the Add Widgets entry. This opens the Add Widgets dialog that lists widgets you can add to the panel (see Figure 8-32). A drop-down menu at the top of the window lets you see different widget categories like Date and Time, Online Services, and Graphics. Another way to open the Add Widgets dialog is to click on the panel toolbox at the right side of the panel and click the Add widgets button

Figure 8-32: KDE Add Widgets for panel

The Plasma panel supports several kinds of Windows and Tasks widgets, including the taskbar (Task Manager) and system tray. To the right of the system tray is the digital clock. The system tray holds widgets for desktop operations like update notifier, the clipboard, Bluetooth, device notifier, sound settings (kmix), media player (if a multimedia player is active), and network manager, as shown here.

The pop-up menu (arrow icon) on the right side of the system tray display widgets that are not in use, or not often used (see Figure 8-33). The Battery and Brightness entry displays a dialog to see battery charges and set screen brightness.

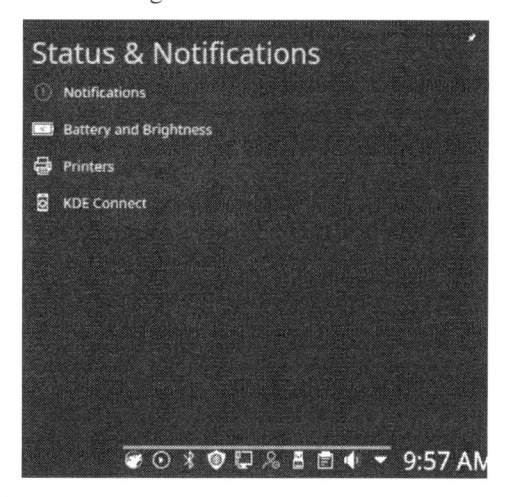

Figure 8-33: System Tray

To configure the system tray, right-click on the system tray menu (arrow icon) and choose System Tray Settings to open the system tray configuration dialog at the General tab, where you can decide what items to display or entries to make visible or remove (see Figure 8-34). In the "Extra Items" list you can check items that you also want displayed on the system tray, such as Printers and Instant Messaging. When you click the Apply button the items are displayed. Items not in use are in the menu. The Entries tab shows how selected items are to be displayed (auto, shown, or hidden).

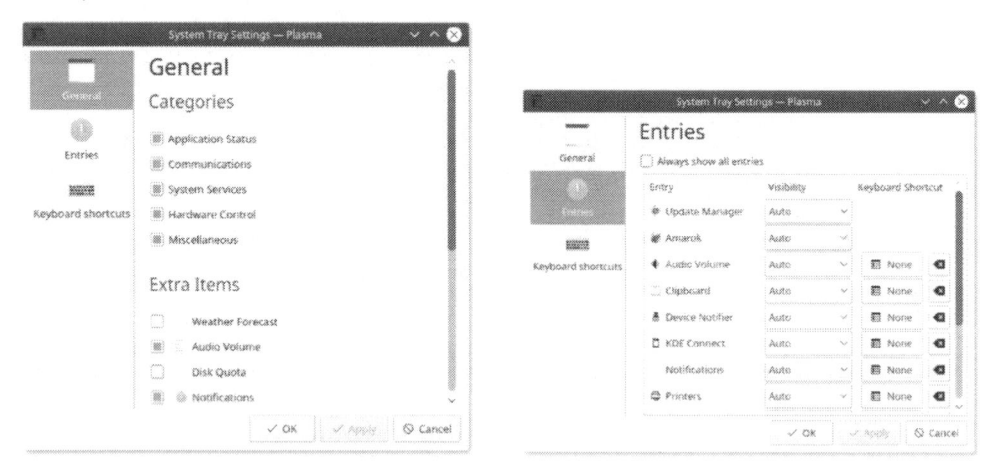

Figure 8-34: KDE panel system tray settings

KDE Panel Configuration

To configure a panel, changing its position, size, and display features, you use the panel's toolbox, located at the right side of the panel. Click on it to open an additional configuration panel with buttons for adding widgets, moving the panel, changing its size, and a More Settings menu for setting visibility and alignment features. Figure 8-35 shows the configuration panel as it will appear on your desktop. Figure 8-36 provides a more detailed description, including the More Settings menu entries.

Figure 8-35: KDE Panel Configuration

With the configuration panel activated, you can also move widgets around the panel. Clicking on a widget will overlay a movement icon, letting you then move the widget icon to a different location on the panel.

As you move your mouse over a widget in the panel, a pop-up dialog opens showing the widget's name, a settings button, and a delete button (see Figure 8-35). To remove the widget from the panel, click its delete button.

The lower part of the configuration panel is used for panel position settings. On the left side is a slider for positioning the panel on the edge of the screen. On the right side are two sliders for the minimum (bottom) and maximum (top) size of the panel.

The top part of the panel has buttons for changing the location and the size of the panel. The Screen Edge button lets you move the panel to another side of the screen (left, right, top, bottom). Just click and drag. The height button lets you change the panel size, larger or smaller. The Add Widgets button will open the Add Widgets dialog, letting you add new widgets to the panel. The Add Spacer button adds a spacer to separate widgets. Right-click on the spacer to set the flexible size option or to remove the spacer.

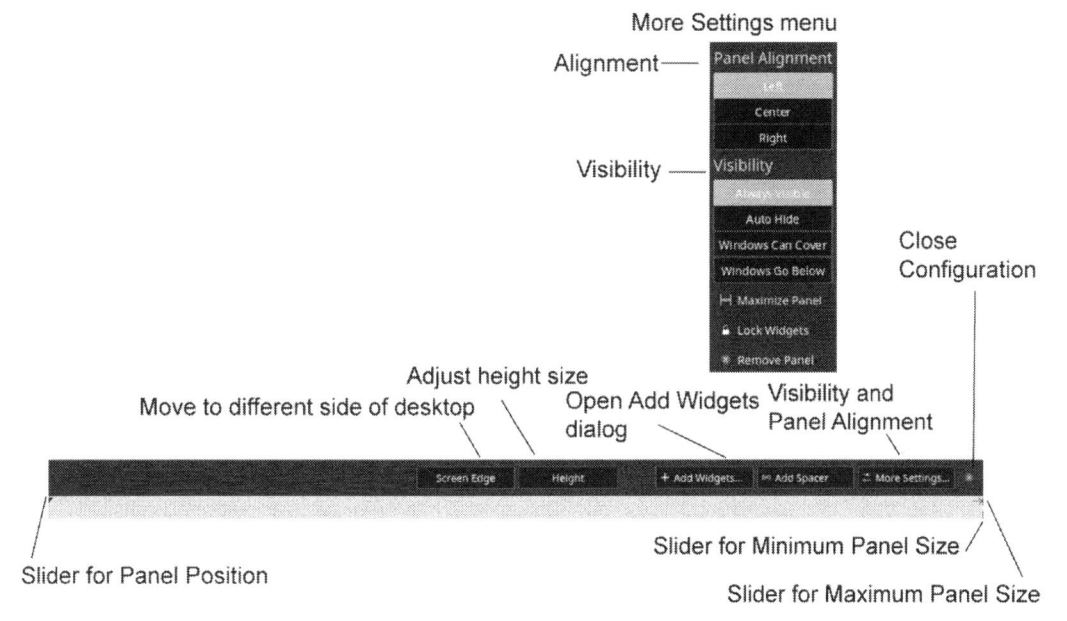

Figure 8-36: KDE Panel Configuration details and display features

The More Setting menu lets you set Visibility and Alignment features. You can choose an AutoHide setting that will hide the panel until you move the mouse to its location. The "Windows can cover" option lets a window overlap the panel. For smaller panels, you can align to the right, left, or center of the screen edge. The More Settings menu also has an entry to remove the panel. Use this entry to delete a panel you no longer want.

When you are finished with the configuration, click the red x icon the upper right side.

Desktop Effects

Desktop effects can be enabled on the System Settings Desktop Effects tab in the Desktop Behavior dialog in the Workspace section (System Settings | Desktop Behavior). For virtual desktop switching you can choose Slide, Fade Desktop, and Desktop Cube Animation (see Figure 8-37). The more dramatic effects are found in the Windows Management section. Desktop Effects requires the support of a capable graphics chip (GPU). You may have to install the proprietary graphics driver (System Settings | Driver Manager).

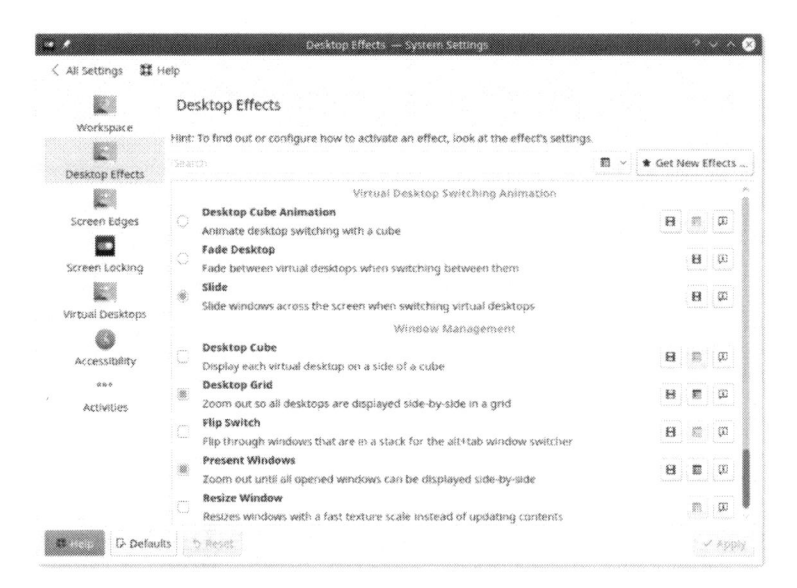

Figure 8-37: Desktop Effects selection

Key	Operation
ALT-TAB	Cover Switch, Thumbnail, or Breeze for open windows
CTRL-F8	Desktop Grid (use mouse to select a desktop)
CTRL-F9	Present Windows Current Desktop
CTRL-F10	Present Windows All Desktops
CTRL-F11	Desktop Cube (use mouse or arrow keys to move, ESC to exit)

Table 8-3: KWin desktop effects keyboard shortcuts

Several Windows effects are selected by default, depending on whether your graphics card can support them. A check box is filled next to active effects. If there is a dialog icon to the right of the effects entry, it means the effect can be configured. Click on the icon to open its configuration dialog. Figure 8-38 shows the configuration dialog for the Desktop Cube effect. For several effects, you use certain keys to start them. The more commonly used effects are Cover Switch, Desktop Grid, Present Windows, and Desktop Cube. The keys for these effects are listed in Table 8-3.

Figure 8-38: Desktop Effects configuration

Window switching using Alt-Tab is controlled on the Windows Management dialog's Task Switcher tab, not from Desktop Behavior's Desktop Effects tab. In the Visualization section, you can choose the window switching effect you want to use from the drop-down menu. These include Breeze, Thumbnails, Grid, Cover Switch, and Flip Switch, as well as smaller listings such as informative, compact, text icons, and small icons. The Alt-Tab keys implement the effect you have chosen. Continually pressing the Tab key while holding down the Alt key moves you through the windows. Thumbnails displays windows in a boxed dialog (see Figure 8-39), whereas Cover Switch arranges windows stacked to the sides, and Flip Switch arranges the windows to one side (see Figure 8-40). The default is Breeze, which arranges the window images to the left side of the screen (see Figure 8-39).

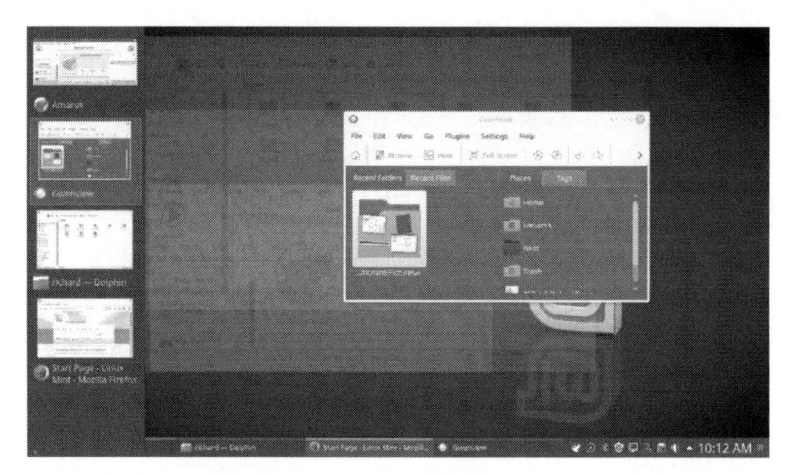

Figure 8-39: Thumbnail and Breeze Switch - Alt-Tab

The Present Windows effect displays images of the open windows on your screen with the selected one highlighted (see Figure 8-41). You can use your mouse to select another. This provides an easy way to browse your open windows. You can also use Ctrl-F9 to display windows on your current virtual desktop statically and use the arrow key to move between them. Use Ctrl-F10 to display all your open windows across all your desktops. Press the ESC key to return to the desktop.

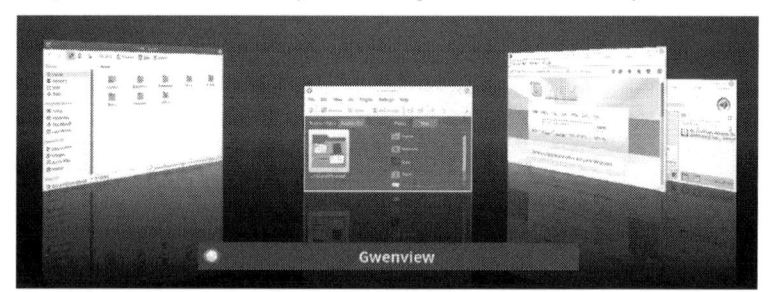

Figure 8-40: Cover Switch - Alt-Tab

Desktop Grid will show a grid of all your virtual desktops (Ctrl-F8), letting you see all your virtual desktops on the screen at once (see Figure 8-42). You can then move windows and open applications between desktops. Clicking on a desktop makes it the current one. The plus and minus keys allow you to add or remove virtual desktops.

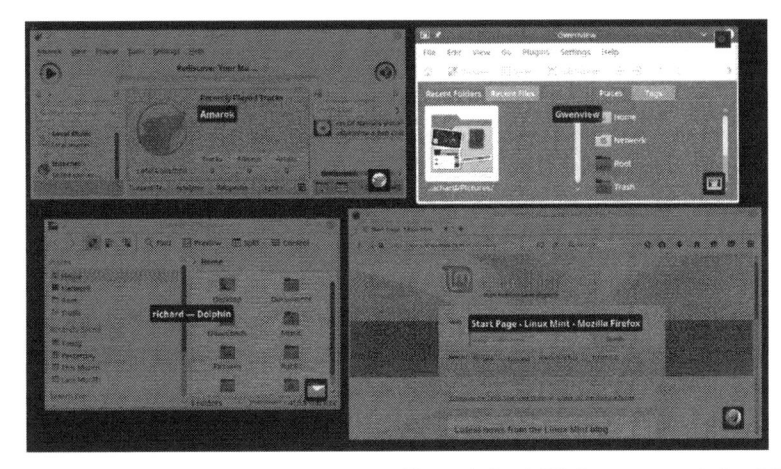

Figure 8-41: Present Windows (Windows effects) Ctrl-F9 for current desktop and Ctrl-f10 for all desktops

Figure 8-42: Desktop Grid - Ctrl-F8

Desktop Cube will show a cube of all your virtual desktops, letting you move to different desktops around a cube (see Figure 8-43). Stop at the side you want to select. Press Ctrl-11 to start the Desktop Cube. You can then move around the cube with the arrow keys or by clicking and dragging your mouse. Alternatively, if you have a touchpad, you can use a two-finger drag to start and move through the Desktop Cube. When you are finished, press the ESC key to return you the desktop. Desktop Cube Animation will use cube animation whenever you switch to a different desktop using the Desktop Pager.

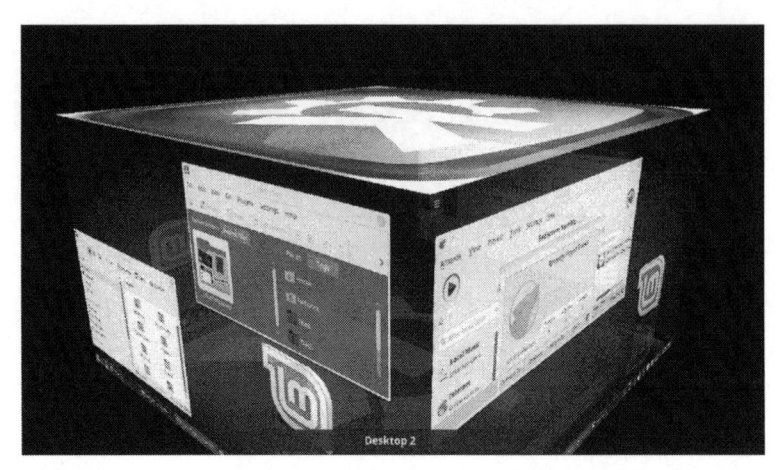

Figure 8-43: Desktop Cube - Ctrl-F11, drag-mouse or right/left arrow keys (or two-finger drag on touchpad)

KDE File Manager: Dolphin

Dolphin is KDE's dedicated file manager (see Figure 8-44). A navigation bar shows the current directory either in a browser or edit mode. In the browse mode it shows icons for the path of your current directory, and in the edit mode, it shows the path name in a text-editable box. You can use either to move to different folders and their subfolders. Use the **Ctrl-l** key or click to the right of the folder buttons to use the edit mode. You can also choose Control | Location Bar | Editable Location. Clicking on the checkmark at the end of the editable text box returns you to the browser mode.

The Dolphin menubar has been hidden by default. The menus are displayed when clicking the Control button on the right end of the toolbar (see Figure 8-45). You can redisplay the menubar by choosing "Show Menubar" from the Control (or View) menu (**Ctrl-m**). You can hide the menubar again by choosing Show Menubar from the Settings menu (or pressing **Ctrl-m**).

You can open a file either by clicking it or by right-clicking it, and choosing the "Open With" submenu to list applications to open it with. If you want to just select the file or folder, you need to hold down the CTRL key while you click it. A single-click will open the file. If the file is a program, that program starts up. If it is a data file, such as a text file, the associated application is run using that data file. Clicking a text file displays it with the Kate editor while clicking an image file displays it with the Gwenview image viewer. If Dolphin cannot determine the application to use, it opens a dialog box prompting you to enter the application name. You can click the Browse button on this box to use a directory tree to locate the application program you want.

Figure 8-44: The KDE file manager (Dolphin)

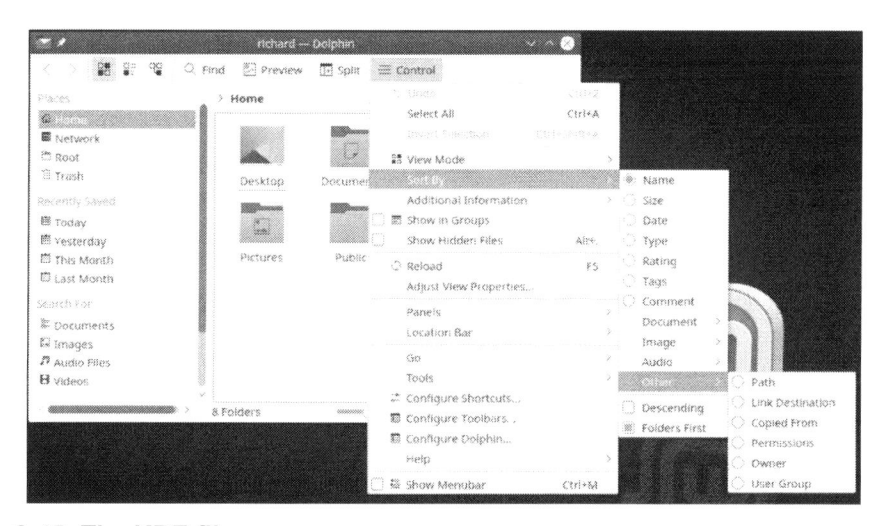

Figure 8-45: The KDE file manager menus

Dolphin can display panels to either side (Dolphin refers to these as panels, though they operate more like stand-alone tabs). The Places panel will show icons for often-used folders like

Home, Network, and Trash, as well as removable devices. To add a folder to the Places panel, just drag it there. The files listed in a folder can be viewed in several different ways, such as icons, detailed listing (Details), and columns (Control | View Mode menu). See Table 8-4 for keyboard shortcuts.

Keys	Description
ALT-LEFT ARROW, ALT-RIGHT ARROW	Backward and Forward in History
ALT-UP ARROW	One directory up
ENTER	Open a file/directory
LEFT/RIGHT/UP/DOWN ARROWS	Move among the icons
PAGE UP, PAGE DOWN	Scroll fast
CTRL-C	Copy selected file to clipboard
CTRL-V	Paste files from clipboard to current directory
CTRL-S	Select files by pattern
CTRL-L	URI text box location bar
CTRL-F	Find files
CTRL-Q	Close window

Table 8-4: KDE File Manager Keyboard Shortcuts

The Additional information submenu in the Control menu (or View menu) lets you display additional information about files such as the size, date, type, and comments. Type specific information can also be displayed such as album, track, and duration for audio files, and word and line counts for documents. You can also display the full path, permissions, and group information (Other submenu).

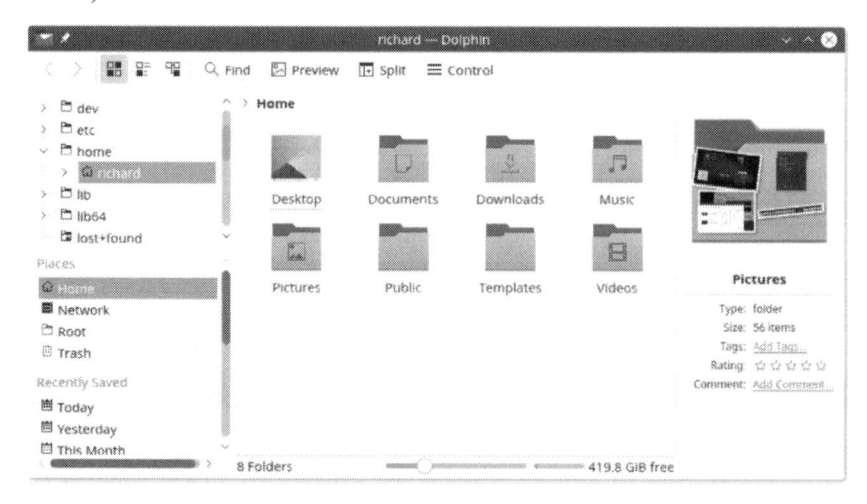

Figure 8-46: The KDE file manager with sidebars

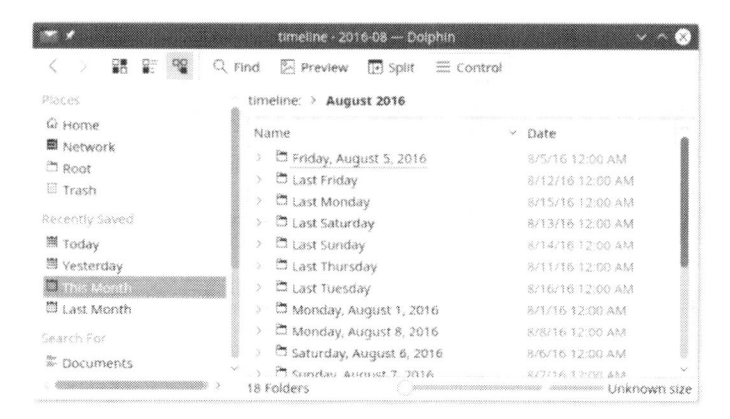

Figure 8-47: The KDE file manager panel Recently Saved

You can display additional panels by selecting them from the Control | Panels submenu. The Information panel displays detailed information about a selected file or folder, and the Folders panel displays a directory tree for the file system. The panels are detachable from the file manager window (see Figure 8-46). Be sure to choose "Unlock Panels" the panels in the Panels menu to make them detachable.

The Places panel makes use of file metadata to provide easy access to files by category and date. The Places panel has four sections: Places, Recently Saved, Search For, and Devices. As in previous versions, the Places section holds your folders, including root, trash, and network, and the Devices section holds your attached devices, including removable devices. The Recently Saved section lets you display files you access fairly recently: today, yesterday, this month, and last month (see Figure 8-47). The Search For section lets you displays files of specified types: documents, images, audio files, and videos.

Dolphin supports split views, where you can open two different folders in the same window. Click the Split button in the toolbar. You can then drag folder and files from one folder to the other (see Figure 8-48).

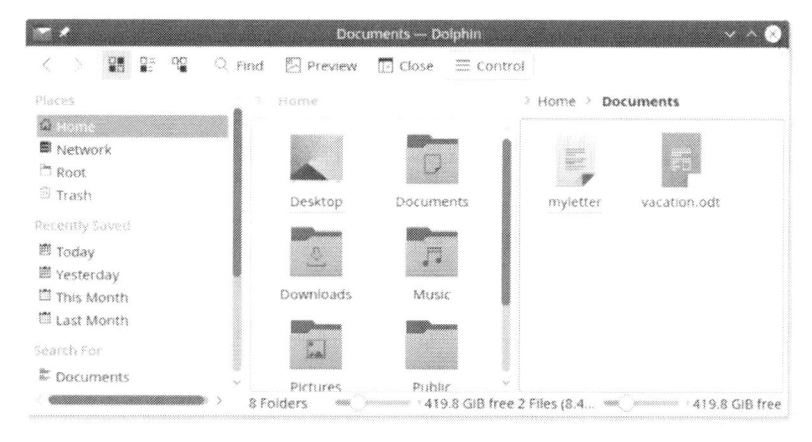

Figure 8-48: The KDE file manager with split views

Dolphin also supports file sharing with Samba. To share a folder, right-click on the folder icon and choose Properties to open the Properties dialog. Then on the Share tab, you can choose to share the folder with Samba (Microsoft Windows). You can also set permissions for users: Read Only, Full Control, and Deny (See Figure 8-49). For the Everyone entry, you would usually set the permission to Read Only.

To configure Dolphin, click Configure Dolphin from the Setting menu to open the Dolphin Preferences dialog with tabs for Startup, View Modes, Navigation, Services, Trash, and General. On the Startup tab, you can specify features like the split view and the default folder to start up with. On the View Modes tab, you can set display features for the different display modes (Icons, Details, and Column), like the icon size, font type, and arrangement. The Navigation tab sets features like opening archives as folders. The Services tab is where you specify actions supported for different kinds of files, like play a DVD with Dragon Player, install a true type font file or display Tiff image files. The Trash tab lets you configure trash settings like deleting items in the trash after a specified time and setting the maximum size of the trash. The General tab has sub-tabs for Behavior, Previews, Confirmations, and Status Bar. The Behavior tab is where you can enable tool tips and show selection markers. Preview lets you choose which type of files to preview. The image, jpeg, and directories types are already selected. On Confirmations, you can require confirmation prompts for file deletion, moving files to the trash, or closing multiple tabs. On the Status tab, you can choose to show the zoom slider and the amount of free storage.

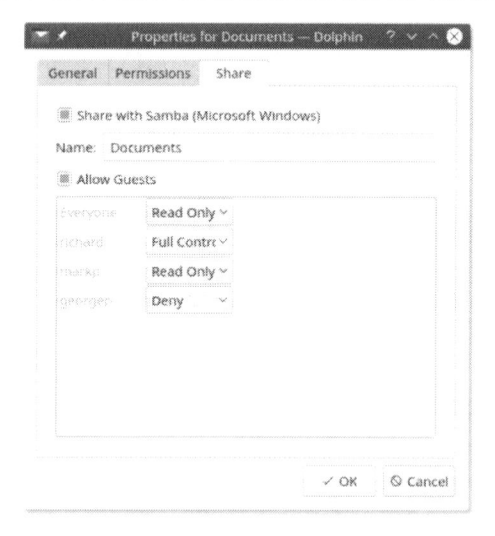

Figure 8-49: The KDE file manager share dialog for folders

Navigating Directories

Within a file manager window, a single-click on a folder icon moves to that folder and displays its file and sub-folder icons. To move back up to the parent folder, you click the back arrow button located on the left end of the navigation toolbar. A single-click on a folder icon moves you down the folder tree, one folder at a time. By clicking the back arrow button, you move up the tree. The Navigation bar can display either the folder path for the current folder or an editable location box where you can enter in a pathname. For the folder path, you can click on any displayed folder name to move you quickly to an upper-level folder. To use the location box, click to the right of the folder path. The Location box is displayed. You can also select Show Full Location in the View | Location Bar | Editable Location menu item (or press Ctrl-L or F6). The navigation bar changes to an editable textbox where you can type a path name. To change back to the folder path, click the check mark to the right of the text box.

Like a Web browser, the file manager remembers the previous folder it has displayed. You can use the back and forward arrow buttons to move through this list of prior folders. You can also use several keyboard shortcuts to perform such operations, like Alt-back-arrow to move up a folder, and the arrow keys to move to different icons.

Copy, Move, Delete, Rename, and Link Operations

To perform an operation on a file or folder, you first have to select it by clicking the file's icon or listing. To select more than one file, hold down the CTRL key down while you click the files you want. You can also use the keyboard arrow keys to move from one file icon to another.

To copy and move files, you can use the standard drag-and-drop method with your mouse. To copy a file, you locate it by using the file manager. Open another file manager window to the folder to which you want the file copied. Then drag-and-drop the file icon to that window. A pop-up menu appears with selections for Move Here, Copy Here, or Link Here. Choose Copy Here. To move a file to another directory, follow the same procedure, but select Move Here from the pop-up menu. To copy or move a folder, use the same procedure as for files. All the folder's files and subfolders are also copied or moved. Instead of having to select from a pop-up menu, you can use the corresponding keys: **Ctrl** for copy, **Shift** for move, and **Ctrl-Shift** for link, same as for GNOME.

To rename a file, Ctrl-click its icon and press F2, or right-click the icon and select Rename from the pop-up menu. A dialog opens where you can enter the new name for the file or folder.

You can delete a file either by selecting it and deleting it, or placing it in the Trash folder to delete later. To delete a file, select it and then choose the Delete entry in the File menu, File | Delete (also SHIFT-DEL key). To place a file in the Trash folder, drag-and-drop it to the Trash icon on the Places panel, or right-click the file and choose "Move To Trash" from the pop-up menu. You can later open the Trash folder and delete the files. To delete all the files in the Trash folder, right-click the Trash icon in Dolphin file manager Places panel, and select Empty Trash from the pop-up menu. To restore files in the Trash bin, open the Trash window and right click on the file to restore and select Restore.

Each file or directory has properties associated with it that include permissions, the filename, and its directory. To display the Properties dialog for a given file, right-click the file's icon and select the Properties entry. On the General tab, you see the name of the file displayed. To change the filename, replace the name there with a new one. Permissions are set on the Permissions tab. Here, you can set read, write, and execute permissions for user, group, or other access to the file. The Group entry enables you to change the group for a file.

Search Bar and Filter Bar

The Dolphin search tool provides a simplified search bar for files and folders. KDE also supports a filter bar to search files and folders in the current folder. You can also use the Filter Panel to refine searches by metadata such as type, date, ratings, and tags. For quick access to basic categories and recent use you can use the Places panel's Recently Accessed and Search For entries, as noted previously.

Search Bar

To search for files, click the Find button on the icon bar to open the search bar, which displays a search text box. You can also choose Find from the Edit menu or press Ctrl-f. The search bar displays a search text box where you enter the pattern of the file or folder you are searching for. Click the red x button to the left to close the find bar, and use the black x button in the text box to clear the search pattern.

Buttons below the search box provide options to qualify the search. The Filename button (the default) searches on the filename. The Content button will search the contents of text files for the pattern. The "From Here" button searches the user's home folders, and the Everywhere button (the default) searches the entire file system (see Figure 8-50).

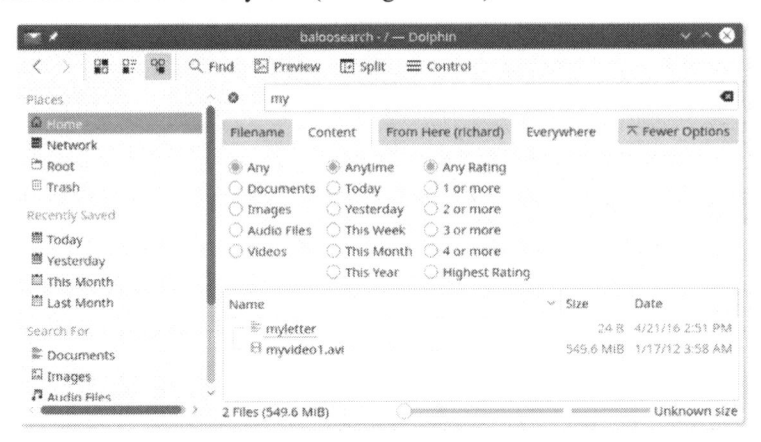

Figure 8-50: The KDE Search Bar

The search results are displayed in the main pane. You can click a file to have it open with its appropriate application. Text files are displayed by the Kate text editor, images by Gwenview, and applications are run. When you are finished searching, click the Close button.

When you pass your mouse over an icon listed in the Query Results, information about it is displayed on the information panel to the right (if the information panel is displayed). Links are shown for adding tags and comments. Right-clicking on this panel lets you open a configure dialog where you can specify what information to display.

The search operation makes use of the KDE implementation of Baloo desktop search. To configure desktop search, choose System Settings | Workspace | Search, File Search tab. On the File Search tab, you can enable or disable file searching, and choose folders not to search.

Filter Bar

For a quick search of the current folder, you can activate the Filter bar (Control | Tools | Show Filter Bar or **Ctrl-i**), which opens a Filter search box at the bottom of the window. Enter a pattern, and only those file and directory names containing that pattern are displayed. Click the x button at the right of the Filter box to clear it (see Figure 8-51).

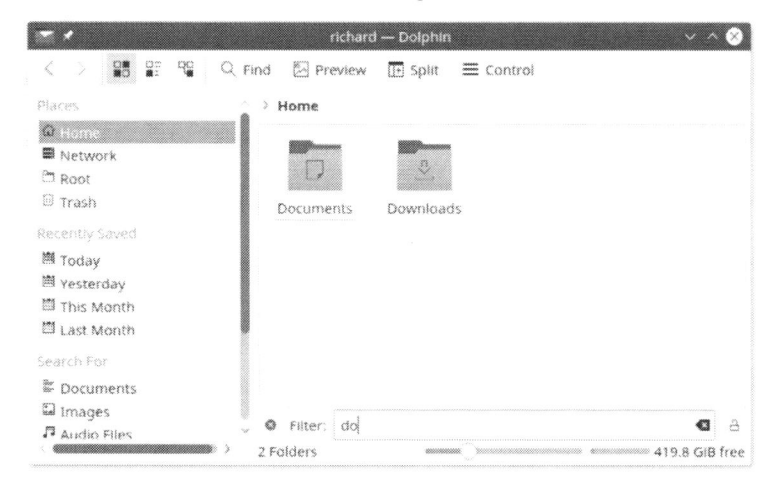

Figure 8-51: The KDE Filter Bar

KDE Configuration: KDE System Settings

With the KDE configuration tools, you can configure your desktop and system, changing the way it is displayed and the features it supports. The configuration dialogs are accessed on the System Settings window (See Figure 8-52). On KDE, you can access System Settings from the System Settings entry in the Kickoff Computer or Favorites menus, or from Applications | Settings | System Settings. On the Application dashboard, you can access it in the Favorites section and in the Settings category.

The System Settings window shows system dialog icons arranged in several sections: Appearance, Workspace, Personalization, Network, and Hardware. Click an icon to display a dialog with a sidebar icon list for configuration tabs, with the tab selected shown on the right. The selected tab may also have tabs on the right side (see Figure 8-53).

The Appearance section lets you set the desktop theme, manage fonts, choose icon sets, and select application and window styles. The Workspace section lets you set desktop effects, virtual desktops, window actions, startup applications, desktop search. The Network section holds icons for configuring networking preferences, Bluetooth connections, and sharing. Personalization lets you set the settings for user management, the date and time, notifications, online accounts, and file/application associations. Hardware lets you set the printer configuration, power management, multimedia devices (sound), your display resolution, and to manage drivers.

Alternatively, you can display the System Settings window using the classic tree format. Click the System Settings Configure button to open the configuration dialog, and select Classic tree on the General tab. Setting sections are displayed as expandable trees on the left pane, with dialogs for a selected section displayed to the right.

Part 3: Desktops

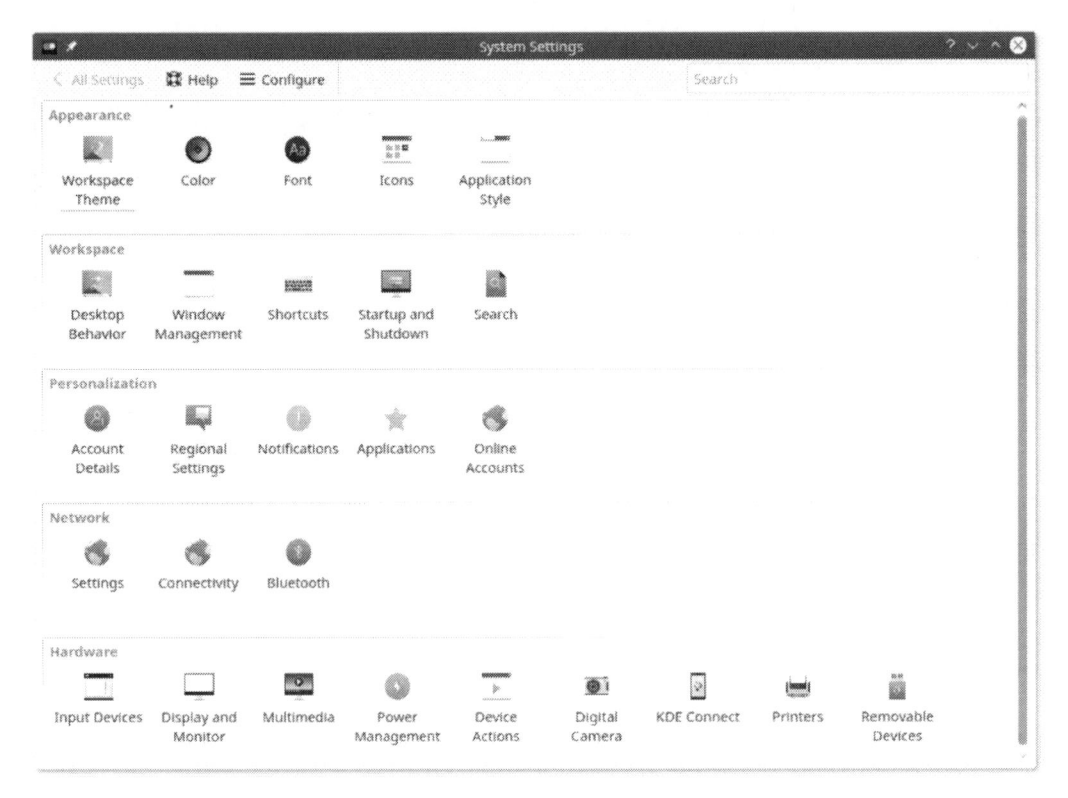

Figure 8-52: KDE System Settings

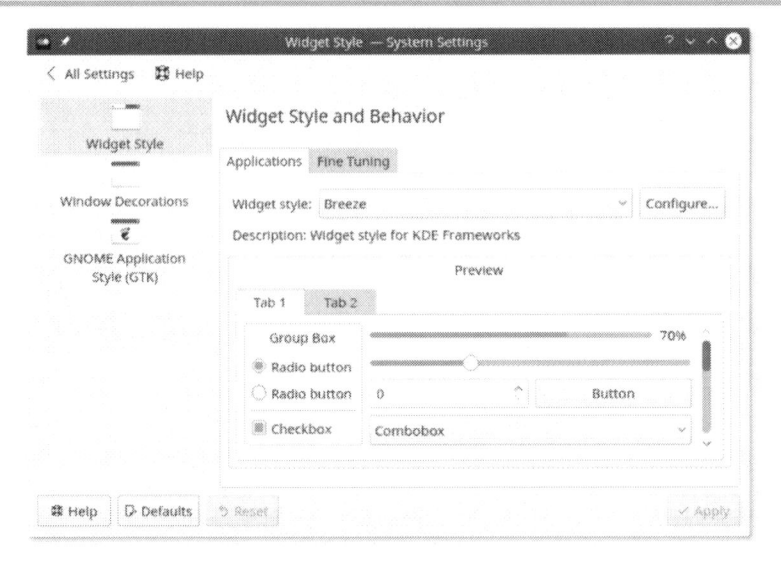

Figure 8-53: KDE System Settings | Application Style, Widget Style

KDE has administration tools comparable to the Cinnamon and Mate desktops. For example, User management is provided by Kuser, accessible from System Settings | Account Details (Personalization section), User Manager tab. It works much the same way as User Accounts on the Mate desktop (see Chapter 14) (see Figure 8-54).

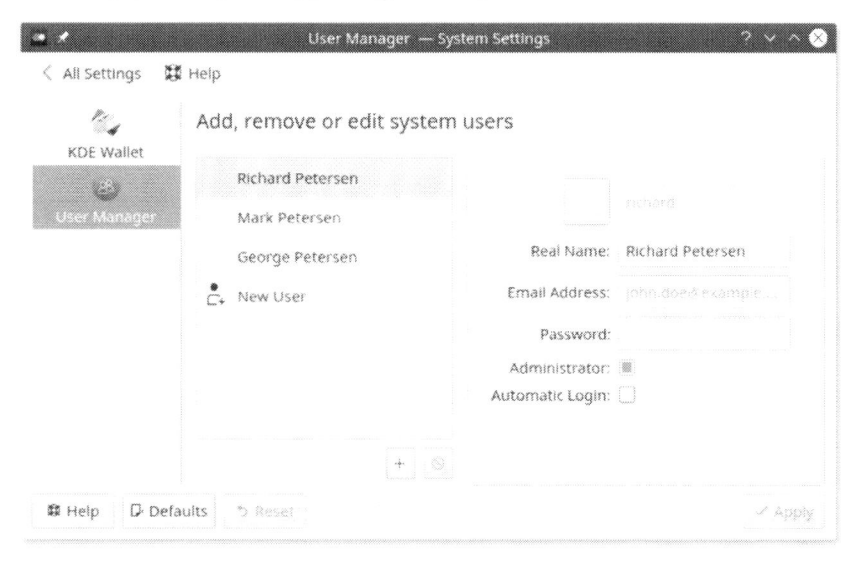

Figure 8-54: KDE System Settings | User Manager

Part 3: Administration

System Tools
System Administration
Network Connections
Shell Configuration

9. System Tools

- GNOME System Monitor
- Scheduling Tasks
- System Log
- Disk Usage Analyzer
- Virus Protection
- Hardware Sensors
- Disk Utility
- Sound (PulseAudio)

Useful system tools, as well as user specific configuration tools, can be found in the Accessories, Preferences, and Administration menus (see Table 9-1). The Administration menu includes tools like the System Monitor and the Disk Usage Analyzer. The Accessories menu holds Disk Utility and the ClamTK Virus Scanner (Virus Scanner). Desktop configuration, such as mouse, keyboard, displays, and sound configuration, are handled by GNOME or KDE directly (System Settings) and can be accessed from the Preferences menu.

Linux Mint System Tools	Name	Description
`gnome-system-monitor`	System Monitor	GNOME System Monitor
`gnome-system-log`	System Log	GNOME System Log
`gnome-terminal`	Terminal	GNOME Terminal Window
`baobab`	Disk Usage Analyzer	Disk usage analyzer with graphic representation
`gnome-nettool`	Network Tools	Network analysis
`KDE task scheduler`	Task Scheduler	KDE schedule manager (KDE desktop only)
`ClamTK`	Virus Scanner	Clam Virus scanner
`Disk Utility`	Disk Utility	Udisks utility for managing hard disks and removable drives
`PulseAudio`	Sound	Sound drivers and server

Table 9-1: Linux Mint System Tools

GNOME System Monitor

Linux Mint provides the GNOME System Monitor for displaying system information and monitoring system processes, accessible from System Tools | System Monitor. There are three tabs: Processes, Resources, and File Systems (see Figure 9-1). The Resources tab displays graphs for CPU History, Memory and Swap History, and Network History. If your system has a multi-core CPU, the CPU History graph shows the usage for each CPU. The Memory and Swap Memory graph shows the amount of memory in use. The Network History graph displays both the amount of sent and received data, along with totals for the current session. The File Systems tab lists your file systems, where they are mounted, and their type, as well as the amount of disk space used and how much is free. Double clicking on a file system entry will open that file system in a file manager window.

The Processes tab lists your processes, letting you sort and search processes. You can use field buttons to sort by name (Process Name), process ID (ID), the percentage of use (%CPU), and memory used (Memory), among others. The menu (right-side of the menu bar) lets you select all processes, just your own (My Processes), or active processes. You can stop any process by selecting it and then clicking the End Process button (lower-right corner) or by right-clicking on it and choosing End. You can right-click a process entry to display a menu with actions you can take on the selected process, such as stopping (Stop), ending (End), killing (Kill), and continuing a process (Continue), as well as changing the priority of the process (Change Priority). The Open Files entry opens a dialog listing all the files, sockets, and pipes the process is using. The Properties entry displays a dialog showing all the details for a process, such as the name, user, status, memory use, CPU use, and priority. Memory Maps display, selected from the Memory Maps entry, shows information on virtual memory, inodes, and flags for a selected process.

Display features such as the colors used for CPU graphs can be set using the dconf editor's gnome-system-monitor keys at org | gnome | gnome-system-monitor.

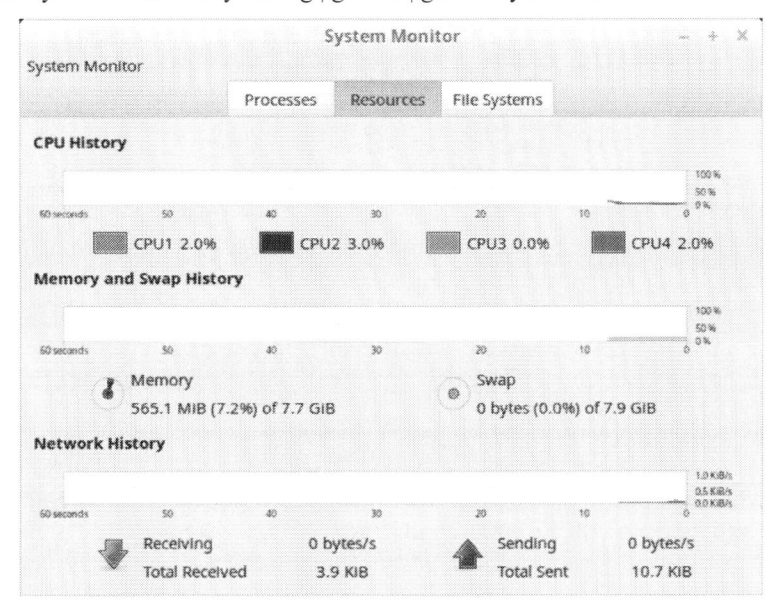

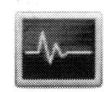

Figure 9-1: GNOME System Monitor: Resources

Managing Processes

Should you have to force a process or application to quit, you can use the Gnome System Monitor Processes tab to find, select, and stop the process. You should be sure of the process you want to stop. Ending a critical process could cripple your system. Application processes will bear the name of the application, and you can use those to force an application to quit. Ending processes manually is usually performed for open-ended operations that you are unable to stop normally. In Figure 9-2, the Firefox application has been selected. Clicking the End Process button on the lower left will then force the Firefox Web browser to end.

The pop-up menu for a process (right-click) provides several other options for managing a selected process: stop, continue, end, kill, and change priority. There are corresponding keyboard keys for most options. The stop and continue operations work together. You can stop (Stop) a process, and then later start it again with the Continue option. The End option stops a process safely, whereas a Kill option forces an immediate end to the process. The End option is preferred, but if it does not work, you can use the Kill option. Change Priority can give a process a lower or higher priority, letting it run faster or slower. The Properties option opens a dialog listing process details such as the name, user, status, different types of memory used, CPU usage, start time, process id, and priority. The Open Files option lists all the files, sockets, and pipes the process is using.

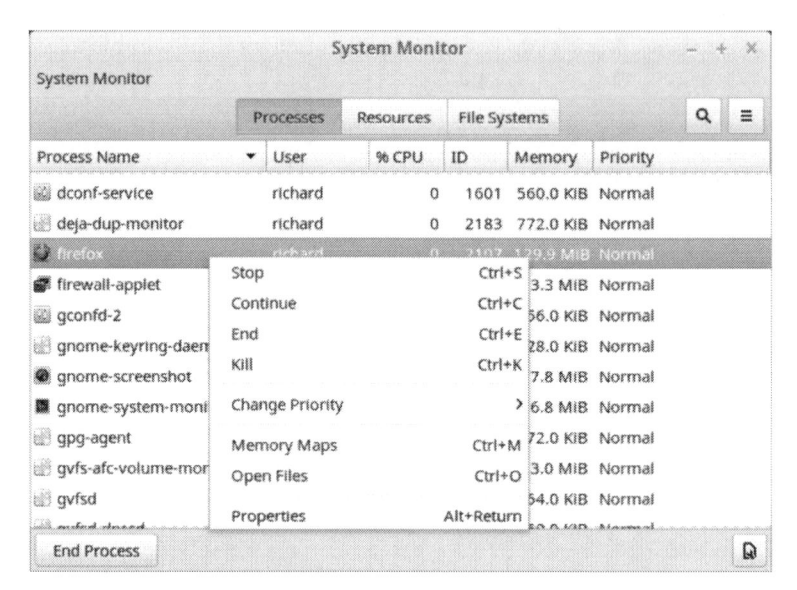

Figure 9-2: GNOME System Monitor: Processes

You can also use the **kill** command in a terminal window to end a process. The **kill** command takes as its argument a process number. Be sure you obtain the correct one. Use the **ps** command to display a process id. Entering in the incorrect process number could cripple your system. The **ps** command with the **-C** option searches for a particular application name. The **-o pid=** option will display only the process id, instead of the process id, time, application name, and tty. Once you have the process id, you can use the **kill** command with the process id as its argument to end the process.

```
$ ps -C firefox -o pid=
5555
$ kill 5555
```

One way to ensure the correct number is to use the **ps** command to return the process number directly as an argument to a **kill** command. In the following example, an open-ended process was started with the **mycmd** command. An open-ended process is one that will continue until you stop it manually.

```
mycmd > my.ts
```

The process is then ended by first executing the **ps** command to obtain the process id for the **mycmd** process (back quotes), and then using that process id in the **kill** command to end the process. The **-o pid=** option displays only the process id.

```
kill `ps -C mycmd -o pid=`
```

Scheduling Tasks

Scheduling regular maintenance tasks, such as backups, is managed by the **cron** service and implemented by a **cron** daemon. These tasks are listed in the **crontab** file. The **cron** daemon constantly checks the user's **crontab** file to see if it is time to take these actions. Any user can set up a **crontab** file of their own. An administrative user can set up a **crontab** file to take system administrative actions, such as backing up files at a certain time each week or month.

Creating cron entries can be a complicated task, using the **crontab** command to make changes to crontab files in the **/etc/crontab** directory. Instead, you can use desktop cron scheduler tools to set up cron actions.

On KDE you can use the KDE Task Scheduler to set up user and system-level scheduled tasks (install the **kde-config-cron** package). You access the Task Scheduler on the KDE System Settings window in the System Administration section as Task Scheduler. The Task Scheduler window will list your scheduled tasks. Task can be either personal or system-wide. Click the New Task button to open a New Task window where you can enter the command to run, add comments, and then specify the time in months, days, hours, and minutes from simple arranged buttons. On the Task Scheduler window, you can select a task and use the side buttons to modify it, delete the task, run it now, or print a copy of it. For tasks using the same complex commands or arguments, you can create a variable, and then use that variable in a command. Variables are listed in the Environment Variables section. To use a variable in a scheduled task, precede its name with the **$** character when you enter the command. Entering just the **$** symbol in the Command text box will display a drop-down list of pre-defined system variables you can use like **$PATH** and **$USER**.

System Log Viewer

Various system logs for tasks performed on your system are stored in the **/var/log** directory. Here you can find logs for mail, news, and all other system operations, such as Web server logs (see Figure 9-3). This usually includes startup tasks, such as loading drivers and mounting file systems. If a driver for a device failed to load at startup, you will find an error message for it here. Logins are also recorded in this file, showing you who attempted to log into what account. The **/var/log/mail.log** file logs mail message transmissions and news transfers.

Figure 9-3: System Log

To view logs, you can use the System Log Viewer accessible as System Log on the Administration menu. A side panel lists different logs. Selecting one displays the log to the right. For **/var/log/syslog**, select **syslog**. You can also choose to display messages in this file just for a specific date. A search button on the top right opens a search box where you can search for messages in the selected log. A tools button on the top right lets you perform tasks such as zooming, copying, selection, and filters.

Disk Usage Analyzer

The disk usage analyzer lets you see how much disk space is used and available on all your mounted hard disk partitions (see Figure 9-4). You can access it from Administration | Disk Usage Analyzer. It will also check all LVM and RAID arrays. Usage is shown in a simple graph, letting you see how much overall space is available and where it is. On the scan dialog you can choose to scan a hard disk (disk drive icon), your home folder, or an attached device like a floppy or USB drive (see Figure 9-5). Clicking on the menu button to the right lets you choose a particular folder to scan, either local for remote. When you scan a directory or the file system, disk usage for your directory is analyzed and displayed. Each file system is shown with a graph for its usage, as well as its size and the number of top-level directories and files. Then the directories are shown, along with their size and contents (files and directories).

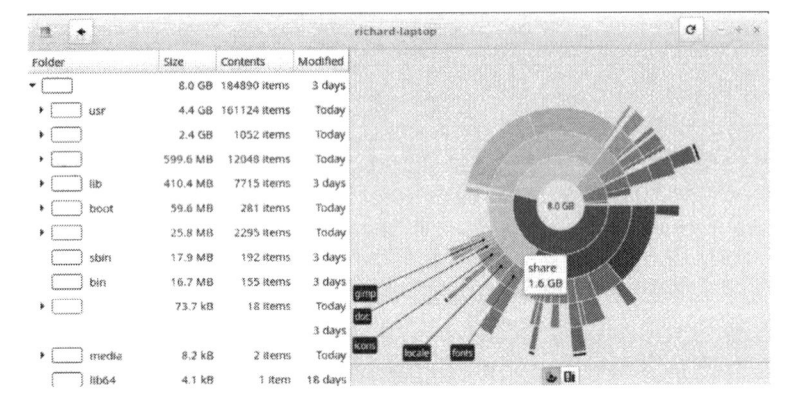

Figure 9-4: Disk Usage Analyzer

A representational graph for disk usage is displayed on the right pane. The graph can be either a Ring Chart or a Treemap. The Ring Chart is the default. Choose the one you want from the buttons on the lower right. For the Ring Chart, directories are shown, starting with the top-level directories at the center and moving out to the subdirectories. Passing your mouse over a section in the graph displays its directory name and disk usage, as well as all its subdirectories. The Treemap chart shows a box representation, with greater disk usage in larger boxes, and subdirectories encased within directory boxes.

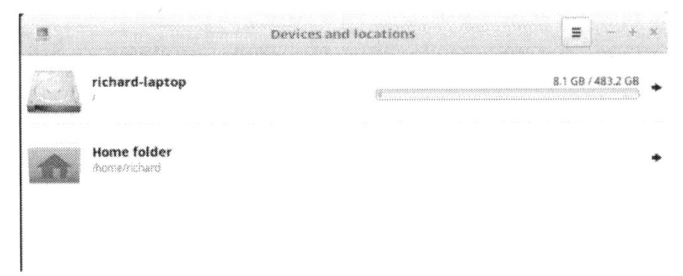

Figure 9-5: Disk Usage Analyzer: Scan dialog

Virus Protection

For virus protection, you can use the Linux version of ClamAV, which uses a GNOME front-end called ClamTK, **https://www.clamav.net**. This Virus scanner is included on the Linux Mint main repository. You can install ClamTK from Software Manager and the Synaptic Package Manager. The supporting ClamAV packages (System category) will also be selected and installed for you (clamav-base and clamav-freshclam). If you have no regular access to the internet you can install the **clamav-data** package for a basic set of virus definition. The **clamav-freshclam** package retrieves current virus definitions from the ClamAV servers. For ClamAV to check your mail messages automatically, you need to install the ClamAV scanner daemon (**clamav-daemon** package).

Figure 9-6: The ClamTK tool for ClamAV virus protection.

You can access ClamTk from the Applications dash, Accessories filter as ClamTk. With ClamTk, you can scan specific files and directories, as well as your home directory (see Figure 9-6). Searches can be recursive, including subdirectories (Settings). You have the option to check configuration files (scan files with a dot). You can also perform quick or recursive scans of your home directory. Infected files are quarantined.

Your virus definitions will be updated automatically. If you want to check manually for virus definitions, you need to click Update Assistant and choose to update the signatures yourself. Then click Updates and click the OK button next to "Check for updates."

Hardware Sensors

A concern for many users is the temperatures and usage of computer components. You can install different software packages to enable certain sensors (see Table 9-2). You can add the applet "CPU Temperature Indicator" to display your CPU temperatures. If your system supports CPU Scaling you can add the CPU Frequency Selector. For CPU, system, fan speeds, and any other motherboard supported sensors, you can use Psensor, Xsensors, or the **lm-sensors** service. Psensors installs the hddtemp hard drive temperature server and displays your CPU, graphics card, and hard drive temperatures. You can set temperature thresholds for alerts. Xsensors displays your CPU temperature.

Sensor application	Description
lm-sensors	Detects and accesses computer (motherboard) sensors like CPU and fan speed. Run **sensors-detect** once to configure.
hddtemp	Detects hard drive temperatures (also detected by Disk Utility)
Disk Utility	Disk Utility provides SMART information for hard disks showing current hard disk temperatures as well as detailed disk health information and checks.
Psensor	Application to detect and display system and hard drive temperatures.
Xsensors	Application to detect and display system temperatures and fans.
indicator-cpufreq	CPU Frequency Scaling Indicator for monitoring and changing CPU frequency.
CPU Frequency Selector	CPU frequency scaling, requires gnome-applets.
CPU Temperature Indicator	Display CPU temperature

Table 9-2: Sensor packages and applications

If not already installed, install the **lm-sensors** package. Then you have to configure your sensor detection. In a terminal window enter following and press ENTER to answer yes to the prompts:

```
sudo sensors-detect
```

Disk Utility (Preferences menu) lets you know your hard disk temperature. Disk Utility uses Udisks to access SMART information about the disk drive, including the temperature and overall health. Open Disk Utility, select the hard disk to check, and then, on the right pane, click on the "SMART Data" link located middle right. A hard disk dialog opens showing the disk temperature along with other details.

Disk Utility and Udisks

Disk Utility is a Udisks supported user configuration interface for your storage media, such as hard disks, USB drives, and DVD/CD drives (**gnome-disk-utility** package, installed by default). Tasks supported include disk labeling, mounting disks, disk checks, and encryption. You can also perform more advanced tasks, like managing RAID and LVM storage devices, as well as partitions. Disk Utility is accessible from the Accessories and Preferences menus as Disks. Users can use Disk Utility to format removable media like USB drives. Disk Utility is also integrated into Nemo and Caja, letting you format removable media directly.

The Disk Utility window shows a sidebar with entries for your storage media (see Figure 9-7). Clicking on an entry displays information for the media on the right pane. Removable devices such as USB drives display an eject button and a task menu with an entry to format the disk. If you are formatting a partition, like that on removable media, you can specify the file system type to use.

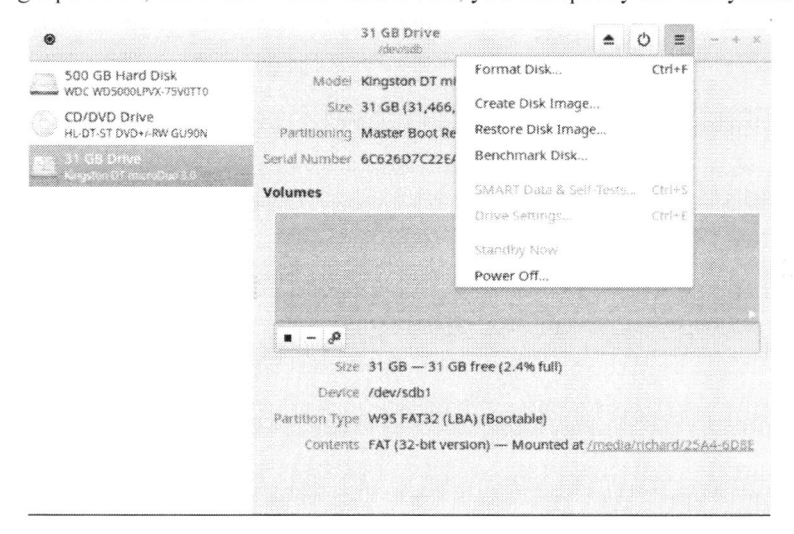

Figure 9-7: Disk Utility

If you select a hard disk device, information about the hard disk is displayed on the right pane in the Drive section, such as the model name, firmware version, serial number, size, device name, and SMART status (see Figure 9-8). Click the task button to display the task menu on the upper right with tasks you can perform on the hard drive: Format, Benchmark, and SMART Data.

The Volumes section on the hard disk pane shows the partitions set up on the hard drive (see Figure 9-9). Partitions are displayed in a graphical icon bar, which displays each partition's size and location on the drive. Clicking on a partition entry on the graphical icon bar displays information about that partition such as the file system type, device name, partition label, and partition size. The "Contents" entry tells if a partition is mounted. If in use, it displays a "Mounted at:" entry with a link consisting of the path name where the file system is mounted. You can click on this path name to open a folder with which you can access the file system. The button bar below the Volumes images provides additional task you can perform, such as unmounting a file system (square button) and deleting a partition (minus button). From the more tasks menu, you can choose entries to change the partition label, type, and mount options. Certain partitions, like extended and swap partitions, display limited information and have few allowable tasks.

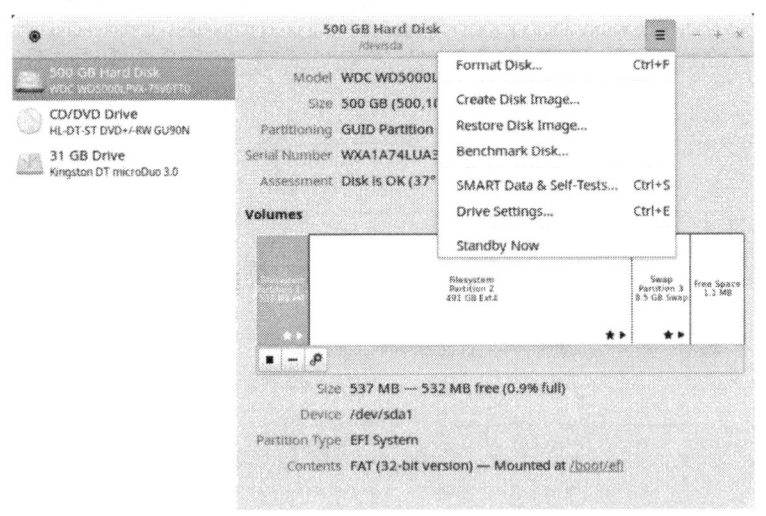

Figure 9-8: Disk Utility, hard drive

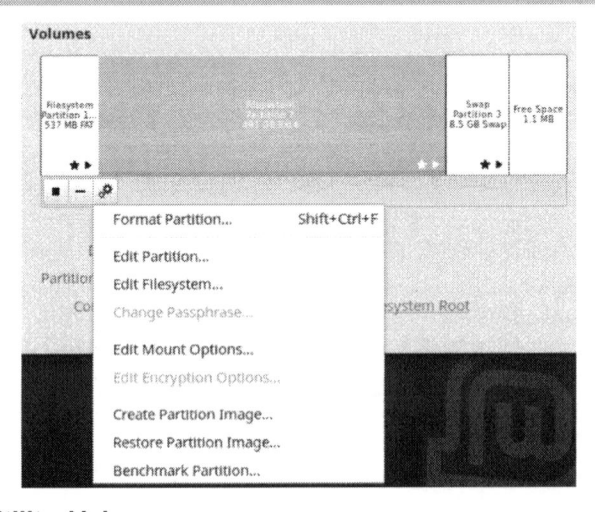

Figure 9-9: Disk Utility, Volumes

For more detailed hardware information about a hard drive, you can click on the "SMART Data and Tests" entry from the task menu in the upper right. This opens a SMART data dialog with hardware information about the hard disk (see Figure 9-10) including temperature, power cycles, bad sectors, and the overall health of the disk. The Attributes section lists SMART details such as the Read Error Rate, Spinup time, temperature, and write error rate. Click the switch to on to enable the tests, and off to disable testing. Click the "Refresh" button to manually run the tests. Click the "Start Self-test" button to open a menu with options for short, extended, and conveyance tests.

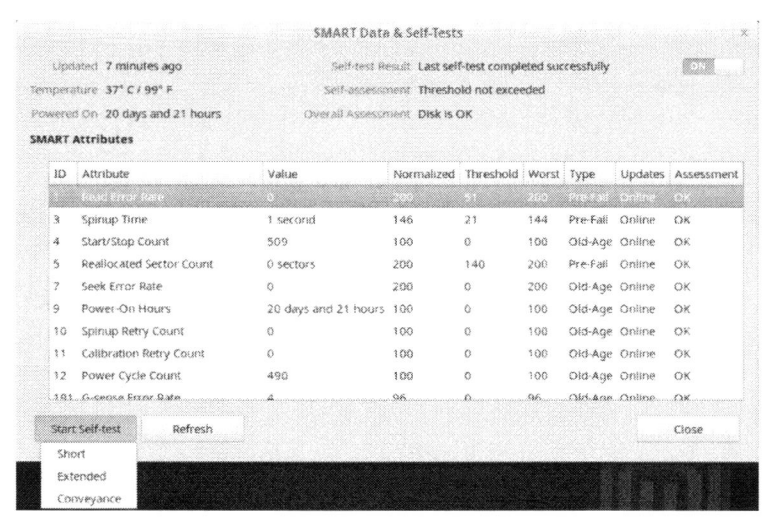

Figure 9-10: Disk Utility: Hard Disk hardware SMART data

Plymouth

Plymouth provides a streamlined, efficient, and faster graphical boot that does not require X server support. It relies on the kernel's Kernel Modesettings (KMS) feature that provides direct support for basic graphics. With the Direct Rendering Manager driver, Plymouth can make use of different graphical plugins. KMS support is currently provided for AMD, Nvidia, and Intel graphics cards. The Plymouth Linux Mint logo theme is installed by default. You can install others like solar, glow, or KDE Linux Mint-logo. The theme packages begin with the prefix **plymouth-theme**. You can search for them on the Synaptic Package Manager. You can also install them from Software Manager (search on Plymouth).

Choosing to use a Plymouth theme involves using the Debian alternatives system, which is designed to designate an application to use when there are several alternative versions to select. A link is set up for the application to use in the **/etc/alternatives** directory. For Plymouth, this link is named **default.plymouth**. You can choose a Plymouth theme by entering the **update-alternatives** command with the **--config** option, the **default.plymouth** link, and the **sudo** command in a terminal window as shown here.

```
sudo update-alternatives --config default.plymouth
```

This displays a numbered menu listing your installed themes. An asterisk indicates the current theme. Enter the number of the theme you want to use. The **default.plymouth** link is then set to the theme you choose. When your system starts up again, it will use that Plymouth theme.

Some of the non-Linux Mint themes may hang on start up. In that case, you can edit the boot kernel line to remove the **splash** option and then boot to your system (see Chapter 3). Then use **update-alternatives** to change your Plymouth theme.

Sound Preferences

Your sound cards are detected automatically for you when you start up your system, by ALSA, which is invoked by udev when your system starts up. Removable devices, like USB sound devices, are also detected. See Table 9-3 for a listing of sound device and interface tools.

Sound tool	Description
KMix	KDE sound connection configuration and volume tool
alsamixer	ALSA sound connection configuration and volume tool
amixer	ALSA command for sound connection configuration
Sound Preferences	GNOME Sound Preferences, used to select and configure your sound interface
PulseAudio	PulseAudio sound interface, the default sound interface for Linux Mint. www.pulseaudio.org
PulseAudio Volume Control	PulseAudio Volume Control, controls stream input, output, and playback, **pavucontrol** package
PulseAudio Volume Meter	Volume Meter, displays active sound levels
PulseAudio Manager	Manager for information and managing PulseAudio, **pman** package
PulseAudio Preferences	Options for network access and virtual output

Table 9-3: Sound device and interface tools

In addition to hardware drivers, sound systems also use sound interfaces to direct encoded sound streams from an application to the hardware drivers and devices. Linux Mint uses the PulseAudio server for its sound interface. PulseAudio aims to combine and consolidate all sound interfaces into a simple, flexible, and powerful server. The ALSA hardware drivers are still used, but the application interface is handled by PulseAudio. PulseAudio is installed as the default set up for Linux Mint and Ubuntu.

Note: Sound devices on Linux are supported by hardware sound drivers. With the Ubuntu kernel, hardware support is implemented by the Advanced Linux Sound Architecture (ALSA) system. You can find more about ALSA at http://alsa-project.org.

PulseAudio is a cross-platform sound server, allowing you to modify the sound level for different audio streams separately. See **https://www.freedesktop.org/wiki/Software/PulseAudio/** for documentation and help. PulseAudio offers complete control over all your sound streams, letting you combine sound devices and direct the stream anywhere on your network. PulseAudio is not confined to a single system. It is network capable, letting you direct sound from one PC to another.

As an alternative, you can use the command-line ALSA control tool, **alsamixer**. This will display all connections and allow you to use keyboard commands to select (arrow keys), mute (m key), or set sound levels (Page Up and Down). Press the ESC key to exit. The **amixer** command lets you perform the same tasks for different sound connections from the command line. To actually play and record from the command-line, you can use the **play** and **rec** commands.

Sound menu (volume control and player access)

The sound menu (speaker icon, sound applet) displays volume control, media player access, sound settings access, and sound device selection entries (see Figure 9-11). You can change your application's sound volume using a sliding bar. When you click on the sound volume slider, you can use your mouse scroll button to adjust the sound volume. To perform volume control for specific devices like a microphone, you use Sound Settings, which you can access from the System Settings, or from the sound menu's Sound Settings entry.

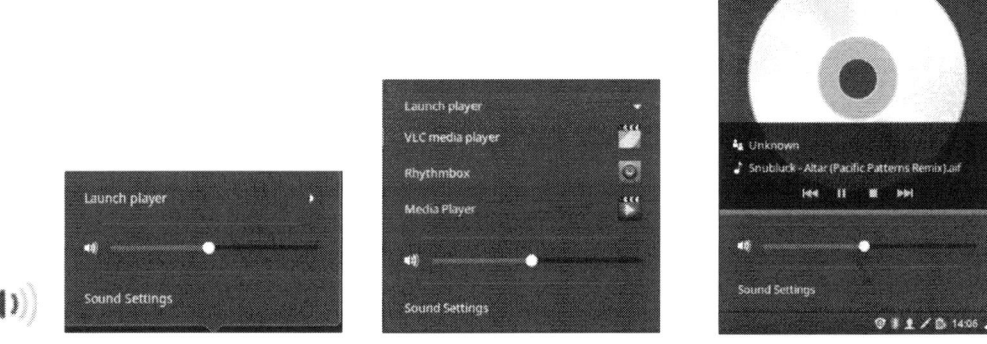

Figure 9-11: Sound Menu

The sound menu provides basic access to the media players, such as Rhythmbox, showing the title of the current track and displaying controls to play, pause, and move to the previous and next tracks. Click the "Launch player" entry to open a listing of your installed players. As you play an audio source, a description of the audio track and basic control buttons are displayed on the sound menu. When you are playing, the sound icon on the panel changes to a music note.

If you wish to mute the sound, you can right-click on the sound icon to display switches for muting the output and input (see Figure 9-12). Click the switch to mute the sound.

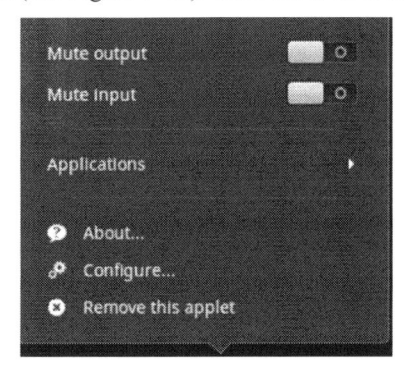

Figure 9-12: Sound Menu, right click, mute options

Sound: PulseAudio

You configure sound devices and set the volume for sound effects, input and output, and applications using GNOME sound tool. Choose Sound on the System Settings dialog. This opens the Sound dialog, which has four tabs: Output, Input, Sound Effects, and Applications (see Figure 9-13).

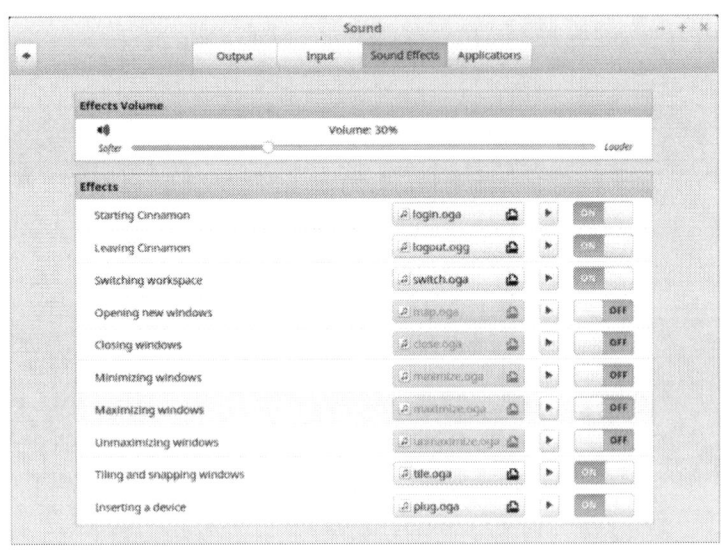

Figure 9-13: Sound Preferences

The Sound Effects tab lets you choose sound effects for different operations such as switching workspaces or closing a window. A play button to the right of each effect lets you play the sound, and a button with the filename of the sound can be clicked to open the **/usr/share/mint-artwork-cinnamon/sounds** folder where you can choose a different sound file to use. You can turn an effect off by clicking the switch to the right of the play button. A sliding bar at the top in the Effects Volume section lets you set the volume for your sound effects.

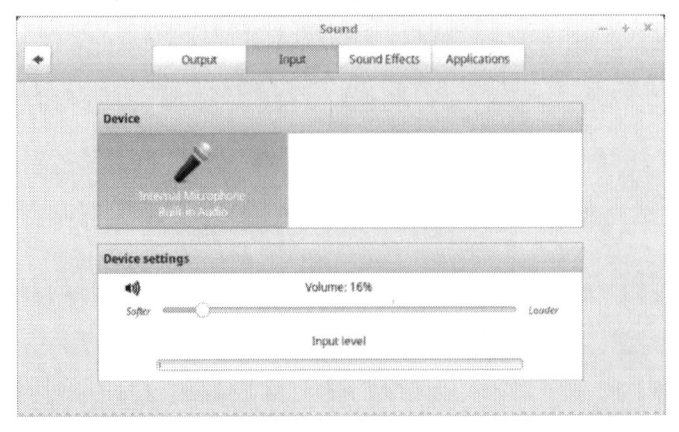

Figure 9-14: Sound Preferences: Input

On the Input tab, you choose the input device and set the input volume. Input devices are listed in the Device section at the top. In the "Device settings" section you can set the volume for a selected device. When speaking or recording, the input level is displayed (see Figure 9-14).

On the Output tab, you can configure settings for a selected device: Digital, Headphones, and Speakers. The available settings will become active according to the device and profile selected. From the "Output profile " menu you can choose from available outputs, if supported, such as analog speakers or surround sound. For a simple Analog Stereo Output, only the Volume and Balance settings are active (see Figure 9-15).

Sound devices that support multiple interfaces like analog surround sound 7.1 or digital SPDIF output, will display a list of interface combinations in the "Output profile" menu. Settings for Fade and Subwoofer are activated. From the menu, you can choose the type of output you want. Configuring digital output for Digital Output (S/PDIF) connectors is a simple matter of selecting the digital output and input entries on the Output and Input tabs. Only the Balance entry will be active.

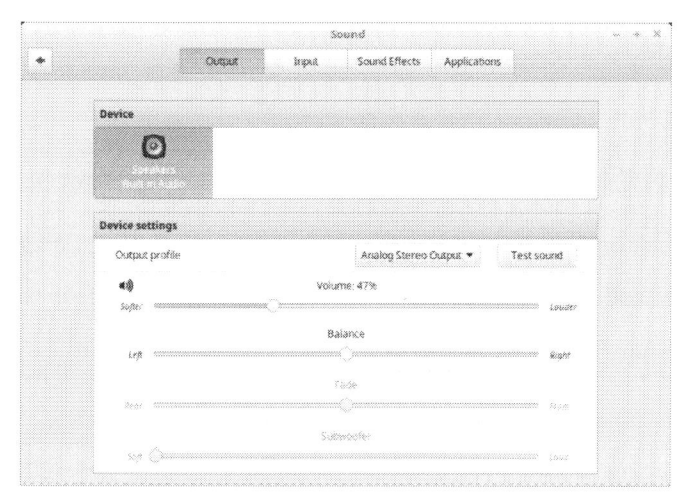

Figure 9-15: Sound Preferences: Output

A laptop may support only a simple internal audio device with left and right balance. Computers with more powerful sound devices have many more options. To test your speakers, click the 'Test sound" button to open the Speakers Testing dialog with test buttons for each speaker.

The Applications tab will show applications currently using sound devices. You can set the sound volume for each (see Figure 9-16).

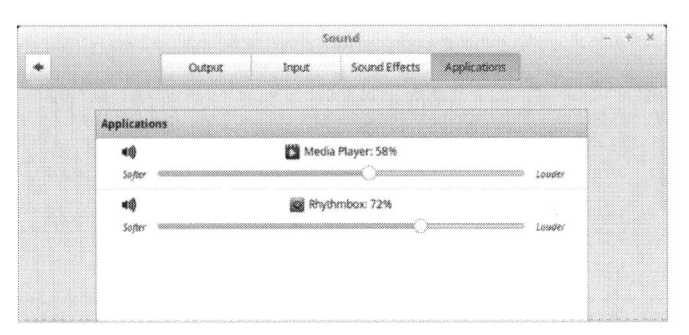

Figure 9-16: Sound Preferences: Applications

Installed with Pulse Audio are the Pulse Audio utilities (**pulseaudio-utils** package). These are command line utilities for managing Pulse Audio and playing sound files (see Table 9-4). The **paplay** and **pacat** will play sound files, **pactl** will let you control the sound server and **pacmd** lets you reconfigure it. Check the Man pages for each for more details. If you change your sound preferences frequently, you could use these commands in a shell script to make the changes, instead of having to use the preferences dialog each time. Some of these commands such as **parec** and **paplay** are links to the **pacat** command, which performs the actual tasks.

Sound tool	Description
pabrowse	List PulseAudio sound servers
pacat	Play, record, and configure a raw audio stream
pacmd	Generates a shell for entering configuration commands
pactl	Control a PulseAudio server, changing input and output sources and providing information about the server
padsp	PulseAudio wrapper for OSS sound applications
pamon	Link to pacat
paplay	Playback audio. The -d option specifies the output device, the -s option specifies the server, and the --volume option sets the volume (link to pacat)
parec	Record and audio stream (link to pacat)
parecord	Record and audio stream (link to pacat)
pasuspender	Suspend a PulseAudio server
pax11publish	Access PulseAudio server credentials

Table 9-4: PulseAudio commands (command-line)

PulseAudio applications

For additional configuration abilities, you can also install the Pulse Audio applications. Most begin with the prefix **pa** in the package name. You can install them from the Software Manager by searching for pulseaudio. Most PulseAudio tools are accessible from the Sound & Video menu. The PulseAudio tools and their command names are shown here.

PulseAudio Volume Control, **pavucontrol**

PulseAudio Volume Meter, **pavumeter**

PulseAudio Manager, **paman**

PulseAudio Preferences, **paprefs**

You can use the PulseAudio Volume Control tool to set the sound levels for different playback applications and sound devices (choose PulseAudio Volume Control in the Sound & Video menu).

The PulseAudio Volume Control applications will show five tabs: Playback, Recording, Output Devices, Input Devices, and Configuration (see Figure 9-17). The Playback tab shows all the applications currently using PulseAudio. You can adjust the volume for each application separately.

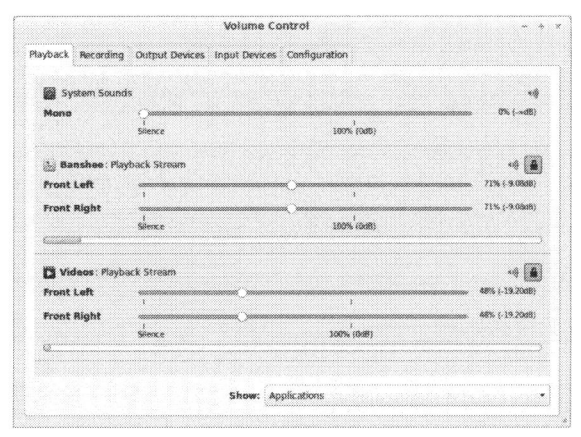

Figure 9-17: PulseAudio Volume Control, Playback

You can use the Output Devices tab panel to set the volume control at the source, and to select different output devices like Headphones (see Figure 9-18). The volume for input and recording devices are set on the Recording and Input Devices tabs. The configuration tab lets you choose different device profiles, like selecting Digital output or Surround Sound 5.1. To find the actual name of the SPDIF output is not always obvious. You may need to run **aplay -L** in a terminal window to see what the name of the digital output device is on your system. It will be the entry with Digital in it.

You can also use the PulseAudio Volume control to direct different applications (streams) to different outputs (devices). For example, you could have two sound sources running, one for video and another for music. The video could be directed through one device to headphones and the music through another device to speakers, or even to another PC. To redirect an application to a different device, right-click its name in the Playback tab. A pop-up menu will list the available devices and let you select the one you want to use.

The PulseAudio Volume Meter tool will show the actual volume of your devices.

The PulseAudio Manager will show information about your PulseAudio configuration (open a terminal window and enter the **paman** command). The Devices tab shows the currently active sinks (outputs or directed receivers) and sources. The Clients tab shows all the applications currently using PulseAudio for sound.

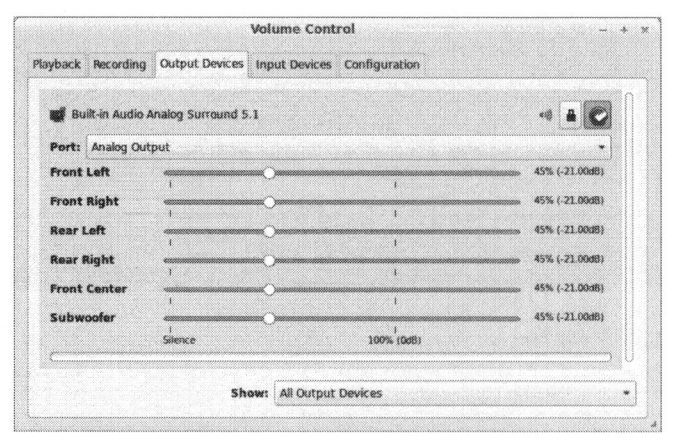

Figure 9-18: PulseAudio Volume Control, Output Devices

To configure network access, you use the PulseAudio Configuration tool, accessible from the Preferences menu. Here you can permit network access, configure the PulseAudio network server, (see Figure 9-19) and enable multicast and simultaneous output. If you are connected to a network with Linux systems also running PulseAudio that have allowed network access to their sound devices, their shared sound devices will be listed in the Sound Preferences Hardware tab, allowing you to access them.

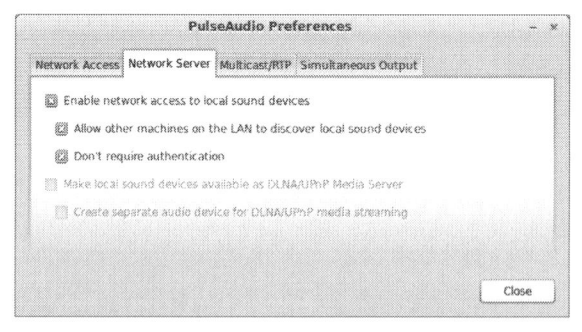

Figure 9-19: PulseAudio Preferences

Simultaneous output creates a virtual output device to the same hardware device. This lets you channel two sources onto the same output. With PulseAudio Volume Control, you could then channel playback streams to the same output device, but using a virtual device as the output for one. This lets you change the output volume for each stream independently. You could have music and voice directed to the same hardware device, using a virtual device for music and the standard device for voice. You can then reduce the music stream, or raise the voice stream.

dconf editor

The dconf editor provides key base configuration options for your GNOME-based desktops (Cinnamon and Mate), GNOME applications, and for X-Apps applications (see Figure 9-20). You can configure both your desktop and GNOME applications, such as the Cinnamon and Mate file managers (nemo and caja), the GNOME system monitor, and X-Apps. Most options deal with display features, such as the default options for Xplayer, the default size for dialogs, or whether to display an application's toolbar.

Configuration with dconf is performed on keys, which can be numbers, checkboxes, text, and menus listing possible options. Text editing supports click-and-drag with the mouse to select text, along with Ctrl-c, Ctrl-x, and Ctrl-v to copy, cut, and paste. Type to insert, use backspace to delete. For very long text entries, a scrollbar appears to let you scroll through the line. Changes take effect immediately. Should you make mistakes you can reset to the default settings by clicking the Set to Default button on the lower right corner.

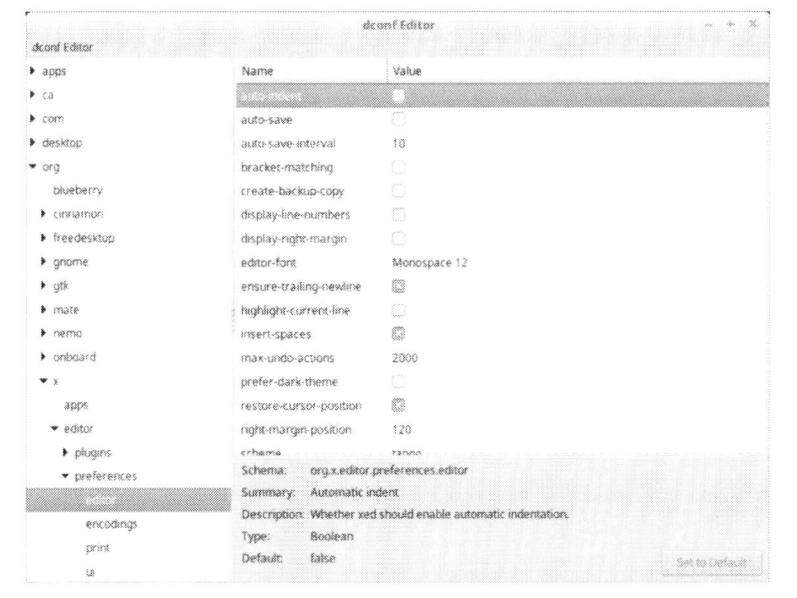

Figure 9-20: dconf editor

The dconf editor organizes keys into schemas, accessible as an expandable tree on the sidebar. The main schemas are apps, ca, com, desktop, org, and system. The org schema is where you will find the Cinnamon configuration keys, with subschemas for desklets, the desktop, background, and the muffin window manager. Here also are the Mate keys (**org.mate**) and the gnome applications keys (**org.gnome**). Under the com schema, you will find linuxmint subschema with a mintmenu subschema for Mint menu keys (**com.linuxmint.mintmenu**). Keep expanding subschemas until you find the key you want, in this case, com.linuxmint.mintmenu.

The keys for GNOME applications are located at **org.gnome**. Most deal with default display options.

The x schema lists the X-Apps application keys. Some let you set application specific options. For player schema (Xplayer) has keys to set contrast, hue, and resizing options (**org.x.plyaer**). The editor (Xed) lets you set margin, save, indent, and font options (**org.x.editor**).

10. System Administration

Linux Mint Administrative Tools
Controlled Administrative Access
Users and Groups (Cinnamon and Mate)
Bluetooth
File System Access
Shared Folders
GRUB Bootloader
Editing Configuration Files Directly
Backup Management
Logical Volume Management

Most administrative configurations tasks are performed for you automatically. Devices like printers, hard drive partitions, and graphics cards are detected and set up for you. There are cases where you may need to perform tasks, manually like adding new users and installing software. Such administrative operations can be performed with user-friendly system tools. Most administration tools are listed in the Administration and System Tools menus.

Linux Mint Administration Tools	Description
Software Manager	Software management using online repositories
Update Manager	Update tool using Linux Mint repositories
Synaptic Package Manager	Software management using online repositories (no longer supported by Linux Mint, available on the Universe repository)
Network Manager	Detects, connects, and configures your network interfaces
clock	GNOME Time & Date tool
Users and Groups	User configuration tool
users-admin	Older User and Group configuration tool, install gnome-system-tools.
system-config-printer	Printer configuration tool
system-config-samba	Configures your Samba server. User level authentication support.
shares-admin	Configures NFS network support, install gnome-system-tools
gnome-language-selector	Selects a language to use
Gufw	Configures your network firewall
FirewallD	FirewallD firewall daemon
Deja-dup	Backup tool using rsync
Backup Tool	Linux Mint backup tool

Table 10-1: Linux Mint Administration Tools

Administrative Tools

Administration is handled by a set of specialized administrative tools, such as those for user management and printer configuration (see Table 10-1). To access the desktop-based administrative tools, you need to log in as a user who has administrative access. You created this user when you first installed Linux Mint. System administrative tools are accessed from the Administration, Preferences, and System Tools menus. On the Cinnamon desktop, you can also access tools from the System Settings dialog. There are tools to set the time and date, manage users, configure printers, and install software. Users and Groups lets you create and modify users. Printing lets you install and reconfigure printers. All tools provide easy-to-use and intuitive desktop interfaces. Tools are identified by simple descriptive terms, whereas their actual names normally begin with terms such as admin or system-config. For example, the printer configuration tool is listed as Printing, but its actual name is **system-config-printer**.

Linux Mint uses the GNOME administrative tools with KDE counterparts, administrative tools adapted from the Fedora distribution supported by Red Hat Linux, and independent tools developed by open source projects. PolicyKit is used for device authorizations, and Linux Mint's Software Manager provides software management. The Printing administrative tool is Fedora's **system-config-printer**. Virus protection is handled by third party application, ClamAV. The Synaptic Package Manager is available, but no longer supported. The older GNOME administrative tools such as Users and Groups are also available, but not installed by default (**gnome-system-tools** package).

Many configuration tasks can also be handled on the command line, invoking programs directly. To use the command line, select the Terminal entry in the Administration menu to open a terminal window with a command line prompt. You will need administrative authorization, so precede the application name with the **sudo** command.

Controlled Administrative Access

To access administrative tools, you have to log in as a user who has administrative permissions. The user that you created during installation is given administrative permissions automatically. Log in as that user. When you attempt to use an administrative tool, a dialog opens prompting you to enter your user password. This is the password for the user you logged in as. Some tools will open without authorization but remain locked, preventing any modifications. These tools may have an Unlock button you can press to gain access. You can use the user management tool, Users and Groups, to grant or deny particular users administrative access.

To perform system administration operations, you must first have to have access rights enabling you to perform administrative tasks. There are several ways to gain such access: login as a sudo supported user, unlocking an administrative tool for access (PolicyKit authorization), and logging in as the root user. PolicyKit is the preferred access method and is used on many administrative tools. The **sudo** granted access method was used in previous Linux Mint releases and is still used for many tasks including software upgrade and installation. The root user access is still discouraged but provides complete control over the entire system.

PolicyKit: Provides access only to specific applications and only to users with administrative access for that application. Requires that the specific application be configured for use by PolicyKit. Linux Mint 18.2 uses a new version of PolicyKit called policykit-1 (Linux Mint repository). The original version, which is named simply policykit, is no longer available.

sudo and **pkexec**: Provides access to any application will full administrative authorization. It imposes a time limit to reduce risk. The **pkexec** command is used for graphical administrative tools like the Synaptic Package Manager. You will still need to use **sudo** to perform any command-line Linux commands at the root level, like moving files to an administrative directory or running the **service** command to start or stop servers. The **gksu** command can still be used, but is not recommended.

root user access, **su**: Provides complete direct control over the entire system. This is the traditional method for accessing administrative tools. It is disabled by default on Linux Mint, but can be enabled. The **su** command will allow any user to log in as the root user if they know the root user password.

nemo as root: From the desktop Cinnamon meu (right-click on the desktop) you can choose the "Open as Root" option to open the Nemo file manager with administrative (root) access. The file manager window displays a red bar below the toolbar showing "Elevated Privileges" title. You can then remove and modify any system files. This remains the most dangerous method of access, as you could easily remove or change critical system files and folders. Deletes are permanent and cannot be undone.

PolicyKit

PolicyKit controls access to certain applications and devices. It is one of the safest ways to grant a user direct access. PolicyKit configuration and support is already set up for you. A new version of PolicyKit, PolicyKit-1, is now used for PolicyKit operations. Configuration files for these operations are held in **/usr/share/polkit-1**. There is, as yet, no desktop tool you can use to configure these settings.

Note: External hard drives, such as USB connected hard drives, are mounted automatically

Difficulties occur if you want to change the authorization setting for certain actions, like mounting internal hard drives. Currently, you can change the settings by manually editing the configuration files in the **/usr/share/polkit-1/actions** directory, but this is risky. To make changes, you first have to know the action to change and the permission to set. The man page for **polkit** lists possible authorizations. The default authorizations are **allow_any** for anyone, **allow_inactive** for a console, and **allow_active** for an active console only (user logged in). These authorizations can be set to the following specific values.

auth_admin	Administrative user only, authorization required always
auth_admin_keep	Administrative user only, authorization kept for a brief period
auth_self	User authorization required
auth_self_keep	User authorization required authorization kept for a brief period
yes	Always allow access
no	Never allow access

You will need to know the PolicyKit action to modify and the file to edit. The action is listed in the PolicyKit dialog that prompts you to enter the password (expand the Details arrow) when you try to use an application. The filename will be the first segments of the action name with the suffix "policy" attached. For example, the action for mounting internal drives is:

`org.freedesktop.udisks2.filesystem-mount-system`

Its file is:

`org.freedesktop.udisks2.policy`

The file is located in the **/usr/share/polkit-1/actions** directory. It's full path name is:

`/usr/share/polkit-1/actions/org.freedesktop.udisks2.policy`

Users with administrative access, like your primary user, can mount partitions on your hard drives automatically. However, users without administrative access require authorization using an administrative password before they can mount a partition (see Figure 10-13). Should you want to allow non-administrative users to mount partitions without an authorization request, the **org.freedesktop.udisks2.policy** file in the **/usr/share/polkit-1** directory has to be modified to change the **allow_active** default for **filesystem-mount-system** action from **auth_admin_keep** to **yes**. The **auth_admin_keep** option requires administrative authorization.

Enter the following to edit the **org.freedesktop.udisks2.policy** file in the **/usr/share/polkit-1/actions** directory:

```
sudo gedit /usr/share/polkit-1/actions/org.freedesktop.udisks2.policy
```

Locate the **action id** labeled as:

```
<action id ="org.feedesktop.udisks2.filesystem-mount-system">
  <description>Mount a filesystem on a system device</description>
```

This is usually the second action id. At the end of that action section, you will find the following entry. It will be located within a defaults subsection, <defaults>.

```
<allow_active>auth_admin_keep</allow_active>
```

Replace **auth_admin_keep** with **yes**.

```
<allow_active>yes</allow_active>
```

Save the file. Non-administrative users will no longer have to enter a password to mount partitions.

sudo

The sudo service provides administrative access to specific users. You have to be a user on the system with a valid username and password that has been authorized by the sudo service for administrative access. This allows other users to perform specific super user operations without having full administrative level control. You can find more about sudo at **https://www.sudo.ws**.

TIP: If you have difficulties with your system configuration, check the Linux Mint forum and community sites for possible solutions, https://forums.linuxmint.com and https://community.linuxmint.com.

sudo command

Some administrative operations require access from the command line in the terminal window. For such operations, you would use the **sudo** command. You can open a terminal window from Accessories menu. On the Cinnamon desktop, you click the terminal icon on the panel or on the favorites bar in the Cinnamon menu.

To use **sudo** to run an administrative command, you would precede the command with the **sudo** command. You are then prompted to enter your password. You will be issued a time-restricted ticket to allow access. The following example sets the system date using the **date** command.

```
sudo date 0406165908
password:
```

You can also use the sudo command to run an application with administrative access. From the terminal window, you would enter the sudo command with the application name as an argument. For example, to use the **nano** editor to edit a system configuration file, you would start **nano** using the **sudo** command in a terminal window, with the **nano** command and the filename as its arguments. This starts up **nano** editor with administrator privileges. The following example will allow you to edit the **/etc/fstab** file to add or edit file system entries. You will be prompted for your user password.

```
sudo nano /etc/fstab
```

sudo configuration

Access for **sudo** is controlled by the **/etc/sudoers** file. This file lists users and the commands they can run, along with the password for access. If the NOPASSWD option is set, then users will not need a password. The ALL option, depending on the context, can refer to all hosts on your network, all root-level commands, or all users. See the Man page for **sudoers** for detailed information on all options.

```
man sudoers
```

To make changes or add entries, you have to edit the file with the special sudo editing command **visudo**. This invokes the nano editor (see Chapter 5) to edit the **/etc/sudoers** file. Unlike a standard editor, **visudo** will lock the **/etc/sudoers** file and check the syntax of your entries. You are not allowed to save changes unless the syntax is correct. If you want to use a different editor, you can assign it to the EDITOR shell variable. Use Ctrl-x to exit and Ctrl-o to save. Be sure to invoke **visudo** with the **sudo** command to gain authorized access.

```
sudo visudo
```

A **sudoers** entry has the following syntax:

```
user    host=command
```

The *host* is a host on your network. You can specify all hosts with the ALL term. The *command* can be a list of commands, some or all qualified by options such as whether a password is required. To specify all commands, you can also use the ALL term. The following gives the user george full root-level access to all commands on all hosts:

```
george  ALL = ALL
```

In addition, you can let a user run as another user on a given host. Such alternate users are placed within parentheses before the commands. For example, if you want to give **george** access to the **beach** host as the user **mydns**, you use the following:

```
george beach = (mydns) ALL
```

To give **robert** access on all hosts to the time tool, you would use

```
robert ALL=/usr/bin/time-admin
```

To specify a group name, you prefix the group with a **%** sign, as in **%mygroup**. This way, you can give the same access to a group of users. By default, **sudo** will grant access to all users in the **admin** group. These are user granted administrative access. The ALL=(ALL) ALL entry allows access by the administrative group users to all hosts as all users to all commands.

```
%admin   ALL=(ALL)   ALL
```

With the NOPASSWD option, you can allow members of a certain group access without a password. A commented **sudo** group is provided in the **/etc/sudoers** file.

```
%sudo    ALL=NOPASSWD:   ALL
```

Though on Linux Mint, sudo is configured to allow **root** user access, Linux Mint does not create a **root** user password. This prevents you from logging in as the **root** user, rendering the sudo root permission useless. The default **/etc/sudoers** file does configure full access for the root user to all commands. The ALL=(ALL) ALL entry allows access by the root to all hosts as all users to all commands. If you were to set up a root password for the root user, the root user could then log in and have full administrative access.

```
root     ALL=(ALL)    ALL
```

If you want to see what commands you can run, you use the **sudo** command with the **-l** option. The **-U** option specifies a particular user. In the following example, the user richard has full administrative access.

```
$ sudo -U richard -l
User richard may run the following commands on this host:
   (ALL) All
```

pkexec

You can use the **pkexec** command in place of **sudo** to run graphical applications with administrative access. The **pkexec** tool is a policykit alternative to **sudo**, and requires that your application has a corresponding policykit action file. Applications like user accounts, Udisks, and NetworkManager already have action files. Others, like Xed, do not. To use **pkexec** with Xed, you have to create a policykit action file for it. This is a simple process, copying most of the entries from the example in the **pkexec** man page. The askubuntu site (**https://askubuntu.com**) also has a detailed explanation on how to do this (search on "pkexec" and open the "How to configure pkexec" entry). The **pkexec** tool will prompt you to enter your password (See Figure 10-1).

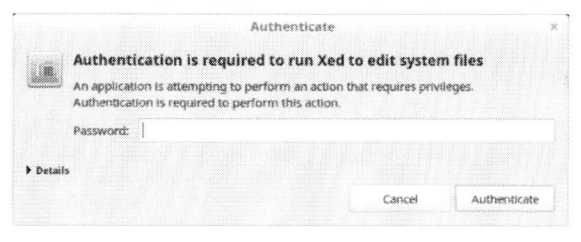

Figure 10-1: pkexec prompt for secure access

You can enter the **pkexec** command in a terminal window with the application as an argument, or set up an application launcher with **pkexec** as the command. The following example will start up the Xed editor with administrative access, allowing you to edit system configuration files directly (see Figure 10-2). A red bar below the toolbar displays an "Elevated Messages" notice so that you know you are running the Xed editor with administrative access.

```
pkexec xed
```

One way to set up a policy file for an application such as Xed is to copy the example in the **pkexec** man page. Change the example entries to xed. For the message entry, you only need a simple message. Be sure to add an annotate line at the end for desktop access, setting the **exec.allow_gui** option to true.

```xml
<annotate key="org.freedesktop.policykit.exec.allow_gui">true</annotate>
```

Alternatively, you could simply copy a simple policy file, change the name, and edit it to replace the program names and the message (for example, making a copy of **com.ubuntu.pkexec.synaptic.policy** located in the **/usr/share/polkit-1/actions** directory). Be sure to use the **sudo** command with **cp** command in a terminal window to perform the copy.

sudo cp com.ubuntu.pkexec.synaptic.policy org.freedesktop.policykit.pkexec.xed.policy

Edit the file and replace **synaptic** with **xed**, and change the message.

A sample policy file for Xed is follows.

org.freedesktop.policykit.pkexec.xed.policy

```xml
<?xml version="1.0" encoding="UTF-8"?>
  <!DOCTYPE policyconfig PUBLIC
    "-//freedesktop//DTD PolicyKit Policy Configuration 1.0//EN"
    "http://www.freedesktop.org/standards/PolicyKit/1/policyconfig.dtd">
<policyconfig>

 <action id="org.freedesktop.policykit.pkexec.xed">
   <description>Run the Xed program</description>
   <message>Authentication is required to run xed to edit system files</message>
   <icon_name>xed</icon_name>
   <defaults>
      <allow_any>auth_admin</allow_any>
      <allow_inactive>auth_admin</allow_inactive>
      <allow_active>auth_self_keep</allow_active>
   </defaults>
   <annotate key="org.freedesktop.policykit.exec.path">/usr/bin/xed</annotate>
   <annotate key="org.freedesktop.policykit.exec.allow_gui">true</annotate>
 </action>

</policyconfig>
```

Note: You can still use the gksu command, which is installed on Linux Mint. It is not recommended. You should use sudo or pkexec instead.

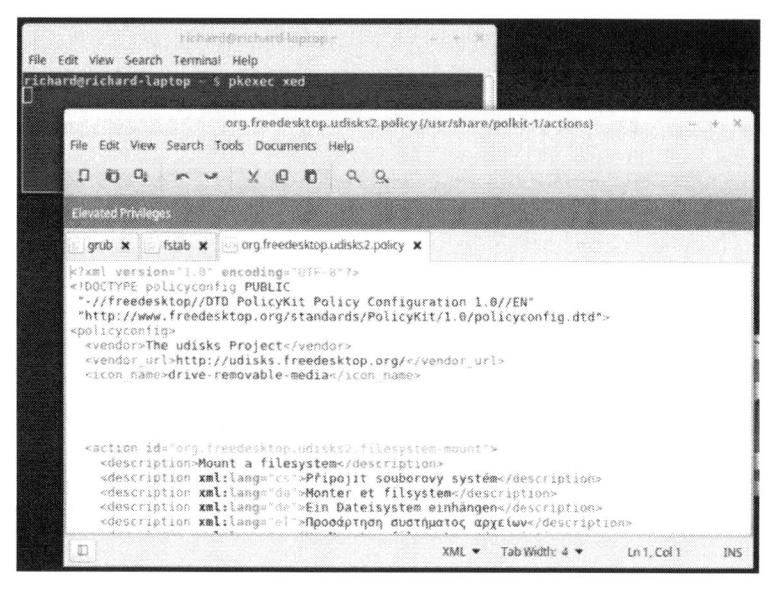

Figure 10-2: Invoking Xed with the pkexec command

Root User Access: root and su

You can access the root user from any normal terminal window using the **sudo** command on the **su** command. The **su** command is the superuser command. Superuser is another name for the **root** user. A user granted administrative access by **sudo** could then become the **root** user. The following logs into the root user.

```
sudo su
```

Like Ubuntu, Linux Mint is designed never to let anyone directly log in as the root user. The **root** user has total control over the entire system. Instead, certain users are given administrative access with which they can separately access administrative tools, performing specific tasks. Even though a **root** user exists, a password for the root user is not defined, never allowing access to it.

You can activate the root user by using the **passwd** command to create a root user password. Enter the **passwd** command with the **root** username in a **sudo** operation.

```
sudo passwd root
```

You are prompted for your administrative password and then prompted by the **passwd** command to enter a password for the **root** user. You are then prompted to repeat the password.

```
Enter new UNIX password:
Retype new UNIX password:
passwd: password updated successfully
```

You can then log in with the **su** command as the root user, making you the superuser (you still cannot login as the root user from the display manager login window). Because a superuser has the power to change almost anything on the system, such a password is usually a carefully guarded secret, changed very frequently, and given only to those whose job it is to manage the system. With the correct password, you can log into the system as a system administrator and configure the system any way you want.

```
su root
```

The **su** command alone will assume the root username.

```
su
```

The **su** command can also be used to login to any user, provided you have that user's password.

```
su richard
```

To exit from a **su** login operation, just enter **exit**.

```
exit
```

Nemo with elevated privileges on Cinnamon desktop

The easiest way to edit system files on the Cinnamon desktop is to open the Nemo file manager with elevated privileges, essentially opening a file manager window that has root (administrative) access. To edit a configuration file in the **/etc** directory, you could then use the file manager to access the **/etc** directory, and then double-click on the file to open it with the Xed editor. This opens the file in Xed with administrative access, letting you change it easily. A red bar below the navigation bar displays an "Elevated Privileges" notice so that you know you are running the file manager with administrative access. To open the file manager with elevated privileges, open the desktop menu (right-click on the desktop) and choose the "Open as Root" entry (see Figure 10-3).

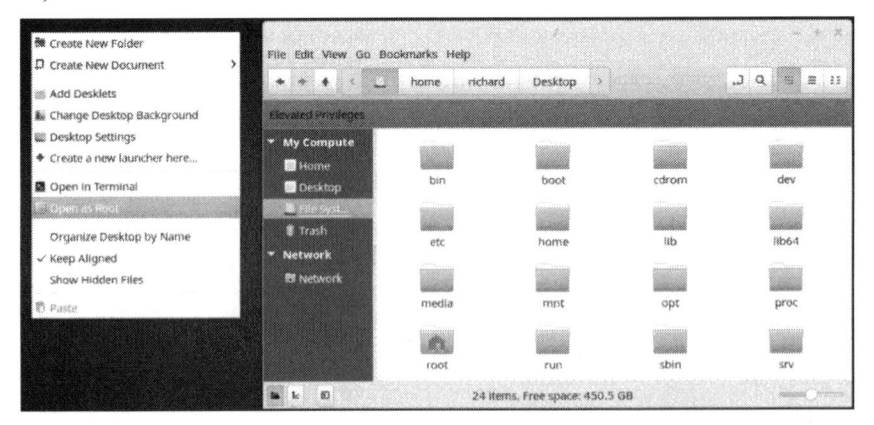

Figure 10-3: Nemo File Manager with Elevated Privileges (as root)

To do this you have to be a user with administrative access (not a standard user). You are first prompted to enter your password (see Figure 10-4). Clicking on the File System entry in the sidebar places you at the root directory where you can access the system folders and files (see Figure 10-3).

Figure 10-4: Prompt to open file manager as root (administrative access)

You can add or remove system folders and files. Be careful of what actions you take. It is very easy to use file manager operations to delete critical system folders and files, which would have catastrophic consequences for your system. Deletes are permanent and cannot be undone. At the same time, if you are careful and know what you want to do, the is an easy way to edit system configuration files. In Figure 10-5, the user has opened the grub configuration file in the /etc/default folder, which can then be edited directly. When invoked from the file manager with elevated privileges, the Xed editor had administrative access letting it change system files. A red bar below the toolbar displays an "Elevated Messages" notice so that you know you are running the Xed editor with administrative access.

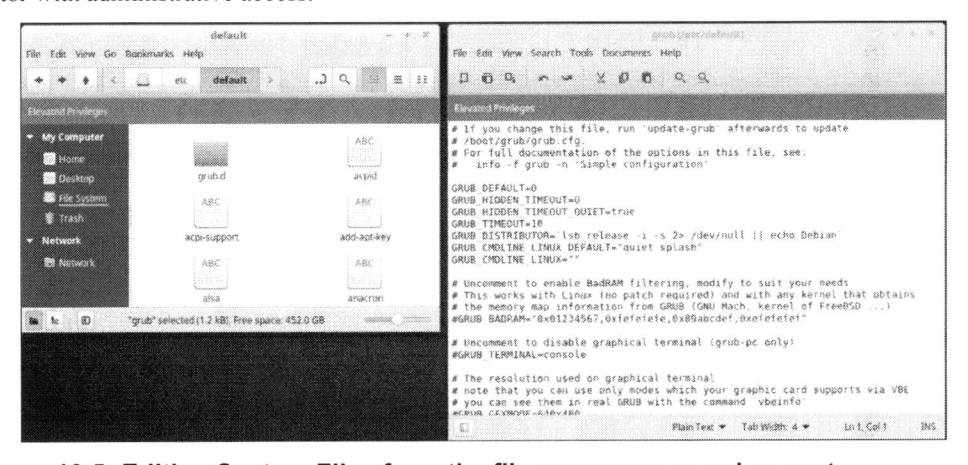

Figure 10-5: Editing System Files from the file manager opened as root

/etc/hostname and hostnamectl

The **/etc/hostname** file contains your hostname. You can use the **hostnamectl** command in a terminal window to display your current hostname and all information pertaining to it such as the machine ID, the kernel used, the architecture, chassis (type of computer), and the operating system (you can add the **status** option if you want). Three different kinds of hostnames are supported: static, pretty, and transient. You can set each with the **hostnamectl**'s **set-hostname** command with the corresponding type. The static hostname is used to identify your computer on the network (usually a fully qualified hostname). You can use the **--static** option to set it. The pretty hostname is a descriptive hostname made available to users on the computer. This can be set by **set-hostname** with the **--pretty** option. The transient hostname is one allocated by a network service such as DHCP, and can be managed with the **--transient** option. Without options, the **set-hostname** command will apply the name to all the hostname types.

```
hostnamectl set-hostname --pretty "my computer"
```

The **set-chassis** command sets the computer type, which can be desktop, laptop, server, tablet, handset, and vm (virtual system). Without a type specified it reverts to the default for the system. The **set-icon-name** command sets the name used by the graphical applications for the host.

Users and Groups (cinnamon-settings-users)

On the Cinnamon desktop, you can configure and create users and groups using the Users and Groups tool accessible from the Administration menu, and also from the System Settings dialog. Users and Groups is the cinnamon-settings-users tool available on the Cinnamon desktop. Users and Groups provides control for both users and groups.

Figure 10-6: Users and Groups (Cinnamon)

The Users and Groups dialog displays two tabs: Users and Groups. The Users tab displays two panes, a left scrollable pane for a list of users, showing their icon and login name and a right pane showing information about a selected user (see Figure 10-6). Below the left pane are buttons for adding and deleting users.

PolicyKit controls administrative access. When you first start up Users and Groups, a dialog appears that asks you to enter your password. Access is granted only to users that are administrators (administrator account type). Once the Users and Groups dialog appears you can then add or delete users, and change the password, name, group, account type, and a picture of any existing user.

When you add a new account, a dialog opens letting you set the account type (standard or administrator), the full name of the user, and the username (see Figure 10-7). Click Add to create the user. The new account appears on the right pane showing the name, icon, account type, password, and groups.

Figure 10-7: Users and Groups: new users

The account remains inactive until you specify a password (see Figure 10-8). The password entry displays the text "No password set." Click on the password entry to open the "Change Password" dialog open where you can enter the new password (see Figure 10-9). The "Show password" checkbox lets you see what the password is. Once the password is selected, the account becomes enabled.

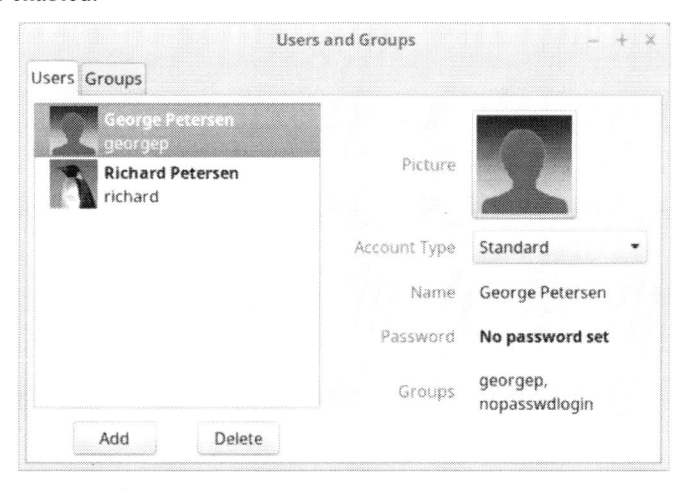

Figure 10-8: Users and Groups: inactive user

To choose an icon, click on the icon image to open an icon selection menu. Choose the one you want, or click on the "Browse for more pictures" entry at the bottom of the menu to open an image selection dialog to locate an image of your own.

You can change the icon, account type, name, password, and group selection by clicking on their entries.

Figure 10-9: Users and Groups: password dialog

To manage groups, click the Groups tab on the Users and Groups window. This displays a list of all groups (see Figure 10-10). To add a new group, click the Add button to open a dialog, where you can specify the group name (see Figure 10-11). If you want to remove a group, just select its entry in the Groups tab window and click the Delete button.

You use the Users tab on the Users and Groups window to add or remove users to or from a group. To add or remove a group for a user, select that user, and then click on the user's group entry. This opens a dialog listing all available groups (see Figure 10-12). Those that the user already belongs to are checked. You can add the users to a group by simply clicking the checkbox for that group. Uncheck groups you want to remove the user from.

Figure 10-10: Users and Groups: Groups tab

Figure 10-11: Users and Groups: add a group

Figure 10-12: Users and Groups: Users group dialog

Users and Groups (Mate)

The Mate desktop uses the older "Users and Groups" application (users-admin), accessible from "User and Groups" on the Administration menu. You can also install it on the Cinnamon desktop by installing the **gnome-system-tools** package. The "Users and Groups" application opens a User Settings window, which displays two panes, a left scrollable pane for a list of users, showing their icon and login name, and a right pane showing information about a selected user. Below the left pane are buttons for adding and deleting users, and for managing groups. At the bottom of the right pane is a button for a selected user's Advanced Settings.

When you start up the users-admin application, only read access is allowed, letting you scroll through the list of users, but not make any changes or add new ones (see Figure 10-13). Read-only access is provided to all users. Users will be able to see the list of users on your system, but they cannot modify their entries, add new ones, or delete current users. Administrative access is required to perform these operations.

Figure 10-13: Users and Groups (Mate)

PolicyKit controls administrative access for the users-admin tool. When you first click a task button, such as Add, Delete, or Advanced Settings, an Authenticate dialog will open and prompt you to enter your user password. You will also be prompted to authenticate if you click a Change link to change a user password, account type, or name.

To change settings for a user, select the user in the User Settings window. On the right pane the username, account type and password access are listed with a Change link to the right of each. Clicking on a Change link lets you change that property. When you click a Change link, an authentication dialog will prompt you to enter an administrative user password. To change a username, click the Change link to the right of the username to open the "Change Username and Login" dialog with a text box for entering the new name.

To change a user password, you would click the Change link to the right of the Password entry to open the "Change User Password" dialog with entries for the current password and the new password (see Figure 10-14). You can also choose to generate a random password.

Figure 10-14: User Settings: Change User Password dialog

Figure 10-15: User Settings: Change User Account Type

An account type can be Administrator, Desktop User, or Custom. When you click the Change link for the Account type, the "Change User Account Type" dialog opens with options for each (see Figure 10-15).

For more detailed configuration, you click the Advanced Settings button to open the "Change Advanced User Settings" dialog, which has tabs for Contact Information, User Privileges, and Advanced (see Figure 10-16. On the Contact tab, you can add basic contact information if you wish, for an office address, as well as work and home phones.

On the User Privileges tab, you can control device access and administrative access (see Figure 10-13). You can restrict or allow access to CD-ROMs, scanners, and external storage like USB drives. You can also determine whether the user can perform administrative tasks.

The Advanced tab lets you select a home directory, the shell to use, a main group, and a user ID. Defaults are already chosen for you. A home directory in the name of the new user is specified and the shell used is the BASH shell. Normally you would not want to change these settings, though you might prefer to use a different shell, like the C-Shell. For the group, the user has a group with its own username (same as the short name).

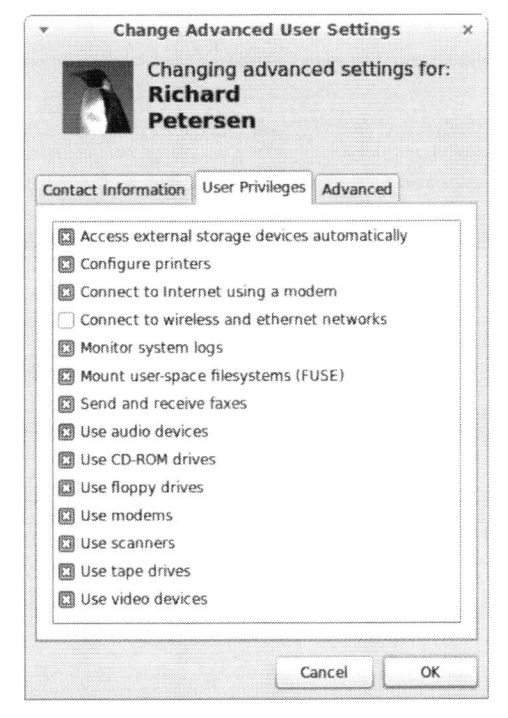

Figure 10-16: Users and Groups: Change User Privileges

Should to you decide to delete a user, you are prompted to keep or delete the user's home directory along with the user's files.

New Users (Users and Groups)

To create a new user, click the Add button in the Users Settings window to open a "Create New User" dialog, where you can enter the username. A short name is automatically entered for you, using the user's first name and the first letter of the last name. You can change the short name if you wish, but it must be in lowercase. The short name is also the name of the new user main group (see Figure 10-17). The new user is then added to the User Settings window.

The "Change User Password" dialog is then displayed, with entries for the new password and confirmation. You can also choose to use a randomly generated password instead (see Figure 10-18). Click the Generate button generate a password.

If you decide not to enter a password (click Cancel), the account will remain disabled. To enable it later, click on the Enable Account button to open the "Change User Password" dialog where you can add the password.

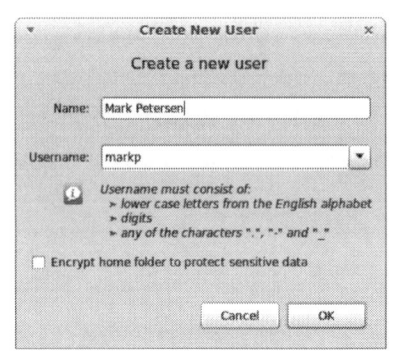

Figure 10-17: Users and Groups: Create New User

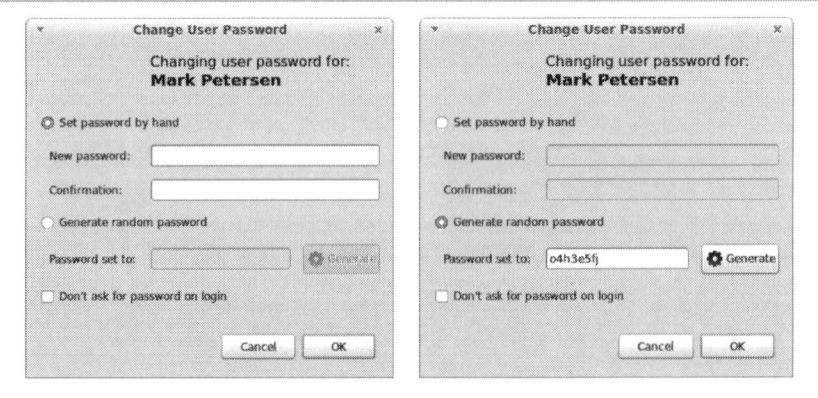

Figure 10-18: Users and Groups: new user password

The Account type is set initially to Desktop user, restricting access by the new user. Should you want to enable administrative access for this user, click the Change link to the right of the Account type entry to open the "Change User Account Type" dialog, where you can change the account type to Administrator (see Figure 10-15). To set more specific privileges and for key user configuration settings such as the home directory and user id, click the Advanced Settings button to open the "Change Advanced User Settings" dialog with Contact Information, User Privileges, and Advanced tabs (see Figure 10-13).

Alternatively, you can use the `useradd` command in a terminal window or command line to add Users and Groups and the `userdel` command to remove them. The following example adds the user **dylan** to the system:

```
$ useradd dylan
```

Groups (Users and Groups)

To manage groups, click the Manage Groups button in the Users Settings window. This opens a Group Settings window that lists all groups (see Figure 10-19). To add or remove users to or from a group, click the group name in the Group Settings window and click Properties. You can then check or uncheck users from the Group Members listing.

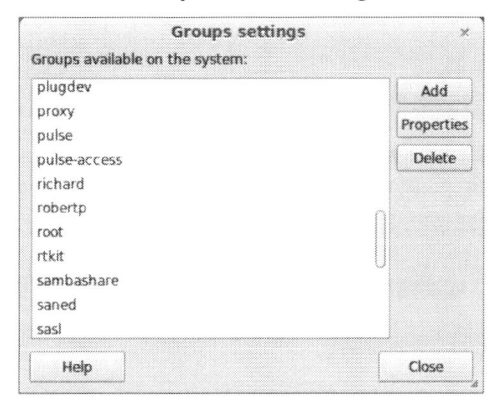

Figure 10-19: Users and Groups: Groups settings

To add a new group, click the Add Group button in the Group Settings window to open a New Group dialog, where you can specify the group name, its id, and select the users to add to the group (see Figure 10-120). If you want to remove a group, just select its entry in the Groups Settings window and click the Delete button.

Figure 10-20: Group Properties: Group Users panel

Passwords

The easiest way to change your password is to use the Users and Groups dialog available from System Settings as Users and Groups, and from the Administration menu. Select your username, then click the button to the right of the Password label to open the Change Password dialog (see Figure 10-7).

Alternatively, you can use the `passwd` command. In a terminal window enter the `passwd` command. The command prompts you for your current password. After entering your current password and pressing ENTER, you are then prompted for your new password. After entering the new password, you are asked to re-enter it. This makes sure you have actually entered the password you intended to enter.

```
$ passwd
Changing password for richard.
(current) UNIX password:
Enter new UNIX password:
Retype new UNIX password:
passwd: password updated successfully
$
```

Managing Services

Many administrative functions operate as services that need to be turned on (see Chapter 13). They are daemons, constantly running and checking for requests for their services. When you install a service, its daemon is normally turned on automatically. You can start, stop, and restart a service from a terminal window using the **service** command with the service name and the commands: **start**, **stop**, **restart**, and **status**. The status command tells you if a service is already running. To restart the Samba file sharing server (**smdb**) you would use the following command.

```
sudo service smbd restart
```

Linux Mint and Ubuntu use systemd to manage services. Systemd services are managed using **.service** configuration files in the **/lib/systemd/system** and **/etc/systemd/system** directories.

File System Access

Various file systems can be accessed on Linux Mint easily. Any additional internal hard drive partitions on your system, both Linux and Windows NTFS, will be detected automatically, but not mounted. In addition, you can access remote Windows shared folders and make your shared folders accessible.

Access to Internal Linux File Systems

Linux Mint will automatically detect other Linux file systems (partitions) on all your internal hard drives. Entries for these partitions are displayed on a file manager sidebar's Computer section. Initially, they are not mounted. Administrative users can mount internal partitions by clicking on its entry or icon, which mounts the file system and displays its icon on the desktop. A file manager window opens displaying the top-level contents of the file system. The file system is mounted under the **/media** directory in a folder named with the file system (partition) label, or, if unlabeled, with the device UUID name.

Non-administrative users (users you create with a standard account type), cannot mount internal partitions unless the task is authenticated using an administrative user's password. An authorization window will appear, similar to that shown in Figure 10-21. You will be asked to choose a user who has administrative access from a drop-down menu, and then enter that user's password. If there is only one administrative user, that user is selected automatically and you are prompted to enter that user's password. Whenever a standard user logs in again, that user will still have to mount the file system, again providing authorization.

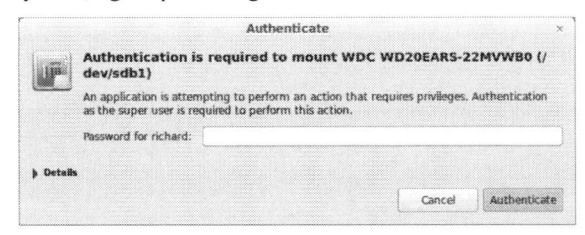

Figure 10-21: Mount authorization request for non-administrative users

Access to Windows NTFS File Systems on Local Drives

If you have installed Linux Mint on a dual-boot system with Windows, Linux NTFS file system support is installed automatically. Your NTFS partitions are mounted using Filesystem in Userspace (FUSE). The same authentication control used for Linux file systems applies to NTFS file systems. Entries for the NTFS partitions are placed on the file manager sidebar's Devices section with an eject button to mount and unmount the file system. If you are a user with administrative access, the file system is mounted (Eject button on file manager sidebar). If you are a user without administrative access, you will be asked to choose a user that has administrative access from a drop-down menu, and then enter that user's password, providing authorization. The NTFS file system is then mounted with icons displayed on the Launcher. You can access the file system by clicking on its desktop icon or its entry in a file manager sidebar Devices section. The partitions will be mounted under the **/media** directory with their UUID numbers or labels used as folder names. The NTFS partitions are mounted using **ntfs-3g** drivers.

Access to Local Network Shared File Systems (Windows)

Shared Windows folders and printers on any of the computers connected to your local network are automatically accessible from any file manager window sidebar under Network. The DNS discovery service (Avahi) automatically detects hosts on your home or local network and will let you access directly any of their shared folders. When you double-click on the file system icon, you will be asked to provide authorization, as in Figure 10-22, specifying the domain and password.

To access the shared network folders, choose "Network" in the Network section of the file manager sidebar. Your connected computers will be listed. If you know the name of the Windows computer you want to access, just click on its icon, otherwise, click on the Windows network icon to see just the Windows machines. Once selected, the shared folders are shown (see Figure 10-23). You can then access a shared folder and it will be mounted automatically on your desktop. The Network section of the file manager sidebar will show an entry for the folder with an Eject button for un-mounting it, as well as an icon for the folder on the desktop. Figure 10-24 shows the

myshared-data shared folder on a Windows system mounted on the Network window and on the desktop.

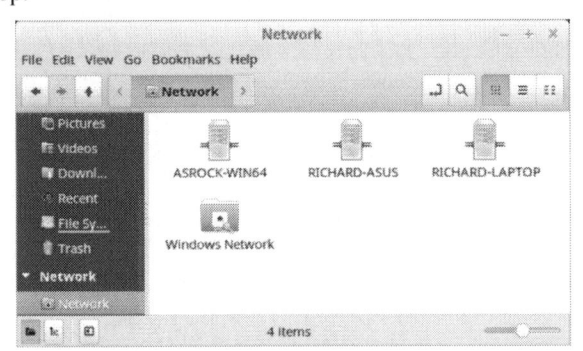

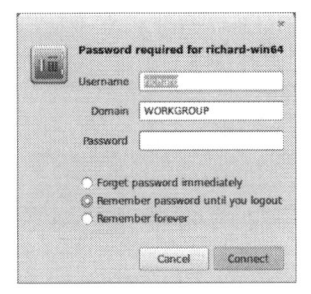

Figure 10-22: Network authorization

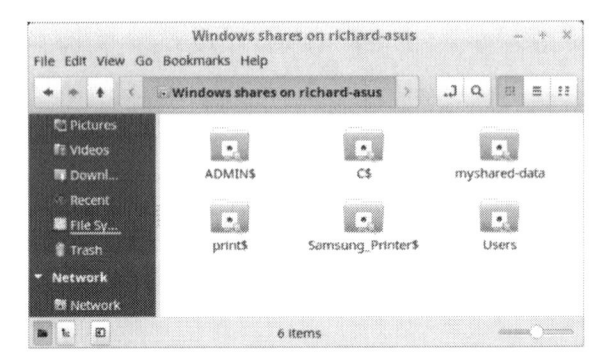

Figure 10-23: Network window

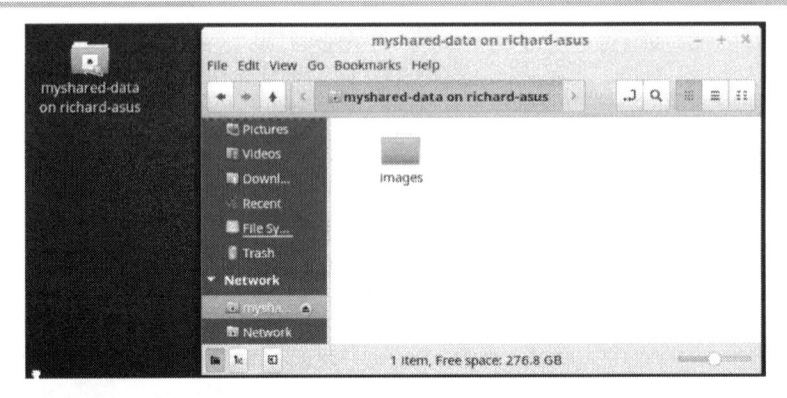

Figure 10-24: Mount remote Windows shares

Other local computers cannot access your shared folders until you install a sharing server, Samba for Windows systems and NFS for Linux/Unix systems. Should you attempt to share a directory, a notice is displayed prompting you to install the sharing service (Samba and NFS). Be sure also to allow firewall access for Samba and desktop browsing (see Chapter 11, Firewalls).

Shared Folders for your network

To share a folder on your Linux Mint system, right-click on it and select Sharing Options. This opens a window where you can allow sharing and choose whether to permit modifying, adding, or deleting files in the folder (see Figure 10-25). You can also use the Share tab on the file's properties dialog (see Figure 10-26). You can allow access to anyone who does not also have an account on your system (guest). Once you have made your selections, click the Create Share button. You can later change the sharing options if you want.

Figure 10-25: Folder Sharing Options

To allow access by other users, permissions on the folder will have to be changed. You will be prompted to allow Nemo or Caja to make these changes for you. Just click the "Add the permissions automatically" button (see Figure 10-26).

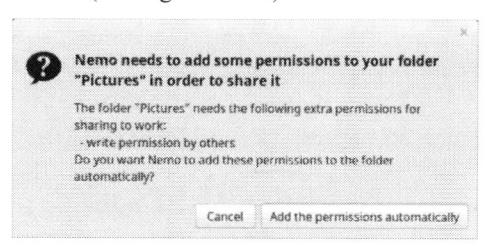

Figure 10-26: Folder Sharing permissions prompt

Note: If you are running a firewall, be sure to configure access for the NFS and Samba services, including browsing support. Otherwise, access to your shared folders by other computers may be blocked (see Chapter 11).

Folders that are shared display a sharing emblem next to their icon on a file manager window, as shown here.

To allow other computers to access your folders be sure the sharing servers are installed, Samba for Windows systems and NFS (**nfs-kernelserver**) for Linux/Unix systems. Once installed, the servers are configured automatically for you and run. You will not be able to share folders until these servers are installed.

You can also install the Samba server directly with the Synaptic Package Manager (**samba** package) and from Software Manager. Two servers are installed and run using the **smbd** and **nmbd** service scripts in the **/etc/init.d** directory (the **samba** service script is no longer used). The **smbd** server is the Samba server, and the **nmbd** server is the network discovery server.

Should the Samba server fail to start, you can start it manually in a terminal window with the commands:

```
sudo service nmbd start
sudo service smbd start
```

You can check the current status with the **status** option and restart with the **restart** option:

```
sudo service nmbd status
sudo service smbd status
```

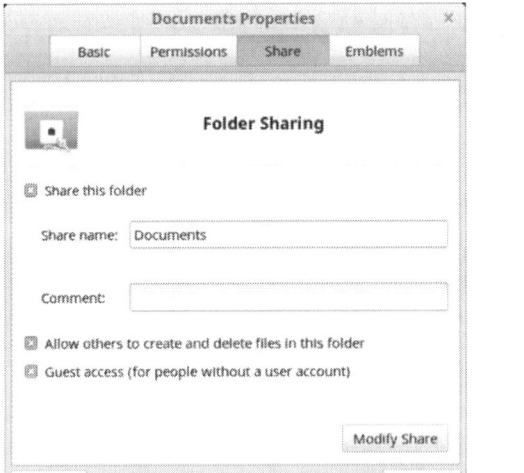

Figure 10-27: Folder Share panel

When first installed, Samba imports the Users and Groups already configured on your Linux Mint system. Corresponding Windows users with the same username and password as a Linux Mint account on your Linux Mint system are connected automatically to the Linux Mint shared folders. Should the Windows user have a different password, that user is prompted on Windows to enter a username and password. This is a Linux Mint username and password. In the case of a Windows user with the same username but different password, the user would enter the same username with a Linux Mint user password, not the Windows password.

Access is granted to all shares by any user. Should you want to implement restricted access by specific users and passwords, you have to configure user level access using a Samba configuration tool such as system-config-samba, as discussed in Chapter 16.

To change the sharing permissions for a folder later, open the folder's Properties window and then select the Share tab. When you make a change, a Modify Share button is displayed. Click it to make the changes. In Figure 10-27 Guest access is added to the Pictures folder.

File and Folder Permissions

On the desktop, you can set a folder or file permission using the Permissions tab in its Properties window (see Figure 10-28). For Files, right-click the icon or entry for the file or directory in the file manager window and select Properties. Then select the Permissions tab. Here you will find menus for read and write permissions, along with rows for Owner, Group, and Other. You can set owner permissions as Read Only or Read And Write. For the group and others, you can also set the None option, denying access. The group name expands to a pop-up menu listing different groups; select one to change the file's group. If you want to execute this file as an application (say, a shell script) check the "Allow executing file as program" entry. This has the effect of setting the execute permission

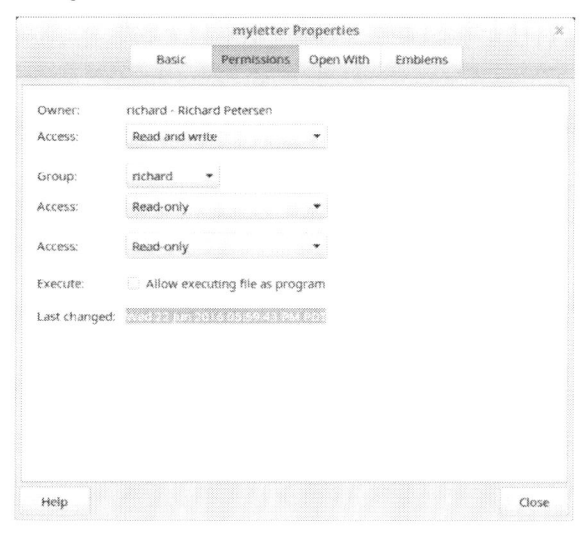

Figure 10-28: File Permissions

The Permissions tab for folders operates much the same way, but it displays two access entries, Folder Access and File Access (see Figure 10-29). The Folder Access entry controls access to the folder with options for List Files Only, Access Files, and Create And Delete Files. These correspond to the read, read and execute, and read/write/execute permissions given to folders. The File Access entry lets you set permissions for all those files in the folder. They are the same as for files: for the owner, Read or Read and Write; for the group and others, the entry adds a None option to deny access. To set the permissions for all the files in the folder accordingly (not just the folder), click the "Apply Permissions To Enclosed Files" button.

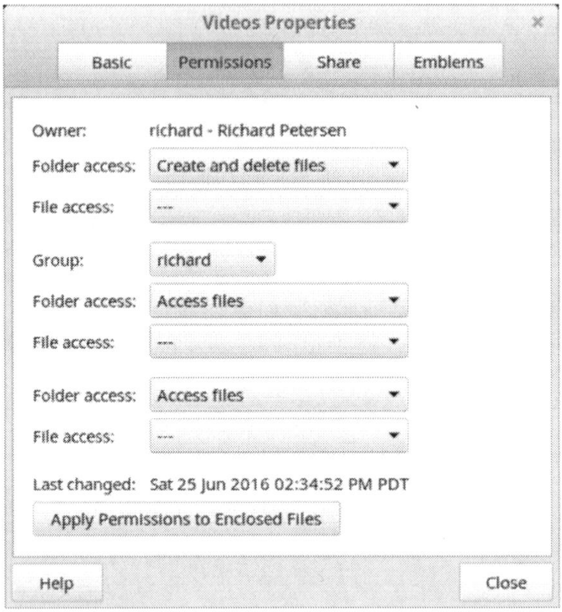

Figure 10-29: Folder Permissions

Automatic file system mounts with /etc/fstab

Though most file systems are automatically mounted for you, there may be instances where you need to have a file system mounted manually. Using the **mount** command you can do this directly, or you can specify the mount operation in the **/etc/fstab** file to have it mounted automatically. Linux Mint file systems are uniquely identified with their UUID (Universally Unique IDentifier). These are listed in the **/dev/disk/by-uuid** directory (or with the **sudo blkid** command). In the **/etc/fstab** file, the file system disk partitions are listed as a comment and then followed by the actual file system mount operation using the UUID. The following example mounts the file system on partition **/dev/sda3** to the **/media/sda3** directory as an **ext4** file system with default options (**defaults**). The UUID for device **/dev/sda3** is b8c526db-cb60-43f6-b0a3-5c0054f6a64a.

```
# /dev/sda3
UUID=b8c526db-cb60-43f6-b0a3-5c0054f6a64a /media/sda3 ext4 defaults 0 2
```

You can also identify your file system by giving it a label. You can use the **ext2label** command to label a file system. In the following **/etc/fstab** file example, the Linux file system labeled **mydata1** is mounted to the **/mydata1** directory as an **ext4** file system type.

Should you have to edit your **/etc/fstab** file, you can use the **sudo** command with the **xed** editor on your desktop. In a terminal window enter the following command. You will first be prompted to enter your password.

```
sudo xed /etc/fstab
```

/etc/fstab

```
# /etc/fstab: static file system information.
#
# <file system> <mount point>   <type>  <options>           <dump> <pass>
proc            /proc           proc    defaults            0      0
# /dev/sda2
UUID=a179d6e6-b90c-4cc4-982d-a4cfcedea7df / ext4 defaults,errors=remount-ro 0 1
# /dev/sda3
UUID=b8c526db-cb60-43f6-b0a3-5c0054f6a64a /media/sda3  ext3 defaults 0 2
# /dev/sda1
UUID=48b96071-6284-4fe9-b364-503817cefb74 none  swap  sw      0 0
/dev/fd0        /media/floppy0  auto    rw,user,noauto,exec 0 0
LABEL=mydata1  /mydata1         ext4    defaults            1 1
```

To mount a partition manually, use the **mount** command and specify the type with the **-t** option. Use the **-L** option to mount by label. List the file system first, and then the directory name to which it will be mounted. For an NTFS partition, you would use the type **ntfs**. For partitions with the Ext4 file system you would use **ext4**, and for older Linux partitions you would use **ext3**. The mount option has the format:

```
mount -t type  file-system  directory
```

The following example mounts the **mydata1** file system to the **/mydata1** directory

```
mount -t ext4  -L mydata1  /mydata1
```

Bluetooth

Linux Mint Linux provides Bluetooth support for both serial connections and BlueZ protocol supported devices. Bluetooth is a wireless connection method for locally connected devices such as keyboards, mice, printers, and cell phones. You can think of it as a small local network dedicated to your peripheral devices, eliminating the need for wires. BlueZ is the official Linux Bluetooth protocol and is integrated into the Linux kernel. The BlueZ protocol was developed originally by Qualcomm and is now an open source project, located at **http://bluez.sourceforge.net**. It is included with Linux Mint in the bluez-utils and bluez-libs packages, among others. Check the BlueZ site for a complete list of supported hardware.

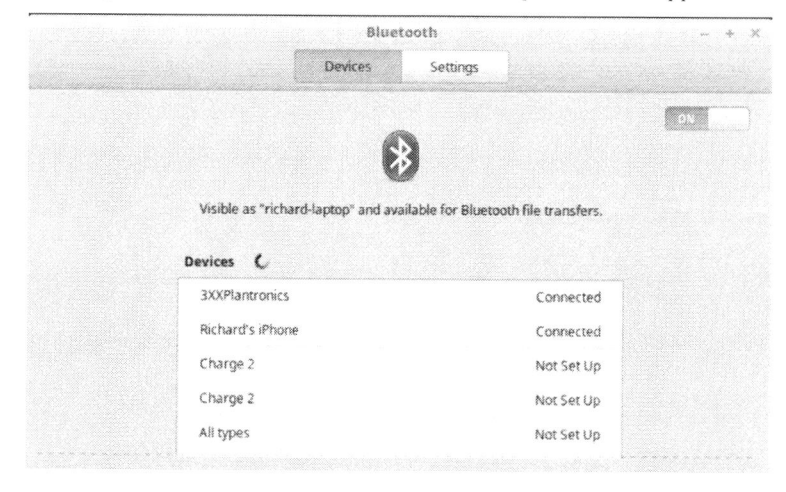

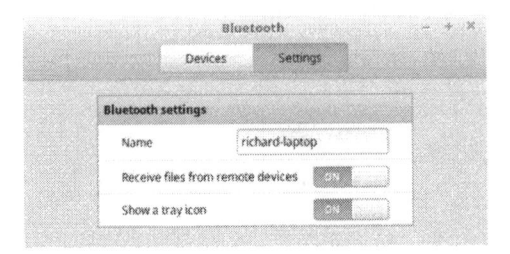

Figure 10-30: Bluetooth Settings (System Settings)

he Bluetooth applet displayed on your panel to the right. Click it to display the Bluetooth dialog (see Figure 10-30). You can also access Bluetooth dialog from the Preferences menu or from the System Settings dialog. The Bluetooth dialog has two tabs: Devices and Settings. On the Settings tab you set the name of your system's Bluetooth service and set switches to show the Bluetooth icon on the panel and whether to receive files from Bluetooth connected devices. To send files to a device, right-click on the Bluetooth icon in the panel and choose "Send files to a device."

On the Devices tab you can connect your system to Bluetooth devices. A Bluetooth switch at the top right lets you turn Bluetooth on or off. Detected devices are listed in the Devices frame at the center. Initially, devices are disconnected (see Figure 10-31). Click on a device entry to connect it. A dialog opens with a detected pin number, which you confirm. Then the device configuration dialog is displayed, with a switch to connect or disconnect the device (see Figure 10-32). Pair, type, and address information are also displayed. If the device supports sound, a Sound Setting button is shown, which opens the PulseAudio Sound Settings dialog for that device (see Figure 10-33). To remove the device configuration, click the Remove button.

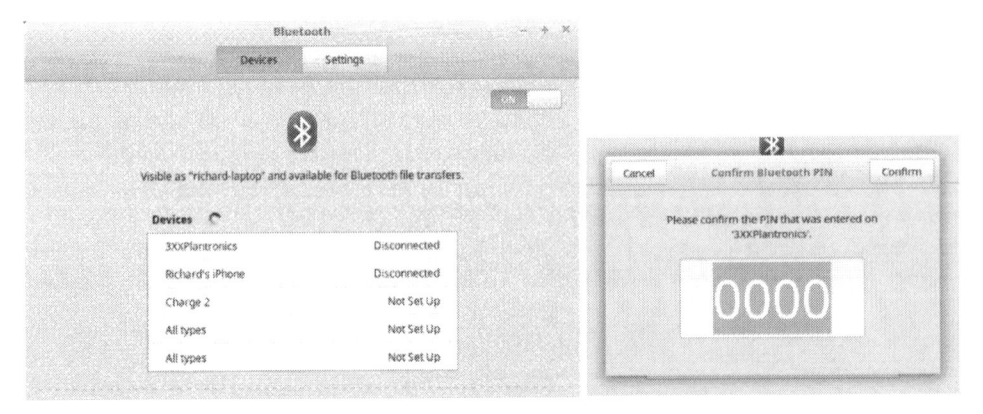

Figure 10-31: Bluetooth Settings: disconnected device

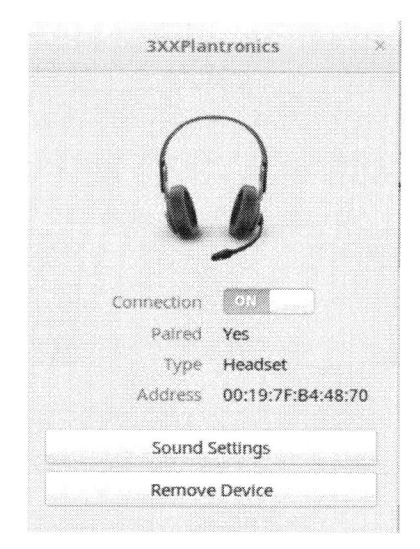

Figure 10-32: Bluetooth Device Configuration

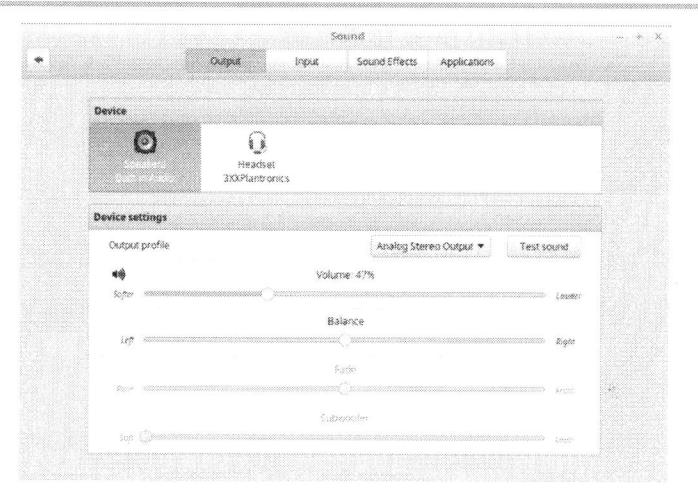

Figure 10-33: Bluetooth Sound

When connecting to a phone (see Figure 10-34), a pin number is detected and displayed. On the configuration dialog, you can choose to connect or disconnect. If you enable a phone to operate as a mobile phone network device (PAN/NAP), then a Mobile Broadband entry is shown on the Network Manager applet's menu.

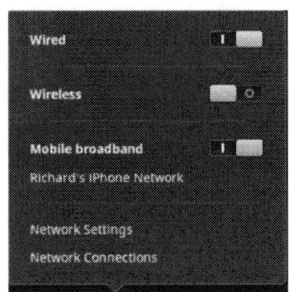

Figure 10-34: Bluetooth Setup Device Wizard: phone

DKMS

DKMS is the Dynamic Kernel Module Support originally developed by DELL. DKMS enabled device drivers can be generated automatically whenever your kernel is updated. This is helpful for proprietary drivers like the Nvidia and AMD proprietary graphics drivers (the X11 open source drivers, Xorg, are automatically included with the kernel package). In the past, whenever you updated your kernel, you also had to download and install a separate proprietary kernel module compiled just for that new kernel. If the module was not ready, then you could not use a proprietary driver. To avoid this problem, DKMS was developed, which uses the original proprietary source code to create new kernel modules as they are needed. When you install a new kernel, DKMS detects the new configuration and compiles a compatible proprietary kernel module for your new kernel. This action is fully automatic and entirely hidden from the user.

On Linux Mint and Ubuntu both the Nvidia and AMD proprietary graphics drivers are DKMS enable packages that are managed and generated by the DKMS service. The generated kernel modules are placed in the **/lib/modules/***kernel-version***/kernel/updates** directory. When you install either graphics proprietary package, their source code is downloaded and used to create a graphics driver for use by your kernel. The source code is placed in the **/usr/src** directory. The DKMS configuration files and build locations for different DKMS-enabled software are located in subdirectories in the **/var/lib/dkms** directory. The subdirectories will have the module name like **fglrx** for the AMD proprietary driver and **NVIDIA** for the Nvidia drivers.

DKMS configuration files are located in the **/etc/dkms** directory. The **/etc/dkms/framework.conf** file holds DKMS variable definitions for directories that DKMS uses, like the source code and kernel module directories. The **/etc/init.d/dkms_autoinstaller** is a script the runs the DKMS operations to generate and install a kernel module. DKMS removal and install directives for kernel updates are maintained in the **/etc/kernel** directory.

Should DKMS fail to install and update automatically, you can perform the update manually using the **dkms** command. The **dkms** command with the **build** action creates the kernel module, and then the **dkms** command with the **install** action installs the module to the appropriate kernel module directory. The **-m** option specifies the module you want to build and the **-k** option is the kernel version (use **uname -r** to display your current kernel version). Drivers like Nvidia and AMD release new versions regularly. You use the **-v** option to specify the driver version you want. See the man page for **dkms** for full details.

Editing Configuration Files Directly

Though the administrative tools will handle all configuration settings for you, there may be times when you will need to make changes by editing configuration files directly. Most system configuration files are text files located in the /**etc** directory. To change any of these files, you will need administrative access, requiring you use the **pkexec** or **sudo** commands.

You can use any standard editor, such as nano or Vi, to edit these files, though one of the easiest ways to edit them is to use the Xed editor on the GNOME desktop. In a terminal window, enter the **sudo** command with the **xed** command. You will be prompted for the root user password. The Gedit window then opens (see Figures 10-2 and 10-3 near the beginning of this chapter). Click Open to open a file browser where you can move through the file system to locate the file you want to edit.

```
gksu gedit
```

Caution: Be careful when editing your configuration files. Editing mistakes can corrupt your configurations. It is advisable to make a backup of any configuration files you are working on first, before making major changes to the original.

Xed (and Pluma) will let you edit several files at once, opening a tab for each. You can use Xed to edit any text file, including ones you create yourself. Two commonly edited configuration files are /**etc/default/grub** and /**etc/fstab**. The /**etc/fstab** file lists all your file systems and how they are mounted, and /**etc/default/grub** file is the configuration file for your Grub 2 boot loader.

You also can specify the file to edit when you first start up the Xed editor (Pluma on Mate).

```
sudo gedit /etc/default/grub
```

User configuration files, dot files, can be changed by individual users directly without administrative access. An example of a user configuration file is the **.profile** file, which configures your login shell. Dot files like **.profile** have to be chosen from the file manager window, not from the Gedit open operation. First configure the file manager to display dot files by opening the Preferences dialog (select Preferences in the Edit menu of any file manager window), then check the Show Hidden Files entry, and close the dialog. This displays the dot files in your file manager window. Double-click the file to open it in Xed.

GRUB 2

The Grand Unified Bootloader (GRUB) is a multiboot boot loader used for most Linux distributions. Linux and Unix operating systems are known as multiboot operating systems and take arguments passed to them at boot time. With GRUB, users can select operating systems to run from a menu interface displayed when a system boots up. Use arrow keys to move to an entry and press ENTER. If instead, you need to edit an entry, press **e**, letting you change kernel arguments or specify a different kernel. The **c** command places you in a command line interface. Provided your system BIOS supports very large drives, GRUB can boot from anywhere on them. For detailed information on Grub2, check the Grub2 Wiki at:

https://wiki.ubuntu.com/Grub2

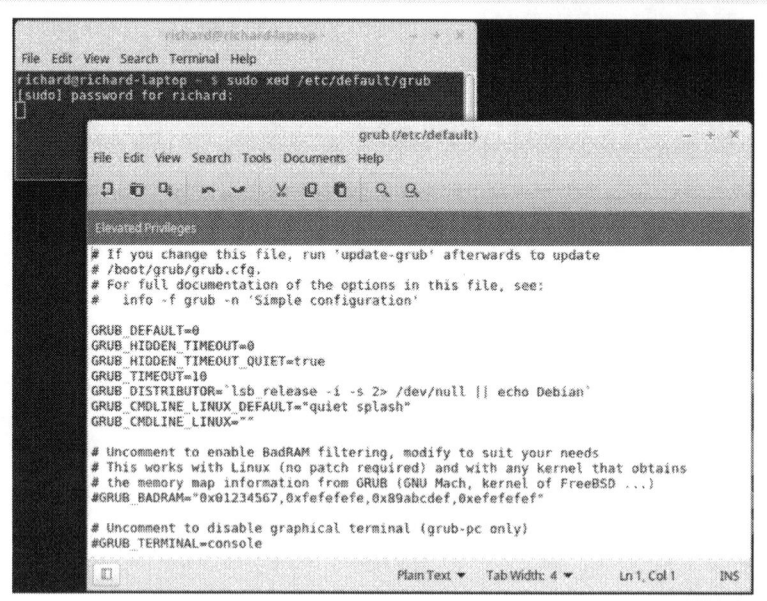

Figure 10-35: Editing the /etc/default/grub file

Check the GRUB Man page for GRUB options. GRUB is a GNU project with its home page at **https://www.gnu.org/software/grub**, the manual at **https://www.gnu.org/software/grub/index.html**. The Ubuntu forums have several helpful threads on using Grub2 on Ubuntu, **https://ubuntuforums.org**. Search on Grub2.

Grub2 detects and generates a menu for you automatically. You do not have to worry about keeping a menu file updated. All your operating systems and Linux Mint kernels are detected when the system starts up, and a menu to display them as boot options is generated at that time.

With Grub2, configuration is placed in user-modifiable configuration files held in the **/etc/default/grub** file and in the **/etc/grub.d** directory. There is a Grub2 configuration file called **/boot/grub/grub.cfg**, but this file is generated by Grub each time the system starts up, and should never be edited by a user. Instead, you would edit the **/etc/default/grub** file to set parameters like the default operating system to boot. To create your own menu entries, you create entries for them in the **/etc/grub.d/40_custom** file.

Grub options are set by assigning values to Grub options in the **/etc/default/grub** file. You can edit the file directly to change these options (see Figure 10-35). To edit the file with the Xed editor (Pluma on Mate), open a terminal window and enter the following command. You will be prompted to enter your password. Alternatively, you can configure Xed to use policykit and run it with **pkexec**. It is also possible to use **gksu**, but not advisable.

```
sudo xed /etc/default/grub
pkexec xed /etc/default/grub
```

You can then edit the file carefully. A red bar below the toolbar displays an "Elevated Messages" notice so that you know you are running the Xed editor with administrative access. The **grub** file used on Linux Mint 18.2 is shown here:

/etc/default/grub

```
# If you change this file, run 'update-grub' afterwards to update
# /boot/grub/grub.cfg.

GRUB_DEFAULT=0
GRUB_HIDDEN_TIMEOUT=0
GRUB_HIDDEN_TIMEOUT_QUIET=true
GRUB_TIMEOUT="10"
GRUB_DISTRIBUTOR=`lsb_release -i -s 2> /dev/null || echo Debian`
GRUB_CMDLINE_LINUX_DEFAULT="quiet splash"
GRUB_CMDLINE_LINUX=""

# Uncomment to enable BadRAM filtering, modify to suit your needs
# This works with Linux (no patch required) and with any kernel that obtains
# the memory map information from GRUB (GNU Mach, kernel of FreeBSD ...)
#GRUB_BADRAM="0x01234567,0xfefefefe,0x89abcdef,0xefefefef"

# Uncomment to disable graphical terminal (grub-pc only)
#GRUB_TERMINAL=console

# The resolution used on graphical terminal
# note that you can use only modes which your graphic card supports via VBE
# you can see them in real GRUB with the command `vbeinfo'
#GRUB_GFXMODE=640x480

# Uncomment if you don't want GRUB to pass "root=UUID=xxx" parameter to Linux
#GRUB_DISABLE_LINUX_UUID=true

# Uncomment to disable generation of recovery mode menu entrys
#GRUB_DISABLE_RECOVERY="true"

# Uncomment to get a beep at grub start
#GRUB_INIT_TUNE="480 440 1"
```

For dual boot systems (those with both Linux Mint and Windows or Mac), the option that users are likely to change is GRUB_DEFAULT, which sets the operating system or kernel to boot automatically if one is not chosen. The option uses a line number to indicate an entry in the Grub boot menu, with numbering starting from 0 (not 1). First, check your Grub menu when you boot up (press any key on boot to display the Grub menu for a longer time), and then count to where the entry of the operating system you want to make the default is listed. If the Windows entry is at 4th, which would be line 3 (counting from 0), to make it the default you would set the GRUB_DEAULT option to 3.

```
GRUB_DEFAULT=3
```

Should the listing of operating systems and kernels change (adding or removing kernels), you would have to edit the **/etc/default/grub** file again and each time a change occurs. A safer way to set the default is to configure GRUB to use the **grub-set-default** command. First, edit the **/etc/default/grub** file and change the option for GRUB_DEFAULT to **saved**.

```
GRUB_DEFAULT=saved
```

Then update GRUB.

```
sudo update-grub
```

The **grub-set-default** command takes as its option the number of the default you want to set (numbering from 0), or the name of the kernel or operating system. The following sets the default to 0, the first kernel entry.

```
sudo grub-set-default 0
```

For a kernel name or operating system, you can use the name as it appears on the GRUB menu (enclosing the name in quotes), such as:

```
sudo grub-set-default 'Windows XP (loader) (on /dev/sda1)'
```

The GRUB_TIMEOUT option sets the number of seconds Grub will wait to allow a user to access the menu, before booting the default operating system. The default options used for Linux Mint kernels are listed by the GRUB_CMDLINE_LINUX_DEFAULT option. Currently, these include the **splash** and **quiet** options to display the Linux Mint emblem on startup (**splash**), but not the list of startup tasks being performed (**quiet**).

Once you have made your changes, you have to run the **update-grub** command with **sudo**, as noted in the first line of the **/etc/default/grub** file. Otherwise, your changes will not take effect. This command will generate a new **/etc/grub/grub.cfg** file, which determines the actual Grub 2 configuration.

```
sudo update-grub
```

You can add your own Grub2 boot entries by placing them in the **/etc/grub.d/40_custom** file. The file is nearly empty except for an initial **exec tail** command that you must take care not to change. After you make your additions to the **40_custom** file, you have to run **sudo update-grub** to have the changes take effect.

When the GRUB package is updated by Linux Mint, you will be given the choice to keep your current local version or use the maintainer's version. Keeping the local version is selected by default. However, unless you have extensively customized your configuration, it is always advisable to select the maintainer's version. The maintainer's version is the most up-to-date. If you had made any changes previously to the **/etc/default/grub** file, you will have to edit that file and make the same changes again, such as setting the default operating system to load. Be sure to run **sudo update-grub** to make the changes take effect.

Backup Management

Backup operations have become an important part of administrative duties. Several backup tools are provided on Linux systems, including Amanda and the traditional dump/restore tools, as well as the **rsync** command used for making individual copies. Linux Mint provides the Backup Tool (mintBackup) for basic backup operations. Deja Dup is a front end for the duplicity backup tool, which uses rsync to generate backup archives. Deja Dup is the recommended default backup tool, available from the System Settings dialog as Backup. Amanda provides server-based backups, letting different systems on a network backup to a central server. BackupPC provides network and local backup using configured **rsync** and **tar** tools. The dump tools let you refine your backup process, detecting data changed since the last backup. Table 10-2 lists websites for Linux backup tools.

Website	Tools
`https://www.linuxmint.com`	mintBackup (Backup Tool)
`https://rsync.samba.org`	rsync remote copy backup
`https://launchpad.net/deja-dup` `http://www.nongnu.org/duplicity`	Deja Dup frontend for duplicity which uses rsync to perform basic backups
`http://www.amanda.org`	Amanda network backup
`http://dump.sourceforge.net`	dump and restore tools
`http://backuppc.sourceforge.net`	BackupPC network or local backup using configured rsync and tar tools.

Table 10-2: Backup Resources

Backup Tool (mintBackup)

The Backup Tool (mintBackup) provides basic backup of files, folders, and file systems, as well as a backup of your currently installed software. Backup Tool is available on both the Cinnamon and Mate desktops (Administration | Backup Tool. The initial dialog displays buttons for the backup options (see Figure 10-36).

Figure 10-36: Backup Tool

When performing a backup, you choose the source, destination, and set advanced options such as preserving permissions (see Figure 10-37). Backups are made to folders or archives.

Figure 10-37: Backup Tool backup

Deja Dup

Deja Dup is a front end for the duplicity backup tool, which uses rsync to generate backup archives (**http://www.nongnu.org/duplicity/**). Once installed, you can access Deja Dup as "Backups" on both the Cinnamon and Mate desktops from the Preferences and Accessories menus. On the Mate desktop you can also access it as Backups on the Control Center, Other section).

The deja-dup settings dialog show tabs for Overview, Folders to save, Folders to ignore, Storage location, and Scheduling (see Figure 10-38). A switch at the top right of the dialog allows you to turn automatic backups on and off. The Overview tab provides information about your backup configuration, showing the folders to backup, those ignored, and the dates of the last and next backups. Click the Help button to display the Deja Dup manual.

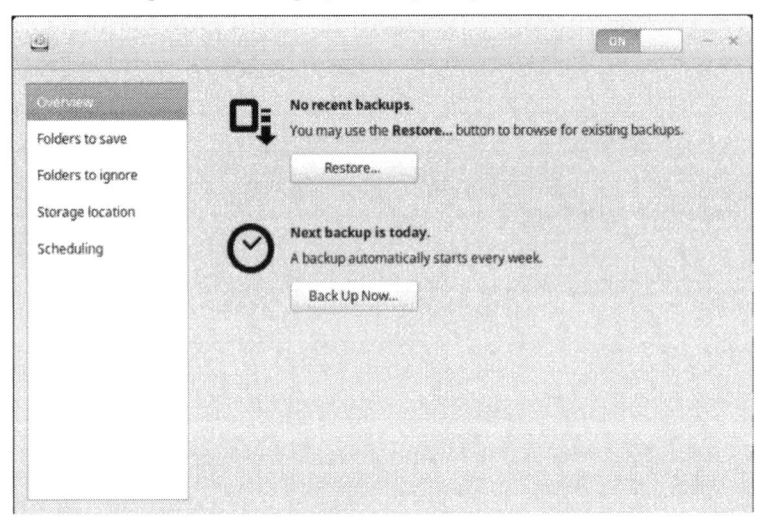

Figure 10-38: Deja Dup settings: overview

The "Folders to save" tab lets you specify folders you want to backup and folders to ignore (see Figure 10-39). Click the plus button (+) at the bottom of the folders list to add a new folder for backup. Do the same to specify folders to ignore. The minus button removes folders from the list. Your home folder has been added already. The "Folders to ignore" tab specifies folders you do not want to back up. The Downloads and Trash folders are selected initially.

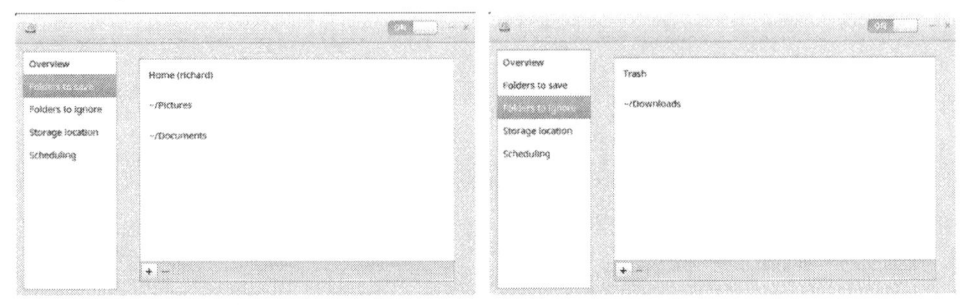

Figure 10-39: Deja Dup settings: Folders to save and ignore

The "Storage Location" tab lets you specify a location to store your backups (see Figure 10-40). You can choose different locations, such as an FTP account, a cloud account, SSH server, Samba (Windows) share, or a local folder. Choose the one you want from the "Backup location" menu. With each choice, you are prompted for the appropriate configuration information.

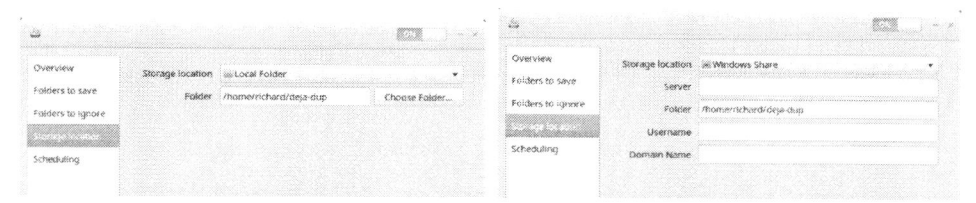

Figure 10-40: Deja Dup settings: storage for Windows share and Local folder

On the Scheduling tab, you can specify the frequency of your backups and how long to keep them (see Figure 10-41). First turn on Automatic backup. Backups can be performed daily, weekly, every two weeks, or monthly. They can be kept for a week, month, several months, a year, or forever.

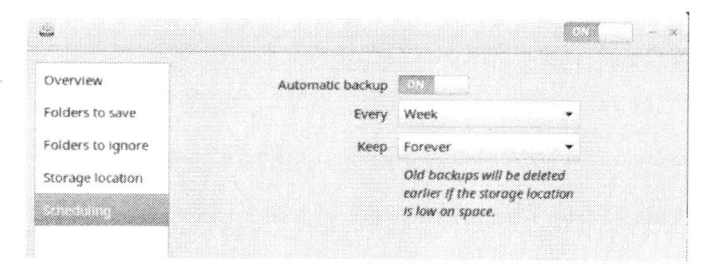

Figure 10-41: Deja Dup settings: backup times

When you perform a backup, you are prompted to backup with or without encryption. For encrypted backups, you are prompted to enter a password, which you will need to restore the files (see Figure 10-42).

Figure 10-42: Deja Dup backup: encryption

When restoring, you are prompted to specify the location you are backing up from, the backup date to restore from, and whether to restore to the original location or a specific folder (see Figure 10-43).

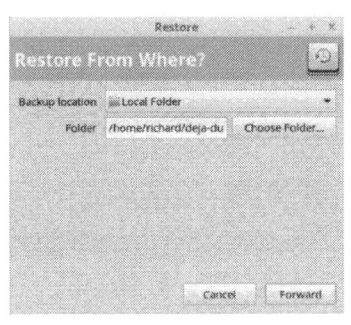

Figure 10-43: Deja Dup restore

Individual Backups: archive and rsync

You can backup and restore particular files and directories with archive tools like `tar`, restoring the archives later. For backups, `tar` is used usually with a tape device. To schedule automatic backups, you can schedule appropriate `tar` commands with the **cron** utility. The archives can be also compressed for storage savings. You can then copy the compressed archives to any medium, such as a DVD disc, a floppy, or tape. On GNOME you can use File Roller (Archive Manager) to create archives easily (Accessories menu), or Engrampa, the MATE archive manager.

File Roller and Engrampa also support LZMA compression, a more efficient and faster compression method. On Archive Manager, when creating a new archive, select "Tar compressed with lzma (.tar.lzma)" for the Archive type. When choosing Create Archive from GNOME Files file manager window on selected files, on the Create Archive dialog, choose the **.lzma** file type for just compression, and the **.tar.lzma** type for a compressed archive.

If you want to remote-copy a directory or files from one host to another, making a particular backup, you can use **rsync**, which is designed for network backups of particular directories or files, intelligently copying only those files that have been changed, rather than the contents of an entire directory. In archive mode, it can preserve the original ownership and permissions, providing corresponding users exist on the host system. The following example copies the **/home/george/myproject** directory to the **/backup** directory on the host **rabbit**, creating a corresponding **myproject** subdirectory. The **-t** specifies that this is a transfer. The remote host is referenced with an attached colon, **rabbit:**

```
rsync -t /home/george/myproject    rabbit:/backup
```

If instead, you wanted to preserve the ownership and permissions of the files, you would use the **-a** (archive) option. Adding a **-z** option will compress the file. The **-v** option provides a verbose mode.

```
rsync -avz /home/george/myproject    rabbit:/backup
```

A trailing slash on the source will copy the contents of the directory, rather than generating a subdirectory of that name. Here the contents of the **myproject** directory are copied to the **george-project** directory.

```
rsync -avz  /home/george/myproject/    rabbit:/backup/george-project
```

The **rsync** command is configured to use Secure Shell (SSH) remote shell by default. You can specify it or an alternate remote shell to use with the **-e** option. For secure transmission, you can encrypt the copy operation with SSH. Either use the **-e ssh** option or set the **RSYNC_RSH** variable to ssh.

```
rsync -avz -e ssh  /home/george/myproject    rabbit:/backup/myproject
```

You can copy from a remote host to the host you are on.

```
rsync -avz  lizard:/home/mark/mypics/   /pic-archive/markpics
```

You can also run rsync as a server daemon. This will allow remote users to synchronize copies of files on your system with versions on their own, transferring only changed files rather than entire directories. Many mirror and software FTP sites operate as rsync servers, letting you update files without have to download the full versions again. Configuration information for rsync as a server is kept in the **/etc/rsyncd.conf** file.

Tip: Though it is designed for copying between hosts, you can also use rsync to make copies within your own system, usually to a directory in another partition or hard drive. Check the rsync Man page for detailed descriptions of each.

BackupPC

BackupPC provides an easily managed local or network backup of your system or hosts, on a system using configured rsync or tar tools. There is no client application to install; just configuration files. BackupPC can back up hosts on a network, including servers, or just a single system. Data can be backed up to local hard disks or to network storage such as shared partitions or storage servers. You can configure BackupPC using your Web page configuration interface. This is the hostname of your computer with the **/backuppc** name attached, like **http://richard1/backuppc**. Detailed documentation is installed at **/usr/share/doc/BackupPC**. You can find out more about BackupPC at **http://backuppc.sourceforge.net**. You can install BackupPC using the Synaptic Package Manager or from Software Manager. Canonical provides critical updates.

BackupPC uses both compression and detection of identical files to reduce the size of the backup, allowing several hosts to be backed up in limited space. Once an initial backup is performed, BackupPC will only back up changed files, reducing the time of the backup significantly.

BackupPC has its own service script with which you start the BackupPC service, **/etc/init.d/backuppc**. Configuration files are located at **/etc/BackupPC**. The **config.pl** file holds BackupPC configuration options and the **hosts** file lists hosts to be backed up.

Amanda

To back up hosts connected to a network, you can use the Advanced Maryland Automatic Network Disk Archiver (Amanda) to archive hosts. Amanda uses **tar** tools to back up all hosts to a single host operating as a backup server. Backup data is sent by each host to the host operating as the Amanda server, where they are written out to a backup medium such as tape. With an Amanda server, the backup operations for all hosts become centralized in one server, instead of each host having to perform its backup. Any host that needs to restore data simply requests it from the

Amanda server, specifying the file system, date, and filenames. Backup data is copied to the server's holding disk and from there, to tapes. Detailed documentation and updates are provided at **http://www.amanda.org**. For the server, be sure to install the amanda-server package, and for clients you use the amanda-clients package. You can install Amanda using the Synaptic Package Manager and from Software Manager. Canonical does not provide critical updates.

Logical Volume Manager

For easier hard disk storage management, you can set up your system to use the Logical Volume Manager (LVM), creating LVM partitions that are organized into logical volumes, to which free space is automatically allocated. Logical volumes provide a more flexible and powerful way of dealing with disk storage, organizing physical partitions into logical volumes in which you can easily manage disk space. Disk storage for a logical volume is treated as one pool of memory, though the volume may, in fact, contain several hard disk partitions spread across different hard disks. Adding a new LVM partition merely increases the pool of storage accessible to the entire system. Check the LVM HOWTO at **www.tldp.org** for detailed examples.

LVM Structure

In an LVM structure, LVM physical partitions, also known as *extents*, are organized into logical groups, which are, in turn, used by logical volumes. In effect, you are dealing with three different levels of organization. At the lowest level, you have physical volumes. These are physical hard disk partitions that you create with partition creation tools such as `parted` or `fdisk`. The partition type will be a Linux LVM partition, **fdisk** code **8e**. These physical volumes are organized into logical groups, known as volume groups that operate much like logical hard disks. You assign collections of physical volumes to different logical groups.

Once you have your logical groups, you can then create logical volumes. Logical volumes function much like hard disk partitions on a standard setup. For example, on the **turtle** group volume, you could create a **/var** logical volume, and on the **rabbit** logical group, you could create **/home** and **/projects** logical volumes. You can have several logical volumes on one logical group, just as you can have several partitions on one hard disk.

You treat the logical volumes as you would any ordinary hard disk partition. Create a file system on it with the `mkfs` command, and then you can mount the file system to use it with the `mount` command. For Linux Mint/Ubuntu the file system type would be **ext4**.

Storage on logical volumes is managed using what are known as extents. A logical group defines a standard size for an extent, say 4MB, and then divides each physical volume in its group into extents of that size. Logical volumes are, in turn, divided into extents of the same size, which are then mapped to those on the physical volumes.

Logical volumes can be linear, striped, or mirrored. The mirror option will create a mirror copy of a logical volume, providing a restore capability. The striped option lets you automatically distribute your Logical volume across several partitions, as you would a RAID device. This adds better efficiency for very large files but is complicated to implement. Like a RAID device, stripe sizes have to be consistent across partitions. As LVM partitions can be of any size, the stripes sizes have to be carefully calculated. The simplest approach is just to use a linear implementation, much like a RAID 0 device, just treating the storage as one large ordinary drive, with storage accessed sequentially.

There is one restriction and recommendation for logical volumes. The boot partition cannot be part of a logical volume. You still have to create a separate hard disk partition as your boot partition with the /**boot** mountpoint in which your kernel and all needed boot files are installed. In addition, it is recommended that you not place your root partition on a logical volume. Doing so can complicate any needed data recovery. This is why a default partition configuration set up during installation for LVM will include a separate /**boot** partition of type **ext4**, whereas the root and swap partitions will be installed on Logical volumes. There will be two partitions, one for the logical group (LVM physical volume, **pv**) holding both swap and root volumes, and another for the boot partition (**ext4**). The logical volumes will in turn both be **ext4** file systems.

LVM Tools: using the LVM commands

Instead of using system-config-lvm, you could use a collection of LVM tools to manage your LVM volumes, adding new LVM physical partitions and removing current ones. The system-config-lvm system tool is actually a GUI interface for the LVM tools. For the LVM tools, you can either use LVM tools directly or use the `lvm` command to generate an interactive shell from which you can run LVM commands. There are Man pages for all the LVM commands. LVM maintains configuration information in the /**etc/lvm/lvm.conf** file, where you can configure LVM options such as the log file, the configuration backup directory, or the directory for LVM devices (see the **lvm.conf** Man page for more details).

Note: For desktop LVM administration, you can try using the system-config-lvm application, but it is an older application that may not work.

Displaying LVM Information

You can use the `pvdisplay`, `vgdisplay`, and `lvdisplay` commands to show detailed information about a physical partition, volume groups, and logical volumes. The `pvscan`, `vgscan`, and `lvscan` commands list your physical, group, and logical volumes.

Managing LVM Physical Volumes with the LVM commands

A physical volume can be any hard disk partition or RAID device. A RAID device is seen as a single physical volume. You can create physical volumes either from a single hard disk or from partitions on a hard disk. On very large systems with many hard disks, you would more likely use an entire hard disk for each physical volume.

You would first use a partition utility like **fdisk**, **parted**, or **gparted** to create a partition of the LVM partition type (**8e**). Then, you can initialize the partition as a physical volume using the **pvcreate** command.

To initialize a physical volume on an entire hard disk, you use the hard disk device name, as shown here:

```
pvcreate /dev/sdc
```

This will initialize one physical partition, **pv**, called **sdc1** on the **sdc** hard drive (the third Serial ATA drive, c).

If you are using a particular partition on a drive, you create a new physical volume using the partition's device name, as shown here:

```
pvcreate /dev/sda3
```

To initialize several drives, just list them. The following create two physical partitions, sdc1 and sdd1.

```
pvcreate /dev/sdc /dev/sdd
```

You could also use several partitions on different hard drives. This is a situation in which your hard drives each hold several partitions. This condition occurs often when you are using some partitions on your hard drive for different purposes like different operating systems, or if you want to distribute your Logical group across several hard drives. To initialize these partitions at once, you simply list them.

```
pvcreate /dev/sda3 /dev/sdb1 /dev/sdb2
```

Once you have initialized your partitions, you have to create LVM groups on them.

Managing LVM Groups

Physical LVM partitions are used to make up a volume group. You can manually create a volume group using the **vgcreate** command and the name of the group along with a list of physical partitions you want in the group.

If you are then creating a new volume group to place these in, you can include them in the group when you create the volume group with the **vgcreate** command. The volume group can use one or more physical partitions. The configuration described in the following example used only one physical partition for the **VolGroup00**. In the following example, a volume group called **mymedia** that is made up two physical volumes, **sdc** and **sdd**.

```
vgcreate mymedia /dev/sdc /dev/sdd
```

The previous example sets up a logical group on two serial ATA hard drives, each with its own single partition. Alternatively, you can set up a volume group to span partitions on several hard drives. If you are using partitions for different functions, this approach gives you the flexibility for using all the space available across multiple hard drives. The following example creates a group called **mygroup** consisting of three physical partitions, **/dev/sda3**, **/dev/sdb4**, and **/dev/sdb4**:

```
vgcreate mygroup /dev/sda3 /dev/sdb2 /dev/sdb4
```

If you later want to add a physical volume to a volume group, you would use the **vgextend** command. The **vgextend** command adds a new partition to a logical group. In the following example, the partition **/dev/sda4** is added to the volume group **mygroup**. In effect, you are extending the size of the logical group by adding a new physical partition.

```
vgextend mygroup /dev/sda4
```

To add an entire new drive to a volume group you would follow a similar procedure. The following example adds a fifth serial ATA hard drive, **sde**, first creating a physical volume on it and then adding that volume, sde, to the **mymedia** volume group.

```
pvcreate /dev/sde
vgextend mymedia /dev/sde
```

To remove a physical partition, first, remove it from its logical group. You may have to use the **pmove** command to move any data off the physical partition. Then use the **vgreduce** command to remove it from its logical group.

You can remove an entire volume group by first deactivating it with **vgchange -a n** and then using the **vgremove** command.

Activating Volume Groups

Whereas in a standard file system structure you mount and unmount hard disk partitions, with an LVM structure, you activate and deactivate entire volume groups. The group volumes are accessible until you activate them with the **vgchange** command with the **-a** option. To activate a group, first, reboot your system, and then enter the **vgchange** command with the **-a** option and the **y** argument to activate the logical group (an **n** argument will deactivate the group).

```
vgchange -a y mygroup
```

Managing LVM Logical Volumes

To create logical volumes, you use the **lvcreate** command and then format your logical volume using the standard formatting command like **mkfs.ext4**. Keep in mind that all these actions can be performed at once by system-config-lvm.

With the **-n** option you specify the volume's name, which functions like a hard disk partition's label. You use the **-L** or **--size** options to specify the size of the volume. Use a size suffix for the measure, **G** for Gigabyte, **M** for megabyte, and **K** for kilobytes. There are other options for implementing features like whether to implement a linear, striped, or mirrored volume or to specify the size of the extents to use. Usually, the defaults work well. The following example creates a logical volume named **projects** on the **mygroup** logical group with a size of 20GB.

```
lvcreate -n projects -L 20GB mygroup
```

The following example sets up a logical volume on the **mymedia** volume group that is 540GB in size. The mymedia volume group is made up of two physical volumes, each on 320GB hard drives. In effect, the two hard drives are logically seen as one.

```
lvcreate -n myvideos -L 540GB mymedia
```

Once you have created your logical volume, you then need to create a file system to use on it. The following creates an ext4 file system on the myvideos logical volume.

```
mkfs.ext4 myvideos
```

You could also use:

```
mkfs -t ext4 myvideos
```

With **lvextend**, you can increase the size of the logical volume if there is unallocated space available in the volume group.

Should you want to reduce the size of a logical volume, you use the **lvreduce** command, indicating the new size. Be sure to reduce the size of any file systems (**ext4**) on the logical volume, using the **resize2fs** command.

To rename a logical volume use the `lvrename` command. If you want to completely remove a logical volume, you can use the `lvremove` command.

Steps to create a new LVM group and volume

Physical Partition First create a physical partition on your hard drive. You can use GParted, QTparted, or fdisk with the disk device name to create the partition. For example, to use fdisk to create a new partition on a new hard drive, whose device name is **/etc/sde**, you would enter:

```
fdisk /etc/sde
```

Then, in the fdisk shell, use the fdisk **n** command to create a new partition, set it as a primary partition (**p**), and make it the first partition. If you plan to use the entire hard drive for your LVM, you would need only one partition that would cover the entire drive.

Then use the **t** command to set the partition type to 8E. The 8E type is the LVM partition type. To make your changes, enter **w** to write changes to the disk.

Physical Volume Next create a physical volume (pv) on the new and empty LVM partition, using the **pvcreate** command and the device name.

```
pvcreate /dev/sde
```

Volume Group Then, create your volume group with **vgcreate** command, with the volume group name and the hard disk device name.

```
vgcreate mynewgroup  /dev/sde
```

Be sure the volume group is activated. Use the **vgs** command to list it. If not listed, use the following command to activate it.

```
vgchange -a  y  mynewgroup
```

Logical Volume Then, create a logical volume, or volumes, for the volume group, using the **lvcreate** command. The **--size** or **-L** options determines the size and the **--name** option specifies the name. To find out the available free space, use the **vgs** command. You can have more than one logical volume in a volume group, or just one if you prefer. A logical volume is conceptually similar to logical volumes in an extended partition on Windows systems.

```
lvcreate --size --name mynewvol1
```

Format the Logical volume. You then use the **mkfs** command with the **-t** option to format the logical volume. The logical volume will be listed in a directory for the LVM group, within the /dev directory, **/dev/mynewgroup/mynewvol1**.

```
mkfs -t ext4 /dev/mynewgroup/mynewgroup-mynewvol1
```

Steps to add a new drive to an LVM group and volume

Physical Partition First create a physical partition on your hard drive. You can use GParted, QTparted, or fdisk with the disk device name to create the partition. For the type specify LVM (**8E**).

Physical Volume Next, create a physical volume (pv) on the new and empty LVM partition, using the pvcreate command and the device name.

```
pvcreate /dev/sdf
```

Add to Logical Group Use the **vgextend** command to add the new physical volume to your existing logical group (LG).

```
vgextend mynewgroup /dev/sdf
```

Add to Logical Volume Then, you can create new logical volumes in the new space, or expand the size of a current logical volume. To expand the size of a logical volume to the new space, first, unmount the logical volume. Then use the **lvextend** command to expand to the space on the new hard drive that is now part the same logical group. With no size specified, the entire space on the new hard drive will be added.

```
umount /dev/mynewgroup/mynewvol1
lvextend /dev/mynewgroup/mynewvol /dev/sdf
```

Use the **-L** option to specify a particular size, **-L +250G** . Be sure to add the + sign to have the size added to the current logical volume size. To find out the available free space, use the **vgs** command.

Add to file system Use the **resize2fs** command to extend the linux file system (ext4) on to logical volume to include the new space, formatting it. Unless you specify a size (second parameter), all the available unformatted space is used.

```
resize2fs /dev/mynewgroup/mynewvol1
```

Note: You can back up volume group metadata (configuration) using the vgcfgbackup command. This does not backup your logical volumes (no content). Metadata backups are stored in /etc/lvm/backup, and can be restored using vgcfgrestore.

Using LVM to replace drives

LVM can be very useful when you need to replace an older hard drive with a new one. Hard drives are expected to last about six years on the average. You could want to replace the older drive with a larger one (hard drive storage sizes double every year or so). Replacing additional hard drives is easy. To replace a boot drive is much more complicated.

To replace the drive, simply incorporate the new drive to your logical volume (see Steps to add a new drive to an LVM group and volume). The size of your logical volume will increase accordingly. You can use the **pmove** command to move data from the old drive to the new one. Then, issue commands to remove the old drive (**vgreduce**) from the volume group. From the user and system point of view, no changes are made. Files from your old drive will still be stored in the same directories, though the actual storage will be implemented on the new drive.

Replacement with LVM become more complicated if you want to replace your boot drive, the hard drive from which your system starts up and which holds your linux kernel. The boot drive contains a special boot partition and the master boot record. The boot partition cannot be part of any LVM volume. You would first have to create a boot partition on the new drive using a partition tool such as Parted or fdisk, labeling it as boot (the boot drive is usually very small, about 200 MB). Then mount the partition on your system, and copy the contents of your **/boot** directory to it. Then add the remainder of the disk to your logical volume and logically remove the old disk, copying the contents of the old disk to the new one. You would still have to boot with linux rescue DVD (or install DVD in rescue mode), and issue the **grub-install** command to install the master boot record on your new drive. You can then boot from the new drive.

LVM Snapshots

A snapshot records and defines the state of the logical volume at a designated time. It does not create a full copy of data on the volume, but only just changes since the last snapshot. A snapshot defines the state of the data at a given time. This allows you to back up the data in a consistent way. Should you need to restore a file to its previous version, you can use the snapshot of it. Snapshots are treated as logical volumes and can be mounted, copied, or deleted.

To create a snapshot, use the lvcreate command with the **-s** option. In this example, the snapshot is given the name mypics-snap1 (**-n** option). You need to specify the full device name for the logical group you want to create the snapshot for. Be sure there is enough free space available in the logical group for the snapshot. In this example, the snapshot logical volume is created in the **/dev/mymedia** logical group. It could just as easily be created in any other logical group. Though a snapshot normally uses very little space, you have to guard against overflows. If the snapshot is allocated the same size as the original, it will never overflow. For systems where little of the original data changes, the snapshot can be very small. The following example allocates one-third the size of the original (60GB).

```
sudo lvcreate -s -n mypics-snap1 -l 20GB /dev/mymedia
```

You can then mount the snapshot as you would any other file system.

```
sudo mount /dev/mymedia/mypic-snap1 /mysnaps
```

To delete a snapshot you use the lvremove command, removing it like you would any logical volume.

```
sudo lvremove -f /dev/mymedia/mypics-nap1
```

Snapshots are very useful for making backups while a system is still active. You can use tar or dump to backup the mounted snapshot to a disk or tape. All the data from the original logical volume will be included, along with the changes noted by the snapshot.

Snapshots also allow you to perform effective undo operations. You can create a snapshot of a logical volume, then unmount the original and mount the snapshot in its place. Any changes you make will be performed on the snapshot, not the original. Should problems occur, unmount the snapshot and then mount the original. This restores the original state of your data. You could also do this using several snapshots, restoring to a previous snapshot. With this procedure, you could test new software on a snapshot, without endangering your original data. The software would be operating on the snapshot, not the original logical volume.

You can also use them as alternative versions of a logical volume. You can read and write to a snapshot. A write will change only the snapshot volume, not the original, creating, in effect, an alternate version.

OpenZFS

The ZFS file system incorporates the features of a logical volume manager (LVM), RAID systems, and file systems. ZFS abstracts a file system, much like LVM, setting up a pool of storage from which a file system can be generated. Checksums for data blocks are saved outside the data blocks and are checked for any corruption within the blocks. This makes ZFS very effective in protecting against silent data corruption from problems such as write interrupts, driver bugs, and access failures. If a RAID-Z support has been set up, corrupted blocks can be recovered. RAID-Z implements a data-oriented RAID-like support with automatic mirroring of your data within the file system. In addition, the LVM-like abstraction of ZFS allows for very large files. Writes are performed with a copy-on-write transaction method, where data is not overwritten directly, but added.

ZFS was developed by SUN, which is now controlled by Oracle. Since 2010, OpenZFS provides an open source version of ZFS for Linux systems. Linux Mint, like Ubuntu, now supports the ZFS file system, using the OpenZFS kernel module. Tools to manage ZFS file systems can be installed with the **zfsutils-linux** package (Universe repository). See the following for more information:

```
https://wiki.ubuntu.com/Kernel/Reference/ZFS
```

Much like an LVM system, you have the physical devices (called virtual devices, VDEVs) that are combined and striped into a data pool (**zpool** command), which can then be used to create the ZFS file system. At the pool level, you can implement RAIDZ options. With the **zfs** command, you can then create file systems in your pool. With the **zfs** command, you can also create snapshots (read-only copy) of a ZFS file system, or a clone (writeable copy). To perform an integrity check of the pool, use the **zpool** command's **scrub** option.

11. Network Connections

Network Connections: Dynamic and Static
GNOME Network (Network Settings)
Network Manager
nm-connection-editor (Network Connections)
Wired and Wireless Configuration
VPN Configuration
nmcli
Dial-up PPP Access: wvdial
Network Configuration with systemd-networkd
Setting up a firewall with Gufw and ufw
Setting up a firewall with FirewallD
Network Information

Linux Mint will automatically detect and configure your network connections with Network Manager. Should the automatic configuration either fail or be incomplete for some reason, you can use Network Manager to perform a manual configuration (choose Network Connections on the Preferences menu, or from the Network Manager panel applet's menu). If you want to make a simple dial-up modem connection, you can use WvDial. Your network will also need a firewall. UFW (with the Gufw interface) or FirewallD is recommended. Table 11-1 lists several network configuration tools. You can also use the GNOME 3 Networking dialog on the Cinnamon desktop (System Settings) for quick wireless and wired connections, as well as proxy configuration (see Chapter 3).

Network Configuration Tool	Description
Network Manager	Automates wireless and wired network connection, selection, and notification (System | Preferences | Network Connections). Used for all network connections including wired, wireless, mobile broadband, VPN, and DSL.
GNOME Network (Network Settings)	GNOME Network connection preferences, allowing quick connection and configuration of wired and wireless networks. Use to set up proxy configuration.
nm-connection-editor (Network Connections)	The Network Manager connection editor for configuring all types of connections. Use for VPN connections. **nmcli** is the command line interface version of Network Manager.
ufw	Sets up a network firewall.
Gufw	GNOME interface for UFW firewall
Firewalld	Sets up a network firewall.
wvdial	PPP dial-up modem connection
systemd-networkd	systemd-based network configuration

Table 11-1: Linux Mint Network Configuration Tools

Network Connections: Dynamic and Static

If you are on a network, you may need to obtain certain information to configure your connection interface. Most networks now support dynamic configuration using either the older Dynamic Host Configuration Protocol (DHCP) or the new IPv6 Protocol and its automatic address configuration. In this case, you need only check the DHCP entry. If your network does not support DHCP or IPv6 automatic addressing, or you are using a static connection (DCHP and IPv6 connections are dynamic), you will have to provide detailed information about your connection. For a static connection, you would enter your connection information manually such as your IP address and DNS servers, whereas in a dynamic connection this information is provided automatically to your system by a DHCP server or generated by IPv6 when you connect to the network. For DHCP, a DHCP client on each host will obtain the information from a DHCP server serving that network. IPv6 generates its addresses directly from the device and router information such as the device hardware MAC address.

In addition, if you are using a dynamic DSL, ISDN, or a modem connection, you will also have to supply provider, login, and password information, and specify whether your system is dynamic or static. You may also need to supply specialized information such as DSL or modem compression methods or dial-up number.

You can obtain most of your static network information from your network administrator, or from your ISP (Internet Service Provider). You would need the following information:

The device name for your network interface   For LAN and wireless connections, this is usually an Ethernet card with the name **eth0** or **eth1**. For a modem, DSL, or ISDN connection, this is a PPP device named **ppp0** (**ippp0** for ISDN).

Hostname   Your computer will be identified by this name on the Internet. Do not use localhost; that name is reserved for special use by your system. The name of the host should be a simple word, which can include numbers, but not punctuation such as periods and backslashes. On a small network, the hostname is often a single name. On a large network that could have several domains, the hostname includes both the name of the host and its domain.

Domain name   This is the name of your network.

The Internet Protocol (IP) address assigned to your machine   This is needed only for static Internet connections. Dynamic connections use the DHCP protocol to assign an IP address for you automatically. Every host on the Internet is assigned an IP address. Small and older network addresses might still use the older IPv4 format consisting of a set of four numbers, separated by periods. The IP protocol version 6, IPv6, uses a new format with a complex numbering sequence that is much more automatic.

Your network IP address   Static connections only. This address is similar to the IP address but lacks any reference to a particular host.

The netmask   IPv4 Static connections only. This is usually 255.255.255.0 for most networks. If, however, you are part of a large network, check with your network administrator or ISP.

The broadcast address for your network, if available (optional)   IPv4 Static connections only. Usually, your broadcast address is the same as your IP address with the number 255 added at the end.

The IP address of your network's gateway computer   Static connections only. This is the computer that connects your local network to a larger one like the Internet.

Name servers   The IP address of the name servers your network uses. These enable the use of URLs.

NIS domain and IP address for an NIS server   Necessary if your network uses an NIS server (optional).

User login and password information   Needed for dynamic DSL, ISDN, and modem connections.

Network Manager

Network Manager detects your network connections automatically, both wired and wireless. It uses the automatic device detection capabilities of udev to configure your connections.

Should you instead need to configure your network connections manually, you can also use GNOME network (Network Settings) or the older nm-connections editor (Network Connections) to enter the required network connection information. Network Manager operates as a daemon with the name Network Manager. It will automatically scan for both wired and wireless connections. Information provided by Network Manager is made available to other applications. The Network Manager monitors your network connection, indicating its status on the Network Manager panel applet.

Network Manager is designed to work in the background, providing status information for your connection and switching from one configured connection to another as needed. For an initial configuration, it detects as much information as possible about a new connection.

Network Manager is also user specific. When a user logs in, wireless connections the user prefers will start up (wired connections are started automatically).

By default, an Ethernet connection will be preferred if available. For wireless connections, you will need to choose the one you want.

Network Manager is designed to work in the background, providing status information for your connection and switching from one configured connection to another as needed. For initial configuration, it detects as much information as possible about the new connection.

Network Manager operates as a daemon with the name NetworkManager. If no Ethernet connection is available, Network Manager will scan for wireless connections, checking for Extended Service Set Identifiers (ESSIDs). If an ESSID identifies a previously used connection, then it is automatically selected. If several are found, then the most recently used one is chosen. If only a new connection is available, then Network Manager waits for the user to choose one. A connection is selected only if the user is logged in. If an Ethernet connection is later made, then Network Manager will switch to it from wireless.

The Network Manager daemon can be turned on or off using the service command as the root user.

```
sudo service NetworkManager start
sudo service NetworkManager stop
```

Network Manager menu

Network Manager displays a network applet on the right side of the Linux Mint panel. The Network Manager icon will vary according to the type of connection. An Ethernet (wired) connection displays two connected plugs. A wireless connection displays a staggered wave graph (see Figure 11-1). If the connection is not active, an empty wave graph is shown. If you have both a wired and wireless connection, and the wired connection is active, the wired connection icon is used.

Figure 11-1: Network Manager wired, wireless, and disconnect icons.

The Network Manager applet menu displays your wired connection as Wired, with a switch to turn it on or off (see Figure11-2). To disconnect your wired connection, you can click the switch, turning it to the off position. Your Network Manager icon on the panel becomes grayed out. To reconnect later, click the switch again.

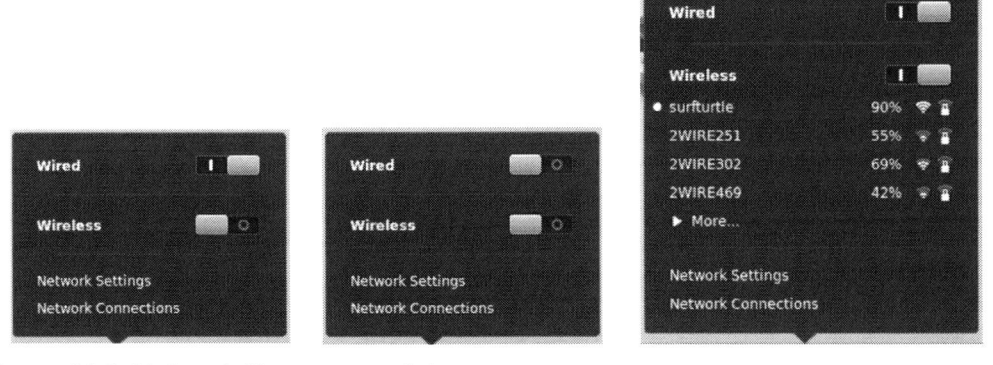

Figure 11-2: Network Manager applet menu

Network Manager will scan for wireless connections, checking for Extended Service Set Identifiers (ESSIDs). If an ESSID identifies a previously used connection, then it is selected by Network Manager. If several are found, then the recently used one is chosen. If only a new connection is available, then Network Manager waits for the user to choose one. A connection is selected only if the user is logged in.

Network Manager manual configuration using GNOME Network (Network Settings)

The GNOME Network tool, available from System Settings as Networking and from the Network Manager menu as Network Settings, can be used to configure your network connections. Automatic wireless and wired connections were covered in Chapter 3. For detailed manual configuration, Network features similar dialogs to those used in Network Connections. When you access GNOME Network, it displays a Network dialog that shows three tabs: Wi-Fi, Wired, and Network Proxy (see Figure 11-3).

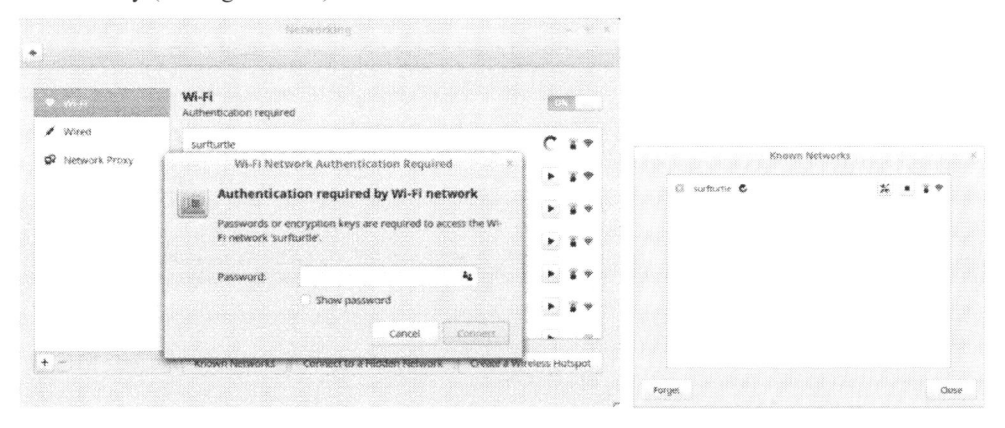

Figure 11-3: Network (System Settings) Wi-Fi Tab and Known Networks

On the Wi-Fi tab, available wireless connections are listed to the right. Selecting an entry will create a gear button for it, which you can click to open the network configuration dialog with tabs for Details, Security, Identity, Ipv4, Ipv6, and Reset. The Details tab show strength, speed, security methods, IP and hardware addresses, routes, and the DNS server IP address. To edit the connection manually you sue the Security, Identity, and IP tabs. The Security tab displays a menu from which you can choose a security method and a password (see Figure 11-4).

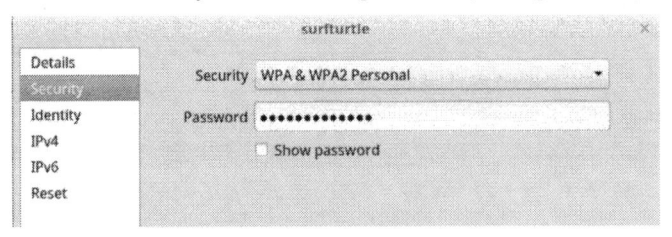

Figure 11-4: Network wireless configuration: Security tab

On the Identity tab you can specify the SSID name, choose a firewall zone, choose to connect automatically when you log in, and whether to make the connection system wide (available to other users (see Figure 11-5).

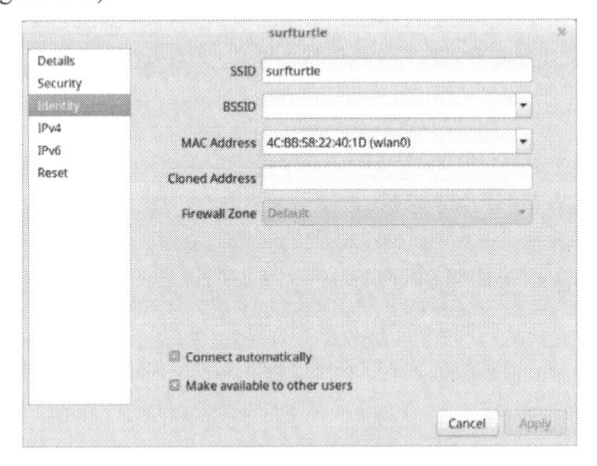

Figure 11-5: Network wireless configuration: Identity tab

On the IPv4 Settings tabs a switch allows you to turn the IP connection on or off. There are sections for Addresses, the DNS servers, and Routes (see Figure 11-6). An Addresses menu lets you choose the type connection you want. By default, it is set to Automatic. If you change it to Manual, new entries appear for the address, netmask, and gateway. On the IPv6 tab, the netmask is replaced by the prefix. You can turn off Automatic switches for the DNS and Routes sections to make them manual. The DNS section has a plus button to let you add more DNS servers.

Figure 11-6: Network wireless configuration: IP tabs, manual

For quick access to networks you have already configured, you can click the Known Networks button to open the Known Networks dialog listing all your configured networks (see Figure 11-3). Use the play button to the right of the network name to start and stop the network. The configuration button opens that network's configuration dialog. To remove a network, click its checkbox, which activates the Forget button at the lower left, then click that button.

The Networking dialog's Wired tab displays information about the wired connection such as the IP, hardware, and DNS server addresses. A gear button is displayed on the lower right. A switch lets you turn the connection on or off (see Figure 11-7). Clicking on the wrench button opens a configuration dialog with tabs for Details, Security, Identity, IPv4, IPv6, and Reset (see Figure 11-8).

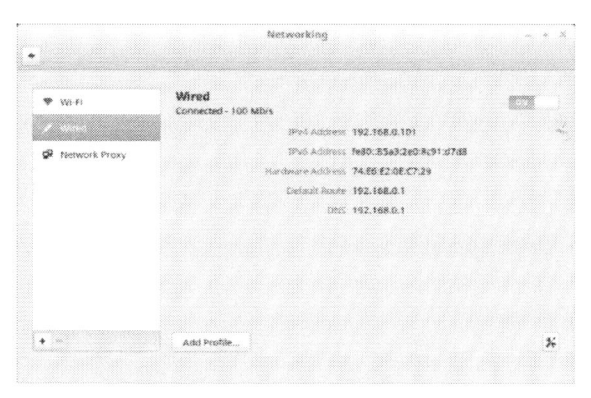

Figure 11-7: Network wired tab

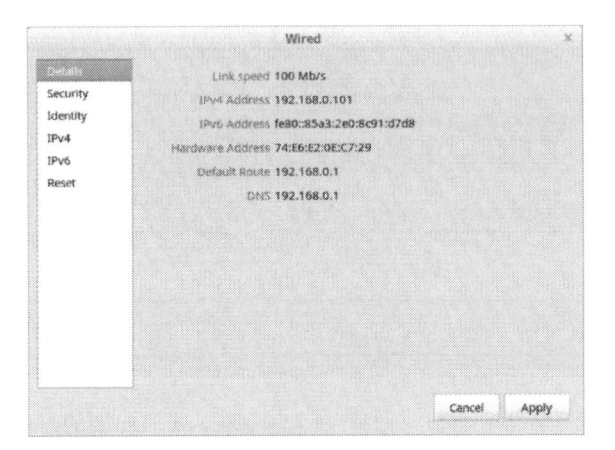

Figure 11-8: Network wired configuration dialog

You can use the Security, Identity, and IP tabs to manually configure the connection. The Security tab lets you turn on 802.1 security and choose an authentication method as well as provide a username and password (see Figure 11-9).

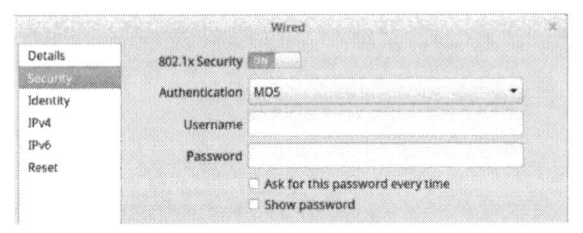

Figure 11-9: Network wired configuration, Security

On the Identity tab you can choose the firewall zone, set the name, choose the hardware address, set the MTU blocks, choose to connect automatically, and whether to make the connection system wide (see Figure 11-10).

Figure 11-10: Network wired configuration, Identity

On the IPv tabs, a switch allows you to turn the connection on or off. The tab has sections for Addresses, DNS servers, and Routes. DNS and Routs have a switch for automatic. Turing the switch off allows you to manually enter a DNS server address or routing information. From the Addresses menu, you can also choose to make the connection automatic or manual. When manual, new entries appear that let you enter the address, netmask, and gateway (see Figure 11-11). On the IPv6 tab, the Netmask entry is replaced by a Prefix entry.

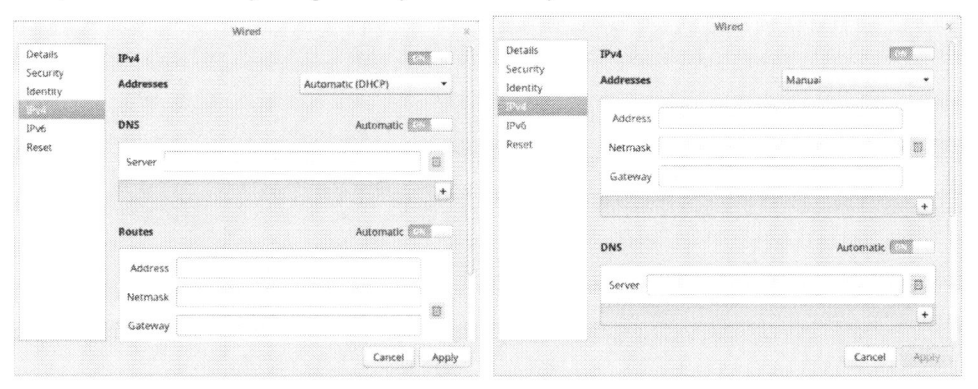

Figure 11-11: Network wired configuration, IPv4

On the Network dialog, you can add a new connection by clicking the plus button on the lower left corner. A dialog opens to let you add a VPN, Bod, Bridge, or VLAN connection. Except for VPN connections, these all open appropriate dialogs in the nm-connections-editor (Network Connections). The VPN connection only opens a dialog where you can load a VPN connection file. For VPN configuration, you should use the nm-connections-editor (Network Connections), described in the following section.

Network Manager manual configuration using the nm-connections-editor (Network Connection)

You can also use the older **nm-connection-editor** (Network Connections) to edit any network connection, accessible from the Network Manager applet's menu as Network Connections, and from the Preferences menu (see Figure 11-2). This opens Network Manager's Network Connections window as shown in Figure 11-12.

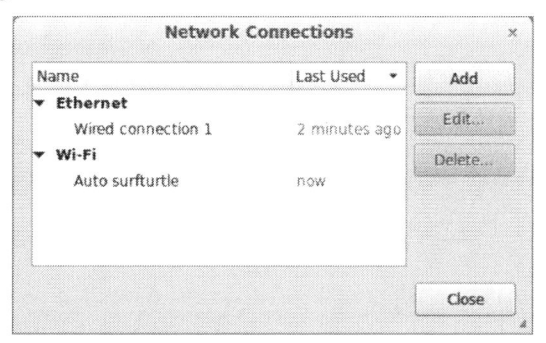

Figure 11-12: Network configuration

Established connections are listed, with Add, Edit, and Delete buttons for adding, editing, and removing network connections. Your current network connections should be listed, having been detected automatically. In Figure 11-3 a wired Ethernet connection referred to as **Wired connection 1** is listed, the first Ethernet connection. This is an automatic configuration set up by Network Manager when it automatically connected to the wired network.

When you add a connection, you can choose the type of connection from a drop-down menu (see Figure 11-13). The menu organizes connection types into three categories: Hardware, Virtual, and VPN (Virtual Private Network) (see Figure 11-14). Hardware connections cover both wired (Ethernet, DSL, and Infiniband) and wireless connections (Wi-Fi, WiMax, and Mobile Broadband). VPN lists the supported VPN types such as OpenVPN, PPTP, and Cisco (install support for additional ones). You can also import a previously configured connection. Virtual supports VLAN, Bridge, and Bond virtual connections.

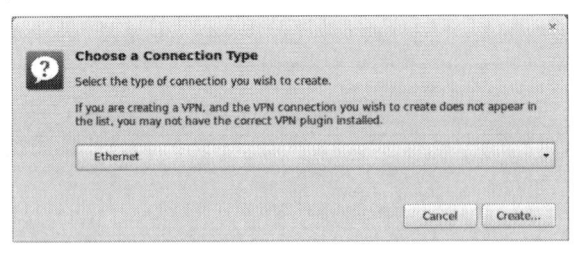

Figure 11-13: Choosing a connection type for a new network connection

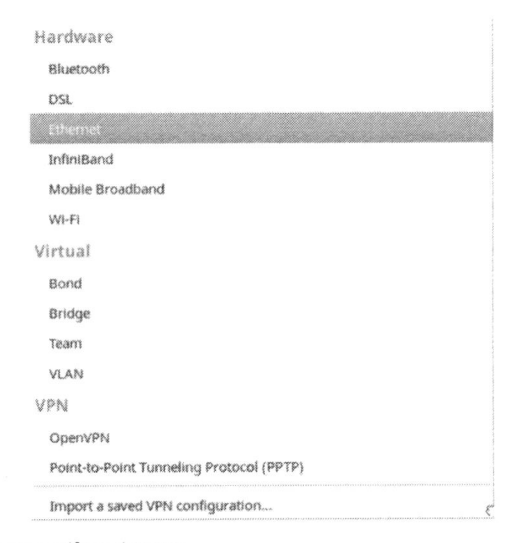

Figure 11-14: New connection types

General tab

Configuration editing dialogs display a General tab where you can make your configuration available to all users, and automatically connect when the network connection is available. You can also choose to use a VPN connection and specify a firewall zone. Figure 11-15 shows the General tab with a wired connection.

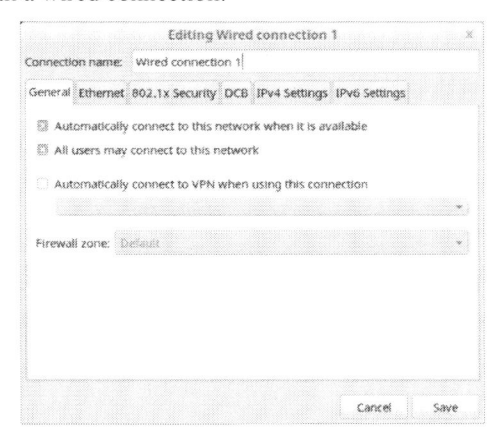

Figure 11-15: General tab

Wired Configuration

To edit a wired connection, select the connection and click the Edit button on the Ethernet tab. This opens an Editing window as shown in Figure 11-16. The Add button is used to add a new connection and opens a similar window, with no settings. There are six tabs: General, Ethernet, 8.02.1x Security, DCB, IPv4 Settings, and IPv6 Settings. The Ethernet tab lists the MAC hardware address and the MTU. The MTU is usually set to automatic. Figure 11-16 shows the standard default configuration for a wired Ethernet connection using DHCP.

Figure 11-16: DHCP Wired Configuration

The IPv4 and IPv6 Settings tabs let you select the kind of protocol your wired connection uses. A check box at the bottom of the dialog lets you require the given protocol to complete the connection. The IPv4 and IPv6 have different entries. The IPv4 options are:

Automatic (DHCP): DHCP connection, address information is blocked out.

Automatic (DHCP) addresses only: DHCP connection that lets you specify your DNS server addresses.

Manual: Enter your IP, network, and gateway addresses along with your DNS server addresses and your network domain name.

Link-local only: IPv6 private local network. All address entries are blocked out.

Shared to other computers: All address entries are blocked out.

The IPv6 options are:

Ignore: Do not use IPv6.

Automatic: IPv6 automatic address detection (similar to DHCP).

Automatic, addresses only: Use IPv6 to determine network addresses, but not DNS (domain) information. You can enter the DNS server addresses and search domains manually.

Manual: Enter your IP, network, and gateway addresses along with your DNS server addresses and your network domain name. IPv6 addresses use an address and a prefix.

Link-local only: IPv6 private local network. All address entries are blocked out.

Figure 11-17 shows the manual configuration entries for an IPv4 wired Ethernet connection. Click the Add button to enter the IP address, network mask, and gateway address. Then enter the address for the DNS servers and your network search domains. The Routes button will open a window where you can manually enter any network routes. Figure 11-18 shows the manual configuration for an IPv6 connection, with address and prefix entries for the address.

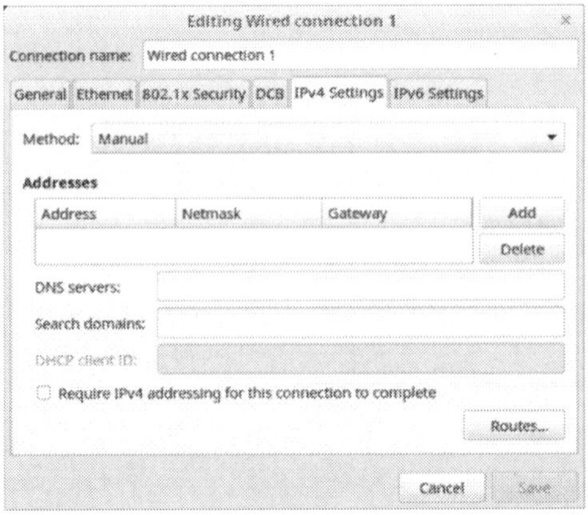

Figure 11-17: Manual IPv4 Wired Configuration

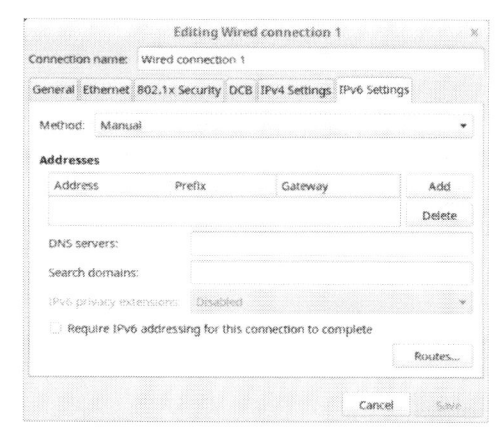

Figure 11-18: Manual IPv6 Wired Configuration

The 802.1 tab allows you to configure 802.1 security if your network supports it (see Figure 11-19). It supports MD5, TLS, FAST, Tunneled TLS, and Protected EAP methods.

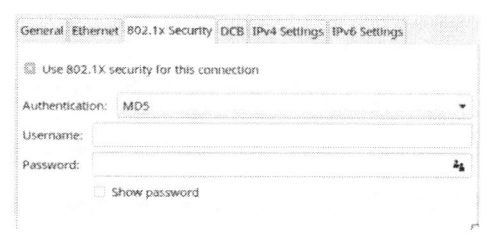

Figure 11-19: 802.1 Security Configuration

The DCB tab allows you to configure Data Center Bridging connections, should your network support them. DCB provides extensions to the Internet protocol to manage high-speed connections better, such as storage area network (SAN) connections and data center fiber channels. Connections supported include Fiber Channel over the Ethernet (FCoE and FIP (Fiber Channel Initialization Protocol)) and iSCSI. For each, you can set the flow control priorities (Priority Pause Transmission) and priority groups priorities.

Wireless Configuration

Wireless connections are listed on the Network Connections window's Wi-Fi listing. To add or edit a wireless connection, use the Add or Edit buttons. When you click the Edit button, the Editing window opens with tabs for your wireless information, security, IPv4, and IPv6 settings (See Figure 11-20). On the Wi-Fi tab, you specify your SSID, along with your Mode and MAC address.

Figure 11-20: Wireless configuration

On the Wi-Fi Security tab, you enter your wireless connection security method (see Figure 11-21). The commonly used method, WEP, is supported, along with WPA personal. The WPA personal method only requires a password. More secure connections like Dynamic WEP and Enterprise WPA are also supported. These will require more configuration information such as authentication methods, certificates, and keys.

On the IPv4 Settings tab, you enter your wireless connection's network address settings. This tab is the same as the IPv4 Setting on the Wired connection (see Figure 11-8). You have the same options: DHCP, DHCP with DNS addresses, Manual, Link-local only, and Shared. If your wireless connection uses the IPv6 protocol, you would use the IPv6 Settings tab, also the same as IPv6 Settings on a wired connection (see Figure 11-18).

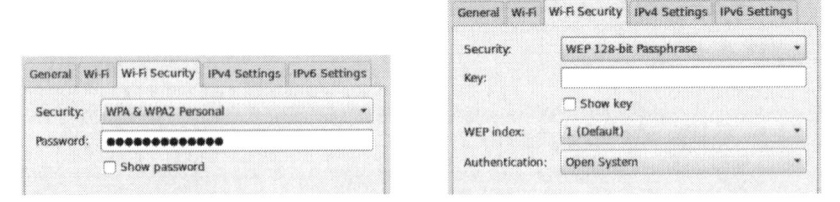

Figure 11-21: Wireless Security: WEP and WPA

DSL Configuration

To add or edit a direct DSL connection, you click the Add or Edit buttons on the Network Connections window's DSL tab. The DSL connection window opens, showing tabs for DSL configuration and for wired, PPP, and IPv4 network connections. On the DSL tab you enter your DSL username, service provider, and password (see Figure 11-22). A wired connection requires a MAC address and MTU byte amount. The PPP tab is the same as that used for Mobile Broadband, and IPv4 is the same as the IPv4 Settings tab used for Wired, Wireless, and Mobile Broadband connections (see Figure 11-17).

Figure 11-22: DSL manual configuration

Mobile Broadband: 3G Support

Mobile Broadband 3G connections are listed in the Mobile Broadband tab. For a new broadband connection, click the Add button. A 3G wizard starts up to help you set up the appropriate configuration for your particular 3G service (see Figure 11-23). Configuration steps are listed on the left pane. If your device is connected, you can select it from the drop-down menu on the right pane. On the next step, you choose your country. The 3G wizard then displays a service provider window listing 3G service providers (see Figure 11-24). You then select the billing plan. For the last step, you are asked to confirm your selections.

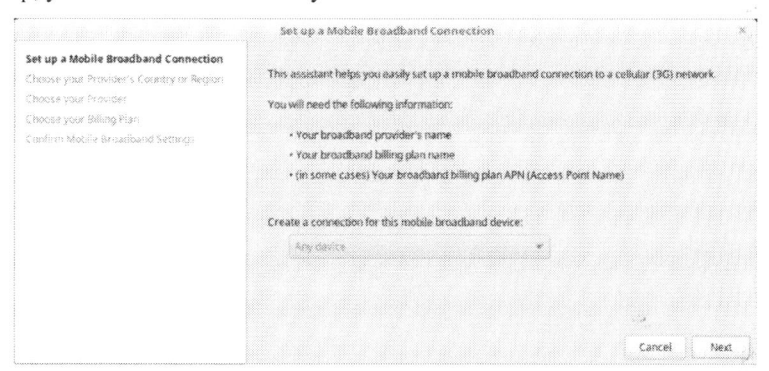

Figure 11-23: 3G Wizard

Once a service is selected, you can further edit the configuration by clicking its entry in the Mobile Broadband tab and clicking the Edit button. The Editing window opens with tabs for Mobile Broadband, PPP, IPv4 settings. On the Mobile Broadband tab, you can enter your number, username, and password. Advanced options include the APN, Network, and PIN (see Figure 11-25). The APN should already be entered.

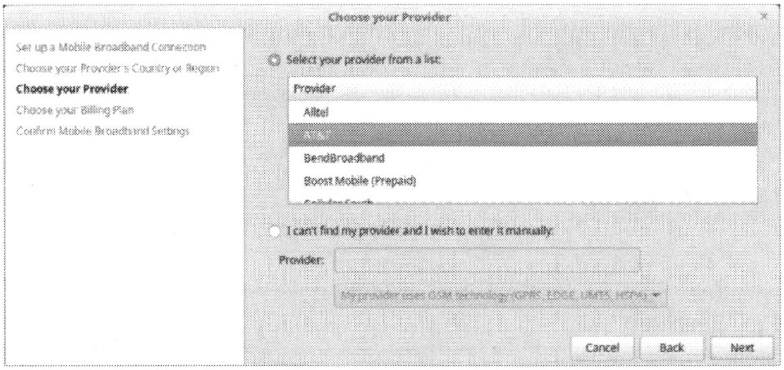

Figure 11-24: 3G Provider Listings

PPP Configuration

For either Wireless Broadband or DSL connections, you also can specify PPP information. The PPP tab is the same for both (see Figure 11-26). There are Authentication, Compression, and the Echo sections. Check the features that are supported by your particular PPP connection. For Authentication, click the Configure Methods button to open a dialog listing possible authentication methods. Check the ones your connection supports.

Figure 11-25: 3G configuration

Figure 11-26: PPP Configuration

Network Manager VPN

On the Network Manager menu, the VPN Connection entry submenu will list configured VPN connections for easy access. The Configure VPN entry will open the Network Connections window to the VPN tab where you can then add, edit, or delete VPN connections. The Disconnect VPN entry will end the current active VPN connection.

Several VPN services are available. The PPTP service for Microsoft VPN connections is installed by default, **network-manager-pptp**. Other popular VPN services include OpenVPN, Cisco Concentrator, and Strongswan (IPSec). For Network Manager support, be sure to install the corresponding Network Manager plugin for these services. The plugin packages begin with the name **network-manager**. To use the **openvpn** service, first, install the **openvpn** software along with the **network-manager-openvpn** plugin (Universe repository). For Cisco Concentrator based VPN, use the **network-manager-vpnc** plugin, and for Cisco OpenConnect use **network-manager-openconnect**. Strongswan uses the **network-manager-strongswan** plugin. To see a list of available VPN services search on vpn in Software Manager or in the Synaptic Package Manager.

To add a VPN connection, choose a VPN Connection type from the connection type menu. (see Figure 11-127).

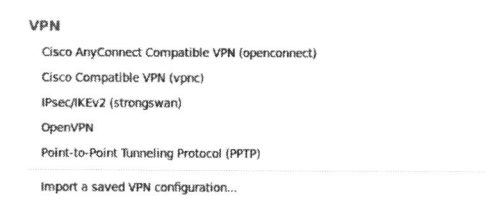

Figure 11-27: VPN connection types

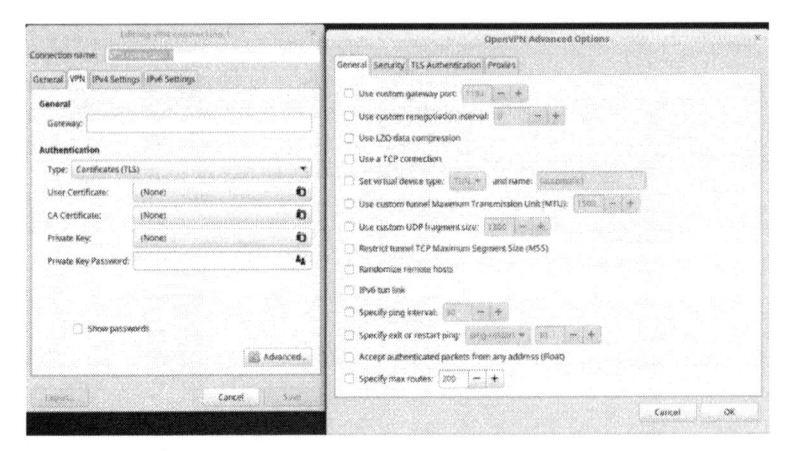

Figure 11-28: VPN configuration (openvpn)

The "Editing VPN connection" dialog then opens with three tabs: General, VPN, and IPv4 Settings. On the VPN tab, you enter VPN connection information such as the gateway address and any additional VPN information that may be required. For an OpenVPN connection, you will need to provide the authentication type, certificates, and keys (see Figure 11-28). Clicking on the Advanced button opens the Advanced Options dialog. An OpenVPN connection will have tabs for General, Security, and TLS Authentication. On the Security tab, you can specify the cipher to use.

Figure 11-29: VPN configuration (pptp)

Options will differ depending on the type of VPN connection you choose. The PPTP connection used on Microsoft networks requires only a gateway address on the VPN tab. Advanced options let you specify the authentication method and security options (see Figure 11-29). Like OpenVPN, a Strongswan IPSec connection also requires certificates and keys. It does not have an Advanced Options dialog. The IPv4 tab lets you specify your DNS servers if you want. The Cisco Connector connection only requires a group name and password. You also can specify the encryption method, domain, and username.

Managing Network Connections with nmcli

The **nmcli** command is NetworkManager Command Line Interface command. Most network configuration tasks can be performed by **nmcli**. The **nmcli** command manages NetworkManager through a set of objects: general (**g**), networking (**n**), radio (**r**), connection (**c**), device (**d**), and agent (**a**). Each can be referenced using the full name or a unique prefix, such as **con** for connection or **dev** for device. The unique prefix can be as short as a single character, such as **g** for general, **c** for connections, or **d** for device. See Table 11-2 for a list of the objects and commonly used options. The **nmcli** man page provides a complete listing with examples.

The general object shows the current status of NetworkManager and what kind of devices are enabled. You can limit the information displayed using the **-t** (terse) and **-f** (field) options. The STATE field show the connection status, and the CONNECTIVITY field the connection.

```
$ nmcli general
STATE       CONNECTIVITY  WIFI-HW  WIFI     WWAN-HW  WWAN
connected   full                   enabled  enabled  enabled  enabled

$ nmcli -t -f STATE general
connected
```

The **connection** object references the network connection and the **show** option displays that information. The following example displays your current connection.

```
nmcli connection show
```

You can use **c** instead of **connection** and **s** instead of show.

```
$ nmcli c s
NAME        UUID                                  TYPE           DEVICE
enp7s0      f7202f6d-fc66-4b81-8962-69b71202efc0  802-3-ethernet enp7s0
AT&T LTE 1  65913b39-789a-488c-9559-28ea6341d9e1  gsm            --
```

As with the general object, you can limit the fields displayed using the **-f** option. The following only list the name and type fields.

```
$ nmcli -f name, type c s
NAME        TYPE
enp7s0      802-3-ethernet
AT&T LTE 1  gsm
```

Object	Description
`general`	NetworkManager status and enabled devices. Use the terse (**-t**) and field (**-f**) option to limit the information displayed.
`networking`	Manage networking, use `on` and `off` to turn networking on or off, and `connectivity` for the connection state.
`radio`	Turns on or off the wireless networking (on or off). Can turn on or off specific kinds of wireless: `wifi`, `wwan` (mobile broadband), and `wimax`. The `all` option turns on or off all wireless.
`connection`	Manage network connections. `show` List connection profiles. With `--active` show only active connections. `up` Activate a connection `down` Deactivate a connection `add` Add a new connection, specifying `type`, `ifname`, `con-name` (profile). `modify` Edit an existing connection, use + and − to add new values to properties `edit` Add a new connection or edit an existing one using the interactive editor `delete` Delete a configured connection (profile) `reload` Reload all connection profiles `load` Reload or load a specific
`device`	Manage network interfaces (devices). `status` Display device status `show` Display device information `connect` Connect the device `disconnect` Disconnect the device `delete` Delete a software device, such as a bridge. `wifi` Display a list of available wifi access points `wifi rescan` Rescan for and display access points `wifi connect` Connect to a wifi network; specify `password`, `wep-key-type`, `ifname`, `bssid`, and `name` (profile name) `wimax` List available WiMAX networks
`agent`	Run as a Network Manager secret agent or polkit agent. `secret` As a secret agent, nmcli listens for secret requests. `polkit` As a polkit agent it listens for all authorization requests.

Table 11-2: The nmcli objects

Adding the **--active** option will only show active connections.

```
nmcli c s --active
```

To start and stop a connection (like **ifconfig** does), use the **up** and **down** options.

```
nmcli con up enp7s0.
```

Use the **device** object to manage your network devices. The **show** and **status** options provide information about your devices. To check the status of all your network devices, use the **device** object and **status** options:

```
nmcli device status
DEVICE   TYPE       STATE         CONNECTION
enp7s0   ethernet   connected     enp7s0
wlp6s0   wifi       disconnected  --
lo       loopback   unmanaged     --
```

You can abbreviate **device** and **status** to **d** and **s**.

```
nmcli d s
```

You also use the **device** object to connect and disconnect devices. Use the **connect** or **disconnect** options with the interface name (ifname) of the device, in this example, **enp7s0**. With the **delete** option, you can remove a device.

```
nmcli device disconnect enp7s0
nmcli device connect enp7s0
```

To turn networking on or off, you use the **networking** object and the **on** and **off** options. Use the **connectivity** option to check network connectivity. The networking object alone tells you if it is enabled or not.

```
$ nmcli networking
enabled

$ nmcli networking on

$ nmcli networking connectivity
full
```

Should you want to just turn on or off the Wifi connection, you would use the **radio** object. Use **wifi**, **wwan**, and **wimax** for a specific type of wifi connection and the **all** option for all of them. The radio object alone shows wifi status of all your wifi connection types.

```
$ nmcli radio
WIFI-HW   WIFI     WWAN-HW   WWAN
enabled   enabled  enabled   enabled

$ nmcli radio wifi on

$ nmcli radio all off
```

nmcli Wired Connections

You can use **nmcli** to add connections, just as you can with the desktop NetworkManager tool. To add a new static connection, use the connection object with the **add** option. Specify the connection's profile name with the **con-name** option, the interface name with the **ifname** option, the **type**, such as Ethernet. For a static connection you would add the IP address (**ipv4** or **ipv6**), and the gateway address (**gw4** or **gw6**). For a DHCP connection simply do not list the IP address and gateway options. The profile name can be any name. You could have several profile names for the same network device. For example, for your wireless device, you could have several wireless connection profiles, depending on the different networks you want to connect to. Should you connect your Ethernet device to a different network, you would simply use a different connection profile that you have already set up, instead of manually reconfiguring the connection. If you do not specify a connection name, one is generated and assigned to you. The connection name can be the same as the device name as shown here, but keep in mind that the connection name refers to the profile and the device name refers to the actual device.

```
$ nmcli c s
NAME      UUID                                   TYPE           DEVICE
enp7s0    f7202f6d-fc66-4b81-8962-69b71202efc0   802-3-ethernet enp7s0
```

For a DHCP connection, specify the profile name, connection type, and ifname. The following example creates an Ethernet connection with the profile name "my-wired."

```
nmcli con add con-name my-wired type ethernet ifname enp7s0
```

For a static connection add the IP (**ip4** or **ip6**) and gateway (**gw4** or **gw6**) options with their addresses.

```
nmcli con add con-name my-wired-static ifname enp7s0 type ethernet ip4 192.168.1.0/24 gw4 192.168.1.1
```

In most cases, the type is Ethernet (wired) or wifi (wireless). Check the **nmcli** man page for a list of other types, such as gsm, infiniband, vpn, vlan, wimax, and bridge.

You can also add a connection using the interactive editor. Use the **edit** instead of the **add** option, and specify the **con-name** (profile) and connection type.

```
nmcli con edit type ethernet con-name my-wired
```

To modify an existing connection, use the **modify** option. For an IP connection, the property that is changed is referenced as part of the IP settings, in this example, **ip4**. The IP properties include addresses, gateway, and method (ip4.addresses, ip4.gateway, and ip4.method).

```
nmcli con mod my-wired ip4.gateway 192.168.1.2
```

To add or remove a value for a property use the + and - signs as a prefix. To add a DNS server address you would use **+ip4.dns**. To remove one use **-ip4.dns**.

```
nmcli con mod my-wired +ip4.dns 192.168.1.5
```

You can also modify a connection using the interactive editor. Use the edit instead of the modify option with the connection name.

```
nmcli con edit enp7s0
```

You are then placed in the interactive editor with an **nmcli>** prompt and the settings you can change are listed. The **help** command lists available commands. Use the **describe** command to show property descriptions.

Use **print** to show the current value of a property and **set** to change its value. To see all the properties for a setting, use the print command and the setting name. Once you have made changes, use the **save** command to effect the changes.

```
print ipv4
print ipv4.dns
print connection
set ipv4.address 192.168.0.1
```

The connection edit command can also reference a profile using the **id** option. The Name field in the connection profile information is the same as the ID. Also, each profile is given a unique system UUID, which can also be used to reference the profile.

Once you are finished editing the connection, enter the **quit** command to leave the editor.

nmcli Wireless Connections

To see a list of all the available wifi connections in your area, you use the **wifi** option with the **device** object. You can further qualify it by interface (if you have more than one) by adding the **ifname** option, and by BSSID adding the **bssid** option.

```
nmcli device wifi
```

To connect to a new Wifi network, use the **wifi connect** option and the SSID. You can further specify a password, wep-key-type, key, ifname, bssid, name (profile name), and if it is private. If you do not provide a name (profile name), nmcli will generate one for you.

```
nmcli dev wifi connect surfturtle password mypass wep-key-type wpa ifname wlp6s0 name my-wireless1
```

To reconnect to a Wifi network for which you have previously set up a connection, use the **connection** object with the **up** command and the **id** option to specify the profile name.

```
nmcli connection up id my-wireless1
```

You can also add a new wireless connection using the **connection** object and the **wifi** type with the **ssid** option.

```
nmcli con add con-name my-wireless2 ifname wlp6s0 type wifi ssid ssidname
```

Then, to set the encryption type use the **modify** command to set the **sec.key-mgmt** property, and for the passphrase set the **wifi-sec.psk** property.

```
nmcli con mod my-wirless2 wifi-sec.key-mgmt wpa-psk
nmcli con modify my-wireless2 wifi-sec.psk mypassword
```

Dial-up PPP Modem Access: wvdial

For direct dial-up PPP modem connections, you can use the wvdial dialer, an intelligent dialer that, not only dials up an ISP service, but also performs login operations, supplying your username and password. The wvdial tool runs on the command line using the wvdial command, and on the desktop with the GNOME PPP application (**gnome-ppp**). The wvdial program first loads its configuration from the **/etc/wvdial.conf** file. In this file, you can place modem and account information, including modem speed, ISP phone number, username, and password.

The **wvdial.conf** file is organized into sections, beginning with a section label enclosed in brackets. A section holds variables for different parameters that are assigned values, such as `username = chris`. The default section holds default values inherited by other sections, so you need not repeat them. Table 11-3 lists the wvdial variables.

You can use the **wvdialconf** utility to create a default **wvdial.conf** file, detecting your modem and setting default values for basic features automatically. You can then edit the **wvdial.conf** file and modify the Phone, Username, and Password entries entering your dial-up information. Remove the preceding semicolon (;) to unquote the entry. Any line beginning with a semicolon is ignored as a comment.

```
wvdialconf
```

Variable	Description
Inherits	Explicitly inherits from the specified section. By default, sections inherit from the [Dialer Defaults] section.
Modem	The device wvdial should use as your modem. The default is **/dev/modem**.
Baud	The speed at which wvdial communicates with your modem. The default is 57,600 baud.
Init1...Init9	Specifies the initialization strings to be used by your modem; wvdial can use up to 9. The default is "ATZ" for Init1.
Phone	The phone number you want wvdial to dial.
Area Code	Specifies the area code, if any.
Dial Prefix	Specifies any needed dialing prefix—for example, 70 to disable call waiting or 9 for an outside line.
Dial Command	Specifies the dial operation. The default is "ATDT".
Login	Specifies the username you use at your ISP.
Login Prompt	If your ISP has an unusual login prompt, you can specify it here.
Password	Specifies the password you use at your ISP.
Password Prompt	If your ISP has an unusual password prompt, you can specify it here.
Force Address	Specifies a static IP address to use (for ISPs that provide static IP addresses to users).
Auto Reconnect	If enabled, wvdial attempts to reestablish a connection automatically if you are randomly disconnected by the other side. This option is on by default.

Table 11-3: Variables for wvdial

You can also create a named dialer. This is helpful if you have different location or services you log in to.

To start wvdial, enter the command **wvdial** in a terminal window, which then reads the connection configuration information from the **/etc/wvdial.conf** file; wvdial dials the location and initiates the PPP connection, providing your username and password when requested.

```
wvdial
```

You can set up connection configurations for any number of connections in the **/etc/wvdial.conf** file. To select one, enter its label as an argument to the **wvdial** command, as shown here:

```
wvdial mylocation
```

Configuring a network with systemd-networkd

The systemd based network manager called **systemd-networkd** can currently be used for basic operations. You would use it as a small, fast, and simple alternative to a larger manager such as NetworkManager. systemd is described in detail in Chapter 5. The service, target, and socket files for systemd-networkd are located in the **/lib/systemd/system**: **systemd-networkd.service**, **systemd-networkd.target**, and **systemd-networkd.socket**. Network resolvconf operations are handled with **systemd-resolved.service**. User configuration files for systemd-networkd are located in /etc/systemd/network.

In the **systemd-networkd.service** file several security features are enabled. A capability bounding set (CapabilityBoundingSet) lets you limit kernel capabilities to those specified. The man page for **capabilities** list the available capabilities. The CAP_NET capabilities limit the networkd service to network operations such as interface configuration, firewall administration, multicasting, sockets, broadcasting, and proxies. The CAP_SET capabilities allow for file and process GID and UIDs. The CAP_CHOWN, CAP_DAC_OVERRIDE, and CAP_FOWNER capabilities deal with bypassing permission checks for files. The CAP_SYS capabilities that provide system administrative capabilities are not included. In addition, the ProtectSystem option (**systemd.exec**) prevents the service from making any changes to the system (/**usr**, /**boot**, and /**etc** directories are read-only for this service). The ProtectHome option makes the /**home**, /**root**, and /**run/user** directories inaccessible. WatchdogSec sets the watchdog timeout for the service. Check the **systemd.directives** man page for a list of all systemd directives.

systemd-networkd.service

```
[Unit]
Description=Network Service
Documentation=man:systemd-networkd.service(8)
ConditionCapability=CAP_NET_ADMIN
DefaultDependencies=no
# dbus.service can be dropped once on kdbus, and systemd-udevd.service can be
# dropped once tuntap is moved to netlink
After=systemd-udevd.service dbus.service network-pre.target systemd-
sysusers.service systemd-sysctl.service
Before=network.target multi-user.target shutdown.target
Conflicts=shutdown.target
Wants=network.target

# On kdbus systems we pull in the busname explicitly, because it
# carries policy that allows the daemon to acquire its name.
Wants=org.freedesktop.network1.busname
```

```
After=org.freedesktop.network1.busname

[Service]
Type=notify
Restart=on-failure
RestartSec=0
ExecStart=/lib/systemd/systemd-networkd
CapabilityBoundingSet=CAP_NET_ADMIN CAP_NET_BIND_SERVICE CAP_NET_BROADCAST
CAP_NET_RAW CAP_SETUID CAP_SETGID CAP_SETPCAP CAP_CHOWN CAP_DAC_OVERRIDE
CAP_FOWNER
ProtectSystem=full
ProtectHome=yes
WatchdogSec=3min

[Install]
WantedBy=multi-user.target
Also=systemd-networkd.socket
```

The **systemd-networkd.socket** file sets **systemd.socket** options for buffer size (ReceiveBuffer), network link (ListenNetlink), passing credentials (PassCredentials). As a condition for starting the service, the CAP_NET_ADMIN capability needs to be set in the capability bounding set (ConditionCapability).

systemd-networkd.socket

```
[Unit]
Description=Network Service Netlink Socket
Documentation=man:systemd-networkd.service(8) man:rtnetlink(7)
ConditionCapability=CAP_NET_ADMIN
DefaultDependencies=no
Before=sockets.target

[Socket]
ReceiveBuffer=8M
ListenNetlink=route 1361
PassCredentials=yes

[Install]
WantedBy=sockets.target
```

The **systemd-resolved.service** provides for the resolvconf operations (DNS server information). It has the same capabilities as **systemd-networkd.service**, except for the network capabilities.

systemd-resolved.service

```
[Unit]
Description=Network Name Resolution
Documentation=man:systemd-resolved.service(8)
After=systemd-networkd.service network.target

# On kdbus systems we pull in the busname explicitly, because it
# carries policy that allows the daemon to acquire its name.
Wants=org.freedesktop.resolve1.busname
After=org.freedesktop.resolve1.busname
```

```
[Service]
Type=notify
Restart=always
RestartSec=0
ExecStart=/lib/systemd/systemd-resolved
CapabilityBoundingSet=CAP_SETUID CAP_SETGID CAP_SETPCAP CAP_CHOWN
CAP_DAC_OVERRIDE CAP_FOWNERs
ProtectSystem=full
ProtectHome=yes
WatchdogSec=3min

[Install]
WantedBy=multi-user.target
```

In addition, the **systemd-networkd-resolvconf-update.service** updates the DNS information. The **systemd-networkd-wait-online.service** delays activation of other services, until **systemd-networkd** service comes online.

You configure a network connection for networkd using **.network** files in the **/etc/systemd/network** directory. Prefix the filename with a number denoting priority. The **10-my-dhcp.network** example sets up a DCHP network connection. The Match section matches on a network device and the Network section configures that connection. You can use Name, Path, or MacAddress Keys to reference the device. Use **ifconfig** or **ip l** to find the name of the device. Use this name for the Name entry. You can also specify the Host, or check for Virtualization or the system Architecture. In the Network section, the DHCP key enables DHCP support. You can further specify IPv4 (**ipv4**) or IPv6 (**ipv6**) support.

The following example configures a wired (ethernet) device for DHCP. The name of the device as used in the Name entry was found using **ifconfig**. In the Network section, the DHCP key is set to yes, turning on DCHP support.

10-my-dhcp.network

```
[Match]
Name=enp7s0

[Network]
DHCP=yes
```

You can use the glob * matching character to reference all devices of a certain kind. The **en*** string will match on all Ethernet (wired) devices. Should your device name change, your **.network** file will still work on it.

10-my-dhcp.network

```
[Match]
Name=en*

[Network]
DHCP=yes
```

A wireless connection with DHCP would use the same entries, but specifying the wireless device for the name.

10-my-wirelss.network

```
[Match]
Name=wlp6s0

[Network]
DHCP=yes
```

To connect all your wireless devices, use **wl** and the * glob matching character, **wl***. A wireless connection with DHCP would use the same entries, but specifying the wireless device for the name.

10-my-wirelss.network

```
[Match]
Name=wl*

[Network]
DHCP=yes
```

With the Address, Gateway, and DNS keys you can set specific addresses for the computer address, the gateway on your network, and the location of the DNS server. This will set up a static connection, instead of a DHCP one.

10-my-static.network

```
[Match]
Name=enp7s0
[Network]
Address=192.168.0.15/24
Gateway=192.168.0.1
DNS=192.168.0.1
```

Additional sections let you add more configuration options. In the Address section, you can add a Broadcast address. The Routes section lets you set source and destination routes. The DHCP section lets you send a hostname and set the MTU transmission limit. If your system has a DHCP server, the DHCPSERVER section lets you configure address pools, leases, and DNS support. The Bridge section configures a bridge network.

To use networkd, you first have to make sure you have disabled Network Manager. These changes are made as the root user. Use **sudo** or login as the root user (**su**).

```
sudo systemctl disable NetworkManager
```

Then enable systemd-networkd.

```
sudo systemctl enable systemd-networkd
```

Also, enable and start **systemd-resolved** to use the DCHP supplied DNS servers.

```
sudo systemctl enable systemd-resolved
```

The **/etc/resolv.conf** file is a link to **/run/resolvconf/resolv.conf**, which lists the DNS servers (nameserver) provided by the DCHP server.

You can check the status of the networkd and NetworkManager using **systemctl** to see which is on.

```
sudo systemctl status systemd-networkd
sudo systemctl status NetworkManager
```

You can also use the **start**, **stop**, and **restart** commands on **systemd-networkd** to start up, stop, and restart networking.

```
sudo systemctl start systemd-networkd
sudo systemctl stop systemd-networkd
sudo systemctl restart systemd-networkd
```

If you are running the desktop and choose to use systemd-networkd, you will notice that nm-applet in the panel is no longer running.

Firewalls

You can choose from several different popular firewall management tools. Linux Mint provides a firewall management tool called the Uncomplicated Firewall (ufw), which is based on IPtables. You can also choose to use other popular management tools like Firewalld and Fwbuilder. FirewallD does not use IPtables but uses a firewall daemon instead. Both ufw and FirewallD are covered in this chapter. Search Software Manager or the Synaptic Package Manager for "firewall" to see a complete listing.

Port number	Service
135,137,138,and 445	Samba ports and Microsoft discovery service (445): 135 and 445 use the TCP Protocol, and 137 and 138 use the UDP protocol.
139	Netbios-ssn
22	Secure SHell, ssh
2049	NFS, Linux and Unix shares
631	IPP, Internet Printing Protocol, access to remote Linux/Unix printers
21	FTP
25	SMTP, forward mail
110	POP3, receive mail
143	IMAP, receive mail

Table 11-4: Service ports

Important Firewall Ports

Commonly used services like Linux and Windows file sharing, FTP servers, BitTorrent, and Secure SHell remote access, use certain network connection ports on your system (see Table 11-4). A default firewall configuration will block these ports. You have to configure your firewall to allow access to the ports these services use before the services will work.

For example, to access a Windows share, you not only have to have the Samba service running, but also have to configure your firewall to allow access on ports 135, 137, 138 (the ports Samba services use to connect to Windows systems), and port 445 used for Microsoft network discovery. In particular, to allow direct access to the detected shares on your system (Avahi), you have to allow access on port 139. Most can be selected easily as preconfigured items in firewall configuration tools, like Gufw and FirewallD. Some, though, may not be listed.

Setting up a firewall with ufw

The Uncomplicated Firewall, ufw, is the supported firewall application for Linux Mint. It provides a simple firewall that can be managed with the Gufw desktop interface or with **ufw** commands. Like all firewall applications, ufw uses IPtables to define rules and run the firewall. The ufw application is just a management interface for IPtables. The IPtables rule files are held in the **/etc/ufw** directory. Default IPtables rules are kept in **before** and **after** files, with added rules in user files. Firewall configuration for certain packages will be placed in the **/usr/share/ufw.d** directory. The ufw firewall is started up using the **ufw.service** file the **/lib/systemd/system** directory. You can find out more about ufw at the Ubuntu Firewall site at **https://wiki.ubuntu.com/UncomplicatedFirewall** and at the firewall section in the Ubuntu Server Guide at **https://help.ubuntu.com/lts/serverguide/**. The Server Guide also shows information on how to implement IP Masquerading on ufw.

Gufw

Gufw provides an easy to use GNOME interface for managing your ufw firewall. A simple interface lets you add rules, both custom and standard. Gufw is installed by default, and can be accessed from the Preferences menu as Firewall Configuration.

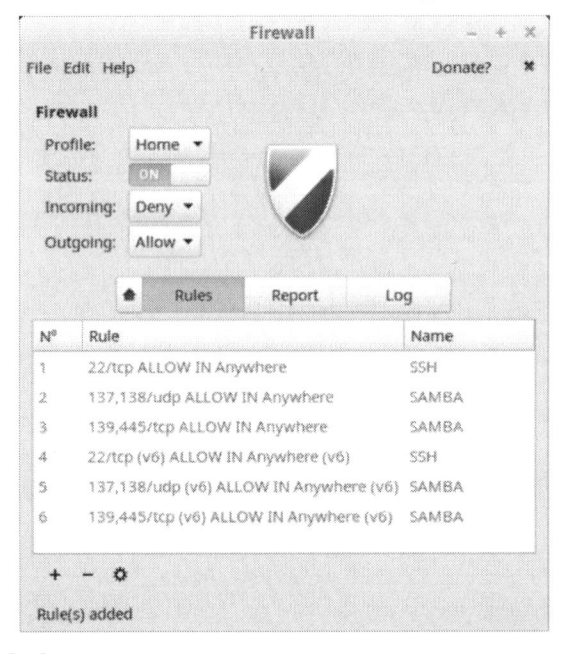

Figure 11-30: Gufw

Gufw will initially open with the firewall disabled, with no ports configured. The Status button is set to off, and the shield image will be gray. To enable the firewall, just click the left side of the Status button, setting the status to on. The shield image will be colored and the firewall rules will be listed. Figure 11-30 shows the firewall enabled and several rules listed Samba ports. Rules for both IPv4 and IPv6 (**v6**) network protocols are listed.

The Gufw dialog has a Firewall section and three tabs: Rules, Report, and Log. The Firewall section has a Status button for turning the firewall on or off. There is a Profile menu for Home, Office, and Public configurations. The Incoming and Outgoing drop down menus for setting the default firewall rules. Options are Deny, Reject, or Allow, and are applied to incoming and outgoing traffic respectively. By default, incoming traffic is denied (Deny), and outgoing traffic is allowed (Allow). Rules you specified in the Rules tab will make exceptions, allowing only certain traffic in or out. Should you select the Allow option, the firewall accepts all incoming traffic. In this case you should set up rules to deny access to some traffic, otherwise, the firewall becomes ineffective, allowing access to all traffic. The Report tab lists active services and ports such as the Samba server (smbd) on port 139. The Log tab list firewall notices. You can copy notices, as well as delete a log. The Home tab provides basic help on how to use Gufw.

To add a rule, click the Rules tab and then click the plus button (+) on the lower left corner of the Rules tab to open the "Add rule" dialog, which has three tabs for managing rules: Preconfigured, Simple, and Advanced (see Figure 11-31). The Preconfigured tab provides five menus: the first for the policy (Allow, Deny, Reject, and Limit), the second for the traffic direction (In or Out), the third for the category of the application and the fourth for a subcategory, and the fifth for the particular application or service for the rule. The main categories are Audio video, Games, Network, Office, and System. The Network category lists most network services like SSH, Samba, and FTP. Should there be a security issue with the rule, a warning is displayed.

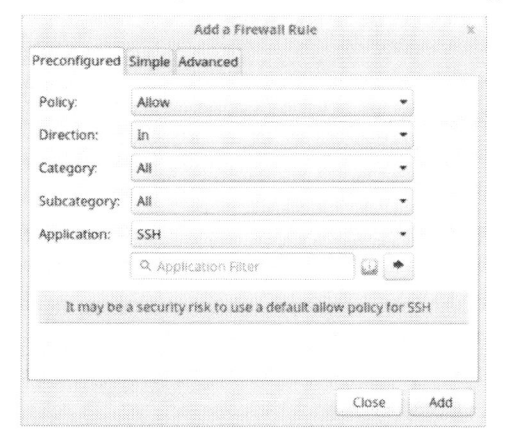

Figure 11-31: Gufw Preconfigured rules

Should you need to modify the default rule for an application, you can click on the arrow button to open the Advanced tab for that rule.

Click the Add button to add the rule. Once added a port entry for the rule appears in the Rules section. In Figure 11-21, the Samba service has been selected and then added, showing up in the Rules section as "137,138/udp ALLOW IN Anywhere." If you need to add several rules at once, you can keep the Add dialog open to select, configure, and add them.

Services can also be blocked. To prevent access by the FTP service, you would first select Deny, then Network, and then the FTP entry.

Besides Allow and Deny, you can also choose a Limit option. The Limit option will enable connection rate limiting, restricting connections to no more than 6 every 30 seconds for a given port. This is meant to protect against brute force attacks.

Should there be no preconfigured entry, you can use the Simple tab to allow access to a port (see Figure 11-32). The first menu is for the rule (Allow, Deny, Reject, and Limit), and the second for the protocol (TCP, UDP, or both). In the Port text box, you enter the port number.

Figure 11-32: Gufw Simple rules

On the Advanced tab, you can enter more complex rules. You can set up allow or deny rules for tcp or udp protocols, and specify the incoming and outgoing host (ip) and port (see Figure 11-33).

Figure 11-33: Gufw Advanced rules

If you decide to remove a rule, select it in the Rules section and then click the minus button in the lower left corner (-). To remove several rules, click and press Shift-click or use Ctrl-click to select a collection of rules, and then click the minus button.

You can edit any rule by selecting it and clicking the edit button (gear image) to open an "Update a Firewall Rule" dialog (see Figure 11-34). For a default or simple rule, you can only change a few options, but you can turn on logging.

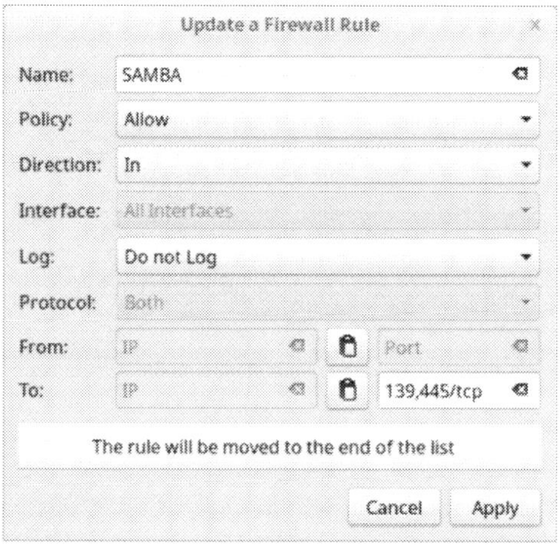

Figure 11-34: Gufw edit a rule

You can also create rules for detected active ports. Click the Report tab and then select a port and click on the plus button at the bottom of the tab. An "Add a Firewall Rule" dialog opens to the Advanced tab with the name of the service active on that port and the port number (see figure 11-35). You can change any of the options. The port number is already entered.

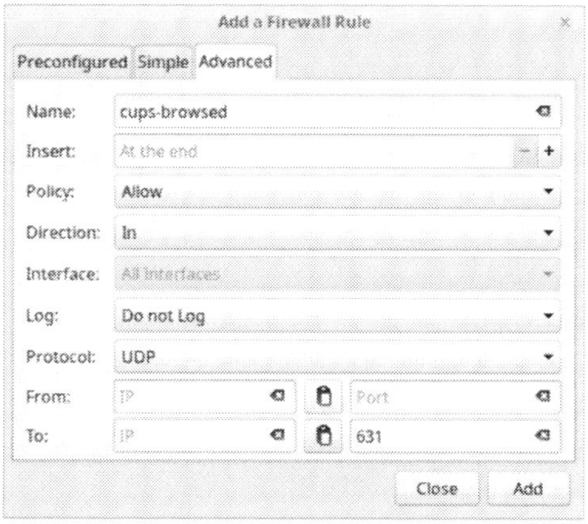

Figure 11-35: Gufw create a rule for an active port

ufw commands

You can also manage your ufw firewall using **ufw** commands entered on a command line in a Terminal window. An **ufw** command requires administrative access and must be run with the **sudo** command. To check the current firewall status, listing those services allowed or blocked, use the **status** command.

```
sudo ufw status
```

If the firewall is not enabled, you first will have to enable it with the **enable** command.

```
sudo ufw enable
```

You can restart the firewall, reloading your rules, using the **service** command with the **restart** option.

```
sudo service ufw restart
```

You can add rules using allow and deny rules and their options as listed in Table 11-5. To allow a service, specify the allow rule and the service name. This is the name for the service listed in the **/etc/services** file. For connection rate limiting, use the **limit** option in place of **allow**. The following allows the ftp service.

```
sudo ufw allow ftp
```

Commands	Description
enable | disable	Turn the firewall on or off
status	Display status along with services allowed or denied.
logging on | off	Turn logging on or off
default allow | deny	Set the default policy, allow is open, whereas deny is restrictive
allow *service*	Allow access by a service. Services are defined in **/etc/services**, which specify the ports for that service.
allow *port /protocol*	Allow access on a particular port using specified protocol.
deny *service*	Deny access by a service
delete *rule*	Delete an installed rule, use allow, deny, or limit and include rule specifics.
proto *protocol*	Specify protocol in allow, deny, or limit rule
from *address*	Specify source address in allow, deny, or limit rule
to *address*	Specify destination address in allow, deny, or limit rule
port *port*	Specify port in allow, deny, or limit rule for from and to address

Table 11-5: UFW firewall operations

If the service you want is not listed in **/etc/services**, and you know the port and protocol it uses, you can specify the port and protocol directly. For example, the Samba service uses port 445 and protocol tcp (among others, see Table 11-4).

```
sudo ufw allow 445/tcp
```

The status operation shows what services the firewall rules allow currently.

```
sudo ufw status
To                      Action          From
21:tcp                  ALLOW           Anywhere
21:udp                  ALLOW           Anywhere
445:tcp                 ALLOW           Anywhere
```

To remove a rule, prefix it with the **delete** command.

```
sudo ufw delete allow 445/tcp
```

More detailed rules can be specified using address, port, and protocol commands. These are very similar to the actual IPtables commands. Packets to and from particular networks, hosts, and ports can be controlled. The following denies ssh access (port 22) from host 192.168.03.

```
sudo ufw deny proto tcp from 192.168.03 to any port 22
```

ufw rule files

The rules you add are placed in the **/lib/ufw/user.rules** file as IPtables rules. The ufw program is just a front end for **iptables-restore**, which will read this file and set up the firewall using **iptables** commands. **ufw** will also have **iptables-restore** read the **before.rules** and **after.rules** files in the **/etc/ufw** directory. These files are considered administrative files that include needed supporting rules for your IPtables firewall. Administrators can add their own IPtables rules to these files for system specific features like IP Masquerading. The **before.rules** file will specify a table with the * symbol, as in ***filter** for the netfilter table. For the NAT table, you would use ***nat**. At the end of each table segment, a COMMIT command is needed to instruct ufw to apply the rules. Rules use **-A** for allow and **-D** for deny, assuming the **iptables** command.

Default settings for ufw are placed in **/etc/default/ufw**. Here you will find the default INPUT, OUTPUT, and FORWARD policies specified by setting associated variables, like DEFAULT_INPUT_POLICY for INPUT and DEFAULT_OUTPUT_POLICY for OUTPUT. The DEFAULT_INPUT_POLICY variable is set to DROP, making DROP the default policy for the INPUT rule. The DEFAULT_OUTPUT_POLICY variable is set to ACCEPT, and the DEFAULT_FORWARD_POLICY variable is set to DROP. To allow IP Masquerading, DEFAULT_FORWARD_POLICY would have to be set to ACCEPT. These entries set default policies only. Any user rules you have set up would take precedence.

FirewallD and firewall-config

Though not supported by Linux Mint directly, you can use the new Firewalld dynamic firewall daemon to set up a firewall. To configure Firewalld you use the **firewalld-config** graphical interface. You can also use **firewalld-cmd** command from the command line. To set up your firewall, run firewall-config, accessible from the Firewall entry on the Preferences menu (see Figure 11-36). Install both the **firewalld** and **firewall-applet** packages. The **firewall-applet** package includes **firewalld-config** and displays a firewall applet on the panel. A right-click on the applet displays a menu with options to edit and configure the firewall. You can start FirewallD from the menu as Administration menu as Firewall.

Figure 11-36: firewall-config: Runtime Configuration

With **firewall-config,** you can configure either a Runtime or Permanent configuration. Select one from the Configuration menu. The Runtime configuration shows your current runtime set up, whereas a Permanent configuration does not take effect until you reload or restart. If you wish to edit your zones and services, you need to choose the Permanent Configuration (see Figure 11-37). This view displays a zone toolbar for editing zone at the bottom of the zone scroll box, and an Edit Services button on the Services tab for editing service protocols, ports, and destination addresses.

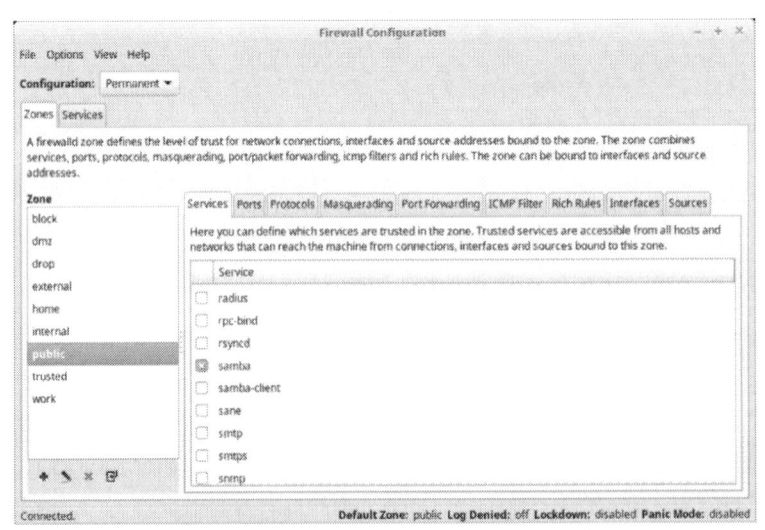

Figure 11-37: firewall-config: Permanent Configuration

Additional tabs can be displayed from the View menu for configuring ICMP types, and for adding firewall rules directly (Direct Configuration).

From the Options menu, you can reload your saved firewall.

A firewall configuration is set up for a given zone, such as a home, work, internal, external, or public zone. Each zone can have its own configuration. Zones are listed in the Zone scroll box on the left side of the firewall-config window (see Figure 11-37). Select the one you want to configure. The firewall-config window opens to the default, Public. You can choose the default zone from the System Default Zone dialog (see Figure 11-38), which you open from the Options menu as "Change Default Zone."

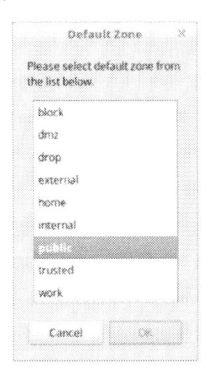

Figure 11-38: Default Zone

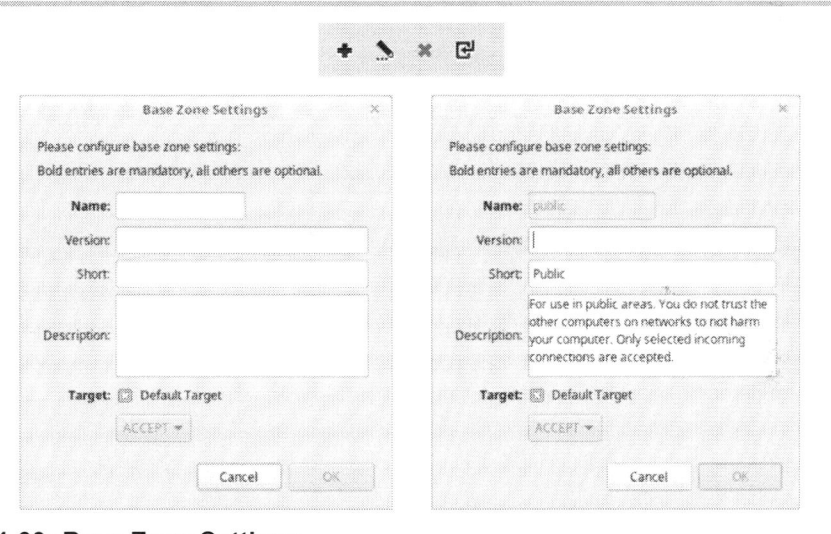

Figure 11-39: Base Zone Settings

If you choose Permanent Configuration from the Current View Menu, a toolbar for zones is displayed below the Zone scroll box, as shown here. The plus button lets you add a zone, minus removes a zone. The pencil button lets you edit a zone. The add and edit buttons open the Base Zone Settings dialog, where you enter or edit the zone name, version, description, and the target (see Figure 11-39). The default target is ACCEPT. Other options are REJECT and DROP. The Load Zone Defaults button (yellow arrow) loads default settings, removing any you have made.

Each zone, in turn, can have one or more network connections. From the Options menu choose "Change Zones of Connections" to open the Network Connections dialog where you can add a network connection.

For a given zone you can configure services, ports, masquerading, port forwarding, and ICMP filter (see Figure 11-40). A Linux system is often used to run servers for a network. If you are creating a strong firewall but still want to run a service such as a Web server, an FTP server, Samba desktop browsing, or SSH encrypted connections, you must specify them in the Services tab. Samba desktop browsing lets you access your Samba shares, like remote Windows file systems, from your GNOME or KDE desktops.

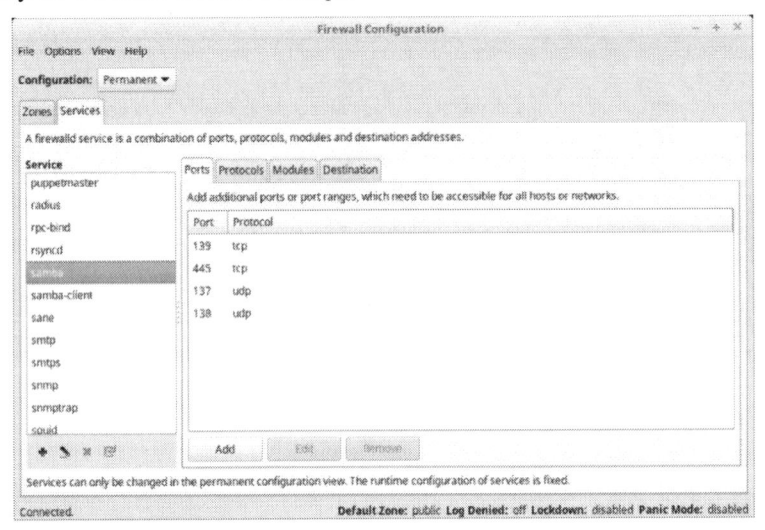

Figure 11-40: Service Settings

For a selected service, you can specify service settings such as ports and protocols it uses, any modules, and specific network addresses. Default settings are already set up for you such as port 139 for Samba, using the TCP protocol. To modify the settings for service, click the Services tab on the Firewall Configuration window to list your services. Choose the service you want to edit from the Service scroll box at the left. For a given service you can then use the Ports and Protocols, Modules, and Destination tabs to specify ports, protocols, modules, and addresses. On the Ports and Protocols tab, click the Add button to open the Port and/or Protocol dialog where you can add a port or port range, and choose a protocol from the Protocol menu (see Figure 11-41). On the Destination tab, you can enter an IPv4 or IPv6 destination address for the service.

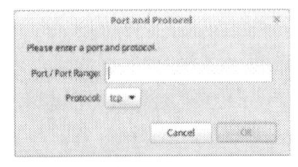

Figure 11-41: Service Protocols and Ports

For Zones, the Ports tab lets you specify ports that you may want opened for certain services, like BitTorrent. Click the Add button to open a dialog where you can select the port number along with the protocol to control (tcp or udp), or enter a specific port number or range.

If your system is being used as a gateway to the Internet for your local network, you can implement masquerading to hide your local hosts from outside access from the Internet. This, though, also requires IP forwarding which is automatically enabled when you choose masquerading. Local hosts will still be able to access the Internet, but they will masquerade as your gateway system. You would select for masquerading the interface that is connected to the Internet. Masquerading is available only for IPv4 networks, not IPv6 networks.

The Port Forwarding tab lets you set up port forwarding, channeling transmissions from one port to another, or to a different port on another system. Click the Add button to add a port, specifying its protocol and destination (see Figure 11-42).

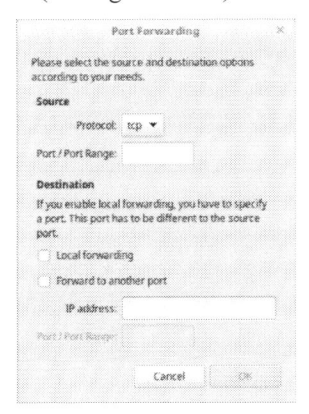

Figure 11-42: Port Forwarding

The ICMP Filters tab allows you to block ICMP messages. By default, all ICMP messages are allowed. Blocking ICMP messages makes for a more secure system. Certain types of ICMP messages are often blocked as they can be used to infiltrate or overload a system, such as the ping and pong ICMP messages (see Figure 11-43).

If you have specific firewall rules to add, use the Direct Configuration tab (displayed from the View | Direct Configuration menu).

Figure 11-43: ICMP Filters

GNOME Nettool

The GNOME Nettool utility (**gnome-nettool**) provides a GNOME interface for network information tools like the ping and traceroute operations as well as Finger, Whois, and Lookup for querying users and hosts on the network (see Figure 11-44). Nettool is accessible from the Administration menu as Network Tools. The first tab, Devices, describes your connected network devices, including configuration and transmission information about each device, such as the hardware address and bytes transmitted. Both IPv4 and IPv6 host IP addresses are listed.

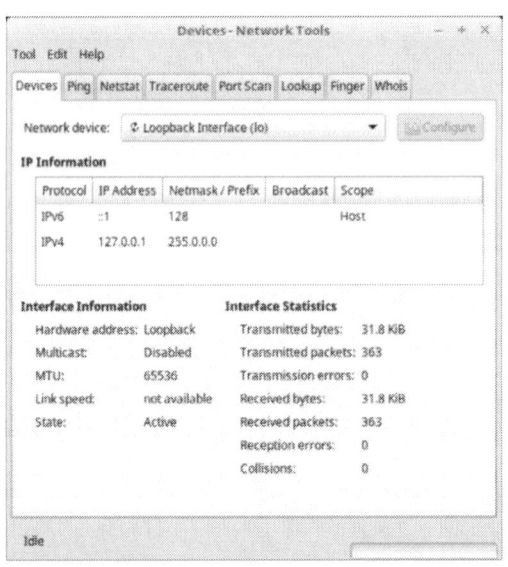

Figure 11-44: Gnome network tool

You can use the ping, finger, lookup, whois, and traceroute operations to find out status information about systems and users on your network. The ping operation is used to check if a remote system is up and running. You use finger to find out information about other users on your network, seeing if they are logged in or if they have received mail. The traceroute tool can be used to track the sequence of computer networks and systems your message passed through on its way to you. Whois will provide domain name information about a particular domain, and Lookup will provide both domain name and IP addresses. Netstat shows your network routing (addresses used) and active service (open ports and the protocols they use). Port Scan lists the ports and services they use on a given connection (address); use 12.0.0.1 for your local computer.

Predictable and unpredictable network device names

Network devices now use a predictable naming method that differs from the older naming method. Names are generated based on the specific device referencing the network device type, its hardware connection and slot, and even its function. The traditional network device names used the **eth** prefix with the number of the device for an Ethernet network device. The name **eth0** referred to the first Ethernet connection on your computer. This naming method was considered unpredictable as it did not accurately reference the actual Ethernet device. The old system relied on probing the network driver at boot, and if you're your system had several Ethernet connections, the names could end up being switched, depending you how the startup proceeded. With systemd udev version 197, the naming changed to a predictable method that specifies a particular device. The predictable method references the actual hardware connection on your system.

The name used to reference predictable device names connection has a prefix for the type of device followed by several qualifiers such as the type of hardware, the slot used, and the function number. Instead of the older unpredictable name like **eth0**, the first Ethernet device is referenced by a name like **enp7s0**. The interface name **enp7s0** references an Ethernet (en) connection, at pci slot 7 (p7) with the hotplug slot index number 0 (s0). **wlp6s0** is a wireless (wl) connection, at pci slot 6 (p6) with the hotplug slot index number 0 (s0). **virvb0** is a virtual (vir) bridge (vb) network interface. Table 11-6 lists predictable naming prefixes.

Unlike the older unpredictable name, the predictable name will most likely be different for each computer. Predictable network names, along with alternatives, are discussed at:

https://www.freedesktop.org/wiki/Software/systemd/PredictableNetworkInterfaceNames/

The naming is carried out by the kernel and is describe in the comment section of the kernel source's **systemd/src/udev/udev-bultin-net_id.c** file.

Network device path names

The directory **/sys/devices** lists all your devices in subdirectories, including your network devices. The path to the devices progresses through subdirectories named for the busses connecting the device. To quickly find the full path name, you can us the **/sys/class** directory instead. For network devices use **/sys/class/net**. Then use the **ls -l** command to list the network devices with their links to the full pathname in the /sys/devices directory (the **../..** path references a cd change up two directories (**class/net**) to the **/sys** directory).

Name	Description
sen	Ethernet
sl	serial line IP (slip)
wl	wlan, wireless local area network
ww	wwan, wireless wide area network (mobile broadband)
p	pci geographical location (pci-e slot)
s	hotplug slot index number
o	onboard cards
f	function (used for cards with more than one port)
u	USB port
i	USB port interface

Table 11-6: Network Interface Device Naming

```
$ cd /sys/class/net
$ ls
enp7s0  lo  wlp6s0
$ ls -l
total 0
lrwxrwxrwx 1 root root 0 Feb 19 12:27 enp7s0 ->
../../devices/pci0000:00/0000:00:1c.3/0000:07:00.0/net/enp7s0
lrwxrwxrwx 1 root root 0 Feb 19 12:27 lo -> ../../devices/virtual/net/lo
lrwxrwxrwx 1 root root 0 Feb 19 12:28 wlp6s0 ->
../../devices/pci0000:00/0000:00:1c.2/0000:06:00.0/net/wlp6s0
```

So the full path name in the /sys/devices directory for enp7s0 is:

/sys/devices/pci0000:00/0000:00:1c.3/0000:07:00.0/net/enp7s0

You can find the pci bus slot used with the lspci command. This command lists all your pci connected devices. In this example, the pci bus slot used 7, which is why the pci part of the name enp7s0 is p7. The s part refers to a hotplug slot, in this example s0.

```
$ lspci
06:00.0 Network controller: Qualcomm Atheros QCA9565 / AR9565 Wireless Network
Adapter (rev 01)
07:00.0 Ethernet controller: Realtek Semiconductor Co., Ltd. RTL8101/2/6E PCI
Express Fast/Gigabit Ethernet controller (rev 07)
```

Devices have certain properties defined by udev, which manages all devices. Some operations, such as systemd link files, make use these properties. The ID_PATH, ID_NET_NAME_MAC, and INTERFACE properties can be used to identify a device to udev. To display these properties, you use the **udevadm** command to query the udev database. With the **info** and **-e** options, properties of all active devices are displayed. You can pipe (|) this output to a **grep** command to display only those properties for a given device. In the following example, the properties for the **enp7s0** device are listed. Preceding the properties for a given device is a line, beginning (^) with a "P" and ending with the device name. The **.*** matching characters match all other intervening characters on that line, **^P.*enp7s0**. The **-A** option displays the specified number of additional lines after that match, **-A 22**.

```
$ udevadm info -e | grep -A 22 ^P.*enp7s0
P: /devices/pci0000:00/0000:00:1c.3/0000:07:00.0/net/enp7s0
E: DEVPATH=/devices/pci0000:00/0000:00:1c.3/0000:07:00.0/net/enp7s0
E: ID_BUS=pci
E: ID_MM_CANDIDATE=1
E: ID_MODEL_FROM_DATABASE=RTL8101/2/6E PCI Express Fast/Gigabit Ethernet
controller
E: ID_MODEL_ID=0x8136
E: ID_NET_DRIVER=r8169
E: ID_NET_LINK_FILE=/lib/systemd/network/99-default.link
E: ID_NET_NAME_MAC=enx74e6e20ec729
E: ID_NET_NAME_PATH=enp7s0
E: ID_OUI_FROM_DATABASE=Dell Inc.
E: ID_PATH=pci-0000:07:00.0
E: ID_PATH_TAG=pci-0000_07_00_0
E: ID_PCI_CLASS_FROM_DATABASE=Network controller
E: ID_PCI_SUBCLASS_FROM_DATABASE=Ethernet controller
E: ID_VENDOR_FROM_DATABASE=Realtek Semiconductor Co., Ltd.
E: ID_VENDOR_ID=0x10ec
E: IFINDEX=2
E: INTERFACE=enp7s0
E: SUBSYSTEM=net
E: SYSTEMD_ALIAS=/sys/subsystem/net/devices/enp7s0
E: TAGS=:systemd:
E: USEC_INITIALIZED=1080179
```

For certain tasks, such as renaming, you many need to know the MAC address. You can find this with the ip link command, which you can abbreviate to ip l. The MAC address is before the brd string. In this example, the MAC address for enp7s0 is 74:e6:e2:0e:c7:29. The ip link command also provides the MTU (Maximum Transmission Unit) and the current state of the connection.

```
$ ip link
1: lo: <LOOPBACK,UP,LOWER_UP> mtu 65536 qdisc noqueue state UNKNOWN mode DEFAULT
group default qlen 1 link/loopback 00:00:00:00:00:00 brd 00:00:00:00:00:00
2: enp7s0: <BROADCAST,MULTICAST,UP,LOWER_UP> mtu 1500 qdisc fq_codel state UP
mode DEFAULT group default qlen 1000 link/ether 74:e6:e2:0e:c7:29 brd
ff:ff:ff:ff:ff:ff
3: wlp6s0: <BROADCAST,MULTICAST> mtu 1500 qdisc noop state DOWN mode DEFAULT
group default qlen 1000 link/ether 4c:bb:58:22:40:1d brd ff:ff:ff:ff:ff:ff
```

Renaming network device names with udev rules

If you should change your hardware, like your motherboard with its Ethernet connection, or, if you use an Ethernet card and simply change the slot it is connected to, then the name will change. For firewall rules referencing a particular Ethernet connection, this could be a problem. You can, if you wish, change the name to one of your own choosing, even using the older unpredictable names. This way you would only have to update the name change, rather than all your rules and any other code that references the network device by name.

You can change device name by adding a user udev rule for network device names. Changes made with udev rules work for both NetworkManager and systemd-networkd. In the **/etc/udev/rules.d** directory, create a file with the .rules extension and prefixed by a number less than 80, such as **70-my-net-names.rules**. The .rules files in **/etc/udev/rules.d** take precedence over those in the udev system directory, **/lib/udev/rules.d**.

In the udev rule, identify the subsystem as net (SUBSYSTEM=="net"), the action to take as add (ACTION=="add)), then the MAC address (ATTR[address}, the address attribute). Use ip link to obtain the mac address. The MAC address is also listed as the ID_NET_NAME_MAC entry in the **udevadm info** output (be sure to remove the prefix and add intervening colons). Use the NAME field to specify the new name for the device. Use the single = operator to make the name assignment.

/etc/udev/rules.d/70-my-net-names.rules

```
SUBSYSTEM=="net", ACTION=="add", ATTR{address}=="74:e6:e2:0e:c7:29", NAME="eth0"
```

To further specify the device you can add the kernel name (KERNEL) of the device. The kernel name is the INTERFACE entry.

```
SUBSYSTEM=="net", ACTION=="add", ATTR{address}=="74:e6:e2:0e:c7:29", KERNEL=="enp7s0", NAME="eth0"
```

Renaming network device names for systemd-networkd with systemd.link

The systemd-networkd manager provides an alternate way to change network device names (keep in mind that an udev rule will also work for systemd-networkd). To change the name you would set up a systemd link file in the /etc/systemd/network directory. The systemd.link man page shows how to do this. A systemd link file consists of Match and Link sections. In the Match section you specify the network device, and in the Link section to specify the name you want to give it. The network device can be referenced by its predictable name (Path) or MAC address (MACAddress).

The default systemd link file is /lib/systemd/network/99-default.link. The file had only a Link section which lists policies to use in determining the name. The NamePolicy key lists the policies to be checked, starting with the kernel, then the udev database, udev firmware onboard information, udev hot-plug slot information, and the device path. In most cases, the slot policy is used. The MACAddressPolicy is set to persistent, for devices that have or need fixed MAC addresses.

99-default.link

```
[Link]
NamePolicy=kernel database onboard slot path
MACAddressPolicy=persistent
```

To rename a device, you would set up a systemd link file in the /etc/systemd/network directory. The /etc/systemd directory takes precedence over the /lib/systemd directory. A link file consists of a priority number, any name, and the .link extension. Lower numbers have a higher priority. In this example, the network device enp7s0 has its named changed to eth0. The Match section uses the Path key to match on the device path, using the ID_PATH property for the device provided by udev.

You can query the udev database for information on your network device using the udevadm info command and match on the device. An added **grep** operation for ID_PATH= will display only the ID_PATH property.

```
$ udevadm info -e | grep -A 22 ^P.*enp7s0 | grep ID_PATH=
E: ID_PATH=pci-0000:07:00.0
```

For the Path key, use the udev ID_PATH value and a * glob matching character for the rest of the path. The Link section uses the Name key to specify the new name. The MacAddressPolicy should be set to persistent, indicating a fixed connection. Start the name of the link file with a number less than 99, so as to take precedence over the 99-default.link file.

10-my-netname.link

```
[Match]
Path=pci-0000:07:00.0-*

[Link]
Name=eth0
MacAddressPolicy=persistent
```

Instead of the Path key, you could use the MACAddress key to match on the hardware address of the network device. The MAC address is udev ID_NET_NAME_MAC property without the prefix and with colons separation. The MAC address in this example is 74:e6:e2:0e:c7:29. You can also use **ip link** to find the MAC address (the numbers before **brd**).

10-my-netname.link

```
[Match]
MACAddress=74:e6:e2:0e:c7:29

[Link]
Name=eth0
MacAddressPolicy=persistent
```

Alternatively, you could use the OriginalName key in the Match section instead of the Path. The original name is the udev INTERFACE property, which also the name of the device as displayed by **ifconfig**.

10-my-netname.link

```
[Match]
OriginalName=enp7s0*

[Link]
Name=eth0
MacAddressPolicy=persistent
```

12. Shell Configuration

Shell Configuration Files
Configuration Directories and Files
Aliases
Controlling Shell Operations
Environment Variables and Subshells: export
Configuring Your Login Shell

Four different major shells are commonly used on Linux systems: the Bourne Again shell (BASH), the AT&T Korn shell, the TCSH shell, and the Z shell. The BASH shell is an advanced version of the Bourne shell, which includes most of the advanced features developed for the Korn shell and the C shell. TCSH is an enhanced version of the C shell, originally developed for BSD versions of UNIX. The AT&T UNIX Korn shell is open source. The Z shell is an enhanced version of the Korn shell. Although their UNIX counterparts differ greatly, the Linux shells share many of the same features. In UNIX, the Bourne shell lacks many capabilities found in the other UNIX shells. In Linux, however, the BASH shell incorporates all the advanced features of the Korn shell and C shell, as well as the TCSH shell. All four shells are available for your use, though the BASH shell is the default.

Command	Description
bash	BASH shell, **/bin/bash**
bsh	BASH shell, **/bin/bsh** (link to **/bin/bash**)
sh	BASH shell, **/bin/sh** (link to **/bin/bash**)
tcsh	TCSH shell, **/usr/tcsh**
csh	TCSH shell , **/bin/csh** (link to **/bin/tcsh**)
ksh	Korn shell, **/bin/ksh** (also added link **/usr/bin/ksh**)
zsh	Z shell, **/bin/zsh**

Table 12-1: Shell Invocation Command Names

The BASH shell is the default shell for most Linux distributions. If you are logging into a command line interface, you will be placed in the default shell automatically and given a shell prompt at which to enter your commands. The shell prompt for the BASH shell is a dollar sign ($). In the GUI interface, such as GNOME or KDE, you can open a terminal window that will display a command line interface with the prompt for the default shell (BASH). Though you log in to your default shell or display it automatically in a terminal window, you can change to another shell by entering its name. Entering tcsh invokes the TCSH shell, bash the BASH shell, ksh the Korn shell, and zsh the Z shell. You can leave a shell by pressing CTRL-D or using the exit command. You only need one type of shell to do your work. Table 12-1 shows the different commands you can use to invoke different shells. Some shells have added links you can use to invoke the same shell, like **sh** and **bsh**, which link to and invoke the **bash** command for the BASH shell.

This chapter describes common features of the BASH shell, such as aliases, as well as how to configure the shell to your own needs using shell variables and initialization files. The other shells share many of the same features and use similar variables and configuration files.

Though the basic shell features and configurations are shown here, you should consult the respective online manuals and FAQs for each shell for more detailed examples and explanations.

Shell Initialization and Configuration Files

Each type of shell has its own set of initialization and configuration files. The TCSH shell uses **.login**, **.tcshrc**, and **.logout** files in place of **.profile** and **.bash_logout**. The Z shell has several initialization files: **.zshenv**, **.zlogin**, **.zprofile**, **.zshrc**, and **.zlogout**. See Table 12-2 for a listing. Check the Man pages for each shell to see how they are usually configured. When you install a shell, default versions of these files are automatically placed in the users' home directories. Except for the TCSH shell, all shells use much the same syntax for variable definitions and assigning values (TCSH uses a slightly different syntax, described in its Man pages).

Filename	Function
BASH Shell	
.profile	Login initialization file
.bashrc	BASH shell configuration file
.bash_logout	Logout name
.bash_history	History file
/etc/profile	System login initialization file
/etc/bash.bashrc	System BASH shell configuration file
/etc/profile.d	Directory for specialized BASH shell configuration files
/etc/bash_completion	Completion options for applications
TCSH Shell	
.login	Login initialization file
.tcshrc	TCSH shell configuration file
.logout	Logout file
Z Shell	
.zshenv	Shell login file (first read)
.zprofile	Login initialization file
.zlogin	Shell login file
.zshrc	Z shell configuration file
.zlogout	Logout file
Korn Shell	
.profile	Login initialization file
.kshrc	KORN shell configuration file

Table 12-2: Shell Configuration Files

Configuration Directories and Files

Applications often install configuration files in a user's home directory that contain specific configuration information, which tailors the application to the needs of that particular user. This may take the form of a single configuration file that begins with a period or a directory that contains several configuration files. The directory name will also begin with a period. For example, Mozilla installs a directory called **.mozilla** in the user's home directory that contains configuration files. On the other hand, many mail applications uses a single file called **.mailrc** to hold alias and feature settings set up by the user, though others like Evolution also have their own, **.evolution**. Most single configuration files end in the letters **rc**. **FTP** uses a file called **.netrc**. Most newsreaders use a file called **.newsrc**. Entries in configuration files are usually set by the application, though you can usually make entries directly by editing the file. Applications have their own set of special variables to which you can define and assign values. You can list the configuration files in your home directory with the ls -a command.

Aliases

You can use the alias command to create another name for a command. The alias command operates like a macro that expands to the command it represents. The alias does not literally replace the name of the command; it simply gives another name to that command. An alias command begins with the keyword alias and the new name for the command, followed by an equal sign and the command the alias will reference.

Note: No spaces should be placed around the equal sign used in the `alias` **command.**

In the next example, list becomes another name for the ls command:

```
$ alias list=ls
$ ls
mydata today
$ list
mydata today
$
```

If you want an alias to be automatically defined, you have to enter the alias operation in a shell configuration file. On Linux Mint, aliases are defined in either the user's **.bashrc** file or in a **.bash_aliases** file. To use a **.bash_aliases** file, you have to first uncomment the commands in the .bashrc file that will read the **.bash_aliases** file. Just edit the **.bashrc** file and remove the preceding # so it appears like the following:

```
if [ -f ~/.bash_aliases ]; then
    . ~/.bash_aliases
fi
```

You can also place aliases in the **.bashrc** file directly. Some are already defined, though commented out. You can edit the **.bashrc** file and remove the # comment symbols from those lines to activate the aliases.

```
# some more ls aliases
alias ll='ls -l'
alias la='ls -A'
alias l='ls -CF'
```

Aliasing Commands and Options

You can also use an alias to substitute for a command and its option, but you need to enclose both the command and the option within single quotes. Any command you alias that contains spaces must be enclosed in single quotes as well. In the next example, the alias lss references the ls command with its -s option, and the alias **lsa** references the ls command with the -

F option. The ls command with the -s option lists files and their sizes in blocks, and ls with the -F option places a slash after directory names. Notice how single quotes enclose the command and its option.

```
$ alias lss='ls -s'
$ lss
mydata 14    today  6    reports  1
$ alias lsa='ls -F'
$ lsa
mydata today reports/
$
```

Aliases are helpful for simplifying complex operations. In the next example, **listlong** becomes another name for the ls command with the -l option (the long format that lists all file information), as well as the -h option for using a human-readable format for file sizes. Be sure to encase the command and its arguments within single quotes so that they are taken as one argument and not parsed by the shell.

```
$ alias listlong='ls -lh'
$ listlong
-rw-r--r--    1 root    root    51K  Sep  18  2008 mydata
-rw-r--r--    1 root    root    16K  Sep  27  2008 today
```

Aliasing Commands and Arguments

You may often use an alias to include a command name with an argument. If you execute a command that has an argument with a complex combination of special characters on a regular basis, you may want to alias it. For example, suppose you often list just your source code and object code files—those files ending in either a **.c** or **.o**. You would need to use as an argument for ls a combination of special characters such as *.[co]. Instead, you can alias ls with the .[co] argument, giving it a simple name. In the next example, the user creates an alias called lsc for the command ls.[co]:

```
$ alias lsc='ls *.[co]'
$ lsc
main.c main.o lib.c lib.o
```

Aliasing Commands

You can also use the name of a command as an alias. This can be helpful in cases where you should use a command only with a specific option. In the case of the rm, cp, and mv commands, the -i option should always be used to ensure an existing file is not overwritten. Instead of always being careful to use the -i option each time you use one of these commands, you can alias the command name to include the option. In the next example, the rm, cp, and mv commands have been aliased to include the -i option:

```
$ alias rm='rm -i'
$ alias mv='mv -i'
$ alias cp='cp -i'
```

The alias command by itself provides a list of all aliases that have been defined, showing the commands they represent. You can remove an alias by using the **unalias** command. In the next example, the user lists the current aliases and then removes the lsa alias:

```
$ alias
lsa=ls -F
list=ls
rm=rm -i
$ unalias lsa
```

Controlling Shell Operations

The BASH shell has several features that enable you to control the way different shell operations work. For example, setting the noclobber feature prevents redirection from overwriting files. You can turn these features on and off like a toggle, using the set command. The set command takes two arguments: an option specifying on or off and the name of the feature. To set a feature on, you use the -o option, and to set it off, you use the +o option. Here is the basic form:

```
$ set -o feature          turn the feature on
$ set +o feature          turn the feature off
```

Features	Description
`$ set -+o feature`	BASH shell features are turned on and off with the `set` command; `-o` sets a feature on and `+o` turns it off: `$ set -o noclobber` *set noclobber on* `$ set +o noclobber` *set noclobber off*
`ignoreeof`	Disables CTRL-D logout
`noclobber`	Does not overwrite files through redirection
`noglob`	Disables special characters used for filename expansion: *, ?, ~, and []

Table 12-3: BASH Shell Special Features

Three of the most common features are ignoreeof, noclobber, and noglob. Table 12-3 lists these different features, as well as the set command. Setting ignoreeof enables a feature that prevents you from logging out of the user shell with CTRL-D. CTRL-D is not only used to log out of the user shell, but also to end user input entered directly into the standard input. CTRL-D is used often for the Mail program or for utilities such as cat. You can easily enter an extra CTRL-D in such circumstances and accidentally log yourself out. The ignoreeof feature prevents such accidental logouts. In the next example, the ignoreeof feature is turned on using the set command with the -o option. The user can then log out only by entering the logout command.

```
$ set -o ignoreeof
$ CTRL-D
Use exit to logout
$
```

Environment Variables and Subshells: export

When you log in to your account, Linux generates your user shell. Within this shell, you can issue commands and declare variables. You can also create and execute shell scripts. When you execute a shell script, however, the system generates a subshell. You then have two shells: the one you logged in to and the one generated for the script. Within the script shell, you can execute another shell script, which then has its own shell. When a script has finished execution, its shell terminates and you return to the shell from which it was executed. In this sense, you can have many shells, each nested within the other. Variables you define within a shell are local to it. If you define a variable in a shell script, then, when the script is run, the variable is defined with that script's shell and is local to it. No other shell can reference that variable. In a sense, the variable is hidden within its shell.

Shell Variables	Description
BASH	Holds full pathname of BASH command
BASH_VERSION	Displays the current BASH version number
GROUPS	Groups that the user belongs to
HISTCMD	Number of the current command in the history list
HOME	Pathname for user's home directory
HOSTNAME	The hostname
HOSTTYPE	Displays the type of machine the host runs on
OLDPWD	Previous working directory
OSTYPE	Operating system in use
PATH	List of pathnames for directories searched for executable commands
PPID	Process ID for shell's parent shell
PWD	User's working directory
RANDOM	Generates random number when referenced
SHLVL	Current shell level, number of shells invoked
UID	User ID of the current user

Table 12-4: Shell Variables, Set by the Shell

You can define environment variables in all types of shells, including the BASH shell, the Z shell, and the TCSH shell. The strategy used to implement environment variables in the BASH shell, however, is different from that of the TCSH shell. In the BASH shell, environment variables are exported. That is to say, a copy of an environment variable is made in each subshell. For example, if the EDITOR variable is exported, a copy is automatically defined in each subshell for you. In the TCSH shell, on the other hand, an environment variable is defined only once and can be directly referenced by any subshell.

In the BASH shell, an environment variable can be thought of as a regular variable with added capabilities. To make an environment variable, you apply the export command to a variable you have already defined. The export command instructs the system to define a copy of that variable for each new shell generated. Each new shell will have its own copy of the environment variable. This process is called exporting variables. To think of exported environment variables as global variables is a mistake. A new shell can never reference a variable outside of itself. Instead, a copy of the variable with its value is generated for the new shell.

Configuring Your Shell with Shell Parameters

When you log in, Linux will set certain parameters for your login shell. These parameters can take the form of variables or features. See the previous section "Controlling Shell Operations" for a description of how to set features. Linux reserves a predefined set of variables for shell and system use. These are assigned system values, in effect, setting parameters. Linux sets up parameter shell variables you can use to configure your user shell. Many of these parameter shell variables are defined by the system when you log in. Some parameter shell variables are set by the shell automatically, and others are set by initialization scripts, described later. Certain shell variables are set directly by the shell, and others are simply used by it. Many of these other variables are application specific, used for such tasks as mail, history, or editing. Functionally, it may be better to think of these as system-level variables, as they are used to configure your entire system, setting values such as the location of executable commands on your system, or the number of history commands allowable. See Table 12-4 for a list of those shell variables set by the shell for shell-specific tasks; Table 12-5 lists those used by the shell for supporting other applications.

A reserved set of keywords is used for the names of these system variables. You should not use these keywords as the names of any of your own variable names. The system shell variables are all specified in uppercase letters, making them easy to identify. Shell feature variables are in lowercase letters. For example, the keyword HOME is used by the system to define the HOME variable. HOME is a special environment variable that holds the pathname of the user's home directory. On the other hand, the keyword noclobber is used to set the noclobber feature on or off.

Shell Parameter Variables

Many of the shell parameter variables automatically defined and assigned initial values by the system when you log in can be changed if you wish. However, some parameter variables exist whose values should not be changed. For example, the HOME variable holds the pathname for your home directory. Commands such as cd reference the pathname in the HOME shell variable to locate your home directory. Some of the more common of these parameter variables are described in this section.

Other parameter variables are defined by the system and given an initial value that you are free to change. To do this, you redefine them and assign a new value. For example, the PATH variable is defined by the system and given an initial value; it contains the pathnames of directories where commands are located. Whenever you execute a command, the shell searches for it in these directories. You can add a new directory to be searched by redefining the PATH variable yourself so that it will include the new directory's pathname.

Still, other parameter variables exist that the system does not define. These are usually optional features, such as the EXINIT variable that enables you to set options for the Vi editor. Each time you log in, you must define and assign a value to such variables. Some of the more common parameter variables are SHELL, PATH, PS1, PS2, and MAIL. The SHELL variable holds the pathname of the program for the type of shell you log in to. The PATH variable lists the different directories to be searched for a Linux command. The PS1 and PS2 variables hold the prompt symbols. The MAIL variable holds the pathname of your mailbox file. You can modify the values for any of these to customize your shell.

Note: You can obtain a listing of the currently defined shell variables using the `env` command. The `env` command operates like the `set` command, but it lists only parameter variables.

Using Initialization Files

You can automatically define parameter variables using special shell scripts called initialization files. An *initialization file* is a specially named shell script executed whenever you enter a certain shell. You can edit the initialization file and place in it definitions and assignments for parameter variables. When you enter the shell, the initialization file will execute these definitions and assignments, effectively initializing parameter variables with your own values. For example, the BASH shell's **.profile** file is an initialization file executed every time you log in. It contains definitions and assignments of parameter variables. However, the **.profile** file is basically only a shell script, which you can edit with any text editor such as the Vi editor; changing, if you wish, the values assigned to parameter variables.

In the BASH shell, all the parameter variables are designed to be environment variables. When you define or redefine a parameter variable, you also need to export it to make it an environment variable. This means any change you make to a parameter variable must be accompanied by an export command. You will see that at the end of the login initialization file, **.profile**, there is usually an export command for all the parameter variables defined in it.

Your Home Directory: HOME

The HOME variable contains the pathname of your home directory. Your home directory is determined by the parameter administrator when your account is created. The pathname for your home directory is automatically read into your HOME variable when you log in. In the next example, the echo command displays the contents of the HOME variable:

```
$ echo $HOME
/home/chris
```

The HOME variable is often used when you need to specify the absolute pathname of your home directory. In the next example, the absolute pathname of **reports** is specified using HOME for the home directory's path:

```
$ ls $HOME/reports
```

Command Locations: PATH

The PATH variable contains a series of directory paths separated by colons. Each time a command is executed, the paths listed in the PATH variable are searched, one by one, for that command. For example, the cp command resides on the system in the directory **/bin**. This directory path is one of the directories listed in the PATH variable. Each time you execute the cp command, this path is searched and the cp command located. The system defines and assigns PATH an initial set of pathnames. In Linux, the initial pathnames are **/bin** and **/usr/bin**.

Shell Variables	Description
BASH_VERSION	Displays the current BASH version number
CDPATH	Search path for the cd command
EXINIT	Initialization commands for Ex/Vi editor
FCEDIT	Editor used by the history fc command.
GROUPS	Groups that the user belongs to
HISTFILE	The pathname of the history file
HISTSIZE	Number of commands allowed for history
HISTFILESIZE	Size of the history file in lines
HOME	Pathname for user's home directory
IFS	Interfield delimiter symbol
IGNOREEOF	If not set, EOF character will close the shell. Can be set to the number of EOF characters to ignore before accepting one to close the shell (default is 10)
INPUTRC	Set the **inputrc** configuration file for Readline (command line). Default is current directory, **.inputrc**. Most Linux distributions set this to **/etc/inputrc**
KDEDIR	The pathname location for the KDE desktop
LOGNAME	Login name
MAIL	Name of specific mail file checked by Mail utility for received messages, if MAILPATH is not set
MAILCHECK	Interval for checking for received mail
MAILPATH	List of mail files to be checked by Mail for received messages
HOSTTYPE	Linux platforms, such as i686, x86_64, or ppc
PROMPT_COMMAND	Command to be executed before each prompt, integrating the result as part of the prompt
HISTFILE	The pathname of the history file
PS1	Primary shell prompt
PS2	Secondary shell prompt
SHELL	Pathname of program for type of shell you are using
TERM	Terminal type
TMOUT	Time that the shell remains active awaiting input
USER	Username
UID	Real user ID (numeric)

Table 12-5: System Environment Variables Used by the Shell

The shell can execute any executable file, including programs and scripts you have created. For this reason, the PATH variable can also reference your working directory; so, if you want to execute one of your own scripts or programs in your working directory, the shell can locate it. No spaces are allowed between the pathnames in the string. A colon with no pathname specified references your working directory. Usually, a single colon is placed at the end of the pathnames as an empty entry specifying your working directory. For example, the pathname **//bin:/usr/bin:** references three directories: **/bin**, **/usr/bin**, and your current working directory.

```
$ echo $PATH
/bin:/usr/sbin:
```

You can add any new directory path you want to the PATH variable. This can be useful if you have created several of your own Linux commands using shell scripts. You can place these new shell script commands in a directory you create, and then add that directory to the PATH list. Then, no matter what directory you are in, you can execute one of your shell scripts. The PATH variable will contain the directory for that script so that directory will be searched each time you issue a command.

You add a directory to the PATH variable with a variable assignment. You can execute this assignment directly in your shell. In the next example, the user **chris** adds a new directory, called **bin,** to the PATH. Although you could carefully type in the complete pathnames listed in PATH for the assignment, you can also use an evaluation of PATH—$PATH—in its place. In this example, an evaluation of HOME is also used to designate the user's home directory in the new directory's pathname. Notice the last colon, which specifies the working directory:

```
$ PATH=$PATH:$HOME/mybin:
$ export PATH
$ echo $PATH
/bin:/usr/bin::/home/chris/mybin
```

If you add a directory to PATH while you are logged in, the directory will be added only for the duration of your login session. When you log back in, the login initialization file, **.profile**, will again initialize your PATH with its original set of directories. The **.profile** file is described in detail a bit later in this chapter. To add a new directory to your PATH permanently, you need to edit your **.profile** file and find the assignment for the PATH variable. Then, you simply insert the directory, preceded by a colon, into the set of pathnames assigned to PATH.

Specifying the BASH Environment: BASH_ENV

The BASH_ENV variable holds the name of the BASH shell initialization file to be executed whenever a BASH shell is generated. For example, when a BASH shell script is executed, the BASH_ENV variable is checked, and the name of the script that it holds is executed before the shell script. The BASH_ENV variable usually holds **$HOME/.bashrc**. This is the **.bashrc** file in the user's home directory. (The **.bashrc** file is discussed later in this chapter.) You can specify a different file if you wish, using that instead of the **.bashrc** file for BASH shell scripts.

Configuring the Shell Prompt

The PS1 and PS2 variables contain the primary and secondary prompt symbols, respectively. The primary prompt symbol for the BASH shell is a dollar sign ($). You can change the prompt symbol by assigning a new set of characters to the PS1 variable. In the next example, the shell prompt is changed to the -> symbol:

```
$ PS1='->'
-> export PS1
->
```

The following table lists the codes for configuring your prompt:

Prompt Codes	Description
\!	Current history number
\$	Use $ as prompt for all users except the root user, which has the # as its prompt
\d	Current date
\#	History command number for just the current shell
\h	Hostname
\s	Shell type currently active
\t	Time of day in hours, minutes, and seconds.
\u	Username
\v	Shell version
\w	Full pathname of the current working directory
\W	Name of the current working directory
\\	Displays a backslash character
\n	Inserts a newline
\[\]	Allows entry of terminal specific display characters for features like color or bold font
\nnn	Character specified in octal format

You can change the prompt to be any set of characters, including a string, as shown in the next example:

```
$ PS1="Please enter a command: "
Please enter a command: export PS1
Please enter a command: ls
mydata /reports
Please enter a command:
```

The PS2 variable holds the secondary prompt symbol, which is used for commands that take several lines to complete. The default secondary prompt is >. The added command lines begin with the secondary prompt instead of the primary prompt. You can change the secondary prompt just as easily as the primary prompt, as shown here:

```
$ PS2="@"
```

Like the TCSH shell, the BASH shell provides you with a predefined set of codes you can use to configure your prompt. With them, you can make the time, your username, or your directory pathname a part of your prompt. You can even have your prompt display the history event number of the current command you are about to enter. Each code is preceded by a \ symbol: \w represents the current working directory, \t the time, and \u your username; \! will display the next history event number. In the next example, the user adds the current working directory to the prompt:

```
$ PS1="\w $"
/home/dylan $
```

The codes must be included within a quoted string. If no quotes exist, the code characters are not evaluated and are themselves used as the prompt. PS1=\w sets the prompt to the characters \w, not the working directory. The next example incorporates both the time and the history event number with a new prompt:

```
$ PS1="\t \! ->"
```

The default BASH prompt is \s-\v\$ to display the type of shell, the shell version, and the $ symbol as the prompt. Some distributions have changed this to a more complex command consisting of the username, the hostname, and the name of the current working directory. A sample configuration is shown here. A simple equivalent is shown here with @ sign in the hostname and a $ for the final prompt symbol. The home directory is represented with a tilde (~).

```
$ PS1="\u@\h:\w$"
richard@turtle.com:~$
```

Linux Mint also includes some complex prompt definitions in the **.bashrc** file to support color prompts and detect any remote user logins.

Specifying Your News Server

Several shell parameter variables are used to set values used by network applications, such as web browsers or newsreaders. NNTPSERVER is used to set the value of a remote news server accessible on your network. If you are using an ISP, the ISP usually provides a Usenet news server you can access with your newsreader applications. However, you first have to provide your newsreaders with the Internet address of the news server. This is the role of the NNTPSERVER variable. News servers on the Internet usually use the NNTP protocol. NNTPSERVER should hold the address of such a news server. For many ISPs, the news server address is a domain name that begins with **nntp**. The following example assigns the news server address **nntp.myservice.com** to the NNTPSERVER shell variable. Newsreader applications automatically obtain the news server address from NNTPSERVER. Usually, this assignment is placed in the shell initialization file, **.profile**, so that it is automatically set each time a user logs in.

```
NNTPSERVER=news.myservice.com
export NNTPSERVER
```

Configuring Your Login Shell: .profile

The **.profile** file is the BASH shell's login initialization file. It is a script file that is automatically executed whenever a user logs in. The file contains shell commands that define system environment variables used to manage your shell. They may be either redefinitions of system-defined variables, or definitions of user-defined variables. For example, when you log in, your user shell needs to know what directories hold Linux commands. It will reference the **PATH** variable to find the pathnames for these directories. However, first, the **PATH** variable must be assigned those pathnames. In the **.profile** file, an assignment operation does just this. Because it is in the **.profile** file, the assignment is executed automatically when the user logs in.

.profile

```
# ~/.profile: executed by the command interpreter for login shells.
# This file is not read by bash(1), if ~/.bash_profile or ~/.bash_login
# exists.
# see /usr/share/doc/bash/examples/startup-files for examples.
# the files are located in the bash-doc package.

# the default umask is set in /etc/profile
#umask 022

# if running bash
if [ -n "$BASH_VERSION" ]; then
    # include .bashrc if it exists
    if [ -f "$HOME/.bashrc" ]; then
      . "$HOME/.bashrc"
    fi
fi

# set PATH so it includes user's private bin directories
PATH="$HOME/bin:$HOME/.local/bin:$PATH"
```

Exporting Variables

Any new parameter variables you may add to the **.profile** file will also need to be exported, using the export command. This makes them accessible to any subshells you may enter. You can export several variables in one export command by listing them as arguments. The **.profile** file contains no variable definitions, though you can add ones of your own. In this case, the **.profile** file would have an export command with a list of all the variables defined in the file. If a variable is missing from this list, you may be unable to access it. The **.bashrc** file contains a definition of the **HISTCONTROL** variable, which is then exported. You can also combine the assignment and export command into one operation as shown here for NNTPSERVER:

```
export NNTPSERVER=news.myservice.com
```

Variable Assignments

A copy of the standard **.profile** file, provided for you when your account is created, is listed in the next example. Notice how PATH is assigned. PATH is a parameter variable the system has already defined. PATH holds the pathnames of directories searched for any command you enter. The assignment PATH="$PATH:$HOME/bin" has the effect of redefining PATH to include your **bin** directory within your home directory so that your **bin** directory will also be searched for any commands, including ones you create yourself, such as scripts or programs.

Should you want to have your current working directory searched also, you can use any text editor to add another PATH line in your **.profile** file PATH="$PATH:". You would insert a colon : after PATH. In fact, you can change this entry to add as many directories as you want to search. Making commands automatically executable in your current working directory could be a security risk, allowing files in any directory to be executed, instead of in certain specified directories. An example of how to modify your **.profile** file is shown in the following section.

```
PATH="$PATH:"
```

Editing Your BASH Profile Script

Your **.profile** initialization file is a text file that can be edited by a text editor, like any other text file. You can easily add new directories to your PATH by editing **.profile** and using editing commands to insert a new directory pathname in the list of directory pathnames assigned to the PATH variable. You can even add new variable definitions. If you do so, however, be sure to include the new variable's name in the export command's argument list. For example, if your **.profile** file does not have any definition of the EXINIT variable, you can edit the file and add a new line that assigns a value to EXINIT. The definition EXINIT='set nu ai' will configure the Vi editor with line numbering and indentation. You then need to add EXINIT to the export command's argument list. When the **.profile** file executes again, the EXINIT variable will be set to the command set nu ai. When the Vi editor is invoked, the command in the EXINIT variable will be executed, setting the line number and auto-indent options automatically.

.profile

```
# ~/.profile: executed by the command interpreter for login shells.
# This file is not read by bash(1), if ~/.bash_profile or ~/.bash_login
# exists.
# see /usr/share/doc/bash/examples/startup-files for examples.
# the files are located in the bash-doc package.

# the default umask is set in /etc/profile
#umask 022

# if running bash
if [ -n "$BASH_VERSION" ]; then
    # include .bashrc if it exists
    if [ -f "$HOME/.bashrc" ]; then
    . "$HOME/.bashrc"
    fi
fi

# set PATH so it includes user's private bin if it exists
if [ -d "$HOME/bin" ] ; then
    PATH="$HOME/bin:$PATH"
fi

HISTSIZE=30
NNTPSERVER=news.myserver.com
EXINIT='set nu ai'
PS1="\w \$"
export PATH HISTSIZE EXINIT PS1 NNTPSERVER
```

In the following example, the user's **.profile** has been modified to include definitions of EXINIT and redefinitions of PATH, PS1, and HISTSIZE. The PATH variable has the ending colon added to it that specifies the current working directory, enabling you to execute commands that may be located in either the home directory or the working directory. The redefinition of

HISTSIZE reduces the number of history events saved, from 1,000 defined in the system's **.profile** file, to 30. The redefinition of the PS1 parameter variable changes the prompt to just show the pathname of the current working directory. Any changes you make to parameter variables within your **.profile** file override those made earlier by the system's **.profile** file. All these parameter variables are then exported with the export command.

Manually Re-executing the .profile script

Although the **.profile** script is executed each time you log in, it is not automatically re-executed after you make changes to it. The **.profile** script is an initialization file that is executed *only* whenever you log in. If you want to take advantage of any changes you make to it without having to log out and log in again, you can re-execute the **.profile** script with the dot (.) command. The **.profile** script is a shell script and, like any shell script, can be executed with the . command.

```
$ . .profile
```

Alternatively, you can use the source command to execute the **.profile** initialization file or any initialization file such as **.login** used in the TCSH shell or **.bashrc**.

```
$ source .profile
```

System Shell Profile Script

Your Linux system also has its own profile file that it executes whenever any user logs in. This system initialization file is simply called **profile** and is found in the **/etc** directory, **/etc/profile**. This file contains parameter variable definitions the system needs to provide for each user. On Linux Mint, the **/etc/profile** script checks the /etc/profile.d directory for any shell configuration scripts to run, and then runs the **/etc/bash.bashrc** script, which performs most of the configuration tasks.

The number of configuration settings needed for different applications would make the **/etc/profile** file much too large to manage. Instead, application task-specific aliases and variables are placed in separate configuration files located in the **/etc/profile.d** directory. There are corresponding scripts for both the BASH and C shells. The BASH shell scripts are run from **/etc/profile** with the following commands. A **for** loop sequentially accesses each script and executes it with the dot (.) operator.

```
for i in /etc/profile.d/*.sh; do
  if [ -r $i ]; then
    . $i
  fi
done
```

For a basic install, you will have only the **gvfs-bash-completion.sh** script. As you install other shells and application there may be more. The **/etc/profile.d** scripts are named for the kinds of tasks and applications they configure. Files run by the BASH shell end in the extension **.sh**, and those run by the C shell have the extension **.csh**. The /etc/profile script will also check first if the **PS1** variable is defined before running any **/etc/profile.d** scripts.

A copy of the system's **profile** file follows

/etc/profile

```
# /etc/profile: system-wide .profile file for the Bourne shell (sh(1))
# and Bourne compatible shells (bash(1), ksh(1), ash(1), ...).

if [ "$PS1" ]; then

  if [ "$BASH" ] && [ "$BASH" != "/bin/sh" ]; then
    # The file bash.bashrc already sets the default PS1.
    # PS1='\h:\w\$ '
    if [ -f /etc/bash.bashrc ]; then
        . /etc/bash.bashrc
    fi
  else
    if [ "`id -u`" -eq 0 ]; then
      PS1='# '
    else
      PS1='$ '
    fi
  fi
fi

# The default umask is now handled by pam_umask.
# See pam_umask(8) and /etc/login.defs.

if [ -d /etc/profile.d ]; then
  for i in /etc/profile.d/*.sh; do
    if [ -r $i ]; then
      . $i
    fi
  done
  unset i
fi
```

The System /etc/bash.bashrc BASH Script

Linux Mint has a system **bashrc** file executed for all users, called **bash.bashrc**. Currently the **/etc/bash.bashrc** file sets the default shell prompt, updates the window size, identifies the root directory, and checks whether a user is authorized to use a command. The beginning of the **bash.bashrc** file is shown here:

```
# System-wide .bashrc file for interactive bash(1) shells.

# To enable the settings / commands in this file for login shells as well,
# this file has to be sourced in /etc/profile.

# If not running interactively, don't do anything
[ -z "$PS1" ] && return

# check the window size after each command and, if necessary,
# update the values of LINES and COLUMNS.
shopt -s checkwinsize
```

```
# set variable identifying the chroot you work in (used in the prompt below)
if [ -z "$debian_chroot" ] && [ -r /etc/debian_chroot ]; then
    debian_chroot=$(cat /etc/debian_chroot)
fi
```

Though commented out, the file also includes statements to set the title of a terminal window to the user, hostname, and directory. Several commands define terminal display features and command operations, including the shell prompt, beginning with **PS1=**.

Aliases that provide color support for the **ls**, **grep**, **fgrep**, and **egrep** commands are listed. An alert alias is also provided which notifies you of long running commands.

```
#alias ll='ls -lF'
#alias la='ls -A'
#alias l='ls -CF'
```

Though not enabled, you can enable the bash completion feature in the **/etc/bash.bashrc** file by removing the comment characters (#). This runs the **/usr/share/bash-completion/bash_completion** script, which makes use of configuration files in its **completions** subdirectory. The **bash.bashrc** file ends with the command-not-found exception handling.

```
# enable bash completion in interactive shells
#if ! shopt -oq posix; then
#  if [ -f /usr/share/bash-completion/bash_completion ]; then
#    . /usr/share/bash-completion/bash_completion
#  elif [ -f /etc/bash_completion ]; then
#    . /etc/bash_completion
#  fi
#fi
```

The BASH Shell Logout File: .bash_logout

The **.bash_logout** file is also a configuration file, but it is executed when the user logs out. It is designed to perform any operations you want to occur whenever you log out. Instead of variable definitions, the **.bash_logout** file usually contains shell commands that form a kind of shutdown procedure, actions you always want taken before you log out. One common logout command is to clear the screen and then issue a farewell message. As with **.profile**, you can add your own shell commands to **.bash_logout**. In fact, the **.bash_logout** file is not automatically set up for you when your account is first created. You need to create it yourself, using the Vi or Emacs editor. You could then add a farewell message or other operations. The default **.bash_logout** file includes instructions to invoke the **clear_console** command to clear the screen.

.bash_logout

```
# ~/.bash_logout: executed by bash(1) when login shell exits.
# when leaving the console clear the screen to increase privacy

    if [ "$SHLVL" = 1 ]; then
        [ -x /usr/bin/clear_console ] && /usr/bin/clear_console -q
    fi
```

Part 4: Shared Resources

Managing Services

Print Services: CUPS

Network File System (NFS), Network Information System (NIS)

Samba (Windows)

13. Managing Services

systemd

systemd unit files: /lib/systemd/system

special targets (runlevels)

managing services

Network Time Protocol, NTP

AppArmor security

OpenSSH

A single Linux system can provide several different kinds of services, ranging from security to administration, and including more obvious Internet services like Web and FTP sites, e-mail, and printing. Security tools, such as the Secure Shell (SSH) and Kerberos run as services, along with administrative network tools, such as Dynamic Host Control Protocol (DHCP) and the BIND Domain Name Server. The network connection interface is itself, a service that you can restart at will. Each service operates as a continually running daemon looking for requests for its particular services. In the case of a web service, the requests come from remote users. You can turn services on or off by starting or shutting down their daemons.

System startup is managed by the **systemd** service. The original System V init system for starting individual services has been phased out. The Upstart service used in previous Ubuntu and Linux Mint releases has been deprecated. For information about changing from Upstart to systemd see:

```
https://wiki.ubuntu.com/SystemdForUpstartUsers
```

systemd

Linux systems traditionally used the Unix System V init daemon to manage services by setting up runlevels at which they could be started or shutdown. Linux has since replaced the System V init daemon with the **systemd** init daemon. Whereas the System V init daemon would start certain services when the entire system started up or shut down using shell scripts run in sequence, **systemd** uses sockets for all system tasks and services. **systemd** sets up sockets for daemons and coordinates between them as they start up. This allows **systemd** to start daemons at the same time (in parallel). Should one daemon require support from another, **systemd** coordinates the data from their sockets (buffering), so that one daemon receives the information from another daemon that it needs to continue. This parallel startup compatibility allows for very fast boot times.

In effect, you can think of **systemd** as a combination of System V init scripts and the inetd daemon (xinetd), using socket activation applied to all system startup tasks and to network servers. The socket activation design was originally inspired by the inetd service that used sockets (AT_INET) to start internet daemons when requested. The socket activation design was used by in Apple's OS X system to apply to all sockets (AF_UNIX). This allowed all start up processes to start at the same time in parallel, making for very fast boot times. Such sockets are set up and managed by **systemd**. When D-BUS needs to write to journald (logging), it writes to the systemd-journald socket managed by **systemd**. It does not have to communicate directly with journald. This means that services no longer have to be started and shutdown in a particular sequence as they were under System V. They can all start and stop at the same time. Also, as **systemd** controls the socket, if a service fails, its socket remains in place. The service can be restarted using the same socket with no loss of information. **systemd** manages all types of sockets including UNIX (system), INET (network), NETLINK (devices), FIFO (pipes), and POSIX (messages). See the following for more details:

```
http://fedoraproject.org/wiki/Systemd
https://wiki.ubuntu.com/SystemdForUpstartUsers
https://www.freedesktop.org/wiki/Software/systemd/
```

systemd sets up sockets for all system tasks and services. Configuration for systemd tasks are defined in unit files in **/lib/systemd/system** directory. In this respect, **systemd** files replace the entries that used to be in the Sys V init's **/etc/inittab** file. **systemd** also has its own versions of **shutdown**, **reboot**, **halt**, **init**, and **telinit**, each with their own man page.

systemd is entirely compatible with both System V scripts in the **/etc/init.d** directory and the **/etc/fstab** file. The SystemV scripts and **/etc/fstab** are treated as additional configuration files for **systemd** to work with. If System V scripts are present in the **/etc/init.d** directory, it will use them to generated a corresponding unit configuration file, if there are no corresponding **systemd** unit configuration files already. **systemd** configuration always takes precedence. **systemd** will also, if needed, use the start and stop priority files in the System V init **/etc/rc.d** directories to determine dependencies. Entries in **/etc/fstab** are used to generate corresponding **systemd** unit files that are then used to manage file systems. **systemd** also supports snapshots that allow restoring services to a previous state.

The systemd configuration (**.service**) files are located in the **/lib/systemd/system** directory and are considered system files that you should not modify. It is possible to copy them to the **/etc/systemd/system** directory and make changes to the copies. Files in the **/etc/systemd/system** file take precedence. The configuration file for the logind daemon, **logind.conf**, is located in the **/etc/systemd** directory. Some software, like the Apache Web server, do not yet have systemd service files. **systemd** automatically generates service files for then in the **/var/run/systemd/generator.late** directory.

Linux Mint also uses systemd services for time (**timedated**), location (**localed**), login (**logind**), and hostname (**hostnamed**) (**systemd-services** package). They can be managed with corresponding systemd control applications: **timedatectl**, **localectl**, and **hostnamectl**.

systemd basic configuration files

You can configure **systemd** for system, login manager, users, and journal service using the configuration files located in the **/etc/systemd** directory. When run for a system service, systemd uses the **system.conf** file, otherwise it uses the **user.conf** file. You can set options such as the log level (LogLevel) and resource size limits. See the man page for **systemd.conf** (**system.conf** and **user.conf**), **logind.conf**, and **journald.conf** for details on the options available.

units

systemd organizes tasks into units, each with a unit configuration file. There are several types of units (see Table 13-1). A unit file will have an extension to its name that specifies the type of unit it is. Service types have the extension **.service**, and mount types have the extension **.mount**. The service type performs much the same function as System V init scripts. Services can be stopped, started and restarted. The **systemctl** command will list all units, including the ones that **systemd** generates.

Units can also be used for socket, device, and mount tasks. The socket type implements the kind of connection used for inetd and xinetd, allowing you to start a service on demand. The device type references devices as detected by udev. The mount type manages a file system's mount point, and automount activates that mount point should it be automounted. An automount unit file has a corresponding mount unit file, which it uses to mount a file system. Similarly, a socket type usually has a corresponding service type file used to perform a task for that socket.

Within each unit are directives that control a service, socket, device, or mount point. Some directives are unique to the type of unit. These are listed in the man page for that service, such as **systemd.service** for the service unit, or **systemd.mount** for a mount unit (see Table 13-1).

```
man systemd.service
```

Options common to units are listed in the **systemd.exec** and **systemd.unit** pages. The **systemd.unit** page lists directives common to all units such as Wants, Conflicts, Before, SourcePath, and Also. The **systemd.exec** pages list options for the execution of a program for a unit, such as the starting of a server daemon. These include options such as User, Group, WorkingDirectory, Nice, Umask, and Environment. The **systemd.exec** page covers options for service, socket, mount, and swap units. The **systemd.directives** man page provides a listing of all systemd unit options and the man page for each option.

Unit Type	Unit Man page	Description
`service`	systemd.service	Services such as servers, which can be started and stopped
`socket`	systemd.socket	Socket for services (allows for inetd like services, AF_INET)
`device`	systemd.device	Devices
`mount`	systemd.mount	File system mount points
`automount`	systemd.automount	Automount point for a file system. Use with mount units.
`target`	systemd.target	Group units
`path`	systemd.path	Manage directories
`snapshot`	systemd.snapshot	Created by systemd using the **systemctl snapshot** command to save runtime states of systemd. Use **systemctl isolate** to restore a state.
`swap`	systemd.swap	Swap unit file generated by systemd for the swap file system.
`timer`	systemd.timer	Time-based activation of a unit. Corresponds to a service file. Time formats are specified on the **systemd.time** man page.
	systemd.unit	Man page with configuration options common to all units
	systemd.exec	Man page for execution environment options for service, socket, mount, and swap units
	systemd.special	Man page for systemd special targets such as multi-user.target and printer.target.
	systemd.time	Time and date formats for **systemd**
	systemd.directives	Listing of all systemd options and the man page they are described on.

Table 13-1: systemd unit types and man pages

The target unit is used to group units. For example, targets are used to emulate runlevels. A multi-user target groups units (services) together that, in System V, would run on runlevel 3. In effect, targets group those services that run on a certain runlevel for a certain task. The printer target activates the CUPS service, and the graphical target emulates runlevel 5. A target can also be used to reference other targets. A default target designates the default runlevel. Some unit files are automatically generated by **systemd**. For example, operations specified in the **/etc/fstab** are performed by mount units, which are automatically generated from the fstab entries.

Units can be dependent on one another, where one unit may require the activation of other units. This dependency is specified using directories with the **.wants** extension. For example, the **poweroff.target** is dependent on the **plymouth-poweroff** service. The directory **poweroff.target.wants** has a symbolic link to this service. Should you want a service dependent on your graphical desktop, you can add symbolic links to it in the **graphical.target.wants** directory.

It is important to distinguish between the wants directories in the **/etc/systemd/system** directory and those in the **/lib/systemd/system** directory. Those in the **/lib/systemd** directory are set up by your system and should be left alone. To manage your own dependencies, you can set up corresponding wants directories in the **/etc/systemd/system** directory. The **/etc/systemd** directory always takes priority. For example, in the **/etc/systemd/system/multi-user.target.wants** directory you can place links to services that you want started up for the multi-user.target (runlevel 3). Your system automatically installs links for services you enable, such as **ufw.service** and **vsftpd.service**. These are all links to the actual service files in the **/lib/systemd/system** directory. The **multi-user.target.wants** directory holds a link to **ufw.sevice**, starting up the firewall. The **printer.target.wants** directory has a link to the cups service.

Disabling a service removes its link from its wants directory in **/etc/systemd/system**. For example, disabling the vsftpd service removes its link from the **/etc/systemd/system/multi-user.target.wants** directory. The original service file, in this case, **vsftpd.service**, remains in the **/lib/systemd/system** directory. If you enable the service again, a link for it is added to the **/etc/systemd/system/multi-user.target.wants** directory.

The **/etc/systemd/system** directory also hold links to services. The **/etc/systemd/system/syslog.service** file is a link to **/lib/systemd/system/rsyslog.service**. The **/etc/systemd/system/dbus-org.freedesktop.Avahi.service** link references **/lib/systemd/system/avahi-daemon.service**.

To manage **systemd** you can use **systemctl**. The older service management tool, **service**, has been modified to use **systemctl** to perform actions on services such as starting and stopping.

unit file syntax

A unit file is organized into sections designated by keywords enclosed in brackets. All units have a unit section, **[Unit]**, and an install section, **[Install]**. The options for these sections are described in the **systemd.unit** Man page. Comments can be written by beginning a line with the # or ; characters. See Table 13-2 for a listing of commonly used Unit and Install section options.

The Unit section of a unit file holds generic information about a unit. The Description option provides information about the task the unit manages, such as the Vsftpd server as shown here.

```
Description=vsftpd FTP server
```

The Documentation option lists URIs for the application's documentation.

```
Documentation=man:dhcpd(8)
```

Note: The syntax for unit file is based on .desktop files, which in turn are inspired by Windows ini files. The .desktop type of file conforms to the XDB Desktop Entry Specification.

Types of dependencies can be specified using the Before, After, Requires, Wants, and Conflicts options in the unit section. After and Before configure the ordering of a unit. In the following After option in the **vsftpd.service** file, the vsftpd service is started after networking.

```
After=network.target
```

Unit options	Description
`[Unit]`	
`Description`	Description of the unit.
`Documentation`	URIs referencing documentation.
`Requires`	Units required by the service. This is a strict requirement. If the required units fail, so will the unit.
`Wants`	Units wanted by the service. This is not a strict requirement. If the required units fail, the unit will still start up. Same functionality as the wants directories.
`Conflicts`	Negative unit dependency. Starting the unit stops the listed units in the Conflicts option.
`Before`	Unit ordering. Unit starts before the units listed.
`After`	Unit ordering. Unit waits until the units listed start.
`OnFailure`	Units to be run if the unit fails.
`SourcePath`	File the configuration was generated from, such as the mount unit files generated from **/etc/fstab**.
`[Install]`	
`WantedBy`	Sets up the unit's symbolic link in listed unit's **.wants** subdirectory. When the listed unit is activated, so is the unit. This is not a strict requirement.
`RequiredBY`	Sets up the unit's symbolic link in listed unit's **.requires** subdirectory. When the listed unit is activated, so is the unit. This is a strong requirement.
`Alias`	Additional names the unit is installed under. The aliases are implemented as symbolic links to the unit file.
`Also`	Additional units to install with this unit.

Table 13-2: systemd Unit and Install section options (common to all units, systemd.unit)

The Requires option sets up a dependency between units. This is a strong dependency. If one fails, so does the other. In the following Requires option from the **graphical.target** unit file, the graphical target can only be started if the multi-user and rescue targets are activated.

```
After=multi-user.target display-manager.service rescue.service rescue.target
```

The Wants option sets up a weaker dependency, requiring activation, but not triggering failure should it occur. This is the case with the graphical target and the display manager service.

```
Wants=display-manager.service
```

Several condition options are available such as ConditionACPower which, if true, checks to see if a system is using AC power. In the following example, ConditionPathExists checks for the existence of a file with runtime options for the DHCP server in the **/etc/default** directory.

```
ConditionPathExists=/etc/default/isc-dhcp-server
```

Some unit files are automatically generated by systemd, allowing you to use older configuration methods. For example, the unit file used to manage the mounting of your file systems is generated from the configuration information in the **/etc/fstab** file. The SourcePath option specifies the configuration file used to generate the unit file. The SourcePath option for the **boot.mount** unit file is shown here.

```
SourcePath=/etc/fstab
```

The Install section provides installation information for the unit. The WantedBy and RequiredBy options specify units that this unit wants or requires. For service units managing servers like Vsftpd and the DCHP servers, the install section has a WantedBy option for the **multi-user.target**. This has the effect of running the server at runlevels 2, 3, 4, and 5. When the multi-user target becomes activated so does that unit.

```
WantedBy=multi-user.target
```

The WantedBy option is implemented by setting up a link to the unit in a wants subdirectory for the wanted by unit. For the **multi-user.target** unit, a subdirectory called **multi-user.target.wants** has symbolic links to all the units that want it, such as **vsftpd.service** for the vsftpd FTP service. These wants symbolic links are set up in the **/etc/systemd/system** directory, which can be changed as you enable and disable a service. Disabling a service removes the link. RequiredBy is a much stronger dependency.

The Alias option lists other unit names that could reference this unit. In the **ssh.service** file you will find an Alias option for **sshd.service**.

```
Alias=sshd.service
```

The Also option lists other units that should be activated when this unit is started. The CUPS service has an Also option to start the CUPS socket and path.

```
Also=cups.socket cups.path
```

Different types of units have their own options. Service, socket, target, and path units all have options appropriate for their tasks.

special targets

A target file groups units for services, mounts, sockets, and devices. **systemd** has a set of special target files designed for specific purposes (see Table 13-3). Some are used for on-demand services such as bluetooth and printer. When a Bluetooth device is connected the bluetooth target becomes active. When you connect a printer, the printer target is activated which, in turn, activates the CUPS print server. The sound target is activated when the system starts and runs all sound-related units. See the **special.target** Man page for more details.

There are several special target files that are designed to fulfill the function of runlevels in System V (see Table 13-4). These include the rescue, multi-user, and graphical targets. On boot,

systemd activates the default target, which is a link to a special target, such as **multi-user.target** and **graphical.target**.

You can override the default target with a **systemd.unit** kernel command line option for GRUB. On the GRUB startup menu, you could edit the kernel boot line and add the following option to boot to the command line instead of the desktop.

```
systemd.unit=multi-user.target
```

The following will start up the rescue target.

```
systemd.unit=rescue.target
```

The following will start up the rescue target.

```
systemd.unit=rescue.target
```

Special units	Description
`basic.target`	Units to be run at early boot
`bluetooth.target`	Starts when a Bluetooth device becomes active
`printer.target`	Starts printer service when a printer is attached.
`sound.target`	Starts when sound device is detected, usually at boot.
`display-manager.service`	Link to display service such as LightDM or KDM.
`ctrl-alt-del.target`	Activated when the user presses Ctrl-Alt-Del keys, this is a link to the reboot.target which reboots the system.
`system-update.target`	Implements an offline system update. After downloading, the updates are performed when your system reboots, at which time it detects the presence of the target.

Table 13-3: special units

Special RunlevelTargets	Description
`default.target`	References special target to be activated on boot
`rescue.target`	Starts up base system and rescue shell
`emergency.target`	Starts base system, with option to start full system
`multi-user.target`	Starts up command line interface, multi-user and non-graphical (similar to runlevel 3)
`graphical.target`	Start graphical interface (desktop) (similar to runlevel 5)

Table 13-4: special runlevel targets (boot)

You could also simply add a 3 as in previous releases, as runlevel links also reference the special targets in **systemd**. The 3 would reference the runlevel 3 target, which links to the multi-user target. A copy of the **multi-user.target** file follows. The multi-user target requires the basic target which loads the basic system (Requires). It conflicts with the rescue target (Conflicts), and it is run after the basic target. It can be isolated allowing you to switch special targets (AllowIsolate).

multi-user.target

```
[Unit]
Description=Multi-User System
Documentation=man:systemd.special(7)
Requires=basic.target
Conflicts=rescue.service rescue.target
After=basic.target rescue.service rescue.target
AllowIsolate=yes
```

The **graphical.target** depends on the **multi-user.target**. A copy of the **graphical.target** unit file follows. It requires that the **multi-user.target** be activated (Requires). Anything run for the multi-user target, including servers, is also run for the graphical target, the desktop. The desktop target is run after the **multi-user.target** (After). It is not run for the **rescue.target** (Conflicts). It also wants the display-manager service to run (GDM or KDM) (Wants). You can isolate it to switch to another target (AllowIsolate).

graphical.target

```
[Unit]
Description=Graphical Interface
Documentation=man:systemd.special(7)
Requires=multi-user.target
Wants=display-manager.service
Conflicts=rescue.service rescue.target
After=multi-user.target rescue.service rescue.target display-manager.service
AllowIsolate=yes
```

Modifying unit files: /etc/systemd/system

systemd uses unit files to manage devices, mounts, and services. These are located in the **/lib/systemd/system** directory and are considered system files that you should not modify. Instead, to modify a unit file, you should copy it to the **/etc/systemd/system** directory. Unit files in this directory take precedence over those in the **/lib/systemd/system** directory. You can then modify the unit file version in **/etc/systemd/system**. Use a **cp** command to copy the file. The following command copies the Samba service unit file.

```
sudo cp /lib/systemd/system/vsftpd.service  /etc/systemd/system/vsftpd.service
```

If you just want to add unit options to a unit file, not changing the original options in the **/lib/systemd/system** version, you do not have to copy the original unit file. Instead, you can set up a corresponding new unit file in **/etc/systemd/system** that has an include option that reads in the original unit file from **/lib/systemd/system**. Then, in the new **/etc/systemd/system** file, you can add the new systemd options.

Keep in mind that most runtime options for a service application, such as the Vsftpd server, are still held in the appropriate **/etc/default** file, such as **/etc/default/vsftpd**. This file is read by the service when it is activated.

The actual enabling or disabling of services such as vsftpd is handled through symbolic links set up or removed from the **multi-user.target.wants** directory in the **/etc/systemd/system** directory. This is considered an administration based modification appropriate for **/etc/systemd/system**.

Execution Environment Options

The unit files of type service, sockets, mount, and swap share the same options for the execution environment of the unit (see Table 13-5). These are found in the unit section for that type such as **[Service]** for service units or **[Socket]** for socket unit. With these options, you can set features such as the working directory (WorkingDirectory), the file mode creation mask (UMask), and the system logging level (SysLogLevel). Nice sets the default scheduling priority level. User specifies the user id for the processes the unit runs.

```
User=mysql
```

Exec options	Description
`WorkingDirectory`	Sets the working directory for an application.
`RootDirectory`	Root directory for an application
`User, Group`	The application's user and group ids.
`Nice`	Sets priority for an application
`CPUSchedulingPriority`	CPU Scheduling priority for the applications.
`UMask`	File mode creation mask, default is 022.
`Environment`	Set environment variables for an application.
`StandardOutput`	Direct standard output a connection such as log, console, or null.
`SysLogLevel`	System logging level such as warn, alert, info, or debug.
`DeviceAllow, DeviceDeny`	Control applications access to a device.
`ControlGroup`	Assign application to a control group.

Table 13-5: systemd exec options (Service, Socket, Mount, Swap) (systemd.exec)

service unit files

A service unit file is used to run applications and commands such as the Samba (smbd) and Web (apache2) servers. They have a **[Service]** section with options specified in the **systemd.service** Man page. See Table 13-6 for a listing of several common service options. A service unit file has the extension **.service** and the prefix is the name of the server program, such as **isc-dhcp-server.service** for the DHCP server and **vsftpd.service** for the Very Secure FTP server. Table 13-7 lists several popular servers.

A copy of the Vsftpd service unit file, **vsftpd.service**, follows. The Vsftpd FTP service is started after the network has started. The server program to run is specified, **/usr/sbin/vsftpd** (ExecStart). The service is installed by the **multi-user.target** (WantedBy), when the system starts up.

vsftpd.service

```
[Unit]
Description=vsftpd FTP server
After=network.target

[Service]
Type=simple
ExecStart=/usr/sbin/vsftpd /etc/vsftpd.conf
ExecReload=/bin/kill -HUP $MAINPID
ExecStartPre=-/bin/mkdir -p /var/run/vsftpd/empty

[Install]
WantedBy=multi-user.target
```

Service options	Description
`ExecStart`	Commands to execute when service starts, such as running an application or server.
`Type`	Startup type such as simple (the default), forking, dbus, notify, or idle
`ExecStartPre`, `ExecStartPost`	Commands executed before and after the ExecStart command.
`TimeStartSec`	Time to wait before starting the ExecStart command.
`Restart`	Restart when the ExecStart command end.
`PermissionsStartOnly`	Boolean value, If true the permission based options are applied, such as User.
`RootDirectoryStartOnly`	Boolean value, if true, the RootDirectory option applies only to the ExecStart option.

Table 13-6: systemd service options [Service] (systemd.service)

The **bind9.service** file is even simpler, incorporating runtime options into the program command. It is run after the network service and is started by the **multi-user.target**.

bind9.service

```
[Unit]
Description=BIND Domain Name Server
Documentation=man:named(8)
After=network.target
[Service]
ExecStart=/usr/sbin/named -f -u bind
ExecReload=/usr/sbin/rndc reload
ExecStop=/usr/sbin/rndc stop
[Install]
WantedBy=multi-user.target
```

Service unit files	Description
`apache2`	Apache Web server
`bind9`	Bind 9 DNS server
`cups`	The CUPS printer daemon
`isc-dhcp-server`	Dynamic Host Configuration Protocol daemon
`mysql`	MySQL database server
`network`	Operations to start up or shut down your network connections.
`nis`	The NIS server
`nfs-server`	Network Filesystem
`postfix`	Postfix mail server
`sendmail`	The Sendmail MTA daemon
`smbd`	Samba for Windows hosts
`squid3`	Squid proxy-cache server
`ssh`	Secure Shell daemon
`systemd-journald`	System logging daemon
`vsftpd`	Very Secure FTP server
`ufw`	Controls the UFW firewall

Table 13-7: Collection of Service unit files

System V Scripts and generated systemd service files: /etc/init.d and /run/systemd/generator.late

Some services are not yet configured natively for use by systemd. They are installed without a systemd service file. Instead, a SysV script is installed in the **/etc/init.d** directory. The **systemd-sysv-generator** tool automatically reads this script and generates a corresponding systemd unit file in the **/var/run/systemd/generator.late** directory, which, in turn, will use the script to manage the service. The Apache Web server is such a service, with an apache2 script in **/etc/init.d** and a corresponding systemd service file in the **/var/run/systemd/generator.late** directory. A copy of the **apache2.service** unit service file follows. It is started before the runlevel targets, which are links to the multi-user and graphical targets (Before), which is the equivalent of runlevels 2, 3, 4, and 5. It is run after network, remote file system mounts, and name service lookup. The server program is run using the **/etc/init.d/apache2** script (ExecStart). The same script is used to reload and stop the server but with different options (ExecReload and ExecStop).

There are **.target.wants** directories for different runlevels in the **/run/systemd/generator.late** directory, which holds links for the services active for a given runlevel. These runlevel target wants directories reference the runlevel targets, which, in turn, are simply links to the systemd multi-user and graphical targets.

apache2.service

```
# Automatically generated by systemd-sysv-generator

[Unit]
Documentation=man:systemd-sysv-generator(8)
SourcePath=/etc/init.d/apache2
Description=LSB: Apache2 web server
Before=multi-user.target
Before=multi-user.target
Before=multi-user.target
Before=graphical.target
Before=shutdown.target
After=local-fs.target
After=remote-fs.target
After=network-online.target
After=systemd-journald-dev-log.socket
After=nss-lookup.target
Wants=network-online.target
Conflicts=shutdown.target

[Service]
Type=forking
Restart=no
TimeoutSec=5min
IgnoreSIGPIPE=no
KillMode=process
GuessMainPID=no
RemainAfterExit=yes
ExecStart=/etc/init.d/apache2 start
ExecStop=/etc/init.d/apache2 stop
ExecReload=/etc/init.d/apache2 reload
```

On Demand and Standalone Services (socket)

The On Demand activation of services, formerly implemented by inetd, is the default in systemd. Should you want a standalone service, you can specify that it is wanted by a special target so that it will be started up at boot time, instead of when it is first activated. In the Install section of a service unit file, a WantedBy option specifying the multi-user target will start the service at boot, making it a standalone service. In the following, the service is wanted by the **multi-user.target**. To put it another way, the service starts at runlevels 2, 3, 4, and 5. Note that the graphical target (5) is dependent on (Requires) the multi-user target (2, 3, and 4), so by specifying the multi-user target, the service is also started with the graphical target.

```
[Install]
WantedBy=multi-user.target
```

The Bluetooth service only wants the **bluetooth.target** which is only activated if a Bluetooth device is present. It is not started at boot.

```
[Install]
WantedBy=bluetooth.target
```

Use the basic target, should you want the service started at all runlevels.

```
[Install]
WantedBy=basic.target
```

To emulate an on-demand server service, as inetd used to do, you would use a **.socket** file to compliment a **.service** file. This is the case with CUPS, which has a cups service file and corresponding cups socket file (CUPS is not installed by default on the Server edition). The WantedBy option for **sockets.target** ties the socket to the special target **sockets.target**, which makes the unit socket-activated.

The Socket section lists options for the socket, usually what socket to listen on (ListenStream). The **systemd.socket** Man page lists socket options. Table 13-8 lists common options.

Socket options	Description
`ListenStream`	Address to listen on for a stream. The address can be a port number, path name for a socket device, or an IPv4 or IPv6 address with a port number.
`Accept`	If true, service instance is set up for each connection; if false, only one service instance is set up for all connections
`MaxConnections`	Maximum number of connections for a service
`Service`	Service unit to run when socket is active. Default is a service name that is the same as the socket name.

Table 13-8: systemd socket file options [Socket] (systemd.socket)

cups.socket

```
[Unit]
Description=CUPS Scheduler

[Socket]
ListenStream=/var/run/cups/cups.sock

[Install]
WantedBy=sockets.target
```

cups.service

```
[Unit]
Description=CUPS Scheduler
Documentation=man:cupsd(8)

[Service]
ExecStart=/usr/sbin/cupsd -l
Type=simple

[Install]
Also=cups.socket cups.path
WantedBy=printer.target
```

Path units

systemd uses path units to monitor a path. Sometimes a service unit has a corresponding path unit to monitor directories, as is the case with **cups.path** and **cups.service**. Options for the Path section are listed in Table 13-9 and on the **systemd.path** Man page. The **cups.path** unit file is shown here. The PathExists option checks if the printer spool files exist.

cups.path

```
[Unit]
Description=CUPS Scheduler

[Path]
PathExists=/var/cache/cups/org.cups.cupsd

[Install]
WantedBy=multi-user.target
```

path options	Description
`PathExists`	Activates if a file exists
`PathExistsGlob`	Activates if there exists a file matching a pattern, such as any file in a specified directory.
`PathModified`	Activates if a file has been modified

Table 13-9: path option (systemd.path)

Template unit files

There is a special type of unit file called a template file, which allow for the generation of several unit files at runtime using one template file. Templates are used for services that generate instances of a service such as a getty terminal, an OpenVPN connection, and an rsync connection. A template filename ends with an @ sign. If a corresponding unit file is not found for a service, **systemd** will check to see if there is a template file that can be applied to it. **systemd** matches the service name with the template name. It then generates an instance unit file for that particular service.

For example, a terminal uses the getty service (get TTY). As you do not know how many terminals you may use, they are generated automatically using the **getty@.service** unit file.

In the configuration file, the **%I** specifier is used to substitute for the service name. Given the service name **getty@tty3**, the **%I** specifier substitutes for **tty3**.

```
ExecStart=-/sbin/agetty --noclear %I $TERM
```

The **getty@.service** template file is shown here.

getty@.service

```
[Unit]
Description=Getty on %I
Documentation=man:agetty(8) man:systemd-getty-generator(8)
Documentation=http://0pointer.de/blog/projects/serial-console.html
After=systemd-user-sessions.service plymouth-quit-wait.service
```

```
After=rc-local.service

# If additional gettys are spawned during boot then we should make
# sure that this is synchronized before getty.target, even though
# getty.target didn't actually pull it in.
Before=getty.target
IgnoreOnIsolate=yes

# On systems without virtual consoles, don't start any getty. Note
# that serial gettys are covered by serial-getty@.service, not this
# unit.
ConditionPathExists=/dev/tty0

[Service]
# the VT is cleared by TTYVTDisallocate
ExecStart=-/sbin/agetty --noclear %I $TERM
Type=idle
Restart=always
RestartSec=0
UtmpIdentifier=%I
TTYPath=/dev/%I
TTYReset=yes
TTYVHangup=yes
TTYVTDisallocate=yes
KillMode=process
IgnoreSIGPIPE=no
SendSIGHUP=yes

# Unset locale for the console getty since the console has problems
# displaying some internationalized messages.
Environment=LANG= LANGUAGE= LC_CTYPE= LC_NUMERIC= LC_TIME= LC_COLLATE=
LC_MONETARY= LC_MESSAGES= LC_PAPER= LC_NAME= LC_ADDRESS= LC_TELEPHONE=
LC_MEASUREMENT= LC_IDENTIFICATION=

[Install]
WantedBy=getty.target
DefaultInstance=tty1
```

Runlevels and Special Targets

Under the old System V, a Linux system could run in different levels, called **runlevels**, depending on the capabilities you want to give it. Under System V, Linux had several runlevels, numbered from 0 to 6. When you power up your system, you enter the default runlevel. Runlevels 0, 1, and 6 are special runlevels that perform specific functions. Runlevel 0 was the power-down state. Runlevel 6 was the reboot state (it shuts down the system and reboots). Runlevel 1 was the single-user state, which allowed access only to the superuser and does not run any network services.

systemd uses special targets instead of runlevels to create the same effect as runlevels, grouping services to run for specified targets. Runlevels are no longer directly implemented. There are two major special targets: multi-user and graphical. The multi-user target is similar to runlevel 3, providing you with a command line login. The graphical target is similar to runlevel 5, providing you with a graphical login and interface.

You set the default target (runlevel) by linking a target's **systemd** service file to the **systemd** default target file. This operation replaces the way inittab was used to specify a default runlevel in previous releases. The following makes the graphical interface the default (runlevel 5).

```
ln -s /lib/systemd/system/graphicl.target  /etc/systemd/system/default.target
```

systemd does provide compatibility support for runlevels. Runlevel compatibility is implemented using symbolic links in **/lib/system/systemd** directory to **systemd** targets. The **runlevel0.target** link references the systemd **poweroff.target**. Runlevel 2, 3, and 4 targets all link to the same **multi-user.target** (command line interface). The **runlevel6.target** links to the reboot target and **runlevel5.target** links to **graphical.target** (desktop interface). The runlevels and their targets are listed in Table 13-10.

System Runlevel links	systemd targets
`runlevel0`	`poweroff.target`
`runlevel1`	`rescue.target`
`runlevel2`	`multi-user.target`
`runlevel3`	`multi-user.target`
`runlevel4`	`multi-user.target.`
`runlevel5`	`graphical.target.`
`runlevel6`	`reboot.target`

Table 13-10: System Runlevels (States)

You can still use the `runlevel` command to see what state you are currently running in. It lists the previous state followed by the current one. If you have not changed states, the previous state will be listed as N, indicating no previous state. This is the case for the state you boot up in. In the next example, the system is running in state 3, with no previous state change:

```
# runlevel
N 3
```

Changing runlevels can be helpful if you have problems at a particular runlevel. For example, if your video card is not installed properly, then any attempt to start up in runlevel 5 (**graphical.target**) will likely fail, as this level immediately starts your graphical interface. Instead, you could use the command line interface, runlevel 3 (**multi-user.target**), to fix your video card installation.

No matter what runlevel you start in, you can change from one runlevel to another with the `telinit` command. If your default runlevel is 3, you power up in runlevel 3, but you can change to, say, runlevel 5 with `telinit 5`. The command `telinit 0` shuts down your system. In the next example, the `telinit` command changes to runlevel 1, the administrative state:

```
telinit 1
```

Before **systemd** was implemented, you could also use `init` to change runlevels. With **systemd**, both `telinit` and `init` are now **systemd** emulation versions of the original Unix commands. The `telinit` command is always used to change runlevels. If you use `init` with a runlevel number, it now merely invokes `telinit` to make the change.

Alternatively, you can use the **systemctl** command directly to change runlevels (targets). The **systemctl** command with the **isolate** option and the name of the target file changes to that target (runlevel). This is what the telinit command actually does. The following command changes to the multi-user target.

```
sudo systemctl isolate multi-user.target
```

You could also use the runlevel link instead.

```
sudo systemctl isolate runlevel3.target
```

systemd and automatically mounting file systems: /etc/fstab

The **systemd** unit files with the extension **.mount** can be used to mount file systems automatically. Normally systemd will read the **/etc/fstab** file for mount information. If a mount unit file exists in the **/etc/systemd** directory, it takes precedence, but **/etc/fstab** takes precedence over any unit mount files in the **/lib/systemd** directory. The **/etc/fstab** file is used for mount configuration information. Most of the options for a mount unit file correspond to those of the **/etc/fstab** file, specifying the device path name, the mount point, file system type, and mount options (see Table 13-11). The entries in the **/etc/fstab** file are converted to mount unit files at boot, which are then used by systemd to perform the actual mount operations. These mount unit files are created by the systemd-fstab-generator and can be found in the **/run/systemd/generator** directory.

The following fstab file entries have corresponding mount files created in the **/run/systemd/generator** directory: **boot.mount** for the boot file system (**boot-efi.mount** for an EUFI boot system), **home.mount** for the home file system, and **-.mount** for the root file system. For the swap file system, a swap unit file is generated.

```
UUID=1059a-4a86-4072-982e-000717229b9f / ext4     errors=remount-ro  0 1
UUID-=5537-AF41 /boot/efi    vfat     umask=0077   0 1
UUID=147b-4a86-4072-982e-000717229b6g /home ext4   default    0 1
UUID=cba958e4-4a86-4072-982e-000717228355 none     swap     sw   0 0
```

For this example, the **-.mount** file used for the root file system will have the following mount options. The root directory is represented in the mount filename as a dash, -, instead of a slash, /. The mount options are listed in a **[Mount]** section.

```
[Mount]
What=/dev/disk/by-uuid/1059a-4a86-4072-982e-000717229b9f
Where=/
Type=ext4
Options=errors=remount-ro
```

The **home.mount** file references partition for the home file system and mounts it to the **/home** directory.

```
[Mount]
What=/dev/disk/by-uuid/147b-4a86-4072-982e-000717229b6g
Where=/home
Type=ext4
FsckPassNo=2
```

The **boot.mount** file mounts the ext4 file system that holds the kernel in the **/boot** directory.

```
[Mount]
What=/dev/disk/by-uuid/e759aa59-4a86-4072-982e-000717229b4a
Where=/boot
Type=ext4
FsckPassNo=2
```

On EFI boot systems, the **boot-efi.mount** file mounts the vfat EFI file system that holds the boot information.

```
[Mount]
What=/dev/disk/by-uuid/5537-AF41
Where=/boot/efi
Type=vfat
Options=umask=0077
```

mount options	Description
What	Path of the device
Where	Directory of the mount point.
Type	File system type
Options	Mount options
DirectoryMode	Permissions for created file system mount directories
TimeoutSec	Time to wait for a mount operation to finish
automount options	Description
Where	Mount point for the file system. If it does not exist, it will be created.
DirectoryMode	Permissions for any directories created.

Table 13-11: systemd mount and automount file options [Mount] [Automount]

All the unit files will designate the **/etc/fstab** file as the SourcePath, the file from which the configuration was generated from.

```
SourcePath=/etc/fstab
```

All are mounted before any local file systems.

```
Before=local-fs.target
```

Local and remote file systems are distinguished by Wants options in their unit files for **local-fs.target** or **remote-fs.target**.

A mount unit file has to be named for the mount point it references. The path name slashes are replaced by dashes in the unit name. For example, the **proc-fs-nfsd.mount** file references the mount point **/proc/fs/nfsd**. The root path name, /, becomes simple a dash, -.

For file systems to be automatically mounted when accessed you can use the automount unit type. An automount unit must have a corresponding mount unit of the same name.

The **systemd-fsck@service** file provides a file system check with fsck, using the disk name as an argument.

```
RequiresOverridable=system-fsck@dev-disk-by\x2duuid-5537\x2dAF41.service
After=system-fsck@dev-disk-by\x2duuid-5537\x2dAF41.service
```

systemd slice and scope units

The slice and scope units are designed to group units to more easily control their processes and resources. The scope units are generated by systemd to manage a process and its subprocesses. An example of a scope unit is a user session scope that groups the processes for a user session together. A slice is used to manage resources for processes, such as the machine slice for virtual machines, the system slice for system services, and the user slice for user sessions.

System V: /etc/init.d

The SysVinit support for services is no longer implemented. There are no **rc.d** scripts for starting services. **systemd** manages all services directly. Check the README file in the **/etc/init.d** directory. For a very few system tasks, you may find System V scripts in the **/etc/init.d** directory. **systemd** will read these scripts as configuration information for a service, generating a corresponding unit configuration file for it. The unit file, in turn, may use the **init.d** script to start, stop, and restart the service. Should there be a unit file already in existence, that unit file is used and the System V script is ignored.

Some servers use unit files generated from System V scripts in the **/etc/init.d** directory. These include Apache (apache2), Samba (smbd and nmbd), Postfix (postfix), NIS (nis), and Squid (squid3). The unit files are generated by systemd-sysv-generator and located in the **/var/run/systemd/generator.late** directory.

An **rc-local.service** unit file in the **/lib/systemd/system** directory will run a **/etc/rc.local** file, if present. This is to maintain compatibility with older System V configuration.

Shutdown and Poweroff

You can use the **shutdown** and **poweroff** commands to power down the system. The **shutdown** command provides more options. Keep in mind that the **shutdown** command used is the **systemd** version, which will use **systemctl** to actually shutdown the system.

You can also shut down your system immediately using the **poweroff** command with the **sudo** command. You will be prompted to enter your password.

```
sudo poweroff
```

To perform a reboot, you can use the **reboot** command.

```
sudo reboot
```

The **shutdown** command has a time argument that gives users on the system a warning before you power down. You can specify an exact time to shut down, or a period of minutes from the current time. The exact time is specified by *hh*:*mm* for the hour and minutes. The period of time is indicated by a + and the number of minutes.

The **shutdown** command takes several options with which you can specify how you want your system shut down. The -h option, which stands for halt, simply shuts down the system, whereas the -r option shuts down the system and then reboots it. In the next example, the system is shut down after ten minutes:

```
shutdown -h +10
```

To shut down the system immediately, you can use **+0** or the word **now**. The shutdown options are listed in Table 13-12. The following example shuts down the system immediately and then reboots:

```
shutdown -r now
```

With the **shutdown** command, you can include a warning message to be sent to all users currently logged in, giving them time to finish what they are doing before you shut them down.

```
shutdown -h +5 "System needs a rest"
```

If you do not specify either the **-h** or the **-r** options, the **shutdown** command shuts down the multi-user mode and shifts you to an administrative single-user mode. In effect, your system state changes from 3 (multi-user state) to 1 (administrative single-user state). Only the root user is active, allowing the root user to perform any necessary system administrative operations with which other users might interfere.

The shutdown process works through systemd using the **systemctl** command. The poweroff, halt, and reboot commands invoke systemd service files activated through corresponding target files. The systemctl command, in turn, uses the **/lib/systemd/system-shutdown** program to perform the actual shut down operation. In the **/lib/systemd/system** directory, the **systemd-poweroff.service** file shows the **systemctl poweroff** command. The man page for the shutdown service is **systemd-halt-service**. Always use the **poweroff**, **reboot**, and **halt** commands to shut down, not the **systemctl** command. The corresponding systemd target and service files for these commands ensure that the shutdown process proceeds safely.

systemd-poweroff.service

```
#  This file is part of systemd.
#
#  systemd is free software; you can redistribute it and/or modify it
#  under the terms of the GNU Lesser General Public License as published by
#  the Free Software Foundation; either version 2.1 of the License, or
#  (at your option) any later version.

[Unit]
Description=Power-Off
Documentation=man:systemd-halt.service(8)
DefaultDependencies=no
Requires=shutdown.target umount.target final.target
After=shutdown.target umount.target final.target

[Service]
Type=oneshot
ExecStart=/bin/systemctl --force poweroff
```

Note: The halt command merely halts the system, it does not turn it off.

Command	Description
`shutdown [-rkhncft]` *time* [*warning*]	Shuts the system down after the specified time period, issuing warnings to users; you can specify a warning message of your own after the time argument; if neither `-h` nor `-r` is specified to shut down the system, the system sets to the administrative mode, runlevel state 1.
Argument	
Time	Has two possible formats: it can be an absolute time in the format *hh*:*mm*, with *hh* as the hour (one or two digits) and *mm* as the minute (in two digits); it can also be in the format +*m*, with *m* as the number of minutes to wait; the word `now` is an alias for +0.
Option	
`-t` *sec*	Tells `init` to wait *sec* seconds between sending processes the warning and the kill signals, before changing to another runlevel.
`-k`	Doesn't actually shut down; only sends the warning messages to everybody.
`-r`	Reboots after shutdown, runlevel state 6.
`-h`	Halts after shutdown, runlevel state 0.
`-n`	Doesn't call `init` to do the shutdown; you do it yourself.
`-f`	Skips file system checking (fsck) on reboot.
`-c`	Cancels an already running shutdown; no time argument.

Table 13-12: System Shutdown Options

Managing Services

You can select certain services to run and the special target (runlevel) at which to run them. Most services are servers like a Web server or FTP server. Other services provide security, such as SSH or Kerberos. You can decide which services to use with the **systemctl** or **service** tools.

Enabling services: starting a service automatically at boot

Services such as the Apache Web server, Samba server, and the FTP server are handled by the **systemd** daemon. You can manage services using the **systemctl** command. The older **service** command is simply a front end to the **systemctl** command.

To have a service start up at boot, you need to first enable it using the **systemctl** tool as the root user. Use the **enable** command to enable the service. The following command enables the vsftpd server and the Samba server (**smbd**). The **systemctl** command uses the service's service configuration file located in the **/lib/systemd/system** or **/etc/systemd/system** directories.

```
sudo systemctl enable vsftpd.service
sudo systemctl enable smbd
```

Managing services manually

Use the **start**, **stop**, and **restart** commands with **systemctl** to manually start, stop, and restart a service. The **enable** command only starts up a service automatically. You could choose to start it manually using the **start** command. You can stop and restart a service any time using the **stop** and **restart** commands. The **condrestart** command only starts the server if it is already stopped. Use the **status** command to check the current status of service.

```
sudo systemctl start vsftpd
sudo systemctl restart vsftpd
sudo systemctl condrestart vsftpd
sudo systemctl stop vsftpd
sudo systemctl status vsftpd
```

The service Command

The **service** command is now simply a front end for the **systemctl** command which performs the actual operation using **systemd**. The **service** command cannot enable or disable services. It only performs management operations such as start, stop, restart, and status. With the `service` command, you enter the service name with the **stop** argument to stop it, the **start** argument to start it, and the **restart** argument to restart it. The **service** command is run from a Terminal window. You will have to use the **sudo** command. The following will start the **vsftpd** FTP service.

```
sudo service vsftpd start
```

The **systemd** version of the **service** command actually invokes the **systemctl** command to run the service's systemd **.servic**e unit file in **/lib/systemd/system**. If a service is not enabled, **systemd** will enable it. You can perform the same operations as the **service** command, using the **systemctl** command. The following is the equivalent of the previous command.

```
sudo systemctl start vsftpd
```

Note: Upstart had been deprecated.

/etc/default

The **/etc/default** directory holds scripts for setting runtime options when a service starts up. For example, the **/etc/default/apache2** script sets cache cleaning options. The **/etc/default/ufw** scripts sets firewall default policies. You can edit these scripts and change the values assigned to options, changing the behavior of a service.

Service Startup Management with rcconf

Linux Mint provides the **rcconf** (Debian) tool which you can use to start or stop services when you boot up your system (see Figure 13-1). The **rcconf** tool was developed by Debian and is used on Debian, Ubuntu, and similar distributions. The **rcconf** tool works both for System V init service scripts located in the **/etc/init.d** directory and for systemd service files, changing appropriate link in the /**etc/systemd/multi-user.target.wants** directory.

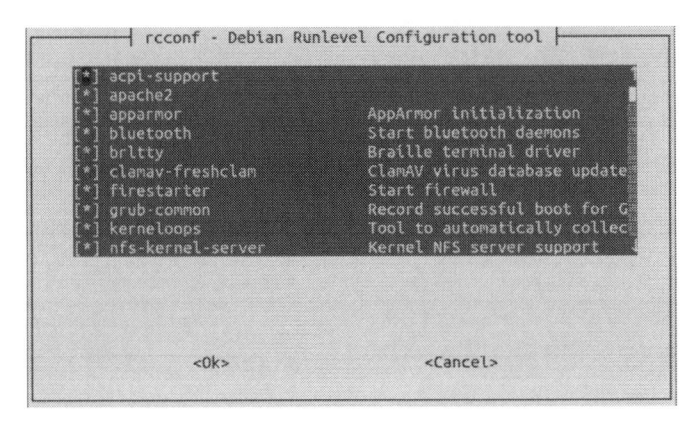

Figure 13-1: rcconf service management

The **rcconf** is run from a terminal window or from the command line and provides an easy cursor-based interface for using arrow keys and the spacebar to turn services on or off.

```
sudo rcconf
```

Network Time Protocol, NTP

For servers to run correctly, they need to always have the correct time. Internet time servers worldwide provide the time in the form of the Universal Time Coordinated (UTC). Local time is then calculated using the local system's local time zone. The time is obtained from Internet time servers from an Internet connection. You have the option of using a local hardware clock instead, though this may be much less accurate.

Normally, the time on a host machine is kept in a Time of Year chip (TOY) that maintains the time when the machine is off. Its time is used when the machine is rebooted. A host using the Network Time Protocol then adjusts the time, using the time obtained from an Internet time server. If there is a discrepancy of more than 1000 seconds (about 15 minutes), the system administrator is required to manually set the time. Time servers in the public network are organized in stratum levels, the highest being 1. Time servers from a lower stratum obtain the time from those in the next higher level.

For servers on your local network, you may want to set up your own time server, ensuring that all your servers are using a synchronized time. If all your servers are running on a single host system that is directly connected to the Internet and accessing an Internet time server, you will not need to set up a separate time server. You can use the **ntpdate** command to update directly from an Internet time server.

```
sudo ntpdate ntp.ubuntu.com
```

If the servers are on different host systems, then you may want a time server to ensure their times are synchronized. Alternatively, you could just use the **ntpdate** command to update those hosts directly at given intervals. You could set up a cron job to perform the **ntpdate** operation automatically.

There are packages on the Ubuntu repository for both the NTP server and its documentation. You can install them with **apt-get**, **aptitude**, or (from the desktop) the Synaptic Package Manager.

```
ntp
ntp-doc
```

The documentation will be located in the **/usr/share/doc/ntp-doc** directory in Web page format.

```
/usr/share/doc/ntp-doc/html/index.html
```

The ntp server

The NTP server name is **ntpd** and is managed by the **/etc/init.d/ntp** script. Use the start, stop, and restart options to manage the server. A corresponding systemd service file, **ntp.service**, is generated in the **/run/systemd/generator.late** directory.

```
sudo service ntp start
```

Your host systems can then be configured to use NTP and access your NTP time server.

To check the status of your time server, you can use the **ntpq** command. With the **-p** option it displays the current status.

```
ntpq -p
```

The ntp.conf configuration file

The NTP server configuration file is **/etc/ntp.conf**. This file lists the Internet time servers that your own time server used to determine the time. Check the **ntp.conf** Man page for a complete listing of the NTP server configuration directives.

In the **ntp.conf** file, the server directive specifies the Internet time server's Internet address that your NTP server uses to access the time. There is a default entry for the Ubuntu time server, but you can add more server entries for other time servers.

```
server ntp.ubuntu.com
```

NTP access controls

Access control to the NTP server is determined by the restrict directives. An NTP server is accessible from the Internet, anyone can access it. You can specify access options and the addresses of hosts allowed access. The **default** option lets you specify the set of default options. The **noquery**, **notrust**, **nopeer**, and **nomodify** option deny all access. The **notrust** option will not trust hosts unless specifically allowed access. The **nomodify** option prevents any modification of the time server. The **noquery** option will not even allow queries from other hosts unless specifically allowed.

```
restrict -4 default kod notrap nomodify nopeer noquery
```

The default **/etc/ntp.conf** file is shown here.

```
#/etc/ntp.conf, configuration for ntpd: see ntp.conf(5) for help
driftfile /ver/lib/ntp/ntp.drift

#Enable this if you want statistics to be logged.
#statsdir /var/log/ntpstats/
statistics loopstats peerstats clockstats
filegen loopstats file loopstats type day enable
filegen peerstats file peerstats type day enable
filegen clockstats file clockstats type day enable
# Use Servers from the NTP Pool Project. Approved by Ubuntu Technical Board
# on 2011-02-08 (LP: #104525). See http://www.pool.ntp.org/join.html for
# more information
pool 0.ubuntu.pool.ntp.org iburst
pool 1.ubuntu.pool.ntp.org iburst
pool 2.ubuntu.pool.ntp.org iburst
pool 3.ubuntu.pool.ntp.org iburst

# Use Ubuntu's ntp server as fallback
server ntp.ubuntu.com

# Access control configuration; see
# /usr/share/doc/ntp-doc/html/accopt.html for
# details.  The web page <http://support.ntp.org/bin/view/Support/AccessRestrictions>
# might also be helpful.
#
# Note that "restrict" applies to both servers and clients, so a configuration
# that might be intended to block requests from certain clients could also end
# up blocking replies from your own upstream servers.

# By default, exchange time with everybody, but don't allow configuration.
restrict -4 default kod notrap nomodify nopeer noquery
restrict -6 default kod notrap nomodify nopeer noquery

# Local users may interrogate the ntp server more closely.
restrict 127.0.0.1
restrict ::1

# Clients from this (example!) subnet have unlimited access, but only if
# cryptographically authenticated.
#restrict 192.168.123.0 mask 255.255.255.0 notrust

# If you want to provide time to your local subnet, change the next
# line. (Again, the address is an example only.)
#broadcast 192.168.123.255

# If you want to listen to time broadcasts on your local subnet,
# de-comment the next lines. Please do this only if you trust everybody
# on the network!
#disable auth
#broadcastclient

#Changes required to use pps synchronisation as explained in documentation:
#http://www.ntp.org/ntpfaq/NTP-s-config-adv.htm#AEN3918

#server 127.127.8.1 mode 135 prefer    # Meinberg GPS167 with PPS
#fudge  127.127.8.1 time1 0.0042       # relative to PPS for my hardware

#server 127.127.22.1                   # ATOM(PPS)
#fudge  127.127.22.1 flag3 1           # enable PPS API
```

Then local users, users on the same host that is running the NTP server, are allowed to access the NTP server. Addresses are specified for both IPv4 and IPv6 localhost, **127.0.0.1** and **::1**.

```
restrict 127.0.0.1
restrict ::1
```

To allow access from hosts on a private local network, you can use the restrict directive to specify the local network address and mask. The following allows access to a local network, 192.168.123, with a network mask of 255.255.255.0 to determine the range of allowable host addresses.

```
restrict 192.168.123.0 mask 255.255.255.0
```

If you want to require the use of encrypted keys for access, add the **notrust** option. Use **ntp-keygen** to generate the required public/private keys.

You can also run the time server in broadcast mode where the time is broadcasted to your network clients (this can involve security risks). Use the broadcast directive and your network's broadcast address. Your host systems need to have the **broadcastclient** setting set, which will listen for time broadcasts.

```
broadcast 192.168.123.255
```

You can also implement support for Pulse Per Second (PPS) API.

```
#server 127.127.8.1 mode 135 prefer    # Meinberg GPS167 with PPS
#fudge  127.127.8.1 time1 0.0042       # relative to PPS for my hardware
```

NTP clock support

You can also list a reference to the local hardware clock, and have that clock be used if your connection to the Internet time server should fail. The hardware clock is referenced by the IP address that has the prefix 127.127 followed by the clock type and instance, as in 127.127.1.1. The type for the local clock is 1.

```
server 127.127.1.1
```

The **fudge** directive is used to specify the time for a hardware clock, passing time parameters for that clock's driver.

AppArmor security

Linux Mint installs AppArmor as its default security system. AppArmor (Application Armor) is designed as an alternative to SELinux (Security-Enhanced Linux, **https://www.nsa.gov/what-we-do/research/selinux/** and **http://selinuxproject.org/page/Main_Page**). It is much less complicated but makes use of the same kernel support provided for SELinux. AppArmor is a simple method for implementing mandatory access controls (MAC) for specified Linux applications. It is used primarily for servers like Samba, the CUPS print servers, and the time server. In this respect, it is much more limited in scope than SELinux, which tries to cover every object. Instead of labeling each object, which SELinux does, AppArmor identifies an object by its path name. The object does not have to be touched. Originally developed by Immunix and later supported for a time by Novell (OpenSUSE), AppArmor is available under the GNU Public License. You can find out more about AppArmor at **http://wiki.apparmor.net**.

AppArmor works by setting up a profile for supported applications. Essentially, this is a security policy similar to SELinux policies. A profile defines what an application can access and use on the system. Linux Mint will install the apparmor and apparmor-utils packages (main repository). Also available are the **apparmor-profiles** (Universe repository) and **apparmor-doc** packages.

AppArmor is still installed with the **/etc/init.d/apparmor** script. You can use the **service** or **systemctl** commands to start, stop, and restart AppArmor.

```
sudo service apparmor start
```

Currently, the generated systemd service file, **apparmor.service** (**/run/systemd/generator.late**), uses the **/etc/init.d/apparmor** script to manage Apparmor.

AppArmor utilities

The **apparmor-utils** packages installs several AppArmor tools, including **enforce**, which enables AppArmor and **complain**, which instructs AppArmor to just issue warning messages (see Table 13-13). The **unconfined** tool will list applications that have no AppArmor profiles. The **audit** tool will turn on AppArmor message logging for an application (uses enforce mode).

The **apparmor_status** tool will display current profile information. The **--complaining** options lists only those in complain mode, and **--enforced** for those in enforcing mode.

```
sudo apparmor_status
```

Utility	Description
apparmor_status	Status information about AppArmor policies
aa-audit *applications*	Enable logging for AppArmor messages for specified applications
aa-complain	Set AppArmor to complain mode
aa-enforce	Set AppArmor to enforce mode
aa-autodep *application*	Generate a basic profile for new applications
aa-logprof	Analyzes AppArmor complain messages for a profile and suggests profile modifications
aa-genprof *application*	Generate profile for an application
aa-unconfined	Lists applications not controlled by AppArmor (no profiles)

Table 13-13: AppArmor Utilities

The **aa-logprof** tool will analyze AppArmor logs to determine if any changes are needed in any of the application profiles. Suggested changes will be presented and the user can allow (**A**) or deny them (**D**). In complain mode, allow is the default, and in enforce mode, deny is the default. You can also make your own changes with the new (**N**) option. Should you want the change applied to all files and directories in a suggested path, you can select the glob option (**G**), essentially replacing the last directory or file in a path with the * global file matching symbol.

The **aa-autodep** tool will generate a basic AppArmor profile for a new or unconfined application. If you want a more effective profile, you can use **aa-genprof** to analyze the application's use and generate profile controls accordingly.

The **aa-genprof** tool will update or generate a detailed profile for a specified application. **aa-genprof** will first set the profile to complain mode. You then start up the application and use it, generating complain mode log messages on that use. Then, **vgenprof** prompts you to either scan the complain messages to further refine the profile (**S**), or to finish (**F**). When scanned, different violations are detected and the user is prompted to allow or deny recommended controls. You can then repeat the scan operation until you feel the profile is acceptable. Select finish (**F**) to finalize the profile and quit.

AppArmor configuration

AppArmor configuration is located in the **/etc/apparmor** directory. Configurations for different profiles are located in the **/etc/apparmor.d** directory. Loaded profile configuration files have the name of their path, using periods instead of slashes to separate directory names. The profile file for the **smbd** (Samba) application is **usr.sbin.smbd**. For CUPS (**cupsd**) it is **usr.sbin.cupsd**. For the time server, it is **user.sbin.ntpd**. Additional profiles like the Samba and Apache profiles are installed with the **apparmor-profiles** package (not installed by default).

```
sudo apt-get install apparmor-profiles
```

Configuration rules for AppArmor profiles consist of a path and permissions allowable on that path. A detailed explanation of AppArmor rules and permissions can be found in the **apparmor.d** Man page, including a profile example. A path ending in a * matching symbol will select all the files in that directory. The ** symbol selects all files and subdirectories. All file matching operations are supported (* || ?). Permissions include **r** (read), **w** (write), **x** (execute), and **l** (link). The **u** permission allows unconstrained access. The following entry allows all the files and subdirectories in the **/var/log/samba/cores/smdb** directory to be written to.

```
/var/log/samba/cores/smbd/** rw,
```

The **/etc/apparmor.d/abstractions** directory has files with profile rules that are common to different profiles. Rules from these files are read into actual profiles using the **include** directive. There are abstractions for applications like audio, samba, and video. Some abstractions will include yet other more general abstractions, like those for the X server (**X**) or GNOME (**gnome**). For example, the profile for the Samba smbd server, **usr.sbin.smbd**, will have an include directive for the **samba** abstraction. This abstraction holds rules common to both the **smbd** and **nmbd** servers, both used by the Samba service. The <> used in an **include** directive indicates the **/etc/apparmor.d** directory. A list of abstraction files can be found in the **apparmor.d** Man page. The **include** directive begins with a # character.

```
#include <abstractions/samba>
```

In some cases, a profile may need access to some files in a directory that it normally should not have access to. In this case, it may need to use a sub-profile to allow access. In effect, the application changes hats, taking on permissions it does not have in the original profile.

The **apparmor-profiles** package will activate several commonly used profiles, setting up profile files for them in the **/etc/apparmor.d** directory, like those for samba (**usr.sbin.nmbd** and **usr.sbin.smbd**), the Dovecot mail pop and imap server (**usr.sbin.dovecot**), and Avahi (**usr.sbin.avahi-daemon**).

The package also will provide profile default files for numerous applications in the **/usr/share/doc/apparmor-profiles/extras** directory, such as the vsftpd FTP server (**usr.sbin.vsftpd**), the ClamAV virus scanner (**usr.bin.freshclam**), and the Squid proxy server (**usr.sbin.squid**). Some service applications are located in the **/usr/lib** directory, and will have **usr.lib** prefix such as those for the Postfix server, which uses several profiles, beginning with **usr.lib.postfix**. To use these extra profiles, copy them to the **/etc/apparmor.d** directory. The following example copies the profile for the vsftpd FTP server.

```
sudo cp /usr/share/doc/apparmor-profiles/extras/usr.sbin.vsftpd /etc/apparmor.d
```

Remote Administration

For remote administration, you can use OpenSSH and Puppet. OpenSSH lets you remotely control and transfer files securely over your network. Puppet lets you manage remote configuration of services.

Puppet

Puppet allows you to configure remote systems automatically, even though they may be running different linux distributions with varying configuration files. Instead of configuring each system on a network manually, you can use Puppet to configure them automatically. Puppet abstracts administration tasks as resources in a resource abstraction layer (RAL). You then specify basic values or operations for a particular resource using a Puppet configuration language. Administration types include services, files, users, and groups. For example, you could use puppet to perform an update for a service (server) on systems using different package managers such as APT or Synaptic.

Puppet configuration can become very complex. Once set up, though, it fully automates configuration changes across all your networked systems. For detailed documentation and guides see the following.

```
https://docs.puppetlabs.com/
```

Puppet configuration is located in the **/etc/puppet** directory. Puppet operations on services are specified in modules programmed in the **init.pp** file located in a **manifests** directory. In the Ubuntu example for Apache (Ubuntu Server Guide, Puppet), the apache module is created in the **init.pp** file in:

```
/etc/puppet/modules/apache2/manifests/init.pp
```

Clients use the puppet client (**puppet** package) and the server uses the puppetmaster daemon (**puppetmaster** package). On puppet clients, use the **service** command to manually start and stop the **puppet** service. For the server, enable the **puppetmaster** service.

On the firewall add access for the Puppet port, 8140.

For the client, the puppet runtime configuration is set in the **/etc/default/puppet** file. Here you set the daemon to start by setting the **START** variable to yes

If your network is running a DNS server, you can set up a CNAME puppet entry for the puppet server. The puppet clients can then use the CNAME to locate the puppet server.

```
puppet    IN    CNAME    turtle.mytrek.com
```

You could also add a host entry for the puppet server in each client's **/etc/host** file.

On the server, the puppetmaster configuration in **/etc/default/puppetmaster** file lets you set port entries and the log service. Default entries are commented out. Remove the comment character, #, to enable.

When you first set up a client server puppet connection, the client and server have to sign the client's SSL certificate. First, run puppet on the client. On the server run the **puppet cert --list** command to see the clients certificate request. Then use **puppet cert --sign** to sign the certificate.

The Secure Shell: OpenSSH

Although a firewall can protect a network from attempts to break into it from the outside, the problem of securing legitimate communications to the network from outside sources still exists. A particular problem is one of the users who want to connect to your network remotely. Such connections could be monitored, and information such as passwords and user IDs used when the user logs in to your network could be copied and used later to break in. One solution is to use SSH for remote logins and other kinds of remote connections such as FTP transfers. SSH encrypts any communications between the remote user and a system on your network.

The SSH protocol has become an official Internet Engineering Task Force (IETF) standard. A free and open source version is developed and maintained by the OpenSSH project, currently supported by the OpenBSD project. OpenSSH is the version supplied with most Linux distributions, including Linux Mint. You can find out more about OpenSSH at **www.openssh.org**, where you can download the most recent version, though Linux Mint and Ubuntu will provide current versions from its repository. Traditionally there were two versions of SSH, the older SSH1 and its replacement SSH2. In the current release of OpenSSH, SSH1 is disabled by default. The OpenSSH server only supports SSH2. Should you need SSH1 tools for accessing an old SSH1 only server, you can install the **openssh-client-ssh1** package.

SSH secures connections by both authenticating users and encrypting their transmissions. The authentication process is handled with public key encryption. Once authenticated, transmissions are encrypted by a cipher agreed upon by the SSH server and client for use in a particular session. SSH supports multiple ciphers. Authentication is applied to both hosts and users. SSH first authenticates a particular host, verifying that it is a valid SSH host that can be securely communicated with. Then the user is authenticated, verifying that the user is who they say they are.

Encryption

The public key encryption used in SSH authentication makes use of two keys: a public key and a private key. The public key is used to encrypt data, while the private key decrypts it. Each host or user has its own public and private keys. The public key is distributed to other hosts, who can then use it to encrypt authenticated data that only the host's private key can decrypt. For example, when a host sends data to a user on another system, the host encrypts the authentication data with a public key, which it previously received from that user. The data can be decrypted only by the user's corresponding private key. The public key can safely be sent in the open from one host to another, allowing it to be installed safely on different hosts. You can think of the process as taking place between a client and a server. When the client sends data to the server, it first encrypts the data using the server's public key. The server can then decrypt the data using its own private key.

It is recommended that SSH transmissions be authenticated with public-private keys controlled by passphrases. Unlike PGP, SSH uses public-key encryption for the authentication process only. Once authenticated, participants agree on a common cipher to use to encrypt transmissions. Authentication will verify the identity of the participants. Each user who intends to use SSH to access a remote account first needs to create the public and private keys along with a passphrase to use for the authentication process. A user then sends their public key to the remote account they want to access and installs the public key on that account. When the user attempts to access the remote account, that account can then use the user's public key to authenticate that the user is who they claim to be. The process assumes that the remote account has set up its own SSH private and public key. For the user to access the remote account, they will have to know the remote account's SSH passphrase. SSH is often used in situations where a user has two or more accounts located on different systems and wants to be able to securely access them from each other. In that case, the user already has access to each account and can install SSH on each, giving each its own private and public keys along with their passphrases.

Authentication

For authentication in SSH, a user creates both public and private keys. For this, you use the **ssh-keygen** command. The user's public key then has to be distributed to those users that the original user wants access to. Often this is an account a user has on another host. A passphrase further protects access. The original user will need to know the other user's passphrase to access it.

When a remote user tries to log into an account, that account is checked to see if it has the remote user's public key. That public key is then used to encrypt a challenge (usually a random number) that can be decrypted only by the remote user's private key. When the remote user receives the encrypted challenge, that user decrypts the challenge with its private key. The remote user will first encrypt a session identifier using its private key, signing it. The encrypted session identifier is then decrypted by the account using the remote user's public key. The session identifier has been previously set up by SSH for that session.

SSH authentication is first carried out with the host, and then with users. Each host has its own host keys, public and private keys used for authentication. Once the host is authenticated, the user is queried. Each user has their own public and private keys. Users on an SSH server who want to receive connections from remote users will have to keep a list of those remote user's public keys. Similarly, an SSH host will maintain a list of public keys for other SSH hosts.

SSH Packages, Tools, and Server

SSH is implemented on Linux systems with OpenSSH. The full set of OpenSSH packages includes the OpenSSH meta-package (ssh), the OpenSSH server (openssh-server), and the OpenSSH client (openssh-clients). These packages also require OpenSSL (openssl), which installs the cryptographic libraries that SSH uses.

The SSH tools are listed in Table 13-7. They include several client programs such as **scp**, **ssh**, as well as the **ssh** server. The **ssh** server (**sshd**) provides secure connections to anyone from the outside using the **ssh** client to connect. Several configuration utilities are also included, such as **ssh-add**, which adds valid hosts to the authentication agent, and **ssh-keygen**, which generates the keys used for encryption.

You can start, stop, and restart the server manually with the **service** or **systemctl** commands.

```
sudo service sshd restart
```

Application	Description
ssh	SSH client
sshd	SSH server (daemon)
sftp	SSH FTP client, Secure File Transfer Program. Version 2 only. Use ? to list sftp commands(SFTP protocol)
sftp-server	SSH FTP server. Version 2 only (SFTP protocol)
scp	SSH copy command client
ssh-keygen	Utility for generating keys. -h for help
ssh-keyscan	Tool to automatically gather public host keys to generate ssh_known_hosts files
ssh-add	Adds RSD and DSA identities to the authentication agent
ssh-agent	SSH authentication agent that holds private keys for public key authentication (RSA, DSA)
ssh-askpass	X Window System utility for querying passwords, invoked by ssh-add (openssh-askpass)
ssh-askpass-gnome	GNOME utility for querying passwords, invoked by ssh-add
ssh-signer	Signs host-based authentication packets. Version 2 only. Must be suid root (performed by installation)
slogin	Remote login (version 1)

Table 13-14: SSH Tools

You have to configure your firewall to allow access to the **ssh** service. The service is set up to operate using the TCP protocol on port 22, tcp/22. If you are managing your IPTables firewall directly, you could manage access directly by adding the following IPtables rule. This accepts input on port 22 for TCP/IP protocol packages.

```
iptables -A INPUT -p tcp --dport 22 -j ACCEPT
```

SSH Setup

Using SSH involves creating your own public and private keys and then distributing your public key to other users you want to access. These can be different users or simply user accounts of your own that you have on remote systems. Often people remotely log in from a local client to an account on a remote server, perhaps from a home computer to a company computer. Your home computer would be your client account, and the account on your company computer would be your server account. On your client account, you need to generate your public and private keys and then place a copy of your public key in the server account. Once the account on your server has a copy of your client user's public key, you can access the server account from your client account. You will be also prompted for the server account's passphrase. You will have to know this to access that account. Figure 13-2 illustrates the SSH setup that allows a user **george** to access the account **cecelia**.

474 Part 4: Shared Resources

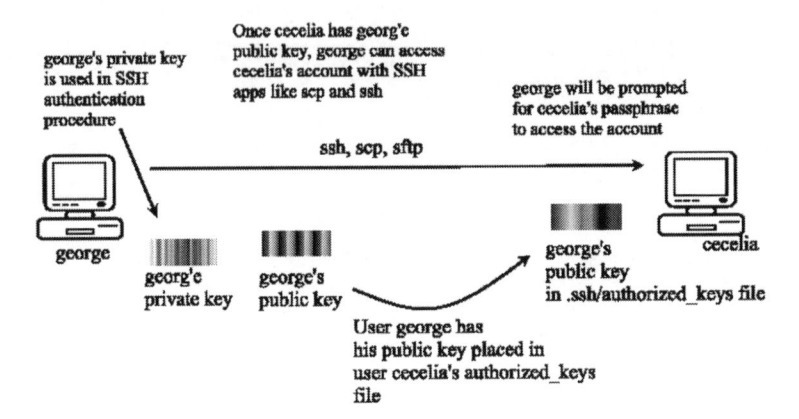

Figure 13-2: SSH setup and access

To allow you to use SSH to access other accounts:

You must create public and private keys on your account along with a passphrase. You will need to use this passphrase to access your account from another account.

You must distribute your public key to other accounts you want to access, placing them in the **.ssh/authorized_keys** file.

Other accounts also have to set up public and private keys along with a passphrase.

You must know the other account's passphrase to access it.

Creating SSH Keys with ssh-keygen

You create your public and private keys using the `ssh-keygen` command. You need to specify the kind of encryption you want to use. You can use either DSA or RSA encryption. Specify the type using the `-t` option and the encryption name in lowercase (**rsa**, **dsa**, **ecdsa**, and **ed25519**). In the following example, the user creates a key with the RSA encryption:

```
ssh-keygen -t rsa
```

The `ssh-keygen` command prompts you for a passphrase, which it will use as a kind of password to protect your private key. The passphrase should be several words long. You are also prompted to enter a filename for the keys. If you do not enter one, SSH will use its defaults. The public key will be given the extension **.pub**. The `ssh-keygen` command generates the public key and places it in your public key file, such as **.ssh/id_dsa.pub** or **.ssh/id_rsa.pub**, depending on the type of key you specified. It places the private key in the corresponding private key file, such as **.ssh/id_dsa** or **.ssh/id_rsa**.

File	Description
$HOME/.ssh/known_hosts	Records host keys for all hosts the user has logged into (that are not in /etc/ssh/ssh_known_hosts).
$HOME/.ssh/random_seed	Seeds the random number generator.
$HOME/.ssh/id_rsa	Contains the RSA authentication identity of the user.
$HOME/.ssh/id_dsa	Contains the DSA authentication identity of the user.
$HOME/.ssh/id_rsa.pub	Contains the RSA public key for authentication. The contents of this file should be added to $HOME/.ssh/authorized_keys on all machines where you want to log in using RSA authentication.
$HOME/.ssh/id_dsa.pub	Contains the DSA public key for authentication.
$HOME/.ssh/config	the per-user configuration file.
$HOME/.ssh/authorized_keys	Lists the RSA or DSA keys that can be used for logging in as this user.
/etc/ssh/ssh_known_hosts	Contains the system-wide list of known host keys.
/etc/ssh/ssh_config	Contains the system-wide configuration file. This file provides defaults for those values not specified in the user's configuration file.
/etc/ssh/sshd_config	Contains the SSH server configuration file.
/etc/ssh/sshrc	Contains the system default. Commands in this file are executed by ssh when the user logs in just before the user's shell (or command) is started.
$HOME/.ssh/rc	Contains commands executed by ssh when the user logs in just before the user's shell (or command) is started.

Table 13-15: SSH Configuration Files

If you need to change your passphrase, you can do so with the `ssh-keygen` command and the `-p` option. Each user will have their own SSH configuration directory, called **.ssh**, located in their own home directory. The public and private keys, as well as SSH configuration files, are placed here. If you build from the source code, the `make install` operation will automatically run `ssh-keygen`. Table 13-15 lists the SSH configuration files.

Authorized Keys

A public key is used to authenticate a user and its host. You use the public key on a remote system to allow that user access. The public key is placed in the remote user account's **.ssh/authorized_keys** file. Recall that the public key is held in the **.ssh/id_dsa.pub** file. If a user wants to log in remotely from a local account to an account on a remote system, they would first place their public key in the **.ssh/authorized_keys** file in the account on the remote system they want to access. If the user **larisa** on **turtle.mytrek.com** wants to access the **aleina** account on **rabbit.mytrek.com**, **larisa**'s public key from **/home/larisa/.ssh/id_dsa.pub** first must be placed in **aleina**'s **authorized_keys** file, **/home/aleina/.ssh/authorized_keys**. User **larisa** can send the key or have it copied over. A simple cat operation can append a key to the authorized key file. In the next example, the user adds the public key for **aleina** in the **larisa.pub** file to the authorized key file. The **larisa.pub** file is a copy of the **/home/larisa/.ssh/id_dsa.pub** file that the user received earlier.

```
cat larisa.pub >>  .ssh/authorized_keys
```

Note: You can also use seahorse to create and manage SSH keys.

Note: The .ssh/identity filename is used in SSH version 1; it may be installed by default on older distribution versions. SSH version 2 uses a different filename, .ssh/id_dsa or .ssh/id_rsa, depending on whether RSA or DSA authentication is used.

Loading Keys

If you regularly make connections to a variety of remote hosts, you can use the `ssh-agent` command to place private keys in memory where they can be accessed quickly to decrypt received transmissions. The `ssh-agent` command is intended for use at the beginning of a login session. For GNOME, you can use the openssh-askpass-gnome utility, invoked by `ssh-add`, which allows you to enter a password when you log in to GNOME. GNOME will automatically supply that password whenever you use an SSH client.

Although the `ssh-agent` command enables you to use private keys in memory, you also must specifically load your private keys into memory using the `ssh-add` command. `ssh-add` with no arguments loads your private key from your private key file, such as. **.ssh/id_rsa**. You are prompted for your passphrase for this private key. To remove the key from memory, use `ssh-add` with the `-d` option. If you have several private keys, you can load them all into memory. `ssh-add` with the `-1` option lists those currently loaded.

SSH Clients

SSH was originally designed to replace remote access operations, such as rlogin, rcp, and Telnet, which perform no encryption and introduce security risks. You can also use SSH to encode X server sessions as well as FTP transmissions (**sftp**). Corresponding SSH clients replace these applications. With **slogin** or **ssh**, you can log in from a remote host to execute commands and run applications, much as you can with rlogin and rsh. With **scp**, you can copy files between the remote host and a network host, just as with rcp. With **sftp**, you can transfer FTP files secured by encryption.

ssh

With **ssh,** you can remotely log in from a local client to a remote system on your network operating as the SSH server. The term local client here refers to one outside the network, such as your home computer, and the term remote refers to a host system on the network to which you are connecting. In effect, you connect from your local system to the remote network host. It is designed to replace rlogin, which performs remote logins, and rsh, which executes remote commands. With ssh, you can log in from a local site to a remote host on your network and then send commands to be executed on that host. The **ssh** command is also capable of supporting X Window System connections. This feature is automatically enabled if you make an ssh connection from an X Window System environment, such as GNOME or KDE. A connection is set up for you between the local X server and the remote X server. The remote host sets up a dummy X server and sends any X Window System data through it to your local system to be processed by your own local X server.

The ssh login operation function is much like the **rlogin** command. You enter the **ssh** command with the address of the remote host, followed by a **-l** option and the login name (username) of the remote account you are logging into. The following example logs into the **aleina** user account on the **rabbit.mytrek.com** host:

```
ssh rabbit.mytrek.com -l aleina
```

You can also use the username in an address format with **ssh**, as in

```
ssh aleian@rabbit.mytrek.com
```

The following listing shows how the user **george** accesses the **cecelia** account on **turtle.mytrek.com**:

```
[george@turtle george]$ ssh turtle.mytrek.com -l cecelia
cecelia@turtle.mytrek.com's password:
[cecelia@turtle cecelia]$
```

A variety of options are available to enable you to configure your connection. Most have corresponding configuration options that can be set in the configuration file. For example, with the **-c** option, you can designate which encryption method you want to use, for instance, **idea**, **des**, **blowfish**, or **arcfour**. With the **-i** option, you can select a particular private key to use. The **-c** option enables you to have transmissions compressed at specified levels (see the **ssh** Man page for a complete list of options).

scp

You use **scp** to copy files from one host to another on a network. Designed to replace rcp, **scp** uses **ssh** to transfer data and employs the same authentication and encryption methods. If authentication requires it, **scp** requests a password or passphrase. The **scp** program operates much like rcp. Directories and files on remote hosts are specified using the username and the host address before the filename or directory. The username specifies the remote user account that **scp** is accessing, and the host is the remote system where that account is located. You separate the user from the host address with an **@**, and you separate the host address from the file or directory name with a colon. The following example copies the file **party** from a user's current directory to the user **aleina**'s **birthday** directory, located on the **rabbit.mytrek.com** host:

```
scp party aleina@rabbit.mytrek.com:/birthday/party
```

Of particular interest is the **-r** option (recursive) option, which enables you to copy whole directories. See the **scp** Man page for a complete list of options. In the next example, the user copies the entire **reports** directory to the user **justin**'s **projects** directory:

```
scp -r reports justin@rabbit.mytrek.com:/projects
```

In the next example, the user **george** copies the **mydoc1** file from the user **cecelia**'s home directory:

```
[george@turtle george]$ scp cecelia@turtle.mytrek.com:mydoc1 .
cecelia@turtle.mytrek.com's password:
mydoc1      0% |                                  |    0  --:--
ETA
mydoc1    100% |*****************************|   17 00:00
[george@turtle george]$
```

sftp and sftp-server

With **sftp**, you can transfer FTP files secured by encryption. The **sftp** program uses the same commands as **ftp**. This client operates much like **ftp**, with many of the same commands.

```
sftp download.ubuntu.com
```

To use the **sftp** to connect to an FTP server, that server needs to be operating the **sftp-server** application. The SSH server invokes **sftp-server** to provide encrypted FTP transmissions to those using the **sftp** client. The sftp server and client use the SSH File Transfer Protocol (SFTP) to perform FTP operations securely.

Port Forwarding (Tunneling)

If for some reason, you can connect to a secure host only by going through an insecure host, SSH provides a feature called port forwarding. With port forwarding, you can secure the insecure segment of your connection. This involves simply specifying the port at which the insecure host is to connect to the secure one. This sets up a direct connection between the local host and the remote host, through the intermediary insecure host. Encrypted data is passed through directly. This process is referred to as tunneling, creating a secure tunnel of encrypted data through connected servers.

You can set up port forwarding to a port on the remote system or to one on your local system. To forward a port on the remote system to a port on your local system, use **ssh** with the **-R** option, followed by an argument holding the local port, the remote host address, and the remote port to be forwarded, each separated from the next by a colon. This works by allocating a socket to listen to the port on the remote side. Whenever a connection is made to this port, the connection is forwarded over the secure channel, and a connection is made to a remote port from the local machine. In the following example, port 22 on the local system is connected to port 23 on the **rabbit.mytrek.com** remote system:

```
ssh -R 22:rabbit.mytrek.com:23
```

To forward a port on your local system to a port on a remote system, use the **-L** option, followed by an argument holding the local port, the remote host address, and the remote port to be forwarded, each two arguments separated by a colon. A socket is allocated to listen to the port on the local side. Whenever a connection is made to this port, the connection is forwarded over the secure channel and a connection is made to the remote port on the remote machine. In the following example, port 22 on the local system is connected to port 23 on the **rabbit.mytrek.com** remote system:

```
ssh -L 22:rabbit.mytrek.com:23
```

You can use the LocalForward and RemoteForward options in your **.ssh/ssh_config** file to set up port forwarding for particular hosts or to specify a default for all hosts you connect to.

SSH Configuration

The SSH configuration file for each user is in their **.ssh/ssh_config** file. The **/etc/ssh/ssh_config** file is used to set site-wide defaults. In the configuration file, you can set various options, as listed in the **ssh_config** Man document. The configuration file is designed to specify options for different remote hosts to which you might connect. It is organized into segments, where each segment begins with the keyword **HOST**, followed by the IP address of the host. The following lines hold the options you have set for that host. A segment ends at the next **HOST** entry. Of particular interest are the **User** and **Ciphers** options. Use the **User** option to specify the names of users on the remote system who are allowed access. With the **Ciphers** option, you can select which encryption method to use for a particular host (the **Cipher** option is an SSH1 option, which is no longer supported) encryption for transmissions:

```
Host turtle.mytrek.com
    User larisa
    Compression no
    Ciphers aes128-ctr
```

Most standard options, including ciphers, are already listed as commented entries. Remove the # to activate.

```
#   Ciphers aes128-ctr,aes192-ctr,aes256-ctr,arcfour256,arcfour128,aes128-cbc,3des-cbc
```

To specify global options that apply to any host you connect to, create a `HOST` entry with the asterisk as its host, **HOST ***. This entry must be placed at the end of the configuration file because an option is changed only the first time it is set. Any subsequent entries for an option are ignored. Because a host matches on both its own entry and the global one, its specific entry should come before the global entry. The asterisk (*) and the question mark (?) are both wildcard matching operators that enable you to specify a group of hosts with the same suffix or prefix.

```
Host *
    PasswordAuthentication yes
    ConnectTimeout 0
    Ciphers aes128-ctr
```

The protocol option lets you specify what version of SSH to use, 1, 2, or both. By default, the Protocol option is set to 2, the SSH2 protocol.

```
Protocol 2
```

You use the **/etc/ssh/sshd_config** file to configure an SSH server. Here you will find server options like the port to use, password requirement, and PAM usage. For the server, only SSH2 is supported. The Protocol option is set to 2.

14. Print Services

Printer Services: CUPS

Printer Devices and Configuration

Configuring Printers on the Desktop (system-config-printer)

CUPS Configuration files

CUPS Command Line Print Clients

CUPS Command Line Administrative Tools

Print services have become an integrated part of every Linux system. They allow you to use any printer on your system or network. Once treated as devices attached to a system directly, printers are now treated as network resources managed by print servers. In the case of a single printer attached directly to a system, the networking features become transparent and the printer appears as just one more device. On the other hand, you could easily use a print server's networking capability to let several systems access the same printer. Although printer installation is almost automatic on most Linux distributions, it helps to understand the underlying process. Printing sites and resources are listed in Table 14-1.

CUPS

The Common Unix Printing System (CUPS) provides printing services, developed by Apple as an open source project, and is freely available under the GNU Public License. CUPS is the primary print server for most Linux distributions, including Linux Mint. The CUPS site at **https://cups.org** provides detailed documentation on installing and managing printers. CUPS is based on the Internet Printing Protocol (IPP), which was designed to establish a printing standard for the Internet (for more information, see **http://pwg.org/ipp**). Whereas the older line printer (LPD) based printing systems focused primarily on line printers, an IPP-based system provides networking, PostScript, and web support. CUPS works like an Internet server and employs a configuration setup much like that of the Apache web server. Its network support lets clients directly access printers on remote servers, without having to configure the printers themselves. Configuration needs to be maintained only on the print servers. GNOME provides integrated support for CUPS, allowing GNOME-based applications to directly access CUPS printers.

Resource	Description
https://cups.org	Common Unix Printing System
http://pwg.org/ipp	Internet Printing Protocol
http://lprng.sourceforge.net/	LPRng print server (Universe repository)

Table 14-1: Print Resources

Once you have installed your printers and configured your print server, you can print and manage your print queue using print clients. A variety of print configuration tools are available for the CUPS server such as system-config-printer, the CUPS configuration tool, and various line printing tools such as **lpq** and **lpc**, described in detail later in this chapter. Check the Ubuntu Server Guide | File Servers | CUPS - Print Server for basic configuration.

https://help.ubuntu.com/stable/serverguide/cups.html

CUPS is managed by systemd using an on demand socket implementation with **cups.service**, **cups.socket**, and **cups.path** files. In addition, a special **printer.target** unit detects when a printer is connected to your system. The **cups.service** file runs the CUPS server, **/usr/sbin/cupsd** (ExecStart). It is run when the **printer.target** is activated, which happens when a user connects a printer (WantedBy). The **cups.socket** unit file has CUPS listen for request at the CUPS socket, **/var/run/cups/cups.sock** (ListenStream). In effect, CUPS runs like the old inetd daemons, activated only when requested. The **cups.path** unit sets up CUPS print directories at **/var/spool/cups** (PathExistsGlob) when the system starts up (WantedBy=multi-user.target).

cups.service

```
[Unit]
Description=CUPS Scheduler
Documentation=man:cupsd(8)

[Service]
ExecStart=/usr/sbin/cupsd -l
Type=simple

[Install]
Also=cups.socket cups.path
WantedBy=printer.target
```

cups.socket

```
[Unit]
Description=CUPS Scheduler

[Socket]
ListenStream=/var/run/cups/cups.sock

[Install]
WantedBy=sockets.target
```

cups.path

```
[Unit]
Description=CUPS Scheduler

[Path]
PathExists=/var/cache/cups/org.cups.cupsd

[Install]
WantedBy=multi-user.target
```

cups-browsed.service

```
[Unit]
Description=Make remote CUPS printers available locally
After=cups.service avahi-daemon.service
Wants=cups.service avahi-daemon.service

[Service]
ExecStart=/usr/sbin/cups-browsed

[Install]
WantedBy=multi-user.target
```

484 Part 4: Shared Resources

Note: Line Printer, Next Generation (LPRng) was the traditional print server for Linux and UNIX systems, but it has since been dropped from many Linux distributions. You can find out more about LPRng at http://lprng.sourceforge.net/.

Printer Devices and Configuration

Before you can use any printer, you first have to install it on a Linux system on your network. A local printer is installed directly on your own system. This involves creating an entry for the printer in a printer configuration file that defines the kind of printer it is, along with other features such as the device file and spool directory it uses. On CUPS, the printer configuration file is **/etc/cups/printers.conf**. Installing a printer is fairly simple. You determine which device file to use for the printer and the configuration entries for it.

Tip: If you cannot find the drivers for your printer, you may be able to download them from OpenPrinting database at http://www.openprinting.org/drivers. The site maintains an extensive listing of drivers.

Printer Device Files

Linux dynamically creates the device names for printers that are installed. USB-connected printers will be treated as a removable device that can easily be attached to other connections and still be recognized. For older printers connected to a particular port, dedicated device files will be generated. As an example, for parallel printers, the device names will be **lp0**, **lp1**, **lp2**, and so on. The number used in these names corresponds to a parallel port on your PC; **lp0** references the LPT1 parallel port and **lp1** references the LPT2 parallel port. Serial printers will use serial ports, referenced by the device files like **ttyS0**, **ttyS1**, **ttyS2**, and so on.

Printer URI (Universal Resource Identifier)

Printers can be local or remote. Both are referenced using Universal Resource Identifiers (URI). URIs support both network protocols used to communicate with remote printers, and device connections used to reference local printers.

Remote printers are referenced by the protocol used to communicate with it, like **ipp** for the Internet Printing Protocol used for UNIX network printers, **smb** for the Samba protocol used for Windows network printers, and **lpd** for the older LPRng Unix servers. Their URIs are similar to a Web URL, indicating the network address of the system the printer is connected to.

```
ipp://mytsuff.com/printers/queue1
smb://guest@lizard/myhp
```

For attached local printers, especially older ones, the URI will use the device connection and the device name. The **usb:** prefix is used for USB printers, **parallel:** for older printers connected to a parallel port, **serial:** for printers connected to a serial port, and **scsi:** for SCSI connected printers.

In the CUPS **/etc/cups/printers.conf** file the DeviceURI entry will reference the URI for a printer. For USB printers, the URI uses **usb:**.

```
DeviceURI usb://Canon/S330
```

Spool Directories

When your system prints a file, it makes use of special directories called spool directories. A print job is a file to be printed. When you send a file to a printer, a copy of it is made and placed in a spool directory set up for that printer. The location of the spool directory is obtained from the printer's entry in its configuration file. On Linux, the spool directory is located at **/var/spool/cups** under a directory with the name of the printer. For example, the spool directory for the **myepson** printer would be located at **/var/spool/cups/myepson**. The spool directory contains several files for managing print jobs. Some files use the name of the printer as their extension. For example, the **myepson** printer has the files **control.myepson**, which provides printer queue control, and **active.myepson** for the active print job, as well as **log.myepson,** which is the log file.

CUPS start and restart: cups init script

You can start, stop, and restart CUPS using the **service** command and the **cups** script. When you make changes or install printers, be sure to restart CUPS to have your changes take effect. You can use the following command:

```
sudo service cups restart
```

The CUPS server is configured to start up when your system boots. The **/etc/default/cups** script holds startup options for the cups server, such as the LOAD_LP_MODULE option to load the parallel printer driver module.

Installing Printers

Several tools are available for installing CUPS printers. The easiest method is to use the **system-config-printer** tool on a desktop system. You can also use the CUPS Web browser-based configuration tools, included with the CUPS software (will work with **lynx** command line browser). Or you can just edit the CUPS printer configuration files directly.

Configuring Printers on the Desktop with system-config-printer (System Settings Printers)

Linux Mint attempts to detect and configure printers automatically. For removable printers, like a USB printer, the printer is detected and configured as soon as you connect your printer. It is configured by System Settings Printers (system-config-printer) and an icon for it appears in the System Settings Printers dialog. If the driver is not available, the printer is not configured and there is no printer icon for it. You will have to manually add and configure the printer.

system-config-printer

To change your configuration or to add a remote printer, you can use the printer configuration tool, system-config-printer, which is accessible from the System Settings dialog as Printers. This utility enables you to select the appropriate driver for your printer, as well as set print options such as paper size and print resolutions. You can configure a printer connected directly to your local computer, or a printer on a remote system on your network. You can start system-config-printer by choosing Printers in the Applications dash, System filter.

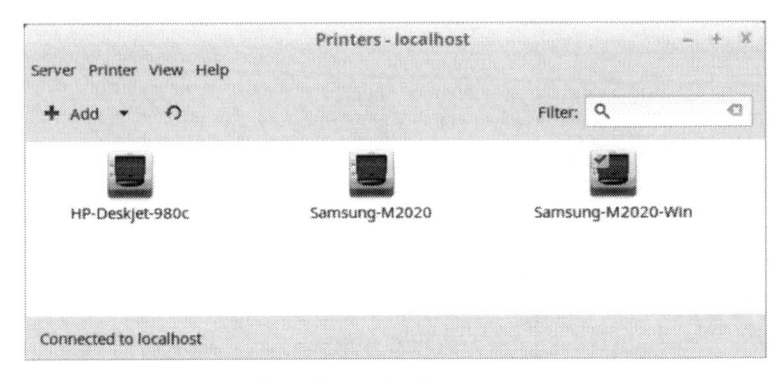

Figure 14-1: system-config-printer tool

The Printing configuration window displays icons for installed printers (see Figure 14-1). The menu bar has menus for Server configuration and selection, Printer features like its properties and the print queue, printer classes, and viewing discovered printers. A toolbar has buttons for adding new printers manually and refreshing print configuration. A Filter search box lets you display only printers matching a search pattern. Click on the x icon in the search box to clear the pattern. Clicking on the Looking glass icon in the File search box will display a pop-up menu that will let you search by Name, Description, Location, and Manufacturer/Model. You can save searches as a search group.

To see the printer settings such as printer and job options, access controls, and policies, double-click on the printer icon or right-click and select Properties. The Printer Properties window opens up with six tabs: Settings, Policies, Access Control, Printer Options, Job Options, and Ink/Toner Levels (see Figure 14-2).

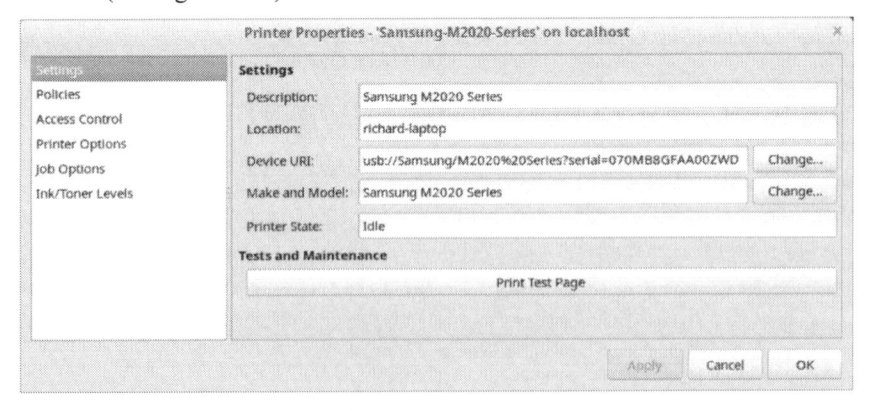

Figure 14-2: Printer properties window

The Printing configuration window's Printer menu lets you rename the printer, enable or disable it, and make it a shared printer. Select the printer icon and then click the Printer menu (see Figure 14-3). You can also display the Printer menu by right-clicking on a printer icon. The Delete entry will remove a printer configuration. Use the Set As Default entry to make the printer a system-wide or your personal default printer. The properties entry opens the printer properties window for that printer. You can also access the print queue for the selected printer. If the printer is already a default, the Set As Default entry is shaded out.

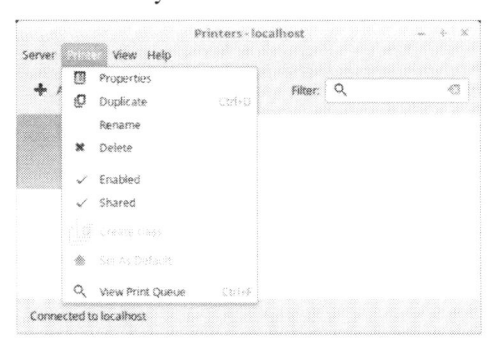

Figure 14-3: Printer configuration window Printer menu

When print jobs are waiting in the print queue, a printer icon will appear on the top panel. Clicking on this icon opens the Document Print Status window listing the pending print jobs. You can also open this window from the system-config-printer's Printer menu, View Print Queue item (Printer | View Print Queue). On the Document Print Status window, you can change a job's queue position as well as stop or delete a job (see Figure 14-4). From the job menu, you can cancel, hold (stop), release (restart), or reprint a print job. Reprint is only available if you have set the preserve jobs option in the printer settings Advanced dialog. You can also authenticate a job. From the View menu, you can choose to display just-printed jobs and refresh the queue.

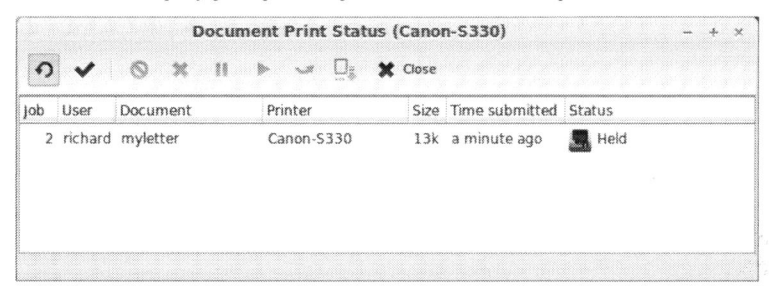

Figure 14-4: Printer queue

To check the server settings, select Settings from the Server menu. This opens a new window showing the CUPS printer server settings (see Figure 14-5). The Advanced expand button displays job history and browser server options. If you want to allow reprinting, then select the "Preserve job files (allow reprinting)" option.

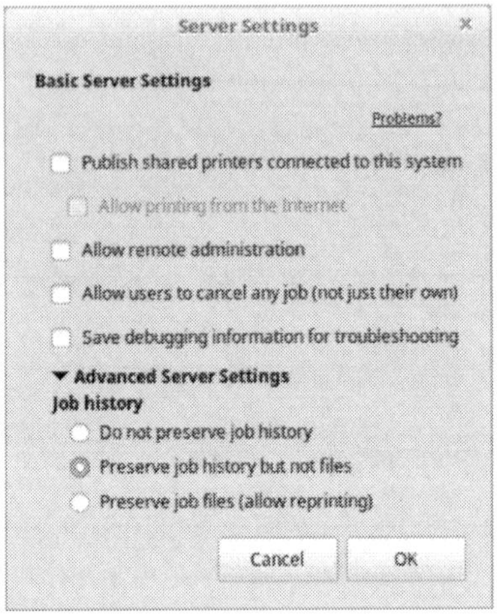

Figure 14-5: Server Settings

To select a particular CUPS server, select the Connect entry in the Server menu. This opens a "Connect to CUPS Server" window with a drop down menu listing all current CUPS servers from which to choose (see Figure 14-6).

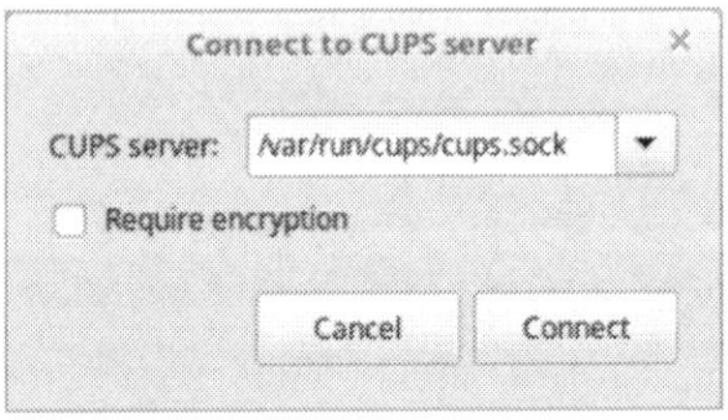

Figure 14-6: Selecting a CUPS server

Editing Printer Configuration

To edit an installed printer, double-click its icon in the Printer configuration window, or right-click and select the Properties entry. This opens a Printer Properties window for that printer. A sidebar lists configuration tabs. Click on one to display that tab. There are configuration tabs for Settings, Policies, Access Control, Printer Options, Job Options, and Ink/Toner Levels (see Figure 14-7).

Once you have made changes, you can click Apply to save your changes and restart the printer daemon. You can test your printer using the Tests and Maintenance tasks on the Settings tab. The Print Test Page prints a page, whereas the Print Self-Test Page also checks the printer hardware such as ink-jet heads.

On the Settings tab, you can change configuration settings like the driver and the printer name, and run test pages (see Figure 14-2). Should you need to change the selected driver, click on the Change button next to the Make and Model entry to open printer model and driver windows like those described in the "Add new printer manually" section. There you can specify the model and driver you want to use, even loading your own driver. Should you have to change the device URI (location and protocol), you can click the Change button to the right of the Device URI entry to open a "Change Device URI" dialog.

The Policies tab lets you enable and disable the printer, determine if it is to be shared, and whether to let it accept jobs or not (you also can enable or share the printer from the Printer menu). You can also specify an error policy, which specifies whether to retry or abort the print job, or stop the printer should an error occur. You can choose to print banners at the start or end indicating the level of security for a document, like confidential and secret.

The Access Control tab lets you deny access to certain users.

The Printer Options tab is where you set particular printing features like paper size and type, print quality, and the input tray to use (see Figure 14-7).

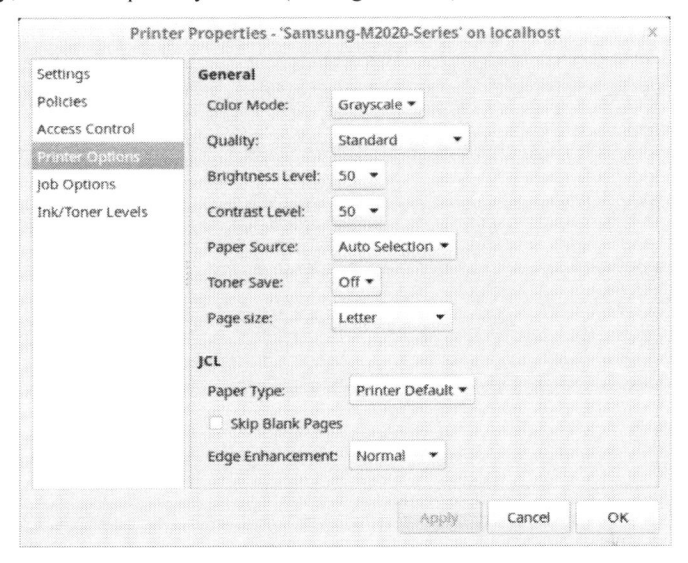

Figure 14-7: Printer Options

On the Job Options tab, you can select default printing features (see Figure 14-8) such as the number of copies, orientation, and single or double-sided printing. Options are arranged into three categories: Common Options, Image Options, and Text Options. Only the more common options are displayed. Each category has an expand button that will display all the options for that category. Double sided, output order, and media are all expanded options in the Common Options category.

The Ink/Toner Levels tab will display Ink or Toner levels for supported printers, along with status messages.

Figure 14-8: Jobs Options

Default System-wide and Personal Printers

To make a printer the default printer, either right-click on the printer icon and select "Set As Default", or single click on the printer icon and then from the Printer configuration window's Printer menu select the "Set As Default" entry (see Figure 14-3). A Set Default Printer dialog open with options for setting the system-wide default or setting the personal default (see Figure 14-9). The system-wide default printer is the default for the system served by your CUPS server.

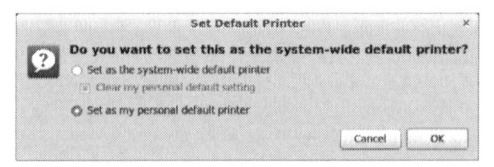

Figure 14-9: Set Default Printer

The system-wide default printer will have a green check mark emblem on its printer icon in the Printing configuration window.

Should you wish to use a different printer yourself (user-specific) as your default printer, you can designate it as your personal default. To make a printer your personal default, select the entry "Set as my personal default printer" in the Set Default Printer dialog. A personal emblem, a yellow star, will appear on the printer's icon in the Printer configuration window. In Figure 14-10, the Samsung M2020 printer is the system-wide default, whereas the HP-DeskJet printer is the personal default.

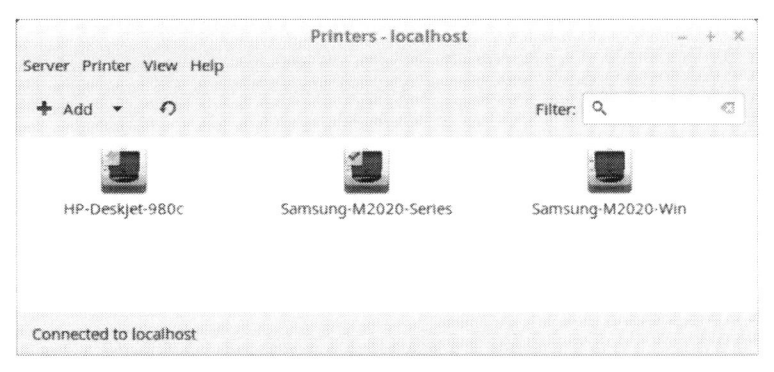

Figure 14-10: System-wide and personal default printers

Adding New Printers Manually

Printers are detected automatically, though, in the case of older printers and network printers, you may need to add the printer manually. In this case, click the Add button and select Printer. A New Printer window opens, displaying a series of dialog boxes where you select the connection, model, drivers, and printer name with location.

On the Select Device dialog, select the appropriate printer connection information. Connected local printer brands will already be listed by name, such as Canon, and a Connection list appears at the lower right of the dialog showing the connection. For remote printers you will specify the type of network connection, like "Windows printers via Samba" for printers connected to a Windows system, "AppSocket/HP Direct" for HP printers connected directly to your network, and the "Internet Printing Protocol (ipp)" for printers on Linux and Unix systems on your network. These connections are displayed under the Network Printer heading. Click the expansion arrow to display them.

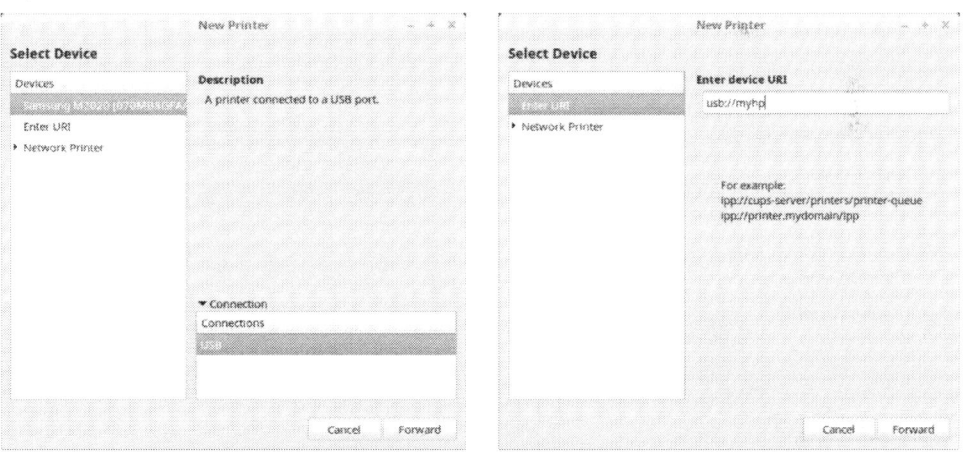

Figure 14-11: Selecting a new printer connection: connected and unconnected

For most connected printers, your connection is usually determined by udev, which now manages all devices. A USB printer will simply be described as a USB printer, using the usb URI

492 Part 4: Shared Resources

designation (see Figure 14-11). For an older local printer, you may have to choose the port the printer is connected to, such as LPT1 for the first parallel port used for older parallel printers, or Serial Port #1 for a printer connected to the first serial port. To add a USB printer manually, you would select the "Enter URI" Entry and enter the URI consisting of the prefix **usb://** and the name you want to give to the printer, like **usb://myhp**.

A search is conducted for the appropriate driver, including downloadable drivers. If the driver is found, the Choose Driver screen is displayed with the appropriate driver manufacturer already selected for you. You need only click the forward button. On the next screen, also labeled Choose Driver, the printer model and driver files are listed and the appropriate one is already selected for you. Just click the Forward button. The Describe Printer screen is then displayed where you can enter the Printer Name, Description, and Location. These are ways you can personally identify a printer. Then click Apply.

If the printer driver is not detected or is detected incorrectly, on the Choose Driver screen you have the options to choose the driver from the printer database, from a PPD driver file, or from a search of the OpenPrinting online repository. The selection display will change according to which option you choose.

Note: Some drivers are installed directly from the printer's company website, such as some of the Samsung drivers. These you may have to install directly, using a shell script run in a terminal window. Once installed, the printer is automatically detected and configured when you connect it. The drivers will also appear on the system-config-printer's Choose Driver local database listing dialog.

The database option lists possible manufacturers. Use your mouse to select the one you want (see Figure 3-12). The search option displays a search box for make and model. Enter both the make (printer manufacturer) and part of the model name (See figure 3-13). The search results will be available in the Printer model drop down menu. Select the one you want. Then click Forward.

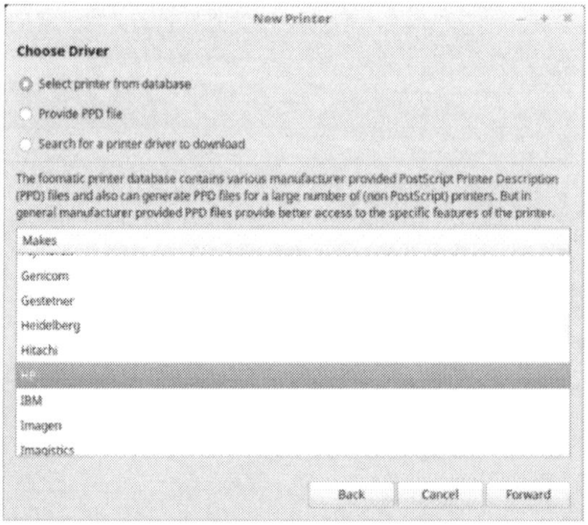

Figure 14-12: Printer manufacturer for new printers

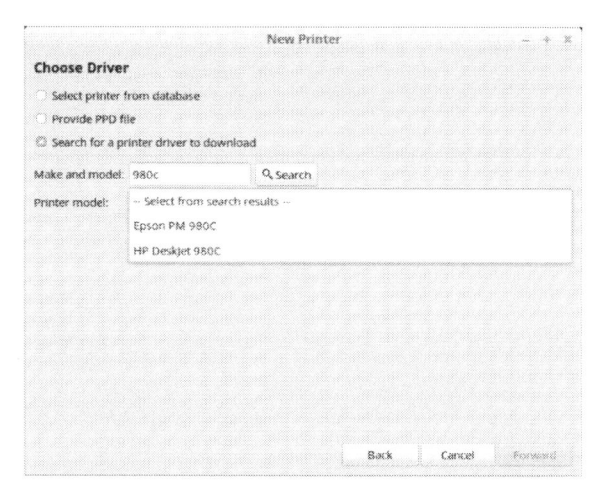

Figure 14-13: Searching for a printer driver from the OpenPrinting repository

The PPD file option displays a file location button that opens a Select file dialog you can use to locate the PPD file on your system.

If you are selecting a printer from the database, on the next screen you select that manufacturer's model along with its driver (see Figure 14-14). For some older printer, though the driver can be located on the online repository, you will still choose it from the local database (the drivers are the same). The selected drivers for your printer will be listed. If there are added options for your printer, the Installable Options screen lists them allowing you to check the ones you want.

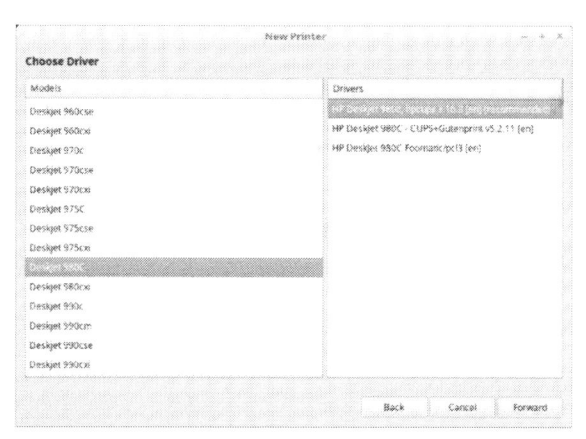

Figure 14-14: Printer Model and driver for new printers using local database

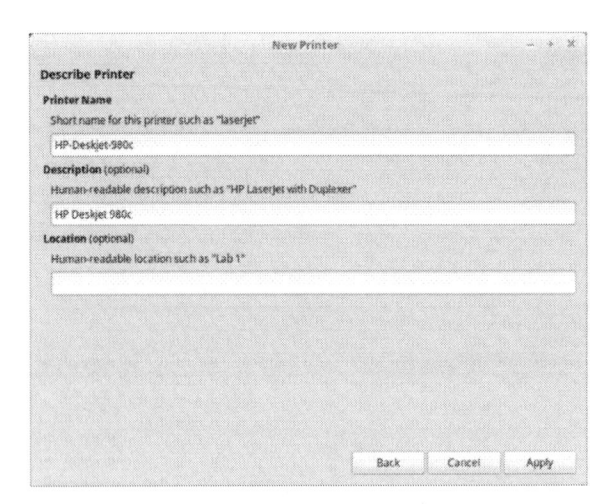

Figure 14-15: Printer Name and Location for new printers

You can then enter your printer name and location (see Figure 14-15). These will be entered for you using the printer model and your system's hostname. You can change the printer name to anything you want. When ready, click Apply. You will be prompted to print a test page. An icon for your printer will be displayed in the Printing configuration window. You are now ready to print.

CUPS Web Browser-based configuration tool

The CUPS configuration Web interface is a web-based tool that can also manage printers and print jobs. A Web page is displayed with tabs for managing jobs and printers and performing administrative tasks. You can access the CUPS configuration tool using the **localhost** address and specifying port **631**. Enter the following URL into your Web browser:

```
http://localhost:631
```

You can also use this CUPS configuration interface with a command line Web browser like **elinks** (install **elinks** first). This allows you to configure a printer from the command line interface. Use the ENTER key to display menus and make selections, and arrow keys to navigate.

```
elinks localhost:631
```

Entering the **localhost:631** URL in your Web browser opens the Home screen for the CUPS Web interface. There are tabs for various sections, as well as links for specialized tasks like adding printers or obtaining help (see Figure 14-16). Tabs include Administration, Classes, Help, Jobs, and Printers. You can manage and add printers on the Administration tab. The Printers tab will list installed printers with buttons for accessing their print queues, printer options, and job options, among others. The Jobs tab lists your print jobs and lets you manage them.

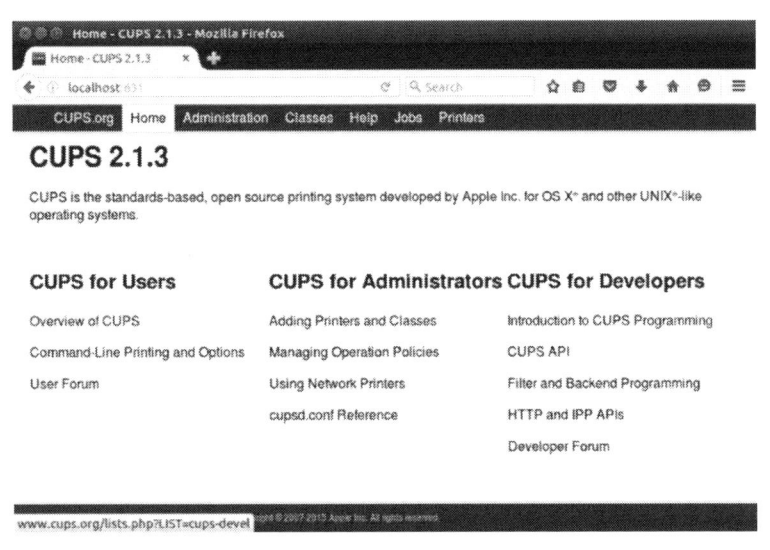

Figure 14-16: CUPS Web-based Configuration Tool: Home tab

When you try to make any changes for the first time during the session, you will first be asked to enter the administrator's username (your username) and password (your user password), just as you would for the **sudo** command.

The Administration tab displays segments for Printers, Classes, Jobs, and the Server (see Figure 14-17). The server section is where you allow printer sharing. Buttons allow you to view logs and change settings.

Figure 14-17: CUPS Web-based Configuration Tool: Administration tab

With the CUPS configuration tool, you install a printer on CUPS through a series of Web pages, each of which requests different information. To install a printer, click the Add Printer button either on the Home page or the Administration page. You must first specify the protocol. On the next screen, you enter a URI to use for the printer. For a local printer, this is the protocol and the hostname. A page is displayed where you enter the printer name and location (see Figure 14-18). A Sharing entry lets you choose to share the printer. The location is the host to which the printer is connected. The procedure is similar to **system-config-printer**. Subsequent pages will prompt you to enter the make and model of the printer, which you select from available listings. You can also load a PPD driver file instead if you have one. Click the Add Printer button when read. On the following page, you then set default options for your printer, like paper size and type, color, print quality, and resolution.

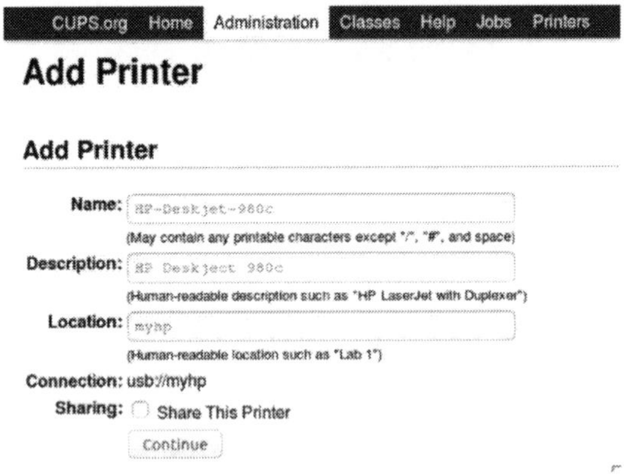

Figure 14-18: Adding a new printer: CUP Web Interface

To manage a printer, click the Printers tab or the Manage Printers button in the Administration page. The Printers page will list your installed printers (see Figure 14-19). Clicking a printer link opens a page for managing your jobs and performing administrative tasks (see Figure 14-20). From the Maintenance drop down menu lets you perform printer and job tasks like pausing the printer, printing a test page, and canceling all jobs. The Administration menu lets you modify the printer, delete it, and set default options. Choosing the Administration menu's Set Default Options entry displays a page can configure how your printer prints (see Figure 14-21). Links at the top of the page display pages for setting certain options like general options, output control, banners, and extra features such as printer direction, ink type, color density, and drop size. The general options are listed first, where you can set basic features like the resolution and paper size.

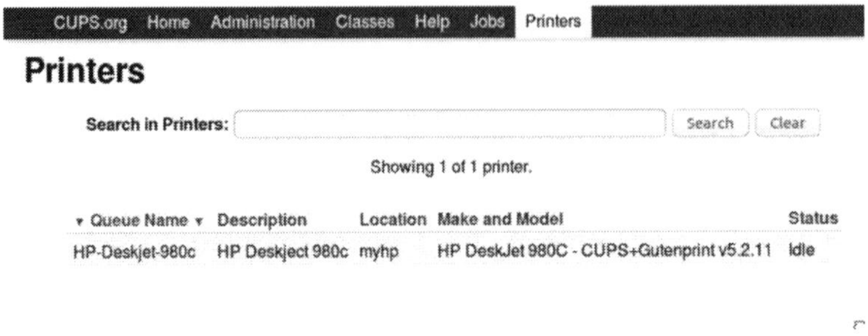

Figure 14-19: CUPS Web-based Configuration Tool: Printers tab

Figure 14-20: CUPS Web-based Configuration Tool: Managing Printers

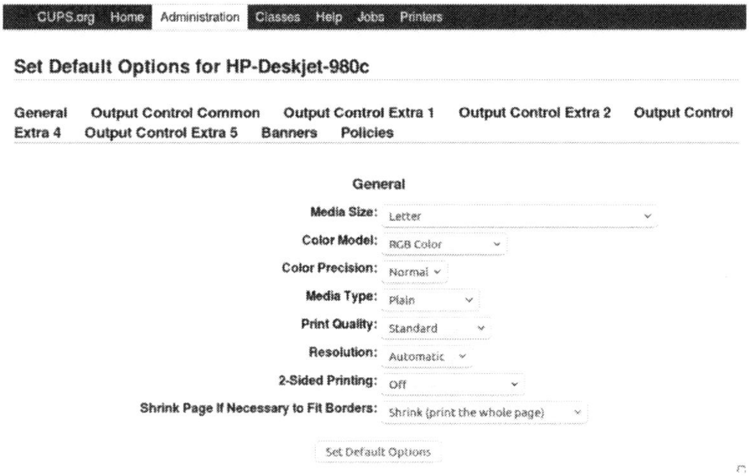

Figure 14-21: CUPS Web-based Configuration Tool: Printer Options

Note: You can perform all administrative tasks from the command line using the lpadmin command. See the CUPS documentation for more details.

Configuring Remote Printers on CUPS

To install a remote printer that is attached to a Windows system or another Linux system running CUPS, you specify its location by using special URL protocols. For another CUPS printer on a remote host, the protocol used is **ipp**, for Internet Printing Protocol, whereas for a Windows printer, it would be **smb**. Older UNIX or Linux systems using LPRng would use the **lpd** protocol.

To use the CUPS configuration tool to install a remote printer, specify the remote printer network protocol on the initial Add Printer page. You can choose from Windows, Internet Printing Protocol (other UNIX or Linux systems), Apple and HP JetDirect connected printers, and the older

LPD line printers (see Figure 14-22). If a network printer is connected currently, it may be listed in the Discovered Network Printers list.

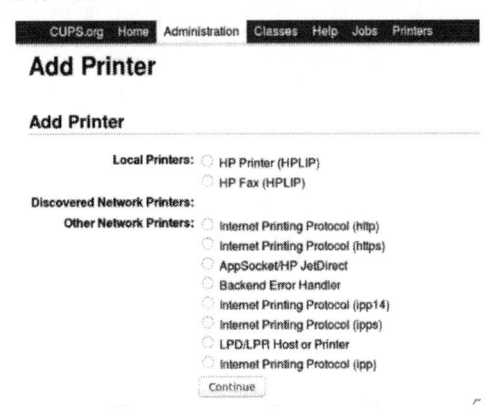

Figure 14-22: CUPS Web-based Configuration Tool: Network Printers

Configuring Remote Printers on the Desktop with system-config-printer

You can use system-config-printer to set up a remote printer on Linux, UNIX, or Windows networks. When you add a new printer or edit one, the New Printer dialog will list possible remote connection types under the Network entry. When you select a remote connection entry, a pane will be displayed to the right where you can enter configuration information.

To find any connected printers on your network automatically, click the Find Network Printer entry. Enter the hostname of the system the remote printer is connected to, then click the Find button. The host is searched and the detected printers are displayed as entries under the Network Printer heading (see Figure 14-23).

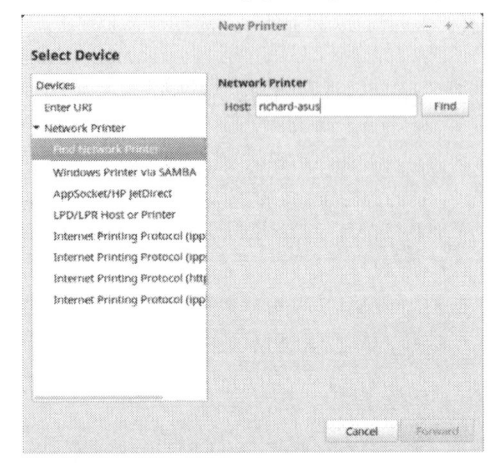

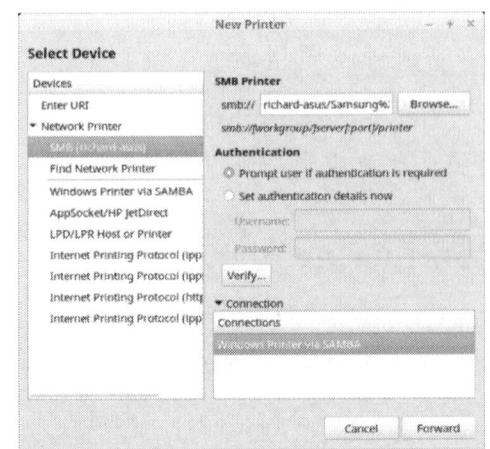

Figure 14-23: Finding a network printer

To configure a specific type of printer, choose from the available entries. For a remote Linux or UNIX printer, select either Internet Printing Protocol (ipp), which is used for newer systems, or LPD/LPR Host or Printer, which is used for older systems. Both panes display entries for the Host name and the queue. For the Host name, enter the hostname of the system that controls the printer. For an Apple or HP jet direct printer on your network, select the AppSocket/HP jetDirect entry.

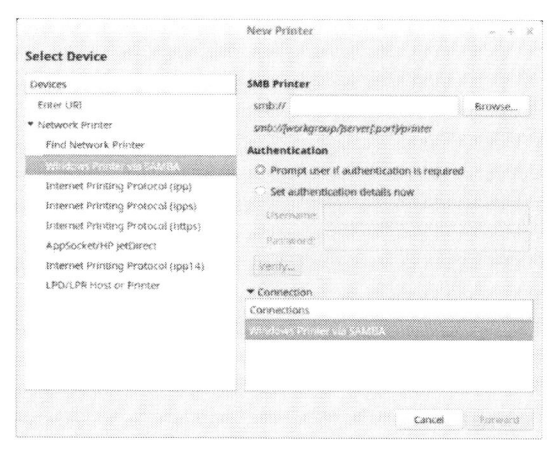

Figure 14-24: Selecting a Windows printer

A "Windows printer via Samba" printer is one located on a Windows network (see Figure 14-24). You need to specify the Windows server (hostname or IP address), the name of the share, the name of the printer's workgroup, and the username and password. The format of the printer SMB URL is shown on the SMP Printer pane. The share is the hostname and printer name in the **smb** URI format *//workgroup/hostname/printername*. The workgroup is the windows network workgroup that the printer belongs to. On small networks, there is usually only one. The hostname is the computer where the printer is located. The username and password can be for the printer resource itself, or for access by a particular user. The pane will display a box at the top where you can enter the share host and printer name as an **smb** URI.

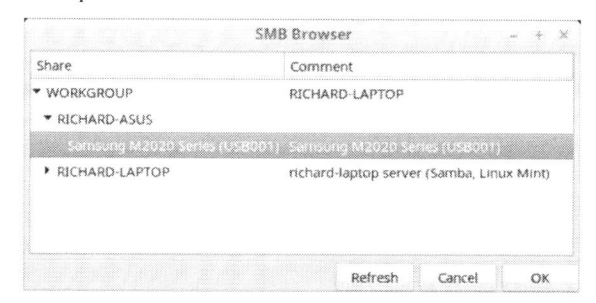

Figure 14-25: SMB Browser, selecting a remote windows printer

Instead of manually entering the URI for a printer, you can use the Browse button to choose from a list of detected Windows printers on your network. Click the Browse button to open an SMB Browser window, where you can select the printer from a listing of Windows hosts (see

Figure 14-25). For example, if your Windows network is WORKGROUP, then the entry WORKGROUP will be shown, which you can then expand to list all the Windows hosts on that network (if your network is MSHOME, then that is what will be listed). If you are using a firewall, be sure to turn it off before browsing a Windows workgroup for a printer, unless the firewall is already configured to allow Samba access.

When you make your selection, the corresponding URI will show up in the **smb://** box (See Figure 14-26). You also can enter in any needed Samba authentication, if required, like username or password. Check "Authentication required" to allow you to enter the Samba Username and Password. The Connections section to the lower right will list "Windows Printer via Samba" as the connection.

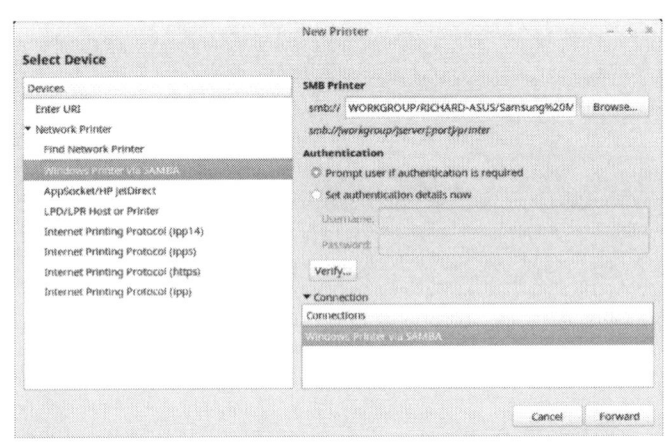

Figure 14-26: Remote Windows printer connection configuration

You then continue with install screens for the printer model, driver, and name. Once installed, you can then access the printer properties just as you would any printer (see Figure 14-27).

Figure 14-27: Remote Windows printer Settings

To access an SMB shared remote printer, you need to install Samba and have the Server Message Block services enabled using the **smbd** and **nmbd** daemons. The Samba service will be enabled by default. You can use the **service** command to restart, stop, and start the services. Printer sharing must be enabled on the Windows network.

```
sudo service smbd restart
sudo service nmbd restart
```

Configuring remote printers manually

In the **printers.conf** file, for a remote printer, instead of listing the device, the DeviceURI entry, will have an Internet address, along with its protocol. For example, a remote printer on a CUPS server (**ipp**) would be indicated as shown here (a Windows printer would use the **smb** protocol):

```
DeviceURI ipp://mytsuff.com/printers/queue1
```

For a Windows printer, you first need to install, configure, and run Samba (CUPS uses Samba to access Windows printers). When you install the Windows printer on CUPS, you specify its location using the URL protocol **smb**. The username of the user allowed to log in to the printer is entered before the hostname and separated from the hostname by an @ sign. On most configurations, this is the **guest** user. The location entry for a Windows printer called **myhp** attached to a Windows host named **lizard** is shown next. It's Samba share reference would be **//lizard/myhp**:

```
DeviceURI smb://guest@lizard/myhp
```

To enable CUPS on Samba, you also have to set the printing option in the **/etc/samba/smb.conf** file to **cups**, as shown here:

```
printing = cups
printcap name = cups
```

CUPS Printer Classes

CUPS lets you select a group of printers to print a job, instead of selecting just one. If one printer is busy or down, another printer can be selected automatically to print the job. Such groupings of printers are called *classes*. Once you have installed your printers, you can group them into different classes. For example, you may want to group all inkjet printers into one class and laser printers to another, or you may want to group printers connected to one specific printer server in their own class.

On system-config-printer, you can set up classes for printers. The Class entry in the Server | New menu lets you create a printer class. You can access the New menu from the Server menu or from the Add button. This feature lets you select a group of printers to print a job, instead of selecting just one. That way, if one printer is busy or down, another printer can be selected automatically to perform the job. Installed printers can be assigned to different classes. When you click the Class entry in the New menu, a New Class window opens. Here you can enter the name for the class, any comments, and the location (your hostname is entered by default). The next screen lists available printers on the right side (Other printers) and the printers you assigned to the class on the left side (Printers in this class). Use the arrow button to add or remove printers to the class. Click Apply when finished. Tabs for a selected class are much the same as for a printer, with a Members tab instead of a Printer Options tab. In the Members tab, you can change which printers belong to the class. You can also select a printer or set of printers and choose "Create class" from the Printer menu, automatically adding them to the new class.

You can also create classes on the CUPS Web Configuration tool. Select the Administration tab, and click the Add Class button. On the Add Class page, you enter the name of the class, its location and then select the printers to add to the class from the Members list. The class will then show up on the Classes tab, showing its members and status.

CUPS Configuration files

CUPS configuration files are placed in the **/etc/cups** directory. These files are listed in Table 14-2. The **classes.conf** and **printers.conf** files can be managed by the web interface. The **printers.conf** file contains the configuration information for the different printers you have installed. Any of these files can be edited manually if you want. Some applications will have their own configuration files like **acroread.conf** for the Adobe Reader.

Filename	Description
classes.conf	Contains configurations for different local printer classes
client.conf	Lists specific options for specified clients
cupsd.conf	Configures the CUPS server, cupsd
printers.conf	Contains printer configurations for available local printers
cups-files.conf	File and directories used by CUPS
cups-browsed.conf	Access to remote and local printers
subscriptions.conf	Subscription controls for printer and print job information
Filename	Description

Table 14-2: CUPS Configuration Files

cupsd.conf

The CUPS server is configured with the **cupsd.conf** file located in **/etc/cups**. You must edit configuration options manually; the server is not configured with the web interface. Your installation of CUPS installs a commented version of the **cupsd.conf** file with each option listed, though most options will be commented out. Commented lines are preceded with a # symbol. Each option is documented in detail. The server configuration uses an Apache web server syntax consisting of a set of directives. As with Apache, several of these directives can group other directives into blocks.

For a detailed explanation of **cupsd.conf** directives check the CUPS documentation for **cupsd.conf**. You can also reference this documentation from the Online Help page | References link on the CUPS browser-based administration tool, **http://localhost:631**.

```
https://www.cups.org/doc/man-cupsd.conf.html
```

The **cupsd.conf** file begins with log settings.

```
LogLevel warn
```

On Linux Mint, CUPS logging is disabled.

```
MaxLogSize 0
```

The Listen directives set the machine and socket on which to receive connections. These are set by default to the local machine, localhost port 631. If you are using a dedicated network interface for connecting to a local network, you would add the network card's IP address, allowing access from machines on your network.

```
# Only listen for connections from the local machine.
Listen localhost:631
Listen /var/run/cups/cups.sock
```

Browsing directives allow your local printers to be detected on your network, enabling them to be shared. For shared printing, the Browsing directive is set to on (it is set to Off by default). A BrowseOrder of allow, deny will deny all browse transmissions, then first check the BrowseAllow directives for exceptions. A reverse order (deny, allow) does the opposite, accepting all browse transmissions, and first checks for those denied by BrowseDeny directives. The default **cupsd.conf** file has a BrowseOrder allow, deny directive followed by a BrowseAllow directive, which is set to **all**. To limit this to a particular network, use the IP address of the network instead of **all**. The BrowseLocalProtocols lists the network protocols to use for advertising the printers on a local network. The BrowseAddress directive will make your local printers available as shared printers on the specified network. It is set to **@LOCAL** to allow access on your local network. You can add other BrowseAddress directives to allow access by other networks.

```
# Show shared printers on the local network.
Browsing On
BrowseOrder allow,deny
BrowseAllow all
BrowseLocalProtocols CUPS dnssd
BrowseAddress @LOCAL
```

CUPS supports both Basic and Digest forms of authentication, specified in the **AuthType** directive. Basic authentication requires a user and password. For example, to use the web interface, you are prompted to enter the root user and the root user password. Digest authentication makes use of user and password information kept in the CUPS **/etc/cups/passwd.md5** file, using MD5 versions of a user and password for authentication. In addition, CUPS also supports a BasicDigest and Negotiate authentication. BasicDigest will use the CUPS md5 password file for basic authentication. Negotiate will use Kerberos authentication. The default authentication type is set, using the DefaultAuthType directive, set to Basic.

```
# Default authentication type, when authentication is required...
DefaultAuthType Basic
```

The Web interface setting is set to yes.

```
WebInterface Yes
```

Location Directives

Certain directives allow you to place access controls on specific locations. These can be printers or resources, such as the administrative tool or the spool directories. Location controls are implemented with the **Location** directive. There are several Location directives that control access.

The first controls access to the server root directory, /. The Order allow, deny entry activates restrictions on access by remote systems. If there are no following Allow or Deny entries then the default is to deny all. There is an implied Allow localhost with the "Order allow, deny" directive, always giving access to the local machine. In effect, access here is denied to all systems, allowing access only by the local system.

```
# Restrict access to the server...
<Location />
  Order allow,deny
</Location>
```

Another **Location** directive is used to restrict administrative access, the **/admin** resource. The **Order allow,deny** directive denies access to all systems, except for the local machine.

```
# Restrict access to the admin pages...
<Location /admin>
  Order allow,deny
</Location>
```

Allow from and **Deny from** directives can permit or deny access from specific hosts and networks. If you wanted to just allow access to a particular machine, you would use an **Allow from** directive with the machine's IP address. CUPS also uses **@LOCAL** to indicate your local network, and **IF(**name**)** for a particular network interface (name is the device name of the interface) used to access a network. Should you want to allow administrative access by all other systems on your local network, you can add the **Allow from @LOCAL**. If you add an **Allow** directive, you also have to explicitly add the **Allow localhost** to ensure access by your local machine.

```
# Restrict access to the admin pages...
<Location /admin>
  Allow from localhost
  Allow from @LOCAL
  Order allow,deny
</Location>
```

The following entry would allow access from a particular machine.

```
Allow From 192.168.0.5
```

The next location directive restricts access to the CUPS configuration files, **/admin/conf**. The **AuthType default** directive refers to the default set by DefaultAuthType. The **Require user** directive references the **SystemGroup** directive, **@SYSTEM** (defined in the **cups-files.conf** file). Only users from that group are allowed access.

```
# Restrict access to configuration files...
<Location /admin/conf>
  AuthType Default
  Require user @SYSTEM
  Order allow,deny
</Location>
```

Default Operation Policy: Limit Directives

A default operation policy is then defined for access to basic administration, printer, print job, and owner operations. The default operation policy section begins with the **<Policy default>** directive. Limit directives are used to implement the directives for each kind of operation. Job operations covers tasks like sending a document, restarting a job, suspending a job, and restarting a job. Administrative tasks include modifying a printer configuration, deleting a printer, managing printer classes, and setting the default printer. Printer operations govern tasks like pausing a printer, enabling or disabling a printer, and shutting down a printer. The owner operations consist of just canceling a job and authenticating access to a job.

See the CUPS documentation on managing operations policies for more details.

```
https://www.cups.org/doc/policies.html
```

On all the default **Limit** directives, access is allowed only by the local machine (localhost), **Order allow,deny**.

The policy section begins with access controls for user and job information. The default for **JobPrivateAccess** limits access to owner, system, and access control lists. **JobPrivateValues** specifies values made private, such as the job name, originating host, and originating user. **SubscriptionPrivateAccess** and **SubscriptionPrivateValues** specify access for subscription attributes such notifications of printer events like job completed or job stopped.

Limit directives are set up to create and print jobs.

```
<Limit Create-Job Print-Job Print-URI Validate-Job>
  Order deny,allow
</Limit>
```

Both the administrative and printer **Limit** directives are set to the **AuthType default** and limited to access by administrative users, **Require user @SYSTEM**. The administrative directive is shown here.

```
# All administration operations require an administrator to authenticate...
<Limit CUPS-Add-Modify-Printer CUPS-Delete-Printer CUPS-Add-Modify-Class CUPS-Delete-Class CUPS-Set-Default CUPS-Get-Devices>
  AuthType Default
  Require user @SYSTEM
  Order deny,allow
</Limit>
```

Both the job related and owner Limit directives require either owner or administrative authentication, **Require user @OWNER @SYSTEM**. The **Owner Limit** directive is shown here.

```
# Only the owner or an administrator can cancel or authenticate a job...
<Limit Cancel-Job CUPS-Authenticate-Job>
  Require user @OWNER @SYSTEM
  Order deny,allow
</Limit>
```

For all other tasks, **<Limit All>**, access is restricted to the local machine (localhost).

```
<Limit All>
 Order deny,allow
</Limit>
```

The **AuthClass** directive can be used within a **Limit** directive to specify the printer class allowed access. The **System** class includes the root, sys, and system users.

An authenticated set of policy directives follows the default policy, with similar entries and an added **AuthType** entry in the Limit directive to create and print jobs.

```
<Limit Create-Job Print-Job Print-URI Validate-Job>
  AuthType Default
  Order deny,allow
</Limit>
```

cupsctl

You can use the **cupsctl** command to modify your **cupsd.conf** file, rather than editing the file directly. Check the **cupsctl** Man page for details. The **cupsctl** command with no options will display current settings.

```
cupsctl
```

The changes you can make with this command are limited turning off remote administration or disabling shared printing. The major options you can set are:

remote-admin   Enable or disable remote administration

remote-any   Enable or disable remote printing

remote-printers   Enable or disable the display of remote printers

share-printers   Enable or disable sharing of local printers with other systems

printers.conf

Configured information for a printer will be stored in the **/etc/cups/printers.conf** file. You can examine this file directly, even making changes. Here is an example of a printer configuration entry. The **DeviceURI** entry specifies the device used, in this case, a USB printer. It is currently idle, with no jobs:

```
# Printer configuration file for CUPS
# Written by cupsd
<Printer mycannon>
Info Cannon s330
Location richard-server
MakeModel Canon S330
DeviceURI usb://Canon/S330
State Idle
StateTime 1166554036
Accepting Yes
Shared Yes
ColorManaged Yes
JobSheets none none
QuotaPeriod 0
PageLimit 0
KLimit 0
OpPolicy default
ErrorPolicy retry-job
</Printer>
```

subscriptions.conf

Configured information for printer and job information is located in the /etc/cups/subscriptions.conf file. Those receiving the information are specified by the **SubscriptionPrivateAccess** and **SubscriptionPrivateValues** directives in the policy section of the **cupd.conf** file. The **Events** directive specifies notifications of events to be sent, events such as job-completed, printer-stopped, and server-started. The **Owner** directive lists the users for this subscription. **LeaseDuration** is the time the subscription remains valid (0 value is the life of the print job or forever). **Interval** is the time between notifications. **Recipient** is the recipient URI for the notification. In the following example it is dbus:// (your desktop).

A sample **subscriptions.conf** file is shown here:

```
# Subscription configuration file for CUPS v2.1.3
NextSubscriptionId 119
<Subscription 118>
Events printer-state-changed printer-restarted printer-shutdown printer-stopped printer-added printer-deleted job-state-changed job-created job-completed job-stopped
Owner richard
Recipient dbus://
LeaseDuration 3600
Interval 0
ExpirationTime 1363212783
NextEventId 1
</Subscription>
```

cups-files.conf

The files and directories that CUPS uses to manage print jobs can be configured in the /etc/cups/cups-files.conf file. The **ErrorLog** directive specifies the CUPS error log file.

```
ErrorLog   /var/log/cups/error_log
```

The SystemGroup directive defines the users referenced by **@SYSTEM** in **cupsd.conf**.

```
SystemGroup lpadmin
```

cups-browsed.conf

The **cups-browsed.conf** file configures the cups-browsed daemon, used for browsing remote and local printers. The BrowseRemoteProtocols defines the protocols to use.

```
BrowseRemoteProtocols   dnssd cups
```

The BrowseAllow directive can be used to restrict browsing to specified servers or networks.

```
BrowseAllow 192.168.1.0/24
```

The CreateIPPPrinterQueues directive allows the detection of non-CUPS IPP printers.

CUPS Command Line Print Clients

Once a print job is placed in a print queue, you can use any of several print clients to manage the jobs on your printer or printers, such as system-config-printer and the CUPS Printer Configuration tool. You can also use several command line print CUPS clients, which include the **lpr**, **lpc**, **lpq**, and **lprm** commands. With these clients, you can print documents, list a print queue, reorder it, and remove print jobs, effectively canceling them. For network connections, CUPS features an encryption option for its commands, **-E**, to encrypt print jobs and print information sent from a network. Table 14-3 shows various printer commands.

Printer Management	Description
GNOME Print Manager	GNOME print queue management tool (CUPS)
CUPS Configuration Tool	Prints, manages, and configures CUPS
`lpr` options file-list	Prints a file, copies the file to the printer's spool directory, and places it on the print queue to be printed in turn. `-P` printer prints the file on the specified printer
`lpq` options	Displays the print jobs in the print queue. `-P` printer prints the queue for the specified printer `-l` prints a detailed listing
`lpstat` options	Displays printer status
`lprm` options printjob-id or printer	Removes a print job from the print queue. You identify a particular print job by its number as listed by `lpq`. `-P` printer removes all print jobs for the specified printer
`lpc`	Manages your printers. At the `lpc>` prompt, you can enter commands to check the status of your printers and take other actions

Table 14-3: CUPS Print Clients

lpr

The **lpr** client submits a job, and **lpd** then takes it in turn, and places it on the appropriate print queue; **lpr** takes as its argument the name of a file. If no printer is specified, the default printer is used. The **-P** option lets you specify a particular printer. In the next example, the user first prints the file **preface** and then prints the file **report** to the printer with the name **myepson**:

```
$ lpr preface
$ lpr -P myepson report
```

lpc

You can use **lpc** to enable or disable printers, reorder their print queues, and re-execute configuration files. To use **lpc**, enter the command **lpc** at the shell prompt. You will see an **lpc>** prompt, where you can enter **lpc** commands to manage your printers and reorder their jobs. The **status** command with the name of the printer displays whether the printer is ready, how many print jobs it has, and so on. The **stop** and **start** commands can stop a printer and start it back up. The printers shown depend on the printers configured for a particular print server. A printer configured on CUPS will appear only if you have switched to CUPS.

```
$ lpc
lpc> status myepson
myepson:
 printer is on device 'usb' speed -1
 queuing is enabled
 printing is enabled
 1 entry in spool area
```

lpq and lpstat

You can manage the print queue using the **lpq** and **lprm** commands. The **lpq** command lists the print jobs currently in the print queue. With the **-P** option and the printer name, you can list the jobs for a particular printer. If you specify a username, you can list the print jobs for that user. With the **-l** option, **lpq** displays detailed information about each job. If you want information on a specific job, simply use that job's ID number with **lpq**. To check the status of a printer, use b.

```
$ lpq
myepson is ready and printing
Rank    Owner  Jobs  File(s)        Total Size
active  chris   1    report         1024
```

lprm

The **lprm** command lets you remove a print job from the queue, deleting the job before it can be printed. The **lprm** command takes many of the same options as **lpq**. To remove a specific job, use **lprm** with the job number. To remove all printing jobs for a particular printer, use the **-P** option with the printer name. **lprm** with no options removes the job printing currently. The following command removes the first print job in the queue (use **lpq** to obtain the job number):

```
lprm 1
```

CUPS Command Line Administrative Tools

CUPS provides command line administrative tools such as **lpadmin**, **lpoptions**, **lpinfo**, **cupsenable**, **cupsdisable**, **accept**, and **reject** (**cups-client** package). The **cupsenable** and **cupsdisable** commands start and stop print queues directly, whereas the **accept** and **reject** commands start and stop particular jobs. The **lpinfo** command provides information about printers, and **lpoptions** lets you set printing options. The **lpadmin** command lets you perform administrative tasks such as adding printers and changing configurations. CUPS administrative tools are listed in Table 14-4.

Note: The command line clients have the same name, and much the same syntax, as the older LPR and LPRng command line clients used in Unix and older Linux systems.

You can use the **lpadmin** command either to set the default printer or configure various options for a printer. You can use the **-d** option to specify a particular printer as the default destination. Here **myepson** is made the default printer:

```
lpadmin -d myepson
```

The **-p** option lets you designate a printer for which to set various options. The following example sets printer description information:

```
lpadmin -p myepson -D Epson550
```

Administration Tool	Description
`lpadmin`	CUPS printer configuration
`lpoptions`	Sets printing options
`cupsenable`	Activates a printer
`cupsdisable`	Stops a printer
`accept`	Allows a printer to accept new jobs
`reject`	Prevents a printer from accepting print jobs
`lpinfo`	Lists CUPS devices available

Table 14-4: CUPS Administrative Tools

Certain options let you control per-user quotas for print jobs. The **job-k-limit** option sets the size of a job allowed per user, **job-page-limit** sets the page limit for a job, and **job-quota-period** limits the number of jobs with a specified time frame. The following command set a page limit of 100 for each user:

```
lpadmin -p myepson -o job-page-limit=100
```

lpadmin

User access control is determined with the **-u** option with an **allow** or **deny** list. Users allowed access are listed following the **allow:** entry, and those denied access are listed with a **deny:** entry. Here access is granted to **chris** but denied to **aleina** and **larisa**.

```
lpadmin -p myepson -u allow:chris deny:aleina,larisa
```

Use **all** or **none** to permit or deny access to all or no users. You can create exceptions by using **all** or **none** in combination with user-specific access. The following example allows access to all users except **justin**:

```
lpadmin -p myepson -u allow:all deny:justin
```

lpoptions

The **lpoptions** command lets you set printing options and defaults that mostly govern how your print jobs will be printed. For example, you can set the color or page format to be used with a particular printer. The **-l** option lists current options for a printer, and the **-p** option designates a printer (you can also set the default printer to use with the **-d** option). The following command lists the current options for the myepson printer.

```
lpoptions -p myepson -l
```

Printer options are set using the **-o** option along with the option name and value, **-o** *option=value*. You can remove a printer option with the **-r** option. For example, to print on both sides of your sheets, you can set the **sides** option to **two-sided**:

```
lpoptions -p myepson -o sides=two-sided
```

To remove the option, use **-r**.

```
lpoptions -p myepson -r sides
```

To display a listing of available options, check the standard printing options **https://www.cups.org/doc/man-lpoptions.html**.

cupsenable and cupsdisable

The **cupsenable** command starts a printer, and the **cupsdisable** command stops it. With the **-c** option, you can cancel all jobs on the printer's queue, and the **-r** option broadcasts a message explaining the shutdown. This command disables the printer named **myepson**.

```
cupsdisable myepson
```

These are CUPS versions of the System V **enable** and **disable** commands, renamed to avoid conflicts.

accept and reject

The **accept** and **reject** commands let you control access to the printer queues for specific printers. The **reject** command prevents a printer from accepting jobs, whereas **accept** allows new print jobs. The following command prevents the **myepson** printer from accepting print jobs:

```
reject myepson
```

The Man pages for accept and reject are **cupsaccept** and **cupsreject**. These names are also links to the **accept** and **reject** commands, allowing you to use them instead.

lpinfo

The **lpinfo** command is a handy tool for letting you know what CUPS devices and drivers are available on your system. Use the **-v** option for devices and the **-m** option for drivers.

```
lpinfo -m
```

15. Network File Systems and Network Information System: NFS and NIS

Network File Systems: NFS and /etc/exports

Setting up NFS Directories with shares-admin: Shared Folders

NFS Configuration: /etc/exports

Controlling Accessing to NFS Servers

Mounting NFS File Systems: NFS Clients

Network Information Service: NIS

Name Service Switch: nsswitch.conf

Linux provides several tools for accessing files on remote systems connected to a network. The Network File System (NFS) enables you to connect to and directly access resources such as files or devices that reside on another machine. The new version, NFS4, provides greater security, with access allowed by your firewall. The Network Information Service (NIS) maintains configuration files for all systems on a network.

Network File Systems: NFS and /etc/exports

NFS enables you to mount a file system on a remote computer as if it were local to your own system. You can then directly access any of the files on that remote file system. This has the advantage of allowing different systems on a network to access the same files directly, without each having to keep its own copy. Only one copy will be on a remote file system, which each computer can then access. You can find out more about NFS at its website at **http://nfs.sourceforge.net**.

To set up the NFS service for your system, install the **nfs-kernel-server** and **nfs-common** packages. You can install with **apt-get**, the Synaptic Package Manager, or Software Manager (mintinstall).

```
sudo apt-get install nfs-kernel-server
```

NFS Daemons

NFS operates over a TCP/IP network using Remote Procedure Calls (RPC) to manage file systems. The remote computer that holds the file system makes it available to other computers on the network. It does so by exporting the file system, which entails making entries in an NFS configuration file called **/etc/exports**, as well as by running several daemons to support access by other systems. These include **rpc.mountd**, **rpc.nfsd**, and **rpc.gssd**. Access to your NFS server can be controlled by the **/etc/hosts.allow** and **/etc/hosts.deny** files. The NFS server daemons provided in the **nfs-kernel-server** package are listed here. You can configure options in the **/etc/default/nfs-kernel-server** file.

rpc.nfsd   Receives NFS requests from remote systems and translates them into requests for the local system.

rpc.mountd   Performs requested mount and unmount operations.

rpc.svcgssd   Performs security for rpc operations (rpcsec_gss protocol).

Additional NFS support daemons are provided by the **nfs-common** package. You can configure options in the **/etc/default/nfs-common** file.

rpc.gssd   Client support for the rpcsec_gss protocol for gss-api security in NFSv4.

rpc.idmapd   Maps user and group IDs to names.

rpc.statd   Provides locking services when a remote host reboots.

The **portmap** server converts remote procedure calls program number to appropriate port numbers.

The NFS daemons are managed by **systemd** using several service unit files located in **/lib/systemd/system**. The NFS daemons and their **systemd** unit files are listed in Table 15-1.

The **nfs-server.service** file is shown here. Runtime configuration information is read from **/etc/default/nfs-kernel-server** (EnvironmentFile).

nfs-server.service

```
[Unit]
Description=NFS server and services
DefaultDependencies=no
Requires= network.target proc-fs-nfsd.mount rpcbind.target
Requires= nfs-mountd.service
Wants=nfs-idmapd.service

After= local-fs.target
After= network.target proc-fs-nfsd.mount rpcbind.target nfs-mountd.service
After= nfs-idmapd.service rpc-statd.service
Before= rpc-statd-notify.service

# GSS services dependencies and ordering
Wants=auth-rpcgss-module.service
After=rpc-gssd.service rpc-svcgssd.service

# start/stop server before/after client
Before=remote-fs-pre.target
Wants=nfs-config.service
After=nfs-config.service

[Service]
EnvironmentFile=-/run/sysconfig/nfs-utils
Type=oneshot
RemainAfterExit=yes
ExecStartPre=/usr/sbin/exportfs -r
ExecStart=/usr/sbin/rpc.nfsd $RPCNFSDARGS
ExecStop=/usr/sbin/rpc.nfsd 0
ExecStopPost=/usr/sbin/exportfs -au
ExecStopPost=/usr/sbin/exportfs -f

ExecReload=/usr/sbin/exportfs -r

[Install]
WantedBy=multi-user.target
```

Use the **service** command to start, stop, and restart the NFS server manually.

```
sudo service nfs-kernel-server start
```

The corresponding **systemd** unit files for the **mountd** and **idmapd** daemons will run these daemons.

To see if NFS is actually running, you can use the **rpcinfo** command with the **-p** option. You should see entries for **mountd** and **nfs**. If not, NFS is not running.

Option for the **nfsd**, **mountd**, **nfsd**, and **svcgssd** daemons are set in the **/etc/default/nfs-kernel-server** file, where you can set options, such as the number of servers, server priority, ports, and whether to use svcgsssd.

/etc/default/nfs-kernel-server

```
# Number of servers to start up
# To disable nfsv4 on the server, specify '--no-nfs-version 4' here
RPCNFSDCOUNT=8

# Runtime priority of server (see nice(1))
RPCNFSDPRIORITY=0

# Options for rpc.mountd.
# If you have a port-based firewall, you might want to set up
# a fixed port here using the --port option. For more information,
# see rpc.mountd(8) or http://wiki.debian.org/?SecuringNFS
RPCMOUNTDOPTS=--manage-gids

# Do you want to start the svcgssd daemon? It is only required for Kerberos
# exports. Valid alternatives are "yes" and "no"; the default is "no".
NEED_SVCGSSD=

# Options for rpc.svcgssd.
RPCSVCGSSDOPTS=

# Options for rpc.nfsd.
RPCNFSDOPTS=
```

The **rpc.statd**, **rpc.idmapd**, and **rpc.gssd** daemons can be accessed using the **service** command.

```
sudo service statd restart
sudo service idmapd restart
sudo service gssd restart
```

To configure whether to start up the **statd**, **idmapd**, and **gssd** daemons, you set options in the **/etc/default/nfs-common** file. By default, the **statd** and **idmapd** daemons are started up.

/etc/default/nfs-common

```
# If you do not set values for the NEED_ options, they will be attempted
# autodetected; this should be sufficient for most people. Valid alternatives
# for the NEED_ options are "yes" and "no".

# Options for rpc.statd.
#   Should rpc.statd listen on a specific port? This is especially useful
#   when you have a port-based firewall. To use a fixed port, set this
#   this variable to a statd argument like: "--port 4000 --outgoing-port 4001".
#   For more information, see rpc.statd(8) or http://wiki.debian.org/?SecuringNFS
STATDOPTS=

# Do you want to start the gssd daemon? It is required for Kerberos mounts.
NEED_GSSD=
```

Setting up NFS Directories on the Desktop with shares-admin

You can set up an NFS shared folder easily using the **shares-admin** tool, which is part of the **gnome-system-tools** package. The gnome-system-tools package is installed by default. The menu entry for shares-admin is Shared Folders and is hidden by default. Open the menu editor in the menu configuration dialog's Menu tab. Then click the checkbox for Shared Folders on the Administration menu.

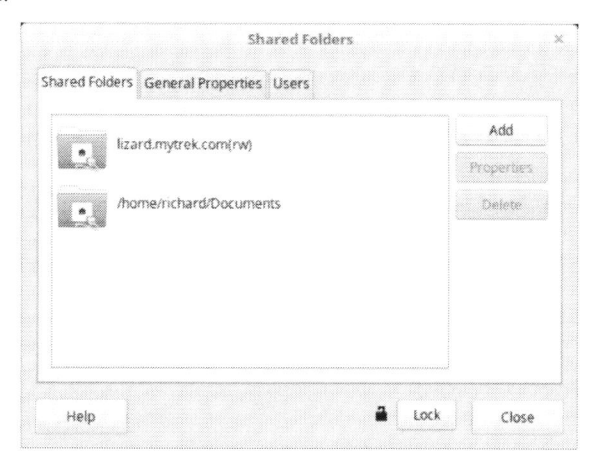

Figure 15-1: Shared Folders tool

The Shared Folders window has three tabs: Shared Folders, General Properties, and Users (see Figure 15-1). On the General tab, you specify the Windows workgroup name, and a WINS server is there is one (see Figure 15-3). On Shared Folders, user access can be configured, but only for all the shares. Use the Users tab to specify which user can have access to the shared folders (see Figure 15-2). You will be prompted for the user's password.

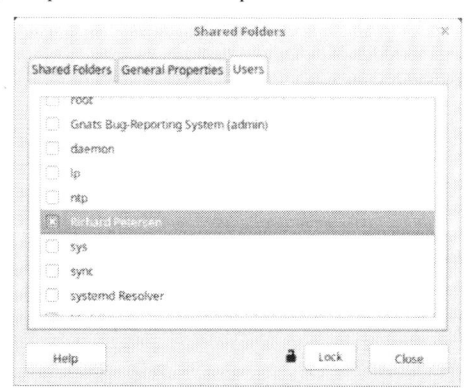

Figure 15-2: Shared Folders User tab

To use shares-admin to manage NFS directories, you first have to unlock it, providing you with administrative access. Click the bottom-left lock button labeled "**Lock**". A PolicyKit authorization dialog will appear, prompting you to enter your password. Upon entering your password, the button label will change to "Lock", and you can now add or modify NFS directories.

Figure 15-3: Adding a new shared folder

To add a new shared folder, click the Add button to open a Share Folder window (see Figure 15-3). On the Path pop-up menu, select the folder you want to share. If the one you want is not listed, select Other to open a file browser for the entire system. You then select the server to share through. For NFS select Unix networks (NFS).

You then select the host or network to allow access to this folder (see Figure 15-4). Click Add to open the Add Allowed hosts window. Here you can select a hostname, IP address, or network address, and then enter the name or address. You can also specify read-only, otherwise, access is writeable.

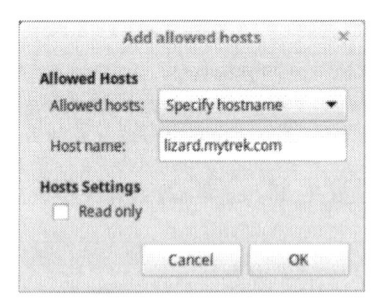

Figure 15-4: Specifying allowed hosts or networks

Figure 15-5: Share Folder with host access

The allowed host will then appear in the Share Folder dialog (see Figure 15-5). You can add more hosts, or delete others to deny access. When finished, click the Share button. The shared folder will then appear in the Shared Folders window.

NFS Configuration: /etc/exports

An entry in the **/etc/exports** file specifies the file system to be exported as well as the hosts on the network that can access it. For the file system, enter its mountpoint (the directory to which it was mounted on the host system). This is followed by a list of hosts that can access this file system along with options to control that access. A comma-separated list of export options placed within a set of parentheses may follow each host. For example, you might want to give one host read-only access and another read and write access. If the options are preceded by an * symbol, they are applied to any host. A list of options is provided in Table 15-1. The format of an entry in the **/etc/exports** file is shown here:

```
directory-pathname    host-designation(options)
```

NFS Host Entries

You can have several host entries for the same directory, each with access to that directory:

```
directory-pathname    host(options) host(options) host(options)
```

You have a great deal of flexibility when specifying hosts. For hosts within your domain, you can just use the hostname, whereas, for those outside, you need to use a fully qualified domain name. You can also use just the host's IP address. Instead of a single host, you can reference all the hosts within a specific domain, allowing access by an entire network. A simple way to do this is to use the * for the host segment, followed by the domain name for the network, such as ***.mytrek.com** for all the hosts in the **mytrek.com** network. Instead of domain names, you can use IP network addresses with a CNDR format where you specify the netmask to indicate a range of IP addresses. You can also use an NIS netgroup name to reference a collection of hosts. The NIS netgroup name is preceded by an @ sign.

```
directory       host(options)
directory       *(options)
directory       *.domain(options)
directory       192.168.1.0/255.255.255.0(options)
directory       @netgroup(options)
```

NFS Options

Options in **/etc/exports** operate as permissions to control access to exported directories. Read-only access is set with the **ro** option, and read/write with the **rw** option. The **sync** and **async** options specify whether a write operation is performed immediately (**sync**) or when the server is ready to handle it (**async**). By default, write requests are checked to see if they are related and if so, they are written together (**wdelay**). This can degrade performance. You can override this default with **no_wdelay** and have writes executed as they are requested. If two directories are exported, where one is the subdirectory of another, the subdirectory is not accessible unless it is explicitly mounted (**hide**). In other words, mounting the parent directory does not make the subdirectory accessible. The subdirectory remains hidden until it is also mounted. You can overcome this restriction with the **no_hide** option (though this can cause problems with some file systems).

General Option	Description
`secure`	Requires that requests originate on secure ports, those less than 1024. This is on by default
`insecure`	Turns off the `secure` option
`ro`	Allows only read-only access. This is the default
`rw`	Allows read/write access
`sync`	Performs all writes when requested. This is the default
`async`	Performs all writes when the server is ready
`no_wdelay`	Performs writes immediately, not checking to see if they are related
`wdelay`	Checks to see if writes are related, and if so, waits to perform them together. Can degrade performance. This is the default.
`hide`	Automatically hides an exported directory that is the subdirectory of another exported directory
`subtree_check`	Checks parent directories in a file system to validate an exported subdirectory. This is the default.
`no_subtree_check`	Does not check parent directories in a file system to validate an exported subdirectory
`insecure_locks`	Does not require authentication of locking requests. Used for older NFS versions
User ID Mapping	**Description**
`all_squash`	Maps all UIDs and GIDs to the anonymous user. Useful for NFS-exported public FTP directories, news spool directories, and so forth
`no_all_squash`	The opposite option to `all_squash`. This is the default setting.
`root_squash`	Maps requests from remote root user to the anonymous UID/GID. This is the default.
`no_root_squash`	Turns off root squashing. Allows the root user to access as the remote root
`anonuid`	Sets explicitly the UID and GID of the anonymous account used for `all_squash` and `root_squash` options. The defaults are nobody and nogroup

Table 15-1: The /etc/exports Options

If an exported directory is actually a subdirectory in a larger file system, its parent directories are checked to make sure that the subdirectory is the valid directory (**subtree_check**). This option works well with read-only file systems but can cause problems for write-enabled file systems, where filenames and directories can be changed. You can cancel this check with the **no_subtree_check** option.

NFS User-Level Access

Along with general options, are options that apply to user-level access. As a security measure, the client's root user is treated as an anonymous user by the NFS server. This is known as squashing the user. In the case of the client root user, squashing prevents the client from attempting to appear as the NFS server's root user. Should you want a particular client's root user to have root-level control over the NFS server, you can specify the **no_root_squash** option. To prevent any client user from attempting to appear as a user on the NFS server, you can classify them as anonymous users (the **all_squash** option). Such anonymous users can access only directories and files that are part of the anonymous group.

Normally, if a user on a client system has a user account on the NFS server, that user can mount and access files on the NFS server. However, NFS requires the User ID for the user be the same on both systems. If this is not the case, the user is considered to be two different users. To overcome this problem, you can use an NIS service, maintaining User ID information in just one place, the NIS password file (see the following section for information on NIS).

NFSv4

NFS version 4 is the latest version of the NFS protocol with enhanced features, such as greater security, reliability, and speed. Most of the commands are the same as the earlier version, with a few changes. For example, when you mount an NFSv4 file system, you need to specify the **nfs4** file type. Also, for NFSv4, in the **/etc/exports** file, you can use the **fsid=0** option to specify the root export location.

```
/home/richlp          *(fsid=0,ro,sync)
```

The preceding entry lets you mount the file system to the **/home/richlp** directory without having to specify it in the mount operation.

```
mount -t nfs4   rabbit.mytrek.com:/   /home/dylan/projects
```

NFSv4 also supports the RPCSEC_GSS (Remote Procedure Call Security, Generic Security Services) security mechanism which provides for private/public keys, encryption, and authentication with support for Kerberos. Kerberos comes in two flavors: **krb5i** which validates the integrity of the data and **krb5p** which encrypts all requests but involves a performance hit. Samples for using the GSS and Kerberos security are listed as comments in the **/etc/exports** file. Instead of specifying a remote location, the rpcsec_gss protocol (**gss**) is used with **krb5i** security, **gss/krb5i**. The directory mounted in the sample is the **/srv/nfs4/homes** directory.

```
# /srv/nfs4/homes   gss/krb5i(rw,sync,no_subtree_check)
```

NFS /etc/exports Example

Examples of entries in an **/etc/exports** file are shown here. Read-only access is given to all hosts to the file system mounted on the **/srv/pub** directory. Users, however, are treated as anonymous users (**all_squash**). The **/srv** directory is used usually for server managed directories and file systems. In the next entry, read and write access is given to the **lizard.mytrek.com** computer for the file system mounted on the **/home/mypics** directory. The next entry allows access by **rabbit.mytrek.com** to the NFS server's DVD-ROM, using only read access. The last entry allows anyone secure access to **/home/richlp**.

/etc/exports

```
/srv/pub                *(ro,insecure,all_squash,sync)
/home/mypics        lizard.mytrek.com(rw,sync)
/media/dvdrom        rabbit.mytrek.com(ro,sync)
/home/richlp          *(secure,sync)
```

The default **/etc/options** file shows examples for using NFSv2, NFSv3, and NFSv4 formats.

/etc/exports

```
# /etc/exports: the access control list for filesystems which may be exported
#               to NFS clients.  See exports(5).
#
# Example for NFSv2 and NFSv3:
# /srv/homes       hostname1(rw,sync,no_subtree_check) hostname2(ro,sync,no_subtree_check)
#
# Example for NFSv4:
# /srv/nfs4        gss/krb5i(rw,sync,fsid=0,crossmnt,no_subtree_check)
# /srv/nfs4/homes  gss/krb5i(rw,sync,no_subtree_check)
#
```

Applying Changes

Each time your system starts up the NFS server (usually when the system starts up), the **/etc/exports** file will be read and any directories specified will be exported. When a directory is exported, an entry for it is made in the **/var/lib/nfs/xtab** file. It is this file that NFS reads and uses to perform the actual exports. Entries are read from **/etc/exports** and corresponding entries made in **/var/lib/nfs/xtab**. The **xtab** file maintains the list of actual exports.

If you want to export added entries in the **/etc/exports** file immediately, without rebooting, you can use the **exportfs** command with the **-a** option. It is helpful to add the **-v** option to display the actions that NFS is taking. Use the same options to effect any changes you make to the **/etc/exports** file.

```
exportfs -a -v
```

If you make changes to the **/etc/exports** file, you can use the **-r** option to re-export its entries. The **-r** option will re-sync the **/var/lib/nfs/xtab** file with the **/etc/exports** entries, removing any other exports or any with different options.

```
exportfs -r -v
```

To export added entries and re-export changed ones, you can combine the **-r** and **-a** options.

```
exportfs -r -a -v
```

Manually Exporting File Systems

You can also use the **exportfs** command to export file systems manually instead of using entries for them in the **/etc/exports** file. Export entries will be added to the **/var/lib/nfs/xtab** file directly. With the **-o** option, you can list various permissions and then follow them with the host and file system to export. The host and file system are separated by a colon. For example, to export the **/home/myprojects** directory manually to **golf.mytrek.com** with the permissions **ro** and **insecure**, you use the following:

```
exportfs -o rw,insecure golf.mytrek.com:/home/myprojects
```

You can also use **exportfs** to un-export a directory that has already been exported, either manually or by the **/etc/exports** file. Just use the **-u** option with the host and the directory exported. The entry for the export will be removed from the **/var/lib/nfs/xtab** file. The following example will un-export the **/home/foodstuff** directory that was exported to **lizard.mytrek.com**:

```
exportfs -u lizard.mytrek.com:/home/foodstuff
```

Controlling Accessing to NFS Servers

You can use several methods to control access to your NFS server, such as using **hosts.allow** and **hosts.deny** to permit or deny access, as well as using your firewall to intercept access.

/etc/hosts.allow and /etc/hosts.deny

The **/etc/hosts.allow** and **/etc/hosts.deny** files are used to restrict access to services provided by your server to hosts on your network or on the Internet (if accessible). For example, you can use the **hosts.allow** file to permit access by certain hosts to your FTP server. Entries in the **hosts.deny** file explicitly denies access to certain hosts. For NFS, you can provide the same kind of security by controlling access to specific NFS daemons.

Portmap Service

The first line of defense is to control access to the portmapper service. The portmapper tells hosts where the NFS services can be found on the system. Restricting access does not allow a remote host to even locate NFS. For a strong level of security, you should deny access to all hosts except those that are explicitly allowed. In the **hosts.deny** file, you should place the following entry, denying access to all hosts by default. ALL is a special keyword denoting all hosts.

```
portmap:ALL
```

The portmapper service is referenced with the **portmap** name. You can set options manually in the **/etc/default/portmap** file.

In the **hosts.allow** file, you can then enter the hosts on your network, or any others that you want to permit access to your NFS server. Again, specify the portmapper service and then list the IP addresses of the hosts you are permitting access. You can list specific IP addresses or a network range using a netmask. The following example allows access only by hosts in the local network, 192.168.0.0, and to the host 10.0.0.43. You can separate addresses with commas:

```
portmap: 192.168.0.0/255.255.255.0, 10.0.0.43
```

The portmapper is also used by other services such as NIS. If you close all access to the portmapper in **hosts.deny**, you will also need to allow access to NIS services in **hosts.allow**, if you are running them. These include ypbind and ypserver. In addition, you may have to add entries for remote commands like **ruptime** and **rusers**, if you are supporting them.

It is also advisable to add the same level of control for specific NFS services. In the **hosts.deny** file, you add entries for each service, as shown here:

```
mountd:ALL
statd:ALL
```

Then, in the **hosts.allow** file, you can add entries for each service:

```
mountd:   192.168.0.0/255.255.255.0, 10.0.0.43
statd:    192.168.0.0/255.255.255.0, 10.0.0.43
```

Netfilter Rules

You can further control access using Netfilter to check transmissions from certain hosts on the ports used by NFS services. The **portmapper** uses port 111, and **nfsd** uses 2049. Netfilter is helpful if you have a private network that has an Internet connection and you want to protect it from the Internet. Usually, a specific network device, such as an Ethernet card, is dedicated to the Internet connection. The following examples assume that device **eth1** is connected to the Internet. Any packets attempting access on port 111 or 2049 are refused.

```
iptables -A INPUT -i eth1 -p 111 -j DENY
iptables -A INPUT -i eth1 -p 2049 -j DENY
```

To enable NFS for your local network, you will have to allow packet fragments. Assuming that **eth0** is the device used for the local network, you could use the following example:

```
iptables -A INPUT -i eth0 -f -j ACCEPT
```

Mounting NFS File Systems: NFS Clients

Once NFS makes directories available to different hosts, those hosts can then mount those directories on their own systems and access them. The host needs to be able to operate as an NFS client. Current Linux kernels all have NFS client capability built in. This means that any NFS client can mount a remote NFS directory that it has access to by performing a simple mount operation.

Mounting NFS Automatically: /etc/fstab

You can mount an NFS directory either by an entry in the **/etc/fstab** file or by an explicit **mount** command. You have your NFS file systems mounted automatically by placing entries for them in the **/etc/fstab** file. An NFS entry in the **/etc/fstab** file has a mount type of **nfs**. An NFS file system name consists of the hostname of the computer on which it is located, followed by the pathname of the directory where it is mounted. The two are separated by a colon. For example, **rabbit.trek.com:/home/project** specifies a file system mounted at **/home/project** on the **rabbit.trek.com** computer. The format for an NFS entry in the **/etc/fstab** file follows. The file type for NFS versions 1 through 3 is **nfs**, whereas for NFS version 4 it is **nfs4**.

```
host:remote-directory    local-directory      nfs    options    0   0
```

You can also include several NFS-specific mount options with your NFS entry. You can specify the size of datagrams sent back and forth, and the amount of time your computer waits for a response from the host system. You can also specify whether a file system is to be hard-mounted or soft-mounted. For a hard-mounted file system, your computer continually tries to make contact if for some reason the remote system fails to respond. A soft-mounted file system, after a specified interval, gives up trying to make contact and issues an error message. A hard mount is the default. A system making a hard-mount attempt that continues to fail will stop responding to user input as it tries continually to achieve the mount. For this reason, soft mounts may be preferable, as they will simply stop attempting a mount that continually fails. Table 15-2 and the Man pages for **mount** contain a listing of these NFS client options. They differ from the NFS server options indicated previously.

Option	Description
`rsize=n`	The number of bytes NFS uses when reading files from an NFS server. The default is 1,024 bytes. A size of 8,192 can greatly improve performance.
`wsize=n`	The number of bytes NFS uses when writing files to an NFS server. The default is 1,024 bytes. A size of 8,192 can greatly improve performance.
`timeo=n`	The value in tenths of a second before sending the first retransmission after a timeout. The default value is seven-tenths of a second.
`retry=n`	The number of minutes to retry an NFS mount operation before giving up. The default is 10,000 minutes (one week).
`retrans=n`	The number of retransmissions or minor timeouts for an NFS mount operation before a major timeout (default is 3). At that time, the connection is canceled or a "server not responding" message is displayed.
`soft`	Mount system using soft mount.
`hard`	Mount system using hard mount. This is the default.
`intr`	Allows NFS to interrupt the file operation and return to the calling program. The default is not to allow file operations to be interrupted.
`bg`	If the first mount attempt times out, continues trying the mount in the background. The default is to fail without backgrounding.
`tcp`	Mounts the NFS file system using the TCP protocol, instead of the default UDP protocol.

Table 15-2: NFS Mount Options

An example of an NFS entry follows. The remote system is **rabbit.mytrek.com**, and the file system is mounted on **/home/projects**. This file system is to be mounted on the local system as the **/home/dylan/projects** directory. The **/home/dylan/projects** directory must already be created on the local system. The type of system is NFS, and the **timeo** option specifies the local system waits up to 20 tenths of a second (two seconds) for a response. The mount is a soft mount and can be interrupted by NFS.

```
rabbit.mytrek.com:/home/projects /home/dylan/projects nfs soft,intr,timeo=20
```

Mounting NFS Manually: mount

You can also use the **mount** command with the **-t nfs** option to mount an NFS file system explicitly. For an NFSv4 file system you use **-t nfs4**. To mount the previous entry explicitly, use the following command:

```
mount -t nfs -o soft,intr,timeo=20 rabbit.mytrek.com:/home/projects /home/dylan/projects
```

You can, of course, unmount an NFS directory with the **umount** command. You can specify either the local mountpoint or the remote host and directory, as shown here:

```
umount  /home/dylan/projects
umount  rabbit.mytrek.com:/home/projects
```

Mounting NFS on Demand: autofs

You can also mount NFS file systems using the automount service, autofs (**autofs** package). This requires added configuration on the client's part. The autofs service will mount a file system only when you try to access it. A directory change operation (**cd**) to a specified directory will trigger the mount operation, mounting the remote file system at that time.

The autofs service is configured using a master file to list map files, which in turn lists the file systems to be mounted. The **/etc/auto.master** file is the autofs master file. The master file will list the root pathnames where file systems can be mounted, along with a map file for each of those pathnames. The map file will then list a key (subdirectory), mount options, and the file systems that can be mounted in that root pathname directory. On some distributions, the **/auto** directory is already implemented as the root pathname for file systems automatically mounted. You can add your own file systems in the **/etc/auto.master** file along with your own map files, if you wish. You will find that the **/etc/auto.master** file contains the following entry for the **/auto** directory, listing **auto.misc** as its map file:

```
/auto    auto.misc    --timeout 60
```

Following the map file, you can add options, as shown in the preceding example. The **timeout** option specifies the number of seconds of inactivity to wait before trying to automatically unmount.

In the map file, you list the key, the mount options, and the file system to be mounted. The key will be the subdirectory on the local system where the file system is mounted. For example, to mount the **/home/projects** directory on the **rabbit.mytrek.com** host to the **/auto/projects** directory, use the following entry:

```
projects    soft,intr,timeo=20    rabbit.mytrek.com:/home/projects
```

You can also create a new entry in the master file for an NFS file system, as shown here:

```
/myprojects    auto.myprojects    --timeout 60
```

You then create an **/etc/auto.myprojects** file and place entries in it for NFS files system mounts, like the following:

```
dylan      soft,intr,rw    rabbit.mytrek.com:/home/projects
newgame    soft,intr,ro    lizard.mytrek.com:/home/supergame
```

Network Information Service: NIS

On networks supporting NFS, many resources and devices are shared by the same systems. Normally, each system needs its own configuration files for each device or resource. Changes entail updating each system individually. However, NFS provides a special service called the Network Information System (NIS) that maintains such configuration files for the entire network. For changes, you need only to update the NIS files. NIS works for information required for most administrative tasks, such as those relating to users, network access, or devices. For example, you can maintain user and password information with an NIS service, having only to update those NIS password files.

The NIS service is configured for use by the **/etc/nsswitch** configuration file. Here are some standard entries:

```
passwd:         compat
shadow:         compat
networks:       files
protocols:      db files
```

Note: NIS+ is a more advanced form of NIS that provides support for encryption and authentication. However, it is more difficult to administer.

NIS was developed by Sun Microsystems and was originally known as Sun's Yellow Pages (YP). NIS files are kept on an NIS server (NIS servers are still sometimes referred to as YP servers). Individual systems on a network use NIS clients to make requests from the NIS server. The NIS server maintains its information on special database files called maps. Linux versions exist for both NIS clients and servers. Linux NIS clients easily connect to any network using NIS.

Note: Instead of NIS, many networks now use LDAP to manage user information and authentication.

The NIS package is part of the Universe repository and can be installed as **nis**, which will also install the **yp-tools** package. NIS client programs and tools are ypbind (the NIS client daemon), ypwhich, ypcat, yppoll, ypmatch, yppasswd, and ypset. Each has its own Man page with details of its use. The NIS server programs and tools are ypserv (the NIS server), ypinit, yppasswdd, yppush, ypxfr, and netgroup. Each has its own Man page. When you install the NIS server (**nis** package) you will be prompted to enter an NIS domain, listing your hostname as the default.

The NIS server is managed by **systemd** using the **nis.service** unit files in the **/run/systemd/generator.late** directory. It is generated by systemd-sysv-generator using the **/etc/init.d/nis** script. The **ypbind.service** and **ypserv.service** files are links to the **nis.service** file.

nis.service

```
# Automatically generated by systemd-sysv-generator

[Unit]
Documentation=man:systemd-sysv-generator(8)
SourcePath=/etc/init.d/nis
Description=LSB: Start NIS client and server daemons.
Before=multi-user.target
Before=multi-user.target
Before=multi-user.target
Before=graphical.target
After=network-online.target
After=rpcbind.target
After=remote-fs.target
Wants=network-online.target

[Service]
Type=forking
```

```
Restart=no
TimeoutSec=5min
IgnoreSIGPIPE=no
KillMode=process
GuessMainPID=no
RemainAfterExit=yes
ExecStart=/etc/init.d/nis start
ExecStop=/etc/init.d/nis stop
ExecReload=/etc/init.d/nis reload
```

/etc/nsswitch.conf: Name Service Switch

Different functions in the standard C Library must be configured to operate on your Linux system. Previously, database-like services, such as password support and name services like NIS or DNS, directly accessed these functions, using a fixed search order. This configuration is carried out by a scheme called the Name Service Switch (NSS), which is based on the method of the same name used by Sun Microsystems Solaris 2 OS. The database sources and their lookup order are listed in the **/etc/nsswitch.conf** file.

File	Description
ethers	Ethernet numbers
group	Groups of users
hosts	Hostnames and numbers
netgroup	Network-wide list of hosts and users, used for access rules; C libraries before glibc 2.1 only support netgroups over NIS
network	Network names and numbers
passwd	User passwords
protocols	Network protocols
publickey	Public and secret keys for SecureRPC used by NFS and NIS+
rpc	Remote procedure call names and numbers
services	Network services
shadow	Shadow user passwords

Table 15-3: NSS-Supported databases

The **/etc/nsswitch.conf** file holds entries for the different configuration files that can be controlled by NSS. The system configuration files that NSS supports are listed in Table 15-3. An entry consists of two fields: the service and the configuration specification. The service consists of the configuration file followed by a colon. The second field is the configuration specification for that file, which holds instructions on how the lookup procedure will work. The configuration specification can contain service specifications and action items. Service specifications are the services to search. Currently, valid service specifications are nis, nis-plus, files, db, dns, and compat (see Table 15-4). Not all are valid for each configuration file. For example, the dns service is valid only for the **hosts** file, whereas nis is valid for all files. The following example will first check the local **/etc/password** file and then NIS.

```
passwd:     files nisplus
```

  For more refined access to passwd, group, and shadow sources, you can use the + and - symbols in file entries to determine if the entry can be accessed by the nsswitch service. The **compat** service provides a compatible mode that will check for such entries. With no such entries, the nis service will be used for all entries. The **compat** service can only be applied to the passwd, group, and shadow databases. This provides the equivalent of the files and nis services.

  If your passwd, group, and shadow files already have + and - entries, and you need to have the file entries take precedence over the nis service, you can specify the files database before the compat entry.

```
passwd:     files compat
```

  An action item specifies the action to take for a specific service. An action item is placed within brackets after a service. A configuration specification can list several services, each with its own action item. In the following example, the entry for the **hosts** file has a configuration specification that says to check the **/etc/hosts** files and **mdns4_minimal** service and, if not found, to check the DNS server and the **mdns4** service (multicast DNS name resolution).

```
hosts:      files mdns4_minimal [NOTFOUND=return] dns mdns4
```

Service	Description
files	Checks corresponding **/etc** file for the configuration (for example, **/etc/hosts** for hosts); this service is valid for all files
db	Checks corresponding **/var/db** databases for the configuration; valid for all files except **netgroup**
compat	Provides **nis** and **files** services, with compatibility support for + and - entries. Valid only for **passwd**, **group**, and **shadow** files
dns	Checks the DNS service; valid only for **hosts** file
nis	Checks the NIS service; valid for all files
nisplus	NIS version 3
hesiod	Uses Hesiod for lookup

Table 15-4: NSS Configuration Services

  An action item consists of a status and an action. The status holds a possible result of a service lookup, and the action is the action to take if the status is true. Currently, the possible status values are SUCCESS, NOTFOUND, UNAVAIL, and TRYAGAIN (service temporarily unavailable). The possible actions are return and continue: return stops the lookup process for the configuration file, whereas continue continues on to the next listed service. In the preceding example, if the record is not found in NIS, the lookup process ends.

  Shown here is a copy of the **/etc/nsswitch.conf** file, which lists commonly used entries. Comments and commented-out entries begin with a # sign:

/etc/nsswitch.conf

```
# /etc/nsswitch.conf
#
# Example configuration of GNU Name Service Switch functionality.
# If you have the `glibc-doc-reference' and `info' packages installed, try:
# `info libc "Name Service Switch"' for information about this file.

passwd:         compat
group:          compat
shadow:         compat
gshadow:        files

hosts:          files mdns4_minimal [NOTFOUND=return] dns
networks:       files

protocols:      db files
services:       db files
ethers:         db files
rpc:            db files

netgroup:       nis
```

16. Samba

Samba Applications

Setting Up Samba with system-config-samba

User Level Security

The Samba smb.conf Configuration File

Testing the Samba Configuration

Domain Logons

Accessing Samba Services with Clients

With Samba, you can connect your Windows clients on a Microsoft Windows network to services such as shared files, systems, and printers controlled by the Linux Samba server and, at the same time, allow Linux systems to access shared files and printers on Windows systems. Samba is a collection of Linux tools that allow you to communicate with Windows systems over a Windows network. In effect, Samba allows a Linux system or network to act as if it were a Windows server, using the same protocols as used on a Windows network. Whereas most UNIX and Linux systems use the TCP/IP protocol for networking, Microsoft networking with Windows uses a different protocol, called the Server Message Block (SMB) protocol that implements a local area network (LAN) of PCs running Windows. SMB makes use of a network interface called Network Basic Input Output System (NetBIOS) that allows Windows PCs to share resources, such as printers and disk space. One Windows PC on such a network can access a folder on another Windows PC's disk drive as if the folder were its own. SMB was originally designed for small LANs. To connect it to larger networks, including those with UNIX systems, Microsoft developed the Common Internet File System (CIFS), which still uses SMB and NetBIOS for Windows networking.

Wanting to connect his Linux system to a Windows PC, Andrew Tridgell wrote an SMB client and server that he called Samba. Samba allows UNIX and Linux systems to connect a Windows network as if they were Windows system. UNIX systems can share resources on Windows systems as if they were just another Windows system. Windows systems can also access resources on UNIX systems as if they were Windows systems. Samba, in effect, has become a professional-level, open source, and free version of CIFS. It also runs much faster than CIFS. Samba lets you use a Linux or UNIX server as a network server for a group of Windows machines operating on a Windows network. You can also use it to share files on your Linux system with other Windows systems, or to access files on a Windows PC from your Linux system, as well as between Windows systems. On Linux systems, the **cifs** file system type enables you, in effect, to mount a remote SMB-shared directory on your own file system. You can then access it as if it were a folder on your local system.

Package name	Description
samba	The Samba server
samba-common	Samba configuration files and support tools
smbclient	Samba clients for accessing Windows shares
system-config-samba	Samba desktop configuration tool from Red Hat
kdenetwork-filesharing	Samba sharing configuration on KDE
nautilus-share	Quick sharing configuration using the GNOME Nautilus file manager

Table 16-1: Samba packages on Linux Mint

You can obtain extensive documentation from the Samba Web and FTP sites at **http://www.samba.org**. Samba HOW-TO documentation is also available at **http://www.tldp.org**. Examples are provided on your system in the **/usr/share/doc/samba** directory.

Samba software is organized into several packages, with configuration tools such as system-config-samba in separate packages (see Table 16-1). By selecting the samba server package, necessary supporting packages such as smbclient and samba-common will be automatically selected. Configuration tools have to be selected manually. Samba software packages can be obtained from the Ubuntu repositories using apt-get, the Synaptic Package Manager, or Software Manager (mintinstall).

. Check the Ubuntu Server Guide | Windows Networking for basic configuration and management.

`https://help.ubuntu.com/lts/serverguide/samba.html`

Samba Applications

The Samba software package consists of two server daemons and several utility programs (see Table 16-2). The **smbd** daemon provides file and printer services to SMB clients and other systems, such as Windows, that support SMB. The **nmbd** daemon provides NetBIOS name resolution and service browser support. Additional packages provide support tools, like **smbclient** which provides FTP-like access by Linux clients to Samba services. The **mount.cifs** and **umount.cifs** commands enable Linux clients to mount and unmount Samba shared directories (used by the **mount** command with the **-t cifs** option). The **smbstatus** utility displays the current status of the SMB server and who is using it. You use **testparm** to test your Samba configuration. **smbtar** is a shell script that backs up SMB/CIFS-shared resources directly to a Unix tape drive. The **nmblookup** command will map the NetBIOS name of a Windows PC to its IP address.

Basic Samba configuration support is already provided by nautilus-share. For a more complex configuration, you can use system-config-samba, a GNOME desktop tool with which you can set up secure access to Samba shares. Configuration files are kept in the **/etc/samba** directory.

Samba provides four main services: file and printer services, authentication and authorization, name resolution, and service announcement. The SMB daemon, **smbd**, provides the file and printer services, as well as authentication and authorization for those services. This means users on the network can share files and printers. You can control access to these services by requiring that users provide a password. When users try to access a shared directory, they are prompted for the password (user mode). The user mode provides a different password for each user. Samba maintains its own password file for this purpose: **/etc/samba/smbpasswd**.

Name resolution and service announcements are handled by the nmbd server. Name resolution essentially resolves NetBIOS names with IP addresses. Service announcements, also known as browsing, are the way a list of services available on the network is made known to the connected Windows PCs (and Linux PCs connected through Samba).

Samba also includes the **winbind** daemon, which allows Samba servers to use authentication services provided by a Windows domain. Instead of a Samba server maintaining its own set of users to allow access, it can make use of a Windows domain authentication service to authenticate users.

Starting up and accessing Samba

Once installed, Samba is normally configured to start up automatically. You can turn this option on or off using **rcconf**. For a simple Samba configuration, you can use **system-config-samba** to configure your **/etc/samba/smb.conf** file. If you make changes, you must restart the Samba server for them to take effect. To restart Samba with your new configuration, use the **service** command. The start, stop, and restart options will start, stop, and restart the server. Run the following command from a terminal window to restart Samba.

```
sudo service smbd restart
sudo service nmbd restart
```

Application	Description
nautilus-share	Basic file sharing configuration built into the GNOME Nautilus file manager
system-config-samba	Samba configuration tool (provided by Red Hat) for configuring **smb.conf** with a GNOME desktop interface
smbd	Samba server daemon that provides file and printer services to SMB clients
nmbd	Samba daemon that provides NetBIOS name resolution and service browser support
winbind	Uses authentication services provided by Windows domain
mount.cifs	Mounts Samba share directories on Linux clients (used by the `mount` command with the `-t cifs` option)
smbpasswd	Changes SMB-encrypted passwords on Samba servers
pdbedit	Edit the Samba users database file. This is a Secure Accounts Manager (SAM) database.
tdbbackup	Backup the Samba **.tdb** database files.
smbcontrol	Send the Samba servers administrative messages, like shutdown or close-share.
smbstatus	Displays the current status of the SMB network connections
testparm	Tests the Samba configuration file, **smb.conf**
nmblookup	Maps the NetBIOS name of a Windows PC to its IP address
/etc/default/samba	Samba startup options

Table 16-2: Samba Server Applications

The Samba server consists of two daemons: **smbd** and **nmbd**. You may have to first enable them with the **systemctl** command, and then start them using the **service** command. At the prompt (on the desktop open a terminal window), use the **sudo** command for administrative access followed by a **systemctl** command for the **smbd** server with the **enable** command to enable the server. Do the same for the **nmbd** server. Then use **service** commands with the **start** command to start them. Once enabled, the server should start automatically whenever your system starts up.

```
sudo systemctl nmbd enable
sudo systemctl smbd enable
service nmbd start
service smbd start
```

Samba is managed by **systemd** using the **smbd.service** and **nmbd.service** unit files in **/run/systemd/generator.late** directory. These files are generated for systemd by the systemd-sysv-generator tool, which generates the unit files from the sysv init files for samba in the **/etc/init.d** directory. The **smbd.service** file is shown here. Samba is started after the networking, file system mounts, and the Cups service (After). It is started before the **multi-user.target** (the runlevel 2, 3, 4 targets are links to the muli-user target) (Before). On the desktop, the **graphical.target** is added (runlevel5.target). The service is started using the **smbd** script in the **/etc/init.d** directory (ExecStart).

smbd.service

```
# Automatically generated by systemd-sysv-generator

[Unit]
Documentation=man:systemd-sysv-generator(8)
SourcePath=/etc/init.d/smbd
Description=LSB: start Samba SMB/CIFS daemon (smbd)
Before=multi-user.target
Before=multi-user.target
Before=multi-user.target
Before=graphical.target
Before=shutdown.target
After=network-online.target
After=local-fs.target
After=remote-fs.target
After=slapd.service
After=cups.service
Wants=network-online.target
Conflicts=shutdown.target

[Service]
Type=forking
Restart=no
TimeoutSec=5min
IgnoreSIGPIPE=no
KillMode=process
GuessMainPID=no
RemainAfterExit=yes
ExecStart=/etc/init.d/smbd start
ExecStop=/etc/init.d/smbd stop
ExecReload=/etc/init.d/smbd reload
```

The NMB daemon is started after networking (After). It starts the **nmbd** server using the **/etc/init.d/nmbd** script.

nmbd.service

```
# Automatically generated by systemd-sysv-generator

[Unit]
Documentation=man:systemd-sysv-generator(8)
SourcePath=/etc/init.d/nmbd
Description=LSB: start Samba NetBIOS nameserver (nmbd)
Before=multi-user.target
Before=multi-user.target
Before=multi-user.target
Before=graphical.target
Before=shutdown.target
After=network-online.target
After=local-fs.target
```

```
After=remote-fs.target
Wants=network-online.target
Conflicts=shutdown.target

[Service]
Type=forking
Restart=no
TimeoutSec=5min
IgnoreSIGPIPE=no
KillMode=process
GuessMainPID=no
RemainAfterExit=yes
ExecStart=/etc/init.d/nmbd start
ExecStop=/etc/init.d/nmbd stop
```

Firewall access

The IPtables firewall prevents browsing Samba and Windows shares from your Linux desktop. To work around this restriction, you need to make sure your firewall treats Samba as a trusted service. To allow firewall access to the Samba ports you should enable access using a firewall configuration tool like ufw. The Samba ports are 125/TCP, 137/UDP, and 138/UDP. In addition, Samba uses the Microsoft Service Discovery service which uses port 445/TCP.

On the command line interface, using the UFW default firewall, you would use the following **ufw** commands. The UFW firewall maintains its IPtables files in **/etc/ufw**.

```
ufw allow 135/tcp
ufw allow 137:138/udp
ufw allow 445/tcp
```

If you are working from a desktop interface, you can use the Gufw tool to set the Samba ports for the UFW firewall. You will have to add the ports as simple rules (see Chapter 17). On the desktop, the UFW firewall blocks remote file browsing from the desktop for Samba (the Network window), because browsing uses additional broadcast packets that have not been allowed. You have to add a rule to allow access to anywhere from port **137/udp** or enter the following command. The rule restricts broadcasts to the local network. Most private networks use the network address **192.168.0.0/24**, as specified in this example (see Chapter 11, Gufw in the Firewall section).

```
sudo ufw allow from 192.168.0.0/24 port 137 proto udp
```

If you are using FirewallD (see Chapter 11, FirewallD in the Firewall section), select the samba entry in the Zone | Services tab. You can configure ports on the Service | Samba tab.

If you are managing your IPtables firewall directly, you could manage access by adding the following IPtables rule. This accepts input on ports 137, 138, and 139 for TCP/IP protocol packages.

```
iptables -A INPUT -p tcp --dport 135 -j ACCEPT
iptables -A INPUT -p udp --dport 137-138 -j ACCEPT
iptables -A INPUT -p tcp --dport 445 -j ACCEPT
```

Setting Up Samba on the Desktop

Folder shares can be set up easily using the folder sharing capability of the GNOME file manager (nautilus-share), see Chapter 3. For more complex configuration you can either edit the **/etc/samba/samba.conf** file or use a desktop configuration tool like system-config-samba, Smb4k, or shares-admin (Chapter 15). The **system-config-samba** tool (see Figure 16-1) provides a basic configuration. The system-config-samba tool is not directly supported by Ubuntu or Linux Mint but is available on the Ubuntu Universe repository. Install the system-config-samba package using the Synaptic Package Manager. Once installed you have to also create an empty **/etc/libuser.conf** file using the **touch** command in a terminal window.

```
sudo touch /etc/libuser.conf
```

You can then run it from the Administration menu as Samba.

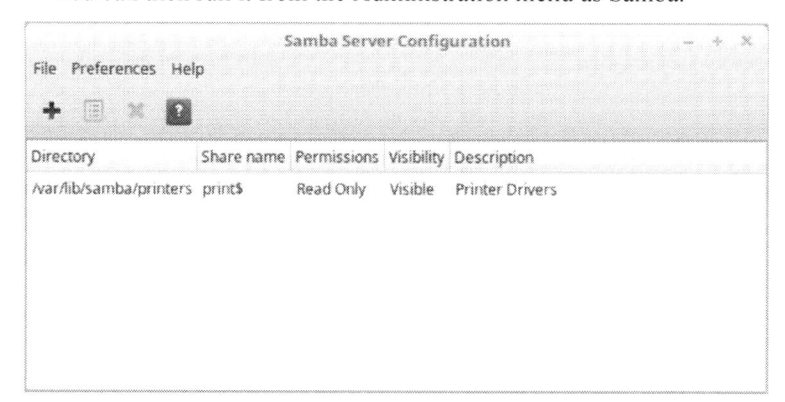

Figure 16-1: Samba server configuration with system-config-samba

Note: If you have already set up file sharing for Windows systems using the Nautilus sharing capability, the configuration information for those Samba shares will be displayed by system-config-samba.

Samba Server Configuration

You will first have to configure the Samba server, designating users that can have access to shared resources like directories and printers. On the Samba Preferences menu, select Server Settings to open the Server Settings dialog. On the Basic tab, enter the name of your Windows network workgroup (see Figure 16-2). The default names given by Windows are MSHOME or WORKGROUP. Use the workgroup name already given to your Windows network. For home networks, you can decide on your own. Just make sure all your computers use the same workgroup name. On a Windows system, the Control Panel's System application will show you the Windows workgroup name. The description is the name you want displayed for your Samba server on your Windows systems.

Figure 16-2: Samba Server Settings, Basic tab

On the Security tab, you can select the kind of authentication you want to use (see Figure 16-3). The authentication mode specifies the access level, which can be user, server (separate authentication server), ADS (Kerberos realm), or domain (Windows domain controller). User-level access restricts access by user password. Normally, you would elect to encrypt passwords, rather than have them passed over your network in plain text. The Guest user is the name of the account used to allow access to shares or printers that you want open to any user, without having to provide a password. The pop-up menu will list all your current users, with "No Guest Account" as the selected default. Unless you want to provide access by everyone to a share, you would not have a Guest account.

Figure 16-3: Samba Server Settings, Security tab

Samba Users

For user authentication, you will want to associate a Windows user with a particular Linux account. Select Samba Users in the Preferences menu to open the Samba Users dialog (see Figure 16-4). Users who were set up on your system when you installed Samba are listed already, using their usernames and password for access by Windows users. If you want to add a new Samba user, click Add User to open the Create New Samba User window. There you can select the Unix Username from a pop-up menu, and then enter the Windows Username and the Samba password to be used for that user (see Figure 16-5). The Unix Username menu lists all the users on your Samba server. Samba maintains its own set of passwords that users on other computers will need to access a Samba share. When a Windows user wants to access a Samba share, they will have to provide their Samba password. If you use a Windows username with spaces, enclose it within quotes.

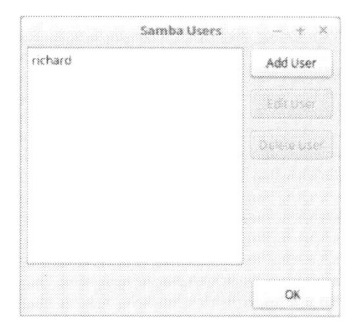

Figure 16-4: Samba Users

Once you create a Samba user, its name will appear in the list of Samba users on the Samba Users window. To later modify or delete a Samba user, use the same Samba Users window, select the user from the list, and click the Edit User button to change entries like the password, or click the Delete User button to remove the Samba user.

Figure 16-5: Create a new samba user

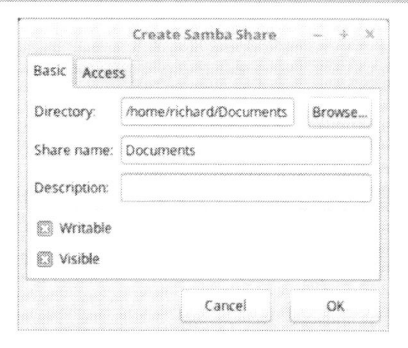

Figure 16-6: New Samba Share, Basic tab

Samba Shares

To set up a simple share, click Add Share in the Samba Server Configuration window, which opens a Create Samba Share window (see Figure 16-6).

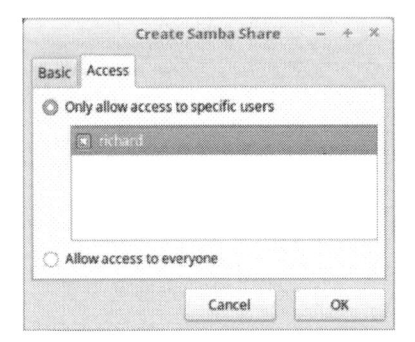

Figure 16-7: Samba share, Access tab

On the Basic tab, select the Linux folder to share (click Browse to find it), and then specify whether it will be writable and visible.

On the Access tab, you can choose to open the share to everyone, or just for specific users (see Figure 16-7). All Samba users on your system are listed with checkboxes where you can select those you want to give access.

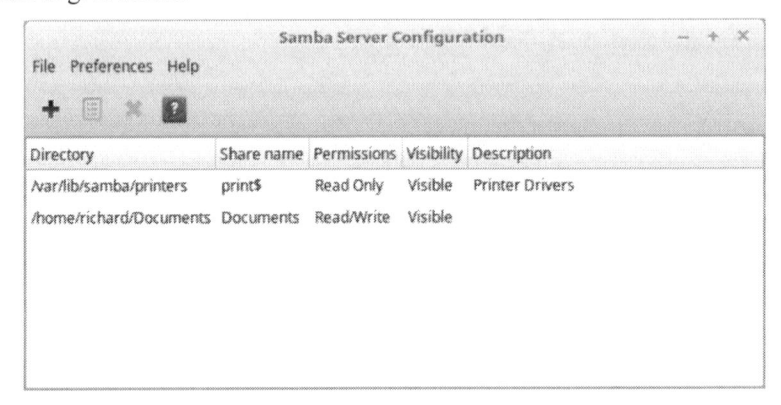

Figure 16-8: Samba with shares

Your new share will be displayed in the Samba Server Configuration window (see Figure 16-8). The share's directory, share name, its visibility, read/write permissions, and description are shown. To modify a share later, click on its entry and then click on the Properties button (or double-click). This opens an Edit samba share window with the same Basic and Access tabs you used to create the share.

User-Level Security

For stand-alone servers, Samba provides user-level security, requiring users on remote systems to log in using Samba-registered passwords. User-level security requires the use of Windows encrypted passwords. Windows uses its own methods of encryption. For Samba to handle such passwords, it has to maintain its own Windows-compatible password database. It cannot use the Linux password databases. Windows also uses additional information for the login process like where the user logged in.

User-level security requires that each user who wants to login to a Samba share from a Windows system have a corresponding user account on the Samba server. These are the users listed in the system-config-samba Samba Users window (see Figure 16-4). In addition, this account has to have a separate Samba password with which to log in to the Samba share. In effect, the user becomes a Samba user.

The account on the Samba server does not need to use the same username as that used on the Windows system. A Windows username can be specified for a Samba user. On system-config-samba, the Create New Samba User window lets you enter a Windows username in the Windows Username entry (see Figure 16-5). This mapping of windows users to Samba (Linux) users is listed in the **/etc/smbusers** file. The following maps the Windows user **rpetersen** to the Samba (Linux) user **richard**.

```
richard = rpetersen
```

When the Windows user in Windows tries to access the Samba share, the user will be prompt to login. The Windows user would then enter **rpetersen** as the username and the Samba password that was set up for **richard**. On system-config-samba, this is the Samba password entered in the Samba Password entries in the Create New Samba Users window (see Figure 16-5)

User-level security is managed by password back-end databases. By default, the **tdbsam** back-end database is used. This is a **tdb** database file (trivial database) that stores Samba passwords along with Windows extended information. The tdbsam database is designed for small networks. For systems using LDAP to manage users, you can use the LDAP-enabled back-end, **ldbsam**. The **ldbsam** database is designed for larger networks. The **smbpasswd** file previously used is still available, but it is included only for backward compatibility. The default configuration entries for user access in the **smb.conf file** are shown here, though, for a standalone server, user security is used and assumed. The security option will not be listed in the **smb.conf** file.

```
security = user
passdb backend = tdbsam
```

The **username map** option specifies the file used to associate Windows and Linux users. Windows users can use the Windows username to log in as the associated user. The username map file is usually **/etc/samba/smbusers**.

```
username map = /etc/samba/smbusers
```

If you are using an LDAP-enabled Samba database, ldbsam, you would use special LDAP Samba tools to manage users. These are provided in the **smbldap-tools** package. They are prefixed with the term smbldap. There are tools for adding, modifying, and deleting users and groups like **smbldap-useradd**, **smbldap-userdelete**, and **smbldap-groupmod**. You use the **sbmldap-passwd** command to manage Samba passwords with LDAP. The **smbldap-userinfo** command is used to obtain information about a user. You configure your LDAP Samba tools support using the **/etc/smbldap-tools/smbldap.conf** file.

Samba also provides its own Samba password Pluggable Authentication Module (PAM) module, **pam_smbpass.so**. With this module, you provide PAM authentication support for Samba passwords, enabling the use of Windows hosts on a PAM-controlled network. The module could be used for authentication and password management configured in your PAM **samba** file. The following entries in the PAM **samba** file would implement PAM authentication and passwords using the Samba password database:

```
auth required pam_smbpass.so nodelay
password required pam_smbpass.so nodelay
```

Be sure to enable PAM in the **smb.conf** file:

```
obey pam restrictions = yes
```

Samba Passwords: smbpasswd

With user-level security, access to Samba server resources by a Windows client is allowed only to users on that client. The username and Samba password used to access the Samba server must be registered in the Samba password database.

You can use either system-config-samba or the smbpasswd tool to manage Samba passwords. On system-config-samba, you use the Samba Users window (Preferences | Samba Users) to add or edit passwords (see Figure 16-4). Alternatively, you can use the **smbpasswd** command in a terminal window to add, or later change, passwords. To add or change a password for a particular user, you use the **smbpasswd** command with the username:

```
$ smbpasswd dylan
New SMB Password: new-password
Repeat New SMB Password: new-password
```

Users can use **smbpasswd** to change their own passwords. The following example shows how you would use **smbpasswd** to change your Samba password. If you have no Samba password, you can press the ENTER key.

```
$ smbpasswd
Old SMB password: old-password
New SMB Password: new-password
Repeat New SMB Password: new-password
```

Should you want to use no passwords, you can use smbpasswd with the **-n** option. The **smb.conf** file will need to have the **null passwords** option set to yes.

If you are using the older smb passwords file, be sure that Samba is configured to use encrypted passwords. Set the **encrypt passwords** option to **yes** and specify the SMB password file.

Managing Samba Users: smbpasswd and pdbedit

To manage users you can use the **smbpasswd** command, the **pdbedit** tool, or system-config-samba. The **smbpasswd** command with the **-a** option will add a user and with the **-x** option will remove one. To enable or disable users you would use the **-e** and **-d** options.

```
smbpasswd -a aleina
```

The smbpasswd command will operate on either the older smbpasswd file or the newer tdbsam backend database files. For the **tdbsam** backend database files, you can use **pdbedit**. To add a user you would use the **-a** option and to remove a user you use the **-x** option.

```
pdbedit -a larisa
```

This is a command line tool with options for adding and removing users, as well as features like changing passwords and setting the home directory. You can also import or export the user entries to or from other back-end databases.

The **pdbedit** command lets you display more information about users. To display users from the back-end database you could use the **-L** option. Add the **-v** option for detailed information. For a particular user, add the username.

```
pdbedit -Lv richard
```

For domain policies such as minimum password lengths or retries, you use the **-P** option.

```
pdbedit -P
```

You use the **-i** and **-e** options to import and export database entries. The following will import entries from the old **smbpasswd** file to the new **tdbsam** back-end database.

```
pdbedit -i smbpasswd -e tdbsam
```

If your system is using an LDAP-enabled Samba database, use the smbldap tools to manage users and groups.

The Samba smb.conf Configuration File

Samba configuration is held in the **smb.conf** file located in the /**etc/samba** directory. Samba configuration tools, such as system-config-samba, will maintain this file for you. Alternatively, you can manually edit the file directly, creating your own Samba configuration. You may have to do this if your Samba configuration proves to be very complex. Direct editing can provide more refined control over your shares.

You use the **testparm** command in a terminal window to check the syntax of any changes you have made to the **/etc/samba/smb.conf** file.

```
testparm
```

The file is separated into two basic parts: one for global options and the other for shared services. Shared services, also known as *shares*, can either be file space services (used by clients as an extension of their native file systems) or printable services (used by clients to access print services on the host running the server). The file space service is a directory to which clients are given access; they can use the space in it as an extension of their local file system. A printable service provides access by clients to print services, such as printers managed by the Samba server.

The **/etc/samba/smb.conf** file holds the configuration for the various shared resources, as well as global options that apply to all resources. Linux installs an **smb.conf** file in your **/etc/samba** directory. The file contains default settings. You can edit the file to customize your configuration to suit your needs. Comments are commented with a # sign and directives that are commented out to deactivate them, are commented with a semicolon, **;**. You can remove a directive's initial semi-colon symbol to make it effective. For a complete listing of the Samba configuration parameters, check the Man page for **smb.conf**.

The **smb.conf** file is organized into two main groups, Global Settings and Share Definitions, each labeled by a comment. The Global Settings section has several subsections for different settings: Browsing/Identification, Networking, Debugging/Accounting, Authentication, Domains, Printing, and Misc. They use shorter comment lines.

In the **smb.conf** file, global options are set first, followed by each shared resource's configuration. The basic organizing component of the **smb.conf** file is called a *section*. Each resource has its own section that holds its service name and definitions of its attributes. Even global options are placed in a section of their own, labeled **global**. For example, each section for a file space share consists of the directory and the access rights allowed to users of the file space. The section of each share is labeled with the name of the shared resource. Special sections called **printers** and **homes**, provide default descriptions for user directories and printers accessible on the Samba server. Following the special sections, other sections are entered for specific services, namely access to specific directories or printers.

A section begins with a section label, consisting of the name of the shared resource encased in brackets. Other than the special sections, the section label can be any name you choose. Following the section label, on separate lines, different parameters for this service are entered. The parameters define the access rights to be granted to the user of the service. For example, for a directory, you may want it to be browseable, but read-only, and use a certain printer. Parameters are entered in the format *parameter name = value*. You can enter a comment by placing a semicolon at the beginning of the comment line.

A simple example of a section configuration follows. The section label is encased in brackets and followed by two parameter entries. The **path** parameter specifies the directory to which access is allowed. The **writeable** parameter specifies whether the user has write access to this directory and its file space.

```
[mysection]
path = /home/chris
writeable = true
```

A printer service has the same format but requires certain other parameters. The path parameter specifies the location of the printer spool directory. The **read-only** and **printable** parameters are set to **true**, indicating the service is read-only and printable. **public** indicates anyone can access the service.

```
[myprinter]
path = /var/spool/samba
read only = true
printable = true
public = true
```

Parameter entries can be synonymous yet use different entries with the same meaning. For example, **read only** = **no**, **writeable** = **yes**, and **write ok** = **yes** all mean the same thing, providing write access to the user.

Variable Substitutions

For string values assigned to parameters, you can incorporate substitution operators. This provides greater flexibility in designating values that may be context-dependent, like usernames. For example, suppose a service needs to use a separate directory for each user who logs in. The path for such directories could be specified using the **%u** variable that substitutes in the name of the current user. The string **path** = **/tmp/%u** would become **path** = **/tmp/justin** for the **justin** user and **/tmp/dylan** for the **dylan** user. Table 16-3 lists several of the more common substitution variables.

Variable	Description
%S	Name of the current service
%P	Root directory of the current service
%u	Username of the current service
%H	Home directory of the user
%h	Internet hostname on which Samba is running
%m	NetBIOS name of the client machine
%L	NetBIOS name of the server
%M	Internet name of the client machine
%I	IP address of the client machine

Table 16-3: Samba Substitution Variables

Tip: The writeable option is an alias for the inverse of the read only option. The writeable = yes entry is the same as read only = no entry.

Global Settings

The Global Settings section determines configuration for the entire server, as well as specifying default entries to be used in the home and directory segments. In this section, you will find entries for the workgroup name, password configuration, and directory settings. Several of the more important entries are discussed here.

Browsing/Identification

The Workgroup entry specifies the workgroup name you want to give to your network. This is the workgroup name that appears on the Windows client's Network window. The default Workgroup entry in the **smb.conf** file is shown here:

```
[global]

# Change this to the workgroup/NT-domain name your Samba server will part of
 workgroup = WORKGROUP
```

The workgroup name has to be the same for each Windows client that the Samba server supports. On a Windows client, the workgroup name is usually found on the Network Identification or General tab in the System tool located in the Control Panel. On many clients, this defaults to WORKGROUP. This is also the default name specified in the **smb.conf** file. If you want to use another name, you have to change the **workgroup** entry in the **smb.conf** file accordingly. The **workgroup** entry in the **smb.conf** file and the workgroup name on each Windows client has to be the same. In this example the workgroup name is **mygroup**.

```
workgroup = mygroup
```

The server string entry holds the descriptive name you want displayed for the server on the client systems. On Windows systems, this is the name displayed on the Samba server icon. The default is Samba Server, but you can change this to any name you want.

```
# server string is the equivalent of the NT Description field
    server string = %h server (Samba, Ubuntu)
```

Note: You can also configure Samba to be a Primary Domain Controller (PDC) for Windows NT networks. As a PDC, Samba sets up the Windows domain that other systems will use, instead of participating in an already established workgroup.

Name service resolution is normally provided by the WINS server (Windows NetBIOS Name Service, **nmbd**). If your local network already has a WINS server, you can specify that instead. The commented default entry is shown here. Replace w.x.y.z with your network's WINS server name.

```
;    wins server = w.x.y.z
```

WINS server support by your Samba **nmbd** server would have to be turned off to avoid conflicts, turning your Samba name resolution server into just a client. The commented entry to turn off WINS support is shown here.

```
#    wins support = no
```

If your network also has its own Domain Name Service (DNS) server that it wants to use for name resolution, you can enable that instead. By default, this is turned off, as shown next. Change the no to yes to allow the use of your network's DNS server for Windows name resolution. Also, WINS server support would have to be turned off.

```
    dns proxy = no
```

Networking

This subsection has interface directives for assigning a network interface device to a particular network to use for your server. The entries are commented out by default. The commented default entry is shown here for localhost on the first Ethernet device. Be sure to replace eth0 with the actual name of your network device (predictable name), such as enp7s0. You can use **ifconfig** to find the name.

```
;    interfaces = 127.0.0.0/8 eth0
```

If the system your Samba server runs on is not protected by a firewall, or the firewall is running on the same system, you should also enable the following.

```
;    bind interfaces only = yes
```

Debugging/Accounting

This section has directives for setting up logging for the Samba server. The log file directive is configured with the **%m** substitution symbol so that a separate log file is set up for each machine that connects to the server.

```
log file = /var/log/samba/log.%m
```

The maximum size of a log file is set to 1000 lines.

```
max log size = 1000
```

To have Samba log only through syslog, set the **syslog only** option to yes.

```
syslog only = yes
```

The syslog directive is set to 0 to just log brief information to the system logs. Detailed logging is handled by the Samba server instead.

```
syslog = 0
```

The panic action directive notifies the administrator in case of a crash.

```
panic action = /usr/share/samba/panic-action %d
```

Authentication

The server role for the Samba server can be standalone, a member server, or a domain controller (primary, backup, or active directory). Usually, the server is a standalone server. The server role determines the security. For standalone server, the security is user, which requires a password login.

```
server role = standalone server
```

Windows clients use encrypted passwords for the login process. Passwords are encrypted by default and managed by the password database. In the following entries, the security is set to the user-level (**user**), and the password database file uses **tdbsam**.

```
passdb backend = tdbsam
```

You can use the security option to specify the security: **user** (user password), **domain** (Windows domain), or **ads** (Kerberos) security. The **auto** setting is the default, which derives the security from the server role. If the server role is **standalone server**, then the security is **user** and is not specified in the **smb.conf** file.

Support for Pluggable Authentication Modules (PAM) security is then turned on.

```
obey pam restrictions = yes
```

Sync unix password with smb password changes.

```
unix password sync = yes
```

When Samba passwords are changed, they need to be synced with UNIX passwords. The **unix password sync** directive turns on syncing, and the **passwd program** and **passwd chat** directives use the **passwd** command and specified prompts to change the password.

```
unix password sync = yes
passwd program = /usr/bin/passwd %u
passwd chat = *Enter\snew\s*\spassword:* %n\n *Retype\snew\s*\spassword:* %n\n *password\supdated\ssuccessfully* .
```

PAM is also used for password changes by Samba clients.

```
pam password change = yes
```

As a security measure, you can restrict access to SMB services to certain specified local networks. On the host's network, type the network addresses of the local networks for which you want to permit access. To deny access to everyone in a network except a few particular hosts, you can use the EXCEPT option after the network address with the IP addresses of those hosts. The localhost (127) is always automatically included. The next example allows access to two local networks:

```
hosts allow = 192.168.1. 192.168.2.
```

The map to guest directive is set to bad user. This will allow any unknown users to log in as guests. Samba users that fail to log in though will not be allowed access, even as guests.

```
map to guest = bad user
```

Domains

The Domains subsection configures your Samba server as a Microsoft Public Domain Controller (PDC). All of these directives are commented out by default. See the section later in this chapter on Public Domain Controller on how to set up your Samba server as a PDC on a Microsoft network.

Misc

The Misc subsection has entries used to customize your server. Most are commented out, except for the **usershare** directive that allows users to create public shares. An include directive lets you set up configuration files for particular machines in the **/home/samba/etc** directory, that are then read when the machine connects.

```
;     include = /home/samba/etc/smb.conf.%m
```

There are also entries for those using the Winbind server, specifying the user and group id ranges, and the shell to use.

```
# Some defaults for winbind (make sure you're not using the ranges
# for something else.)
;    idmap uid = 10000-20000
;    idmap gid = 10000-20000
;    template shell = /bin/bash
```

The usershare directives allow non-root users to share folders. A commented entry for user max shares can be use to limit the number of shares a user can set up.

```
;     usershare max shares = 100
```

The **user allow guests** directive permits users to create public shares, allowing guests to access the shares.

```
# Allow users who've been granted usershare privileges to create
# public shares, not just authenticated ones
usershare allow guests = yes
```

You can use a guest user login to make resources available to anyone without requiring a password. A guest user login would handle any users who log in without a specific account. Samba is usually set up to use the **nobody** user as the guest user. Alternatively, you can set up and designate a specific user to use as the guest user. You can designate the guest user with the **guest ok** and **guest account** entries in the **smb.conf** file. Be sure to add the guest user to the password file (you can also set up the guest user on the system-config-samba Server Settings dialog, Security tab, Guest Account menu).

```
guest ok = yes
guest account = nobody
```

In addition, this section provides several performance tweaks, such as setting socket options for Linux systems.

Share Definitions

The Share Definitions part will hold sections for the definition of commonly used shares, as well as any shares you have set up yourself, like shared directories or printers. There are three special sections: homes, netlogon, and profiles that are used for special purposes.

Homes Section

The Homes section specifies default controls for accessing a user home directory through the SMB protocols by remote users. Setting the **browseable** entry to **no** prevents the client from listing the files in a file browser. The **read only** entry specifies whether users have read access to files in their home directories. The **create mask** and **directory mask** entries set default permissions for new files and directories. The permission is 0700, which allows owner read/write/execute permission. The **valid users** entry uses the **%S** macro to map to the current service. You can add the **writeable** directive to allow write access.

```
writeable = yes
```

All these entries are commented out, disabling access to user home directories by default. To enable access to home directories, remove the semi-colon comment in front of each entry in the **smb.conf** file. If you are setting up a PDC and chose to save user profiles in the user home directories, then the homes section and its entries have to be un-commented.

```
[homes]
 comment = Home Directories
 browseable = no
 read only = yes
 create mask = 0700
 directory mask = 0700
 valid users = %S
```

The printers and print$ Sections

The printers section specifies the default controls for accessing printers. These are used for printers for which no specific sections exist. Setting **browseable** to **no** simply hides the Printers section from the client, not the printers. The **path** entry specifies the location of the spool directory Samba will use for printer files. To enable printing at all, the **printable** entry must be set to yes. To allow guest users to print, set the **guest ok** entry to **yes**. The standard implementation of the Printers section is shown here:

```
[printers]
comment = All Printers
browseable = no
path = /var/spool/samba
printable = yes
guest ok = no
read only = yes
create mask = 0700
```

The **print$** section, shown next, specifies where a Windows client can find a print driver on your Samba server. The printer drivers are located in the **/var/lib/samba/printers** directory and are read-only. The browseable, read-only, and guest directives are commented out. They can be enabled to allow browsing of the drivers. The **write list** directive would allow you to remotely administer the Windows print drivers. **lpadmin** is the name of your administrator group.

```
# Windows clients look for this share name as a source of downloadable
# printer drivers
[print$]
   comment = Printer Drivers
   path = /var/lib/samba/printers
  browseable = yes
  read only = yes
  guest ok = no
;  write list = root, @lpadmin
```

Shares

Sections for specific shared resources, such as directories on your system, are placed after the Homes and Printers sections. For a section defining a shared directory, enter a label for the share. Then, on separate lines, enter options for its pathname and the different permissions you want to set. In the **path** = *option,* specify the full pathname for the directory. The **comment** = *option* holds the label to be given the share. You can make a directory writeable, public, or read-only. You can control access to the directory with the **valid users** entry, which you can use to list those users permitted access. For those options not set, the defaults entered in the Global, Homes, and Printers segments are used.

The following example is the **myprojects** share. Here the **/myprojects** directory is defined as a shared resource that is open to any user with guest access.

```
[myprojects]
    comment = Great Project Ideas
    path = /myprojects
    read only = no
    guest ok = yes
```

To limit access to certain users, you can list a set of valid users. Setting the **guest ok** option to **no** closes it off from access by others.

```
[mynewmusic]
comment =  New Music
path = /home/specialprojects
valid users = mark, richard
guest ok = no
read only = no
```

The following example makes the Documents folder accessible and writeable to the georgep and richard users.

```
[Documents]
path = /home/richard/Documents
writeable = yes
browseable = yes
valid users = georgep, richard
```

To allow complete public access, set the **guest ok** entry to **yes**, with no valid users entry.

```
[newdocs]
comment =  New Documents
path = /home/newdocs
guest ok = yes
read only = no
```

To set up a directory that can be shared by more than one user, where each user has control of the files he or she creates, simply list the users in the Valid Users entry. Permissions for any created files are specified in the Advanced mode by the Create Mask entry (same as create mode). In this example, the permissions are set to 765, which provides read/write/execute access to owners, read/write access to members of the group, and only read/execute access to all others (the default is 744, read-only for group and other permission):

```
[myshare]
 comment = Writer's projects
 path = /usr/local/drafts
 valid users = Justin, chris, dylan
 guest ok = no
 read only = no
 create mask = 0765
```

Printer shares

Access to specific printers is defined in the Printers section of the **smb.conf** file. For a printer, you need to include the Printer and Printable entries, as well as specify the type of Printing server used. With the Printer entry, you name the printer, and by setting the Printable entry to yes, you allow it to print. You can control access to specific users with the **valid users** entry and by setting the Public entry to no. For public access, set the **public** entry to yes. For the CUPS server, set the printing option to **cups**.

The following example sets up a printer accessible to guest users. This opens the printer to use by any user on the network. Users need to have write-access to the printer's spool directory, located in **/var/spool/samba**. Keep in mind that any printer has to first be installed on your system. The following printer was already installed as **myhp**. You use the CUPS administrative tool to set up printers for the CUPS server. The Printing option can be inherited from the Printers share.

```
[myhp]
    path = /var/spool/samba
    read only = no
    guest ok = yes
    printable = yes
    printer = myhp
    oplocks = no
    share modes = no
    printing = cups
```

As with shares, you can restrict printer use to certain users, denying it to public access. The following example sets up a printer accessible only by the users **larisa** and **aleina** (you could add other users if you want). Users need to have write access to the printer's spool directory.

```
[larisalaser]
    path = /var/spool/samba
    read only = no
    valid users = larisa aleina
    guest ok = no
    printable = yes
    printing = cups
    printer = larisalaser
    oplocks = no
    share modes = no
```

Testing the Samba Configuration

After you make your changes to the **smb.conf** file, you can then use the **testparm** program to see if the entries are correctly entered. **testparm** checks the syntax and validity of Samba entries. By default, testparm checks the **/etc/samba/smb.conf** file. If you are using a different file as your configuration file, you can specify it as an argument to testparm. You can also have testparm check to see if a particular host has access to the service set up by the configuration file.

To check the real-time operation of your Samba server, you can log in to a user account on the Linux system running the Samba server and connect to the server.

Samba Public Domain Controller: Samba PDC

Samba can also operate as a Public Domain Controller (PDC). The domain controller will be registered and advertised on the network as the domain controller. The PDC provides a much more centralized way to control access to Samba shares. It provides the netlogon service and a NETLOGON share. The PDC will set up machine trust accounts for each Windows and Samba client. Though you can do this manually, Samba will do it for you automatically. Keep in mind that Samba cannot emulate a Microsoft Active PDC, but can emulate a Windows NT4 PDC. You can find out more about Samba PDC at:

```
https://www.samba.org/samba/docs/man/Samba-HOWTO-Collection/samba-pdc.html
```

For basic configuration check the Ubuntu Server Guide | Windows Networking | Samba as a Domain Controller.

```
https://help.ubuntu.com/lts/serverguide/samba-dc.html
```

Microsoft Domain Security

As noted in the Samba documentation, the primary benefit of Microsoft domain security is single-sign-on (SSO). In effect, logging into your user account also logs you into access to your entire network's shared resources. Instead of having to be separately authenticated any time you try to access a shared network resource, you are already authenticated. Authentication is managed using Security IDs (SID) that consists of a network ID (NID) and a relative ID (RID). The RID references your personal account. A separate RID is assigned to every account, even those for groups or system services. The SID is used to set up access control lists (ACL) the different shared resources on your network, allowing a resource to automatically identify you.

Essential Samba PDC configuration options

To configure your PDC, edit the **Domains** section in the **smb.conf** file. Here you will find entries for configuring your Samba PDC options. Certain other entries are found elsewhere. The domain master entry is located in the Misc section.

The essential PDC options are shown here.

```
workgroup = myworkgroup
domain logons = yes
domain master = yes
security = user
```

If the netbios name is different from the hostname on which the server is run, you can add a **netbios name** option to specify it.

```
netbios name = myserver
```

Basic configuration

Like most Samba configurations, the PDC requires a Samba back-end. The **tdbsam** is already configured for you. The security level should be **user**. This is normally the default and is already be set. The **smb.conf** entry is shown here:

```
passdb backend = tdbsam
```

The PDC must also be designated the domain master. This is set to auto by default. For a PDC, set it to yes, and for a BDC (backup domain controller) set it to no.

```
domain master = yes
```

The PDC has browser functionality, with which it locates systems and shares on your network. These features are not present in the **smb.conf** file, but you can add them if needed. The **local master** option is used only if you already have another PDC that you want to operate as the local master. You could have several domain controllers operating on your network. Your Microsoft network holds an election to choose which should be the master. The **os level** sets the precedence for this PDC. It should be higher than 32 to gain preference over other domain controllers on your network, ensuring this PDC's election as the primary master controller. The **preferred master** option starts the browser election on startup.

```
;       local master = no
os level = 33
preferred master = yes
```

Domain Logon configuration

Samba PDC uses the domain logons service whereby a user can log on to the network. The domain logon service is called the netlogon service by Microsoft. The samba share it uses is also called netlogon. To configure the domain logon service, you set the **domain logons** option to yes, or if you set the **server role** option to "primary classic domain controller" or to "backup domain controller."

```
domain logons = yes
```

The logon path references the profile used for a user. The **%N** will be the server name, and the **%U** references the username. Profiles can be set up either in a separate profiles share or in the user home directories. The following would reference user profiles in the profiles share. You would also have to define the profiles share by un-commenting the profiles share entries in the **smb.conf** file.

```
logon path = \\%N\Profiles\%U
```

If the profile is stored in the user's home directory instead of the Profiles share, you would uncomment the following entry instead. You will also have to allow access to user home directories, un-commenting the homes share entries.

```
logon path = \\%N\%U\profile
```

The **logon drive** and **logon home** specify the location of the user's home directory. The logon drive is set as the H: drive. The **%N** evaluates to the server name and **%U** to the user.

```
logon drive = H:
logon home = \\%N\%U
```

The login script can be one set by the system or by users.

```
# the login script name depends on the machine name
logon script = logon.cmd
```

You can then enable user add operations for adding users, groups, and machines to the PDC. The add machine entry allows Samba to automatically add trusted machine accounts for Windows systems when they first join the PDC controlled network.

```
add user script = /usr/sbin/adduser --quiet --disabled-password --gecos "" %u
add machine script = /usr/sbin/useradd -g machines -c "%u machine account" -d /var/lib/samba -s /bin/false %u
add group script = /usr/sbin/addgroup --force-badname %g
```

You then need to set up a netlogon share in the **smb.conf** file. This share holds the **netlogon** scripts, in this case, the **/var/lib/samba/netlogon** directory, which should not be writable, but should be accessible by all users (Guest OK). In the share definitions section of the **smb.conf** file, you will find the **[netlogon]** section commented. Remove the semi-colon comments from the entry, as shown here.

```
# Un-comment the following and create the netlogon directory for Domain Logon
# (you need to configure Samba to act as a domain controller too.)
[netlogon]
comment = Network Logon Service
path = /home/samba/netlogon
guest ok = yes
read only = yes
```

If you choose to use a profiles share to store user profiles in, then you should enable the **profiles** share. Un-comment the following (remove the preceding semi-colon) to define a **profiles** share. The entries are located just after the **netlogon** shares.

```
[profiles]
comment = Users profiles
path = /home/samba/profiles
guest ok = no
browseable = no
create mask = 0600
directory mask = 0700
wins support = no
username map = /etc/samba/smbusers
security = user
encrypt passwords = yes
guest ok = no
guest account = nobody
```

The **profile** share is where user netlogon profiles are stored. If instead, you are using the user's home directories to store their profiles, you will not need to define and use a **profiles** share. If you choose to store user profiles in the user home directories, you would un-comm

ent the **homes** share entries instead.

Accessing Samba Services with Clients

Client systems connected to the SMB network can access the shared services provided by the Samba server. Windows clients should be able to access shared directories and services automatically through the My Network Places or Network on a Windows desktop. For Linux systems connected to the same network, Samba services can be accessed using the GNOME Nautilus file manager and KDE file manager, as well as special Samba client programs.

With the Samba smbclient, a command line client, a local Linux system can connect to a shared directory on the Samba server and transfer files and run shell programs. Using the **mount** command with the **-t cifs** option, directories on the Samba server can be mounted to local directories on the Linux client. The **cifs** option invokes **mount.cifs** to mount the directory.

Accessing Windows Samba Shares from GNOME

On the desktop, you can use a file manager like GNOME Files to access your Samba shares. Open the Network window (Network on the sidebar) to display the icons for your network. In this window, open the Windows Network folder to list folders for your Windows network groups, such as WORKGROUP. Opening up a Windows group folder will list the hosts in that group. These will show host icons for your shared Windows hosts. Clicking a host icon will list all the shared resources on it.

Alternatively, you can enter the **smb:** protocol in the file manager's Location box to display all the Samba and Windows networks, from which you can access the Samba and Windows shares.

smbclient

The smbclient utility operates like FTP to access systems using the SMB protocols. With smbclient, you can access SMB-shared services, either on the Samba server or on Windows systems. Many smbclient commands are similar to those of FTP, such as **mget** to transfer a file or **del** to delete a file. The smbclient program has several options for querying a remote system, as well as connecting to it. See the **smbclient** Man page for a complete list of options and commands. The smbclient program takes as its argument a server name and the service you want to access on that server. A double slash precedes the server name, and a single slash denotes the service. The service can be any shared resource, such as a directory or a printer. The server name is its NetBIOS name, which may or may not be the same as its IP name. For example, to specify the **myreports** shared directory on the server named **turtle.mytrek.com**, use **//turtle.mytrek.com/myreports**. If you must specify a pathname, use backslashes for Windows files and forward slashes for Unix/Linux files:

```
//server-name/service
```

You can also supply the password for accessing the service. Enter it as an argument following the service name. If you do not supply the password, you are prompted to enter it.

You can then add several options to access shares, such as the remote username or the list of services available. With the **-I** option, you can specify the system using its IP address. You use the **-U** option and a login name for the remote login name you want to use on the remote system. Attach **%** with the password if a password is required. With the **-L** option, you can obtain a list of the services provided on a server, such as shared directories or printers. The following command will list the shares available on the host **turtle.mytrek.com**:

```
smbclient -L turtle.mytrek.com
```

To access a particular directory on a remote system, enter the directory as an argument to the **smbclient** command, followed by any options. For Windows files, you use backslashes for the pathnames, and for Unix/Linux files, you use forward slashes. Once connected, an SMB prompt is displayed and you can use smbclient commands such as **get** and **put** to transfer files. The **quit** and **exit** commands quit the smbclient program. In the following example, smbclient accesses the directory **myreports** on the **turtle.mytrek.com** system, using the **dylan** login name:

```
smbclient //turtle.mytrek.com/myreports -I 192.168.0.1 -U dylan
```

In most cases, you can simply use the server name to reference the server, as shown here:

```
smbclient //turtle.mytrek.com/myreports -U dylan
```

If you are accessing the home directory of a particular account on the Samba server, you can simply specify the **homes** service. In the next example, the user accesses the home directory of the **aleina** account on the Samba server, after being prompted to enter that account's password:

```
smbclient //turtle.mytrek.com/homes -U aleina
```

You can also use smbclient to access shared resources located on Windows clients. Specify the computer name of the Windows client along with its shared folder. In the next example, the user accesses the **windata** folder on the Windows client named **lizard**. The folder is configured to allow access by anyone, so the user just presses the ENTER key at the password prompt.

```
$ smbclient //lizard/windata
```

Once logged in, you can execute smbclient commands to manage files and change directories. Shell commands can be executed with the ! operator. To transfer files, you can use the **mget** and **mput** commands, much as they are used in the FTP program. The **recurse** command enables you to turn on recursion to copy whole subdirectories at a time. You can use file-matching operators, referred to here as *masks*, to select a certain collection of files. The file-matching (mask) operators are *, ||, and ? (see Chapter 19). The default mask is *, which matches everything. The following example uses **mget** to copy all files with a **.c** suffix, as in **myprog.c**:

```
smb> mget *.c
```

mount.cifs: mount -t cifs

Using the **mount** command with the **-t cifs** option, a Linux client can mount a shared directory onto its local system. The **cifs** option invokes the **mount.cifs** command to perform the mount operation. The syntax for the **mount.cifs** command is similar to that for the **smbclient** command, with many corresponding options. The **mount.cifs** command takes as its arguments the Samba server and shared directory, followed by the local directory where you want to mount the directory. Instead of using **mount.cifs** explicitly, you use the **mount** command with the file system type **cifs**. The **mount** command will then run the **/sbin/mount.cifs** command, which will invoke **smbclient** to mount the file system. The following example mounts the **myreports** directory onto the **/mnt/myreps** directory on the local system.

```
mount -t cifs //turtle.mytrek.com/myreports /mnt/myreps -U dylan
```

To unmount the directory, use the **umount** command with the **-t cifs** option and the directory name. This will invoke the **umount.cifs** command which performs the unmount operation.

```
umount -t cifs /mnt/myreps
```

To mount the home directory of a particular user on the server, specify the **homes** service and the user's login name. The following example mounts the home directory of the user **larisa** to the **/home/chris/larisastuff** directory on the local system:

```
mount -t cifs //turtle.mytrek.com/homes /home/chris/larisastuff -U larisa
```

You can also mount shared folders on Windows clients. Specify the computer name of the Windows client along with its folder. If the folder name contains spaces, enclose it in single quotes. In the following example, the user mounts the **windata** folder on **lizard** as the **/mylinux** directory. For a folder with access to anyone, just press ENTER at the password prompt:

```
$ mount -t cifs //lizard/windata /mylinux
Password:
$ ls /mylinux
_hi_mynewdoc.doc_myreport.txt
```

To unmount the shared folder when you are finished with it, use the **umount** command and the **-t cifs** option.

```
umount -t cifs /mylinux
```

You could also specify a username and password as options if user-level access is required:

```
mount -t cifs -o username=chris passwd=mypass //lizard/windata /mylinux
```

You can also use the **cifs** type in an **/etc/fstab** entry to have a Samba file system mounted automatically:

```
//lizard/windata /mylinux cifs defaults 0 0
```

Table Listing

Table 1-1: Linux Mint Editions 30

Table 1-2: Linux Mint resources and help 33

Table 1-3: Linux Mint Welcome Screen resources 34

Table 1-4: Ubuntu help and documentation 35

Table 3-1: Window and File Manager Keyboard shortcuts 70

Table 4-1: Linux Software Package File Extensions 122

Table 4-2: apt-get commands 123

Table 5-1: X-App Applications 131

Table 5-2: LibreOffice Applications 132

Table 5-3: Calligra Applications 132

Table 5-4: GNOME Office and Other Office Applications for GNOME 133

Table 5-5: PostScript, PDF, and DVI viewers 134

Table 5-6: Ebook Readers 134

Table 5-7: Desktop Editors 135

Table 5-8: Database Management Systems for Linux 136

Table 5-9: Linux Mail Clients 137

Table 5-10: Linux Newsreaders 139

Table 5-11: Graphics Tools for Linux 141

Table 5-12: Music players, editors, and rippers 144

Table 5-13: Video and DVD Projects and Applications 146

Table 5-14: CD/DVD Burners 147

Table 5-15: Web browsers 148

Table 5-16: Java Packages and Java Web Applications 149

Table 5-17: Linux FTP Clients 150

Table 5-18: Instant Messenger, Talk, and VoIP Clients 152

Table 6-1: Cinnamon Keyboard Shortcuts 162

Table 6-2: File Manager View Menu 186

Table 6-3: File Manager File Menu 187

Table 6-4: File Manager Edit Menu	188
Table 6-5: File Manager Pop-up Menu	189
Table 6-6: File Manager Go Menu	190
Table 6-7: The File Manager Sidebar Pop-Up Menu	191
Table 6-8: The File and Directory Pop-Up Menu	193
Table 6-9: Desktop System Settings	200
Table 7-1: The Desktop Menu	221
Table 7-2: File Manager Go Menu	237
Table 7-3: File Manager File Menu	238
Table 7-4: File Manager View Menu	242
Table 7-5: File Manager Edit Menu	243
Table 7-6: File Manager Pop-up Menu	244
Table 7-7: The File Manager Side Pane Pop-Up Menu	244
Table 7-8: The File and Directory Pop-Up Menu	246
Table 7-9: The Mate Preferences	251
Table 8-1: KDE Websites	262
Table 8-2: Desktop, Plasma, and KWin Keyboard Shortcuts	265
Table 8-3: KWin desktop effects keyboard shortcuts	290
Table 8-4: KDE File Manager Keyboard Shortcuts	296
Table 9-1: Linux Mint System Tools	308
Table 9-2: Sensor packages and applications	314
Table 9-3: Sound device and interface tools	318
Table 9-4: PulseAudio commands (command-line)	322
Table 10-1: Linux Mint Administration Tools	328
Table 10-2: Backup Resources	361
Table 11-1: Linux Mint Network Configuration Tools	376
Table 11-2: The nmcli objects	394
Table 11-3: Variables for wvdial	398
Table 11-4: Service ports	403
Table 11-5: UFW firewall operations	408
Table 11-6: Network Interface Device Naming	416

Table 12-1: Shell Invocation Command Names	422
Table 12-2: Shell Configuration Files	423
Table 12-3: BASH Shell Special Features	426
Table 12-4: Shell Variables, Set by the Shell	427
Table 12-5: System Environment Variables Used by the Shell	430
Table 13-1: systemd unit types and man pages	444
Table 13-2: systemd Unit and Install section options (common to all units, systemd.unit)	446
Table 13-3: special units	448
Table 13-4: special runlevel targets (boot)	448
Table 13-5: systemd exec options (Service, Socket, Mount, Swap) (systemd.exec)	450
Table 13-6: systemd service options [Service] (systemd.service)	451
Table 13-7: Collection of Service unit files	452
Table 13-8: systemd socket file options [Socket] (systemd.socket)	454
Table 13-9: path option (systemd.path)	455
Table 13-10: System Runlevels (States)	457
Table 13-11: systemd mount and automount file options [Mount] [Automount]	459
Table 13-12: System Shutdown Options	462
Table 13-13: AppArmor Utilities	468
Table 13-14: SSH Tools	473
Table 13-15: SSH Configuration Files	475
Table 14-1: Print Resources	482
Table 14-2: CUPS Configuration Files	502
Table 14-3: CUPS Print Clients	508
Table 14-4: CUPS Administrative Tools	510
Table 15-1: The /etc/exports Options	520
Table 15-2: NFS Mount Options	525
Table 15-3: NSS-Supported databases	528
Table 15-4: NSS Configuration Services	529
Table 16-1: Samba packages on Linux Mint	532
Table 16-2: Samba Server Applications	534
Table 16-3: Samba Substitution Variables	545

Figure Listing

Figure 1-1: Linux Mint 18.2 Cinnamon Desktop 29

Figure 1-2: Linux Mint 18.2 Cinnamon Live DVD 31

Figure 1-3: Linux Mint Welcome dialog 33

Figure 2-1: Live DVD (Desktop) with Install icon. 43

Figure 2-2: Install Third-Party Software 44

Figure 2-3: No detected operating systems 45

Figure 2-4: Manually partitioning a new hard drive 49

Figure 2-5: Select free space on a blank hard drive 49

Figure 2-6: Hard drive with windows on part of the drive 50

Figure 2-7: Create a new swap partition 50

Figure 2-8: Create a new root partition 51

Figure 2-9: Manual partitions 51

Figure 2-10: Where Are You, Time zone 53

Figure 2-11: Keyboard Layout 54

Figure 2-12: Who are you? 55

Figure 2-13: Install progress slide show 55

Figure 2-14: Recovery options 56

Figure 3-1: Linux Mint GRUB menu 60

Figure 3-2: Editing a GRUB menu item 61

Figure 3-3: LightDM Login Screen with user list 62

Figure 3-4: LightDM Login Screen with Shut Down options 62

Figure 3-5: LightDM Login screen with desktop choices 63

Figure 3-6: Login Window Preferences 64

Figure 3-7: Login Window with no grid and no hostname 64

Figure 3-8: Lock Screen 65

Figure 3-9: Shut Down and Restart dialog 66

Figure 3-10: Log Out dialog 66

Figure 3-11: Linux Mint Cinnamon desktop 68

Figure 3-12: Linux Mint Cinnamon menu 68

Figure 3-13: Nemo File manager 70

Figure 3-14: Linux Mint Mate desktop 71

Figure 3-15: Linux Mint Menu (Mate) 72

Figure 3-16: Caja File manager 73

Figure 3-17: KDE Linux Mint desktop 74

Figure 3-18: KDE Menu 74

Figure 3-19: Dolphin File manager 75

Figure 3-20: Xfce desktop 76

Figure 3-21: Xfce Whisker menu 77

Figure 3-22: Xfce Settings Manager 78

Figure 3-23: Network Manager connections menu 83

Figure 3-24: Network Manager connections menu: wired and wireless 83

Figure 3-25: Network Manager wireless authentication 84

Figure 3-26: System Settings Networking wireless connections (Cinnamon) 85

Figure 3-27: System Settings Networking wireless Known Networks (Cinnamon) 85

Figure 3-28: System Settings Networking wireless information (Cinnamon) 86

Figure 3-29: Proxy settings (System Settings Networking) (Cinnamon) 87

Figure 3-30: Connect to a Hidden Wireless Network 87

Figure 3-31: Hardware Drivers: Driver Manager 88

Figure 3-32: Proprietary video driver: Software Sources, Device Drivers tab 89

Figure 3-33: Displays 90

Figure 3-34: Color Management dialog 91

Figure 3-35: Linux Mint User Guide 93

Figure 3-36: Linux Mint User Guide Topic 93

Figure 3-37: Linux Mint User Guide: All Documents 94

Figure 3-38: Terminal Window 95

Figure 3-39: Terminal Window without menubar 96

Figure 3-40: Terminal Window Profile configuration 96

Figure 4-1: Software Sources Linux Mint Official Repositories. 105

Figure Listing **565**

Figure 4-2: Software Sources Mirrors...105
Figure 4-3: Software Sources Additional Repositories..106
Figure 4-4: Software Sources PPA 106
Figure 4-5: Software Sources Authentication Keys..107
Figure 4-6: Update Policy...108
Figure 4-7: Update Manager update icon and package information dialog......................108
Figure 4-8: Update Manager with selected packages..109
Figure 4-9: Update download and install..110
Figure 4-10: Update Manager Preferences 111
Figure 4-11: Software Manager..112
Figure 4-12: Software Manager sub-categories...112
Figure 4-13: Software Manager package listing 113
Figure 4-14: Software Manager application 114
Figure 4-15: Software Manager and Launcher item download and install progress........114
Figure 4-16: Software Manager installed application...115
Figure 4-17: Software Manager search..115
Figure 4-18: Synaptic Package Manager: Quick search 116
Figure 4-19: Synaptic Package Manager: Sections 117
Figure 4-20: Synaptic Package Manager: Status 118
Figure 5-1: Xreader X-App Document Viewer 133
Figure 5-2: Xed X-App editor...135
Figure 5-3: Xviewer X-App Image Viewer 140
Figure 5-4: Pix X-App Image Viewer, Organizer, and Editor 140
Figure 5-5: Linux Mint codec wizard selection 142
Figure 5-6: Xplayer X-App Video Player...144
Figure 5-7: GNOME FTP access Connect to Server dialog 151
Figure 5-8: GNOME FTP access with Connect to Server and the file manager................152
Figure 6-1: Cinnamon desktop...156
Figure 6-2: Cinnamon desktop with Cinnamon Menu and Nemo file manager...............157
Figure 6-3: System Settings Desktop 158
Figure 6-4: Desklets on the desktop...158

Figure 6-5: Desklets Installed tab 159

Figure 6-6: Desklets "Get more online" tab 159

Figure 6-7: System Settings Hot Corners 160

Figure 6-8: System Settings Keyboard, Keyboard Shortcuts................................ 161

Figure 6-9: Cinnamon menu 162

Figure 6-10: Cinnamon menu search 163

Figure 6-11: Cinnamon menu favorites.. 163

Figure 6-12: Cinnamon menu 164

Figure 6-13: Cinnamon menu applet menu... 165

Figure 6-14: Cinnamon menu Main Menu editor 165

Figure 6-15: Windows Settings: Titlebar tab 166

Figure 6-16: Windows Settings: Behavior tab 167

Figure 6-17: Windows Settings: Alt-tab tab 167

Figure 6-18: Window Tiling and Edge Flip 168

Figure 6-19: Window List menus and configuration 169

Figure 6-20: Windows QuickList menu.. 170

Figure 6-21: Scale: zoomed windows to switch windows (Hot corners, Show all windows) 171

Figure 6-22: Window switching with Alt-Tab (Icons and Thumbnails)............... 172

Figure 6-23: Window switching with Alt-Tab (Coverflow 3D) 172

Figure 6-24: System Settings Effects: Enable effects tab................................... 173

Figure 6-25: System Settings Effects: Customize tab... 173

Figure 6-26: Workspace Switcher applet... 174

Figure 6-27: Hot Corner with Expo enabled 174

Figure 6-28: Expo workspace configuration (square grid).................................. 175

Figure 6-29: Expo workspace configuration (no grid) 175

Figure 6-30: System Settings Workspaces: OSD and Settings tabs 176

Figure 6-31: The Linux Mint panel with menu, window list, and applets, at the bottom of Linux Mint desktop 177

Figure 6-32: The panel pop-up menu (right-click on middle) and panel applet menu 177

Figure 6-33: The panel menu Troubleshoot and Modify submenus 178

Figure 6-34: The Linux Mint panel in edit mode 178

Figure 6-35: The panel settings dialog 179
Figure 6-36: The Applets Dialog Installed tab 179
Figure 6-37: The Applets dialog "Available applets (online)" tab 180
Figure 6-38: Panel Launchers applet 181
Figure 6-39: Nemo file manager home folders 182
Figure 6-40: File manager with sidebar 182
Figure 6-41: File manager sidebar with bookmarks menu 183
Figure 6-42: File manager sidebar Places menus, expanded and unexpanded 184
Figure 6-43: File manager sidebar Treeview menus, expanded and unexpanded 184
Figure 6-44: File manager window with tabs 185
Figure 6-45: File manager File, View, and Edit menus 187
Figure 6-46: File manager navigation 189
Figure 6-47: Expanded and unexpanded paths and location 190
Figure 6-48: Nemo File Manager Search 191
Figure 6-49: Nemo Plugins and Extensions 192
Figure 6-50: File properties on Nemo 195
Figure 6-51: System Settings dialog (Appearance and Preferences) 197
Figure 6-52: System Settings dialog (Hardware and Administration) 197
Figure 6-53: Backgrounds: Images tab 201
Figure 6-54: Backgrounds: Settings tab 201
Figure 6-55: Fonts 202
Figure 6-56: Themes 203
Figure 6-57: Themes (Installed Themes) 203
Figure 6-58: Themes (Online Themes) 204
Figure 6-59: Themes (Settings tab) 204
Figure 6-60: Preferred Applications 205
Figure 6-61: Preferred Applications: Removable media 206
Figure 6-62: Calendar applet 206
Figure 6-63: Time & Date settings, network time 207
Figure 6-64: Calendar applet 207
Figure 6-65: Screensaver 208

Figure 6-66: Screensaver: Settings tab 209

Figure 6-67: Languages 210

Figure 6-68: Accessibility 210

Figure 6-69: Startup Applications Preferences 211

Figure 6-70: System Info 211

Figure 6-71: System Settings, Mouse and Touchpad 212

Figure 6-72: GNOME Power Manager menu and applet configuration 213

Figure 6-73: GNOME Power Manager 213

Figure 6-74: GNOME Power Manager: Brightness tab 214

Figure 6-75: Keyboard Typing 214

Figure 6-76: Keyboard: Layouts tab 215

Figure 6-77: Keyboard Layout Options 215

Figure 6-78: Notifications 216

Figure 6-79: Privacy 216

Figure 7-1: Mate desktop and panel 218

Figure 7-2: Mate with Linux Mint menu and Caja file manager 219

Figure 7-3: Mate Desktop Settings 220

Figure 7-4: Mate window 222

Figure 7-5: Switching Windows with thumbnails 222

Figure 7-6: Window List applet 223

Figure 7-7: Window List Preferences 223

Figure 7-8: Workspace switcher, one row and two rows 224

Figure 7-9: Switching workspaces, Ctrl-Alt-arrow 224

Figure 7-10: Workspace Switcher Preferences 224

Figure 7-11: Linux Mint Menu for Mate 225

Figure 7-12: Linux Mint Menu search 226

Figure 7-13: Linux Mint Menu Applications pop-up menu. 226

Figure 7-14: Linux Mint Menu Favorites 227

Figure 7-15: Linux Mint Menu Preferences dialog 228

Figure 7-16: Linux Mint Menu with Recent Documents plugin 228

Figure 7-17: Mate Panel 229

Figure Listing **569**

Figure 7-18: Mate Panel pop-up menu 230

Figure 7-19: Mate Panel Properties 230

Figure 7-20: Mate Panel "Add to Panel" dialog for panel applets 233

Figure 7-21: Caja file manager home folders...235

Figure 7-22: Caja file manager with sidebar 236

Figure 7-23: Caja navigation buttons: back, forward, parent, home, computer...............236

Figure 7-24: Caja locations: unexpanded, expanded, and location path 237

Figure 7-25: File manager side pane menu and views 238

Figure 7-26: File manager side pane with bookmarks menu 239

Figure 7-27: File manager window with tabs..240

Figure 7-28: File manager File, Edit, and View menus 241

Figure 7-29: File manager File | Open with submenu for folders and files 243

Figure 7-30: File properties on Caja 247

Figure 7-31: GNOME Control Center..249

Figure 7-32: Keyboard Preferences 251

Figure 7-33: About Me information: Preferences | About Me 252

Figure 7-34: Selecting GNOME themes...253

Figure 7-35: Choosing a desktop background, System | Preferences | Appearance 254

Figure 7-36: Fonts..255

Figure 7-37: Mate Power Manager 256

Figure 7-38: Preferred Applications tool...257

Figure 7-39: File Management Preferences for Media 258

Figure 7-40: Screensaver Preferences 259

Figure 7-41: Assistive Technologies Preferences 260

Figure 8-1: SDDM Display Manager, login screen 264

Figure 8-2: The KDE desktop..266

Figure 8-3: KDE Help Center 267

Figure 8-4: Default Desktop Settings, wallpaper..268

Figure 8-5: Default Desktop Settings, Get New Wallpapers 268

Figure 8-6: System Settings | Workspace Theme | Desktop Theme, Get New Themes ..269

Figure 8-7: The Kickoff Menu Leave 270

Figure 8-8: Shutdown and Logout dialog 270

Figure 8-9: The Application Dashboard Menu Power/Session 271

Figure 8-10: The Kickoff Menu Favorites 272

Figure 8-11: The Kickoff Menu Computer 272

Figure 8-12: The Kickoff Menu Applications 273

Figure 8-13: The Application Dashboard Menu: Office 274

Figure 8-14: Application Dashboard Menu: All Applications 274

Figure 8-15: Krunner application search 275

Figure 8-16: Device Notifier and its panel widget icon 276

Figure 8-17: Network Manager connections and panel icons. 276

Figure 8-18: KDE Network Manager connection information: speed and details. 276

Figure 8-19: KDE connection editor and KDE Network Manager 277

Figure 8-20: Clock Widget with task sidebar and configuration dialog 278

Figure 8-21: Adding a widget: Widgets dialog 278

Figure 8-22: Folder, Calculator, Digital clock, CPU Load monitor, and Notes widgets ... 279

Figure 8-23: Folder and Icon widgets. 279

Figure 8-24: Activity toolbar and icons 281

Figure 8-25: Create an activity 281

Figure 8-26: stop Activity icons 282

Figure 8-27: Activity Manager and screen of selected activity 282

Figure 8-28: Window tiles 284

Figure 8-29: Virtual desktop configuration (Desktop Behavior) and Pager widget icon.
.... 285

Figure 8-30: Pager Settings. 286

Figure 8-31: KDE panel 286

Figure 8-32: KDE Add Widgets for panel 287

Figure 8-33: System Tray 287

Figure 8-34: KDE panel system tray settings 288

Figure 8-35: KDE Panel Configuration 288

Figure 8-36: KDE Panel Configuration details and display features 289

Figure 8-37: Desktop Effects selection 290

Figure 8-38: Desktop Effects configuration 291

Figure 8-39: Thumbnail and Breeze Switch - Alt-Tab 292

Figure 8-40: Cover Switch - Alt-Tab 292

Figure 8-41: Present Windows (Windows effects) Ctrl-F9 for current desktop and Ctrl-F10 for all desktops 293

Figure 8-42: Desktop Grid - Ctrl-F8 293

Figure 8-43: Desktop Cube - Ctrl-F11, drag-mouse or right/left arrow keys (or two-finger drag on touchpad) 294

Figure 8-44: The KDE file manager (Dolphin) 295

Figure 8-45: The KDE file manager menus 295

Figure 8-46: The KDE file manager with sidebars 296

Figure 8-47: The KDE file manager panel Recently Saved 297

Figure 8-48: The KDE file manager with split views 297

Figure 8-49: The KDE file manager share dialog for folders 298

Figure 8-50: The KDE Search Bar 300

Figure 8-51: The KDE Filter Bar 301

Figure 8-52: KDE System Settings 302

Figure 8-53: KDE System Settings | Application Style, Widget Style 302

Figure 8-54: KDE System Settings | User Manager 303

Figure 9-1: GNOME System Monitor: Resources 309

Figure 9-2: GNOME System Monitor: Processes 310

Figure 9-3: System Log 311

Figure 9-4: Disk Usage Analyzer 312

Figure 9-5: Disk Usage Analyzer: Scan dialog 312

Figure 9-6: The ClamTK tool for ClamAV virus protection 313

Figure 9-7: Disk Utility 315

Figure 9-8: Disk Utility, hard drive 316

Figure 9-9: Disk Utility, Volumes 316

Figure 9-10: Disk Utility: Hard Disk hardware SMART data 317

Figure 9-11: Sound Menu 319

Figure 9-12: Sound Menu, right click, mute options 319

Figure 9-13: Sound Preferences 320

Figure 9-14: Sound Preferences: Input 320

Figure 9-15: Sound Preferences: Output...321
Figure 9-16: Sound Preferences: Applications 322
Figure 9-17: PulseAudio Volume Control, Playback..323
Figure 9-18: PulseAudio Volume Control, Output Devices 324
Figure 9-19: PulseAudio Preferences...324
Figure 9-20: dconf editor...325
Figure 10-1: pkexec prompt for secure access...333
Figure 10-2: Invoking Xed with the pkexec command...335
Figure 10-3: Nemo File Manager with Elevated Privileges (as root) 336
Figure 10-4: Prompt to open file manager as root (administrative access).........337
Figure 10-5: Editing System Files from the file manager opened as root............337
Figure 10-6: Users and Groups (Cinnamon)...338
Figure 10-7: Users and Groups: new users 339
Figure 10-8: Users and Groups: inactive user 339
Figure 10-9: Users and Groups: password dialog...340
Figure 10-10: Users and Groups: Groups tab 340
Figure 10-11: Users and Groups: add a group 340
Figure 10-12: Users and Groups: Users group dialog..341
Figure 10-13: Users and Groups (Mate)..341
Figure 10-14: User Settings: Change User Password dialog.................................342
Figure 10-15: User Settings: Change User Account Type......................................342
Figure 10-16: Users and Groups: Change User Privileges 343
Figure 10-17: Users and Groups: Create New User 344
Figure 10-18: Users and Groups: new user password 344
Figure 10-19: Users and Groups: Groups settings 345
Figure 10-20: Group Properties: Group Users panel 345
Figure 10-21: Mount authorization request for non-administrative users 347
Figure 10-22: Network authorization..348
Figure 10-23: Network window 348
Figure 10-24: Mount remote Windows shares 348
Figure 10-25: Folder Sharing Options 349

Figure Listing **573**

Figure 10-26: Folder Sharing permissions prompt 349

Figure 10-27: Folder Share panel 350

Figure 10-28: File Permissions 351

Figure 10-29: Folder Permissions 352

Figure 10-30: Bluetooth Settings (System Settings) 354

Figure 10-31: Bluetooth Settings: disconnected device 354

Figure 10-32: Bluetooth Device Configuration 355

Figure 10-33: Bluetooth Sound 355

Figure 10-34: Bluetooth Setup Device Wizard: phone 356

Figure 10-35: Editing the /etc/default/grub file 358

Figure 10-36: Backup Tool 361

Figure 10-37: Backup Tool backup 361

Figure 10-38: Deja Dup settings: overview 362

Figure 10-39: Deja Dup settings: Folders to save and ignore 362

Figure 10-40: Deja Dup settings: storage for Windows share and Local folder 363

Figure 10-41: Deja Dup settings: backup times 363

Figure 10-42: Deja Dup backup: encryption 363

Figure 10-43: Deja Dup restore 364

Figure 11-1: Network Manager wired, wireless, and disconnect icons. 378

Figure 11-2: Network Manager applet menu 379

Figure 11-3: Network (System Settings) Wi-Fi Tab and Known Networks 379

Figure 11-4: Network wireless configuration: Security tab 380

Figure 11-5: Network wireless configuration: Identity tab 380

Figure 11-6: Network wireless configuration: IP tabs, manual 381

Figure 11-7: Network wired tab 381

Figure 11-8: Network wired configuration dialog 382

Figure 11-9: Network wired configuration, Security 382

Figure 11-10: Network wired configuration, Identity 382

Figure 11-11: Network wired configuration, IPv4 383

Figure 11-12: Network configuration 383

Figure 11-13: Choosing a connection type for a new network connection 384

Figure 11-14: New connection types	384
Figure 11-15: General tab	385
Figure 11-16: DHCP Wired Configuration	385
Figure 11-17: Manual IPv4 Wired Configuration	386
Figure 11-18: Manual IPv6 Wired Configuration	387
Figure 11-19: 802.1 Security Configuration	387
Figure 11-20: Wireless configuration	388
Figure 11-21: Wireless Security: WEP and WPA	388
Figure 11-22: DSL manual configuration	389
Figure 11-23: 3G Wizard	389
Figure 11-24: 3G Provider Listings	390
Figure 11-25: 3G configuration	390
Figure 11-26: PPP Configuration	391
Figure 11-27: VPN connection types	391
Figure 11-28: VPN configuration (openvpn)	392
Figure 11-29: VPN configuration (pptp)	392
Figure 11-30: Gufw	404
Figure 11-31: Gufw Preconfigured rules	405
Figure 11-32: Gufw Simple rules	406
Figure 11-33: Gufw Advanced rules	406
Figure 11-34: Gufw edit a rule	407
Figure 11-35: Gufw create a rule for an active port	407
Figure 11-36: firewall-config: Runtime Configuration	410
Figure 11-37: firewall-config: Permanent Configuration	410
Figure 11-38: Default Zone	411
Figure 11-39: Base Zone Settings	411
Figure 11-40: Service Settings	412
Figure 11-41: Service Protocols and Ports	412
Figure 11-42: Port Forwarding	413
Figure 11-43: ICMP Filters	414
Figure 11-44: Gnome network tool	414

Figure Listing

Figure 13-1: rcconf service management 464
Figure 13-2: SSH setup and access 474
Figure 14-1: system-config-printer tool 486
Figure 14-2: Printer properties window 486
Figure 14-3: Printer configuration window Printer menu 487
Figure 14-4: Printer queue 487
Figure 14-5: Server Settings 488
Figure 14-6: Selecting a CUPS server 488
Figure 14-7: Printer Options 489
Figure 14-8: Jobs Options 490
Figure 14-9: Set Default Printer 490
Figure 14-10: System-wide and personal default printers 491
Figure 14-11: Selecting a new printer connection: connected and unconnected 491
Figure 14-12: Printer manufacturer for new printers 492
Figure 14-13: Searching for a printer driver from the OpenPrinting repository 493
Figure 14-14: Printer Model and driver for new printers using local database 493
Figure 14-15: Printer Name and Location for new printers 494
Figure 14-16: CUPS Web-based Configuration Tool: Home tab 495
Figure 14-17: CUPS Web-based Configuration Tool: Administration tab 495
Figure 14-18: Adding a new printer: CUP Web Interface 496
Figure 14-19: CUPS Web-based Configuration Tool: Printers tab 496
Figure 14-20: CUPS Web-based Configuration Tool: Managing Printers 497
Figure 14-21: CUPS Web-based Configuration Tool: Printer Options 497
Figure 14-22: CUPS Web-based Configuration Tool: Network Printers 498
Figure 14-23: Finding a network printer 498
Figure 14-24: Selecting a Windows printer 499
Figure 14-25: SMB Browser, selecting a remote windows printer 499
Figure 14-26: Remote Windows printer connection configuration 500
Figure 14-27: Remote Windows printer Settings 500
Figure 15-1: Shared Folders tool 517
Figure 15-2: Shared Folders User tab 517

Figure 15-3: Adding a new shared folder 518
Figure 15-4: Specifying allowed hosts or networks 518
Figure 15-5: Share Folder with host access... 518
Figure 16-1: Samba server configuration with system-config-samba 537
Figure 16-2: Samba Server Settings, Basic tab 538
Figure 16-3: Samba Server Settings, Security tab 538
Figure 16-4: Samba Users 539
Figure 16-5: Create a new samba user 539
Figure 16-6: New Samba Share, Basic tab 539
Figure 16-7: Samba share, Access tab 540
Figure 16-8: Samba with shares.. 540

Index

.bash_logout, 438
.mount, 458
.path, 455
.profile, 433, 434
.service, 450
.socket, 453
.target, 447, 456
.wine, 120
/etc/apparmor, 469
/etc/apparmor.d, 469
/etc/apt/sources.list, 103
/etc/bash.bashrc, 437
/etc/default, 463
/etc/fstab, 458
/etc/hostname, 337
/etc/init.d, 460
/etc/init.d/apparmor, 468
/etc/nsswitch.conf, 528
/etc/profile, 436
/etc/profile.d, 436
/etc/ssh/ssh_config, 479
/etc/systemd/system, 445, 449
/lib/systemd/system, 442, 445
/media, 346

A

aa-genprof, 469
Activities
  KDE, 280
Administration
  Disk Usage Analyzer, 312
  GNOME System Monitor, 308
  Linux Mint Administrative Tools, 328
  Linux Mint System Tools, 307
  Mate Control Center, 248
  new printers, 491
  pkexec, 333
  PolicyKit, 330
  Puppet, 470
  root user, 335
  services, 346, 442
  Services, 462
  Software Manager, 111
  su, 335
  sudo, 331
  Synaptic Package Manager, 116
  System Settings (Cinnamon), 196
  systemd, 346, 442
  Tools
    Gufw, 404
    Services, 346
    shares-admin, 517
    System Monitor, 308
    system-config-printer, 485
    system-config-samba, 537
    terminal window, 95
    Update Manager, 107
    virus protection, 313
Administrative Tools, 328
Adobe, 133
Advanced Linux Sound Architecture, 318
Advanced Package Tool, 100
Aliases, 424
alien, 127
ALSA, 318
  alsamixer, 318
  amixer, 318
alsamixer, 318
Amanda, 365
AMD
  DKMS, 356
amixer, 318
AppArmor, 467
  /etc/apparmor.d, 469
  aa-genprof, 469
  apparmor_status, 468
apparmor_status, 468
Appearance, 200, 252
  System Settings, 200
applets, 179, 234

network, 82
sound menu, 319
time & date menu, 206
Application Dashboard (KDE), 273
Applications
administration, 328
burners, 147
defaults, 194, 245
defaults (Cinnamon), 205
email, 137
FTP, 149
Internet, 148
KDE, 284
Krunner, 274
mail, 137
multimedia, 141
music, 143
networks, 376
newsreaders, 138
Office, 131
panel, 180
removable media, 205
Software Manager, 111
Synaptic Package Manager, 116
TV, 146
APT, 100
apt-get, 123
apt cache tools, 125
apt-cache, 125
apt-get, 123
install, 123
update, 124
upgrade, 124
Archive Mounter, 80
auth_admin_keep, 330
Authentication
root user, 335
su, 335
sudo, 331

B

backgrounds
Cinnamon, 200
KDE, 267
Mate, 254
Backports

repository, 102, 103
backup, 360
Amanda, 365
Backup Tool, 361
BackupPC, 365
Deja Dup, 360, 362
duplicity, 360, 362
rsync, 364
tar, 364
BackupPC, 365
bad
Gstreamer, 143
Baloo, 300
base
Gstreamer, 143
bash.bashrc, 437
bash_completion, 436
BASH_ENV, 431
bash_logout, 438
battery, 257
BitTorrent, 149
Transmission, 149
Bluetooth, 353
bookmarks, 182, 235
boot
fstab mount units, 458
graphical.target, 449
runlevels, 456
special targets, 456
Bootloader
configuration, 358
edit, 60
GRUB, 60, 357
GRUB_DEFAULT, 359
grub-install, 57
Plymouth, 61, 317
re-install, 57
update-grub, 360
box switch, 291
Brasero, 147
brightness
System Settings, 208, 259

C

Caja, 72, 234
bookmarks, 235

desktop settings, 235
displaying files and folders, 240
File Manager search, 244
file properties, 247
media, 258
navigation, 241
preferences, 248
side pane, 239
tabs, 239
xdg-user-dirs, 234
calendar, 206
calendar menu, 206
Calligra Suite, 132
CD Burners and Rippers, 147
CD burning, 80
CD/DVD disc images
   Archive Mounter, 80
cifs, 557
Cinnamon, 67, 156
   Appearance, 200
   applets, 179
   application defaults, 205
   backgrounds, 200
   calendar, 206
   date, 206
   dconf, 325
   desklets, 158
   desktop icons, 158
   documentation, 92
   expo, 160
   Expo, 174
   Expo applet, 174
   favorites, 163
   File Manager, 70
   FTP, 183
   Help, 32, 92
   keyboard, 214
   keyboard shortcuts, 160
   languages, 209
   Linux Mint User Guide, 32, 92
   menu (Cinnamon), 162
   menu (edit), 165
   Nemo, 181
   notifications, 215
   panel, 176
   privacy, 216
   removable media, 205

   Startup Applications, 210
   switching windows, 171
   system info, 211
   System Settings, 196
   themes, 202
   tiles, 170
   time, 206
   universal access, 210
   Users and Groups, 338
   window list, 169
   windows, 166
   windows quicklist menu, 170
   workspace switcher applet, 174
Cinnamon Power Manager, 212
cinnamon-settings-users, 338
ClamAV
   virus protection, 313
clocks
   GNOME Clocks, 134
codecs, 107
   Matroska, 147
   MPEG-4, 147
   Xvid, 147
color profiles, 90
command line, 97
   terminal window, 95
command line interface, 66
commands, 97
Common Unix Printing System (CUPS), 482
Common User Directory Structure, 181, 234
compression
   LZMA, 364
configuration, 502
   dconf editor, 325
   networks, 377
   system-config-printer, 485
Configuration files
   editing, 357
configuring users, 338, 341
Connect to Server
   FTP, 151
connections
   hidden wireless, 87
   networks, 81
   options, 85
   wired, 82
   wireless, 83

580 Index

Control Center
  Mate, 248
copy, 299
cron
  KDE Task Scheduler, 311
CUPS, 482
  configuration, 502
  cups-browsed.conf, 507
  cupsctl, 506
  cupsd.conf, 502
  cups-files.conf, 507
  lpadmin, 509
  print clients, 508
  printers.conf, 506
  subscription.conf, 507
  system-config-printer, 485
cups-browsed.conf, 507
cupsctl, 506
cupsd.conf, 501, 502
cupsdisable, 511
cupsenable, 511
cups-files.conf, 507

D

Database Management Systems, 135
database servers
  MySQL, 135
  PostgreSQL, 135
Databases
  LibreOffice, 136
  MySQL, 136
  PostgreSQL, 136
  SQL Databases, 136
date
  timedatectl, 208
dconf editor, 325
DEB, 122
Debian alternatives system, 317
default applications
  MATE, 258
  System Settings (Cinnamon), 205
default.plymouth, 317
Deja Dup, 360, 362
desklets, 158
Desktop
  Activities (KDE), 280

Appearance, 200
backgrounds (Cinnamon), 200
backgrounds (Mate), 254
Cinnamon, 67, 156
copy, 299
dconf, 325
default applications, 194, 245
desklets, 158
desktop settings (Mate), 220
displaying files and folders, 185, 240
documentation, 32, 92
Dolphin, 294
expo, 160
Expo, 174
Expo applet, 174
favorites, 163, 225
file manager, 70, 72, 75
file properties, 194, 247
fonts (Mate), 255
FTP, 183
icons
  Cinnamon, 158
  Mate, 220
KDE, 73, 265
KDE configuration, 265
keyboard (Cinnamon), 214
keyboard shortcuts, 160
Linux Mint Administrative Tools, 328
Linux Mint User Guide, 32, 92
Linx Mint menu (Mate), 225
Mate, 71, 218
menu, 165
menu (Cinnamon), 162
menu (Mate), 225
Nemo, 181
notifications (Cinnamon), 215
panel (Cinnamon), 176
panel (Mate), 229
Plasma 5.8, 262
Power Manager (Cinnamon), 212
Power Manager (Mate), 256
privacy (Cinnamon), 216
Removable media, 79
shut down, 65
spices, 156
startup applications (Cinnamon), 210
switching windows (Cinnamon), 171

Index 581

System Settings (Cinnamon), 196
themes (Cinnamon), 202
themes (Mate), 253
tiles, 170
window list, 223
windows, 166, 221
workspace switcher applet, 174, 224
workspaces (Mate), 224
XFce, 75
desktop cube, 293
desktop effects
   box switch, 291
   desktop cube, 293
   desktop grid, 292
   KDE, 289
   present windows, 292
desktop grid, 292
device notifier (KDE), 275
Devices
   KDE device notifier, 275
   Udisks, 315
Disk Usage Analyzer, 312
display
   configuration, 87
   Displays, 87
   HiDPI settins, 90
   System Settings, 89
   vendor drivers, 88
display manager
   LightDM, 61
   SDDM, 264
DivX, 147
   Xvid, 147
dkms, 356
DKMS, 356
   dkms command, 356
Document Viewers, 133
   Evince, 133
   Okular, 133
   Xreader, 133
documentation
   GNOME, 92
   info pages, 94
   Linux Mint User Guide, 92
   Man pages, 94
Dolphin, 75, 294
download, 149

dpkg, 123, 125, 126
   alien, 127
dpkg-query, 125
Dragon Player, 146
drawers, 233
DSL, 388
dual-booting, 40
duplicity, 360, 362
DVB
   Kaffeine, 147
DVD
   burning, 80
      K3b, 147
   Linux Mint, 30
DVI, 133
   Evince, 133
   Okular, 133
Dynamic IP Address, 376
Dynamic Kernel Module Support, 356

E

ecryptfs, 91
edit
   GRUB, 60
editions
   Linux Mint, 28
Editors, 129, 134
   Xed, 134
Email, 137
Encryption
   ecryptfs, 91
   Port Forwarding, 478
   private encrypted directory, 91
   SSH, 471
   ssh-keygen, 474
Engrampa, 364
Environment Variables, 426
Evince, 133
Expo, 160, 174
   Expo applet, 174
export, 426
exports, 519

F

favorites
   Cinnamon, 163
   Mate, 225
File Manager, 191, 244
   bookmarks, 182, 235
   Caja, 234
   Caja preferences, 248
   default applications (MATE), 258
   desktop icons, 182
   desktop settings, 235
   displaying files and folders, 185
   displaying files and folders (Caja), 240
   Dolphin, 294
   navigation (Caja), 241
   navigation (Nemo), 189
   Nemo, 181
   preferences (Nemo), 196
   side pane (Caja), 239
   sidebar, 183
   tabs, 185, 239
   xdg-user-dirs, 181, 234
file permission
   GNOME, 351
File Roller, 364
file systems, 346, 458
   fstab, 352
   Linux, 346
   LVM, 366
   NTFS, 347
   Windows, 346
   ZFS, 366, 373
Files
   copy, 299
   default applications, 194, 245
   display, 185, 240
   move, 299
   properties, 194, 247
   rename, 299
filter bar (KDE), 300
Firefox
   FTP, 150
Firewall, 403
   firewall-config, 409
   FirewallD, 409
   Gufw, 404
   masquerading, 413
   ports, 403, 413
   Samba, 536
   ufw, 404, 408
firewall-config, 409
FirewallD, 409
folders
   display, 185, 240
   properties, 195, 247, 248
fonts
   Mate, 255
fstab, 352, 458, 524
FTP, 150
   Cinnamon, 183
   Connect to Server, 151
   Linux Mint desktop, 183, 236
   Nemo, 151
   sftp, 478
   SSH, 151
FTP Clients, 149

G

gcj, 149
GIMP, 139
GNOME
   Clocks, 134
   dconf, 325
   display configuration, 87
   display manager (LightDM), 61
   documentation, 92
   DVD/CD burner, 80
   file permission, 351
   folder properties, 195, 247, 248
   groups, 340, 345
   Gufw, 404
   Panel Objects, 232
   Photos, 139
GNOME Control Center, 248
GNOME Media Player, 145
GNOME movie player, 145
GNOME Office, 133
GNOME System Monitor, 308
   Processes, 309
gnome-nettool, 414
GNU General Public License, 36

good

Gstreamer, 143
GPar2, 138
Grand Unified Bootloader, 357
graphical.target, 449
Graphics
    default applications (MATE), 258
    GIMP, 139
    Inkscape, 139
    Pix, 139
    Xviewer, 139
groups
    managing, 340, 345
    Users and Groups (GNOME), 340, 345
GRUB, 60, 357
    configuration, 358
    editing, 60
    grub-install, 57
    grub-set-default, 359
    re-installing the boot loader, 57
    update-grub, 360
GRUB 2, 357
GRUB_DEFAULT, 359
grub-install, 57
grub-set-default, 359
GStreamer, 142
    bad, 143
    base, 143
    good, 143
    Plug-ins, 143
    ugly, 143
Gufw, 404

H

hard drives
    SMART information, 316
hardware sensors, 314
HDTV, 146
    Kaffeine, 147
Help
    info pages, 94
    Linux Mint, 33
    Linux Mint User Guide, 32, 92
    Man pages, 94
    Mate, 94
    Unity, 32, 92
    X-Apps, 94
help.ubuntu.com, 35
hidden wireless networks, 87
High Dots per Inch, 90
HOME, 429
hostname, 337
hostnamectl, 337
hosts.allow, 523

I

icons
    desktop
        Cinnamon, 158
        Mate, 220
import
    repository, 102
info, 94
info pages, 94
inittab, 442
Inkscape, 139
install, 123
Installation
    computer name, 54
    help, 41
    Linux Mint, 40
    Live DVD, 43
    overview, 41
    partitions, 44
    Prepare disk space, 44
    reuse existing Linux partitions, 52
    specify partitions manually, 48
    upgrade from 17, 40
    upgrade from 18, 40
    USB, 31
    user, 54
IPv6, 386

J

Java, 149
    gcj, 149
    GNU Java compiler, 149
    OpenJDK, 149
Java Runtime Environment, 149
JRE, 149

K

K3b, 147
Kaffeine, 145, 146, 147
KDE, 28, 73
   Activities, 280
   Application Dashboard, 273
   applications, 284
   Baloo, 300
   box switch, 291
   configuration, 265, 301
   copy, 299
   desktop backgrounds, 267
   desktop cube, 293
   desktop effects, 289
   desktop grid, 292
   desktop pager, 284
   device notifier, 275
   Dolphin, 294
   file manager, 75
   filter bar, 300
   Help Center, 266
   Kaffeine, 145
   KDE Desktop, 265
   KickOff, 271
   Krunner, 274
   Linux Mint, 73, 263
   move, 299
   Network Manager, 276
   panel, 286
   panel configuration, 288
   Plasma, 286
   Plasma 5.6, 262
   Plasmoids, 277
   present windows, 292
   rename, 299
   SDDM, 264
   search bar, 300
   shutdown, 269
   System Settings, 301
   Task Scheduler, 311
   themes, 268
   tiles, 283
   virtual desktops, 284
   wallpaper, 267
   Widgets, 277
   windows, 282
keyboard, 53
   Cinnamon, 214
   Mate, 250
   System Settings (Cinnamon), 214
keyboard layout
   localectl, 215
keyboard shortcuts, 160
keys
   ssh-keygen, 474
KickOff, 271
kill, 310
Krunner, 274
KWin
   box switch, 291
   desktop cube, 293
   desktop grid, 292
   present windows, 292

L

languages
   System Settings (Cinnamon), 209
laptop, 81
   brightness, 208, 259
   Network Manager, 81
   power management, 81
   wireless networks, 81
libdvdcss, 107
LibreOffice, 131
LibreOffice Base, 136
libxvidcore, 147
LightDM, 61
   configuration, 63
LightDM display Manager, 61
Linux, 36
   Man pages, 94
Linux Mint, 263
   Administrative Tools, 328
   Cinnamon, 67, 156
   editions, 28
   help, 33
   Help, 32, 92
   Installation, 40
   installation help, 41
   Introduction, 27
   KDE, 73, 263

laptop, 81
LightDM, 63
Live DVD, 30
login window, 63
LTS, 28
Mate, 71, 218
menu (Mate), 225
recovery, 56
releases, 28
software packages, 32
Spices, 156
Synaptic Package Manager, 116
System Settings (Cinnamon), 196
update, 107
upgrade, 40
welcome dialog, 33
Linux Mint Desktop
   Cinnamon, 67, 156
   display configuration, 87
   Displays, 87
   folder properties, 195, 247, 248
   FTP, 236
   KDE, 73
   Mate, 71, 218
   spices, 156
   Users, 338
   Users and Groups (Mate), 341
Linux Mint Live DVD, 30
Linux Mint official-pakcages-repositories.list, 103
Linux Mint repositories, 101, 102
Linux Mint Software manager, 111
Linux Mint User Guide, 32, 92
lm-sensors, 314
localectl
   keyboard layout, 215
   location, 215
location
   localectl, 215
lock
   System Settings, 208, 259
Logical Volume Manager, 366
login
   LightDM display manager, 61
   logind, 60
login window
   preferences, 63

logind, 60
lpadmin, 509
lpc, 508
lpinfo, 511
lpoptions, 509, 510
lpq, 508
lpr, 508
lprm, 508
LVM, 366
   commands, 367
   groups, 368
   Logical Volumes, 369
   physical volume, 367
   snapshots, 372
   vgcreate, 368
lynx, 485
LZMA, 364

M

Mail, 137
Mail applications, 137
main
   repository, 102
man, 94
Man pages, 94
MariaDB, 137
masquerading, 413
Mate, 71, 218
   about me, 252
   adding panel objects, 232
   Appearance, 252
   Applets, 234
   backgrounds, 254
   Caja, 72, 234
   desktop icons, 220
   desktop settings, 220
   Desktop User Guide, 94
   drawers, 233
   favorites, 225
   fonts, 255
   Help, 94
   keyboard, 250
   menu, 225
   menu (edit), 227
   panel, 229
   panel objects, 232

Index

personal information, 252
preferences, 249
Preferred Applications, 257
themes, 253
universal access, 259
users and groups, 341
window list, 223
windows, 221
workspace switcher applet, 224
workspaces, 224
Mate Power Manager, 256
Matroska, 147
menu
    Application Dashboard (KDE), 273
    Cinnamon, 162
    edit, 165
    KickOff, 271
    Linux Mint menu, 225
    Mate, 225
    panel (Mate), 233
    preferences (Mate), 227
    window list, 169
    windows quicklist menu, 170
me-tv, 146
Microsoft Domain Security, 553
mintBackup, 361
mintinstall, 111
mint-meta-codecs, 107
mintupgrade, 40
mint-upgrade-info, 40
mkv
    Matroska, 147
Mobile Broadband, 389
mount
    cifs, 557
move
    KDE, 299
MP3, 143
MPEG-4, 147
    Matroska, 147
MPlayer, 145, 146
Multimedia, 141
    applications, 143
    CD Burners and Rippers, 147
    codecs, 107, 142
    default applications (MATE), 258
    DVD, 145

GNOME Media Player, 145
GStreamer, 142
HDTV, 146
Kaffeine, 145, 147
Matroska, 147
mint-meta-codecs, 107
MPEG-4, 147
MPlayer, 145
Photos, 139
PiTiVi Video editor, 145
Sound Preferences, 318
Totem, 145
TV Players, 146
VideoLAN, 145
vlc, 145
Xplayer, 145
Xvid, 147
multiverse
    repository, 102
Music Applications, 143
MySQL, 135, 136
Mythbuntu
    MythTV, 146
MythTV, 146

N

Name Service Switch, 528
Nemo, 70, 181
    bookmarks, 182
    Connect to Server, 151
    desktop icons, 182
    File Manager search, 191
    file properties, 194
    FTP, 151
    navigation, 189
    preferences, 196
    xdg-user-dirs, 181
NetBIOS, 532
Nettool, 414
Network Configuration, 375
Network File System (NFS), 514
Network Information, 376
Network Information System (NIS), 526
Network Object Model Environment, 218
Network Time Protocol, 464
    ntp, 465

ntp.conf, 465
ntpupdate, 464
TOY, 464
Universal Time Coordinated, 464
UTC, 464
Networking
   link files, 418
   nmcli, 393
   predictable network device names, 415
   renaming device names, 417
   renaming network device names, 417, 418
   systemd-networkd, 399, 418
   udev, 417
NetworkManager, 81, 377
   3G, 389
   connections, 81
   device names, 415
   DSL, 388
   hidden wireless, 87
   IPv6, 386
   KDE, 276
   laptop, 81
   manual configuration, 379
   Mobile Broadband, 389
   Network (System Settings), 85
   network menu, 82
   nmcli, 393
   PPP, 390
   udev, 417
   VPN, 391
   wired configuration, 384, 385
   wired connection, 82
   wireless configuration, 387
   wireless connections, 83
   wireless security, 388
NetworkManager Command Line Interface (**nmcli**), 393
Networks
   3G, 389
   configuration, 377
   connections, 81
   device names, 415
   firewall, 409
   hidden wireless networks, 87
   manual configuration, 379, 383
   Mobile Broadband, 389
   Nettool, 414

Network (System Settings), 85
network connections, 81
NetworkManager, 81, 377
nework menu, 82
nmcli, 393
PPP, 390
proxies, 86
renaming device names, 417, 418
renaming network device names, 417
shared file systems, 347
shared folders, 349
SSID, 87
System Settings, 85
system-config-samba, 537
systemd link files, 418
udev, 417
wired configuration, 384, 385
wired connections, 82
wireless configuration, 387
wireless connections, 83
newsreaders
   NNTPSERVER, 138
   par2, 138
NFS, 350, 514
   /etc/exports, 519
   fstab, 524
   hosts.allow, 523
   nfs4, 521
   options, 519
   portmapper, 523
   shared folders, 517
   shares-admin, 517
nfs4, 521
NIS
   Name Service Switch, 528
nmbd, 350, 500
nmcli, 393
NNTPSERVER, 138, 433
notifications
   Cinnamon, 215
   System Settings (Cinnamon), 215
NTFS, 347
ntp, 465
NTP, 464
ntp.conf, 465
ntpupdate, 464
Nvidia

588 Index

DKMS, 356
nvidia-settings, 89

O

Office
    GNOME Clocks, 134
Office Suites, 131
    Calligra, 132
    GNOME Office, 133
    LibreOffice, 131
    OpenOffice, 131
Okular, 133
Open Source, 36
OpenJDK, 149
openjdk-8-jre, 149
OpenOffice, 131
OpenSSH, 471
OpenZFS, 373

P

Package Management Software, 101
packages
    software, 32, 130
packages.mint.com, 122
Panel
    adding objects (Mate), 232
    application launchers, 180
    Cinnamon, 176
    drawers (Mate), 233
    KDE, 286
    KDE configuration, 288
    Mate, 229
    menus, 233
    panel objects (Mate), 232
par2, 138
Partitions, 44
    blank hard drive, 48
    new partitions, 48
    reusing, 52
passwd, 346
Passwords, 346
PATH, 429
pdbedit, 542
PDC, 552

logon configuration, 554
PDF, 133
    Adobe, 133
    Evince, 133
    Okular, 133
    Xreader, 133
permissions
    files (GNOME), 351
personal information, 252
Photos
    GNOME Photos, 139
    Pix, 139
    Shotwell, 139
Photoshop, 120
physical volume, 367
PiTiVi Video editor, 145
Pix, 139
pkexec, 333
    policy file, 333
    Xed, 333
Plasma, 286
Plasma 5.8, 262
plasmoids, 277
Plymouth, 61, 317
    default.plymouth, 317
    update-alternatives, 317
PolicyKit, 330
    auth_admin_keep, 330
    pkexec, 333
    PolicyKit-1, 330
polkit-1, 330
Port Forwarding, 478
portmapper, 514, 523
ports
    firewall, 403, 413
PostgreSQL, 135, 136
PostScript, 133
power management
    laptop, 81
Power Manager
    GNOME Power Manager (Cinnamon), 212
    laptop, 213, 257
    Mate Power Manager (Mate), 256
poweroff, 460
PPP, 390, 397

predictable network device names, 415, 417, 418
   link files, 418
   systemd-networkd, 418
   udev, 417
Preferences
   file manager (Caja), 248
   file manager (Nemo), 196
   Linux Mint menu (Mate), 227
   Mate, 249
      Control Center, 248
   monitors, 87
   Software Sources, 106
   sound, 318, 320
   windows, 166
Preferred Applications
   Mate, 257
present windows, 292
presentation
   LibreOffice Impress, 132
Print server
   configuration, 502
   CUPS, 482
   cupsd.conf, 501, 502
   lpadmin, 509
   remote printer, 501
   system-config-printer, 485, 498
Print services, 482
Printers
   default personal printer, 490
   default system printer, 490
   editing printers, 488
   installing. *See*
   job options, 489
   new printers, 491
   options, 489
   print queue, 487
   remote printer, 498
   Samba, 499, 551
   system-config-printer, 485
   Windows, 499
printers.conf, 506
privacy
   Cinnamon, 216
   System Settings (Cinnamon), 216
private encrypted directory, 91
processes, 309

Gnome System Monitor, 309
   kill, 310
   ps, 310
profile, 433, 436
Prompt, 431
properties
   files, 194, 247
   folders, 195, 247, 248
proprietary graphics drivers, 356
Proxy
   Network (System Settings), 86
ps, 310
Psensor, 314
Public Domain Controller, 552
PulseAudio, 318, 322
   PulseAudio Configuration, 324
   PulseAudio Volume Control, 323
   PulseAudio Volume Meter, 323
   Sound Preferences, 318
PulseAudio Volume Control, 323
Puppet, 470
puppetmaster, 470

R

Recovery, 56
re-install bootloader, 57
reject, 511
remote printer, 501
removable media, 79
   System Settings, 205
rename, 299
repositories, 101, 102, 103
   /etc/apt/sources.list, 103
   Backports, 102, 103
   import, 102
   main, 102
   multiverse, 102
   official-package-repositories.list, 103
   restricted, 102
   Security updates, 103
   sources.list, 104
   universe, 102
   Updates, 103
   upstream, 102
restricted
   repository, 102

root user, 335
  su, 335
rsync, 364
runlevels, 456

S

Samba, 350, 499, 532
  cifs, 557
  firewall, 536
  Microsoft Domain Security, 553
  nmbd, 350
  pdbedit, 542
  PDC, 552
  printers, 499
  Printers, 551
  Public Domain Controller, 552
  restart, 500
  server configuration, 537
  shares, 539, 550
  smb.conf, 543
  smbclient, 556
  smbd, 350
  smbpasswd, 533, 542
  system-config-samba, 537
  user level security, 538, 540
  user-level access, 517
  winbind, 533
scanner, 134
schedule tasks
  KDE Task Scheduler, 311
scope unit files, 460
scp, 477
Screensaver, 208
SDDM, 264
search
  Baloo, 300
  File Manager search (Caja), 244
  File Manager search (Nemo), 191
  filter bar, 300
  software, 119
search bar (KDE), 300
Secure Shell, 471
Security
  AppArmor, 467
  OpenSSH, 471
  pkexec, 333

  PolicyKit, 330
  virus protection, 313
Security updates
  repository, 103
sensors, 314
  Disk Utility, 314
  lm-sensors, 314
  Psensor, 314
  Xsensors, 314
Server Message Block (SMB), 532
service, 346, 462, 463
Services, 346, 441, 462
  /etc/systemd/system, 445
  /lib/systemd/system, 442, 445
  execution environment options, 450
  graphical target, 449
  mount units, 458
  path units, 455
  runlevels, 456
  service, 463
  service command, 346
  service units, 450
  socket units, 453
  systemd, 346, 442
  target units, 447, 456
  template units, 455
  unit files, 443
sessions
  Startup Applications (Cinnamon), 210
sftp, 478
shared file systems, 347
shared folders, 349
  NFS, 350, 517
  Samba, 537
  shares-admin, 517
  system-config-samba, 539
  user-level access, 517
  Windows, 537
Shared resources
  NFS, 514
shares, 550
shares-admin, 517
  shared folders, 517
Shell
  .profile, 434
  Aliases, 424
  bash.bashrc, 437

Index

bash_logout, 438
   Environment Variables, 426
   HOME, 429
   PATH, 429
   profile, 433, 436
Shell Configuration, 421
Shell Configuration Files, 423
Shell Initialization, 422
Shell Prompt, 431
Shell Variables, 427
Shut down, 65
   KDE, 269
shutdown, 460
side pane, 239
sidebar, 183
Simple Desktop Display Manager (SDDM), 264
slice unit files, 460
SMART, 314, 316
smb.conf, 543
smbclient, 556
smbd, 350, 500
smbpasswd, 542
Snapshots
   LVM, 372
Social networking, 152
software
   /etc/apt/sources.list.d/official-package-repositories.list, 103
   alien, 127
   APT, 100
   apt-cache, 125
   apt-get, 123
   DEB, 122
   dpkg, 126
   Linux Mint, 32
   Linux Mint Software manager, 111
   mintinstall, 111
   open source, 36
   packages, 32, 130
   remove
      Synaptic Package Manager, 119
   search, 119
   Software Manager, 111
   Software Sources, 106
   Synaptic Package Manager, 116
   Ubuntu, 32

Software Manager, 111
software package types, 121
Software Sources, 106
sound
   alsamixer, 318
   amixer, 318
   preferences, 318
   PulseAudio, 318, 322
   PulseAudio Configuration, 324
   PulseAudio Volume Control, 323
   PulseAudio Volume Meter, 323
   sound interfaces, 322
   sound menu, 319
   Sound Preferences, 318
   SPDIF, 321
   volume control, 319
Sound Effects, 320
Sound Preferences, 318, 320
   PulseAudio, 318
Source code, 121
sources.list, 104
SPDIF, 321
Spices, 156
spreadsheet
   LibreOffice Calc, 132
SQL Databases, 136
ssh, 476
SSH
   authentication, 472
   configuration, 479
   FTP, 151
   OpenSSH, 471
   Port Forwarding, 478
   scp, 477
   Secure Shell, 471
   sftp, 478
   ssh, 476
   ssh/ssh_config, 479
   ssh-agent, 476
   ssh-keygen, 474
ssh-agent, 476
ssh-keygen, 474
SSID, 87
Startup Applications, 210
startup-animation
   Plymouth, 61, 317
Static IP address, 376

su, 335
subscription.conf, 507
Subshells, 426
sudo, 331
   configuration, 332
Synaptic Package Manager, 116
system administration, 327
   Mate Control Center, 248
System Environment Variables, 430
system info
   System Settings (Cinnamon), 211
System Settings, 196
   Appearance, 200
   brightness, 208, 259
   color, 90
   default applications, 205
   displays, 89
   General, 90
   Hi-DPI, 90
   keyboard, 214
   languages, 209
   lock, 208, 259
   network, 85
   notifications, 215
   privacy, 216
   removable media, 205
   screen, 208, 259
   system info, 211
   universal access, 210, 259
   User and Groups, 338
System Tools, 307
   Disk Usage Analyzer, 312
   Disk Utility, 315
   GNOME System Monitor, 308
System V, 460
system-config-printer, 485, 498
system-config-samba, 537
systemd, 346, 442
   /etc/systemd/system, 445
   /lib/systemd/system, 442, 445
   execution enironment options, 450
   file systems, 458
   graphical target, 449
   logind, 60
   mount units, 458
   path units, 455
   runlevels, 456

   scope units, 460
   service units, 450
   slice units, 460
   socket units, 453
   special targets, 456
   systemd-networkd, 399
   target units, 447
   template units, 455
   unit files, 443
systemd-networkd, 399
   renaming device names, 418

T

tabs
   File Manager (Caja), 239
   File Manager (Nemo), 185
   terminal window, 95
tar, 364
targets
   graphical, 449
temperature
   Disk Utility, 314
template unit files, 455
terminal window, 95
   configuration, 97
   tabs, 95
themes
   Cinnamon, 202
   KDE, 268
   Mate, 253
   sound, 320
tiles
   Cinnamon, 170
   KDE, 283
time
   Cinnamon, 206
   GNOME Clocks, 134
   timedatectl, 208
timedatectl, 208
   time and date, 208
timer
   GNOME Clocks, 134
Totem, 145, 146
   totem plugins, 145
Transmission, 149
TV Players, 146

Kaffeine, 147
MythTV, 146
tvtime, 146

U

Ubuntu, 34
  help, 35
  repository, 102
  software, 32
udev
  predictable network device names, 415, 417
Udisks, 315
  SMART, 316
ufw, 404, 408
  commands, 408
  Gufw, 404
ugly
  Gstreamer, 143
unexpanded panels
  movable and fixed, 231
units
  execution environment, 450
  fstab, 458
  mount units, 458
  paths, 455
  runlevels, 456
  scope, 460
  service, 450
  slice, 460
  sockets, 453
  special targets, 456
  targets, 447
  templates, 455
  unit files, 443
universal access
  System Settings (Cinnamon), 210
  System Settings (Mate), 259
Universal Time Coordinated, 464
universe
  repository, 102
update, 124
  software, 107
Update Manager, 107
update-alternatives, 317
update-grub, 360

Updates
  repository, 103
upgrade, 124
upgrade from 18, 40
upstream
  repository, 102
USB
  installation, 31
  Live drive, 31
Usenet News, 138
user level security
  Samba, 540
useradd, 345
Users, 341
  cinnamon-settings-users, 338
  groups, 340, 345
  installation, 54
  managing users, 338, 341
  new users, 344
  Passwords, 346
  root user, 335
  Samba, 538
  su, 335
  System Settings, 338
  User and Groups (Cinnamon), 338
  Users and Groups (Mate), 341
  users-admin, 341
Users and Groups (Cinnamon), 338
users-admin, 341
UTC, 464

V

vendor display drivers, 88
vgcreate, 368
Video
  default applications (MATE), 258
  GNOME Media Player, 145
  Kaffeine, 145
  MPEG-4, 147
  MPlayer, 145
  PiTiVi Video editor, 145
  Totem (GNOME movie player), 145
  VideoLAN, 145
  vlc, 145
  Xplayer, 145
VideoLAN, 145, 146

594 Index

virtual desktops
    KDE, 284
virus protection, 313
vlc, 145
volume control, 319
VPN, 391

W

wallpaper
    KDE, 267
Web Browser, 148
Welcome dialog
    Linux Mint, 33
widgets, 277
winbind, 533
window list, 223
windows, 166, 221
    configuration, 166
    KDE, 282
    preferences, 166
    switching, 171
    tiles, 170
    tiles (KDE), 283
    window list, 169
    windows quicklist menu, 170
Windows
    file systems, 347
    fonts, 121
    printers (Samba), 499
    Samba, 532
    user-level access, 517
    Windows compatibility layer, 120
    Wine, 120
Windows compatibility layer
    Wine, 120
wired
    configuration, 384, 385
    Network (System Settings), 85
    network connections, 82
    nmcli, 395

wired configuration
    IPv6, 386
wireless
    laptop, 81
    network connections, 83
    nmcli, 397
wireless configuration, 387
wireless security, 388
Workspaces
    Expo, 174
    Mate, 224
    workspace switcher applet, 174, 224
wvdial, 397

X

X Window System
    Displays, 87
    RandR, 87
    vendor drivers, 88
X-Apps, 130
    documentation, 94
    Linux Mint User Guide, 94
    Pix, 139
    Xed, 134
    Xplayer, 145
    Xreader, 133
    Xviewer, 139
Xed, 134
    pkexec, 333
XFce, 75
Xplayer, 145
Xreader, 133
Xsensors, 314
Xvid, 147
Xviewer, 139

Z

ZFS, 373